Nonadditive Entropies and Nonextensive Statistical Mechanics—Dedicated to Professor Constantino Tsallis on the Occasion of His 80th Birthday

Nonadditive Entropies and Nonextensive Statistical Mechanics—Dedicated to Professor Constantino Tsallis on the Occasion of His 80th Birthday

Guest Editors

Ugur Tirnakli
Christian Beck
Hans J. Herrmann
Airton Deppman
Henrik Jeldtoft Jensen
Evaldo M. F. Curado
Fernando D. Nobre
Angelo Plastino
Astero Provata
Andrea Rapisarda

MDPI

Basel • Beijing • Wuhan • Barcelona • Belgrade • Novi Sad • Cluj • Manchester

Guest Editors

Ugur Tirnakli
Izmir University of Economics
Izmir
Turkey

Christian Beck
Queen Mary University of London
London
UK

Hans J. Herrmann
ESPCI
Paris
France

Airton Deppman
The São Paulo University
São Paulo
Brazil

Henrik Jeldtoft Jensen
Imperial College London
London
UK

Evaldo M. F. Curado
Centro Brasileiro de Pesquisas Físicas
Rio de Janeiro
Brazil

Fernando D. Nobre
Centro Brasileiro de Pesquisas Físicas and National Institute of Science and Technology for Complex Systems
Rio de Janeiro
Brazil

Angelo Plastino
Universidad Nacional de La Plata
La Plata
Argentina

Astero Provata
National Center for Scientific Research "Demokritos"
Athens
Greece

Andrea Rapisarda
University of Catania
Catania
Italy

Editorial Office

MDPI AG
Grosspeteranlage 5
4052 Basel, Switzerland

This is a reprint of the Special Issue, published open access by the journal *Entropy* (ISSN 1099-4300), freely accessible at: https://www.mdpi.com/journal/entropy/special_issues/1USSCI9ZU4.

For citation purposes, cite each article independently as indicated on the article page online and as indicated below:

Lastname, A.A.; Lastname, B.B. Article Title. *Journal Name* **Year**, *Volume Number*, Page Range.

ISBN 978-3-7258-3999-5 (Hbk)
ISBN 978-3-7258-4000-7 (PDF)
https://doi.org/10.3390/books978-3-7258-4000-7

Contents

Muhammad Waqas, Abd Haj Ismail, Haifa I. Alrebdi and Muhammad Ajaz
Centrality and System Size Dependence among Freezeout Parameters and the Implications for EOS and QGP in High-Energy Collisions
Reprinted from: *Entropy* **2023**, *25*, 1586, https://doi.org/10.3390/e25121586 . . . . **173**

Mansour Shrahili and Mohamed Kayid
Some New Results Involving Past Tsallis Entropy of Order Statistics
Reprinted from: *Entropy* **2023**, *25*, 1581, https://doi.org/10.3390/e25121581 . . . . **183**

Pei-Pin Yang, Fu-Hu Liu and Khusniddin K. Olimov
Rapidity and Energy Dependencies of Temperatures and Volume Extracted fromIdentified Charged Hadron Spectra in Proton–Proton Collisions ata Super Proton Synchrotron (SPS)
Reprinted from: *Entropy* **2023**, *25*, 1571, https://doi.org/10.3390/e25121571 . . . . **195**

Princy Thankamani, Nicy Sebastian and Hans J. Haubold
On Complex Matrix-Variate Dirichlet Averages and Its Applications in Various Sub-Domains
Reprinted from: *Entropy* **2023**, *25*, 1534, https://doi.org/10.3390/e25111534 . . . . **227**

Denisse Pasten, Eugenio E. Vogel, Gonzalo Saravia, Antonio Posadas and Oscar Sotolongo
Tsallis Entropy and Mutability to Characterize Seismic Sequences: The Case of 2007–2014 Northern Chile Earthquakes
Reprinted from: *Entropy* **2023**, *25*, 1417, https://doi.org/10.3390/e25101417 . . . . **241**

Harun Yaşar Köse and Serhat İkizoğlu
Nonadditive Entropy Application to Detrended Force Sensor Data to Indicate Balance Disorder of Patients with Vestibular System Dysfunction
Reprinted from: *Entropy* **2023**, *25*, 1385, https://doi.org/10.3390/e25101385 . . . . **257**

Zhipeng Liu
Effects of Nonextensive Electrons on Dust–Ion Acoustic Waves in a Collisional Dusty Plasma with Negative Ions
Reprinted from: *Entropy* **2023**, *25*, 1363, https://doi.org/10.3390/e25091363 . . . . **273**

D. Monteoliva, A. Plastino and A. R. Plastino
Magic Numbers and Mixing Degree in Many-Fermion Systems
Reprinted from: *Entropy* **2023**, *25*, 1206, https://doi.org/10.3390/e25081206 . . . . **285**

Mohamed Kayid and Mashael A. Alshehri
Tsallis Entropy of a Used Reliability System at the System Level
Reprinted from: *Entropy* **2023**, *25*, 550, https://doi.org/10.3390/e25040550 . . . . **296**

entropy

MDPI

Editorial

Nonadditive Entropies and Nonextensive Statistical Mechanics

Ugur Tirnakli

Department of Physics, Faculty of Arts and Sciences, Izmir University of Economics, Izmir 35330, Turkey; ugur.tirnakli@ieu.edu.tr

The centennial Boltzmann–Gibbs statistical mechanics [1], which are based on the additive Boltzmann–Gibbs–von Neumann–Shannon entropy [2], have had undeniable success in an extremely large class of physical systems [3]. This theory is generically designed for systems in equilibrium, and is deeply related to chaotic non-linear dynamics [4]. This implies, for classical systems, that the maximal Lyapunov exponent is expected to be positive. However, in many complex systems, where this exponent becomes vanishingly small, the need emerges for non-additive entropies and consistent generalizations of quantities such as the Maxwellian distributions of velocities [5,6], the celebrated Boltzmann–Gibbs weight for energies [7,8], the standard Fokker–Planck equation [9–11], and Pesin-like identities [12,13]. As a whole, this amounts to generalized statistical mechanics based on nonadditive entropies [14,15].

One of the possible such generalizations, known in the literature as nonextensive statistical mechanics, was proposed in 1988 by Constantino Tsallis [16] and, since then, has received many applications in the natural, artificial, and social sciences. Nowadays, Professor Constantino Tsallis has an outstanding global impact on physics, astrophysics, geophysics, economics, mathematics, chemistry, and computational sciences, among others (see the bibliography at https://tsallis.cbpf.br/biblio.htm (accessed on 5 November 2024)). In recognition of his extraordinarily creative and productive scientific life and innumerable contributions to the field of statistical physics of complex systems, this Special Issue is dedicated to him on the occasion of his 80th birthday (5 November 2023).

Several manuscripts were selected for publication in this Special Issue, which I will attempt to describe in this article. All of these manuscripts were prepared by researchers who are working all around the world in related areas.

In this Special Issue, we have 21 articles in total, with two of them being review articles and the rest being research articles. Let us now describe these articles briefly.

For the first review article, we have the privilege of having a contribution from C. Tsallis himself [17]. In this article, one can follow the development of the theory over the years, adorned with historical anecdotes. This invaluable contribution can be considered as yet another example in which one can see the progress of new ideas that enable us to understand nature better.

The second review article in this SI is the one where K. Nelson has concentrated on some related open problems [18]. Rephrasing the terminology of the framework based on scale-shape distributions, several interesting remarks and research questions have been discussed.

The contributions of the research articles in this SI starts with [19], which is an application of the Tsallis entropy to an engineering problem. The performance and quantification of uncertainties over the lifetime of a system is critical from engineering point of view. The authors develop a useful criterion for measuring the predictability of the lifetime of a coherent system.

Received: 7 January 2025
Accepted: 13 January 2025
Published: 20 January 2025

Citation: Tirnakli, U. Nonadditive Entropies and Nonextensive Statistical Mechanics. *Entropy* **2025**, 27, 93. https://doi.org/10.3390/e27010093

In [20], the authors provide some valuable insights into the interplay between quantum mixing, magic numbers, and thermodynamic properties in many-fermion systems at low temperatures. It is shown that the utilization of Tsallis entropy and an exactly solvable model offer a powerful framework for understanding complex fermionic behavior and its observable consequences.

The contribution to the SI from Liu essentially highlights the crucial role of nonextensive electrons in modifying dust-ion acoustic wave dynamics within collisional dusty plasmas containing negative ions [21]. The obtained results have implications for understanding wave phenomena in various space and laboratory plasma environments where deviations from Maxwellian electron distributions are observed.

In [22], the authors aim to demonstrate the potential for Tsallis entropy analyses of insole pressure data as a quick and accurate tool for identifying vestibular system dysfunction. The proposed detrending algorithm effectively separates balance-related fluctuations from individual walking habits, improving diagnostic accuracy. It is argued that further research with a larger participant pool is needed to validate these findings and refine the diagnostic process.

The next contribution by Pasten et al., in [23], presents a compelling case for the combined use of Tsallis entropy and mutability (dynamical entropy) to analyze seismic sequences and potentially identify pre-earthquake signals. The identified potential indicators offer a promising route for further research in seismic risk assessment and forecasting.

In [24], the authors make a significant contribution to the theory of Dirichlet averages by extending them to the complex domain for matrix-variate cases. This generalization establishes a relationship between Tsallis entropy and Dirichlet averages. It provides a mathematical tool for analyzing and understanding a wide range of phenomena across various disciplines, from special functions and fractional calculus to statistical mechanics and gene expression modeling.

In [25], the reader can find an investigation of the thermodynamic properties of the system created in proton–proton collisions at the Super Proton Synchrotron by analyzing the transverse momentum spectra of identified charged hadrons. Standard Bose–Einstein and Fermi–Dirac distributions are utilized to extract related parameters. These findings are expected to contribute to our understanding of particle production mechanisms and the evolution of the collision system.

In their contributions [26], Shrahili and Kayid offer valuable insights into the past Tsallis entropy of order statistics, providing a framework for understanding and analyzing the uncertainty associated with past events in systems with various structures. Obtained results and derived tools seem to have potential for applications in reliability engineering, lifetime analysis, and broader information theory contexts.

The authors of [27] analyze the transverse momentum spectra of positive pions in high-energy heavy ion collisions using a modified Hagedorn function to extract freeze-out parameters. Their efforts reveal how these parameters depend on both collision centrality and system size. The obtained results are compared to data from the PHENIX and BRAHMS collaborations, and discussed in the context of nonextensive statistical mechanics.

Another interesting contribution by Lenzi et al. [28] demonstrates the significant impact of stochastic resetting on nonlinear diffusion processes. The interplay between these mechanisms leads to non-Gaussian distributions, transient anomalous diffusion, and the emergence of power-law stationary states, which provide valuable insights into systems exhibiting complex diffusion behavior and have potential applications in diverse fields.

In [29], the authors provide a first-principles validation of Fourier's law in a classical inertial Heisenberg model. The results highlight the relevance of nonextensive statistical mechanics, specifically the stretched q-exponential function, in describing the thermal transport properties of complex systems.

Another contribution to this SI investigates Kleiber's law, which describes the 3/4 power-law relationship between organism mass and metabolic rate [30]. The authors propose a nonlinear dynamical model, grounded in statistical mechanics and renormalization group theory, to explain this law across plant and animal kingdoms. The model uses Tsallis entropy and connects to concepts of rank distributions and conjugate pairs of power-law exponents. The findings offer a unified explanation for Kleiber's law based on nonlinear dynamics and nonextensive statistical mechanics.

In their article [31], Biro and collaborators explore the mathematical relationships between non-additive entropy formulas such as Tsallis entropy and the Gini index, a measure of inequality. A dynamical model, illustrating the time evolution of the Gini index, is presented.

In [32], Jensen and Tempesta present a group-theoretic approach to classifying entropies, focusing on how the number of system states grows with the number of components. This approach, emphasizing composability and extensivity, leads to a systematic framework encompassing known entropies, such as Boltzmann–Gibbs–Shannon and Tsallis, and introduces new ones. The framework is applied to data analysis, offering improved methods for characterizing complexity in time series data.

Another research article here explores relativistic thermodynamics within the framework of special relativity, examining different viewpoints on how heat and temperature transform under Lorentz boosts [33]. It then investigates the Maxwell–Jüttner distribution, and proposes a connection between the Tsallis distribution, quantum statistics, and the cosmological constant. The study uses de Sitter space-time as a model to achieve this connection, presenting the Tsallis distribution as a deformation of the Maxwell–Jüttner distribution.

In [34], Yoon et al. examine the non-thermal velocity distribution of solar wind electrons. The authors build upon prior research linking this non-thermal distribution to Langmuir turbulence, proposing a model that incorporates whistler-mode turbulence and thermal fluctuations. The model uses a combination of theoretical calculations and particle-in-cell simulations. A key aspect is the consideration of spontaneous thermal fluctuations alongside the background turbulence in shaping the electron distribution. The resulting distribution, determined numerically, exhibits a distinct core and halo electron population, aligning with observational data.

Barauna and collaborators introduce a method for classifying spatiotemporal patterns in complex systems using entropy measures [35]. The authors propose a parameter space based on Shannon permutation entropy and Tsallis spectral permutation entropy to distinguish between various processes. This approach shows promising results in distinguishing various classes of dynamic processes, and paves the way for further research and applications in data-driven science.

Another contribution by Eroglu et al. [36] provides a compelling quantitative analysis of the impact and influence of nonextensive statistical mechanics and the pivotal role of Constantino Tsallis in its development. The study underscores the importance of scientometric methods in understanding the dynamics of scientific knowledge dissemination, and the impact of individual researchers and their collaborations.

In the final article in this SI, the authors provide valuable insights into the statistical properties of Sicilian precipitation data, highlighting the presence of scale-invariant behavior, long-range correlations, and potential climate change impacts [37]. The application of nonextensive statistical mechanics offers a powerful tool for understanding the complexities of evolving precipitation patterns.

We hope that this volume will be of interest not only to physicists, but also to mathematicians and complex systems scientists.

Acknowledgments: I would like to sincerely express my personal gratitute to C. Tsallis for his neverending support and friendship. U.T. is a member of the Science Academy, Bilim Akademisi, Turkey.

Conflicts of Interest: The author declares no conflicts of interest.

References

1. Gibbs, J.W. *Elementary Principles in Statistical Mechanics*; Charles Scribner's Sons: New York, NY, USA, 1902.
2. Boltzmann, L. *Studien Über das Gleichgewicht der Lebendigen Kraft Zwischen bewegten Materiellen Punkten*; Aus der kaiserlich-königlichen Hof-und Staatsdruckerei: Wien, Austria, 1877.
3. Pathria, R.K.; Beale, P.D.; *Statistical Mechanics*; Elsevier: Amsterdam, The Netherlands, 2011; Volume 3.
4. Beck, C.; Schlogl, F. *Thermodynamics of Chaotic Systems*; Cambridge University Press: Cambridge, UK, 1993.
5. Wild, R.; Notzold, M.; Simpson, M.; Tran, T.D.; Wester, R. Tunnelling measured in a very slow ion-molecule reaction. *Nature* **2023**, *615*, 425. [CrossRef]
6. Beck, C.; Tsallis, C. Anomalous velocity distributions in slow quantum-tunneling chemical reactions. *arXiv* **2024**, arXiv 2411.16428.
7. Cirto, L.J.L.; Rodriguez, A.; Nobre, F.D.; Tsallis, C. Validity and failure of the Boltzmann weight. *EPL* **2018**, *123*, 30003. [CrossRef]
8. Wong, C.Y.; Wilk, G.; Cirto, L.J.L.; Tsallis, C. From QCD-based hard-scattering to nonextensive statistical mechanical descriptions of transverse momentum spectra in high-energy pp and $p\bar{p}$ collisions. *Phys. Rev. D* **2015**, *91*, 114027. [CrossRef]
9. Plastino, A.R.; Plastino, A. Non-extensive statistical mechanics and generalized Fokker-Planck equation. *Physica A* **1995**, *222*, 347. [CrossRef]
10. Tsallis, C.; Bukman, D.J. Anomalous diffusion in the presence of external forces: Exact time-dependent solutions and their thermostatistical basis. *Phys. Rev. E* **1996**, *54*, R2197. [CrossRef] [PubMed]
11. Combe, G.; Richefeu, V.; Stasiak, M.; Atman, A.P.F. Experimental validation of nonextensive scaling law in confined granular media. *Phys. Rev. Lett.* **2015**, *115*, 238301. [CrossRef] [PubMed]
12. Latora, V.; Baranger, M.; Rapisarda, A.; Tsallis, C. The rate of entropy increase at the edge of chaos. *Phys. Lett. A* **2000**, *273*, 97. [CrossRef]
13. Baldovin, B.; Robledo, A.; Nonextensive Pesin identity - Exact renormalization group analytical results for the dynamics at the edge of chaos of the logistic map. *Phys. Rev. E* **2004**, *69*, 045202(R). [CrossRef]
14. Tsallis, C. *Introduction to Nonextensive Statistical Mechanics—Approaching a Complex World*, 2nd ed.; Springer-Nature: New York, NY, USA, 2023.
15. Umarov, S.; Tsallis, C. *Mathematical Foundations of Nonextensive Statistical Mechanics*; WSPC: Singapore, 2022.
16. Tsallis, C. Possible generalization of Boltzmann-Gibbs statistics. *J. Stat. Phys.* **1988**, *52*, 479. [CrossRef]
17. Tsallis, C. Reminiscences of Half a Century of Life in the World of Theoretical Physics. *Entropy* **2024**, *26*, 158. [CrossRef] [PubMed]
18. Nelson, K.P. Open Problems within Nonextensive Statistical Mechanics. *Entropy* **2024**, *26*, 118. [CrossRef] [PubMed]
19. Kayid, M.; Alshehri, M.A. Tsallis Entropy of a Used Reliability System at the System Level. *Entropy* **2023**, *25*, 550. [CrossRef] [PubMed]
20. Monteoliva, D.; Plastino, A.; Plastino, A.R. Magic Numbers and Mixing Degree in Many-Fermion Systems. *Entropy* **2023**, *25*, 1206. [CrossRef] [PubMed]
21. Liu, Z. Effects of Nonextensive Electrons on Dust–Ion Acoustic Waves in a Collisional Dusty Plasma with Negative Ions. *Entropy* **2023**, *25*, 1363. [CrossRef] [PubMed]
22. Kose, H.Y.; Ikizoglu, S. Nonadditive Entropy Application to Detrended Force Sensor Data to Indicate Balance Disorder of Patients with Vestibular System Dysfunction. *Entropy* **2023**, *25*, 1385. [CrossRef]
23. Pasten, D.; Vogel, E.E.; Saravia, G.; Posadas, A.; Sotolongo, O. Tsallis Entropy and Mutability to Characterize Seismic Sequences: The Case of 2007–2014 Northern Chile Earthquakes. *Entropy* **2023**, *25*, 1417. [CrossRef]
24. Thankamani, P.; Sebastian, N.; Haubold, H.J. On Complex Matrix-Variate Dirichlet Averages and Its Applications in Various Sub-Domains. *Entropy* **2023**, *25*, 1534. [CrossRef] [PubMed]
25. Yang, P.P.; Liu, F.H.; Olimov, K.K. Rapidity and Energy Dependencies of Temperatures and Volume Extracted from Identified Charged Hadron Spectra in Proton–Proton Collisions at a Super Proton Synchrotron (SPS). *Entropy* **2023**, *25*, 1571. [CrossRef]
26. Shrahili, M.; Kayid, M. Some New Results Involving Past Tsallis Entropy of Order Statistics. *Entropy* **2023**, *25*, 1581. [CrossRef] [PubMed]
27. Waqas, M.; Ismail, A.H.; Alrebdi, H.I.; Ajaz, M. Centrality and System Size Dependence among Freezeout Parameters and the Implications for EOS and QGP in High-Energy Collisions. *Entropy* **2023**, *25*, 1586. [CrossRef] [PubMed]

28. Lenzi, E.K.; Zola, R.S.; Rosseto, M.P.; Mendes, R.S.; Ribeiro, H.V.; Silva, L.R.D.; Evangelista, L.R. Results for Nonlinear Diffusion Equations with Stochastic Resetting. *Entropy* **2023**, *25*, 1647. [CrossRef]
29. Lima, H.S.; Tsallis, C.; Nobre, F.D. First-Principle Validation of Fourier's Law: One-Dimensional Classical Inertial Heisenberg Model. *Entropy* **2024**, *26*, 25. [CrossRef] [PubMed]
30. Camacho-Vidales, L.J.; Robledo, A. A Nonlinear Dynamical View of Kleiber's Law on the Metabolism of Plants and Animals. *Entropy* **2024**, *26*, 32. [CrossRef] [PubMed]
31. Biró, T.S.; Telcs, A.; Jakovác, A. Analogies and Relations between Non-Additive Entropy Formulas and Gintropy. *Entropy* **2024**, *26*, 185. [CrossRef] [PubMed]
32. Jensen, H.J.; Tempesta, P. Group Structure as a Foundation for Entropies. *Entropy* **2024**, *26*, 266. [CrossRef] [PubMed]
33. Gazeau, J.P. Tsallis Distribution as a Λ-Deformation of the Maxwell–Jüttner Distribution. *Entropy* **2024**, *26*, 273. [CrossRef] [PubMed]
34. Yoon, P.H.; López, R.A.; Salem, C.S.; Bonnell, J.W.; Kim, S. Non-Thermal Solar Wind Electron Velocity Distribution Function. *Entropy* **2024**, *26*, 310. [CrossRef]
35. Barauna, L.O.; Sautter, R.A.; Rosa, R.R.; Rempel, E.L.; Frery, A.C. Characterizing Complex Spatiotemporal Patterns from Entropy Measures. *Entropy* **2024**, *26*, 508. [CrossRef] [PubMed]
36. Eroglu, D.; Boghosian, B.M.; Borges, E.P.; Tirnakli, U. The Statistics of q-Statistics. *Entropy* **2024**, *26*, 554. [CrossRef] [PubMed]
37. Pecorino, V.; Pluchino, A.; Rapisarda, A. Tsallis q-Statistics Fingerprints in Precipitation Data across Sicily. *Entropy* **2024**, *26*, 623. [CrossRef] [PubMed]

entropy

MDPI

Review

Reminiscences of Half a Century of Life in the World of Theoretical Physics

Constantino Tsallis [1,2,3,4]

[1] Centro Brasileiro de Pesquisas Físicas and National Institute of Science and Technology of Complex Systems, Rua Xavier Sigaud 150, Rio de Janeiro 22290-180, RJ, Brazil; tsallis@cbpf.br
[2] Santa Fe Institute, 1399 Hyde Park Road, Santa Fe, NM 87501, USA
[3] Complexity Science Hub Vienna, Josefstädter Strasse 39, 1080 Vienna, Austria
[4] Sistemi Complessi per le Scienze Fisiche, Socio-Economiche e della Vita, Dipartimento di Fisica e Astronomia Ettore Majorana, Università degli Studi di Catania, Via S. Sofia 64, 95123 Catania, Italy

Abstract: Selma Lagerlöf said that culture is what remains when one has forgotten everything we had learned. Without any warranty, through ongoing research tasks, that I will ever attain this high level of wisdom, I simply share here reminiscences that have played, during my life, an important role in my incursions in science, mainly in theoretical physics. I end by presenting some perspectives for future developments.

Keywords: critical phenomena; graph theory; nonlinear dynamical systems; nonadditive entropies; nonextensive statistical mechanics

Citation: Tsallis, C. Reminiscences of Half a Century of Life in the World of Theoretical Physics. *Entropy* **2024**, *26*, 158. https://doi.org/10.3390/e26020158

Academic Editor: Yong Deng

Received: 18 January 2024
Revised: 5 February 2024
Accepted: 9 February 2024
Published: 11 February 2024

Yo soy yo y mi circunstancia
[José Ortega y Gasset]

1. The Leitmotif

Let me start this narrative backwards. While trying to organize a plethora of reminiscences from my scientific life, a single aspect vividly came to my mind that percolates through it all: the intuitive or conscious search for beauty, either primordial or actual. Insistent thoughts and feelings such as "This way it is not well expressed", "It must be possible to present it, to think of it, in a more powerful, more general form", "Yes, now it is perfect, there is no way to present it or to think about it more beautifully or more simply" have been recurrent along my entire life, the *leitmotif* of my research activities. It is, almost always, through this path that I imagine—sometimes successfully—the correct scenario, the correct outcome, for a given issue. I have no doubts that such experiences are currently shared with virtually all scientists and artists. They are, in any case, shared with A. K. Rajagopal, with whom I lengthily discussed, many years ago, precisely this point.

The earliest memory that I have of some sort of conscious search for aesthetics goes back to my childhood. Every day, I used to commute between my residence and school in Mendoza, Argentina, using the tramway. Every tram ticket had a unique five-digit number. I had immense pleasure in utilizing every travel duration to play with the digits, rearranging them or performing various simple arithmetic operations so that the number would finally be written in a more beautiful manner. I would not stop until the number reappeared, in my child mind, in an *aesthetic* form.

For Plato, *Truth* and *Beauty* were two inseparable aspects of the same reality.

John Keats wrote, in 1819,
Beauty is truth, truth is beauty
that is all Ye know on earth, and all Ye need to know.

A few years later, Emily Dickinson, in her lonely style, insisted

I died for beauty, but was scarce
Adjusted in the tomb,
In an adjoining room.
He questioned softly why I failed?
"For beauty", I replied.
"And I for truth,—the two are one;
We brethren are", he said.
And so, as kinsmen met at night,
We talked between the rooms,
Until the moss had reached our lips,
And covered up our names.

The *Academy of Athens* (in Greece, just *Academy*) is not an Academy of Sciences or of Arts, it is just *The Academy*, originally founded by Plato. And, in front of it, two big columns stand up, dedicated, one of them, to Pallas Athena, the Goddess of Wisdom and Science—the utopia of which is Truth, and the other one to Apollo, the God of Art—the utopia of which is Beauty—(see Figure 1).

Figure 1. The Academy of Athens. Centered between the two columns of Pallas Athena and Apollo, we see the statues of Socrates and of his disciple Plato, the founder of the original Academy, where Aristotle studied for twenty years.

A few months ago, while lecturing in Princeton University, I had a pleasant surprise: the symbol of the celebrated Institute for Advanced Study where Einstein spent many years of his life precisely joins, hand in hand, Truth and Beauty (see Figure 2).

Figure 2. Symbol of the Institute for Advanced Study, in Princeton, New Jersey.

2. Early Years

After finishing my high-school studies, I first registered, at the National University of Cuyo, in San Juan, Argentina, on the course of Chemical Engineering at the (immature) age of 15 and, at the age of 16, I started to follow with enthusiasm the lessons in mathematics, physics and chemistry. During the first two years, the obligatory disciplines were the basic ones and I was enchanted. But, in the third year, the technological disciplines themselves started with all their weight and my interest definitively declined. Coincidentally, I heard a presentation by Alberto P. Maiztegui at the Institute of Physics Balseiro, part of the same University but located in the beautiful Bariloche. Fellowships were accessible through a national competition in Buenos Aires, one of the requirements being to have completely finished two full years of studies in exact or technological sciences. This is how I shifted from engineering to physics. I finished in 1965 and eventually moved to France, supported by a French fellowship, to take a doctorate degree (Doctorat d' État ès Sciences Physiques).

After some initial years of research in experimental physics (the construction, in 1968, at the Laboratoire de Spectroscopie Moléculaire headed by Gilbert Amat at the University of Paris in Jussieu, of a molecular laser working on the CO and CO_2 states, and, in 1969, impedance measurements of complex perovskites supervised by Claude Rocchiccioli-Deltcheff [1] at the Laboratoire de Magnétisme et Physique des Solides/Centre National de la Recherche Scientifique in Bellevue-Paris), I definitively turned the focus of my research onto theoretical physics. However, that early experience in experimental physics indelibly marked my entire understanding of science.

My first theoretical steps were taken, in the area of ferroelectricity in perovskites [2,3], with Jacques Bouillot and Roland Machet, who were starting to work at the University of Dijon, France. We three together discovered with perplexity the beauty and power of the sum rules in physics.

Those years were marked by the May 1968 student generalized movements in Paris and elsewhere. I moved to the Service de Physique du Solide et Resonance Magnétique—Commissariat à l'Énergie Atomique, in Saclay-Paris (Jacques Villain had just moved from Saclay to Grenoble and I inherited his office room). There, by meditating on the fascinating mathematical and physical mysteries of phase transitions and critical phenomena, I had the invaluable fortune to learn priceless insights from Nino Boccara and Gobalakichena Sarma.

I still remember today that one of my first personal theoretical efforts had a definitively aesthetic motivation. K. Kobayashi [4,5] had proposed an interesting model for KDP-like ferroelectric crystals. There was, however, an issue of his theory that strongly bothered me: the order parameter and the frequency of the associated soft mode did *not* vanish at the same temperature. Since, within such simple theoretical approaches, I considered the order parameter and the corresponding soft mode to be two faces of the same coin, that discrepancy appeared to me as inadmissible. I thought that the simplest and most beautiful scenario was that the two main "consequences" of the same "cause"—the thermodynamical inclination of the system to make a phase transition—emerged together, at a *single* temperature. Then, by including some specific configuration energy within Kobayashi's theory, it came out that, as desired, the order parameter and the soft mode frequency indeed vanish at precisely the *same* temperature. Satisfied with this result, I then published this, so corrected, theory [6]. The 1972 paper's Figure 1 exhibits the critical temperature as a function of a scaled molecular field Γ. This particular dependence was, some time later, experimentally confirmed at the Institute of Physics of the University of Campinas-Unicamp. Unfortunately, I have not succeeded in finding the corresponding plot but I still remember Sergio Porto showing it to me at the University of Brasilia while, smiling, he told me "You propose and Unicamp checks!" That was my first experience where some theoretical effort of mine was experimentally validated. I was fascinated by this experimental verification which, for me, was close to a miracle. Beauty was showing its power in science...

This fact was somehow consistent with the two most influential lessons—one from Guido Beck (distinguished German physicist, former assistant of Werner Heisenberg, having lived part of his life in Argentina and Brazil, where he currently taught the theory of relativity and quantum mechanics; his quantum mechanics first lesson was simply unforgettable: he entered the classroom and, to our enormous perplexity, said abruptly "Do you think that an electron is a hard black little ball? Noooo, an electron is a distribution of amplitudes of probabilities!"), at the time I was his student at the Balseiro Institute of Physics in Bariloche, Argentina, and the other one from Pierre-Gilles de Gennes (French physicist, 1991 Nobel laureate in Physics), when I was following, at Orsay-Paris, his regular course on Solid State Physics—that I was fortunate to receive during my student times, before my initiation as a researcher.

Guido Beck was teaching us some simple features about the real and imaginary parts of some basic dissipative coefficient, and, in the middle of long mathematical calculations, a zero emerged. At this point he said "Because of this zero, if you put your finger into shoe polish, when you get your finger out, *the hole remains*". Indeed, if you put your finger into water, the hole then disappears! That was like a sudden flash of lightening in my mind: *the good mathematical theory ought to reflect the empirical fact!* The protagonists of Raffaello Sanzio's *School of Athens* in the Vatican are Plato and Aristotle. Plato point to the heavens (*topos Uranos*), in contrast to Aristotle who points towards the ground (*topos Physis*). In their search for truth, they were both right: the theoretical truth must correspond to the empirical truth, two faces of the same coin! The perfect balance between Poetry and History. From Aristotle's thoughts: *Poetry is more philosophical and more elevated than history; for poetry expresses the universal, and history only the particular. History tells us the events as they happened, whereas poetry tells them as they could or should have happened.* ("Elevated" is to be understood here as closer to "philosophy", which occupies, in the Aristotelian thinking, the highest place in the hierarchy of the forms of knowledge.)

In a different realm, in his teaching, Pierre-Gilles de Gennes solved concrete physical problems by using generic intuitive and scaling arguments. So, in a few minutes, he would find the correct answer (excepting perhaps for a pure number of the order of unity). At home, after many-hour calculations, we students verified systematically that his answer indeed was the correct one! This opened in my mind a completely new perspective: *It is possible to find the correct theoretical description and understanding without doing tedious mathematical calculations, just by focusing on what is a must, or nearly so, for that specific physical problem!* (It is within this respect that *abduction*, the Charles Sanders Peirce favorite form of logical inference, plays its central role, the one which enables Sherlock Holmes to identify the murderer, through the "relevant details"!).

Bond percolation is an interesting geometrical critical phenomenon based on *independent bond-occupancy probabilities* on a given structure, e.g., a square lattice. If we have a *series* array of two bonds whose occupancy probabilities are p_1 and p_2, the overall occupancy probability is given by

$$p_s = p_1 p_2 \,, \tag{1}$$

where s stands for *series*. If the array is a *parallel* one, then the overall occupancy probability is given by

$$p_p = p_1 p_2 + p_1(1-p_2) + p_2(1-p_1) = p_1 + p_2 - p_1 p_2 \,, \tag{2}$$

where p stands for *parallel*. But, already at this elementary stage, aesthetics may come in! We may say that Equation (2) is *not* written in a beautiful manner. Indeed, it can be rewritten in a much more elegant way, namely

$$1 - p_p = (1-p_1)(1-p_2) \,. \tag{3}$$

Now, all variables are written in *one and the same form*. On top of this, Equation (3) trivially transforms the parallel composition into the *same form* as the series one. This leads us naturally to a deep transformation which we will name *duality*, i.e., $p \leftrightarrow (1-p)$. It is from these very elementary seeds that a powerful graph calculation algorithm, currently referred to in the literature as the *Break-Collapse Method*, was developed, valid for a model, namely the q_P-state Potts model (where P stands here for *Potts*). This model is sensibly more general than bond percolation, which is therein recovered as the particular case $q_P = 1$. A very elegant method was born and an important unification was achieved based on the above very simple considerations [7,8]. Incidentally, a very useful variable currently referred to as *thermal transmissivity* t was concomitantly introduced (it was Robin B. Stinchcombe, during a car ride in Rio de Janeiro, who helped me, with his beautiful Oxford English, to decide whether to call it *transmissivity* or *transmittivity*); this variable precisely becomes the above bond occupancy probability p when $q_P = 1$ (I once had an unforgettable conversation with my friend and outstanding statistical mechanicist Antonio Coniglio: with his *red bonds*, he had arrived at essentially the same understanding of this beautiful geometrical–thermal problem). The square lattice is a self-dual (infinite) graph in the sense that, if we cut each of its bonds by one and only one dual bond, we recover once again the square lattice. Because of this crucial topological property, its bond-percolation critical point p_c must satisfy $p_c = 1 - p_c$; hence, $p_c = \frac{1}{2}$ (see [9,10]). Along totally analogous lines, it can be shown that the critical thermal transmissivity t_c of the square-lattice q_P-state Potts ferromagnet is given by $t_c = \frac{1}{1+\sqrt{q_P}}$. I then introduced a convenient new variable, namely

$$s \equiv \frac{\ln[1 + (q_P - 1)t]}{\ln q_P} \tag{4}$$

It is straightforward to verify that the duality (i.e., series–parallel) transformation now becomes $s \leftrightarrow (1-s)$, *one and the same for all values of* q_P! Consequently, the square-lattice critical point is given by $s_c = \frac{1}{2}$ ($\forall q_P$) and the q_P-state Potts ferromagnetic model becomes, in this sense, collapsed in the bond percolation model, *for all values of* q_P. I believe that this simplicity illustrates well what makes the beauty of unification!

Notice, by the way, that definition (4) satisfies, in the $q_P \to 1$ limit,

$$s \sim \frac{\ln[1 + (q_P - 1)t]}{q_P - 1} \sim t \,. \tag{5}$$

Amazingly enough, we shall later on see [11] that this transformation is precisely the one which, through $(q_P - 1) \leftrightarrow (1-q)$, connects the Rényi entropic functional S_q^R (R standing for *Rényi*) and the nonadditive entropic functional S_q, which will play a major role in generalizing the Boltzmann–Gibbs statistical mechanics; s plays here the role of S_q^R and t that of S_q, the $q_P \to 1$ (hence $q \to 1$) limit corresponding to the Boltzmann–Gibbs entropic functional S_{BG} (Per Bak, the "father" of the concept of *self-organized criticality*, once shared with me a curious statement, "Every man has only one idea in his life; if he has many, he has none". Many years later, at the Santa Fe Institute, NM, the Nobel laureate Murray Gell-Mann and I lengthily discussed, just for pleasure, this point: he disagreed with Bak's statement, whereas I was inclined to agree with it).

Diverse real-space renormalization groups and other theoretical techniques were implemented on the Potts-model above grounds. This perspective enabled many doctoral theses to be worked out as well as several papers to be published. Also, basically due to these developments in theoretical physics, I had in 1982 the good fortune to become a Fellow of the John Simon Guggenheim Foundation (USA), which allowed me to have enriching post doc periods at Oxford, Boston and Cornell Universities.

The unification implied in any generalization always involves some form of simple beauty. Indeed, within a generalization, diverse physical situations emerge as particular instances of a more powerful, more "universal", theory, a sort of metaphor.

It is a memory of this kind which points to the calculation that Anibal Omar Caride and myself performed in 1984 [12]. It concerned the quantum specific heat of an anisotropic rigid rotor whose inertial tensor has a revolution symmetry. This approach unified three different symmetries, namely the spherical, oblate ("flying disk" like) and prolate ("cigar" like) ones. The quantum nature of the problem ensures that the various rotational degrees of freedom are activated at possibly different temperatures T. In the extreme prolate case, rotations around the symmetry axis might be frozen until very high temperatures are achieved, due to its nearly vanishing moment of inertia I. Indeed, in such a case, the first excited state of rotation around that axis becomes thermally activated only at extremely high temperatures. This yields a nonuniform convergence related to the *ordering* of $T \to \infty$ and $I \to 0$. This fact elegantly clarifies the perplexity felt by Josiah Willard Gibbs concerning the specific heat of diatomic molecules calculated, naturally in his time, on *classical* grounds: quantum mechanics did not even exist! To be more precise, in the Preface of his celebrated 1902 book [13], he writes: *Even if we confine our attention to the phenomena distinctively thermodynamic, we do not escape difficulties in as simple a matter as the number of degrees of freedom of a diatomic gas. It is well known that while theory would assign to the gas six degrees of freedom per molecule, in our experiments on specific heat we cannot account for more than five. Certainly, one is building on an insecure foundation, who rests his work on hypotheses concerning the constitution of matter. Difficulties of this kind have deterred the author from attempting to explain the mysteries of nature...*

Another memory along similar lines refers to the 1987 discussion by Maria da Conceição de Sousa Vieira and myself focusing on the thermal equilibrium of a D-dimensional ideal gas in Gentile parastatistics [14]. Each parastatistics is characterized by the *maximal allowed number* p_G of particles per state (G stands for *Gentile*); hence, $p_G = 1$ and $p_G \to \infty$, respectively, recover Fermi–Dirac (FD) and Bose–Einstein (BE) statistics; in the BE case, a finite-temperature macroscopic condensation on the ground state occurs at a sufficiently high dimension D, whereas no such phenomenon is possible for the FD case. The central issue of that paper concerns whether such macroscopic condensation is or is not possible for $1 < p_G < \infty$. The answer is that *it is not*. This strong result is once again related to an elegant nonuniform convergence, this time involving the ordering of the $p_G \to \infty$ and the chemical potential $\mu \to 0$ limits. An analysis of this result on aesthetical grounds is available in [15].

3. Nonadditive-Entropy Years

As a consequence of the French–Brazilian *Colloquium on Phase Transitions (Critical Phenomena)* that I organized in November 1981 in Rio de Janeiro, a French–Mexican–Brazilian similar event, the *First Workshop on Statistical Mechanics*, was held in September 1985 in Mexico City. France provided important financial support. The French delegation was led by Édouard Brézin and the Brazilian one by myself. During a morning coffee break, while the participants were outside chatting, I remained resting inside the lecture room. Brézin was at the blackboard with a Mexican student whose name I do not remember. Their conversation was about something related to multifractals. I could not hear them because of the distance, but I could see that Brézin was writing on the blackboard various expressions containing p^q, well known to naturally appear in the theory of multifractals. Then, it suddenly came to my mind that it would be possible with p^q to generalize Boltzmann entropy and therefore the entire standard statistical mechanics. Back home, I simply wrote down the expression of the following entropic functional:

$$S_q = k\frac{1 - \sum_{i=1}^{W} p_i^q}{q-1} \quad (q \in [-\infty, \infty])\,. \tag{6}$$

If this expression, which trivially contains the Bolzmann–Gibbs–von Neumann–Shannon functional $S_{BG} = -k\sum_{i=1}^{W} p_i \ln p_i$ as the $q \to 1$ instance, was adopted as a postulate, then *it would be possible to generalize the entire BG statistical mechanics* [13,16–19]! (Years later, I gradually learnt from Silvio R.A. Salinas, Richard N. Silver and others that similar entropic functionals had previously been advanced in the literature of cybernetics and related mathematical formalisms. But, seemingly, no one ever addressed the possibility of generalizing, on such grounds, the entire BG theory itself. Historical details can be found in [20] and references therein.) During three years I did not feel like publishing anything along this line because I had no clarity about what could be the physical interpretation of S_q. Obviously, ideas related to hierarchical space–time structures were lurking. Also, for whatever reason, the thought emerged insistently that a small probability p_i $(0 < p_i \ll 1)$ may be considerably magnified through the *biased* probability p_i^q (more precisely, $p_i^q / \sum_{j=1}^{W} p_j^q$) if $q < 1$, i.e., basically, $(0.01)^{1/2} = 0.1 \gg 0.01$. The image that appeared in my mind was the calm and gigantic vortices that I had seen in the bottom of the river at the fascinatingly hectic Iguaçu Falls: zillions of water molecules slowly turning around, just one after the other. An astronomically low a priori probability, stable and peaceful, quasi-stationary state in the middle of Hesiodic Chaos! (In fact, many years later, various connections of turbulent systems did appear with theoretical approaches involving $q \neq 1$, e.g., [21–23]).

Time goes by and, in 1987, Enaldo F. Sarmento, myself and a few other colleagues met, for a few days (*Encontro de Trabalho sobre Autômatas Celulares*, 24 to 28 August 1987, Maceió, Alagoas), at the Federal University of Alagoas in Maceió with the purpose of launching in Brazil the area of cellular automata. During a free-time period, on a blackboard, I presented the entropy S_q to Hans J. Herrmann and Evaldo M. F. Curado, and we searched, without particular success, for possible physical applications. Next day, there were too many mosquitoes in the hotel where I was sleeping and I decided to go back to Rio de Janeiro. During the air flight I optimized the functional S_q with the standard norm and energy constraints, and I found the now well-known q-exponential distribution. I was delighted by the fact that this distribution unified exponential, asymptotic power-law and cut-off behaviors, depending on whether $q = 1$, $q > 1$ or $q < 1$.

Some time later on, virtually all the best statistical physicists of Brazil happened to be in my office at CBPF to discuss the organizational issues of the upcoming IUPAP Statphys 17 meeting to be held in 1989 in Rio de Janeiro. At the end of our discussion, I briefly presented to them, on the blackboard, the main lines of the S_q proposal, and asked them whether it would be worthy or not to make this proposal in a standard international journal. The unanimous opinion was favorable to submitting it outside Brazil. I still remember the words of Silvio R. A. Salinas, at the time Chief Editor of the Brazilian Journal of Physics (BJP): "I would send it to a good journal outside Brazil, but if you want to submit it to BJP, it is already accepted!".

I first wrote a Centro Brasileiro de Pesquisas Físicas preprint (*Notas de Física CBPF-NF-062/87*), published in 1987. Eventually, I submitted the manuscript to the *Journal of Statistical Physics* [11] (this paper is, at the date I write these lines, the most cited one in the entire life of the journal, born in 1969, with 7164 citations at the Web of Science (All Databases), the second one, with 2715 citations, being the well-known 1978 article by Mitchell J. Feigenbaum, in **19**, 25–52), at the time edited by Joel L. Lebowitz. The submission letter, sent on my birthday, 5 November 1987, included the lines "Well, the last few months I have been working in a 'crazy' idea: a possible generalization of Boltzmann–Gibbs statistics! [. . .]. I did not succeed in finding a direct and useful application to an already known system. Nevertheless, the generalization has—at least to my eyes!—an internal elegance, which, I think, makes it worthy to be published: maybe somebody else will find the desired applications!". As far as I can tell, the manuscript was sent to two reviewers and neither of them showed any enthusiasm. The first reviewer wrote "Although the ideas of this paper are not tremendously new, I recommend publication in the Journal of Statistical Physics". The second reviewer appreciated the content of the paper even less. The report is here reproduced in Figure 3. It seemingly confuses S_q with Rényi's entropic functional $\bar{S}_q$ (independently rediscovered in Equation (8) of the 1988 paper), and ends with "I don't believe that what appears here demonstrates that this generalized canonical ensemble is of any significance for statistical physics. Thus I don't believe this manuscript should be accepted for publication in J. S. P.". The editor, Lebowitz, sent to me these two reports on 14 January 1988. He wrote "My suggestion would be that you certainly include references to the Renyi entropy. I really do not know any offhand, but I certainly have seen it in the literature. I particularly remember seeing it mentioned in papers by Hao Bai-lin, but I believe that you will have any trouble finding it. Given that, you may want to shorten the paper and emphasize point D. I will be happy to go along with publication after I get your revised and shortened version". I submitted my revised version on 28 January 1988 (misprinted as 1987): see Figure 4. The editor, Lebowitz, formally accepted its publication on 15 March 1988 and it was published in July 1988 (the differences between the original and the revised versions are the following ones: (1) after further discussions, "I am very indebted to E.M.F. Curado and H.J. Herrmann for very stimulating discussions" (in the 1987 version) became "I am very indebted to E.M.F. Curado, H.J. Herrmann, R. Maynard and A. Coniglio for very stimulating discussions" (in the 1988 version); (2) for reasons that are not present in my memory any more and in surprising contrast with what I practice in virtually all my publications, "We postulate for the entropy. . ." (in the 1987 version) became "I postulate for the entropy. . ." (in the 1988 version); (3) after learning of the existence of the Rényi entropy, I added (in the 1988 version) "For arbitrary q, $\bar{S}_q$ reproduces the Renyi entropy. [(2)]" and consistently added the reference 2. A. Rényi, *Probability Theory*, (North Holland, 1970)"), three years after I started thinking about such a generalization of the celebrated centennial BG theory.

A few months later I was scheduled to deliver an invited talk at the *International Workshop on Fractals* organized by Luciano Pietronero and held during 10–15 October 1988 in Erice, Italy. Renowned scientists were also present, such as Michael E. Fisher, Benoit Mandelbrot and Shlomo Alexander, among others. I asked Pietronero whether I could talk for a few minutes on a topic that was not in my initial Abstract. He told me to feel free to use my time as I preferred. I then briefly presented the content of my 1988 paper during the last 10 min of my talk. Mandelbrot was ostensively showing his disapproval by negatively moving his head just in front of me. At the coffee break I approached him and gave a reprint of my article which had just arrived in my hands, while telling him "This is what I talked about". He took the reprint and, in front of me, went directly to the references to check whether his name was there. As he did not find it, he gave me, on the spot, the reprint back and told me "*Tout ceci a été fait il y a bien longtemps*" (all this has been carried out a long time ago). It can be trivially checked that his discouraging statement was completely gratuitous. At the end of the meeting there was a collective appreciation of what the audience had liked the most. Hans J. Herrmann said "The last 10 min of Constantino".

REPORT ON "POSSIBLE GENERALIZATION OF BOLTZMANN-GIBBS STATISTICS" BY C. TSALLIS (JSP 87-267).

THIS PAPER DEFINES A GENERALIZED ENTROPY, $S_q \equiv k[1-\sum_i p_i^q]/(q-1)$ (WHERE THE p_i's ARE PROBABILITIES) AND THEN DISCUSSES SUCH ISSUES AS

(A) $\lim_{q\to 1} S_q \equiv S_1$ = USUAL ENTROPY $\equiv -k\sum p_i \ln p_i$

(B) S_q IS EXTREMIZED (SUBJECT TO $\sum p_i = 1$) FOR EQUIPROBABILITY

(C) CONVEXITY/CONCAVITY PROPERTIES OF $S_q(\{p_i\})$

(D) HOW TO EXTREMIZE S_q SUBJECT TO $\sum p_i = 1$ AND $\sum p_i \epsilon_i = U_q$ ("GENERALIZATION OF CANONICAL ENSEMBLE")

THE AUTHOR SEEMS UNAWARE THAT THIS S_q IS ALREADY KNOWN WITHIN THE INFORMATION/PROBABILITY THEORY LITERATURE. I BELIEVE IT'S OFTEN REFERRED TO AS "RENYI INFORMATION" SINCE IT WAS INTRODUCED BY RENYI MANY YEARS AGO. I AM SURE THAT ITEMS (A), (B) AND (C) ARE ALREADY KNOWN IN THE LITERATURE. I ALSO SUSPECT THAT ITEM (D) IS KNOWN, BUT I AM LESS CONFIDENT ABOUT THIS. EVEN IF IT ISN'T KNOWN, I DON'T BELIEVE THAT WHAT APPEARS HERE DEMONSTRATES THAT THIS GENERALIZED CANONICAL ENSEMBLE IS OF ANY SIGNIFICANCE FOR STATISTICAL PHYSICS. THUS I DON'T BELIEVE THIS MANUSCRIPT SHOULD BE ACCEPTED FOR PUBLICATION IN J.S.P.

Figure 3. Report of the second reviewer of [11].

CNPq
CONSELHO NACIONAL
DE DESENVOLVIMENTO
CIENTIFICO E TECNOLOGICO

Rio de Janeiro, January 28, 1987

Prof. Joel L. Lebowitz
Journal of Statistical Physics
Department of Mathematics
Rutgers University
New Brunswick, NJ 08903 USA

Ref.: JSP 87-267

Dear Joel,

Thank you for your letter of 14 January 1988 including two reports on my manuscript "Possible generalization...".

Indeed my $\bar{S}_q$ (not my Sq) essentially reproduces Renyi entropy, a fact which is now duly inserted in the new version. Consistently the first part of the paper has been shortened. However, the use Renyi does of his entropy is completely different from mine. In particular, the discussion I present for the Canonical Ensemble follows a path very different from those followed in his important works. To be more concrete, I found nowhere in his (or subsequent) works the central result of the present manuscript, namely distribution of Eq.(11) and related properties. In addition to that, Renyi is essentially concerned with $q>0$, whereas in the present manuscript I discuss $q \gtrless 0$ (as commonly done nowadays in multifractal research).

I thank you and one of the referees for stressing my attention onto Renyi entropy. I hope the revised version herein enclosed (3 copies) is suitable for your further consideration. Thanks again for your kind attention.

With warm wishes for a happy 1988,

Sincerely Yours,

Constantino

Constantino Tsallis

CBPF - CENTRO BRASILEIRO DE PESQUISAS FISICAS

Figure 4. Submission of my revised version (the correct date is 28 January 1988, not 1987).

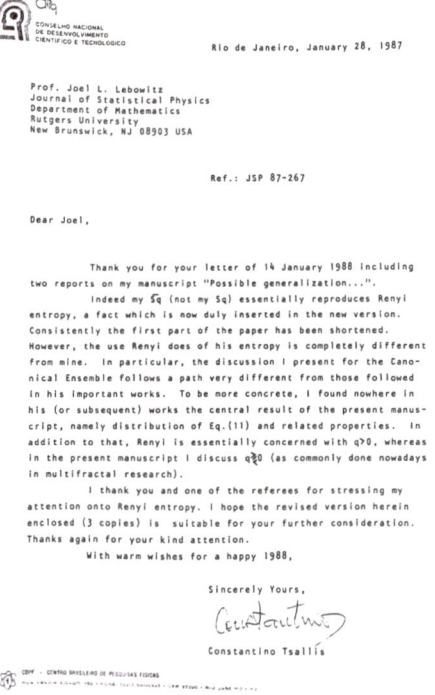

On 18 November 1988, S. Alexander sent to me from the University of California, Los Angeles, a long letter with his opinion on my Erice presentation. He included therein: "You presented it as a new path in statistical physics—in my view without any justification. My guess would be that the chances that this will prove useful are about equal to those of other attempts to violate the second law of thermodynamics—or generalize it. If I prove wrong I will concede that this is the greatest contribution to physics since Einstein".

The next relevant step of q-statistics was performed thanks to Evaldo M.F. Curado: the article [24] established the first connection with thermodynamics through a q-generalized partition function and consistently generalized the third axiom of the celebrated Shannon theorem. (A rather funny incident occurred with this paper. We had used in it the word "holistic" in a sort of intuition that this theory, one day maybe, could be useful for globally correlated systems, a well-established fact nowadays. One of the reviewers strongly criticized the inclusion of that word (which was "esoteric" in his/her understanding) in a scientific paper. We did not agree with him/her, especially because in Greek this word is simply a sort of antonym of "atomistic". But, to avoid an irrelevant controversy, we eliminated the word from our revised text. It was with amused surprise that we discovered, several months later, that the word reappeared in the published version, most probably due to some mild inadvertence at the production level of the journal!)

Then, in 1993, a long-awaited result appeared. Angel R. Plastino and his father, A. Plastino, published [25] the first application to a physical system, namely the stellar polytropes, introduced by Lord Kelvin in 1862. It was since long known that the extremization of the entropic functional S_{BG} leads to a distribution which is characterized by an *infinite* total mass. This unphysical result disappears when it is S_q which is extremized with q sensibly differing from unity. A. Plastino's genuine interest in S_q started during a long and relaxed conversation he and I had at the hotel swimming pool in San Juan, Puerto Rico, during the XVI International Workshop on Condensed-Matter Theories (1 to 5 June 1992). The Plastinos' paper became accessible to me and Roger Maynard during the International Workshop on Nonlinear Phenomena, held during 7 to 9 December 1992 in Florianopolis, Brazil. During three or four hours, we peripatetically discussed it trying to understand why S_q does the correct job where S_{BG} fails. We concluded that it was due to the fact that gravitation is a *long-range* interaction. The door was open.

A couple of years later, on 4 April 1995, I delivered a talk at the Physics Department of the Boston University at the invitation of Harry Eugene Stanley. Bruce M. Boghosian was in the audience. Soon after, he produced a new bridge with a concrete physical system [26]: a non-neutral electronic plasma, where the Coulombian interactions play a role similar to the gravitational ones in stellar polytropes. Boghosian showed that the empirical distribution emerging in two-dimensional turbulence in a pure-electron plasma column precisely corresponds to $q = 1/2$.

Concomitantly with the worldwide spread of scientific articles focusing on diverse aspects of q-statistics (at the date I am writing these lines, they surpass 10,000 articles authored by nearly 17,000 scientists from 112 countries, as they appear in the Bibliography at [27]), a wave of some opponents grew up around the world. Among them, it is possible to distinguish Joel L. Lebowitz—ironically enough, precisely the *Journal of Statistical Physics* Editor who accepted my 1988 paper for publishing, Itamar Procaccia—who, in March 2002, declared without any justification, to a Brazilian newspaper that all this was nothing but "mindless fitting", Roger Balian—who was very fundamentally critical (Balian sent, nearly 25 years ago, a private letter to A.K. Rajagopal criticizing q-statistics and telling him that, in the 1978 Balian–Balazs paper, it was proved that basically no other statistical mechanics was possible outside the BG one; Rajagopal and Sumiyoshi Abe studied carefully the Balian–Balazs 48-page paper and then published, in [28], their mathematically consistent q-generalization of it; they naturally quoted the Balian–Balazs paper and sent to Balian their recently published paper together with a letter thanking his indication of the 1978 Balian–Balazs paper and its content; as far as I know, they never received an answer back from Balian) but declined the formal invitation from the President of the *Société*

Française de Physique (SFP) to have, in Paris, a free public debate with me, organized by the SFP itself (some time after Balian's declination, his own laboratory at L'Orme des Mérisiers, Commissariat à l'Énergie Atomique, France, invited me to deliver a seminar on 9 March 2009 on nonadditive entropies and the associated statistical mechanics; while the loudspeakers were announcing the beginning of the seminar, Balian was at his office, 5–6 m away from the seminar room, but he did not show; I cannot say that his attitude was a surprise to me; in contrast, the audience was quite interested and asking many questions, very especially Serge Aubry, who openly manifested his appreciation of the theory and its physical consequences), Michael Nauenberg—whom I invited, with all traveling and hosting expenses covered, to freely present his objections at the International Summer School and Workshop on "Complex Systems—Nonextensive Statistical Mechanics", held during 30 July to 8 August 2006, in Trieste, Italy, sponsored by the International Centre for Theoretical Physics/ICTP Director Katepalli R. Sreenivasan (free time was given to Nauenberg to publicly present his viewpoints and criticism, and possibly hear some of the dozens of talks by all kinds of speakers focusing on q-statistics: he went to none), Peter Grassberger—who, both in private and publicly, confused S_q with Renyi's entropy in spite of the fact that the intervals of q for which these two entropic functionals are concave considerably differ, and a few others. With quite rare exceptions, such claims are not accompanied by concrete technical papers, which could in principle be answered/rebutted through other technical papers. This hardly constitutes a surprise: opinative claims are always by far easier than rigorously founded ones. This is but the old Greek distinction between *doxa* and *episteme*!

A contrasting and interesting case is that of Joseph I. Kapusta. On 19 May 2021, Kapusta delivered an online talk within the Theoretical Physics Colloquium series that Igor Shovkovy was hosting at the Arizona State University (ASU), USA. His talk was titled "A Primer on Tsallis Statistics for Nuclear and Particle Physics". It started with a pedagogical introductory attempt and ended with skeptical comments about the q-generalized statistical mechanics being useful for discussing physical phenomena. I discovered, on the internet, the existence of Kapusta's talk many months after it was delivered. I had plenty of reasons to disagree with him, and therefore I suggested to Shovkovy that he organized at ASU a in-person or online open debate with Kapusta, or at least a seminar by myself focusing on the points that Kapusta had criticized in his seminar. Shovkovy showed no special interest in organizing such (reciprocal) activity, so I decided to rebut, on general grounds, Kapusta's views in an online seminar of mine at the Santa Fe Institute, New Mexico, which was delivered on 12 April 2022 [29]. The whole issue is focused on in an article of mine titled *Enthusiasm and skepticism: Two pillars of science—A nonextensive statistics case* [30].

As it happens, we may also identify scientists who have expressed diametrically opposite opinions. These include Murray Gell-Mann—1969 Nobel laureate, who, after hearing my talk at the IIIrd Gordon Research Conference on "Modern Developments in Thermodynamics", 18 to 23 April 1999 in Il Ciocco-Barga, Italy, stood up from his seat and came to the front of the auditorium exclaiming "Wonderful, absolutely wonderful!", Pierre-Gilles de Gennes—1991 Nobel laureate, who, after a 40 min conversation during the International Conference on "Scaling Concepts and Complex Fluids", 4 to 8 July 1994 in Catanzaro, Italy, shared with me that "a nonadditive entropy seems to me quite natural for gravitational systems.", László Tisza—who kindly signed for me a copy of his book "Generalized Thermodynamics" [31] with the words "With best wishes to Constantino Tsallis for his bold enterprise to generalize Generalized Thermodynamics on a broad front. Laszlo Tisza. 8 April 1995" (I was introduced to László Tisza—highly esteemed, by the way, by Murray Gell-Mann, who considered him a top master in thermodynamics—by Gene Stanley, who invited him to his Boston University office in 1995 to introduce us to each other; on that occasion, Tisza was nearly 90 years old and we had a lengthy and delightful conversation; at the end, Tisza told me "How cute! I stopped working in statistical mechanics because I did not know which way to go. And, certainly, I never thought about generalizing entropy."), Leo P. Kadanoff—who, after hearing the seminar that I delivered on

4 May 2005 at the University of Chicago at his invitation, told me, while going for dinner, "Everything that you said seems to me quite natural and not controversial at all.", Athanassios S. Fokas—who, at the end of the talk that, through his invitation, I delivered on 15 November 2012 at the Department of Applied Mathematics and Theoretical Physics, Cambridge University, England, loudly exclaimed "Unbelievable, unbelievable!", Ezequiel G. D. "Eddie" Cohen—who emphatically included q-statistics in his Boltzmann Medal reception lecture in Statphys 22/IUPAP, during 4 to 9 July 2004 in Bangalore, India [32], see Figure 5, George Contopoulos—who, on two different occasions, invited me to become a full member of the Academy of Athens; since I could not accept this tempting position because I would be unable to stay long enough per year in Greece due to my family in Rio de Janeiro, he eventually honored me, as President of the Academy of Athens, with its highest distinction, namely the *Aristion* (Excellence), Michel J. L. Baranger—who, during a workshop at the New England Complex Systems Institute in the 1990s, after we lengthily discussed nonlinear dynamical consequences of S_q, told me "I learnt something about physics today. It does not happen often to me." [33], Bruce B. Boghosian—who, walking around within MIT, told me "General Relativity became possible through Riemannian geometry, which violates Euclid's 5th postulate. You generalized the BG theory by violating the additivity of the usual entropic functional. It is but a neat illustration of Kuhn's *Structure of Scientific Revolutions*" [34], Peter T. Landsberg—who once told me, walking around the São Conrado beach in Rio de Janeiro, "In the first pages of all books on thermodynamics it should be written that the content is valid only for short-range interactions, but it is not" and, smiling, he added "In mine it is.", Roger Maynard, Christian Beck, Hans J. Haubold, J. Doyne Farmer, Shun'ichi Amari, Alan R. Bishop, H. Eugene "Gene" Stanley, Thomas A. "Tom" Kaplan, Grzegorz Wilk, Tamás S. Biró, Gergely G. Barnaföldi, Jan Naudts, Stefan Thurner, Rudolf Hanel, Andrea Rapisarda, Alessandro Pluchino, Alberto Robledo, Renio S. Mendes, Ugur Tirnakli, Sabir Umarov, Giorgio Benedek, Guiomar Ruiz, Antonio Rodriguez, Piergiulio Tempesta and definitively many others.

The whole situation might be accurately described through the acute Gregoire Nicolis and David Daems' words [35] "*It is the strange privilege of statistical mechanics to stimulate and nourish passionate discussions related to its foundations, particularly in connection with irreversibility. Ever since the time of Boltzmann it has been customary to see the scientific community vacillating between extreme, mutually contradicting positions.*".

It could even be described through Niccolò Machiavelli's words: see Figure 6.

PRAMANA — journal of physics | © Indian Academy of Sciences | Vol. 64, No. 5 May 2005 pp. 635–643

Boltzmann and Einstein: Statistics and dynamics – An unsolved problem

E G D COHEN
The Rockefeller University, 1230 York Avenue, New York, NY 10021, USA
E-mail: egdc@rockefeller.edu

1. **Boltzmann's struggle**
2. **Einstein**
3. **Tsallis**
4. **Superstatistics [23]**

Will the essence of the present molecular theory, in spite of all amplifications and modifications, yet remain, or will one day an atomism totally different from the present prevail. . . . (Or, I could add, will entropy and statistics continue to play their present dominant role or will dynamics become more essential for the description of the properties of macroscopic systems?)" Boltzmann concludes his lecture by: "Indeed interesting questions! One almost regrets to have to die long before they are settled.

O! immodest mortal! Your fate is the joy of watching the ever-shifting battle!" (not to see its outcome).

Figure 5. Basic content of Ezequiel G. D. "Eddie" Cohen's Boltzmann Medal reception lecture in Statphys 22/IUPAP, held during 4 to 9 July 2004 in Bangalore, India. The red underlines are mine.

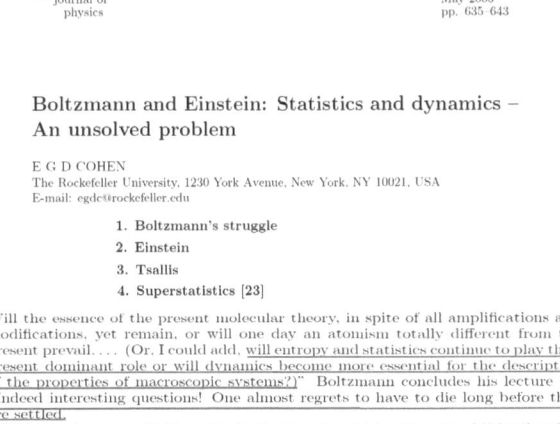

E debbasi considerare come non è cosa più difficile a trattare, né più dubia a riuscire, né più pericolosa a maneggiare, che farsi capo ad introdurre nuovi ordini. Perché lo introduttore ha per nimici tutti quelli che delli ordini vecchi fanno bene, et ha tepidi defensori tutti quelli che delli ordini nuovi farebbono bene. La quale tepidezza nasce, parte per paura delli avversarii, che hanno le leggi dal canto loro, parte dalla incredulità delli uomini; li quali non credano in verità le cose nuove, se non ne veggono nata una ferma esperienza.

Niccolò Machiavelli (1469-1527)

Il Principe (Capitolo VI)

We must consider that nothing is harder to implement, of more uncertain success, nor more dangerous to deal with, than to initiate a new order of things. Because the one who introduces the novelties finds enemies in all those who profit from the old order and tepid defenders in all those who would profit from the new order. This tepidity comes in part from their fear of their adversaries, who have the laws on their side, and in part from the incredulity of people, who do not really believe in new things until they have solid experience of them.

(Translation: C. Tsallis and M. Gell-Mann)

Figure 6. Text from Nicolas Machiavelli (translated into English by M. Gell-Mann and myself during a pleasant afternoon at the Santa Fe Institute, New Mexico).

4. Perspectives

I was chatting one day at tea time with Gell-Mann at the Santa Fe Institute (see Figure 7) and he shared with me that he was traveling to California to deliver a talk on the *Laws of creativity*. I inquired: *Oh, how interesting! Tell me about these laws.* He continued: *The first of them is: If you have good reasons to believe in something, you must believe in all of its consequences, no matter how strange or foolish these consequences might a priori seem to you! If you believe that the molecules of the air of this room are in Brownian motion, you must believe that they are all the time hitting in the cheeks of your face as well!* I would say that this "law" is true more generally than just for physical phenomena. Reviewers of my 1988 manuscript were skeptical about the validity or usefulness of a nonadditive entropy in physics. After four decades of all kinds of applications, and of experimental and analytical validations in both inanimate and living matter (my friend and distinguished chemist Ricardo de Carvalho Ferreira, whose name is for ever linked to the asteroid 158520 (2002 FR1), generously told me once "You did for living matter what Boltzmann did for inanimate matter"; a similar view was kindly expressed to me by Aneta Stefanovska during the Medyfinol 2012 meeting in Santiago de Chile; she then invited me to publish a paper in Contemporary Physics, which was indeed implemented [36]; living matter frequently involves complex stationary or quasi-stationary states; what is currently referred to as *thermal equilibrium*, quite frequent in inanimate matter, may be seen as a particular case of stationary state; see also [37]), it is definitively allowed to think that those JSP reviewers were wrong, and so were, at least in their initial thoughts, Mandelbrot and Alexander and various others. At variance, Herrmann, Curado, Plastino Sr. and Plastino Jr., Boghosian, Beck, Gell-Mann, de Gennes, Tisza, Cohen, Landsberg, Kadanoff, Maynard, Haubold, Tirnakli, Nobre, Borges, Deppman and many others, were right!

After all, $S_{BG}(A+B)$ is symmetric (with regard to $A \leftrightarrow B$) and, for independent A and B, it is *additive* [38] in $S_{BG}(A)$ and $S_{BG}(B)$. S_q is symmetric and *multilinear* (the importance of a strategic multilinearity property was emphasized to me, four or five decades ago, by Carlos Guido Bollini during a quick chat at CBPF) in $S_q(A)$ and $S_q(B)$ (trivial consequences of the specific p_i^q-dependence postulated in definition (6)). Just a "small" logical step further! But so amazingly powerful!

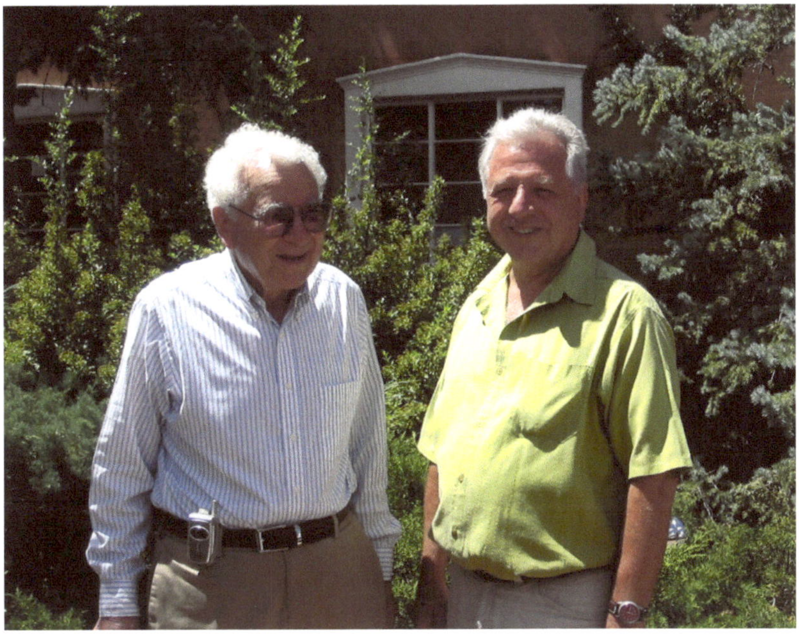

Figure 7. With M. Gell-Mann at the Santa Fe Institute, New Mexico (2005).

This is perhaps not the appropriate place for registering the many (impressive) validations of the present thermostatistical theory that are available in the literature: they can be found in [20,39–41], for instance. But it might be appropriate to mention at this point a few illustrative ongoing issues.

(i) Long-range-interacting many-body Hamiltonian systems undoubtedly need to be revisited. Let us focus on d-dimensional classical systems with two-body attractive power-law interactions whose potential decays with distance r like $1/r^{\alpha}$, where $\alpha \geq 0$. I initially thought, for many years, that $0 \leq \alpha/d \leq 1$ required $q \neq 1$, whereas systems with $\alpha/d > 1$ were fully correctly described within BG statistical mechanics. This belief was based on the elementary fact that $\alpha/d > 1$ potentials are integrable. But increasing evidence is growing nowadays that this integrability is *necessary but not sufficient* for the BG theory to be applicable. It appears that *all* momenta of $1/r^{\alpha}$ need to be *finite* and not only the lower-order ones. Consequently, only when $\alpha/d \to \infty$ should we use $q = 1$ if we wish that *all* thermostatistical (e.g., energy and velocity distributions) and nonlinear dynamical (e.g., size dependence of the maximal Lyapunov exponent) properties are adequately handled within the BG theory. Consistently, $q = 1$ is also fully correct if the two-body interaction potential decays exponentially with distance or if it is nonzero only between near-neighboring bodies. For the power-law case, the energy distribution may be reasonably conjectured to be given by a q-exponential form (the q-exponential function is defined as $e_q \equiv [1 + (1-q)x]_+^{\frac{1}{1-q}}$ with $[\ldots]_+ = [\ldots]$ if $[\ldots] > 0$ and zero otherwise; $e_1^x = e^x$; its inverse function is given by $\ln_q x \equiv \frac{x^{1-q}-1}{1-q}$; $\ln_1 x = \ln x$) with q given by say $q = \frac{4}{3}$ for $0 \leq \alpha/d \leq 1$ and $q = 1 + \frac{1}{3}e^{1-\alpha/d}$ for $\alpha/d > 1$. In such power-law systems, only the $\alpha/d \to \infty$ limit is to be considered, as mentioned above, as rigorously *short-range* interactions, belonging therefore to the BG world.

Moreover, it would be wonderful to (analytically and/or numerically) check whether, for $\alpha/d \in [0, \infty)$, a nonuniform convergence occurs at the $t \to \infty$ and $N \to \infty$ limits, something like the existence, in the (N, t) space, of a curve (probably of the type $1/N \propto (1/t)^{\gamma}$, with $\gamma > 0$) such that on one side ($1/t^{\gamma} \ll 1/N$) BG statistics prevails, whereas on the other side ($1/t^{\gamma} \gg 1/N$) q-statistics prevails (see, for instance, [42]).

The rigorous approach of this class of systems would provide an analytical confirmation that Boltzmann–Gibbs statistical mechanics is *sufficient but not necessary* for the validity of (properly scaled) thermodynamics and its Legendre-transform structure (see [43,44] as well as pioneering studies such as [45,46] and references therein).

(ii) For the astonishing quantum chemical reaction studied in [47], it has been conjectured [48] that the index q associated with the distribution of velocities nearly satisfies $(q-1) \propto n^{1/4}$, where n is the H_2 density. Further experimental work would be very welcome to check the possible validity of this conjecture.

(iii) A "dream" theorem [49] is waiting to be proved, namely, what would be the necessary and sufficient conditions for a q-generalized Central Limit Theorem whose attractors (in the space of probability distributions) would be q-Gaussians instead of the usual Gaussians. Both of them are ubiquitously found in nature.

(iv) The elegant q-generalization of the product frequently referred to, in the literature, as the *q-product* [50,51] has been recently shown to be consistent with an entire new q-generalized *algebra* [52,53]. Could some sort of q-generalized *vector space* be defined on this basis? Such an achievement could be of great operational utility in areas such as theoretical chemistry where q-Gaussians are known to play a sensibly more efficient numerical role than Gaussians, as Kleber C. Mundim has repeatedly shown.

(v) Triangles and more triangles! Andrea Rapisarda invited me in 2003 to deliver a seminar at the Dipartimento di Fisica e Astronomia of the Università di Catania, Italy. At the end of the presentation, a student expressed his curiosity with regard to the fact that I had mentioned different values of q for the same physical system. I clarified that, for a complex system, it was possible that different physical properties behave q-exponentially *with different values of* q, whereas a system well described within BG statistical mechanics currently exhibits only one value of q, namely $q=1$. I then illustrated that with a triplet, more precisely $(q_{sen}, q_{rel}, q_{stat})$ (*sen*, *rel* and *stat* stand for *sensitivity*, *relaxation* and *stationary state*, respectively): the q-triplet was born. See Figure 8 and [54].

Figure 8. Seminar in Catania, 2003, with Andrea Rapisarda. On the blackboard we see the proposal of the q-triplet, profusely found afterwards in nature and nonlinear dynamical systems. Such a possibility was based on possible physical interpretations of the ordinary differential equation $dy/dx = ay^q$ [$y(0) = 1$ yields $y = e_q^{ax}$], thought up in May 1988 on the train from Bayreuth back to Copenhagen (where I was visiting Per Bak at the Niels Bohr Institutet) to provide an analytical basis for the re-association in folded proteins [55]. It was George Bemski who drew my attention to this peculiar biophysical phenomenon, telling me that it could well be related to q-statistics: he was right!

A couple of years later, in January 2005, NASA invited me to deliver some talks at the Goddard Space Flight Center, Greenbelt, Maryland. It was terribly cold but the warm hospitality of Leonard F. Burlaga and Adolfo Figueroa Viñas balanced that! Len Burlaga showed to me the clock where data from the Voyager 1 spacecraft were arriving. To see directly online those numbers sent to the Earth from near Pluto meant for me an unforgettable experience. Then, in his office, Len showed to me corresponding time series of the solar wind. It struck me that these data could perhaps reveal the empirical existence in nature of the q-triplet conjectured in Catania. He asked me how to obtain these three numbers from his Voyager 1 data. I explained to him with all details how this might possibly be carried out. A few weeks later I received at the Santa Fe Institute-SFI, New Mexico, where I was spending a long sabbatical period, an email that Len sent me with wonderful news: $(q_{sen}, q_{rel}, q_{stat}) = (-0.6 \pm 0.2, 3.8 \pm 0.3, 1.75 \pm 0.06)$. See Figure 9 and [56]. The first q-triplet ever detected in nature was found, amazingly enough, in the solar wind! I immediately gave a seminar at SFI. Murray Gell-Mann became intrigued with these numbers arriving from outer space and came to my office on a Friday afternoon, just before the party at which his 75th birthday was going to be celebrated. Through a several-hour discussion, we succeeded in finding simple relations between those three numbers, based on the *additive duality* $q \leftrightarrow (2-q)$ and the *multiplicative duality* $q \leftrightarrow 1/q$. The theoretical proposal was $(q_{sen}, q_{rel}, q_{stat}) = (-1/2, 4, 7/4)$. That was the beginning of an entire algebra of indices q! [20,57]. I asked Murray why he was so fond of triangles. His answer was "You ask *me* why I like triangles? To start with, it is the simplest possible polygon!" From that moment on, a plethora of q-triplets started being observed around the world in very diverse complex systems. I conjecturally proposed some possible logical frame to those empirical sets of q-triplets and advanced a connection with the Moebius group of transformations in [58,59], but the real step forward [60] was made by Jean-Pierre Gazeau, my teaching colleague at the University of Paris, close to 55 years ago! Consistently with that first triangular structure, all kinds of triangles emerged within q-statistics. An important one is indicated in Figure 10, which illustrates the Enciso–Tempesta theorem [61], proving that the only entropic functional which simultaneously is trace-form and composable, and contains the BG entropy as a particular case is S_q as given in Equation (6). In the realm of nonlinear dynamical systems, we may think of the three classical roads to chaos (period doubling, quasi-periodicity and intermittency) as one more triplet deeply related to q-statistics, as profusely shown by Robledo, Tirnakli, Beck, Jensen and their collaborators (see [62–67] and references therein), among others. Another interesting triangle emerged in [68] in connection with molecular kinetics as shown in Figure 11. Finally, a beautiful metaphor for complex systems was recently presented by Henrik J. Jensen at the IIIrd International Workshop on Statistical Physics, held from 13 to 15 December 2023 in Antofagasta, Chile: see Figure 12.

On top (or, rather, *at the basis*) of all the above, let us remind the reader of a distinguished and crucial triplet upon which nonextensive statistical mechanics is constructed. We refer to the behavior of the q-exponential function e_q^{-x}, which straightforwardly emerges through the optimization of S_q under simple constraints. Indeed, e_q^{-x} decays exponentially for $q = 1$, as an asymptotic power-law $x^{-\frac{1}{q-1}}$ for $q > 1$, and presents a cutoff for $q < 1$.

(vi) A *nonadditive* entropic functional differing from S_q, namely

$$S_\delta = k \sum_{i=1}^{W} p_i [\ln(1/p_i)]^\delta \quad (\delta > 0; S_1 = S_{BG}), \tag{7}$$

was introduced in [69,70], which, *for equal probabilities*, satisfies $S_\delta = k(\ln W)^\delta$. The quantum version of S_δ was advanced in [20,71] as a *thermodynamically admissible* alternative to the Bekenstein–Hawking entropy S_1 for black holes as well as for cosmological holographic models. Indeed, for such deeply gravitational systems (*if* thought of as $(3+1)$-dimensional ones), S_1 is well known to be proportional to the black hole area A and not to its volume. Therefore, S_1 is *not* extensive and violates, consequently, the Legendre structure of thermodynamics. (Two decades ago, during a garden cocktail in a scientific event in Germany, Antonio Coniglio asked me "Since you have generalized the entropy, why don't you generalize the Legendre structure of thermodynamics itself?". His provocative question haunted my thoughts for many years, until I became deeply convinced that the specific form of the entropic functional acts on an epistemological level *less fundamental* than the elegant and powerful Legendre-transform structure of macroscopic phenomena. Unless new deep and solid empirical evidence emerges, this structure can (and should), through proper and natural scalings, be maintained in theoretical physics as it stands today, *even if the entropic functional differs from the usual BG one*. The basic dilemma for complex systems is whether to keep the *additive* entropic functional S_{BG} and violate the entropic extensivity mandated by the thermodynamical Legendre structure, or the other way around. It turns out eventually that violating the usual entropic additivity is a small price to pay in order to preserve the important Legendre structure. The situation is totally analogous to the special relativity dilemma of preserving the Galilean additivity of composition of velocities and violating the Lorentz transformation, or the other way around. It was clear to Einstein that violating the lovely Galilean additivity was a small price to pay for preserving the Lorentz transformation, which enabled nothing less than the unification of Maxwell electromagnetism and mechanics!) It was claimed in [71] that S_δ with $\delta = 3/2$ could solve the serious thermodynamical difficulty of S_1. (The idea of using S_δ for black holes emerged at the closed International Symposium on "Sub-nuclear Physics: Past, Present and Future" organized by Antonino Zichichi at the Pontifical Academy of Sciences during 30 October to 2 November 2011. After my presentation and that of Michael J. Duff, we had an interesting coffee-break conversation focusing on the thermodynamical requirement of entropic extensivity for all macroscopic systems, mandated by the Legendre structure of thermodynamics. Motivated by our discussion, I went back to my room at Saint Martha's House inside the Vatican and started investigating which value of $q \neq 1$ could possibly make S_q overcome the inadmissible lack of extensivity of the well-known Bekenstein–Hawking entropy (which corresponds to $q = 1$). It took me two research evenings to suddenly realize that perhaps no such value of q did exist: I had to use an entropic functional different from S_q! I then remembered about S_δ, which I had introduced, as a mere mathematical possibility, in [69]. The path was open and eventually led to $\delta = 3/2$ for (3+1)-dimensional black holes.) Basically, if $\ln W \propto A$, then $S_{\delta=3/2} \propto A^{3/2}$, which, as desired, is *extensive*. Recent observational results are accumulating [72–74] which indeed indicate $\delta \simeq 3/2$. (Ref. [72] indicates $\delta = 1.565$ for neutrinos as detected at the IceCube Neutrino Observatory at the South Pole. Ref. [73] indicates $\delta = 1.87$ and $\delta = 1.26$ through two different theoretical processings of the data collected at the outer-space Planck Observatory/ESA; amazingly enough, the mean value of 1.87 and 1.26 precisely yields $\delta = 1.565$! Ref. [74] indicates, from the Big Bang nucleosynthesis and the relic abundance of cold dark matter particles, $\delta = 1.499$.) This appears to neatly exclude, for such systems, the Bekenstein–Hawking entropy S_1 (i.e., $\delta = 1$), *enfant aimé* of string theorists and others (see, for example, [75]). The scientific importance of such timely issue surely deserves a re-analysis in the light of *nonadditive entropic functionals* adequately chosen so as to satisfy *entropic extensivity*.

Human memory is like a fractal, one reminiscence endlessly pulling another one, and another and another. Still, I hope that, through these lines, I could share with the reader a few illustrative facets of what it is possible to learn and appreciate during half a century of theoretical physics.

In the present manuscript, I mainly focused on concepts—*truth and beauty*—that may be thought of as primarily belonging to what is currently referred to as the *objective* world. There are others, equally important, such as *curiosity and enthusiasm* (from Greek *enthousiasmós*, divine inspiration), *focus and resilience*, which primarily belong to the *subjective* world ... but that is another story!

At this point, as final words, it might be proper to emphasize that, in science and elsewhere, the concepts of *objective* and *subjective* themselves surely are strangely entangled. In the prologue of Miguel de Unamuno's wonderful *Niebla* (1935) we can read: *Don Quijote me ha revelado íntimos secretos suyos que no reveló a Cervantes.* (Don Quixote revealed to me intimate secrets of himself that he did not reveal to Cervantes).

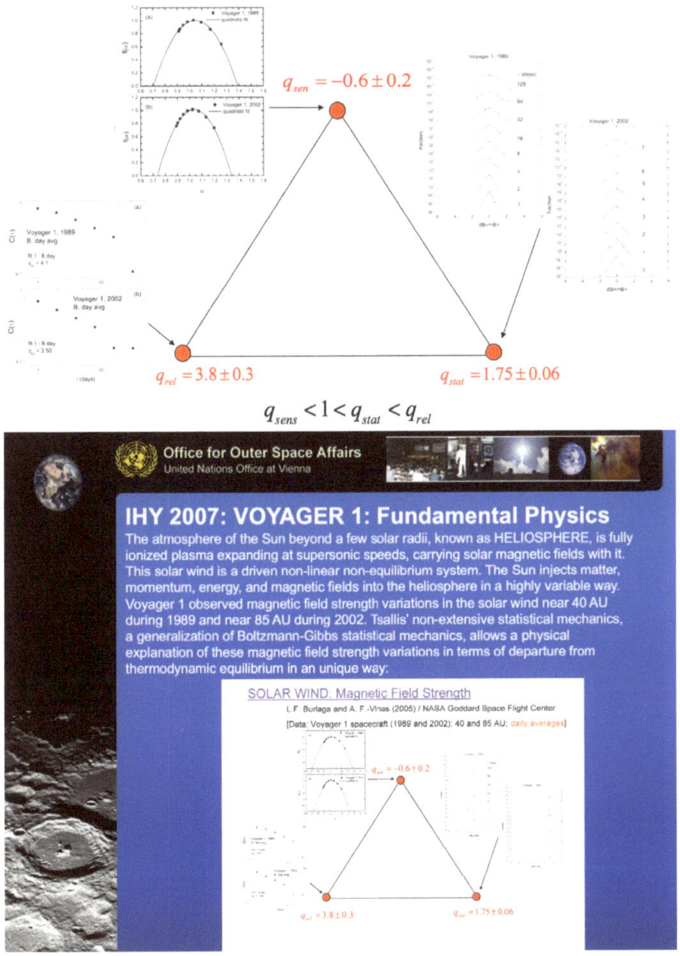

Figure 9. **Top**: Slide exhibiting the NASA results on the solar wind q-triplet ($q_{sensitivity} < 1 < q_{stationary\,state} < q_{relaxation}$ was the expectation in [54]). **Bottom**: With my consent for using the slide, this poster was prepared, selected and exhibited by the United Nations Office for Outer Space Affairs for the Opening Ceremony of the United Nations International Heliophysical Year exhibit (19 February 2007, Vienna).

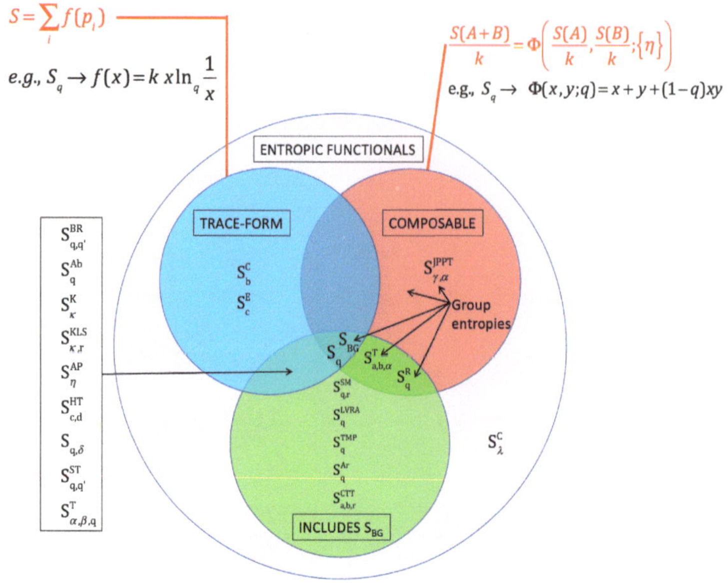

Figure 10. Scheme of the Enciso–Tempesta theorem [61] proving the uniqueness of S_q for simultaneously being trace-form and composable, and containing S_{BG} as a particular case. For further details, see [20].

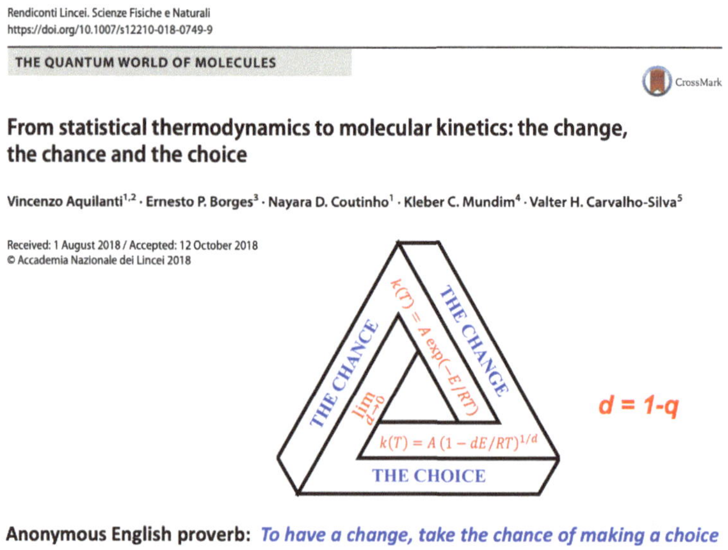

Figure 11. Triangle from [68], reflecting the q-exponential generalization of the Arrhenius law for chemical kinetics. Experimental validations of $q \neq 1$ can be found in [68] and references therein.

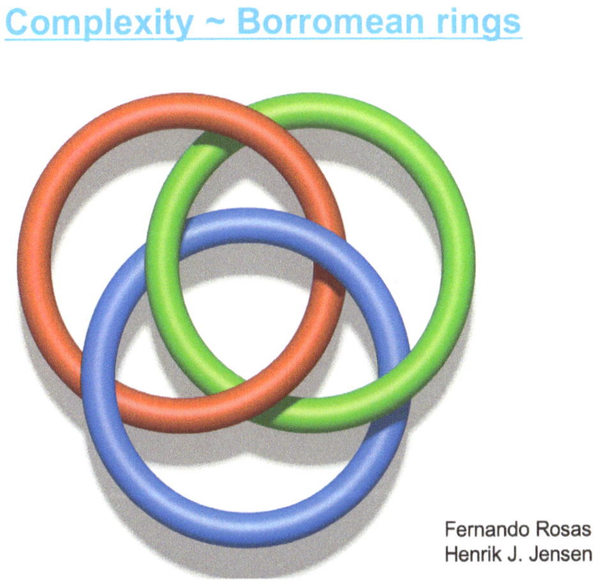

Figure 12. Borromean rings are three elementary rings that are two-by-two free but not so when the three of them are entangled. This expressive metaphor for complex systems was recently presented in a lecture by Henrik J. Jensen, in co-authorship with Fernando Rosas.

Funding: This research received no external funding.

Acknowledgments: I am deeply indebted to Marisa Lopes, Décio O. S. da Rocha, Ernesto P. Borges, Evaldo M. F. Curado, Airton Deppman, Henrik J. Jensen, Fernando D. Nobre and Ugur Tirnakli for very valuable remarks, and to Juan M. Maldacena for a recent fruitful conversation at the Princeton Institute for Advanced Study. Partial financial support by CNPq and FAPERJ (Brazilian agencies) is acknowledged as well.

Conflicts of Interest: The author declares no conflicts of interest.

References

1. Rocchiccioli-Deltcheff, C.; Tsallis, C. Étude de propriétés ferroélectriques de perovskites complexes. *C. R. L'Académie Sci.* **1969**, *269*, 1198–1201.
2. Bouillot, J.; Machet, R.; Tsallis, C. Electrostatic field in a slightly orthorhombic ionic crystal. Application to the calculation of tetragonal $BaTiO_3$ and $PbTiO_3$ birefringence. *Phys. Status Solidi* **1970**, *38*, 313–316. [CrossRef]
3. Tsallis, C.; Machet, R.; Bouillot, J. Electrostatic field in a pseudo-cubic ionic structure. Application to all $BaTiO_3$ structure-types. *J. Phys.* **1971**, *32*, 171–175. [CrossRef]
4. Kobayashi, K. Dynamical aspects of the phase transition in KH_2PO_4-type ferroelectric crystals. *Phys. Lett. A* **1967**, *26*, 55. [CrossRef]
5. Kobayashi, K. Dynamical theory of the phase transition in KH_2PO_4-type ferroelectric crystals. *J. Phys. Soc. Jpn.* **1968**, *24*, 497. [CrossRef]
6. Tsallis, C. Dynamics of KH_2PO_4 type ferroelectric phase transitions. *J. Phys.* **1972**, *33*, 1121–1127. [CrossRef]
7. Tsallis, C.; Levy, S.V.F. Simple method to calculate percolation, Ising and Potts clusters—Renormalization group applications. *Phys. Rev. Lett.* **1981**, *47*, 950–953. [CrossRef]
8. Tsallis, C.; de Magalhaes, A.C.N. Pure and random Potts-like models: Real-space renormalization-group approach. *Phys. Rep.* **1996**, *268*, 305–430. [CrossRef]
9. Sykes, M.F.; Essam, J.W. Some exact critical percolation probabilities for bond and site problems in two dimensions. *Phys. Rev. Lett.* **1963**, *10*, 3. [CrossRef]
10. Sykes, M.F.; Essam, J.W. Exact critical percolation probabilities for site and bond problems in two dimensions. *J. Math. Phys.* **1964**, *5*, 1117–1127. [CrossRef]
11. Tsallis, C. Possible generalization of Boltzmann-Gibbs statistics. *J. Stat. Phys.* **1988**, *52*, 479–487. [CrossRef]
12. Caride, A.O.; Tsallis, C. Specific heat of the anisotropic rigid rotator. *J. Stat. Phys.* **1984**, *35*, 187–190. [CrossRef]

13. Gibbs, J.W. *Elementary Principles in Statistical Mechanics—Developed with Especial Reference to the Rational Foundation of Thermodynamics*; Scribner's Sons, C.: New York, NY, USA, 1902.
14. Vieira, M.C.S.; Tsallis, C. D-dimensional ideal gas in parastatistics: Thermodynamic properties. *J. Stat. Phys.* **1987**, *48*, 97–120. [CrossRef]
15. Robertson, H.S. *Statistical Thermophysics*; Prentice-Hall: Hoboken, NJ, USA, 1993.
16. Boltzmann, L. Weitere Studien uber das Wármegleichgewicht unter Gas molekulen [Further Studies on Thermal Equilibrium Between Gas Molecules, The Kinetic Theory of Gases]. *Sitzungsberichte Akad. Wiss.* **1872**, *66*, 275–370.
17. Boltzmann, L. Uber die Beziehung eines allgemeine mechanischen Satzes zum zweiten Haupsatze der Warmetheorie. In *Sitzungberichte der Akademie der Wissenschaften II* ; De Gruyter: Berlin, Germany; Boston, MA, USA, 1877; Volume 75, pp. 67–73.
18. Gibbs, J.W. The collected works. In *Thermodynamics*; Yale University Press: New Haven, CT, USA, 1948; Volume 1.
19. Gibbs, J.W. *Elementary Principles in Statistical Mechanics*; OX Bow Press: Woodbridge, CT, USA, 1981.
20. Tsallis, C. *Introduction to Nonextensive Statistical Mechanics—Approaching a Complex World*, 2nd ed.; Springer: New York, NY, USA, 2023.
21. Arimitsu, T.; Arimitsu, N. Analysis of fully developed turbulence in terms of Tsallis statistics. *Phys. Rev.* **2000**, *61*, 3237. [CrossRef]
22. Daniels, K.E.; Beck, C.; Bodenschatz, E. Defect turbulence and generalized statistical mechanics. *Phys. Nonlinear Phenom.* **2004**, *193*, 208–217. [CrossRef]
23. Swinney, H.L.; Tsallis, C. Anomalous Distributions, Nonlinear Dynamics and Nonextensivity. *Phys. Nonlinear Phenom.* **2004**, *193*, 1–2. [CrossRef]
24. Curado, E.M.F.; Tsallis, C. Generalized statistical mechanics: Connection with thermodynamics. *J. Phys. A Math. Gen.* **1991**, *24*, L69–L72; Erratum in *J. Phys. A Math. Gen.* **1992**, *25*, 1019. [CrossRef]
25. Plastino, A.R.; Plastino, A. Stellar polytropes and Tsallis' entropy. *Phys. Lett. A* **1993**, *174*, 384. [CrossRef]
26. Boghosian, B.M. Thermodynamic description of the relaxation of two-dimensional turbulence using Tsallis statistics. *Phys. Rev. E* **1996**, 53, 4754. [CrossRef]
27. Regularly Updated Bibliography. Available online: https://tsallis.cbpf.br/biblio.htm (accessed on 1 December 2023).
28. Abe, S.; Rajagopal, A.K. Microcanonical foundation for systems with power-law distributions. *J. Phys. A* **2000**, 33, 8733. [CrossRef]
29. Seminar by C. Tsallis at the Santa Fe Institute, NM. Available online: https://www.youtube.com/watch?v=uQGN2PThukk (accessed on 1 December 2023).
30. Tsallis, C. Enthusiasm and skepticism: Two pillars of science—A nonextensive statistics case. *Physics* **2022**, *4*, 609–632. [CrossRef]
31. Tisza, L. *Generalized Thermodynamics*; MIT Press: Cambridge, MA, USA, 1977.
32. Cohen, E.G.D. Boltzmann and Einstein: Statistics and dynamics—An unsolved problem, Boltzmann Award Lecture at Statphys-Bangalore-2004. *Pramana* **2005**, *64*, 635–643. [CrossRef]
33. Baranger, M. Why Tsallis statistics? In *Non Extensive Statistical Mechanics and Physical Applications—Physica A*; Kaniadakis, G., Lissia, M., Rapisarda, A., Eds.; Elsevier: Amsterdam, The Netherlands, 2002; Volume 305, p. 27.
34. Kuhn, T.S. *The Structure of Scientific Revolutions*; The University of Chicago Press: Chicago, IL, USA, 1962.
35. Nicolis, G.; Daems, D. Probabilistic and thermodynamics aspects of dynamical systems. *Chaos* **1998**, 8, 311–320. [CrossRef]
36. Tsallis, C. An introduction to nonadditive entropies and a thermostatistical approach of inanimate and living matter. *Contemp. Phys.* **2014**, *55*, 179–197. [CrossRef]
37. Tsallis, C. Approach of complexity in nature: Entropic nonuniqueness. *Axioms* **2016**, *5*, 20. [CrossRef]
38. Penrose, O. *Foundations of Statistical Mechanics: A Deductive Treatment*; Pergamon: Oxford, UK, 1970; p. 167.
39. Tsallis, C. Entropy. *Encyclopedia* **2022**, *2*, 264–300. [CrossRef]
40. Ramirez-Reyes, A.; Hernandez-Montoya, A.R.; Herrera-Corral, G.; Dominguez-Jimenez, I. Determining the entropic index q of Tsallis entropy in images through redundancy. *Entropy* **2016**, *18*, 299. [CrossRef]
41. Umarov, S.; Tsallis, C. *Mathematical Foundations of Nonextensive Statistical Mechanics*; World Scientific: Singapore, 2022.
42. Christodoulidi, H.; Tsallis, C.; Bountis, T. Fermi-Pasta-Ulam model with long-range interactions: Dynamics and thermostatistics. *Europhys. Lett.* **2014**, *108*, 40006. [CrossRef]
43. Tsallis, C.; Cirto, L.J.L. Thermodynamics is more powerful than the role to it reserved by Boltzmann-Gibbs statistical mechanics. *Eur. Phys. J. Spec. Top.* **2014**, 223, 2161. [CrossRef]
44. Tsallis, C.; Haubold, H.J. Boltzmann-Gibbs entropy is sufficient but not necessary for the likelihood factorization required by Einstein. *Europhys. Lett.* **2015**, *110*, 30005. [CrossRef]
45. Plastino, A.; Plastino, A.R. On the universality of Thermodynamics' Legendre transform structure. *Phys. Lett. A* **1997**, *226*, 257. [CrossRef]
46. Mendes, R.S. Some general relations in arbitrary thermostatistics. *Physica A* **1997**, *242*, 299. [CrossRef]
47. Wild, R.; Notzold, M.; Simpson, M.; Tran, T.D.; Wester, R. Tunnelling measured in a very slow ion-molecule reaction. *Nature* **2023**, *615*, 425. [CrossRef]
48. Tsallis, C. Online Comment on "Tunnelling measured in a very slow ion-molecule reaction". *Nature* **2023**, *615*, 425–429. [CrossRef]
49. Tsallis, C. Open mathematical issues in nonextensive statistical mechanics. *Mat. Contemp.* **2023**, 58, 316–337.
50. Nivanen, L.; Mehaute, A.L.; Wang, Q.A. Generalized algebra within a nonextensive statistics. *Rep. Math. Phys.* **2003**, *52*, 437. [CrossRef]
51. Borges, E.P. A possible deformed algebra and calculus inspired in nonextensive thermostatistics. *Physica A* **2004**, *340*, 95–101. [CrossRef]

52. Borges, E.P.; da Costa, B.G. Deformed mathematical objects stemming from the q-logarithm function. *Axioms* **2022**, *11*, 138. [CrossRef]
53. Borges, E.P.; Kodama, T.; Tsallis, C. Along the lines of nonadditive entropies: q-prime numbers and q-zeta functions. *Entropy* **2022**, *24*, 60. [CrossRef]
54. Tsallis, C. Dynamical scenario for nonextensive statistical mechanics. *Physica A* **2004**, 340, 1–10. [CrossRef]
55. Tsallis, C.; Bemski, G.; Mendes, R.S. Is re-association in folded proteins a case of nonextensivity? *Phys. Lett. A* **1999**, *257*, 93–98. [CrossRef]
56. Burlaga, L.F.; Vinas, A.F. Triangle for the entropic index q of non-extensive statistical mechanic observed by Voyager 1 in the distant heliosphere. *Physica A* **2005**, *356*, 375. [CrossRef]
57. Tsallis, C.; Gell-Mann, M.; Sato, Y. Asymptotically scale-invariant occupancy of phase space makes the entropy S_q extensive. *Proc. Natl. Acad. Sci. USA* **2005**, *102*, 15377. [CrossRef] [PubMed]
58. Tsallis, C. Generalization of the possible algebraic basis of q-triplets. *Eur. Phys. J. Spec. Top.* **2017**, *226*, 455–466. [CrossRef]
59. Tsallis, C. Statistical mechanics for complex systems: On the structure of q-triplets. In *Physical and Mathematical Aspects of Symmetries, Proceedings of the 31st International Colloquium in Group Theoretical Methods in Physics, Rio de Janeiro, Brazil, 20–24 June 2016*; Duarte, S., Gazeau, J.-P., Faci, S., Micklitz, T., Scherer, R., Toppan, F., Eds.; Springer: Cham, Switzerland, 2017; pp. 51–60.
60. Gazeau, J.-P.; Tsallis, C. Moebius transforms, cycles and q-triplets in statistical mechanics. *Entropy* **2019**, *21*, 1155. [CrossRef]
61. Enciso, A.; Tempesta, P. Uniqueness and characterization theorems for generalized entropies. *J. Stat. Mech.* **2017**, *2017*, 123101. [CrossRef]
62. Robledo, A.; Velarde, C. How, why and when Tsallis statistical mechanics provides precise descriptions of natural phenomena. *Entropy* **2022**, *24*, 1761. [CrossRef]
63. Camacho-Vidales, L.J.; Robledo, A. A nonlinear dynamical view of Kleiber's law on the metabolism of plants and animals. *Entropy* **2014**, *26*, 32. [CrossRef]
64. Tirnakli, U.; Borges, E.P. The standard map: From Boltzmann-Gibbs statistics to Tsallis statistics. *Sci. Rep.* **2016**, *6*, 23644. [CrossRef]
65. Cetin, K.; Tirnakli, U.; Oliveira, D.F.M.; Leonel, E.D. Statistical mechanical characterization of billiard systems. *Chaos Solitons Fractals* **2014**, *178*, 114331. [CrossRef]
66. Tirnakli, U.; Jensen, H.J.; Tsallis, C. Restricted random walk model as a new testing ground for the applicability of q-statistics. *Europhys. Lett.* **2011**, *96*, 40008. [CrossRef]
67. Zand, J.; Tirnakli, U.; Jensen, H.J. On the relevance of q-distribution functions: The return time distribution of restricted random walker. *J. Phys. A Math. Theor.* **2015**, *48*, 425004. [CrossRef]
68. Aquilanti, V.; Borges, E.P.; Coutinho, N.D.; Mundim, K.C.; Carvalho-Silva, V.H. From statistical thermodynamics to molecular kinetics: The change, the chance and the choice. *Rendiconti Lincei, Scienze Fisiche e Naturali* **2018**, *29*, 787. [CrossRef]
69. Tsallis, C. *Introduction to Nonextensive Statistical Mechanics —Approaching a Complex World*, 1st ed.; Springer: New York, NY, USA, 2009.
70. Ubriaco, M.R. Entropies based on fractional calculus. *Phys. Lett. A* **2009**, *373*, 2516. [CrossRef]
71. Tsallis, C.; Cirto, L.J.L. Black hole thermodynamical entropy. *Eur. Phys. J. C* **2013**, *73*, 2487. [CrossRef]
72. Jizba, P.; Lambiase, G. Tsallis cosmology and its applications in dark matter physics with focus on IceCube high-energy neutrino data. *Eur. Phys. J. C* **2022**, *82*, 1123. [CrossRef]
73. Salehi, A.; Pourali, M.; Abedini, Y. Search for neutrino masses in the Barrow holographic dark energy cosmology with Hubble horizon as IR cutoff. *Gen. Relativ. Gravit.* **2023**, *55*, 57. [CrossRef]
74. Jizba, P.; Lambiase, G. Constraints on Tsallis cosmology from Big Bang nucleosynthesis and the relic abundance of cold dark matter particles. *Entropy* **2023**, *25*, 1495. [CrossRef]
75. Maldacena, J.M.; Strominger, A. Statistical entropy of four-dimensional extremal black holes. *Phys. Rev. Lett.* **1996**, *77*, 428. [CrossRef]

entropy

MDPI

Review
Open Problems within Nonextensive Statistical Mechanics

Kenric P. Nelson

Photrek, LCC, Watertown, MA 02472, USA; kenric.nelson@photrek.io or kenric.nelson@gmail.com

Abstract: Nonextensive statistical mechanics has developed into an important framework for modeling the thermodynamics of complex systems and the information of complex signals. To mark the 80th birthday of the field's founder, Constantino Tsallis, a review of open problems that can stimulate future research is provided. Over the thirty-year development of NSM, a variety of criticisms have been published ranging from questions about the justification for generalizing the entropy function to the interpretation of the generalizing parameter q. While these criticisms have been addressed in the past and the breadth of applications has demonstrated the utility of the NSM methodologies, this review provides insights into how the field can continue to improve the understanding and application of complex system models. The review starts by grounding q-statistics within scale-shape distributions and then frames a series of open problems for investigation. The open problems include using the degrees of freedom to quantify the difference between entropy and its generalization, clarifying the physical interpretation of the parameter q, improving the definition of the generalized product using multidimensional analysis, defining a generalized Fourier transform applicable to signal processing applications, and re-examining the normalization of nonextensive entropy. This review concludes with a proposal that the shape parameter is a candidate for defining the statistical complexity of a system.

Keywords: complexity; nonextensive; Pareto; student's t; Fourier; entropy

Citation: Nelson, K.P. Open Problems within Nonextensive Statistical Mechanics. *Entropy* **2024**, *26*, 118. https://doi.org/10.3390/e26020118

Academic Editors: Andrea Rapisarda, Airton Deppman, Astero Provata, Evaldo M. F. Curado, Christian Beck, Hans J. Herrmann, Henrik Jeldtoft Jensen, Ugur Tirnakli, Fernando D. Nobre and Angelo Plastino

Received: 31 December 2023
Revised: 21 January 2024
Accepted: 23 January 2024
Published: 29 January 2024

1. Introduction

Nonextensive statistical mechanics (NSM) [1–3] has developed into an important framework for modeling the thermodynamics of complex systems [4–6] and the information of complex signals [7–9]. The methodology ties together heavy-tailed statistics derived from a generalized entropy function and the resultant analysis, modeling, and design methods for systems impacted by nonlinear dynamics. To mark the 80th birthday of the field's founder, Constantino Tsallis, I reflect on open problems that will stimulate future investigation and development of NSM. While there is much to celebrate in the applications of NSM, a review of open problems requires examination of some of the criticism [10–15] the field has received over its thirty-year development [16]. The criticism ranges from questions about the interpretation of the generalizing parameter q to the justification for modifying the entropy function. In this paper, I will carefully examine several key concerns with the aim of motivating the further improvement and applicability of NSM.

Inspection of a few applications of NSM introduces the challenges of characterizing the properties of complex systems using q-statistics. Table 1 lists seven examples in which a theoretical underpinning is available to explain experimental observations. However, in each case, the mapping between the physical phenomena and the parameter q requires unexplained constants that detract from the ability of NSM to describe the physics of those systems. The relationship $q = 1 + x$, in which x (or its inverse) is a physical property, is common since x often defines a property of the system that induces nonlinearity. This property changes to zero (or infinity for inverse) when $q = 1$. Another typical relationship is $q = 2 - y$, since this is the reflection of $q = 1$. If NSM was defined in terms of the physical property x, the reflection of 0 would simply be $x = -y$. However, the full review of open problems in NSM will show that this simple translation is not adequate to account for multidimensional systems and the effects of other nonlinear elements.

Table 1. Applications of nonextensive statistical mechanics. A variety of complex systems, such as atomic gases, space plasma velocities, financial volatility, cellular mobility, wavelets, and heat baths, can be modeled using NSM. In each case, the mapping between the physical property and the parameter q requires numerical constants that diminish the ability of q-statistics to describe the physical phenomena.

Applications	**Physical Property**	**Relation to q**
Entropy of Hydrogen Atoms [17]	M, number of atoms	$q = 1 + \frac{1}{M}$
Space Plasma Velocities [18,19]	$\kappa = \nu$, spectral index	$q = 1 + \frac{1}{\kappa}$
Volatility of Financial Markets [7,20]	ν, nonlinear Fokker-Plank	$q = 2 - \nu$
Hydra-Cell Velocity [21,22]	ν, nonlinear Kramers Equ	$q = 2 - \nu$
Wavelet Analysis [23]	i, wavelet scale index	$q = 1 - 2i$
Heat Bath Thermodynamics [24,25]	n, degrees of freedom, $n = \frac{d\,N}{2}$, d dimensions, N particles	$q = \frac{n}{n-1}$
Superstatistic Fluctuations [5]	n, Chi-square deg. of freedom	$q = 1 + \frac{2}{n+1}$

The analysis in this review is grounded in the role heavy-tailed statistics plays in modeling the nonlinear dynamics of complex systems. It will be shown that by decomposing the NSM parameter q into more direct physical properties, interpretations of NSM are clarified and the connections with the tail shape of distributions, such as the generalized Pareto distribution and the Student t distribution, are simplified. This approach has been called *nonlinear statistical coupling* (NSC). Here, I refer to the theory as NSM and reserve NSC or simply the coupling for the shape parameter, which may also be a candidate for quantifying statistical complexity. For simplification, I will assume that distributions have a location of zero throughout. Also not included in the discussion are distributions, such as the Weibull distribution, which introduce modifications to the skew of the distribution.

Each section addresses a fundamental question and defines an open problem. In some cases, a comment will be provided suggesting directions for investigation. Solutions are specifically not provided because although the author has, in some cases, previously recommended a solution, the future direction of NSM is ultimately a community decision made by the investigators pushing the field forward. Section 2 reviews how q relates to the traditional parameters of heavy-tailed and compact-support distributions. Section 3 discusses the question of generalizing entropy. Section 4 examines the difference between mathematical fits and physical theories, as well as the role of independent random variables in clarifying the physical property of q. Section 5 highlights some inconsistencies in how the q-product is defined and applied. Section 6 explains the limitations in the use of the q-Fourier transform as a physical model. Section 7 considers three different normalizations of the nonextensive entropy. Finally, Section 8 asks whether a definition for statistical complexity is possible.

2. How Is q-Statistics Related to Traditional Definitions of Heavy-Tailed Distributions?

NSM began [16,26] with a proposal to generalize Boltzmann–Gibbs statistics by examining the properties of systems with a distribution of states modified by the power of q. This modified distribution with the elements p_i^q is referred to as the escort distribution; however, it is unfortunate that the NSM literature has not been explicit that this expression necessarily defines q as a real number of independent random variables sharing the same state. If q is an integer n, elementary probability theory establishes that p^n is the probability of n independent random variables, each with probability p. Fractional random variables are discussed further in Section 4. From this start, the Tsallis entropy and its maximizing distribution were derived as follows:

$$S_q^T \equiv \frac{1 - \sum_i p_i^q}{q-1} \tag{1}$$

$$p_i = \frac{(1-\beta(q-1)x_i)^{\frac{1}{q-1}}}{\sum_{j=1}^{N}(1-\beta(q-1)x_j)^{\frac{1}{q-1}}} \tag{2}$$

Warm-Up Problem: *The first problem is not so much open as a warm-up to ground the discussion of the other problems. How does the NSM parameter q relate to the shape of a distribution? And how does the Lagrange multiplier β relate to the scale of a distribution?*

I will address this question via the examination of the generalized Pareto and Student t distributions. Both the probability density function (pdf) and the survival function (sf) are provided since the sf will provide insights into the definition of a generalized exponential function. To unify the discussion, both distributions will be defined in terms of the shape parameter κ, though the Student t is traditionally defined in terms of its reciprocal, the degrees of freedom, $\nu = \frac{1}{\kappa}$. The shape parameter is also referred to as the nonlinear statistical coupling or coupling due to its connection with nonlinearity; further, the final problem will consider whether it is a candidate for quantifying statistical complexity. The distributions have three domains:

$$\begin{array}{cc} \text{Compact} - \text{Support} & -1 < \kappa < 0 \\ \text{Exponential} & \kappa = 0 \\ \text{Heavy} - \text{Tail} & \kappa > 0 \end{array} \tag{3}$$

Definition 1: *Generalized Pareto Distribution*

The survival function (cf) is one minus the cumulative distribution function (cdf), $\overline{F} = 1 - F$. The Pareto Type IV with a location of zero is defined in terms of a scale,σ, and two shape parameters,κ and α.

$$\overline{F}(x;\sigma,\ \kappa,\alpha) = \left[1+\kappa\left(\frac{x}{\sigma}\right)^{\alpha}\right]^{-\frac{1}{\alpha\kappa}};x \geq 0,\ \kappa,\ \alpha > 0 \tag{4}$$

The probability distribution function (pdf) is the derivative of the cdf

$$(x;\sigma,\ \kappa,\alpha) = \frac{1}{\sigma}\left(\frac{x}{\sigma}\right)^{\alpha-1}\left[1+\kappa\left(\frac{x}{\sigma}\right)^{\alpha}\right]^{-\left(\frac{1}{\alpha\kappa}+1\right)};x \geq 0,\ \kappa,\ \alpha > 0 \tag{5}$$

For Pareto Type II $\alpha = 1$and the cf and pdf reduce to

$$\overline{F}(x;\sigma,\ \kappa) = \left[1+\kappa\frac{x}{\sigma}\right]^{-\frac{1}{\kappa}};x \geq 0,\ \kappa > 0 \tag{6}$$

$$f(x;\sigma,\ \kappa) = \frac{1}{\sigma}\left[1+\kappa\frac{x}{\sigma}\right]^{-\left(\frac{1}{\kappa}+1\right)};x \geq 0,\ \kappa > 0 \tag{7}$$

Comment on Definition 1: *The definition for Type IV is modified from the traditional approach to clearly distinguish between the decay of the tail in the limit as x changes to infinity, κ, and the raising of the variable to the power α. Thus, the outer exponent is $-\frac{1}{\alpha\kappa}$, meaning that $-\frac{1}{\kappa}$ is the asymptotic power. Nevertheless, the emphasis here will be on questions about NSM and connections to the long-standing traditions in statistical analysis.*

Definition 2: *Generalized Student t Distribution*

The Student t distribution is traditionally defined in terms of the degrees of freedom, ν; however, to unify the discussion, the reciprocal shape parameter, $\kappa = \frac{1}{\nu}$, is used. The survival function of the generalized Student t distribution, which depends on the Gauss hypergeometric function, ${}_2F_1$, and the Beta function, B, is

$$\overline{F}(x;\sigma,\kappa,\alpha) \\ = -\frac{1}{2} \\ -\frac{\sigma\sqrt{|\kappa|}}{B\left(\frac{1}{2},\ \frac{\kappa-\mathrm{sign}(\kappa)(\kappa-2)}{4\kappa}\right)}\,{}_2F_1\left(\frac{1}{2},\ \frac{1+\kappa}{2\kappa};\ \frac{3}{2};\min\left(1,-\kappa\frac{x^2}{\sigma^2}\right)\right);\ \begin{cases} 0 \le |x| \le \sqrt{-\kappa} & -1<\kappa<0 \\ 0 \le |x| < \infty & \kappa \ge 0 \end{cases} \tag{8}$$

$$\begin{gathered} {}_2F_1(a,b;c;z) = \sum_{n=0}^{\infty} \frac{(a)_n(b)_n}{(c)_n}\frac{z^n}{n!}; \\ (a)_n = \begin{cases} 1 & n=0 \\ a(a+1)\cdots(a+n-1) & n>0 \end{cases}; \\ B(z_1,z_2) = \int_0^1 t^{z_1-1}(t-1)^{z_2-1}dt. \end{gathered} \tag{9}$$

The Student t probability density function is:

$$f(x;\sigma,\ \kappa) = \begin{cases} \frac{\sqrt{|\kappa|}}{\sigma B\left(\frac{1}{2},\ \frac{\kappa-\mathrm{sign}(\kappa)(\kappa-2)}{4\kappa}\right)}\left[1+\kappa\left(\frac{x}{\sigma}\right)^2\right]_+^{-\frac{1}{2}\left(\frac{1}{\kappa}+1\right)} & \kappa \neq 0,\ \kappa \ge -1 \\ \frac{1}{\sigma\sqrt{2\pi}}\exp\left(-\frac{1}{\alpha}\left(\frac{x}{\sigma}\right)^2\right) & \kappa = 0. \end{cases} \tag{10}$$

Warm-Up Solution: *The exponent of the Pareto ($\alpha = 1$) and Student t ($\alpha = 2$) distributions determines the relationship between q and the shape κ:*

$$q = 1 + \frac{\alpha\kappa}{1+\kappa};\ \kappa = \frac{q-1}{\alpha+1-q}. \tag{11}$$

From this relationship, the escort probability or density can be defined in terms of the following shape:

$$p_i^{(\alpha,\kappa)} \equiv \frac{p_i^{1+\frac{\alpha\kappa}{1+\kappa}}}{\sum_{j=1}^{N} p_j^{1+\frac{\alpha\kappa}{1+\kappa}}};\ f^{(\alpha,\kappa)}(x) \equiv \frac{f^{1+\frac{\alpha\kappa}{1+\kappa}}(x)}{\int_{x\in X} f^{1+\frac{\alpha\kappa}{1+\kappa}}(x)dx} \tag{12}$$

The multiplicative term of the variable determines the relationship between the Lagrange multiplier β and the scale σas follows:

$$\beta = \frac{(1+\kappa)}{\alpha\sigma^\alpha};\ \sigma = \left(\frac{1}{(\alpha+1-q)\beta}\right)^{\frac{1}{\alpha}}. \tag{13}$$

Open Problem 1: *We notice that the Pareto Type II survival function is in the form of the generalized exponential function*

$$\exp_\kappa(z) \equiv \begin{cases} (1+\kappa z)_+^{\frac{1}{\kappa}} & \kappa \neq 0,\ (a)_+ \equiv \max(0,a) \\ e^x & \kappa = 0. \end{cases} \tag{14}$$

This leads to a question regarding the definitions for the generalized algebra of NSM. In the development of NSM, the generalization of the exponential function has been applied to the pdf; however, would the sf be the more natural function to generalize? If so, the shape parameter rather than q becomes the fundamental parameter of the NSM generalization of statistical mechanics. We will see that this modification leads to a clearer definition of the multivariate distributions and more direct physical interpretations. A related issue is that $exp_\kappa(-z) \neq exp_\kappa^{-1}(z)$ for $\kappa \neq 0$.

This is important in the definition of distributions since it is the reciprocal of the exponential function rather than the negative of the argument that is important.

Before continuing, the inverse of the generalized exponential function is defined as the generalized logarithm as follows:

$$\log_\kappa z \equiv \begin{cases} \frac{1}{\kappa}(z^\kappa - 1) & \kappa \neq 0,\ z > 0 \\ e^z & \kappa = 0,\ z > 0. \end{cases} \tag{15}$$

3. Is a Generalization of Entropy Necessary?

One of the challenges of statistical mechanics is that it is quite difficult even for seasoned experts to formulate an intuitive framework for its foundational concept, entropy. To address the question of the need for a generalized entropy, we will describe the issue in terms of a distribution's average density (or probability for non-continuous distributions). While most concepts in statistics are framed in terms of densities/probabilities (y-axis of distribution) and estimates of the random variable (x-axis of distribution), entropy is based on the logarithm of the probabilities. This transformation, $p \to \log p$, is essential to providing an additive scale, meaning that the arithmetic average is the central tendency of the uncertainty, leading to the definition of entropy, $S = -\sum_{i=1}^{N} p_i \log p_i$. This is the informational entropy, which will be used in this paper, while the physical entropy includes multiplication using the Boltzmann constant. We must notice, however, that the logarithm can be separated from the aggregation of the probabilities using the weighted geometric mean $S = \log \prod_{i=1}^{N} p_i^{-p_i}$. For the continuous distributions, the entropy is $S = -\int_{x \in X} f(x) \log f(x) dx$, and the equivalent of the weighted geometric mean of the density is $\exp(-S)$, known as the log-average. Therefore, the weighted geometric mean can be used to examine the *average density or probability* without resorting to the logarithmic transformation. Using Equations (12)–(15), the log-average is generalized to a function that I will refer to as the coupled log-average.

$$f_{\text{avg}}(x; \alpha, \kappa) \equiv \left(\exp_\kappa \left(\int_{x \in X} f^{(\alpha,\kappa)}(x) \log_\kappa f^{-\frac{\alpha}{1+\kappa}}(x) dx \right) \right)^{-\frac{1+\kappa}{\alpha}}, \tag{16}$$

where the factor $-\frac{\alpha}{1+\kappa}$ and its inverse are determined using the exponent of the distribution *f*. For discrete functions, (9) reduces to the generalized mean, as derived from Definition 3 of [27].

$$p_{\text{avg}}(\mathbf{p}; \alpha, \kappa) \equiv \left(\sum_{i=1}^{N} p_i^{(\alpha,\kappa)} p_i^{-\frac{\alpha\kappa}{1+\kappa}} \right)^{-\frac{1+\kappa}{\alpha\kappa}} = \left(\sum_{i=1}^{N} p_i^{1+\frac{\alpha\kappa}{1+\kappa}} \right)^{\frac{1+\kappa}{\alpha\kappa}}. \tag{17}$$

Figure 1 shows the Gaussian, $\kappa = 0$, and three heavy-tailed coupled Gaussians, $\kappa = \{0.5, 1, 2\}$. The distributions are normalized by their couple average density, which is highlighted in the figure by a horizontal line. The couped average density is computed for each density with the matching coupling value, κ. Furthermore, the matching coupled average of the density is always equal to the density at $x = \mu \pm \sigma$. As the coupling or shape increases, the tail becomes heavier, and the log-average ($\kappa = 0$), shown as dashed horizontal lines, approaches zero. Thus, the entropy, which is the logarithm of the average density, approaches infinity. Nevertheless, the Student t distribution has a structure that is quite different from the variance of the Gaussian changing to infinity. Something has clearly been lost in summarizing the uncertainty of the Student t with just the entropy.

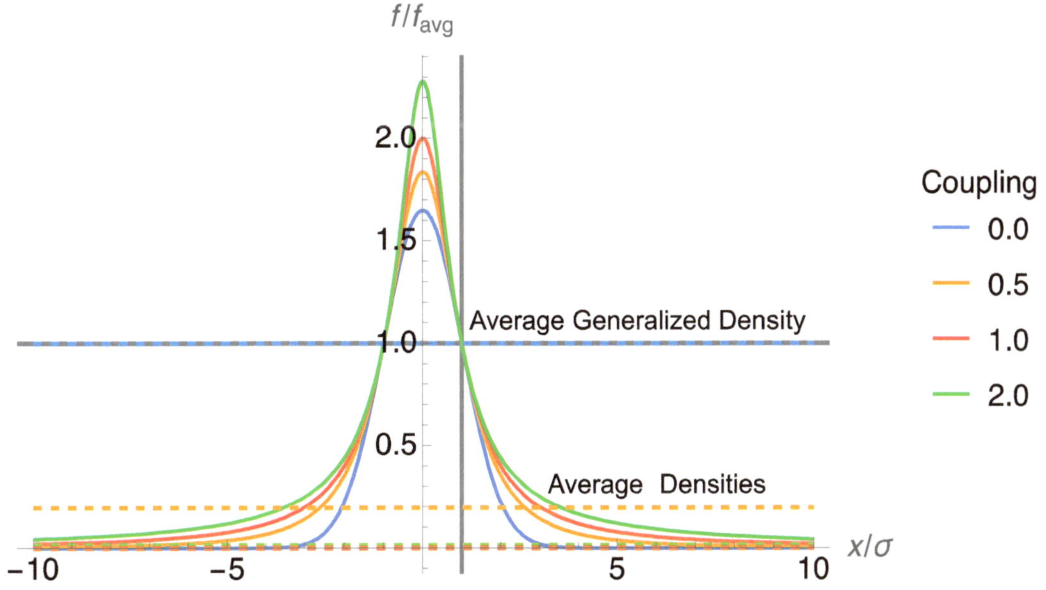

Figure 1. Contrast between the average density and average generalized density.

In particular, the scale σ of the Student t distribution, which generalizes the standard deviation of the Gaussian and is referred to as the *q-standard deviation* in NSM, remains finite. The analysis shows that the generalized mean can be used to separate the effect that the shape and the scale have on measures of the uncertainty.

Open Problem 2: *Given that the average generalized density is equal to the density at the mean plus/minus the scale for the coupled Gaussian and the location plus the scale for the coupled exponential, can the relationship between the average generalized density and the average density be quantified in a manner that strengthens the explanation of how the generalized entropy complements the entropy function in describing the uncertainty of a system? For instance, given that entropy is a measure of the degrees of freedom of a system, and the coupling is the inverse of the degrees of freedom, can the difference between the coupled entropy and the entropy be quantified in terms of the degrees of freedom?*

Comment on Problem 2: *An important aspect of the investigation of statistical degrees of freedom is its relationship with the thermodynamic degrees of freedom. As noted in Table 1 and described in* [25], *q is determined by the degrees of freedom, n, of a temperature bath. Substituting (11), the shape, which is the reciprocal of the statistical degrees of freedom, is related by*

$$n = \frac{d\,N}{2} = \frac{q}{q-1} = 2 + \frac{1}{\kappa}, \tag{18}$$

Taking $\alpha = 1$*, given that the distribution is based on the energy. d is the dimensions of translational degrees of freedom, though rotational and vibrational could also be considered. N is the number of molecules.*

4. NSM: Mathematical Fit or Physical Theory?

A common criticism of the NSM has been that it is merely a mathematical fit to physical phenomena given a free parameter rather than a physical theory that provides an explanatory description of complex systems [10,12,14,28]. While this claim has been refuted by investigators in the NSM community [2,29–31], we should take a moment to consider what distinguishes a physical theory from a mathematical fit. Firstly, mathematical theories build from assumed axioms and deductively prove derivative theories. Physical theories are a subset of mathematical theories that are constrained by physical measurements of the world. So, demonstrating a fit between a mathematical theory and physical measurement is a crucial step toward a physical theory. But is a fit sufficient to qualify a relationship as a physical theory? In physics, we are seeking models that provide explanatory power in describing a system. As such, each term (variables and constants) in a physical theory must have a clear definition of its role in the physical model; otherwise, the model loses its ability to be explanatory.

Further, an effective model must fulfill the requirement of being the simplest representation of a phenomenon. Occam's razor [32,33] was one of the first articulations of this principle, and Bayes' Theorem quantifies this property by specifying the uncertainty created by the overfitting of more complex models (see Ch. 28 of [34]). In the context of NSM, these criteria establish a requirement that its defining parameter q has a clear physical definition and this property provides a simpler explanation of the statistics of complex systems than the shape or degrees of freedom parameters that it seeks to replace. For even in the case where the equations of NSM can be derived from first principles [35,36], if the defining parameter does not have a physical definition, the derivation still lacks a physical interpretation.

Furthermore, as noted in the introduction, q does in fact have a straightforward interpretation based on the escort distribution. The original motivation of q-statistics was the consideration of systems defined by an escort distribution with probabilities $\frac{p_i^q}{\sum_{i=1}^N p_i^q}$. The quantity p_i^q defines the probability of q random variables that occupy the same state i. Thus, the necessary starting point for defining a physical property of q is the number of independent random variables sharing the same state. For continuous random variables, we can consider an approximate threshold to discretize the limit. The relevance to complex systems is that the independent components of a multivariate heavy-tailed distribution are nevertheless correlated (or conversely, if linearly uncorrelated the components are dependent). Due to the nonlinear dependence between the dimensions of a heavy-tailed distribution, there is a higher occurrence of discrete variables that are equal or continuous variables that are approximately equal than would occur for distributions with exponential decay. This property has recently been explored as an approach to filtering heavy-tailed samples to facilitate the estimation of their distribution [37].

Nevertheless, the question remains whether the property of equal-valued independent random variables is central to describing the statistics of complex systems. Several investigators have suggested other interpretations, but close examination shows that the descriptions are equal to $q-1$ or another function of q, rather than q itself. For instance, Wilk and Włodarczyk [38,39] show how the fluctuations (relative variance) of an inverse scale parameter $\left(\frac{1}{\lambda}\right)$ are equal to $q-1$. The problem is this does not provide an interpretation of q's statistical property; rather, it shows that q is misaligned by -1 with a possible interpretation. The relative variance is indeed a useful property, and, thus, the variable $a = q - 1$ is a candidate for an approach to defining nonextensive statistical mechanics. But, as we will see in the following section, multidimensional analysis shows that neither q nor $q-1$ are fundamental.

Open Problem 3: *We must define and provide evidence for a physical definition of the parameter q. Included in this definition must be an explanation of the role of the number of independent random variables via the expression p^q. We must demonstrate that this physical property simplifies and/or improves the description of the statistics of complex systems in comparison to the shape or the shape's inverse, the degrees of freedom.*

5. The q-Product Does Not Construct the Multivariate Distributions

Borges [26] initiated and other investigators [40–42] further developed a q-algebra to encapsulate the core functions of nonextensive statistical mechanics. The foundational functions are a generalization of addition and multiplication, though the two do not form a generalized distributive property. The lack of distribution property was in part caused by the q-sum being primarily relevant to the combining of q-logarithms, while the q-product was primarily relevant to the combining of q-exponentials. Here are the definitions in those contexts:

$$\begin{aligned} \ln_q x \oplus_q \ln_q y \equiv \left(\tfrac{x^{1-q}-1}{1-q}\right) + \left(\tfrac{y^{1-q}-1}{1-q}\right) + (1-q)\left(\tfrac{x^{1-q}-1}{1-q}\right)\left(\tfrac{y^{1-q}-1}{1-q}\right) \\ = \left(\tfrac{(xy)^{1-q}-1}{1-q}\right) = \ln_q xy; \end{aligned} \tag{19}$$

$$\begin{aligned} &\exp_q(x) \otimes_q \exp_q(y) \\ &\equiv \left(\left((1+(1-q)x)_+^{\frac{1}{1-q}}\right)^{1-q} + \left((1+(1-q)y)_+^{\frac{1}{1-q}}\right)^{1-q} - 1\right)^{\frac{1}{1-q}} \\ &= (1+(1-q)(x+y))_+^{\frac{1}{1-q}} = \exp_q(x+y). \end{aligned} \tag{20}$$

While these constructions provide a useful shorthand for some of the complex relationships in nonextensive statistical mechanics, when applied to statistical analysis, a significant shortcoming is evident. A bedrock principle of probability theory, which was discussed in the last section, is that independent probabilities multiply to form the joint probability. Thus, a natural question arises regarding the properties of the q-product of probabilities. Putting aside for a moment the normalization of the q-exponential and q-Gaussian distributions, which add a further complication, how does the q-product of their distributions relate to the multivariate forms of these distributions? From the definition of the q-product, we have

$$\exp_q\left(\frac{1}{\alpha}x^{\alpha}_{1_1}\right) \otimes_q \exp_q\left(\frac{1}{\alpha}x_2^{\alpha}\right) \ldots \otimes_q \exp_q\left(\frac{1}{\alpha}x_n^{\alpha}\right) = \exp_q\left(\sum_{i=1}^{n} x_i^{\alpha}\right). \tag{21}$$

where α is one for the q-exponential distribution and two for the q-Gaussian. Unfortunately, the expression on the right has very little to do with the multivariate form of these distributions when no cross-terms $x_i^{\alpha}x_j^{\alpha}$ exist. This is because the exponents of the distribution include both a dimensional term and α. Even for just the one-dimensional case, this led investigators to define $1-Q \equiv 2(1-q)$ to account for the distinctions. The multivariate form of these distributions [43] is proportional to the following:

$$f(\mathbf{x}) \propto \left[1 + \kappa \frac{\sum_{i=1}^{n} x_i^{\alpha}}{\sigma^{\alpha}}\right]^{-\frac{1}{\alpha}\left(\frac{1}{\kappa}+d\right)}. \tag{22}$$

From this expression, it is evident that trying to force the multiplicative term inside the brackets and the exponent to be $1-q$ and $\frac{1}{1-q}$, respectively, results in several distortions of the physical properties. Firstly, in NSM, the physical scale of the distributions σ is typically buried in a parameter referred to as the generalized inverse temperature, $\beta_q = \frac{\kappa}{(1-q)\sigma^{\alpha}}$. And from the exponent, q is defined by the relationship $\frac{1}{1-q} = -\frac{1}{\alpha}\left(\frac{1}{\kappa}+d\right)$.

$$q = 1 + \frac{\alpha\kappa}{1+d\kappa} \tag{23}$$

To address the multivariate case, Umarov and Tsallis [44] formulated the following definitions for the multivariate Gaussian case ($\alpha = 2$):

$$q_k^d \equiv q_{kd} \equiv \frac{2q - kd(q-1)}{2 - kd(q-1)}. \tag{24}$$

Far from illuminating the multivariate statistics of complex systems, these types of expressions provide evidence that q is not aligned with the statistical properties of complex systems. Again, to interpret such an expression, it is not enough to understand that q is the number of equal-valued independent random variables; rather, we also need to explain the physical role of each term in the right-hand expression. Without these explanations, the relationship fulfills a mathematical fit but falls short of a physical theory.

Open Problem 4: *While the q-product is often referenced regarding its role in defining q-independence, the form does not lead to the structure of the multivariate heavy-tailed distributions in the manner that the product of distributions equates with the multivariate distribution of independent variables. A definition of the generalized product for NSM is needed that is based on the properties of the multivariate distributions, as was proposed in* [43].

6. Does the q-Fourier Transform Model the Properties of Complex Signals?

One of the celebrated results of NSM is the proof of a generalized central limit theorem (q-CLT) [45] that converges to q-Gaussians for random variables found to have a property of *q-independence*. The nonlinear dependence described by q-independence relies on a generalization of the Fourier transform that maps q-Gaussians to a q^*-Gaussians. Given a more general form of the Fourier transforms, a natural application would be the design of filters for signals with long-range correlations and/or fluctuations, the tell-tale characteristic of signals from a complex system. And yet, to date, there appear to be no applications of the q-Fourier transform to signal processing. Related to the lack of applications is the lack of a symmetric inverse [46–48], one of the key properties that has made the Fourier transform the foundation of signal processing. To frame this problem, I will examine the Fourier transform in the context of the symmetry between the compact-support and heavy-tailed functions of NSM [49].

The gap in what should be a straightforward application of NSM results from the disconnect between the mathematical relationships for the q-CLT and the physics of signal processing. We must recall that the Fourier transform takes a function as an input (called the signal) and outputs another function (called the image) that preserves all the information about the original function. The process can be inverted with a function that has the same structural form. The image has been proven to represent the sinusoidal frequencies of the original signal and is used throughout engineering and science to craft filters for noise reduction, match filtering, and countless other purposes. As the name "image" implies, the FT is a kind of mirror. When applied to probability distributions, the FT mirror has the property of transforming wide, high-entropy distributions into narrow, low-entropy image functions. The Gaussian turns out to be the symmetrical function of this process, whereby the FT of a Gaussian is also Gaussian (though no longer normalized to integrate to one). And the variance of the image is proportional to the inverse of the signal's variance.

Unfortunately, as currently defined, the q-FT violates this basic relationship between a signal and its image. The q-FT transforms both the tail shape and the scale of the distribution. Focusing on the tail shape, the transformed value of q and its translation into the shape parameter are determined from the definition of q-FT to be

$$q_1 = \frac{1+q}{3-q};\ \kappa_1 = \frac{\kappa}{1-\kappa}. \tag{25}$$

Table 2 shows how different domains of the heavy-tailed q-Gaussian distributions are transformed by the q-FT into wider-tailed images. The Cauchy distribution ($\kappa = 1,\ q = 2$) highlights the difficulties involved in applying the q-FT to signal processing since the image function is an impulse function ($\kappa = \infty,\ q = 3$). This suggests that the Cauchy distribution is the limit of physically realizable distributions. There are systems such as the Standard Map in which the Cauchy does act as a limiting distribution [50,51]. At the same time, the coherent noise model [52] and the Erhenfest dog–flea model [53] have been measured to have q-Gaussians with the shape/q values ($\kappa = 1.53,\ q = 2.21$) and ($\kappa = 2.08,\ q = 2.35$), respectively. And yet, distributions in this domain of very slow tail decay ($1 < \kappa < \infty,\ 2 < q < 3$) have a q-FT image function with a divergent integral ($-\infty < \kappa < -1,\ 3 < q < \infty$), suggesting that these would not arise in physically realizable systems.

Table 2. Description of the q-Gaussian domains and their associated q-FT image. The q-FT transforms have functions such as the q-FT to images with slower decaying tails. So, for example, the last row is the domain of distributions with an undefined mean, which has an image with a divergent integral.

q-Gaussian Domain			q-FT Image		
Description	**Shape, κ**	**q**	**Description**	**Shape**	**q**
Finite Mean Finite Var.	[0, 1/3)	[1, 3/2)	Finite Mean Finite Var.	[0, 1/2)	[1, 5/3)
Finite Mean Finite Var.	[1/3, 1/2)	[3/2, 5/3)	Finite Mean Div. Variance	[1/2 , 1)	[5/3, 2)
Finite Mean Div. Variance	[1/2 , 1)	[5/3, 2)	Undefined Mean Div. Variance	[1, ∞)	[2, 3)
Undefined Mean Div. Variance	[1, ∞)	[2, 3)	Div. Integral	[−∞, −1)	[3, ∞)

In contrast to the q-FT, the Fourier transform maps heavy-tailed q-Gaussians into functions that are a product of a power-law term and a modified second-order Bessel function, which has an exponential tail decay.

$$\mathcal{F}\left[\left[1+\kappa x^2\right]_+^{-\frac{1}{2}\left(\frac{1}{\kappa}+1\right)}\right] \propto \left(\frac{|t|}{\sqrt{\kappa}}\right)^{\frac{1}{2\kappa}} K_{1/2}\left(\frac{|t|}{\sqrt{\kappa}}\right). \tag{26}$$

The power-law term increases with x but is sharply dampened by and in the limit of $x \to \infty$ dominated by the exponential decay of the Bessel function. It is noteworthy that the exponent of the power-law term $\frac{1}{2\kappa}$ turns out to be a conjugate mapping between the exponents of the heavy-tailed and compact-support q-Gaussians. That is, for $\kappa > 0$, the heavy-tail and compact-support domains are related by

$$\begin{array}{cc} \text{Heavy}-\text{tailed} & \text{Compact}-\text{support} \\ \left[1+\kappa x^2\right]_+^{-\frac{1}{2}\left(\frac{1}{\kappa}+1\right)} & \left[1-\frac{\kappa}{1+\kappa}x^2\right]_+^{\frac{1}{2\kappa}}. \end{array} \tag{27}$$

In [49], I proposed a symmetrical generalization of the Fourier transform that maps the q-Gaussians between their compact-support and heavy-tailed domains. However, the transform included a mapping of the q parameter that did not generalize to other functions. A requirement for a complete definition is a mathematically rigorous mapping between the infinite domain of the heavy-tailed distributions and the finite-domain compact-support functions.

Open Problem 5: *As currently defined, the q-Fourier transform of NSM has limited physical applications, since (a) the inverse is not symmetric and (b) the image function has slower decaying tails. Can these limitations be validated by limits within physical applications of heavy-tailed distributions, or can a symmetric generalization of the Fourier transform be defined? A candidate for a symmetric Fourier transform maps q-Gaussians between their heavy-tailed and compact-support domains but currently lacks a general mapping between these domains. Can a mathematically rigorous mapping between the compact-support and heavy-tailed domains be defined that would qualify as a generalization of the Fourier transform?*

7. How Should Nonextensive Entropy Be Normalized?

During the early investigations of nonextensive entropy, a question arose regarding the proper probability required to weight the generalized entropy. Tsallis entropy, $S_q^T \equiv \frac{1-\sum_i p_i^q}{q-1} = -\sum_i p_i^q ln_q p_i$ (Tsallis, 2009), is weighted by p_i^q; however, this form does not make use of the escort probability $\frac{p_i^q}{\sum_i p_i^q}$ normalization used for defining the constraints for the generalized maximum entropy formalism. For this reason, the normalized Tsallis entropy [54,55] $S_q^{NT} \equiv \frac{S_q^T}{\sum_j p_j^q} = \frac{-1+\frac{1}{\sum_i p_i^q}}{q-1} = -\sum_i \frac{p_i^q}{\sum_j p_j^q} ln_q p_i$ was investigated. The normalized Tsallis entropy was found not to satisfy the Lesche stability requirement [56–58] and has since been dismissed in favor of the original Tsallis entropy form.

However, given the insight regarding the distinction between the power and normalization for the generalized exponential and logarithms discussed in Section 5, another normalization can be considered. The coupled entropy [27,59] is defined as follows:

$$
\begin{aligned}
S_\kappa^C(\mathbf{p}; d, \alpha) &\equiv \sum_i \frac{p_i^{1+\frac{\alpha\kappa}{1+d\kappa}}}{\alpha \sum_j p_j^{1+\frac{\alpha\kappa}{1+d\kappa}}} \ln_\kappa p_i^{\frac{-\alpha}{1+d\kappa}} \\
&= \sum_i \frac{1}{\alpha\kappa} \frac{p_i^{1+\frac{\alpha\kappa}{1+d\kappa}}}{\sum_j p_j^{1+\frac{\alpha\kappa}{1+d\kappa}}} \left(p_i^{\frac{-\alpha\kappa}{1+d\kappa}} - 1 \right).
\end{aligned} \tag{28}
$$

In [27], it was found that the coupled and Tsallis entropy are (constant, asymptotically constant) a function of the coupling for the generalized Pareto distribution with the matching coupling value and a scale equal to (one, non-one), respectively. However, for the matched coupled Gaussian, the coupled entropy rose in value, while the Tsallis entropy decayed with the increasing coupling value, i.e., the more heavy-tailed distributions.

The issue of normalization for a generalized entropy comes into sharper focus when considering the role of a generalized sum in defining the nonlinear combination of entropies. Substituting for q the relationship between the coupled, normalized, and Tsallis entropies results in the following expression:

$$
S_\kappa^C(\mathbf{p}; d, \alpha) = \frac{S_\kappa^{NT}(\mathbf{p}; d, \alpha)}{1 + d\kappa} = \frac{S_\kappa^T(\mathbf{p}; d, \alpha)}{(1 + d\kappa) \sum_j p_j^{1+\frac{\alpha\kappa}{1+d\kappa}}}. \tag{29}
$$

While the q-sum of q-entropies has been defined as (using the coupling notation)

$$
\begin{aligned}
& S^T_{1+\frac{\alpha\kappa}{1+d\kappa}}(\mathbf{p}_A) \oplus_{1+\frac{\alpha\kappa}{1+d\kappa}} S^T_{1+\frac{\alpha\kappa}{1+d\kappa}}(\mathbf{p}_B) \\
&\quad \equiv S^T_{1+\frac{\alpha\kappa}{1+d\kappa}}(\mathbf{p}_A) + S^T_{1+\frac{\alpha\kappa}{1+d\kappa}}(\mathbf{p}_B) \\
&\quad -\frac{\alpha\kappa}{1+d\kappa} S^T_{1+\frac{\alpha\kappa}{1+d\kappa}}(\mathbf{p}_A) S^T_{1+\frac{\alpha\kappa}{1+d\kappa}}(\mathbf{p}_B),
\end{aligned} \tag{30}
$$

the coupled sum removes the dependency on $\frac{1}{1+d\kappa}$

$$
S_\kappa^C(\mathbf{p}_A) \bigoplus_{\alpha\kappa} S_\kappa^C(\mathbf{p}_B) \equiv S_\kappa^C(\mathbf{p}_A) + S_\kappa^C(\mathbf{p}_B) + \alpha\kappa\, S_\kappa^C(\mathbf{p}_A) S_\kappa^C(\mathbf{p}_B). \tag{31}
$$

Notably, the B-G-S entropy scales with the degrees of freedom, and the nonextensive entropies modify this scaling [35,60]. Given that κ is the inverse of the statistical degrees of freedom, the coupled sum of the coupled entropies directly expresses this modification.

Open Problem 6: *What is the proper normalization of a generalized entropy, and how does the normalization impact the relationship between a generalized entropy and the statistical degrees of freedom? Stability issues caused a rejection of the normalized Tsallis entropy; however, neither the normalized nor the unnormalized Tsallis entropy consider how converting the derivatives of a cdf into a pdf impacts the relationship between the definition of the generalized exponential and logarithmic functions and the structure of a pdf and its generalized entropy. When this is accounted for, the nonlinear term combining a nonextensive entropy (coupled entropy) is precisely the inverse of the statistical degrees of freedom. Does this suggest a criterion for the normalization?*

Comment on Problem 6: *There are a variety of applications that may be impacted by the normalization of the NSM entropy. For instance, the robustness of machine learning algorithms have been improved using both q-entropy* [61,62] *and coupled entropy* [59] *generalizations. A careful analysis of whether the difference in normalization impacts the performance improvements would contribute to determining the importance of the normalization. Entropic analysis has been shown to be an effective measure of financial market volatility, but greater detail is needed to determine the relative advantages of different forms of generalized entropy* [63,64].

8. A Measure of Complexity

The derivation of nonextensive entropy began with the investigation of systems with a modified distribution, in which the probability of a state is raised to the power q. As discussed in Sections 2 and 4, this necessitates a physical interpretation of q as the number of independent random variables sharing the same state. Unfortunately, clarifying this interpretation raises questions as to whether q is a fundamental or secondary property of complex systems. The more fundamental question is as follows: how should the statistical complexity of a system be quantified? The mismatch between q's physical interpretation and the fundamental properties of complex systems may explain why the field has avoided addressing this issue.

Nevertheless, an approach to quantifying the statistical complexity of a system may be quite simple. The property nonlinear statistical coupling was first introduced with the candidate $1 - q$, which fulfilled the need for the linear domain to have a value of zero; however, multidimensional analysis exposed that isolating the nonlinear properties required decomposition. As shown in Equation (23), q is dependent on three properties, the dimension d, the nonlinearity of the random variable α, and the redefined nonlinear statistical coupling κ. The coupling term is not new; in fact, it has a long tradition within statistical analysis as the shape parameter defining the deviation from exponential decay, and it is the inverse of the degrees of freedom used to define the Student t distribution. And so, the final open problem for the reader to consider is whether the coupling or shape parameter is an appropriate measure of a system's statistical complexity.

Open Problem 7: *Does the shape parameter, also referred to as the nonlinear statistical coupling, provide a quantification of a system's statistical complexity? Can this definition of statistical complexity be related to other forms of complexity, such as algorithmic complexity? Explain the statistical complexity in terms of its inverse, the statistical degrees of freedom. For instance, given samples from which to determine a model, does the nonlinearity of the function define the deterministic complexity of the model? And do the statistical degrees of freedom (samples minus model parameters) determine the inverse of the statistical complexity of the model?*

9. Conclusions

While NSM has advanced the modeling of uncertainty within complex systems, there remain many open problems worthy of investigation. In this paper, issues arising from the use of the parameter q as a focal point for modeling complex systems are examined. These issues are framed in terms of a set of open problems, including the following:

1. Should the generalized exponential function, originally proposed by (Borges, 2004) [26], be applied to the survival function rather than the probability density functions?
2. Can the difference between generalized entropy and BGS entropy be explained in terms of the degrees of freedom and its inverse, the nonlinear statistical coupling?
3. For NSM to be a complete physical theory, a clear physical interpretation of q is required. We must determine whether the number of independent random variables sharing the same state is the appropriate interpretation of q.
4. We must define the q-product using the properties of the multivariate distributions of q-statistics.
5. The q-Fourier transform does not seem to model the physical image of a heavy-tailed signal. For example, the Cauchy distribution is transformed into a delta function,

which could not be used for real-world signal processing. Can a generalization of the Fourier transform be defined that utilizes the complementary properties of the compact-support and heavy-tailed domains?

6. The normalization of the coupled entropy differs from both the normalized and unnormalized Tsallis entropy. Is there a criterion that would clarify a preference between these three normalizations of the generalized entropy for complex systems?
7. We must define a measure of statistical complexity.

The author has proposed that the nonlinear statistical coupling, which is equal to the shape parameter and the inverse of the degrees of freedom, is a measure of statistical complexity. It is left to the reader to examine this set of open problems, determine satisfactory solutions, and consider whether a reframing of nonextensive statistical mechanics leads to a focus on the fundamental properties of complex systems.

Funding: This research received no external funding.

Conflicts of Interest: Author Kenric P. Nelson was employed by the company Photrek, LLC. The author declares that the research was conducted in the absence of any commercial or financial relationships that could be construed as a potential conflict of interest.

References

1. Tsallis, C. *Introduction to Nonextensive Statistical Mechanics: Approaching a Complex World*; Springer Science & Business Media: Berlin/Heidelberg, Germany, 2009. [CrossRef]
2. Umarov, S.; Constantino, T. *Mathematical Foundations of Nonextensive Statistical Mechanics*; World Scientific: Singapore, 2022; ISBN 9789811245176. [CrossRef]
3. Abe, S.; Okamoto, Y. (Eds.) *Nonextensive Statistical Mechanics and Its Applications*; Lecture Notes in Physics; Springer: Berlin/Heidelberg, Germany, 2001; Volume 560, ISBN 978-3-540-41208-3. [CrossRef]
4. Abe, S.; Martínez, S.; Pennini, F.; Plastino, A. Nonextensive Thermodynamic Relations. *Phys. Lett. A* **2001**, *281*, 126–130. [CrossRef]
5. Beck, C. Dynamical Foundations of Nonextensive Statistical Mechanics. *Phys. Rev. Lett.* **2001**, *87*, 180601. [CrossRef]
6. Tsallis, C.; Baldovin, F.; Cerbino, R.; Pierobon, P. Introduction to Nonextensive Statistical Mechanics and Thermodynamics. *arXiv* **2003**, arXiv:cond-mat/0309093. [CrossRef]
7. Plastino, A.R.; Plastino, A. Non-Extensive Statistical Mechanics and Generalized Fokker-Planck Equation. *Phys. A Stat. Mech. Its Appl.* **1995**, *222*, 347–354. [CrossRef]
8. Rajagopal, A.K.; Rendell, R.W. Nonextensive Statistical Mechanics: Implications to Quantum Information. *Europhys. News* **2005**, *36*, 221–224. [CrossRef]
9. Ruseckas, J.; Gontis, V.; Kaulakys, B. Nonextensive Statistical Mechanics Distributions and Dynamics of Financial Observables from the Nonlinear Stochastic Differential Equations. *Advs. Complex. Syst.* **2012**, *15*, 1250073. [CrossRef]
10. Hilhorst, H.J.; Schehr, G. A Note on Q-Gaussians and Non-Gaussians in Statistical Mechanics. *J. Stat. Mech.* **2007**, *2007*, P06003. [CrossRef]
11. Ou, C.; Chen, J. Two Long-Standing Problems in Tsallis' Statistics. *Phys. A Stat. Mech. Its Appl.* **2006**, *370*, 525–529. [CrossRef]
12. Dauxois, T. Non-Gaussian Distributions under Scrutiny. *J. Stat. Mech.* **2007**, *2007*, N08001. [CrossRef]
13. Shalizi, Cosma, R. Tsallis Statistics, Statistical Mechanics for Non-Extensive Systems and Long-Range Interactions. *arXiv* **2021**, arXiv:math/0701854. [CrossRef]
14. Nauenberg, M. Critique of q-Entropy for Thermal Statistics. *Phys. Rev. E* **2003**, *67*, 036114. [CrossRef]
15. Zanette, D.H.; Montemurro, M.A. A Note on Non-Thermodynamical Applications of Non-Extensive Statistics. *Phys. Lett. A* **2004**, *324*, 383–387. [CrossRef]
16. Tsallis, C. Possible Generalization of Boltzmann-Gibbs Statistics. *J. Stat. Phys.* **1988**, *52*, 479–487. [CrossRef]
17. Drzazga, E.A.; Szczęśniak, R.; Domagalska, I.A.; Durajski, A.P.; Kostrzewa, M. Non-Parametric Application of Tsallis Statistics to Systems Consisting of M Hydrogen Molecules. *Phys. A Stat. Mech. Its Appl.* **2019**, *518*, 1–12. [CrossRef]
18. Livadiotis, G.; McComas, D.J. Beyond Kappa Distributions: Exploiting Tsallis Statistical Mechanics in Space Plasmas. *J. Geophys. Res.* **2009**, *114*, 2009JA014352. [CrossRef]
19. Pavlos, G.P.; Karakatsanis, L.P.; Iliopoulos, A.C.; Pavlos, E.G.; Tsonis, A.A. Non-Extensive Statistical Mechanics: Overview of Theory and Applications in Seismogenesis, Climate, and Space Plasma. In *Advances in Nonlinear Geosciences*; Tsonis, A.A., Ed.; Springer International Publishing: Cham, Switzerland, 2018; pp. 465–495. ISBN 978-3-319-58895-7. [CrossRef]
20. Devi, S. Financial Market Dynamics: Superdiffusive or Not? *J. Stat. Mech.* **2017**, *2017*, 083207. [CrossRef]
21. Upadhyaya, A.; Rieu, J.-P.; Glazier, J.A.; Sawada, Y. Anomalous Diffusion and Non-Gaussian Velocity Distribution of Hydra Cells in Cellular Aggregates. *Phys. A Stat. Mech. Its Appl.* **2001**, *293*, 549–558. [CrossRef]
22. Mendes, G.A.; Ribeiro, M.S.; Mendes, R.S.; Lenzi, E.K.; Nobre, F.D. Nonlinear Kramers Equation Associated with Nonextensive Statistical Mechanics. *Phys. Rev. E* **2015**, *91*, 052106. [CrossRef] [PubMed]

23. Akıllı, M.; Yılmaz, N.; Akdeniz, K.G. The 'Wavelet' Entropic Index q of Non-Extensive Statistical Mechanics and Superstatistics. *Chaos Solitons Fractals* **2021**, *150*, 111094. [CrossRef]
24. Potiguar, F.; Costa, U. Thermodynamics Arising from Tsallis' Thermostatistics. *arXiv* **2002**, arXiv:cond-mat/0208357. [CrossRef]
25. Potiguar, F.Q.; Costa, U.M.S. Fluctuation of Energy in the Generalized Thermostatistics. *Phys. A Stat. Mech. Its Appl.* **2003**, *321*, 482–492. [CrossRef]
26. Borges, E.P. A Possible Deformed Algebra and Calculus Inspired in Nonextensive Thermostatistics. *Phys. A Stat. Mech. Its Appl.* **2004**, *340*, 95–101. [CrossRef]
27. Nelson, K.P.; Umarov, S.R.; Kon, M.A. On the Average Uncertainty for Systems with Nonlinear Coupling. *Phys. A Stat. Mech. Its Appl.* **2017**, *468*, 30–43. [CrossRef]
28. Cartwright, J. Roll Over, Boltzmann. *Physics World*, 29 May 2014; pp. 31–35. Available online: https://physicsworld.com/a/roll-over-boltzmann/ (accessed on 22 January 2024)
29. Tsallis, C. Comment on "Critique of q-Entropy for Thermal Statistics". *Phys. Rev. E* **2004**, *69*, 038101. [CrossRef] [PubMed]
30. Baranger, M. Why Tsallis Statistics? *Phys. A Stat. Mech. Its Appl.* **2002**, *305*, 27–31. [CrossRef]
31. Tsallis, C. T. Dauxois' "Non-Gaussian Distributions Under Scrutiny" Under Scrutiny. In Proceedings of the Third UN/ESA/NASA Workshop on the International Heliophysical Year 2007 and Basic Space Science, Japan, Tokyo, 18–22 June 2007; Springer: Berlin/Heidelberg, Germany, 2009. [CrossRef]
32. Domingos, P. The Role of Occam's Razor in Knowledge Discovery. *Data Min. Knowl. Discov.* **1999**, 3, 409–425. [CrossRef]
33. Standish, R.K. Why Occam's Razor. *Found. Phys. Lett.* **2004**, *17*, 255–266. [CrossRef]
34. MacKay, D.J.C. *Information Theory, Inference and Learning Algorithms*; Cambridge University Press: Cambridge, UK, 2003; ISBN 978-0-521-64298-9. [CrossRef]
35. Thurner, S.; Hanel, R. The Entropy of Non-Ergodic Complex Systems—A Derivation from First Principles. *Int. J. Mod. Phys. Conf. Ser.* **2012**, *16*, 105–115. [CrossRef]
36. Saadatmand, S.N.; Gould, T.; Cavalcanti, E.G.; Vaccaro, J.A. Thermodynamics from First Principles: Correlations and Nonextensivity. *Phys. Rev. E* **2020**, *101*, 060101. [CrossRef]
37. Nelson, K.P. Independent Approximates Enable Closed-Form Estimation of Heavy-Tailed Distributions. *Phys. A Stat. Mech. Its Appl.* **2022**, *601*, 127574. [CrossRef]
38. Wilk, G.; Włodarczyk, Z. Interpretation of the Nonextensivity Parameter q in Some Applications of Tsallis Statistics and Lévy Distributions. *Phys. Rev. Lett.* **2000**, *84*, 2770–2773. [CrossRef]
39. Wilk, G.; Włodarczyk, Z. Fluctuations, Correlations and the Nonextensivity. *Phys. A Stat. Mech. Its Appl.* **2007**, *376*, 279–288. [CrossRef]
40. Pennini, F.; Plastino, A.; Ferri, G.L. Fisher Information, Borges Operators, and q-Calculus. *Phys. A Stat. Mech. Its Appl.* **2008**, *387*, 5778–5785. [CrossRef]
41. Nivanen, L.; Le Méhauté, A.; Wang, Q.A. Generalized Algebra within a Nonextensive Statistics. *Rep. Math. Phys.* **2003**, *52*, 437–444. [CrossRef]
42. Cardoso, P.G.S.; Borges, E.P.; Lobão, T.C.P.; Pinho, S.T.R. Nondistributive Algebraic Structures Derived from Nonextensive Statistical Mechanics. *J. Math. Phys.* **2008**, *49*, 093509. [CrossRef]
43. Nelson, K.P. A Definition of the Coupled-Product for Multivariate Coupled-Exponentials. *Phys. A Stat. Mech. Its Appl.* **2015**, *422*, 187–192. [CrossRef]
44. Umarov, S.; Tsallis, C. On Multivariate Generalizations of the q-central Limit Theorem Consistent with Nonextensive Statistical Mechanics. *AIP Conf. Proc.* **2007**, *965*, 34–42. [CrossRef]
45. Umarov, S.; Tsallis, C.; Steinberg, S. On a q-Central Limit Theorem Consistent with Nonextensive Statistical Mechanics. *Milan J. Math.* **2008**, *76*, 307–328. [CrossRef]
46. Jauregui, M.; Tsallis, C. q-Generalization of the Inverse Fourier Transform. *Phys. Lett. A* **2011**, *375*, 2085–2088. [CrossRef]
47. Umarov, S.; Tsallis, C. The Limit Distribution in the q-CLT for $q >= 1$ Is Unique and Can Not Have a Compact Support. *J. Phys. A Math. Theor.* **2016**, *49*, 415204. [CrossRef]
48. Umarov, S.; Tsallis, C. On a Representation of the Inverse Fq-Transform. *Phys. Lett. A* **2008**, *372*, 4874–4876.
49. Nelson, K.P.; Umarov, S. The Relationship between Tsallis Statistics, the Fourier Transform, and Nonlinear Coupling. *arXiv* **2008**, arXiv:0811.3777. [CrossRef]
50. Cetin, K.; Tirnakli, U.; Boghosian, B.M. A Generalization of the Standard Map and Its Statistical Characterization. *Sci. Rep.* **2022**, *12*, 8575. [CrossRef]
51. Ruiz, G.; Tirnakli, U.; Borges, E.P.; Tsallis, C. Statistical Characterization of the Standard Map. *J. Stat. Mech. Theory Exp.* **2017**, *2017*, 063403. [CrossRef]
52. Celikoglu, A.; Tirnakli, U.; Queirós, S.M.D. Analysis of Return Distributions in the Coherent Noise Model. *Phys. Rev. E* **2010**, *82*, 021124. [CrossRef] [PubMed]
53. Bakar, B.; Tirnakli, U. Analysis of Self-Organized Criticality in Ehrenfest's Dog-Flea Model. *Phys. Rev. E* **2009**, *79*, 040103. [CrossRef] [PubMed]
54. Rajagopal, A.K.; Abe, S. Implications of Form Invariance to the Structure of Nonextensive Entropies. *Phys. Rev. Lett.* **1999**, *83*, 1711–1714. [CrossRef]
55. Lenzi, E.K.; Mendes, R.S.; da Silva, L.R. Normalized Tsallis Entropy and Its Implications for the Nonextensive Thermostatistics. *Phys. A Stat. Mech. Its Appl.* **2001**, *295*, 230–233. [CrossRef]

56. Abe, S. Stability of Tsallis Entropy and Instabilities of Rényi and Normalized Tsallis Entropies: A Basis for q -Exponential Distributions. *Phys. Rev. E* **2002**, *66*, 046134. [CrossRef] [PubMed]
57. Abe, S.; Kaniadakis, G.; Scarfone, A.M. Stabilities of Generalized Entropies. *J. Phys. A Math. Gen.* **2004**, *37*, 10513–10519. [CrossRef]
58. Lesche, B. Instabilities of Rényi Entropies. *J. Stat. Phys.* **1982**, *27*, 419–422. [CrossRef]
59. Cao, S.; Li, J.; Nelson, K.P.; Kon, M.A. Coupled VAE: Improved Accuracy and Robustness of a Variational Autoencoder. *Entropy* **2022**, *24*, 423. [CrossRef] [PubMed]
60. Hanel, R.; Thurner, S.; Gell-Mann, M. How Multiplicity Determines Entropy and the Derivation of the Maximum Entropy Principle for Complex Systems. *Proc. Natl. Acad. Sci. USA* **2014**, *111*, 6905–6910. [CrossRef] [PubMed]
61. Kobayashi, T.; Watanuki, R. Sparse Representation Learning with Modified Q-VAE towards Minimal Realization of World Model. *Adv. Robot.* **2023**, *37*, 1–21. [CrossRef]
62. Kobayashis, T. Q-VAE for Disentangled Representation Learning and Latent Dynamical Systems. *IEEE Robot. Autom. Lett.* **2020**, *5*, 5669–5676. [CrossRef]
63. Bentes, S.R.; Menezes, R. Entropy: A New Measure of Stock Market Volatility? *J. Phys. Conf. Ser.* **2012**, *394*, 012033. [CrossRef]
64. Drzazga-Szczęśniak, E.A.; Szczepanik, P.; Kaczmarek, A.Z.; Szczęśniak, D. Entropy of Financial Time Series Due to the Shock of War. *Entropy* **2023**, *25*, 823. [CrossRef]

entropy

MDPI

Article

The Statistics of q-Statistics

Deniz Eroglu [1], Bruce M. Boghosian [2,3], Ernesto P. Borges [4,5] and Ugur Tirnakli [6,*]

1 Faculty of Engineering and Natural Sciences, Kadir Has University, Istanbul 34083, Turkey; deniz.eroglu@khas.edu.tr
2 American University of Armenia, Yerevan 0019, Armenia; bruce.boghosian@tufts.edu
3 Department of Mathematics, Tufts University, Medford, MA 02155, USA
4 Instituto de Fisica, Universidade Federal da Bahia, Rua Barão de Jeremoabo, Salvador 40170-115, Brazil; ernesto@ufba.br
5 National Institute of Science and Technology of Complex Systems, Rua Xavier Sigaud 150, Rio de Janeiro 22290-180, Brazil
6 Department of Physics, Faculty of Arts and Sciences, Izmir University of Economics, Izmir 35330, Turkey
* Correspondence: ugur.tirnakli@ieu.edu.tr

Abstract: Almost two decades ago, Ernesto P. Borges and Bruce M. Boghosian embarked on the intricate task of composing a manuscript to honor the profound contributions of Constantino Tsallis to the realm of statistical physics, coupled with a concise exploration of q-Statistics. Fast-forward to Constantino Tsallis' illustrious 80th birthday celebration in 2023, where Deniz Eroglu and Ugur Tirnakli delved into Constantino's collaborative network, injecting renewed vitality into the project. With hearts brimming with appreciation for Tsallis' enduring inspiration, Eroglu, Boghosian, Borges, and Tirnakli proudly present this meticulously crafted manuscript as a token of their gratitude.

Keywords: q-Statistics; nonextensive statistical mechanics; generalized entropies; complex networks

1. Introduction

Statistical physics has profoundly enhanced our understanding of nature, life, and physical phenomena by revolutionizing our comprehension of macroscopic phenomena—the observable properties of materials—through their connection to microscopic laws, which govern the behavior of individual atoms and molecules. This bridging of the microscopic and macroscopic worlds has enabled scientists to predict and explain macroscopic phenomena such as temperature, pressure, and entropy based on the statistical behavior of microscopic constituents [1,2]. Statistical physics has provided a robust microscopic foundation for thermodynamics. The statistical interpretation of entropy, in particular, has deepened our understanding of the second law of thermodynamics and the direction of natural processes [3]. The field has greatly advanced our knowledge of phase transitions, such as the change from solid to liquid or liquid to gas, explaining critical phenomena and the nature of phase changes through concepts like critical exponents and scaling laws [4]. In the quantum realm, these principles have been extended to systems governed by quantum mechanics, elucidating phenomena such as superconductivity, superfluidity, and the behavior of Bose–Einstein condensates [5]. Concepts like entropy have also become fundamental to understanding information processing and transmission, leading to applications in information theory and computational complexity [6]. In materials science, statistical physics has provided insights into the properties of new materials, such as polymers, glasses, and complex fluids, driving the development of new technologies and materials with tailored properties [7,8]. On the largest scales, statistical physics has contributed to our understanding of the structure of the universe, the distribution of galaxies, and the thermodynamic history of the cosmos, including the study of black holes and the early universe [9]. Moreover, the methods and concepts of statistical physics have influenced various other disciplines, including chemistry, biology, and economics. In biology, for example, it aids in

Citation: Eroglu, D.; Boghosian, B.M.; Borges, E.P.; Tirnakli, U. The Statistics of q-Statistics. *Entropy* **2024**, *26*, 554. https://doi.org/10.3390/e26070554

Academic Editor: Antonio M. Scarfone

Received: 28 May 2024
Revised: 24 June 2024
Accepted: 26 June 2024
Published: 28 June 2024

understanding processes like protein folding and the behavior of biological membranes [10]. Overall, statistical physics has transformed physics by providing a powerful framework to understand and predict the behavior of complex systems, making it an essential pillar of modern science [11].

Statistical physics is indeed largely founded upon the framework of Boltzmann–Gibbs (BG) statistics, which emerged in the late 19th century. Ludwig Boltzmann's introduction of entropy and its correlation with the microscopic states of a system laid the groundwork for statistical mechanics [12]. Subsequently, Josiah Willard Gibbs expanded upon Boltzmann's ideas, formulating a more rigorous mathematical framework known as Gibbs statistical mechanics [13]. This framework became instrumental in relating the macroscopic properties of a system, such as temperature, pressure, and energy, to the microscopic configurations of its constituent particles. Boltzmann–Gibbs statistics provides a robust framework for describing the behavior of large systems composed of numerous particles. Considering the statistical distribution of these microscopic states enables the calculation of thermodynamic quantities and the prediction of macroscopic behavior. However, Boltzmann–Gibbs statistics alone was insufficient to address the entire puzzle of bridging the macroscopic and microscopic worlds. In certain non-equilibrium and complex systems contexts, Boltzmann–Gibbs statistics exhibit limitations. To address these challenges, Constantino Tsallis proposed a generalization of the BG formalism, known now as q-Statistics, which is based upon a non-additive entropy having the BG entropy as a special case. These kinds of generalized entropies have already been introduced in the literature, particularly within the context of information theory [14], but they had never been used for the generalization of statistical mechanics. Tsallis' q-Statistics offer a broader framework applicable to systems with long-range interactions and non-equilibrium dynamics, providing insights into phenomena beyond the scope of traditional statistical mechanics [15,16].

The well-deserved success of statistical physics is not only evident in its transformative insights into the behavior of complex systems, but also in the robust acknowledgment it receives through scholarly citations. In the scientific community, acknowledgment of scholarly contributions is quintessentially expressed through citations, encapsulating the cumulative impact of scientific endeavors. The statistics of these citations serve as barometers of influence within the scientific world, reflecting the reach, significance, and enduring legacy of research contributions. This quantitative analysis of scientific citations and related data falls within the purview of scientometrics, which aims to objectively quantify the impact of scientific outcomes, whether in the form of scientific papers or the corpora of an individual scientist or even a group of scientists. Despite the inevitable inaccuracies and biases inherent in these measures and methods, various indexes have gained widespread usage among the scientific community and funding agencies. It is implicitly assumed that such indexes can capture universal behaviors, at least within specific domains, such as scientific fields.

In this article, the collective measures of q-Statistics, a branch of statistical physics initiated by Tsallis' landmark 1988 paper [15], are examined. Additionally, Tsallis' collaboration network, which significantly shaped the q-Statistics community, is reconstructed to understand how q-Statistics has spread globally and been influenced by key contributors. Functions emerging within this area provide statistical descriptions of the field's time evolution and the geographical distribution of contributors, among other metrics. The outcome of the analysis shows the remarkable success of the field and its strong impact on the scientific community. While these observations are notable, they align with the broader understanding that numerous complex phenomena in the physical, biological, computational, and social domains exhibit behaviors accurately described by q-Statistics.

2. Diffusion of q-Statistics Ideas

Aiming to understand natural phenomena through statistical approaches has extended into the intriguing research field of statistically analyzing complex social systems by identifying the distributions within a given context. First, attention is specifically drawn to two particular examples of the diffusion of ideas within a social community, focusing on their "success":

(i) *The distribution of the number of citations of scientific papers.* In ref. [17], this scientometric feature was addressed, and it was concluded that highly cited papers follow a power-law distribution, while low-cited papers follow a stretched exponential distribution, suggesting that different phenomena govern these two regimes. In ref. [18], it was found that the same data could be represented by a single distribution, namely, a q-exponential distribution:

$$\exp_q(x) \equiv [1 + (1-q)x]_+^{1/(1-q)} \quad (q \in \mathcal{R}) \tag{1}$$

where $[\cdots]_+$ means that $\exp_q(x) = 0$ if $[1 + (1-q)x] \leq 0$. This finding suggests that both high- and low-cited papers may follow the same rules;

(ii) *The distribution of the number of weeks that pop musicians stay in Britain's top-selling lists.* In ref. [19], the top-75 best-selling musicians on a week-by-week basis from 1950 to 2000 in the UK were analyzed, and it was found that a stretched exponential can fit the data. In ref. [20], it was shown that the same data could be equally well-fitted with a function that displays an intermediate power-law regime and presents a crossover to an exponential tail. This function, introduced by [21] within a different context (reassociation of carbon monoxide in folded myoglobin), is given by

$$f(x) \equiv \left[1 - \frac{\beta_q}{\beta_1} + \frac{\beta_q}{\beta_1} e^{(q-1)\beta_1 x}\right]^{1/(1-q)} \quad (\beta_q > \beta_1 \geq 0; q > 1), \tag{2}$$

that is, a generalization of the q-exponential, as it reduces to $f(x) = \exp_q(-\beta_q x)$ in the limit $\beta_1 \to 0$.

These two examples of a measure of success that can be represented by q-exponentials or functions that belong to the family of q-exponentials support a conjecture that these social phenomena have a nonextensive nature.

In the present work, the growth and spread of nonextensive ideas among scientists are considered as an instance of the diffusion of knowledge within a social community. The time evolution of the number of papers on q-Statistics (including printed or electronic papers, books, theses, etc.) is regarded as the dynamical aspect of the diffusion process. The scientific community is viewed as a "phase-space" of the system. The geographical distribution of the scientists represents a measure of the filling of the phase-space. The spatial spread is indicated by the distribution of countries to which the authors of those papers belong. Country rank one is assigned to the country with the highest number of different authors within the q-Statistics literature. Different statistical measures of the diffusion of q-Statistics are found, with some satisfactorily described by q-exponentials or functions belonging to the q-exponential family.

Figure 1 illustrates the cumulative number of papers per year, revealing three distinct regimes. Initially, the linear regime spans from 1988, coinciding with Tsallis' first paper on the subject, to approximately 1992. The onset of the first q-exponential regime ($f(t) = A\exp_q(\lambda_q t)$, $q < 1$, $\lambda_q > 0$) is observed around 1992 ($q = 0.75$), indicated by the red dashed line in Figure 1. Notably, this period marked the establishment of the connection between nonextensive statistical mechanics and thermodynamics [22], as well as the first connection to a physical system, namely, self-gravitating stellar polytropes [23]. A bibliography on the theme of q-Statistics has been continously updated by Constantino Tsallis since 1995. The name of the file available at the `URL` [24], `TEMUCO.pdf`, was chosen in honor of the city that held the *IX Taller Sur de Física del Sólido*, 26–29 April 1995, Misión Borea, Temuco, Chile. The two above important papers and the continuously updated bibliography likely facilitated the transition from linear growth to the q-exponential regime. Subsequently, a second q-exponential regime emerged around 2004 and persisted until December 2023, with $q = 0.625$. It is worth noting that, to maintain analogy with the current nonextensive nomenclature, the index associated with the time evolution, q_{sen}, denotes sensitivity to initial conditions ($q_{sen} < 1$), as depicted in Figure 1.

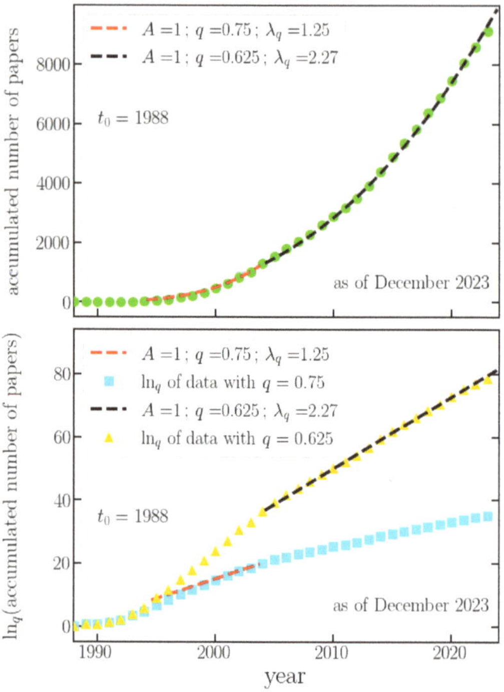

Figure 1. Cumulative number of published papers per year. The cumulative number of papers related to q-Statistics published each year (as of December 2023) is depicted, where the data follows two distinct q-exponential regimes ($f(t) = A \exp_q(\lambda_q t)$) for two different time spans. (**Top Panel**) The red dashed line represents the regime from 1992 to 2004 ($q = 0.625$), and the black dashed line represents the regime from 2004 to the present ($q = 0.75$). Each regime's trend is well-approximated by a q-exponential with the parameters provided in the figure. (**Bottom Panel**) The top panel is in linear–linear scale, while the bottom panel is in mono-q-log scale: the ordinate is represented in q-log scale, with the q-values 0.625 (yellow triangles) and 0.75 (blue squares). The same q-log functions are applied to the fitting curves in the top panel, represented again by dashed red and black lines in the bottom one.

Figure 2 presents the (unnormalized) decreasing cumulative distribution of the number of scientists that collaborated to q-Statistics per country. The dashed line indicates a fitting with a generalization of a q-exponential with two power-law regimes. In light of [16,21], one can write

$$\frac{dy}{dx} = -\beta_r y^r - (\beta_q - \beta_r) y^q \quad (r \leq q) \tag{3}$$

with $y(0) = 1$, whence

$$x = \int_y^1 \frac{du}{\beta_r u^r + (\beta_q - \beta_r) u^q} \tag{4}$$

can be obtained. Here, x denotes the number of scientists and $y \equiv R/C$, where R is the rank of countries. In the $r = 1$ case, Equation (4) recovers Equation (2). Notably, a q-value larger than 1 is found, with $q = 2.75$, where the index associated with geographical distributions is analogous to the index q_{stat} ($q_{stat} > 1$), indicating a stationary state. For a given complex system, there typically exist several indices q, depending on the class of properties that are being analyzed. This is frequently referred in the literature as the q-triplet and analogous structures [25]. One of these indices is the so-called q_{sen}, which is typically $q_{sen} \leq 1$. Another one of these indices is q_{stat}, which can be, depending on the system, either $q_{stat} \geq 1$ or $q_{stat} < 1$. Further details can be found in [16].

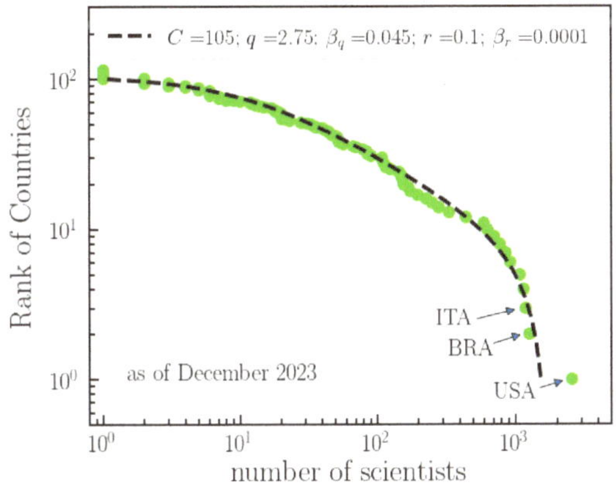

Figure 2. National researcher contributions to q-Statistics. The collective involvement and impact of researchers from different countries in the field of q-Statistics, as reflected by the number of scientists with published papers in the field. The figure illustrates the ranking of countries by the total number of scientists with published papers on q-Statistics. The dashed line corresponds to the fitting of the data with a (q,r)-exponential (see text), with the parameters indicated in the figure. The figure highlights the varying levels of participation and influence of researchers from different nations in advancing the understanding and development of q-Statistics. As of December 2023, the USA, Brazil, and Italy are the three major contributors to the field.

The distribution of scientific journals that have been used as vehicles for work on q-Statistics is shown in Figure 3. Two power-law regimes are identified, with a cross-over at about 10 papers per journal.

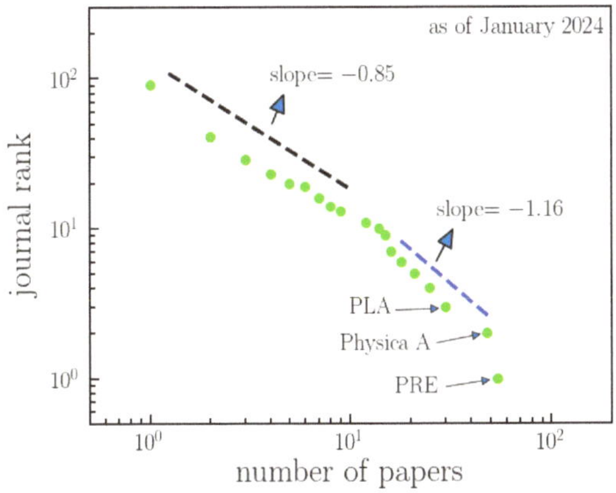

Figure 3. Ranking of journals with publications in q-Statistics. This figure presents the arrangement of journals based on the number of articles that they have published related to q-Statistics. The data exhibit two distinct power-law regimes: one for journals with a relatively small number of papers (slope = −0.85) and another for journals with a higher number of papers on q-Statistics (slope = −1.16). This offers an overview of the distribution of publications across different journals in the field. As of January 2024, among 91 journals, Physical Review E, Physica A, and Physics Letters A have the highest number of published papers on q-Statistics.

The statistics of q-Statistics indicate a q-exponential growth in the number of publications over the years, characterized by shifting regimes. Leading contributors to q-Statistics include the United States, Brazil, and Italy, with manuscripts predominantly published in impactful and longstanding journals such as Physical Review E, Physica A, and Physics Letters A. The primary architects of this success are undoubtedly Constantino Tsallis and his collaborators. Therefore, the subsequent section is dedicated to exploring the collaboration network of Tsallis.

3. Collaboration Network of C. Tsallis

The collaboration network of Constantino Tsallis comprises autonomous individuals collaborating to address research problems, particularly in statistical mechanics. Remarkably, researchers are located in diverse geographic regions and represent various disciplines, including fundamental sciences, computer sciences, psychology, and even art. This dynamic collaboration network has evolved over many years, culminating in the configuration depicted in Figure 4, facilitating the sharing and dissemination of scientific knowledge. The network's formation is not solely attributed to technological advancements but also to progress in international research and camaraderie.

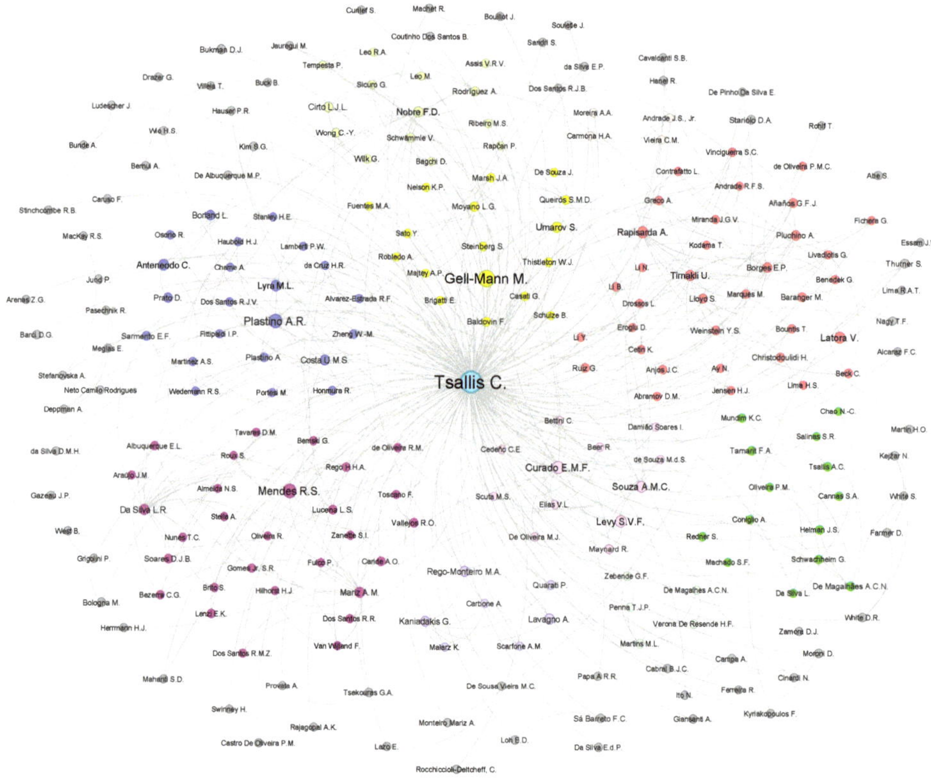

Figure 4. Constantino Tsallis' collaboration network. Illustration of Constantino Tsallis' collaboration network, encompassing all researchers (included in the Scopus database) who collaborated with him throughout his research career. The network comprises 236 researchers with 436 publications and 543 edges linking authors who have joint papers within the network. Node sizes are proportional to the number of citations of coauthored papers, reflecting the impact of researchers on the scientific community through their collaboration with C. Tsallis. Notably, the network reveals the presence of 11 distinct communities, each denoted by a unique color.

Data containing joint papers, author names, and Scopus IDs were initially collected from the Scopus database (on 17 January 2024) to reconstruct Constantino Tsallis's collaboration network. Utilizing unique Scopus IDs allowed for the differentiation of homonym author names. Notably, some significant contributions by Tsallis, such as the book titled "Nonextensive Entropy: Interdisciplinary Applications" by M. Gell-Mann and C. Tsallis, published by Oxford University Press, were absent from the Scopus database. These important contributions were integrated into the parsed Scopus data, completing the data preprocessing approach.

The finalized publication record of C. Tsallis indicates a total of 438 publications and 28,039 citations. The cumulative increase in publications (orange) and citations (red) is depicted in Figure 5. Additionally, Figure 5 presents the cumulative citation distribution of papers relative to the year of publications (blue line). The most-cited paper by C. Tsallis, titled "Possible generalization of Boltzmann-Gibbs statistics" [15], is prominently highlighted by a significant increase in the blue curve, denoted by an arrow and the text "Tsallis 1988".

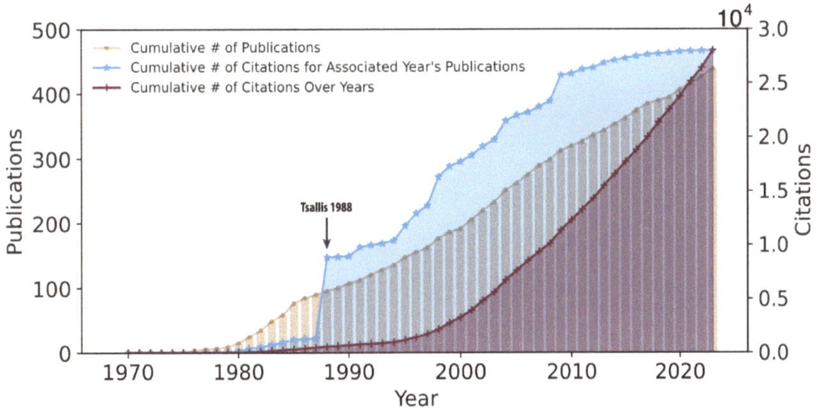

Figure 5. Constantino Tsallis' Publications and Citations. Illustrations depict the cumulative number of publications (orange) and citations (red) throughout the academic career of C. Tsallis, spanning from 1970 to the present. Cumulative plots of the total number of citations for papers published in each respective year are also provided (blue). The seminal article by C. Tsallis on q-Statistics, published in 1988, stands out as a highly cited paper, marked by the arrow denoted "Tsallis 1988".

Authors of coauthored articles or books were considered connected; in essence, if two authors published a joint paper, they were linked in the network structure. As the dataset encompasses all of C. Tsallis' works, Tsallis is considered a (co)author of all the papers, thereby linked to all other researchers within the network. Links between other researchers indicate that the connected authors have joint paper(s) with C. Tsallis. Consequently, the collaboration network comprises 236 nodes, indicating that C. Tsallis has 235 coauthors and 543 links. In Figure 4, node sizes are proportional to the total number of citations received from coauthored papers with C. Tsallis. Thus, large nodes do not signify that the author has numerous papers with Tsallis; rather, they have a substantial number of citations together.

In addition, a community detection algorithm was employed to discern 11 distinct clusters, each delineated by different colors, as depicted in Figure 4. These clusters are based on the coauthorships among C. Tsallis' collaborators, where nodes represent authors and edges represent shared publications with Tsallis. Each cluster also features leading authors; for instance, M. Gell-Mann is a prominent node in the yellow cluster, indicating that researchers in the yellow cluster share a common coauthoring basis. This applies to all other clusters, including important and impactful leading collaborators such as E.M.F. Curado, R.S. Mendes, A.R. Plastino, A. Rapisarda, U. Tirnakli, E.P. Borges, and others.

The clusters not only reflect the frequency of coauthorship, but also sometimes align with specific research fields and geographic locations. For example, distinct communities may emerge from authors working in similar research areas but are not strictly grouped by this criterion. Geographic factors also influence clustering, with authors from the same research field but different countries or continents often appearing in separate clusters. This global reach highlights the diverse and extensive nature of Tsallis' collaborative network.

The nodes in the gray cluster contain researchers who had a few joint works with C. Tsallis, and they have no significant collaborations with the rest of the network to be assigned to a specific community. Although intuitively detectable from the network visualization, these insights underscore the broad and varied impact of Tsallis' collaborations across different research fields and international borders. This information has now been incorporated to provide a clearer understanding of the community structures within the network.

Figure 6 shows the distribution of citations with coauthors—equivalent to the node sizes in Figure 4. In order to fit the data, we once again utilize Equations (3) and (4), where x now represents the citations of papers and $y \equiv R/C'$, with R denoting the coauthor's citations rank. As the number of citations is significantly larger than the number of papers, authors, or countries, the distribution is more saturated. Consequently, we were able to fit it with a single distribution with better accuracy.

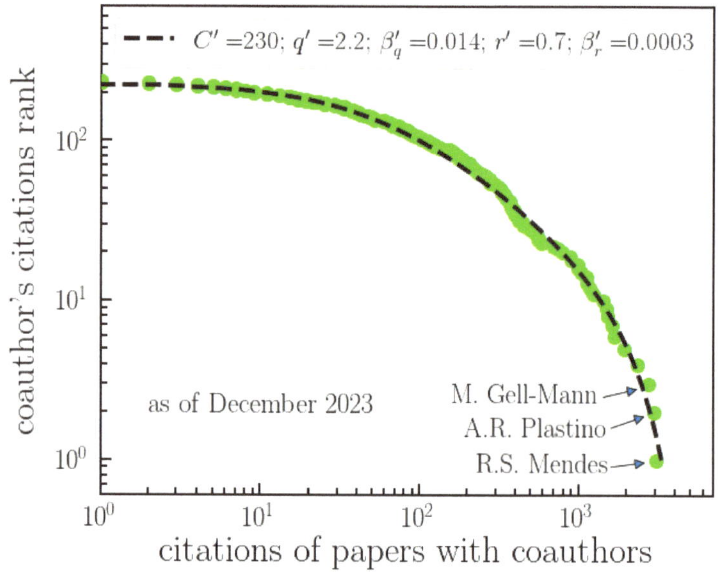

Figure 6. Ranking of Tsallis' citations with coauthors. The analysis of citations received by articles authored by Tsallis in collaboration with other researchers. This figure displays the unnormalized decreasing cumulative distribution of citations for papers with coauthors. The data are fitted with a (q,r)-exponential model, with parameters indicated by Equations (3) and (4). The figure involves ranking these citations based on the number of times they have been cited, providing insights into the impact and influence of Tsallis' collaborative work. The top-three most-cited coauthors with joint papers, Mendes, Plastino and Gell-Mann, are indicated.

The distribution of the number of papers with coauthors is illustrated in Figure 7. Unlike Figure 6, this distribution is not described by a q-exponential function. Instead, it exhibits two distinct power-law regimes with a transition point between them. The number of joint papers with a given coauthor is influenced by different factors than the number of citations of those joint papers. Psychological or personal aspects, such as friendship or proximity, among others, may play a more significant role in shaping the behavior observed in Figure 7 compared to Figure 6, as citations are generally less personal than collaborations.

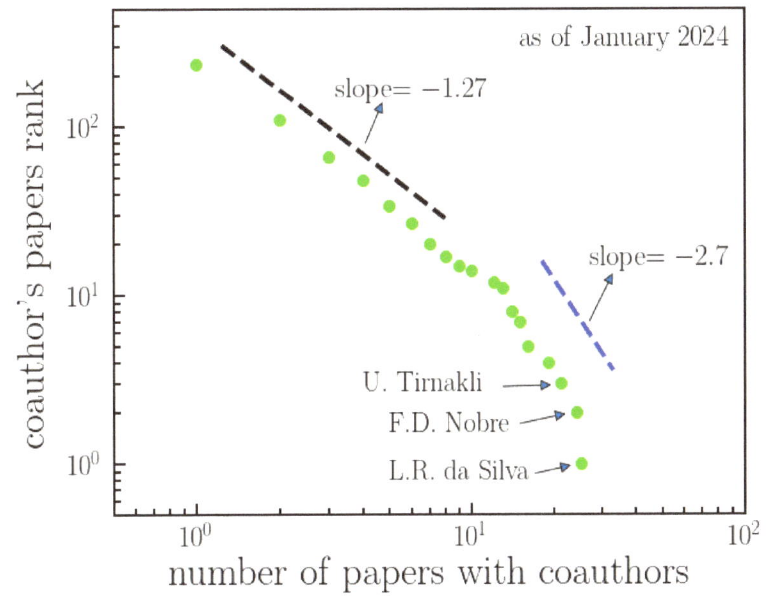

Figure 7. Ranking of Tsallis' papers with coauthors. This analysis focuses on articles authored by Tsallis in collaboration with other researchers, specifically examining the frequency of coauthorship. The figure illustrates the unnormalized decreasing cumulative distribution of the number of papers authored by Tsallis in collaboration with others. It identifies two distinct power-law regimes, with a transition regime between them (slopes indicated). This ranking offers insights into the collaborative research efforts involving Tsallis. Additionally, the figure highlights the top-three most-frequent collaborators: da Silva, Nobre, and Tirnakli.

The citations of papers (co)authored by Constantino Tsallis are displayed in Figure 8, depicted as a Pareto-like plot, where the citations of each paper are plotted as a function of their respective rank, representing an unnormalized decreasing cumulative distribution. The log–log scale provides a clear visualization of the fitting of a q-exponential with parameters $A = 437$, $b = 0.07$, and $q = 1.86$. A widely adopted measure is the h-index [26], proposed in 2005 to quantify the importance, significance, and impact of an individual researcher's corpus. The definition of h-index is such that a researcher has an h-index of n if their top-n most-cited papers have been cited at least n times each, and the remaining papers have been cited fewer than n times each. Tsallis' h-value, reaching a relatively large number of 67, is illustrated in Figure 8, indicating the average relevance of his scientific contributions. In contrast, the q-parameter reveals extraordinary contributions. Notably, the increase in citations of top-cited papers does not immediately affect the h-index, while the q-parameter increases. Tsallis' top-ranked paper [15] appears as an outlier, akin to phenomena like highly energetic cosmic rays described as an "ankle" (see Figure 1 of [27]), where the ankle signifies extraordinarily highly cited papers.

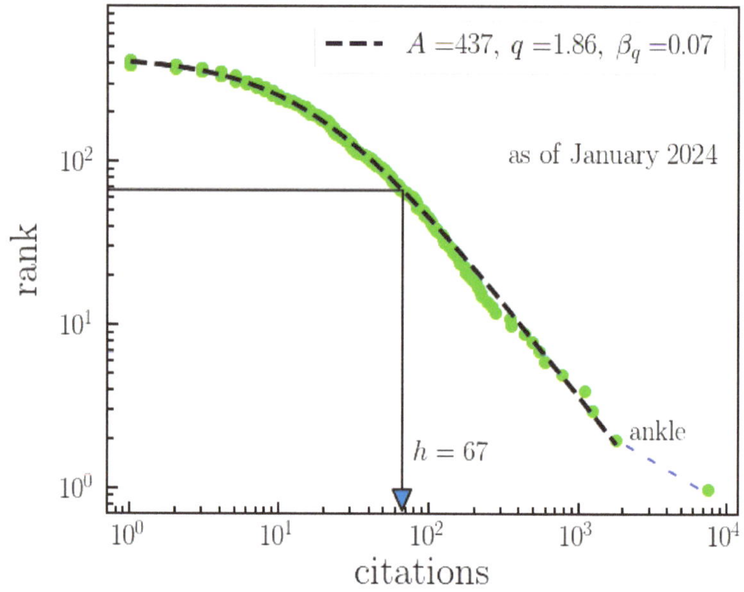

Figure 8. Ranking of citations of Tsallis' papers. This figure presents an analysis of the citations received by papers authored by Tsallis. It illustrates the unnormalized decreasing cumulative distribution of citations for Tsallis' papers, effectively fitted with a q-exponential distribution ($A\exp_q(-\beta_q x)$). The displayed index $h = 67$ indicates the citation count at which the papers achieve an h-index of 67. This ranking offers insights into the impact and influence of Tsallis' publications based on their citation counts. Furthermore, Tsallis' seminal paper from 1988 stands out as an outlier, significantly contributing to the ankle point shown in the figure, which highlights its exceptionally high citation impact.

4. Concluding Remarks

Constantino Tsallis' remarkable contributions to science and the q-Statistics are investigated by considering the meta-data of the associated articles and collaborators, which was collected from the Scopus database. We have presented scientometric indexes that express additional features to the difficult task of objectively, quantitatively, and unbiasedly classifying his activity. Furthermore, we have also compared the nominal citations of a non-exhaustive list of scientists with remarkable contributions to thermal physics throughout history and other relatively known scientists within the current statistical mechanics community (Figure 9). By nominal citation, we mean the appearance of the name of the scientist in the topic, title, or abstract, rather than in the authorship, of a cited paper, according to Web of Science. Scientists like K.E. Wilson, M.E. Fisher, and H.E. Stanley clearly belong to this group. However, their names are not included because of the very large number of homonyms. If the results we have found are replicated to other scientists and fields (especially for scientists with major contributions, for which fluctuations due to poor statistics tend to be minimized), we believe the characterization of scientific activity will be better described.

In conclusion, Constantino Tsallis has made significant contributions to the field of statistical physics, with 438 publications amassing a total of 28,000 citations, according to Scopus data (as of May 2024, 461 publications, according to Web of Science (All Databases) data; 44,146 citations according to Google Scholar citations data). He has also supervised and continues to supervise numerous students and colleagues, including the authors of this article. His love for science, a deep curiosity about nature, and friendly mentorship, coupled with wise advice, have consistently inspired us. This harmonious blend of motivation, passion, and enthusiasm for statistical physics continues to drive our collective efforts in the field.

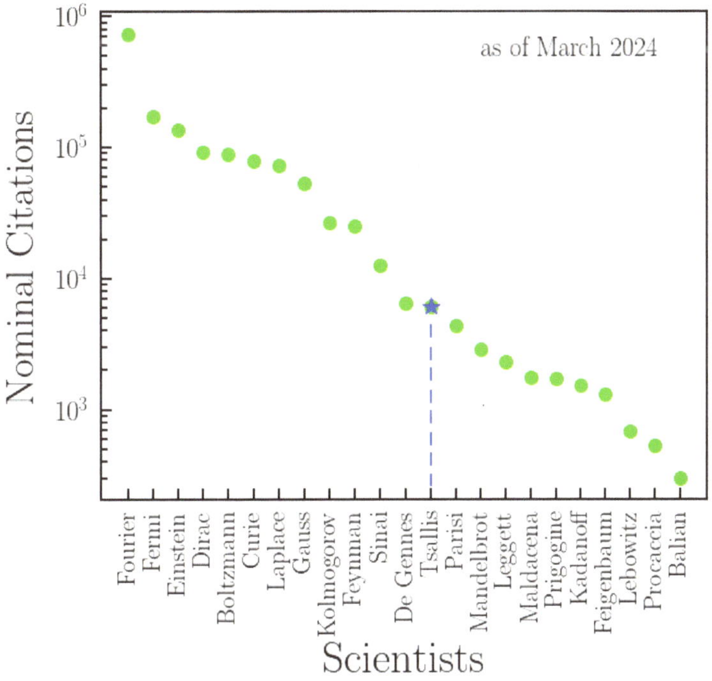

Figure 9. Nominal citations in thermal physics: Comparison with titans. A comparison of nominal citations is conducted for a non-exhaustive list of scientists with remarkable contributions to thermal physics throughout history and other relatively well-known scientists within the current statistical mechanics community. The numbers presented here are obtained from WoS by employing a search of each name in "All Databases", including "Preprint Citation Index" in "Topic". Tsallis is among the most-cited scientists in the field of thermal physics, providing insights into his relative impact and influence compared to other luminaries in the field.

Author Contributions: All authors contributed to conceptualization, methodology and formal analysis. Software was provided by D.E. and U.T. All authors worked in the process of writing—review and editing, and finally have read and agreed to the published version of the manuscript.

Funding: This research received no external funding

Data Availability Statement: The data used in this study to analyze the contributions, collaborations, and citations of Professor C. Tsallis are sourced from Web of Science (WoS) and Scopus. The majority of the data were obtained from Scopus by searching "Constantino Tsallis" with Author ID 7006572244. Additional data were included to address gaps in the Scopus data, as detailed in the main text. Data for Figure 9, related to nominal citations in thermal physics, were downloaded from WoS using the keyword "Thermal Physics". Researchers can access the original data through these databases. For detailed information or specific data requests, please contact the corresponding author.

Acknowledgments: We sincerely thank Tsallis for his long-standing and ongoing encouragement and support throughout many years. D.E., U.T., and E.P.B. express their gratitude to the organizers of the Conference on Tsallis' 80th birthday, especially E. M. F. Curado, where they were graciously hosted and had the opportunity to engage in enriching discussions with all participants, reminiscing about memorable moments with Constantino, delving into the diffusion of q-Statistics ideas, and exploring the complexity of Tsallis' collaboration network structure. U.T. is a member of the Science Academy, Bilim Akademisi, Turkey.

Conflicts of Interest: The authors declare no conflicts of interest.

References

1. Reif, F. *Fundamentals of Statistical and Thermal Physics*; McGraw-Hill Education: New York, NY, USA, 1965.
2. Huang, K. *Statistical Mechanics*; John Wiley & Sons: Hoboken, NJ, USA, 1987.
3. Landau, L.D.; Lifshitz, E.M. *Statistical Physics*; Elsevier: Oxford, UK, 1980; Volume 1.
4. Kubo, R. *Statistical Mechanics: An Advanced Course with Problems and Solutions*; North-Holland: Amsterdam, The Netherlands, 1965.
5. Kardar, M. *Statistical Physics of Particles*; Cambridge University Press: Cambridge, UK, 2007.
6. Jaynes, E.T. Information theory and statistical mechanics. *Phys. Rev.* **1957**, *106*, 620–630. [CrossRef]
7. Kawakatsu, T. *Statistical Physics of Polymers: An Introduction*; Springer Science & Business Media: Berlin, Germany, 2004.
8. Mauro, J.C.; Smedskjaer, M.M. Statistical mechanics of glass. *J. Non-Cryst. Solids* **2014**, *396*, 41–53. [CrossRef]
9. Pietronero, L.; Labini, F.S. Statistical physics for cosmic structures. In *Complexity, Metastability and Nonextensivity*; World Scientific: Singapore, 2005; pp. 91–101.
10. Nelson, P. *Biological Physics: Energy, Information, Life*; W. H. Freeman: New York, NY, USA, 2004.
11. Pathria, R.K.; Beale, P.D. *Statistical Mechanics*; Elsevier: Amsterdam, The Netherlands, 2011; Volume 3.
12. Boltzmann, L. *Studien Über das Gleichgewicht der Lebendigen Kraft Zwischen bewegten Materiellen Punkten*; Aus der Kaiserlich-Königlichen Hof und Staatsdruckerei: Wien, Austria, 1877.
13. Gibbs, J.W. *Elementary Principles in Statistical Mechanics*; Charles Scribner's Sons: New York, NY, USA, 1902.
14. Havrda, J.; Charvat, F. Quantification method of classification processes. Concept of structural a-entropy. *Kybernetika* **1967**, *3*, 30.
15. Tsallis, C. Possible generalization of Boltzmann-Gibbs statistics. *J. Stat. Phys.* **1988**, *52*, 479. [CrossRef]
16. Tsallis, C. *Introduction to Nonextensive Statistical Mechanics—Approaching a Complex World*, 2nd ed.; Springer-Nature: New York, NY, USA, 2023.
17. Redner, R. How popular is your paper? An empirical study of the citation distribution. *Eur. Phys. J. B* **1998**, *4*, 131. [CrossRef]
18. Tsallis, C.; de Albuquerque, M.P. Are citations of scientific papers a case of nonextensivity? *Eur. Phys. J. B* **2000**, *13*, 777. [CrossRef]
19. Davies, J.A. The individual success of musicians, like that of physicists, follows a stretched exponential distribution. *Eur. Phys. J. B* **2002**, *27*, 445. [CrossRef]
20. Borges, E.P. The individual success of musicians, like that of physicists, follows a stretched exponential distribution by JA Davies. *Eur. Phys. J. B* **2002**, *30*, 593. [CrossRef]
21. Tsallis, C.; Bemski, G.; Mendes, R.S. Is re-association in folded proteins a case of nonextensivity? *Phys. Lett. A* **1999**, *257*, 93. [CrossRef]
22. Curado, E.M.F.; Tsallis, C. Generalized statistical mechanics: Connection with thermodynamics. *J. Phys. A* **1991**, *24*, L69; Corrections in *J. Phys. A* **1991**, *24*, 3187 and *J. Phys. A* **1992**, *25*, 1019. [CrossRef]
23. Plastino, A.R.; Plastino, A. Stellar polytropes and Tsallis' entropy. *Phys. Lett. A* **1993**, *174*, 384. [CrossRef]
24. Available online: https://tsallis.cbpf.br/TEMUCO.pdf (accessed on 5 January 2024).
25. Gazeau, J.P.; Tsallis, C. Moebius transforms, cycles and q-triplets in statistical mechanics. *Entropy* **2019**, *21*, 1155. [CrossRef]
26. Hirsh, J.E. An index to quantify an individual's scientific research output. *Proc. Natl. Acad. Sci. USA* **2005**, *102*, 16569. [CrossRef] [PubMed]
27. Tsallis, C.; Anjos, J.C.; Borges, E.P. Fluxes of cosmic rays: A delicately balanced stationary state. *Phys. Lett. A* **2003**, *310*, 372. [CrossRef]

Article

Tsallis q-Statistics Fingerprints in Precipitation Data across Sicily

Vera Pecorino [1], Alessandro Pluchino [1,2,*] and Andrea Rapisarda [1,2,3]

1 Dipartimento di Fisica e Astronomia "Ettore Majorana", Università di Catania, 95123 Catania, Italy; pecov1800@gmail.com (V.P.); andrea.rapisarda@ct.infn.it (A.R.)
2 INFN Sezione di Catania, 95123 Catania, Italy
3 Complexity Science Hub, 1080 Vienna, Austria
* Correspondence: alessandro.pluchino@ct.infn.it

Abstract: Precipitation patterns are critical for understanding the hydrological and climatological dynamics of any region. Sicily, the largest island in the Mediterranean sea, with its diverse topography and climatic conditions, serves as an ideal case study for analyzing precipitation data, to gain insights into regional water resources, agricultural productivity, and climate change impacts. This paper employs advanced statistical physics methods, particularly Tsallis q-statistics, to analyze sub-hourly precipitation data from 2002 to 2023, provided by the Sicilian Agrometeorological Informative System (SIAS). We investigate several critical variables related to rainfall events, including duration, depth, maximum record, and inter-event time. The study spans two decades (2002–2012 and 2013–2023), analyzing the distributions of relevant variables. Additionally, we examine the simple returns of these variables to identify significant temporal changes, fitting these returns with q-Gaussian distributions. Our findings reveal the scale-invariant nature of precipitation events, the presence of long-range interactions, and memory effects, characteristic of complex environmental processes.

Keywords: Tsallis q-statistics; Sicily rainfall data; climate change

Citation: Pecorino, V.; Pluchino, A.; Rapisarda, A. Tsallis q-Statistics Fingerprints in Precipitation Data across Sicily. *Entropy* **2024**, *26*, 623. https://doi.org/10.3390/e26080623

Academic Editor: Yong Deng

Received: 28 May 2024
Revised: 20 July 2024
Accepted: 23 July 2024
Published: 24 July 2024

Copyright: © 2024 by the authors. Licensee MDPI, Basel, Switzerland. This article is an open access article distributed under the terms and conditions of the Creative Commons Attribution (CC BY) license (https://creativecommons.org/licenses/by/4.0/).

1. Introduction

Precipitation patterns play a crucial role in understanding the hydrological and climatological dynamics of any region. In the context of Sicily, an island characterized by diverse topographical and climatic conditions, analyzing precipitation data provides valuable insights into regional water resources, agricultural productivity, and climate change impacts. Being the largest island in the Mediterranean sea and located in the middle of it, Sicily is also of great interest for the entire Mediterranean area.

A robust statistical approach is essential for uncovering the underlying patterns and anomalies in precipitation data, thereby enabling more accurate predictions and effective water management strategies. In recent years, the application of advanced statistical physics methods has provided new insights into the analysis of complex environmental data [1–3]. In particular, various studies have emphasized the importance of different probability distributions in rainfall analysis. For instance, the Poisson Hurwitz–Lerch zeta distribution has been used to model the frequency of interarrival times and rainfall depths [4]. Some studies assumed that the daily precipitation intensities are distributed according to a Gamma [5] or a mixed exponential [6], light-tailed or heavy tailed distributions [7,8], while other authors found a log-normal [9] or a stretched exponential [10] distribution. Probability distributions of daily rainfall extremes have also been studied to make rainfall inferences [11], and entropy-based derivations of probability distributions have been applied to daily rainfall data [12]. Understanding the fundamental probability distribution for heavy rainfall can provide insights into extreme weather events [10], and analyzing extreme rainfall trends is crucial for evaluating depth–duration–frequency curves in climate change scenarios [13].

In this context, q-statistics offer a robust framework for analyzing the variability and distribution of complex environmental data, as they are particularly effective in capturing the non-linear and multi-scalar nature of such events. Raw data often follow power law distributions, indicating the presence of scale-invariant processes and the frequent occurrence of extreme events [14]. For instance, Yang et al. demonstrated the power-law behavior of hourly precipitation intensity and dry spell duration over the United States, highlighting the scale-invariant nature of these phenomena [15]. Additionally, studies have focused on the use of probability distributions in rainfall analysis [16], and memory in volatility return intervals and a decumulative probability function, following the methodologies usually employed in the study of financial markets [17]. Decumulated data can be effectively modeled using Tsallis exponential distributions, which account for long-range interactions and memory effects typical of many natural processes. Pluchino et al. showed the applicability of Tsallis statistics in capturing long-term correlations at the edge of chaos [18]. Similarly, Ludescher et al. described the universal behavior of interoccurrence times between losses in financial markets using Tsallis statistics [19], emphasizing the presence of memory effects [20]. Furthermore, the simple returns of these events, representing changes over time, conform to q-Gaussian distributions [21], which better capture the heavy tails and non-Gaussian behavior observed in the data. Recently, Tsallis statistics were also successfully applied by Greco et al. to study acoustic emissions close to the rupture point of compressed rocks of various natures [22,23]. Bogachev and Bunde (2008) discussed memory effects in the statistics of interoccurrence times between large returns in financial markets, demonstrating the relevance of q-Gaussian distributions in modeling heavy tails and non-Gaussian behaviors [24]. Yamasaki et al. also highlighted scaling and memory in volatility return intervals in financial markets, further supporting the use of q-Gaussian distributions for this kind of analysis [25].

In this paper, we present a comprehensive analysis of precipitation data through the lens of q-statistics. Specifically, we analyzed sub-hourly precipitation data from 2002 to 2023, provided by the Sicilian Agrometeorological Informative System (SIAS). The considered dataset comprises records from 107 meteorological stations, with a focus on nine key rain gauges located in Messina, Catania, Siracusa, Ragusa, Enna, Caltanissetta, Agrigento, Trapani, and Palermo. We examined several key variables related to rainfall events, including

- Duration [minutes], the length of consecutive wet records;
- Depth [mm], the total amount of precipitation during an event;
- Maximum record [mm/10′], the highest recorded precipitation in a 10 min interval during an event.

To investigate the temporal evolution of these variables, we analyzed their distributions over two decades (2002–2012 and 2013–2023). We also explored simple returns of these variables. In order to characterize our distributions and to identify any significant changes over time, we considered Tsallis q-statistics [19].

Our analysis aimed to uncover patterns and trends in Sicilian precipitation data, providing insights into regional climate dynamics and potential impacts of climate change. This study could offer valuable information to scientists, policymakers, and stakeholders involved in environmental and water resource management in Sicily.

2. Dataset and Relevant Variables

This study is based on precipitation records from 2002 to 2023 provided by a robust and extensive rain gauge network under the maintenance of the Sicilian Agrometeorological Informative System (SIAS), which comprises 107 meteorological stations. We included in our study the rain gauges of Messina, Catania, Siracusa, Ragusa, Agrigento, Trapani, and Palermo, which are the most populated cities on the coastline (Istat—Statistical National Insitute—report 2018/2019). In order to include the midland area, we added two more cities, namely Enna and Caltanissetta. We analyzed precipitation time series with a 10 min basis across the nine selected rain gauge stations, see Figure 1. The minimum quantity observable with the SIAS's pluviometers was 0.2 mm and, as we mentioned, the time resolution was 10 min; we used such granular data per station and built a new time series based on rainfall events.

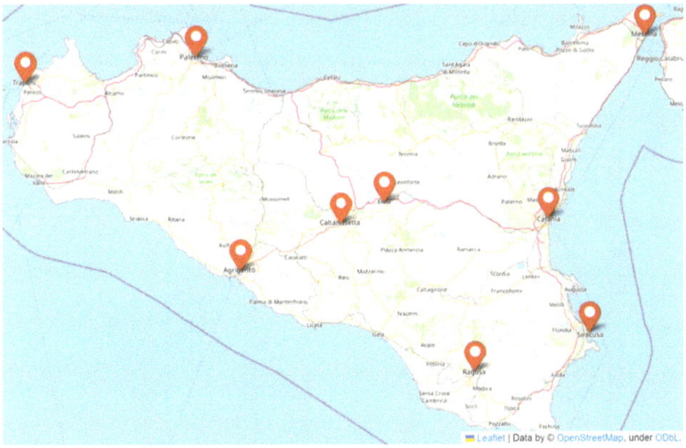

Figure 1. SIAS meteorological network: location of the nine rain gauge stations considered in this paper. See text for more details.

A rainfall event over a rain gauge in our dataset is an episode of consecutive wet records, i.e., the consecutive not null rows. It follows that each rainfall event can be characterized by two quantities: a duration [in minutes] and a depth [in mm]. The duration of an event is the length of consecutive wet records or, in other words, the number of consecutive not null rows. The rainfall depth relative to an event is the sum of precipitation amount over the corresponding event duration, in other words, how much it rained during the event. Each rainfall event is formed by one or more not null records, and one of those values is the maximum value recorded during the event. We focused our study on the previous relevant variables related to rainfall events: depth [mm], maximum record [mm/10′], and duration [minutes]. The first two variables are related to the amount of precipitation, whilst the duration is a temporal variable. We grouped results following such criteria. As the whole dataset covers a time span of 22 years, we arbitrarily chose to perform our analysis with a 11-year scale. We adopted a seasonal approach exploring the principal features of the distributions of these variables, in order to evaluate the presence of certain temporal trends across decades.

3. Statistical Analysis of Precipitation Events

3.1. Probability Density Functions

First, we analyzed the probability density function (PDF) for our relevant variables, considering both seasonal and decade variations. This approach helps in managing the complexity and volume of the data, while still providing clear insights into the overall trends.

Due to the extensive number of reports generated for each season, variable, and decade, we present only a few selected plots, then we can summarize all the results in a more compact way. Figures 2–4 illustrate PDFs of the events' rainfall depth, maximum record, and duration, respectively, cumulated over all the gauge stations for the autumn season in each of the two decades, 2002–2012 (left panel) and 2013–2023 (right panel). All the distributions can be well fitted by power-law functions $y \sim x^{-b}$. Performing a χ^2 test, the power-law fit always resulted in a p-value < 0.05, indicating the scale-invariant nature of the precipitation data, but with different slopes (reported in the legends).

In Figure 5, we compare, as bar charts, the slopes of all the power-law fits performed on the seasonal distributions of the same three variables for the two considered decades. Bars are colored in blue for 2002–2012 and in green for 2013–2023. The analysis of rainfall depth and maximum record (top and central panel, respectively) revealed a sensitive increase in extreme events, indicated by a lower absolute value of the slopes, only for summer and autumn of the second decade. A slight increase in the events' duration for the second decade can also be appreciated (bottom panel), but only for spring and summer. The winter behavior remained largely unchanged from one decade to another, even if a small decrease in rainfall depth together with a slight increase in the max intensity are visible for this season (in the top and central panels, respectively).

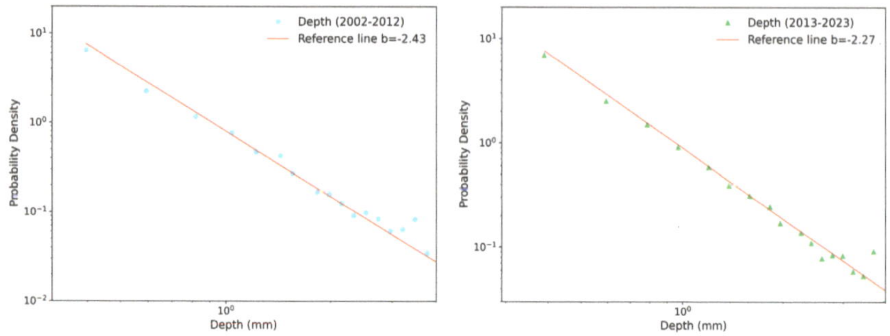

Figure 2. Probability density function of autumn rainfall depth in log–log scale and its fits with a power law (red line) for the two decades considered: 2002–2012 (**left** panel) and 2013–2023 (**right** panel). The slopes of the fits are also reported, see text for more details.

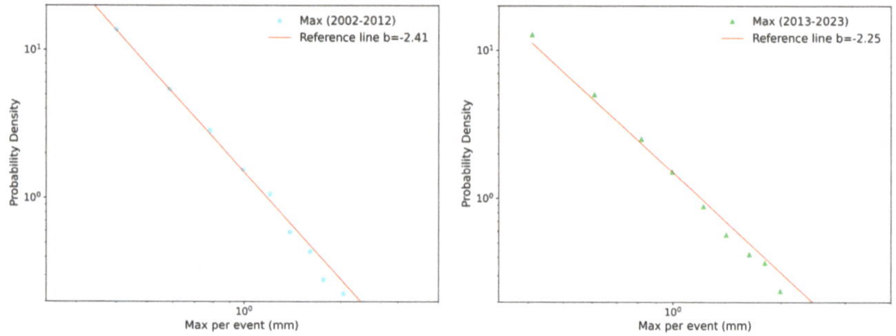

Figure 3. Probability density function of autumn max per event in log–log scale and the fit with a power law (red line) for the two decades considered: 2002–2012 (**left** panel) and 2013–2023 (**right** panel). The slopes of the fits are also reported, see text for more details.

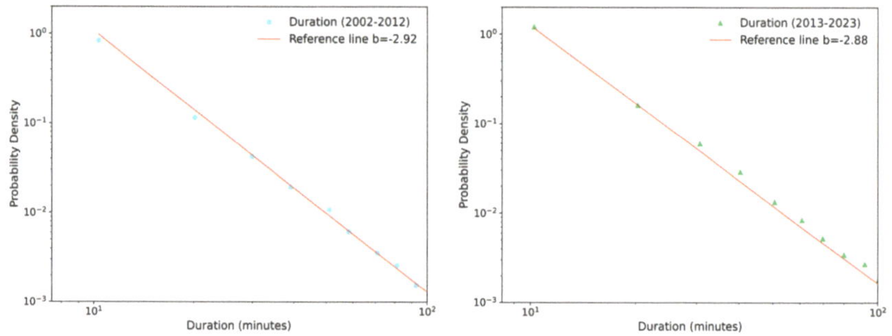

Figure 4. Probability density function of autumn rainfall event duration in log–log scale and its fits with a power law (red line) for the two decades considered: 2002–2012 (**left** panel) and 2013–2023 (**right** panel). The slopes of the fits are also reported, see text for more details.

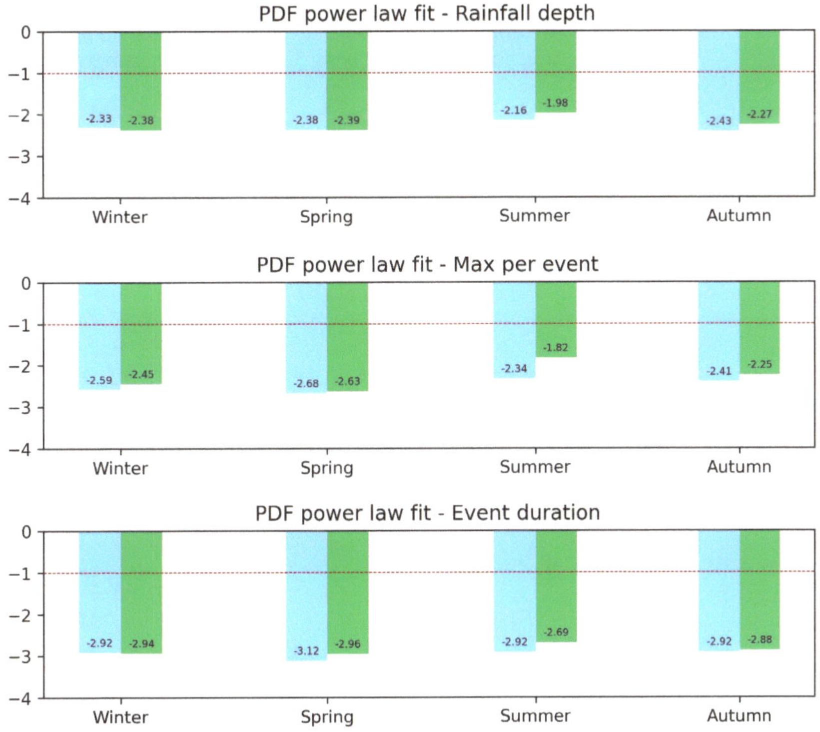

Figure 5. We report the values of the slopes of the power-law fits for the events' rainfall depth (**top** panel), maximum record (**central** panel), and duration (**bottom** panel). The different colors refer to the two decades studied: blue for the period 2002–2012 and green for the period 2013–2023. Differences between the two decades can be appreciated, in particular for summer. An horizontal red dotted line has been added as reference for the eye. See text for more details.

The observed changes in the slopes over the decades indicate a possible increase in the frequency and intensity of extreme precipitation events, which might be attributed to changing climate patterns affecting atmospheric turbulence and energy distribution.

3.2. Decumulative Probability Distributions

In this section, we investigate the decumulative probability distributions for our three relevant variables in the four seasons and the two decades by means of q-statistics. For each variable, we plot the fraction of precipitation events (collected for all the gauge stations), with values above the threshold reported on the x-axis. As in the previous section, we start by presenting some selected examples of these distributions in the two decades. In particular, in Figures 6 and 7 we analyzed the rainfall depth and the maximum record in winter, while in Figure 8 we focused on the event duration in summer. All the distributions resulted as well fitted by Tsallis q-exponential functions in the usual form [19]:

$$e_q(x) = [1 + (1-q)kx]^{\frac{1}{1-q}}, \quad (1)$$

where q is the entropic index and k is a constant that controls the inflection point of the curve. For $q = 1$, the standard exponential function is recovered. Values of the entropic index greater than 1 indicate fat tailed tails and typically quantify the degree of long-range correlations and memory effects present in the system, expressed by the entity of the deviation from unit. Applying the χ^2 test, the Tsallis q-exponential fit consistently yields a

p-value lower than 0.05. In these examples, the entropic index shows a slight difference between the two decades only for winter rainfall depth, while the winter maximum intensity and summer duration remained largely unchanged.

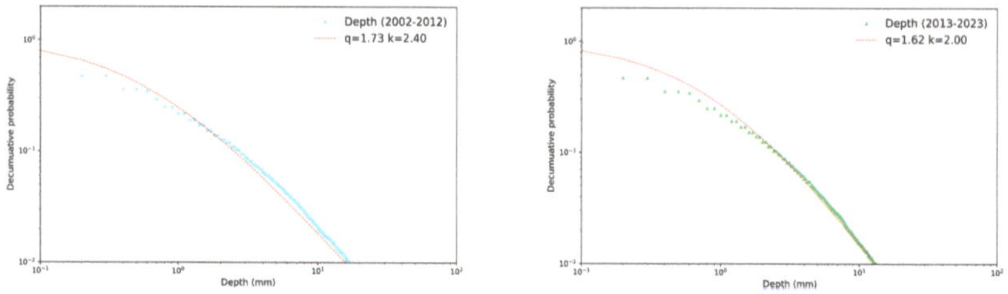

Figure 6. Decumulative probability distributions in log–log scale of winter rainfall depth per event and their q-exponential fits. Comparison between decades: 2002–2012 (**left** panel) and 2013–2023 (**right** panel).

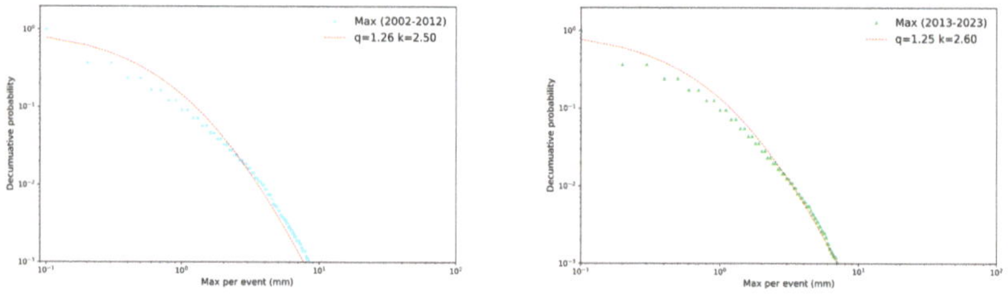

Figure 7. Decumulative probability distributions in log–log scale of winter maximum per event and their q-exponential fits. Comparison between decades: 2002–2012 (**left** panel) and 2013–2023 (**right** panel).

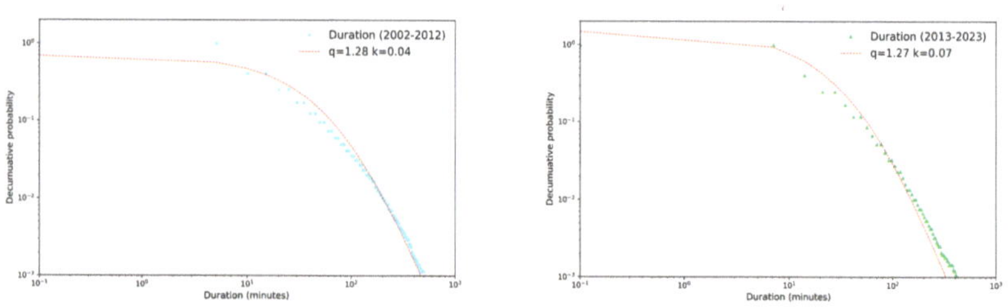

Figure 8. Decumulative probability distributions in log–log scale of winter event duration and their q-exponential fits. Comparison between decades: 2002–2012 (**left** panel) and 2013–2023 (**right** panel).

The use of Tsallis q-statistics with $q > 1$ indicated that the precipitation events exhibited long-range correlations and memory effects, deviating from classical exponential behavior. This is consistent with systems that have persistent interactions over time, suggesting that atmospheric processes have significant temporal dependencies.

Detailed results of the values of the entropic index q for each variable and each season are reported in the three panels of Figure 9, where bar charts are again colored in blue and green for 2002–2012 and 2013–2023, respectively.

The changes in the entropic index q across different decades and seasons imply variations in the degree of correlations and memory effects within the atmospheric system. This may be indicative of evolving climatic conditions and their impact on the statistical properties of precipitation events.

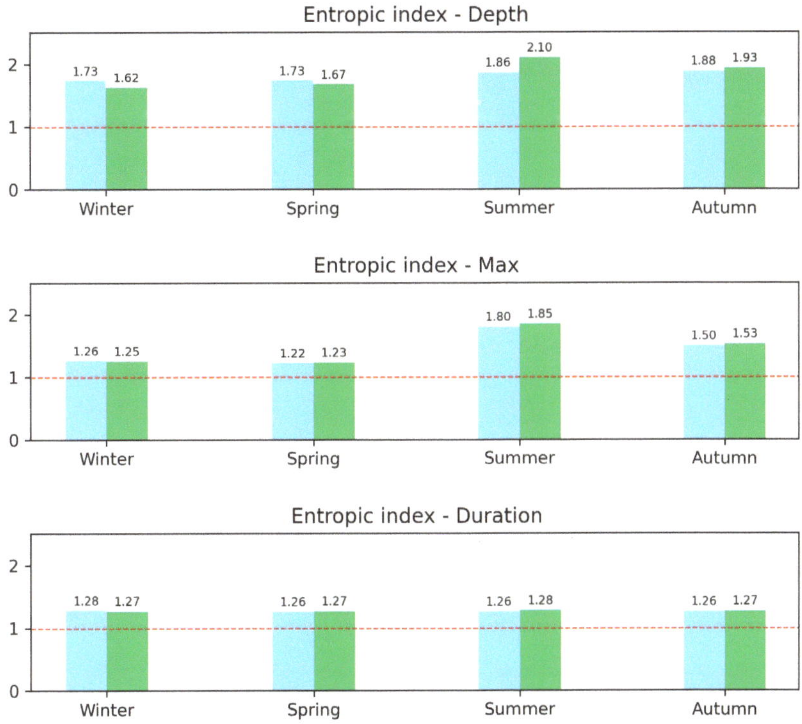

Figure 9. Seasonal bar chart of the entropic index q calculated for the rainfall depth, maximum intensity per event, and duration decumulative distributions. Comparison between decades: 2002–2012 (blue) and 2013–2023 (green). A red dotted line as be added as reference for $q = 1$. See text for more details.

In the top panel, the comparison of entropic indexes for the events' rainfall depth revealed an increase in correlations in the second decade for summer and autumn only, while a decrease was observed for winter and spring. A slight increase in the index q among decades can also be observed only in summer for the maximum per event intensity (central panel). All the other comparisons in both the central and bottom panels only show very similar values for the entropic index.

The observed variations in the entropic index q for different seasons and decades suggest that the degree of correlation and memory in precipitation events has changed over time, potentially due to climatic changes. Increases in q indicate stronger correlations and memory effects, particularly in summer and autumn, reflecting changes in atmospheric dynamics.

3.3. Returns Distribution

Finally, in this section, we investigate the behavior of simple returns distributions for each relevant variable, for the different seasons and decades studied. We consider normalized simple returns R defined as follows:

$$R = \frac{[(x_{n+1} - x_n) - x_{mean}]}{\sigma_{std.dev}}. \tag{2}$$

With the distributions of returns being symmetric, they are well fitted by Tsallis q-Gaussian curves defined as [19]:

$$G_q(x) = A\left[1 - (1-q)\beta x^2\right]^{\frac{1}{1-q}}, \tag{3}$$

where A is a normalization parameter, q is the entropic index, and β is a parameter related to the spread around the mean. Values of entropic index greater than unit quantify deviations from a Gaussian behavior, also indicating a violation of the standard central limit theorem due to correlations present in the system. In Figures 10–12, we report, as in the previous sections, some seasonal examples of distributions of simple returns for our three variables, comparing the two decades: the spring season was chosen for both rainfall depth and duration, with the winter season for the maximum recorded value. No relevant differences among decades are visible in any case for the entropic index q, although different values of β were obtained. Such an absence of any change in q during 2002–2012 and 2013–2023 can be also appreciated in the summary presented in Figure 13, where we report the bar charts of the entropic index values extracted from q-Gaussian fits. For both rainfall depth (top panel) and maximum intensity (central panel), the fitted entropic index does not vary significantly across decades and seasons, suggesting a consistent statistical behavior over time. However, the event duration (bottom panel) shows a substantial increase in winter and, in particular, in summer and autumn, indicating potential changes in the dynamics of rainfall events in these seasons over the considered decades.

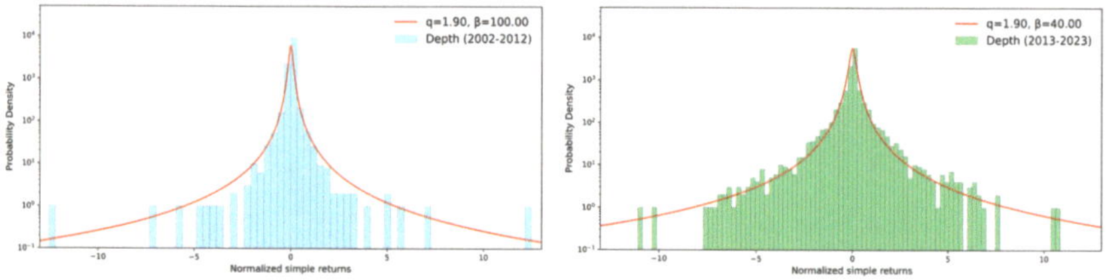

Figure 10. Simple returns in log–lin scale: data and q-Gaussian fits of spring events' rainfall depth. The comparison between the two considered decades, i.e., 2002–2012 (**left** panel) and 2013–2023 (**right** panel), does not show any relevant differences in the entropic index q.

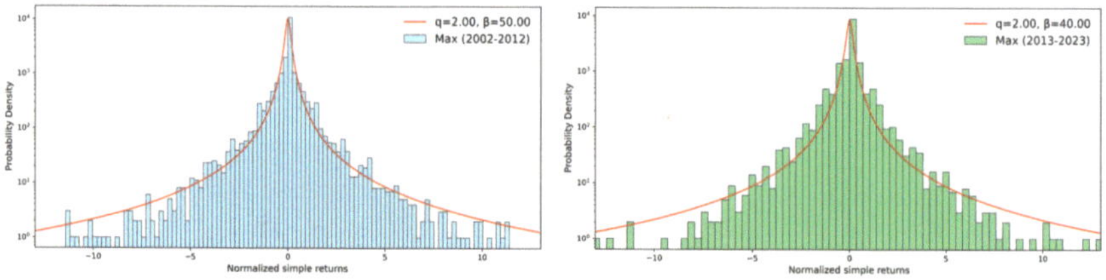

Figure 11. Simple returns in log–lin scale: data and q-Gaussian fits of winter maximum per event. In the **left** panel, we report the 2002–2012 decade, while the **right** panel shows the 2013–2023 decade. See text for more details.

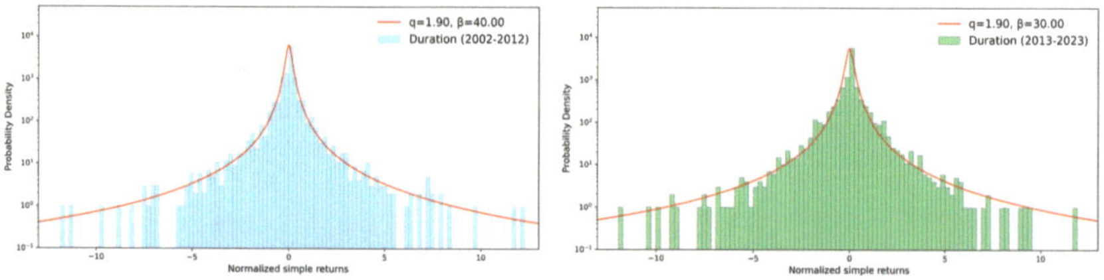

Figure 12. Simple returns in log–lin scale: data and q-Gaussian fits of spring rainfall event duration. In the **left** panel we report the 2002–2012 decade, while the **right** panel shows the 2013–2023 decade. See text for more details.

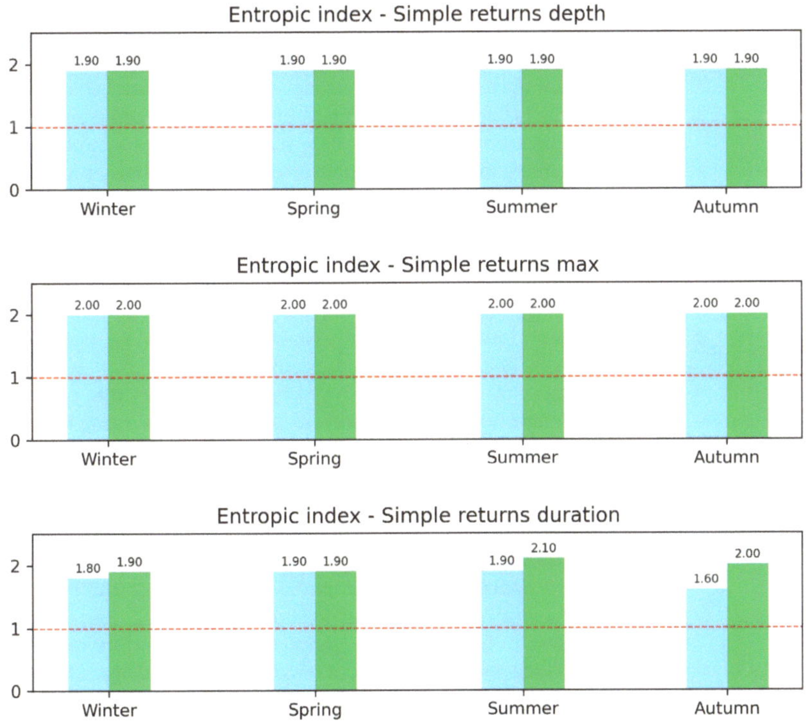

Figure 13. Bar chart of entropic index q for rainfall depth (**top** panel), maximum intensity recorded per event (**central** panel), and event duration (**bottom** panel) are reported for decade (2002–2012 in green and 2013–2023 in blue) and season. A red dotted line as be added as reference for $q = 1$. See text for more details.

The χ^2 test of fitting of simple returns with Tsallis q-Gaussian curves yielded a p-value < 0.05. We observe that the exponent q is always greater than one, indicating the presence of correlations and deviations from the Gaussian distribution. This suggests that the precipitation events exhibit complex dynamics and memory effects, not fully captured by traditional Gaussian statistics. The lack of significant changes in q across decades for rainfall depth and maximum intensity suggests that these aspects of precipitation events have remained statistically stable. However, the increase in q for event duration indicates evolving dynamics in how long precipitation events last, potentially reflecting changes in atmospheric conditions over time.

These results highlight the complexity and evolving nature of precipitation event dynamics. The consistent behavior in the entropic index q for rainfall depth and maximum intensity suggests a stable underlying process, whereas the increase in q for event duration points to changes in how precipitation events are temporally distributed, possibly due to shifts in atmospheric dynamics or climate change.

4. Discussion and Conclusions

In this study, we analyzed sub-hourly precipitation data from nine rain gauge stations located in the main cities of Sicily over two decades, 2002–2012 and 2013–2023. Our analysis focused on several key features of rainfall events: depth, maximum recorded value of the event, and duration of the event. The aim was to understand the statistical properties of these variables and possible changes over time.

Our analysis provided, for the first time, a comprehensive quantitative analysis of precipitation data across Sicily using Tsallis q-statistics, revealing significant insights into the statistical properties of rainfall events. The power law distributions of the relevant variables suggest the presence of scale-invariant behavior: in fluid dynamics, this points to the influence of turbulence and fractal-like atmospheric phenomena. The q-exponential and q-Gaussian distributions highlight the presence of long-range correlations and memory effects in the data, suggesting that atmospheric processes are influenced by persistent interactions over time.

The application of Tsallis q-statistics in this context has proven to be particularly valuable. By comparing the deviation from exponential and Gaussian behavior among decades and seasons, we were able to capture the deep out-of-equilibrium nature of the precipitation data, which classical statistics often fail to describe accurately. Tsallis q-statistics, with a foundation in non-extensive entropy, provide a more flexible and encompassing framework that accounts for the complex dynamics and interactions inherent in environmental data. This non-extensive behavior indicates that precipitation events have significant long-range dependencies and correlations, reflecting the complex, interconnected nature of atmospheric dynamics.

Our findings indicate, in several cases, notable changes among the two decades considered, particularly during the summer and—to a lesser extent—the autumn seasons. We observed an increase in correlations, on one hand, in the decumulative distributions for rainfall depth and the maximum intensity of events and, on the other hand, in the normalized returns distributions for the event duration. This increase in correlations and memory effects, as indicated by the higher entropic index q, suggests that the precipitation system has become more interconnected and influenced by long-term climatic factors, which could be a result of ongoing climate change. These quantitative changes, if correctly interpreted, could have significant implications for water resource management and agricultural planning in Sicily, especially in the context of climate change adaptation. In fact, the investigation of the underlying mechanisms driving the observed changes in rainfall patterns could offer valuable insights for developing adaptive strategies to mitigate the impacts of climate variability and change.

By providing a straightforward and accessible approach, q-statistics offer valuable insights into complex hydrometeorological processes, especially in regions with prevalent non-equilibrium conditions like the Mediterranean.

Overall, this study contributes to the growing body of knowledge on precipitation variability and its impacts, offering a valuable resource for scientists, policymakers, and stakeholders involved in environmental and water resource management in Sicily. The application of q-statistics reveals richer structures and long-range dependencies in precipitation data, aiding in better risk analysis, modeling, and decision support.The use of Tsallis q-statistics provides a robust tool for understanding the complexity of precipitation patterns and their broader climatic implications. By revealing the non-Gaussian nature and the long-range correlations in precipitation data, this approach helps in better modeling and predicting extreme weather events, which are crucial for effective climate change adaptation strategies. Future research should focus on extending this analysis to other regions and incorporating additional climatic variables, to provide a more detailed understanding of precipitation dynamics.

Author Contributions: Conceptualization, V.P., A.P. and A.R.; Methodology, V.P., A.P. and A.R.; Formal analysis, V.P., A.P. and A.R.; Writing—original draft, V.P., A.P. and A.R. All authors have read and agreed to the published version of the manuscript.

Funding: This study was funded by the European Union—NextGenerationEU, in the framework of the GRINS—Growing Resilient, INclusive and Sustainable project (GRINS PE00000018—CUP E63C22002120006). The views and opinions expressed are solely those of the authors and do not necessarily reflect those of the European Union, nor can the European Union be held responsible for them.

Institutional Review Board Statement: Not applicable.

Data Availability Statement: Data are available on request.

Acknowledgments: Authors thank L. Pasotti and C. Tsallis for useful discussions.

Conflicts of Interest: The authors declare no conflicts of interest.

References

1. Fan, J.; Meng, J.; Ludescher, J.; Chen, X.; Ashkenazy, Y.; Kurths, J.; Havlin, S.; Schellnhuber, H.J. Statistical physics approaches to the complex Earth system. *Phys. Rep.* **2021**, *896*, 1–84. [CrossRef] [PubMed]
2. Bunde, A.; Ludescher, J.; Schellnhuber, H.J. How to determine the statistical significance of trends in seasonal records: Application to Antarctic temperatures. *Clim. Dyn.* **2022**, *58*, 1349–1361. [CrossRef]
3. Bunde, A.; Ludescher, J.; Schellnhuber, H.J. Evaluation of the real-time El Niño forecasts by the climate network approach between 2011 and present. *Theor. Appl. Climatol.* **2024** . [CrossRef]
4. Agnese, C.; Baiamonte, G.; Nardo, E.D.; Ferraris, S.; Martini, T. Modelling the Frequency of Interarrival Times and Rainfall Depths with the Poisson Hurwitz-Lerch Zeta Distribution. *Fractal Fract.* **2022**, *6*, 509. [CrossRef]
5. Buishand, T. Some remarks on the use of daily rainfall models. *J. Hydrol.* **1978**, *36*, 295–308. [CrossRef]
6. Wilks, D.S.; Wilby, R.L. The weather generation game: A review of stochastic weather models. *Prog. Phys. Geogr.* **1999**, *23*, 329–357. [CrossRef]
7. Mielke, P.W.; Johnson, E.S. Some generalized beta distributions of the second kind having desirable application features in hydrology and meteorology. *Water Res.* **1974**, *10*, 223–226. [CrossRef]
8. Papalexiou, S.; Koutsoyiannis, D.; Makropoulos, C. How extreme is extreme? An assessment of daily rainfall distribution tails. *Hydrol. Earth Syst. Sci.* **2013**, *17*, 851–862. [CrossRef]
9. Swift, L.W.; Schreuder, H.T. Fitting daily precipitation amounts using the SB distribution. *Mon. Weather Rev.* **1981**, *109*, 2535–2540. [CrossRef]
10. Wilson , P.S.; Toumi, R. A fundamental probability distribution for heavy rainfall. *Geophys. Res. Lett.* **2005**, *32*, L14812 . [CrossRef]
11. Moccia, B.; Mineo, C.; Ridolfi, E.; Russo, F.; Napolitano, F. Probability distributions of daily rainfall extremes in Lazio and Sicily, Italy, and design rainfall inferences. *J. Hydrol. Reg. Stud.* **2021**, *33*, 100771. [CrossRef]
12. Papalexiou, S.M.; Koutsoyiannis, D. Entropy based derivation of probability distributions: A case study to daily rainfall. *Adv. Water Res.* **2011**, *45*, 51–57. [CrossRef]
13. Liuzzo, L.; Freni, G. Analysis of Extreme Rainfall Trends in Sicily for the Evaluation of Depth-Duration-Frequency Curves in Climate Change Scenarios. *J. Hydrol. Eng.* **2015**, *20*, 04015036. [CrossRef]
14. Bunde, A.; Kropp, J.; Schellnhuber, H.J. *The Science of Disasters: Climate Disruptions, Heart Attacks, and Market Crashes*; Springer: Berlin/Heidelberg, Germany, 2002.
15. Yang, L.; Franzke, C.L.E.; Fu, Z. Power-law behaviour of hourly precipitation intensity and dry spell duration over the United States. *Int. J. Climatol.* **2019**, *40*, 2429–2444. [CrossRef]
16. Sharma, M.A.; Singh, J.B. Use of Probability Distribution in Rainfall Analysis. *N. Y. Sci. J.* **2010**, *3*, 40–49.
17. Bunde, A.; Eichner, J.F.; Kantelhardt, J.W.; Havlin, S. The effects of multifractality on the statistics of return intervals. *Phys. Rev. Lett.* **2005**, *161*, 181–193.
18. Pluchino, A.; Rapisarda, A.; Tsallis, C. Noise, synchrony and correlations at the edge of chaos. *Phys. Rev. E* **2013**, *87*, 022910. [CrossRef]
19. Tsallis, C. *Introduction to Nonextensive Statistical Mechanics: Approaching a Complex World*, 2nd ed.; Springer: Berlin/Heidelberg, Germany, 2023.
20. Ludescher, J.; Tsallis, C.; Bunde, A. Universal behaviour of interoccurrence times between losses in financial markets: An analytical description. *Europhys. Lett.* **2011**, *95*, 68002. [CrossRef]
21. Tsallis, C.; Mendes, R.S. The role of constraints within generalized nonextensive statistics. *Physica A* **1998**, *261*, 534–554. [CrossRef]
22. Greco, A.; Tsallis, C.; Rapisarda, A.; Pluchino, A.; Fichera, G.; Contrafatto, L. Acoustic emissions in compression of building materials: *q*-statistics enables the anticipation of the breakdown point. *Eur. Phys. J. Spec. Top.* **2020**, *229*, 841–849. [CrossRef]
23. Vinciguerra, S.C.; Greco, A.; Pluchino, A.; Rapisarda, A.; Tsallis, C. Acoustic emissions in rock deformation and failure: New insights from q-statistical analysis. *Entropy* **2023**, *25*, 701. [CrossRef] [PubMed]
24. Bogachev, M.I.; Bunde, A. Memory effects in the statistics of interoccurrence times between large returns in financial markets. *Phys. Rev. E* **2008**, *78*, 036114. [CrossRef] [PubMed]
25. Yamasaki, K.; Muchnik, L.; Havlin, S.; Bunde, A.; Stanley, H.E. Scaling and memory in volatility return intervalsin financial markets. *Proc. Natl. Acad. Sci. USA* **2005**, *102*, 9424–9428. [CrossRef] [PubMed]

entropy

MDPI

Article

Characterizing Complex Spatiotemporal Patterns from Entropy Measures

Luan Orion Barauna [1,*], Rubens Andreas Sautter [1], Reinaldo Roberto Rosa [1,2], Erico Luiz Rempel [3] and Alejandro C. Frery [4]

[1] Applied Computing Graduate Program (CAP), National Institute for Space Research, Av. dos Astronautas, 1.758, Jardim da Granja, São José dos Campos 12227-010, SP, Brazil; rubens.sautter@gmail.com (R.A.S.); reinaldo.rosa@inpe.br (R.R.R.)

[2] Laboratory for Computing and Applied Math, National Institute for Space Research, Av. dos Astronautas, 1.758, Jardim da Granja, São José dos Campos 12227-010, SP, Brazil

[3] Mathematics Department, Aeronautics Institute of Technology, Praça Marechal Eduardo Gomes, 50, Vila das Acácias, São José dos Campos 12228-900, SP, Brazil; erico.rempel@ita.br

[4] School of Mathematics and Statistics, Victoria University of Wellington, P.O. Box 600, Wellington 6140, New Zealand; alejandro.frery@vuw.ac.nz

* Correspondence: luanorion1@gmail.com

Abstract: In addition to their importance in statistical thermodynamics, probabilistic entropy measurements are crucial for understanding and analyzing complex systems, with diverse applications in time series and one-dimensional profiles. However, extending these methods to two- and three-dimensional data still requires further development. In this study, we present a new method for classifying spatiotemporal processes based on entropy measurements. To test and validate the method, we selected five classes of similar processes related to the evolution of random patterns: (i) white noise; (ii) red noise; (iii) weak turbulence from reaction to diffusion; (iv) hydrodynamic fully developed turbulence; and (v) plasma turbulence from MHD. Considering seven possible ways to measure entropy from a matrix, we present the method as a parameter space composed of the two best separating measures of the five selected classes. The results highlight better combined performance of Shannon permutation entropy (S_H^p) and a new approach based on Tsallis Spectral Permutation Entropy (S_q^s). Notably, our observations reveal the segregation of reaction terms in this $S_H^p \times S_q^s$ space, a result that identifies specific sectors for each class of dynamic process, and it can be used to train machine learning models for the automatic classification of complex spatiotemporal patterns.

Keywords: nonlinear dynamics; spatiotemporal patterns; turbulence; Shannon entropy; Tsallis entropy; gradient pattern analysis

Citation: Barauna, L.O.; Sautter, R.A.; Rosa, R.R.; Rempel, E.L.; Frery, A.C. Characterizing Complex Spatiotemporal Patterns from Entropy Measures. *Entropy* **2024**, *26*, 508. https://doi.org/10.3390/e26060508

Academic Editors: Ugur Tirnakli, Christian Beck, Hans J. Herrmann, Airton Deppman, Henrik Jeldtoft Jensen, Evaldo M. F. Curado, Fernando D. Nobre, Angelo Plastino, Astero Provata and Andrea Rapisarda

Received: 31 January 2024
Revised: 2 March 2024
Accepted: 8 March 2024
Published: 12 June 2024

1. Introduction

The intricate relationship between probability and entropy is a cornerstone in information theory and statistical thermodynamics, providing a robust framework for analyzing a multitude of phenomena ranging from data transmission processes to the behavior of many physical systems. Entropy, derived from the probability distribution of the states of a process or system, can be interpreted as a quantitative measure of randomness or disorder, offering deep insights into the underlying dynamics of several complex systems (see, for instance, Refs. [1–6]).

From a thermodynamic perspective, the entropy concept is intimately tied to the statistical mechanics of microstates. Entropy, S, is defined by Boltzmann's entropy equation, $S = k_B \ln \Omega$, where k_B is the Boltzmann constant and Ω represents the number of microstates. This relationship can be interpreted as the degree of disorder or randomness in a system's microscopic configurations, drawing a direct connection between the macroscopic observable properties and the statistical behavior of microstates. Complementarily, in the realm of information theory, entropy is fundamentally concerned with quantifying the expected level of "information", "surprise", or "uncertainty" in the potential outcomes of a system [7]. This quantification is intricately linked to the probability distribution of these outcomes. It essentially measures the average unpredictability or the requisite amount of information needed to describe a random event, thereby providing a metric for the efficiency of data transmission and encoding strategies. Therefore, the duality of the entropy interpretation works as a bridge between the abstract realm of information and the tangible world of the statistics of physical systems. It encapsulates the essence of entropy as a fundamental measure, providing a unifying lens through which the behavior of complex systems, whether in the context of information processing or thermodynamics, can be coherently understood and analyzed. This interdisciplinary approach not only deepens our understanding of individual phenomenon but also reveals the underlying universality of the concepts of randomness and information across diverse scientific domains.

In the scenario described above, it is necessary to identify entropy measures that are effective in characterizing the spatiotemporal patterns of complex processes typically observed or simulated in $3D + 1$: following the notation of the amplitude equation theory, where D corresponds to the spatial dimension in which the amplitude of a variable fluctuates over time. This need is justified by the great advances in the generation of big data in computational physics, with emphasis on the direct numerical simulation (DNS) of turbulence [8,9], ionized fluids [10–14], and reactive–diffusive processes [15] to highlight a few.

Our main objective in this work is to present and evaluate the performance of a set of information entropy measurements, conjugated two by two, in order to characterize different classes of 3D structural patterns arising from nonlinear spatiotemporal processes. To this end, the article is organized as follows: The analytical methodology is presented in Section 2, and the data are presented in Section 3. The results, in the context of a benchmark based on the generalization of the silhouette score, are presented and interpreted in Section 4. Our concluding remarks, with emphasis on pointing out the usability of the method in the context of data-driven science, are presented in Section 6.

2. Methods

Various entropy metrics have been proposed in the literature, including spectral entropy, permutation entropy, and statistical complexity.

The process of defining a new metric typically involves two fundamental steps: (i) establishing the probability definition and (ii) determining the entropic form. This framework allows for the generalization of any new metric by specifying these two steps (code publicly available at https://github.com/rsautter/Eta (14 January 2024)).

In Sections 2.1 and 2.2, we present, respectively, the key techniques for defining probabilities and entropic forms. Subsequently, in Section 2.3, we introduce a methodology to assess these metrics using criteria that are commonly applied to clustering techniques.

2.1. Probabilities

Probability is a concept that quantifies the likelihood of an event occurring. It is expressed as a numerical value between 0 and 1. Here, 0 signifies the complete impossibility of an event, while 1 denotes absolute certainty. Mathematically, if we consider a process with a finite number of possible outcomes, the probability $\Pr(E)$ of an event E is defined by the following ratio:

$$\Pr(E) = \frac{\text{Number of favorable outcomes}}{\text{Total number of possible outcomes}}. \quad (1)$$

This definition is useful for gaining insight of systems that produce discrete real-valued outcomes. In such a case, a histogram of proportions of observed events is the usual tool for estimating the underlying probability distribution of such outcomes.

Many systems produce continue-valued multidimensional outcomes, and the observer needs to define methods for estimating a useful probability that is able to characterize their behavior. Approaches such as permutation and spectral analysis incorporate spatial locality and scale considerations to elucidate the occurrence of specific patterns.

In the permutation approach, local spatial differences (increase, decrease, or constancy) represent the states. New states can be generated by permuting the array elements. Thus, the probabilities account for the occurrences of those states. To extend this definition to multiple dimensions, a given array is flattened. Further details of this technique have been explored by Pessa and Ribeiro [16].

Another methodology involves spectral analysis, wherein the probability is computed as the power spectrum density (PSD) of the signal $P(\omega)$, which is normalized accordingly. Since this approach considers the probability associated with a given frequency ω, it explores the scaling relation of the signal. For instance, white noise, characterized by equal power across all frequencies, represents a type of signal exhibiting maximum entropy. In contrast, red noise presents a higher PSD for lower frequencies, leading to lower entropy values. This approach has been popularized in the literature to study time series [2,17]. The probabilities presented in this section describe the possible spatial states, while the subsequent subsection elaborates on the entropic characterization of this system.

2.2. Entropic Forms

Several entropy equations and generalizations have been proposed, such as Boltzmann–Gibbs entropy (also known as Shannon entropy), Tsallis entropy, and Rényi entropy. The most common form is Shannon entropy, which is expressed as follows:

$$S_H = -\sum_{i=1}^{W} p_i \log p_i. \tag{2}$$

Here, p_i is the probability of state i, which can also comprise complex numbers [18], and W is the size of the set of possible events. The value of S_H depends on the distribution. Notably, S_H is at the maximum when all probabilities are equal, i.e., under the uniform distribution; in this case, $S_H = -\log W$, and it is at the minimum when p_i is Dirac's delta. To account for this maximum value, normalized Shannon entropy is given by the following:

$$S_H = -\frac{\sum_{i=1}^{W} p_i \log p_i}{\log W}. \tag{3}$$

Another significant entropic form is Tsallis entropy, proposed as a generalization of Boltzmann–Gibbs entropy [19]:

$$S_q = \frac{1 - \sum_{i=1}^{W} p_i^q}{q-1}, \tag{4}$$

where $q \in \mathbb{R}$ is the entropic index or nonextensivity parameter, and it plays a crucial role in determining the degree of nonextensivity in Tsallis entropy.

It is important to explore a range of values for the parameter q to derive a metric distinct from Shannon entropy since $\lim_{q \to 1} S_q = S_H$. Therefore, we suggest exploring values for q in the range of $1 < q < 5$ and seek a relationship denoted by α, where $\log S_q = \alpha \log q$. This approach enables the examination of this generalization of S_H.

A unique strategy for characterizing complex nonlinear systems is gradient pattern analysis (GPA). This technique involves computing a set of metrics derived from the gradient lattice representation and the gradient moments (see Appendix A). Specifically, we highlight G_4, which is determined as the Shannon entropy from the complex representation of the gradient lattice:

$$G_4 = \left| \sum_{j=0}^{V_A} \frac{z_j}{z} \ln \frac{z_j}{z} \right|. \tag{5}$$

In the lattice context, the gradient signifies the local variation of amplitudes, computed as the spatial derivative at every embedding dimension. From these spatial derivatives, the following complex representation is formed:

$$z_j = |v_j| e^{i\theta_j}, \tag{6}$$

It comprises both the modulus ($|v_j|$) and phases (θ_j). To obtain a probability, the complex notation is normalized by $z = \sum z_j$. For an in-depth review of this metric, please refer to [18,20]. Table 1 provides a summary of all combinations of entropic forms with associated probabilities, along with the GPA metric, that were examined in this study.

Table 1. Entropy measures.

Measure	Probability	Entropic Form	Reference
S_H^h	histogram	Shannon, Equation (3)	Lesne [21]
S_H^p	permutation	Shannon, Equation (3)	Pessa, Ribeiro [16]
S_H^s	spectral	Shannon, Equation (3)	Abdelsamie et al. [9], Abdullah et al. [3]
S_q^h	histogram	Tsallis q-law, Equation (4)	Li and Shang [22]
S_q^p	permutation	Tsallis q-law, Equation (4)	Li and Shang [22]
S_q^s	spectral	Tsallis q-law, Equation (4)	This paper
G_4	gradient	Complex Shannon, Equation (5)	Ramos et al. [18]

To assess the efficacy of each metric and explore the impact of various combinations of probability definitions with entropic forms, we introduce a criterion outlined in the subsequent section. This criterion is formulated with a focus on clustering the entropy measures of the dataset.

2.3. Silhouette Score and Generalized Silhouette Score

Non-supervised algorithms face unique challenges, and a remarkable one is defining their efficiency. The silhouette score is a criterion for defining if a set has been well clusterized [23]. Given an element x_i in a cluster π_k, this metric is computed as follows [3,24]:

$$s(x_i) = \frac{b(x_i) - a(x_i)}{\max\{b(x_i), a(x_i)\}}, \tag{7}$$

where $a(x_i)$ is the average dissimilarity, which is the average distance of x_i to all other elements in the cluster π_k, and $b(x_i)$ is the average distance to the elements of other clusters. The greater the $s(x_i)$ value, the better performance of the clustering algorithm because it has produced groups with low dissimilarities and large distances between clusters. This technique can be extended to feature extractions if one considers the individual datasets as the clusters π_k. However, it is equally essential to account for the potential correlation between metrics, as metrics may inadvertently capture the same data aspects, which is undesirable. To mitigate this, we use the modulus of the Pearson correlation $|r|$ to form the penalty term $1 - |r|$ as follows:

$$s'(x_i) = (1 - |r|) \frac{b(x_i) - a(x_i)}{\max\{b(x_i), a(x_i)\}}, \tag{8}$$

which we call the generalized silhouette score (GSS).

After defining a group of entropy measurements and the tool (GSS), which allows the determination of the best pair of measurements to compose a 2D parameter space, we selected the dataset to test and validate our methodological approach.

3. Data

Our main objective is to test the performance of a space composed of two entropy measures in which it is possible to distinguish different classes of complex spatiotemporal processes. For this first study, we chose turbulence-related processes and simulated dynamic colored noises.

We employ simulated data related to the following processes: (i) white noise; (ii) colored noise; (iii) weak turbulence; (iv) hydrodynamic turbulence; and (v) magnetohydrodynamic turbulence (MHD). The main reason for choosing these processes, except colored noise, is that they all present random-type patterns with underlying dynamic characteristics based on physical processes described by partial differential equations (diffusion, reaction, and advection). Each was obtained from simulations identified in Table 2.

Based on the power-law-scaling algorithm technique [25], we created our noise simulator [26]. The data representing weak turbulence (also called chemical or reactive–diffusive turbulence) were obtained from the solution of the Ginzburg–Landau complex equation [15,27]. The hydrodynamic turbulence patterns were selected from the John Hopkins database (JHTDB) [28], and the MHD turbulence was simulated using the PENCIL code [12]. Details regarding the simulations are provided in the Supplementary Materials in the GitHub repository.

To test the approach based on entropy measurements, we selected a total of 25 snapshots representing the evolution of each chosen process. After selecting the middle slice of the hypercube, we uniformly resized all snapshots to 64×64 byte-valued pixels using nearest neighbor interpolation; while this resizing expedites the analysis, it does entail a loss in resolution. The snapshots were extracted from 3D simulations, taking the analysis of the central slice of each hypercubeas a criterion as the measurement technique used to act on matrices within a two-dimensional approach.

Table 2. Datasets and references.

Simulation	Process	Reference
White Dynamic Noise	Spatiotemporal stochastic	Timmer et al. [25]
Red Dynamic Noise	Spatiotemporal stochastic	Timmer et al. [25]
CGL [1]	Weak turbulence	Sautter [26], Sautter et al. [27]
JHTDB	Fully developed turbulence	Brandenburg et al. [12]
PENCIL	MHD turbulence	Brandenburg et al. [12]

[1] Our 3D simulator is public available at https://github.com/rsautter/Noisy-Complex-Ginzburg-Landau (14 January 20224).

Figure 1 shows representative snapshots of the respective spatiotemporal processes. These visualizations provide a compelling narrative of the dynamic behavior of each system, highlighting the wide variety of patterns that emerge through temporal dynamics in the phase space.

The numerical procedures and/or technical acquisition details related to the data shown in Figure 1 are available in the Supplementary Materials in the repository (https://github.com/rsautter/Eta/ (14 January 2024)) and in the section entitled "Data Simulations".

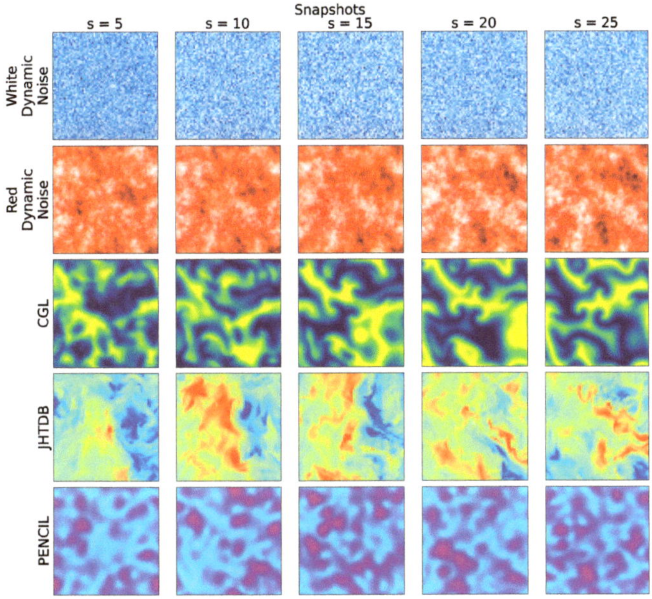

Figure 1. Snapshots of the spatiotemporal evolution of each selected system class, listed in Table 2. Each row shows one of the simulations, rendered at time steps that show representative pattern dynamics: dynamic white noise ($\beta = 0$ represented by colormap `'Blues'`) on the 1st row; random red noise ($\beta = 2$, represented by colormap `'Reds'`) on the 2nd row; weak turbulence from the reaction–diffusion complex Ginzburg–Landau dynamics on the 3rd row (represented by colormap `'viridis'`); fully developed turbulence from JHTDB on the 4th row (represented on colormap `'rainbow'`) and MHD turbulence from PENCIL on the 5th row (represented by colormap `'cool'`).

4. Results and Interpretation

The analyses in this study were conducted within 2D metric spaces, encompassing all possible entropy measure combinations. Based on the minimum information principle, this configuration offers advantages in terms of interpretability, considering the minimum set of parameters that can be addressed as labels within a possible machine learning interpretation. Our approach to measuring entropies from the data follows the following steps:

- Input of a snapshot;
- Pre-processing for which its output is a 64×64 matrix with amplitudes ranging from 0 to 255;
- Generation of three matrix data outputs: 2D histogram, 2D permutation, and 2D FFT spectra;
- For each of the three domains, the entropy measures are calculated.

Given the definition of the three types of domains interpreted as probabilities (from histogram, permutation, and spectrum), we have six entropy variations, as detailed in Section 2. To distinguish these metrics, we introduced superscripts denoted by h for histogram probability, p for permutation probability, and s for spectral probability. The GPA analysis yields another metric, resulting in 21 scores, as illustrated in Figure 2.

As a result, the most effective combination is the following pair: spectral Tsallis entropy (S_q^s) and Shannon permutation entropy (S_H^p). A visual representation of this space, accompanied by some snapshots, is presented in Figure 3. In this space, the metrics reveal a constant Shannon permutation entropy dynamical noise system, which is solely distinguished by spectral Tsalllis entropy, indicating the differences in the scaling effects in pattern formation. Conversely, the distinct complex nonlinear characteristics and reaction terms observed in MHD simulations are more pronounced in Shannon permutation entropy, accentuating the diversity of localized patterns alongside the larger-scale ones.

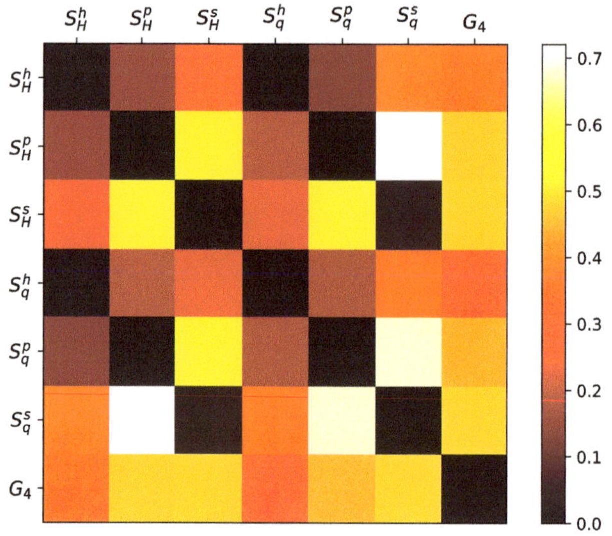

Figure 2. Generalized silhouette score for all 2D metric combinations. Higher values on the heatmap indicate superior metric performance. The optimal result is achieved with the pairing of spectral Tsallis entropy and Shannon permutation entropy ($S_q^s \times S_H^p$).

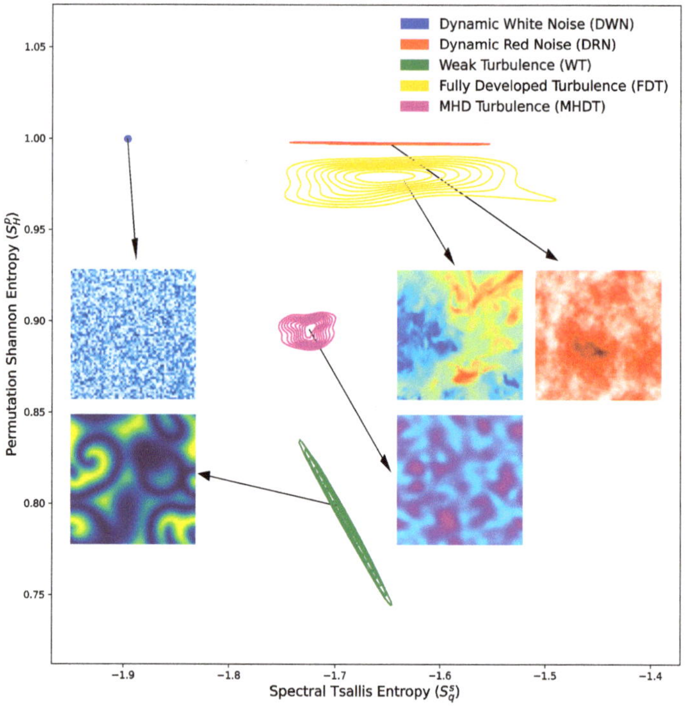

Figure 3. Optimal outcomes achieved are assessed through the generalized silhouette score criterion. The method achieves its best performance in the ($S_q^s \times S_H^p$) parameter space.

The analysis of entropy distribution is essential in a classification context, as it offers insights into the similarity between a new dataset and various models. However, carefully analysing the entropy metrics over time can highlight important aspects of the underlying physical processes. For instance, the transition from initial conditions to an oscillatory relaxation state is evident in Figure 4. This outcome aligns with expectations in the context of the CGL system due to the periodic nature of the reaction term. However, it is essential to highlight that in this introductory study, we avoided simulations with more complex regimes (such as relaxations) as the primary purpose here is to present a new method, and the objective here is not to use it to deepen the physical interpretation of each process.

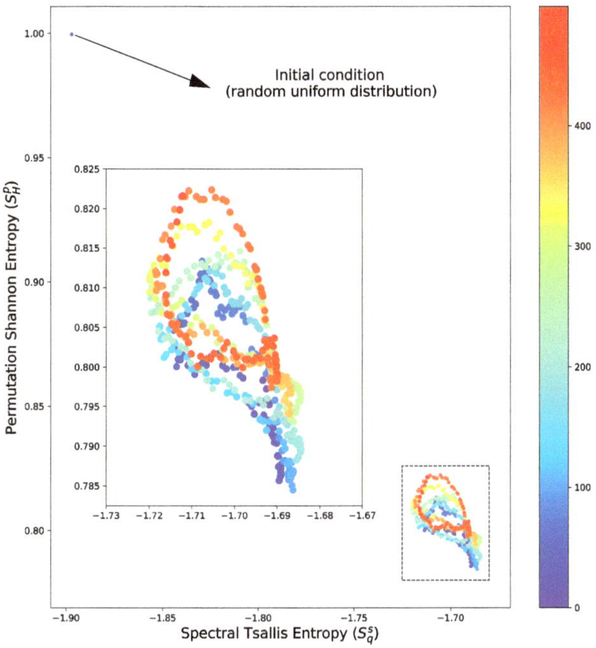

Figure 4. Best entropy set according to the generalized silhouette score (see Figure 2) for the 3D-CGL solution over time, where the oscillatory dynamic of the system is highlighted. The color indicates the snapshot, where 500 samples are presented.

5. Outlook

Based on the study and approach presented here, we defined a methodological pipeline for the spatiotemporal characterization of simulated and/or observed complex processes (Figure 5). The method can be applied to identify and segregate different classes of processes and to classify isolated patterns when necessary. In a context where measured and simulated data may exist, it also serves to validate models. Likewise, the pair of entropy measurements can also serve as a binomial label for training deep learning architectures for automatic classification.

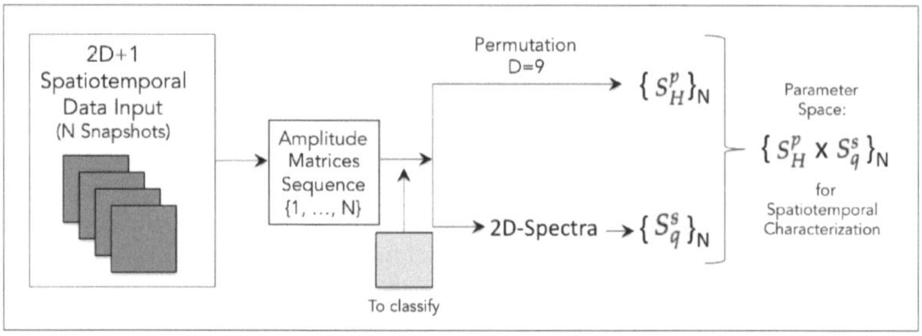

Figure 5. Pipeline of the method proposed in this study based on the best results found: A sequence of snapshots from the simulation of a given process (in the $2D+1$ or $3D+1$ domains) comprises the input from which entropy measurements will be obtained. To calculate the respective Shannon permutation entropy values S_H^p, the permutation values are obtained (see Appendix B). To calculate the spectral Tsallis entropy S_q^s, the respective spectra are obtained. From the calculated values, the parameter space is constructed where where it is proposed to characterize the underlying process. The space also works for classifying isolated patterns, taking as reference the distinct processes that have already been characterized.

6. Concluding Remarks

This work carried out a comprehensive analysis of entropy metrics and their application to complex extended nonlinear systems. The study explored new approaches, including different entropy measures and a new *generalized silhouette score* for measurement evaluation.

Through the meticulous consideration of *canonical* datasets, distinct patterns have been characterized in terms of entropy metrics. The pivotal finding was the identification of the optimal pair: spectral Tsallis entropy (S_q^s) and Shannon permutation entropy (S_H^p), yielding superior outcomes in the generalized silhouette score. This combination showcased efficacy in distinguishing spatiotemporal dynamics coming from different classes of turbulent-like processes, including pure stochastic 2D $1/f^{-\beta}$ (colored) noise.

The new method contributes valuable insights into applying entropy probabilistic measures, providing a foundation for future studies in terms of extended complex system pattern formation characterization.

Initial work considering entropy measurements for training machine learning models is underway. In this context, it also includes a study of the computational complexity of the method for a benchmark with other measures and approaches that may emerge. This strategy is fundamental when we think about the presented method being applied in a data science context.

Author Contributions: Conceptualization, R.R.R., L.O.B. and R.A.S.; methodology, R.R.R., L.O.B. and R.A.S.; software, L.O.B. and R.A.S.; validation, R.R.R., L.O.B., R.A.S., A.C.F. and E.L.R.; formal analysis, R.A.S. and L.O.B.; investigation, R.A.S. and L.O.B.; resources, R.R.R., L.O.B. and A.C.F.; data curation, E.L.R. and R.A.S.; writing—original draft preparation, R.R.R., L.O.B. and R.A.S.; writing—review and editing, R.R.R., L.O.B., R.A.S., A.C.F. and E.L.R.; visualization, L.O.B. and R.A.S.; supervision, R.R.R.; project administration, R.R.R.; funding acquisition, R.R.R., L.O.B., R.A.S. and A.C.F. All authors have read and agreed to the published version of the manuscript.

Funding: R.R.R. thanks FAPESP under Grant No. 2021/15114-8 for partial financial support. L.O. Barauna and R.A.S were supported by the Federal Brazilian Agency-CAPES. E.L.R. acknowledges financial support from CNPq (Brazil) under Grant No. 306920/2020-4. Te Herenga Waka–Victoria University of Wellington partially funded this publication through Read & Publish agreements negotiated by the Council of Australian University Librarians (CAUL) Consortium.

Institutional Review Board Statement: Not applicable.

Data Availability Statement: All the mathematical content and data used in this work in a GitHub repository (https://github.com/rsautter/Eta/ (14 January 2024)) to guarantee the reproducibility of this experiment.

Acknowledgments: The authors thank the Brazilian Space Agency (AEB) for the payment of APC (Article Processing Charge) costs.

Conflicts of Interest: The authors declare no conflict of interest.

Appendix A. Gradient Pattern Analysis

Gradient pattern analysis (GPA) represents a paradigm shift in data analysis, focusing on the spatiotemporal dynamics of information rather than static values. This innovative approach emphasizes the examination of gradients within datasets—dynamic vectors that encode the rate of change—thereby revealing patterns and structures that are often obscured by traditional analytical methods.

From a mathematical perspective, GPA utilizes a series of gradient moments to quantify the smoothness and alignment of these vectors within the data lattice:

$$G_1 = \frac{N_C - N_V}{N_V}, \tag{A1}$$

$$G_2 = \frac{V_A}{V}\left(1 - \frac{\left|\sum_{j=0}^{V_A} v_j\right|}{2\sum_{j=0}^{V_A}|v_j|}\right), \tag{A2}$$

$$G_3 = \frac{1}{2}\left(\frac{V_A}{V} + \frac{1}{2V_A}\sum_{j=0}^{V_A} u_j.v_j + 1\right), \tag{A3}$$

and

$$G_4 = \left|\sum_{j=0}^{V_A} \frac{z_j}{z} \ln \frac{z_j}{z}\right|. \tag{A4}$$

where N_C and N_V are the connections in the Delaunay triangulation and the number of vertices; V_A is the number of asymmetrical vectors, V is the total number of vectors in the lattice, and v_j^A is an asymmetrical vector; $u_j = (\cos(\phi_j), \sin(\phi_j))$ and $z_j = |vi| \exp(i\theta_j)$, where $|vi|$ represents the modulus and θ_j represents the phase and

$$z = \sum_{j}^{V_A} z_j. \tag{A5}$$

These moments provide a distinctive signature that characterizes the inherent patterns in the data, and they are applicable across various domains. This versatility enables GPA's application in diverse fields, ranging from time-series analysis in climatology to image recognition in computer vision.

One of the notable strengths of GPA is its capacity for efficient data compression. By discerning and eliminating redundant information while retaining the essential gradient characteristics, GPA achieves data compression without losing the dataset's critical structural and dynamic properties. This aspect of GPA is particularly advantageous for storing, transmitting, and analysing large-scale datasets in numerous scientific and engineering disciplines. For a complete review, see Refs. [18,20].

Appendix B. Two-Dimensional Permutation Entropy

Based on the concept of permutation entropy [29], two-dimensional multiscale sample entropy has been proposed as a new texture algorithm [30,31] and has therefore been used to evaluate the complexity of 2D patterns [32]. In a simplified way, the technique is based on the following steps:

- Step 1: Obtain the coarse-grained image as an $N \times N$ matrix;
- Step 2: Apply a window of size $d \times d$ to it;
- Step 3: Carry out $d!$ reshape permutations to obtain the probabilities of each local pattern;
- Step 4: Repeat the last procedure, scanning the entire matrix;
- Step 5: Apply the probability values as input to the chosen entropy formula.

In our application, we use $d = 9$ since it is the minimum kernel size encompassing a central pixel. This value corresponds to a kernel of $dx = dy = 3$.

References

1. Tsallis, C. When may a system be referred to as complex? An entropic perspective. *Front. Complex Syst.* **2023**, *1*, 1284458. [CrossRef]
2. Zhang, A.; Yang, B.; Huang, L. Feature Extraction of EEG Signals Using Power Spectral Entropy. In Proceedings of the International Conference on BioMedical Engineering and Informatics, Sanya, China, 27–30 May 2008.
3. Raja Abdullah, R.S.A.; Saleh, N.L.; Syed Abdul Rahman, S.M.; Zamri, N.S.; Abdul Rashid, N.E. Texture classification using spectral entropy of acoustic signal generated by a human echolocator. *Entropy* **2019**, *21*, 963. [CrossRef]
4. Mattedi, A.P.; Ramos, F.M.; Rosa, R.R.; Mantegna, R.N. Value-at-risk and Tsallis statistics: Risk analysis of the aerospace sector. *Phys. A Stat. Mech. Its Appl.* **2004**, *344*, 554–561. [CrossRef]
5. Ramos, F.M.; Rosa, R.R.; Rodrigues Neto, C.; Bolzan, M.J.A.; Abren Sá, L.D. Nonextensive thermostatistics description of intermittency in turbulence and financial markets. *Nonlinear Anal. Theory Methods Appl.* **2001**, *47*, 3521–3530. [CrossRef]
6. Ramos, F.M.; Bolzan, M.J.A.; Abreu Sá, L.D.; Rosa, R.R. Atmospheric turbulence within and above an Amazon forest. *Phys. D Nonlinear Phenom.* **2004**, *193*, 278–291. [CrossRef]
7. Brissaud, J. The meanings of entropy. *Entropy* **2005**, *7*, 68–96. [CrossRef]
8. Gotoh, T.; Kraichnan, R.H. Turbulence and Tsallis statistics. *Physica D* **2004**, *193*, 231–244. [CrossRef]
9. Abdelsamie, A.; Janiga, G.; Thévenin, D. Spectral entropy as a flow state indicator. *Int. J. Heat Fluid Flow* **2017**, *68*, 102–113. [CrossRef]
10. Mignone, A.; Bodo, G.; Massaglia, S.; Matsakos, T.; Tesileanu, O.; Zanni, C.; Ferrari, A. PLUTO: A numerical code for computational astrophysics. *ApJS* **2007**, *170*, 228–242. [CrossRef]
11. Franci, L.; Hellinger, P.; Guarrasi, M.; Chen, C.H.K.; Papini, E.; Verdini, A.; Matteini, L.; Landi, S. Three-dimensional simulations of solar wind turbulence. *J. Phys. Conf. Ser.* **2018**, *1031*, 012002. [CrossRef]
12. The Pencil Code Collaboration; Brandenburg, A.; Johansen, A.; Bourdin, P.A.; Dobler, W.; Lyra, W.; Rheinhardt, M.; Bingert, S.; Haugen, N.E.L.; Mee, A.; et al. The Pencil Code, a modular MPI code for partial differential equations and particles: Multipurpose and multiuser-maintained. *J. Open Source Softw.* **2021**, *6*, 2807.
13. Veronese, T.B.; Rosa, R.R.; Bolzan, M.J.A.; Rocha Fernandes, F.C.; Sawant, H.S.; Karlicky, M. Fluctuation analysis of solar radio bursts associated with geoeffective X-class flares. *J. Atmos. Sol.-Terr. Phys.* **2011**, *73*, 1311–1316. [CrossRef]
14. Bolzan, M.J.A.; Sahai, Y.; Fagundes, P.R.; Rosa, R.R.; Ramos, F.M.; Abalde, J.R. Intermittency analysis of geomagnetic storm time-series observed in Brazil. *J. Atmos. Sol.-Terr. Phys.* **2005**, *67*, 1365–1372. [CrossRef]
15. Lu, H.; Lü, S.J.; Zhang, M.J. Fourier spectral approximations to the dynamics of 3D fractional complex Ginzburg-Landau equation. *Discret. Contin. Dyn. Syst.* **2017**, *37*, 2539–2564. [CrossRef]
16. Pessa, A.A.B.; Ribeiro, H.V. ordpy: A Python package for data analysis with permutation entropy and ordinal network methods. *Chaos Interdiscip. J. Nonlinear Sci.* **2021**, *31*, 063110. [CrossRef]
17. Xiong, P.Y.; Jahanshahi, H.; Alcarazc, R.; Chud, Y.M.; Gómez-Aguilar, J.F.; Alsaadi, F.E. Spectral Entropy Analysis and Synchronization of a Multi-Stable Fractional-Order Chaotic System using a Novel Neural Network-Based Chattering-Free Sliding Mode Technique. *Chaos Solitons Fractals* **2021**, *144*, 110576. [CrossRef]
18. Ramos, F.M.; Rosa, R.R.; Rodrigues Neto, C.; Zanandrea A. Generalized complex entropic form for gradient pattern analysis of spatio-temporal dynamics. *Physica A* **2000**, *283*, 171–174. [CrossRef]
19. Tsallis, C. Possible generalization of Boltzmann-Gibbs statistics. *J. Stat. Phys.* **1998**, *52*, 479–487. [CrossRef]
20. Rosa, R.R.; de Carvalho, R.R.; Sautter, R.A.; Barchi, P.H.; Stalder, D.H.; Moura, T.C.; Rembold, S.B.; Morell, D.R.F.; Ferreira, N.C. Gradient pattern analysis applied to galaxy morphology. *Mon. Not. R. Astron. Soc. Lett.* **2018**, *477*, L101–L105. [CrossRef]
21. Lesne, A. Shannon entropy: A rigorous notion at the crossroads between probability, information theory, dynamical systems and statistical physics. *Math. Struct. Comput. Sci.* **2014**, *24*, e240311. [CrossRef]

22. Li, C.; Shang, P. Multiscale Tsallis permutation entropy analysis for complex physiological time series. *Physica A* **2019**, *523*, 10–20. [CrossRef]
23. Kaufman, L.; Rousseeuw, P. *Finding Groups in Data: An Introduction to Cluster Analysis*; Wiley and Sons: Hoboken, NJ, USA, 2005.
24. Shutaywi, M.; Kachouie, N.N. Silhouette analysis for performance evaluation in machine learning with applications to clustering. *Entropy* **2021**, *23*, 759. [CrossRef] [PubMed]
25. Timmer, J.; Koenig, M. On generating power law noise. *Astron. Astrophys.* **1995**, *300*, 707.
26. Sautter, R.A. Gradient Pattern Analysis: Enhancements and Applications Including the Influence of Noise on Pattern Formation. Ph.D. Thesis, National Institute for Space Research, São José dos Campos, Brazil, 2023.
27. Sautter, R.; Rosa, R.; Pontes, J. *Incremental Gradient Pattern Analysis of Stochastic Complex Ginzburg-Landau Dynamics*; ResearchGate: Berlin, Germany, 2023. [CrossRef]
28. Li, Y.; Perlman, E.; Wan, M.; Yang, Y.; Meneveau, C.; Burns, R.; Chen, S.; Szalay, A.; Eyink, E. A public turbulence database cluster and applications to study Lagrangian evolution of velocity increments in turbulence. *J. Turbul.* **2008**, *9*, N31. [CrossRef]
29. Bandt, C.; Pompe, B. Permutation entropy: A natural complexity measure for time series. *Phys. Rev. Lett.* **2002**, *88*, 174102. [CrossRef] [PubMed]
30. Silva, L.; Duque, J.; Felipe, J.; Murta, L.; Humeau-Heurtier, A. Two-dimensional multiscale entropy analysis: Applications to image texture evaluation. *Signal Process.* **2018**, *147*, 224–232. [CrossRef]
31. Humeau-Heurtier, A.; Omoto, A.C.M.; Silva, L.E. Bi-dimensional multiscale entropy: Relation with discrete Fourier transform and biomedical application. *Comput. Biol. Med.* **2018**, *100*, 36–40. [CrossRef]
32. Morel, C.; Humeau-Heurtier, A. Multiscale permutation entropy for two-dimensional patterns. *Pattern Reg. Lett.* **2021**, *150*, 139–146. [CrossRef]

entropy

MDPI

Article

Non-Thermal Solar Wind Electron Velocity Distribution Function

Peter H. Yoon [1,*], Rodrigo A. López [2], Chadi S. Salem [3], John W. Bonnell [3] and Sunjung Kim [4]

1 Institute for Physical Science and Technology, University of Maryland, College Park, MD 20742, USA
2 Research Center in the Intersection of Plasma Physics, Matter, and Complexity (P^2mc), Comisión Chilena de Energía Nuclear, Casilla 188-D, Santiago 7600713, Chile; rodrigo.lopez@cchen.cl
3 Space Sciences Laboratory, University of California, Berkeley, CA 94720, USA; salem@ssl.berkeley.edu (C.S.S.); jwbonnell@berkeley.edu (J.W.B.)
4 Astronomy and Space Sciences, Kyung Hee University, Yongin 17104, Gyeonggi, Republic of Korea; sunjungkim1982@gmail.com
* Correspondence: yoonp@umd.edu

Abstract: The quiet-time solar wind electrons feature non-thermal characteristics when viewed from the perspective of their velocity distribution functions. They typically have an appearance of being composed of a denser thermal "core" population plus a tenuous energetic "halo" population. At first, such a feature was empirically fitted with the kappa velocity space distribution function, but ever since the ground-breaking work by Tsallis, the space physics community has embraced the potential implication of the kappa distribution as reflecting the non-extensive nature of the space plasma. From the viewpoint of microscopic plasma theory, the formation of the non-thermal electron velocity distribution function can be interpreted in terms of the plasma being in a state of turbulent quasi-equilibrium. Such a finding brings forth the possible existence of a profound inter-relationship between the non-extensive statistical state and the turbulent quasi-equilibrium state. The present paper further develops the idea of solar wind electrons being in the turbulent equilibrium, but, unlike the previous model, which involves the electrostatic turbulence near the plasma oscillation frequency (i.e., Langmuir turbulence), the present paper considers the impact of transverse electromagnetic turbulence, particularly, the turbulence in the whistler-mode frequency range. It is found that the coupling of spontaneously emitted thermal fluctuations and the background turbulence leads to the formation of a non-thermal electron velocity distribution function of the type observed in the solar wind during quiet times. This demonstrates that the whistler-range turbulence represents an alternative mechanism for producing the kappa-like non-thermal distribution, especially close to the Sun and in the near-Earth space environment.

Keywords: Kappa distribution; solar wind electrons; whistler-mode waves; turbulence; thermal fluctuations; electromagnetic; electrostatic; plasma; kinetic

Citation: Yoon, P.H.; López, R.A.; Salem, C.S.; Bonnell, J.W.; Kim, S. Non-Thermal Solar Wind Electron Velocity Distribution Function. *Entropy* **2024**, *26*, 310. https://doi.org/10.3390/e26040310

Academic Editors: Ugur Tirnakli, Christian Beck, Hans J. Herrmann, Airton Deppman, Henrik Jeldtoft Jensen, Evaldo M. F. Curado, Fernando D. Nobre, Angelo Plastino, Astero Provata and Andrea Rapisarda

Received: 21 February 2024
Revised: 24 March 2024
Accepted: 27 March 2024
Published: 30 March 2024

1. Introduction

In situ measurements of charged particles in the near-Earth space environment by artificial satellite became possible during the decade of the 1960s. It was realized then that the velocity space distributions of charged particles that make up the space plasma deviate from the expected Maxwell–Boltzmann–Gauss statistics; instead, the observed distributions typically feature a suprathermal (or non-thermal) component with inverse power-law "tail" characteristics for the suprathermal velocity regime, $f \propto v^{-\gamma}$ for $v \gg \alpha$, where v represents the particle speed, f is the charged particle velocity distribution function, γ is the inverse power-law index, and α denotes the thermal speed [1–3]. Recent inner heliospheric missions, the Parker Solar Probe and Solar Orbiter, further confirm that such a non-thermal feature persists even for heliospheric environments much closer to the

Sun [4–6]. The physical origin of such a feature was not understood then. Instead, Olbert and Vasyliunas [7–10] introduced an empirical model known as the kappa distribution,

$$f_\kappa(v) \propto \left(1 + \frac{v^2}{\kappa\alpha^2}\right)^{-(\kappa+1)}, \tag{1}$$

to fit the observation. Here, $\alpha = (2k_B T/m)^{1/2}$ is the Maxwellian thermal speed, meaning that α is the thermal speed had $f(v)$ been given by the Maxwell–Boltzmann distribution. $k_B = 1.3806503 \times 10^{-23}\,\mathrm{m}^2\,\mathrm{kg}\,\mathrm{s}^{-2}\,\mathrm{K}^{-1}$ is the Boltzmann constant, which can replaced by unity if we adopt the unit of eV for thermal energy. That is, if the temperature T is expressed in eV instead of Kelvins (K), then we may take $k_B = 1$. Hereafter, we shall adopt such a convention. The mass of the charged particles is denoted by m. The free parameter κ determines the degree to which the observed distribution deviates from the Maxwellian–Boltzmann (MB or thermal) distribution in that if $\kappa \to \infty$, then the model reduces to the thermal distribution, $f_{MB}(v) \propto \exp(-v^2/\alpha^2)$, while for $v \gg \alpha$, the kappa model depicts an inverse power-law velocity distribution, $f_\kappa(v) \propto v^{-2(\kappa+1)}$. It is to be noted that, regardless of the value of the κ index, the kappa distribution approximates the MB distribution for $v \leq \alpha$—to be more precise, for a low v, the kappa distribution approaches the MB distribution with a sightly lower thermal speed, by a factor of $\sqrt{\kappa/(\kappa+1)}$. That is, the kappa model naturally encompasses the quasi-Maxwellian feature in the "core" part of the velocity distribution characterized by $v \leq \alpha$ and the inverse power-law tail portion of the distribution for the suprathermal regime, $v \gg \alpha$.

A sample non-thermal charged particle velocity distribution function in space is shown in Figure 1. Specifically, Figure 1 plots the typical electron velocity distribution function measured in the near-Earth space environment during quiet-time conditions. Figure 1 is a reproduction of Figure 4 of Ref. [11], and it shows two typical electron velocity distribution functions (eVDFs) in the solar wind at 1 au (astronomical unit) measured by the Wind/3DP electrostatic analyzers EESA-L and EESA-H. The left panels (a) and (c) show an eVDF in the slow solar wind (at 1995-06-19/00:06:38), and the right panels (b) and (d) show an eVDF in the fast solar wind (at 1995-06-19/23:13:59). The top panels (a) and (b) show cuts through the eVDF in one of the two directions perpendicular to the local magnetic field **B**: the diamonds are data points from EESA-L and the asterisks are data points from EESA-H. The dotted lines represent the one-count level for EESA-L and EESA-H. The blue dashed line in Figure 1a,b represents the sum of Maxwellian and kappa distributions (indicated in blue). The red line represents the fit to the measured perpendicular eVDF cut; the resulting fit parameters are indicated in red. The bottom panels (c) and (d) show cuts through the eVDF in the direction parallel to **B**. The perpendicular fit is shown in red, and the perpendicular fit parameters are used to initialize the parallel eVDF fit. The blue dashed line in Figure 1a,b represents the sum of Maxwellian and kappa distributions calculated using independent measurements of the core and halo densities and temperatures obtained from the fit of the spectrum of quasi-thermal fluctuations around the electron plasma frequency measured by the Wind/Waves electric field antennas. This "quasi-thermal noise" (QTN) technique is immune to spacecraft potential and therefore offers an independent and highly accurate measure of the core electron density and temperature, which are used as a reference to initiate the nonlinear least squares fitting of the measured VDF, resulting in the red curve fit, whose fit parameters are indicated in red as well. For more details, see Ref. [11] and Figure 4 therewith, including the accompanying description.

It is well known that the MB distribution corresponds to the maximum entropic (or the most probable) state as defined through the textbook Boltzmann–Gibbs (BG) definition for the entropy [12–14], namely,

$$S_{BG} = -k_B \int d\mathbf{x} \int d\mathbf{v} f(\mathbf{v}) \ln f(\mathbf{v}),$$

where $\int d\mathbf{x}$ is the spatial integration normalized to the total volume, $\int d\mathbf{x} \to \mathscr{V}^{-1} \int d\mathbf{x}$, and $f(\mathbf{v})$ is the velocity distribution function. The Boltzmann–Gibbs (BG) entropy, which is additive and extensive, applies to an ideal gas or systems dictated by short-range interactions. The suitability of BG entropy for systems interacting through long-range forces, such as the plasma or gravitational systems, has been questioned since the inception of the BG entropy in the first place [15–17]. The additive property relates to the BG entropy of a total system being equal to the entropies of subsystems. The extensivity means that the entropy is proportional to the total number of particles. The non-additive/non-extensive entropy, which presumably may be applicable to systems governed by long-range forces, violates these properties [18]. The mathematical form of non-extensive entropy, which became well-known thanks to the work by Tsallis [19], was apparently independently discovered several times over, as entry 107 in Ref. [18], p. 347, describes. Specifically, it is mentioned there that several authors have independently rediscovered the form of entropy

$$S_q = k\,\frac{1-\sum_{i=1}^{W} p_i^q}{q-1}.$$

The list includes J. Havrda and F. Charvat, Kybernetika **3**, 30 (1967); I. Vajda, Kybernetika **4**, 105 (1968); Z. Daroczy, Inf. Control **16**, 36 (1970); J. Lindhard and V. Nielsen, *Studies in statistical mechanics*, Det Kongelige Danske Videnskabernes Selskab Matematisk-fysiske Meddelelser (Denmark) **38** (9), 1 (1971); B. D. Sharma and D. P. Mittal, J. Math. Sci. **10**, 28 (1975); J. Aczel and Z. Daroczy, *On Measures of Information and Their Characterization*, in *Mathematics in Science and Engineering*, ed. R. Bellman (Academic Press, New York, 1975); A. Wehrl, Rev. Mod. Phys. **50**, 221 (1978); and G. P. Patil and C. Taillie, An overview of diversity, in *Ecological Diversity in Theory and Practice*, eds. J. F. Grassle, G. P. Patil, W. Smith, and C. Taillie (Int. Cooperat. Publ. House, Maryland, 1979), pp. 3–27.

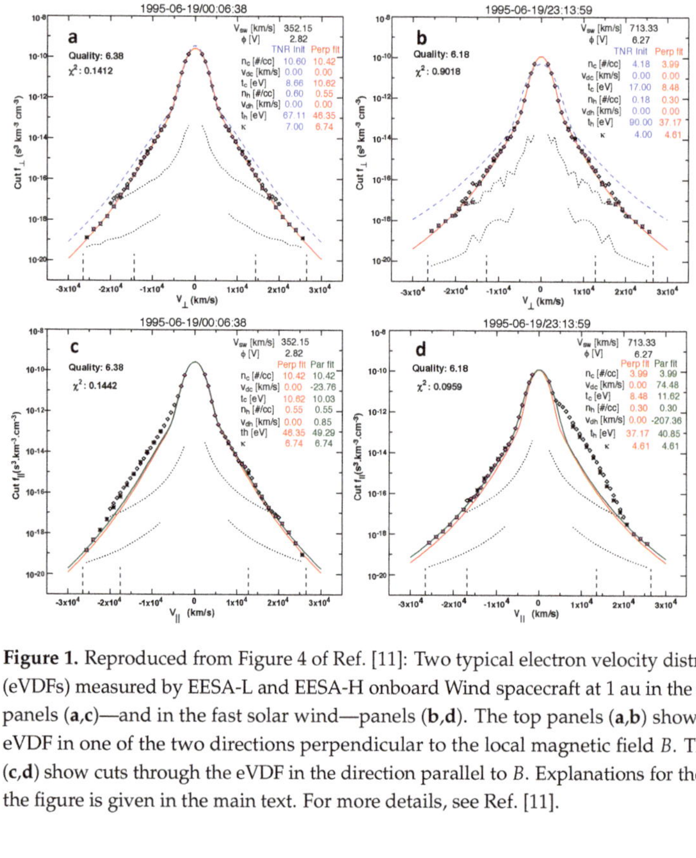

Figure 1. Reproduced from Figure 4 of Ref. [11]: Two typical electron velocity distribution functions (eVDFs) measured by EESA-L and EESA-H onboard Wind spacecraft at 1 au in the slow solar wind—panels (**a**,**c**)—and in the fast solar wind—panels (**b**,**d**). The top panels (**a**,**b**) show cuts through the eVDF in one of the two directions perpendicular to the local magnetic field B. The bottom panels (**c**,**d**) show cuts through the eVDF in the direction parallel to B. Explanations for the different lines in the figure is given in the main text. For more details, see Ref. [11].

These earlier works notwithstanding, it is Tsallis's model [19] that is most well known, and it has triggered an explosive growth of recent interest in the topic of non-extensive thermostatics, in the space plasma context as well as in other applications [10,20,21]. The celebrated Tsallis entropy in continuum form is defined by

$$S_q = -\frac{k_B}{1-q}\int d\mathbf{x}\int d\mathbf{v}\{f(\mathbf{v}) - [f(\mathbf{v})]^q\},$$

and the velocity distribution that corresponds to the maximum entropic (or the most probable) state is given by

$$f_q(\mathbf{v}) \propto \left(1 + \frac{(1-q)\,v^2}{\alpha^2}\right)^{-1/(1-q)}. \tag{2}$$

Upon identifying $\kappa = 1/(1-q)$ or alternatively $\kappa = q/(1-q)$, one finds that the solution reduces to either $f \sim \left[1 + v^2/(\kappa\alpha^2)\right]^{-\kappa}$ or $f \sim \left\{1 + v^2/[(\kappa+1)\alpha^2]\right\}^{-\kappa-1}$, respectively. Strictly speaking, neither is exactly identical to the kappa distribution since f_κ is defined with a mixed κ and $\kappa+1$—see Equation (1). Nonetheless, this convergence of Tsallis's non-extensive entropic principle and the kappa model has led to the space physics community embracing the notion that the space plasma may be in a state of non-extensive statistical quasi-equilibrium [10,20,22–24].

From the microscopic plasma physics, it is known that the electron kappa distribution can be regarded as an end product of the weak electrostatic Langmuir turbulence [25,26]. The initial findings involved a numerical study of a gentle weak electron beam–plasma (or bump-on-tail) instability and subsequent saturation of the Langmuir turbulence. It was found that the quasi-steady state of the Langmuir turbulence is characterized by the formation of a non-thermal, kappa-like velocity distribution function. Subsequently, more rigorous theoretical analysis revealed that the kappa distribution belongs to a family of unique solutions that characterize a steady-state electrostatic plasma turbulence [27,28]. This finding implies that a profound inter-relationship may exist between the non-extensive statistical state and the turbulent quasi-equilibrium, but the precise mathematical formulation to establish such a connection does not yet exist at present.

The findings in Refs. [27,28] directly relate to the solar wind electrons [11,29], which can be interpreted as velocity distribution functions made of multiple subcomponents. The primary component is the quasi-Maxwellian core population ($\sim$90–95% of the density, with $\sim$10 eV). The hotter and tenuous halo electron population can be distinguished from the core population by its distinct velocity profile, which can be modeled by an inverse power law. Other distinct populations can also be identified. For high-speed solar wind streams, a highly field-aligned strahl component can be separately classified from the halo electrons by their narrow pitch-angle distribution. The halo/strahl density is about $\sim$5–10% of the total density with a $\sim$50 eV energy range. Also, the highly energetic superhalo electrons (with a typical energy in the $\sim$2 keV range but extending up to 100 keV), which are observed in nearly all solar wind conditions, including the inner heliosphere [4,5] with a nearly invariant velocity power-law index, are a distinct component [29–31]. The core, halo/strahl, and superhalo electron populations are sometimes associated with their respective slight temperature anisotropy, although the superhalo is almost completely isotropic, and relative drifts between the core and halo can also be detected. In the present discussion, however, we idealize the situation by considering that the velocity distribution is isotropic and without any net drifts.

In the present paper, we will first briefly overview the previous weak turbulence theory of electron kappa distribution [27], but, thereafter, we will discuss a new development, which involves the whistler-mode fluctuations and turbulence. For the near-Earth space plasma environment as well as for the inner heliosphere close to the Sun, the effects of wave–particle resonant interaction that involves the whistler-mode waves, instability, and fluctuations on the electrons are important [6,32–35]. As such, we consider the consequence of the electrons undergoing wave–particle resonant interactions with the background turbulence in the whistler-mode frequency range in the present paper. As will be shown, the impact of such interactions is none other than the formation of a non-thermal velocity distribution function for the electrons, which is not necessarily the kappa distribution but rather a more general one that must be generated by a numerical indefinite velocity integration. However, in the theoretical formalism of the present paper, it turns out that thermal fluctuations play an important role. A finite-temperature plasma constantly spontaneously emits and reabsorbs electromagnetic fluctuations—the fluctuation–dissipation theorem. A correct self-consistent theory of steady-state plasma particle velocity distribution based upon the steady-state Fokker–Planck particle kinetic equation thus requires the computation of thermal fluctuations. We thus begin the discourse by considering the thermal fluctuations emitted by the core electrons and the modification of the fluctuation spectrum by the presence of background turbulence.

2. Thermal Fluctuations Emitted by Maxwellian Core Electrons in the Background of Solar Wind Turbulence

In this section, we discuss the quasi-steady-state spectrum of the electrostatic and electromagnetic fluctuations in the background of solar wind turbulence. We assume that the thermal fluctuations are spontaneously emitted and reabsorbed predominantly by the Maxwellian core electrons. The background large-amplitude turbulence is assumed to be of the transverse electromagnetic type, with its characteristic frequency that encompasses the whistler-mode frequency range. The combined fluctuations and turbulence spectra determine the quasi-steady-state velocity distribution function for the solar wind halo electrons. As already discussed, the solar wind electrons are observed to be made of several distinct components, but the simplest description pertains to the two-component model, in which these electrons comprise dense Maxwellian core electrons and a tenuous but energetic halo electron population. It turns out that the halo electrons immersed in the field of thermal fluctuations alone will be organized in velocity space into a Maxwellian distribution. Thus, in this case, there will be no distinction between the core and halo so that both species will form one continuous thermal population. However, if there exist turbulent wave spectra for the whistler mode, then as the electrons interact with these combined spontaneously generated fluctuations and turbulence, they will organize into a non-thermal velocity distribution function, which manifests a clear demarcation between the core population and a tail component. The spontaneous emission is important because these background fluctuations provide the basis upon which non-thermal distribution can be built.

The electrostatic component of the spontaneous emission [36,37] is the well-known quasi-thermal noise [38], but the solar wind core electrons should also emit electromagnetic emissions as well, although a clear identification of such a transverse quasi-thermal noise is difficult because it will be partially occulted by the background turbulence. However, with improved future detection techniques, identifying the transverse quasi-thermal noise may become possible. Although we expect the electric and magnetic fields associated with the whistler-mode fluctuations to partially overlap with the frequency range of the background solar wind turbulence, the spectrum should extend to slightly higher frequencies so that with sufficiently sensitive instruments, the identification could be possible. Even with today's technology, if one analyzes the data with sufficient accuracy for the high-frequency end of the spectrum, one should be able to discern the characteristic signature associated with the whistler-mode thermal spectrum. Regardless, from a theoretical perspective, consideration of the emission of electromagnetic fluctuations in the whistler mode is important. In the presence of the combined background spectrum of Langmuir and whistler-mode fluctuations as well as the whistler wave turbulence, it will be shown that the solar wind electrons naturally form a non-thermal velocity distribution function of the type observed in space, but it is not necessarily the kappa model in the analytic sense. Rather, the model distribution will be obtained by a numerical indefinite velocity integration.

The first step in the present discussion is to consider the spectrum of electrostatic and electromagnetic fluctuations emitted by the thermal core electrons. In Ref. [39], the formulae for these fluctuation spectra are derived. For electromagnetic fluctuations propagating in a parallel direction with respect to the ambient magnetic field vector, the transverse electric and magnetic field spectra are designated as $\langle \delta E_\perp^2 \rangle_{k,\omega}$ and $\langle \delta B_\perp^2 \rangle_{k,\omega}$, while for electrostatic fluctuations characterized by propagation parallel to the ambient magnetic field, the electric field spectrum is denoted by $\langle \delta E_\parallel^2 \rangle_{k,\omega}$. These are given by [39–41].

$$
\begin{aligned}
\langle \delta E_\perp^2 \rangle_{k,\omega} &= \frac{2k_m^2 e^2}{\omega^2 |\epsilon_\perp(k,\omega) - c^2k^2/\omega^2|^2} \int d\mathbf{v}\, v_\perp^2\, \delta(\omega - kv_\parallel - \Omega_e) f, \\
\langle \delta B_\perp^2 \rangle_{k,\omega} &= \frac{c^2k^2}{\omega^2} \langle \delta E_\perp^2 \rangle_{k,\omega}, \\
\langle \delta E_\parallel^2 \rangle_{k,\omega} &= \frac{2k_m^2 e^2}{k^2 |\epsilon_\parallel(k,\omega)|^2} \int d\mathbf{v}\, \delta(\omega - kv_\parallel) f, \\
\epsilon_\perp(k,\omega) &= 1 + \frac{\omega_{pe}^2}{\omega^2} \int d\mathbf{v}\, \frac{v_\perp/2}{\omega - kv_\parallel - \Omega_e} \left((\omega - kv_\parallel) \frac{\partial f}{\partial v_\perp} + kv_\perp \frac{\partial f}{\partial v_\parallel} \right), \\
\epsilon_\parallel(k,\omega) &= 1 + \frac{\omega_{pe}^2}{k} \int d\mathbf{v}\, \frac{\partial f/\partial v_\parallel}{\omega - kv_\parallel},
\end{aligned}
\tag{3}
$$

where e is the unit electric charge; $\omega_{pe} = (4\pi n/m_e)^{1/2} e$ is the plasma frequency, with n and m_e being the ambient density and electron mass, respectively; $\Omega_e = eB/(m_e c)$ is the electron cyclotron frequency, with B and c being the ambient magnetic field intensity and the speed of light, respectively; and $k_m^2 = \Omega_e^2/\alpha_e^2$ is the maximum perpendicular wave length, which results from the integration over the perpendicular wave number, with $\alpha_e = (2T/m_e)^{1/2}$ being the electron thermal speed [40]. Here, $f = f(v_\perp, v_\parallel)$ represents the electron velocity distribution function (normalized to unity, $\int d\mathbf{v} f = 1$), with $v_\perp$ and $v_\parallel$ denoting the velocity component perpendicular and parallel to the ambient magnetic field. The angular frequency and the parallel wave number are defined by ω and k, respectively.

For the Maxwellian thermal velocity distribution function, these are given as shown below:

$$
\begin{aligned}
\langle \delta E_\perp^2 \rangle_{k,\omega} &= \frac{\omega_{pe}^2 k_m^2 T_e e^{-\zeta^2}}{4\pi^{3/2} \omega^2 k \alpha_e |\epsilon_\perp(k,\omega) - c^2k^2/\omega^2|^2}, \qquad \langle \delta B_\perp^2 \rangle_{k,\omega} = \frac{c^2k^2}{\omega^2} \langle \delta E_\perp^2 \rangle_{k,\omega}, \\
\langle \delta E_\parallel^2 \rangle_{k,\omega} &= \frac{\omega_{pe}^2 k_m^2 T_e e^{-\xi^2}}{\pi^{3/2} k^3 \alpha_e^3 |\epsilon_\parallel(k,\omega)|^2}, \\
\epsilon_\perp(k,\omega) &= 1 - \frac{c^2k^2}{\omega^2} + \frac{\omega_{pe}^2}{\omega^2} \xi Z(\zeta), \qquad \zeta = \frac{\omega - \Omega_e}{k\alpha_e}, \\
\epsilon_\parallel(k,\omega) &= 1 - \frac{\omega_{pe}^2}{k^2\alpha_e^2} Z'(\xi), \qquad \xi = \frac{\omega}{k\alpha_e},
\end{aligned}
\tag{4}
$$

where $Z(\zeta) = \pi^{-1/2} \int_{-\infty}^{\infty} dx e^{-x^2} (x - \zeta)^{-1}$, $\mathrm{Im}(\zeta) > 0$, is the plasma dispersion function with the prime indicating the derivative with respect to the argument.

Figure 2 plots the electrostatic and electromagnetic spectra, $\langle \delta E_\parallel^2 \rangle_{k,\omega}$ and $\langle \delta E_\perp^2 \rangle_{k,\omega}$, respectively, computed from the theoretical formulae (4), versus ck/ω_{pe} (horizontal axis) and ω/Ω_e (vertical axis). The color scale is relative in that the maximum value for each panel is represented by red and the minimum intensity is plotted as a blue backdrop. The left-hand top and bottom panels correspond to the electrostatic and electromagnetic fluctuation spectra, respectively. The input parameters are $\omega_{pe}/\Omega_e = 5$ and $\beta_e = 1$, where $\beta_e = 8\pi n T_e/B^2$ is the electron beta (ratio of electron thermal energy to the magnetic field energy). In order to verify that the theoretical formalism (4) is indeed reliable, we have also carried out a one-dimensional particle-in-cell (PIC) simulation. We have used a simulation box of $L_x = 512\,c/\Omega_{pe}$ and $n_x = 4096$ grid points, with 2000 particles per grid per species. The time step used was $\Delta t = 0.01\,/\omega_{pe}$, and the simulation ran until $t = 2621.44\,/\omega_{pe}$. The ratio of plasma frequency to electron gyro frequency was $\omega_{pe}/\Omega_e = 5$. This ratio is somewhat lower than the actual value typical of the solar wind at 1 au, which is close to $\omega_{pe}/\Omega_e \sim \mathcal{O}(10)$–$\mathcal{O}(10^2)$, but for the sake of illustration we have chosen a relatively low value of ω_{pe}/Ω_e. Otherwise, the spectral peak at $\omega \sim \omega_{pe}$ associated with the electrostatic thermal fluctuations (upper panels) and the spectral characteristics associated with the transverse-mode fluctuations around the electron cyclotron frequency and below would have been separated by a wide gap, which would have made visual inspection quite challenging. Also, if the separation between the two frequencies is too high, it becomes very challenging for the simulations, too, because we need to resolve both time scales. Other parameters were electron and proton betas, which were taken to be $\beta_e = \beta_p = 0.1$. These choices are not atypical of the solar wind conditions at 1 au. The simulated electrostatic and electromagnetic fluctuation spectra are plotted in the top and bottom right-hand panels, respectively. As the readers may appreciate, the theoretical plots compare very well with the simulated spectra, which indicates that the theoretical method is a reliable tool for describing the spontaneously emitted thermal spectra in magnetized plasmas accurately.

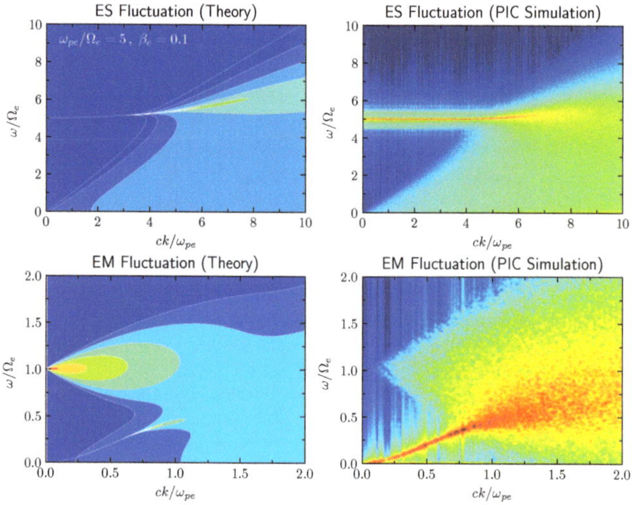

Figure 2. **[Upper-left]** Electrostatic fluctuation spectrum $\langle \delta E_\parallel^2 \rangle_{k,\omega}$ computed from theory; **[upper-right]** simulated electrostatic fluctuation spectrum; **[lower-left]** electromagnetic fluctuation spectrum $\langle \delta E_\perp^2 \rangle_{k,\omega}$ computed from theory; **[lower-right]** simulated electromagnetic fluctuation spectrum. These spectra are plotted as a function of ck/ω_{pe} (horizontal axis) and ω/Ω_e (vertical axis), with their relative intensities indicated by color maps in arbitrary scales.

The electrostatic fluctuation spectrum is enhanced along the Langmuir wave dispersion curve but broadens in frequency somewhat for shorter wavelengths. In the simulated spectrum, the enhanced fluctuation along the Langmuir wave dispersion curve is broader than that of the theoretical spectrum, but, otherwise, the overall agreement is excellent. For the electromagnetic spectrum, it is seen that the fluctuation spectrum is enhanced along the whistler-mode dispersion curve, but the triangular (or conical) emission pattern that converges to the electron cyclotron frequency, $\omega = \Omega_e$ at the $k \to 0$ limit, is also prominent in both the theoretical emission spectrum and the simulated spectrum. Such a feature is associated with the virtual (or higher-order) modes, that is, heavily damped solutions of the linear dispersion relation [42–44]. Both the theoretical and simulated spectra accurately reproduce the emission characteristics associated with such modes. Note, however, that the simulation does not completely demonstrate the intensification of the higher-order mode as k approaches a zero value. This is owing to the limited resolution in the simulation spectrum. As will be discussed, this limitation further affects the k-integrated wave spectra for the electric and magnetic fields.

Shown in Figure 3 are wave number-integrated ($\int dk \cdots$) spectra. The left-hand panel shows the k-integrated magnetic and transverse electric field fluctuation spectra $\int dk \langle \delta B^2 \rangle_{k,\omega}$ (red) and $\int dk \langle \delta E_\perp^2 \rangle_{k,\omega}$ (blue) that were computed from theory, plotted against ω/Ω_e. The right-hand panel displays the same spectra constructed from the PIC simulation result and integrated over the wave numbers. Both the theoretical and simulated spectra exhibit the behavior of increasing intensities, for both magnetic and electric spectra, over an increasing frequency, up to $\omega \sim 0.5\Omega_e$ or so. However, some differences in the behavior are also evident. For instance, in the theoretical integrated spectra, both the electric and magnetic field intensify around the electron cyclotron frequency, $\omega \sim \Omega_e$, but the simulated spectra do not exhibit such a behavior. Clearly, the peak at $\omega/\Omega_e = 1$ in the theoretical spectrum is associated with the contribution from the higher-order mode. In the simulated spectrum, the higher-order mode for the low k regime is not as clearly enhanced, which explains the absence of such a peak. This is due to the limited resolution in the simulation. Such an increasing behavior as a function of frequency for the fluctuation spectra in the low-frequency regime is a characteristic of the plasma, and it is the baseline spectral behavior associated with the thermal motion of plasma particles. It is interesting to note that in many PIC simulations of low-frequency turbulence, such an increasing intensity can be seen at the high end of the simulation spectrum. In a typical kinetic simulation of the low-frequency turbulence, the MHD-like regime corresponding to $\omega^2 \ll \Omega_p^2 \ll \Omega_e^2$, where $\Omega_i = eB/(m_p c)$ is the proton cyclotron frequency, is characterized by a Kolmogorov type of inverse power-law spectrum, $k^{-5/3}$ [45–47], but as k increases, in some cases, the intensity actually rises again [47,48]. In the literature, such a behavior is not clearly explained nor understood. However, it is entirely possible that the simulation system is automatically generating the background thermal spectrum.

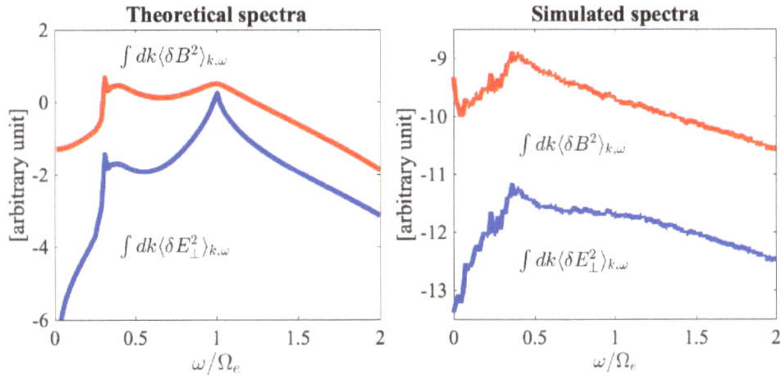

Figure 3. **[Left]** k-integrated magnetic and transverse electric field fluctuation spectra $\int dk \langle \delta B^2 \rangle_{k,\omega}$ (red) and $\int dk \langle \delta E_\perp^2 \rangle_{k,\omega}$ (blue) computed from theory. **[Right]** Simulated fluctuation spectra integrated over k. The integrated spectra are plotted against ω/Ω_e.

As confirmed by Figures 2 and 3, the theoretical description of thermal fluctuations is consistent with the simulation result. Thus, we now focus on the analytical approach. Furthermore, henceforth, we are interested in the fluctuations associated with the eigen modes. For the electrostatic fluctuation, we are concerned with the spectral wave intensity along the Langmuir mode dispersion relation, $\omega = \omega_L(k)$, where $\omega_L = \omega_{pe}\left[1 + 3k^2\alpha_e^2/(4\omega_{pe}^2)\right]$. Likewise, for the electromagnetic fluctuations, we pay attention to the whistler-mode dispersion relation, $\omega = \omega_W(k)$, where $\omega_W = \Omega_e c^2 k^2/(\omega_{pe}^2 + c^2k^2)$. Then, by expanding the denominators by $\epsilon_\parallel \approx (\omega - \omega_L + i0)(\partial\,\mathrm{Re}\,\epsilon_\parallel/\partial\omega_L) + i\,\mathrm{Im}\,\epsilon_\parallel$

and $\Lambda_+ \approx (\omega - \omega_W + i0)(\partial \operatorname{Re} \Lambda_+ / \partial \omega_W) + i \operatorname{Im} \Lambda_+$ while ignoring the contribution from the term associated with Λ_-, it is possible to obtain

$$\begin{aligned} \langle \delta E_\parallel^2 \rangle_{k,\omega} &= I_L(k)\, \delta(\omega - \omega_L), \\ \langle \delta E_\perp^2 \rangle_{k,\omega} &= I_W(k)\, \delta(\omega - \omega_W), \qquad \langle \delta B_\perp^2 \rangle_{k,\omega} = M_W(k)\, \delta(\omega - \omega_W), \end{aligned} \tag{5}$$

where

$$\begin{aligned} I_L(k) &= \frac{k_m^2 T_e}{4\pi}, \\ I_W(k) &= \frac{k_m^2 T_e}{4\pi} \frac{\omega_{pe}^2 \omega_W^3}{c^4 k^4} = \frac{k_m^2 T_e}{4\pi} \frac{\Omega_e^2 \omega_{pe}^2 c^2 k^2}{(\omega_{pe}^2 + c^2 k^2)^3}, \\ M_W(k) &= \frac{k_m^2 T_e}{4\pi} \frac{\omega_{pe}^2 \omega_W}{c^2 k^2} = \frac{k_m^2 T_e}{4\pi} \frac{\omega_{pe}^2}{\omega_{pe}^2 + c^2 k^2}. \end{aligned} \tag{6}$$

For more details regarding the derivation of this result, see [39–41].

In the solar wind, there exists a permanent low-frequency turbulence of a solar origin. Such turbulence is commonly believed to be generated on the surface of the Sun through various mechanisms, including the solar surface convection and small reconnection near the lower corona, and convected to outer space [49]. The solar wind turbulence for a low-MHD frequency regime is hydromagnetic in nature and is characterized by a Kolmogorov-like inertial range spectrum but with a spectral break in the kinetic regime. That is, for the frequency range above the nominal proton cyclotron frequency and below the electron cyclotron frequency, $\Omega_p < \omega < |\Omega_e|$, the turbulence exhibits a spectral break. Such a frequency range can be characterized as the whistler turbulence range. For an even higher frequency $\omega > |\Omega_e|$, another spectral break is present. We may model such a multi-scale spectral behavior by adopting an analytical model first suggested by von Kármán [50] and generalizing to reflect the multiple spectral breaks,

$$I_{\text{turb}}(k) = \frac{k_m^2 I_0}{(1 + k^2 l^2)^\alpha (1 + c^2 k^2 / \omega_{pi}^2)^{\beta - \alpha} (1 + c^2 k^2 / \omega_{pe}^2)^{\gamma - \beta}}, \tag{7}$$

where $l \gg c/\omega_{pi}$. Here, we explicitly extracted out the factor k_m^2 since this is related to the integration over $k_\perp$ [40]. The solar wind turbulence spectrum appears to behave as $\omega^{-5/3}$ in the frequency range corresponding to the MHD regime. If we make use of the Taylor hypothesis [51], then ω can be trivially replaced by k, but in the kinetic regime, beyond the ion skin depth, c/ω_{pi} or shorter, and much more so for the electron skin depth, c/ω_{pe} or shorter, the Taylor hypothesis may not be valid. Moreover, since we are interested in the parallel wave vector and the turbulence intensity integrated over $k_\perp$, the inverse power-law index α may not be the same as that of the Kolmogorov value, namely $\alpha = 5/6$. Nevertheless, we may model the MHD regime by the Kolmogorov type of spectrum. In any event, the model spectrum (8) describes a finite and maximum turbulence level at $k = 0$, and for $0 < k < \omega_{pi}/c$ it describes the $k^{-2\alpha}$ behavior. For the wave number regime corresponding to $\omega_{pi}/c < k < \omega_{pe}/c$, the model depicts a $k^{-2\beta}$ behavior. For $k > \omega_{pe}/c$, the spectrum behaves as $k^{-2\gamma}$. We illustrate this by choosing $\alpha = 5/6$, $\beta = 1.2$, and $\gamma = 2$, which are admittedly arbitrary. We also choose the MHD scale factor $l = 10^2(m_p/m_e)$, which is again arbitrary.

In Figure 4, we demonstrate the influence of the whistler-mode fluctuation spectrum on the background turbulence spectrum by considering the superposition of the model turbulence spectrum and the whistler-mode fluctuation spectrum, $I_{\text{turb}}(k) + I_W(k)$, where the whistler-mode fluctuation spectrum $I_W(k)$ is defined in Equation (6) and the model turbulence spectrum $I_{\text{turb}}(k)$ is given by Equation (7). Figure 4 plots the spectral factor that defines the combined spectrum, namely,

$$\begin{aligned} S(q) &= \frac{q^2}{(1+q^2)^3} + \frac{R}{(1+Mlq^2)^\alpha(1+Mq^2)^{\beta-\alpha}(1+q^2)^{\gamma-\beta}}, \\ q &= \frac{ck}{\omega_{pe}}, \qquad M = \frac{m_p}{m_e} = 1836, \qquad R = \frac{4\pi I_0}{T_e}\frac{\omega_{pe}^2}{\Omega_e^2}, \end{aligned} \tag{8}$$

where $\alpha = 5/6$, $\beta = 1.2$, $\gamma = 2$, and $l = 10^2(m_p/m_e)$, as already noted above. The first term on the right-hand, $q^2/(1+q^2)^3$, denotes the spontaneously emitted whistler-mode thermal fluctuation spectrum. The second term on the right-hand side is the model spectrum with multiple spectral breaks. In Figure 4, the dashed magenta-colored curve represents the spontaneously emitted whistler-mode fluctuation spectrum, $q^2/(1+q^2)^3$. The dashed black curves represent the background turbulence spectrum without the influence of the fluctuation, for two cases of $R = 10^6$ and $R = 10^7$. The total spectral factor for the two cases is plotted with thick blue ($R = 10^6$) and red ($R = 10^7$) curves. It is evident that the model turbulence spectrum (8) depicts a flat spectrum for a $q \to 0$ regime; a Kolmogorov-type of spectrum in the "MHD" regime, $(Ml)^{-1/2} < q < M^{-1/2}$; a slightly steeper spectrum of $k^{-2.4}$ in the "kinetic proton" regime, $M^{-1/2} < q < 1$; and a yet steeper spectrum, k^{-4}, in the whistler turbulence regime, $q > 1$. It is in this wave number regime where the presence of the thermal fluctuation spectrum should be discernible. Specifically, in the case of a relatively low turbulence level, as indicated by $R = 10^6$, we expect that the actual solar wind turbulence should reveal the presence of the fluctuation. However, for higher turbulence levels (as denoted by $R = 10^7$), the intensity of fluctuation will be partially hidden so that a clear identification might not be so straightforward.

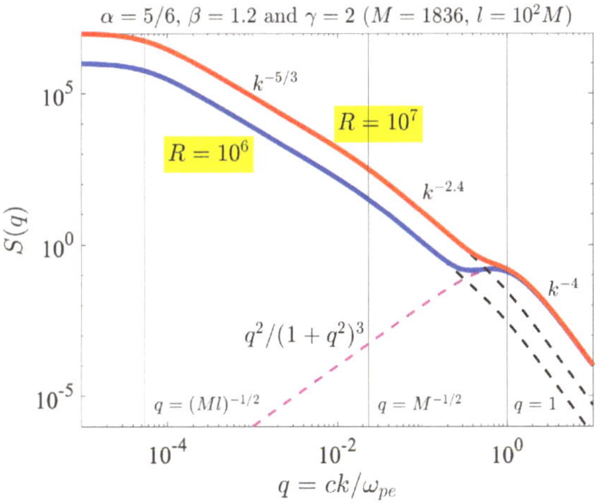

Figure 4. Model spectral factor, $S(q)$, versus q in logarithmic horizontal and vertical scales. The magenta dashes represent the spontaneous whistler-mode fluctuation, while the black dashes denote the background turbulence for two cases of $R = 10^6$ and $R = 10^7$. The combined spectra are plotted with thick blue ($R = 10^6$) and red ($R = 10^7$) curves. For a low turbulence level ($R = 10^6$), the presence of fluctuation should be more evident, but if the turbulence level is high ($R = 10^7$), then the fluctuation will be partially hidden.

As an example of actual solar wind turbulence spectra measured in the near-Earth environment, we reproduce a figure taken from Ref. [52]. The result is Figure 5, which is constructed from the measurements made by *Cluster* spacecraft. The location of the spacecraft is at 1 au during a quiet-time condition on 30 January 2003. The detailed discussion of the instrumentation and data analysis method can be found in Ref. [52], but the main focus of the present paper is bring the readers' attention to the spectral flattening behavior for the high-frequency end of the turbulence spectra, especially for the electric field. According to the theory—see Equation (6)—and the model spectrum shown in Figure 4, the spontaneously emitted thermal fluctuations should affect the high end of the solar wind turbulence spectra, especially if the turbulence level is sufficiently low. Admittedly, just what exactly it means by "sufficiently low" is not entirely clear, and further study is called for. Nevertheless, the identification of the spontaneous quasi-thermal whistler-mode fluctuations based on observation could be an intriguing and innovative research topic. In any case, Figure 5 displays the Kolmogorov-like spectrum in the low-frequency band while also showing a spectral break at frequency f_b, which represents the "break" frequency for the transition of one spectral slope to another. This frequency could be associated with the kinetic proton effects. The whistler-mode thermal noise, however, is supposed to be associated with the electron kinetic effects, which are believed to be related to a much higher frequency. However, before one could reach such a frequency, the instrument noise floor would contaminate the data, so it is very challenging to delineate the noise effects versus the baseline thermal noise.

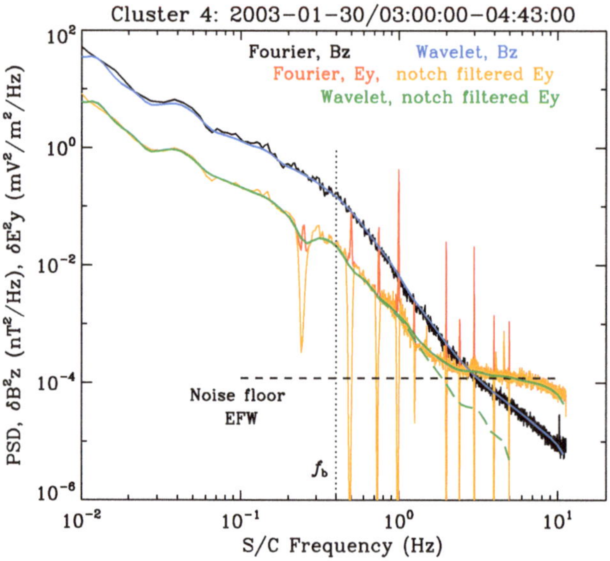

Figure 5. Magnetic (black) and electric (red) field spectra taken by *Cluster* spacecraft [reproduced from Ref. [52]].

Specifically, a key element that should be accounted for before one can definitely extract the theoretical signature, i.e., the whistler-mode thermal fluctuation, from the data is for the model turbulence spectrum of the type shown in Figure 4 to be translated into the spacecraft frame frequency using the appropriate solar wind speed and electron inertial length, as well as to properly scale the normalized amplitude $S(q)$ to physical units. This includes translating the "R" parameter into actual units. The flattening of the E-field spectrum shown in Figure 5 could be entirely due to the instrumental artifact. In spite of this, however, the thermal noise associated with the whistler-mode fluctuations could partly contribute to the observed flattening of the spectrum, if not for this particular event, then at least for some other events. As will be shown in the next section, the combination of the quasi-thermal whistler noise and the background turbulence can account for the observed non-thermal electron velocity distribution function. We thus proceed with the discussion of the theory for the formation of the electron velocity distribution function under the influence of background whistler-mode turbulence and the quasi-thermal noise spectrum, which contains both electrostatic Langmuir-type and whistler-mode-type electromagnetic fluctuations.

3. Formation of Kappa Electron Distribution by Langmuir Turbulence

In this section, we briefly overview the previous theory of kappa electron distribution by Langmuir turbulence advanced by Yoon [27]. The full discourse of this theory is quite complex and requires a detailed exposition of kinetic weak plasma turbulence theory [37,53–65], but, in its essence, it boils down to the modification of the spontaneously emitted Langmuir fluctuations to reflect the influence of the steady-state weak Langmuir turbulence spectrum. It was shown by considering the balance of the nonlinear wave kinetic equation for Langmuir turbulence that, in the steady state, the electrostatic fluctuation spectrum should be modified to include the effects of turbulence in the following form:

$$I_L(k) = \frac{k_m^2 T_e}{4\pi}\left(1 + \frac{k_L^2}{k^2}\right). \tag{9}$$

The modification factor k_L^2/k^2 leads to the kappa electron distribution function when this spectrum is inserted into the diffusion coefficient of the steady-state electron distribution function computed from the kinetic theory.

Reference [40] derives the Fokker–Planck electron kinetic equation with waves and fluctuations that have a wave vector lying in the parallel direction defined with the ambient magnetic field vector. We summarize the equation for the electron velocity distribution function f,

$$\begin{aligned} \frac{\partial f}{\partial t} &= \frac{1}{v^2}\frac{\partial}{\partial v}(v^2 A_v f) + \frac{1}{v}\frac{\partial}{\partial \mu}(A_\mu f) \\ &+ \frac{1}{v^2}\frac{\partial}{\partial v}\left(v^2 D_{vv}\frac{\partial f}{\partial v}\right) + \frac{1}{v^2}\frac{\partial}{\partial v}\left(v D_{v\mu}\frac{\partial f}{\partial \mu}\right) \\ &+ \frac{1}{v}\frac{\partial}{\partial \mu}\left(D_{v\mu}\frac{\partial f}{\partial v}\right) + \frac{1}{v^2}\frac{\partial}{\partial \mu}\left(D_{\mu\mu}\frac{\partial f}{\partial \mu}\right), \end{aligned} \tag{10}$$

where the right-hand side of the kinetic equation is expressed in a velocity-space spherical coordinate system, in which $v = \sqrt{v_\perp^2 + v_\parallel^2}$ is the magnitude and $\mu = v_\parallel/v$ is the cosine of the pitch angle. Under the assumption of primarily electrostatic interaction, the velocity space friction and diffusion coefficients are given by

$$\begin{aligned} \begin{pmatrix} A_v \\ A_\mu \end{pmatrix} &= \frac{e^2 k_m^2}{2\pi m_e}\int dk \int d\omega \, \mathrm{Im}\left(\frac{1}{k\epsilon_\parallel(k,\omega)}\right)^* \begin{pmatrix} \mu \\ 1-\mu^2 \end{pmatrix} \delta(\omega - kv\mu), \\ \begin{pmatrix} D_{vv} \\ D_{v\mu} \\ D_{\mu\mu} \end{pmatrix} &= \frac{\pi e^2}{m_e^2}\int dk \int d\omega \, \langle \delta E_\parallel^2 \rangle_{k,\omega} \begin{pmatrix} \mu^2 \\ \mu(1-\mu^2) \\ (1-\mu^2)^2 \end{pmatrix} \delta(\omega - kv\mu). \end{aligned} \tag{11}$$

We assume steady state, $\partial/\partial t \to 0$, and isotropy, $\partial f/\partial \mu = 0$. Then, we average over μ. Then, we obtain the steady-state solution for the electron velocity distribution function,

$$\begin{aligned} f &= \mathrm{const}\exp\left(-\int^v dv' \frac{A(v')}{D(v')}\right), \\ A(v) &= \int_{-1}^{1} d\mu A_v, \qquad D(v) = \int_{-1}^{1} d\mu D_{vv}. \end{aligned} \tag{12}$$

We should note that this type of steady-state solution of the Fokker–Planck equation is found in the literature [66–68], so the basic concept is not new. Making use of the property

$\text{Im}\,\epsilon_{\|}(k,\omega)^{-1*} = \frac{1}{2}\pi\omega_{pe}\,\delta(\omega-\omega_L)$ and expressing $\langle\delta E_{\|}^2\rangle_{k,\omega} = I_L(k)\,\delta(\omega-\omega_L)$, where $I_L(k)$ is given by Equation (9), then we have

$$A = \frac{e^2k_m^2}{2m_e}\int_0^1 d\mu\mu, \qquad D = \frac{T_e}{m_e v}\frac{e^2k_m^2}{2m_e}\left(\int_0^1 d\mu\mu + \frac{k_L^2}{\omega_{pe}^2}v^2\int_0^1 d\mu\mu^3\right). \tag{13}$$

From this, we obtain the desired electron kappa velocity distribution function,

$$f = \text{const}\,\exp\left(-\frac{m_e}{T_e}\int^v dv'\,\frac{v'}{1+k_L^2v'^2/(2\omega_{pe}^2)}\right) = \text{const}\left(1+\frac{v^2}{\kappa\alpha^2}\right)^{-\kappa}, \tag{14}$$

if we identify

$$\frac{k_L^2\alpha^2}{2\omega_{pe}^2} = \frac{1}{\kappa}, \qquad \text{and} \qquad \alpha^2 = \frac{\kappa+1}{\kappa}\frac{2T_e}{m_e}. \tag{15}$$

In this version of the theory, the formation of a non-thermal (kappa) electron distribution is attributed to the Langmuir turbulence in the asymptotical steady state. According to this theory, no clear separation of the core and halo electrons is made, but, instead, both populations are treated as a single kappa distribution function with the low end of the velocity spectrum mimicking the Maxwellian thermal core, while the suprathermal high-velocity regime represents the inverse power-law tail population. The brief overview of this section is not new, and a full discourse can be found in Refs. [27,37,53–65]. In the remaining part of the present manuscript, we put forth a new model for which the role of whistler turbulence is emphasized.

4. Formation of Non-Thermal Electron Distribution by Combined Background Turbulence and Thermal Fluctuations

Section 2 discussed the thermal fluctuations spontaneously emitted by Maxwellian core electrons. We also discussed the effects of pre-existing solar wind turbulence and how the combined model may relate to the existing literature on low-frequency turbulence simulations. We also discussed how the effects of baseline quasi-thermal spontaneous emission fluctuations may impact the observations, although we noted that the unambiguous identification of the predicted spectral features associated with thermal fluctuations in the observation may depend on the level of turbulence. In this section, we proceed to discuss the combined impact of the quasi-thermal whistler-mode fluctuations and the background turbulence on the electron velocity distribution function.

In Section 3, the steady-state electron distribution function subject only to the Langmuir turbulence was discussed, and it was shown that the result is the kappa electron velocity distribution. For the kappa model, however, no distinction is made between the core and halo populations. Moreover, the spontaneously emitted transverse fluctuations in the whistler-mode frequency are ignored. Further, the presence of background solar wind turbulence is not taken into consideration either. As such, the kappa distribution and Langmuir turbulence problem may pertain to the outer heliosphere where the local ambient magnetic field strength is sufficiently low so that the whistler-mode frequency range effects can be ignored and the underlying plasma may be treated as essentially unmagnetized.

For the near-Earth space environment, however, the whistler-mode dynamics may be an integral part of wave–particle interaction with the electrons [32,33]. Thus, this section discusses the formation of the non-thermal electron velocity distribution function in the presence of spontaneous thermal fluctuations in both the longitudinal Langmuir and transverse whistler modes and also under the influence of background turbulence [52,69–74]. As will be shown, under such a physical environment, the self-consistent steady-state solution for the electron velocity distribution function will be characterized by a distinct core and halo populations, which is consistent with observations.

The notion of the pre-existing whistler-mode turbulence affecting the solar wind electron dynamics, resulting in a non-thermal velocity distribution function, has been discussed in the literature. For instance, Refs. [75–78] carried out extensive and detailed numerical simulation based on the quasilinear velocity diffusion theory where the diffusion coefficient is computed from the model whistler wave turbulence spectrum. It was shown in these references that the resonant wave–particle interaction between the solar wind electrons and the pre-existing turbulence in the whistler-mode frequency range leads to the gradual formation of a non-thermal energetic tail. The present paper is similar in conceptual background in that we are also seeking to find a non-thermal electron velocity distribution function that is a result of resonant wave–particle interaction with the background whistler wave turbulence. However, the main distinction between the present approach and those of previous works is twofold. Firstly, unlike the previous works, which relate to the dynamical evolution of the velocity distribution function, we are concerned with the steady-state solution. This aspect leads to the second distinction. That is, in order to obtain the steady-state solution, the effects of spontaneous thermal fluctuation are essential. The effects of spontaneous thermal fluctuations and the related velocity friction effects are not considered in the dynamical theories of solar wind electron distribution function in the above references. For dynamical problems, the velocity friction, which is intimately related to the spontaneous thermal fluctuations, is indeed relatively unimportant, but for the theory of an asymptotic steady state, the balance of velocity friction coefficient **A** and velocity diffusion coefficient D is crucially important—see Equation (12). Reference [67], however, considered a steady-state solution of a magnetospheric electron velocity distribution in resonant wave–particle interaction with the background whistler-mode waves. Their solution is very similar in conceptual background and mathematical methodology to the present work, except that, in their approach, the velocity friction coefficient is replaced by the collisional drag coefficient.

We again start from the Fokker–Planck electron kinetic equation with waves and fluctuations where a wave vector lying in the parallel direction is defined with the ambient magnetic field vector, that is, Equation (10) or the steady-state solution (12), except that now the electrons are immersed in the bath of thermal fluctuations of both Langmuir and whistler types and also the background turbulence. As a result, the velocity friction and the diffusion coefficients now contain contributions from both longitudinal and transverse modes,

$$\begin{aligned}\begin{pmatrix} A_v \\ A_\mu \end{pmatrix} &= \frac{e^2k_m^2}{4\pi m_e}\int dk\int d\omega\,\mathrm{Im}\left(\frac{1}{\omega^2\epsilon_\perp(k,\omega)-c^2k^2}\right)^* \\ &\quad\times\begin{pmatrix} \omega \\ kv-\omega\mu \end{pmatrix} v(1-\mu^2)\delta(\omega-kv\mu-\Omega_e) \\ &\quad+\frac{e^2k_m^2}{2\pi m_e}\int dk\int d\omega\,\mathrm{Im}\left(\frac{1}{k\epsilon_\parallel(k,\omega)}\right)^*\begin{pmatrix} \mu \\ 1-\mu^2 \end{pmatrix}\delta(\omega-kv\mu), \\ \begin{pmatrix} D_{vv} \\ D_{v\mu} \\ D_{\mu\mu} \end{pmatrix} &= \frac{\pi e^2}{4m_e^2}\int dk\int d\omega\,\langle\delta E_\perp^2\rangle_{k,\omega}\begin{pmatrix} \omega^2 \\ (kv-\omega\mu)\omega \\ (kv-\omega\mu)^2 \end{pmatrix} \\ &\quad\times\frac{1-\mu^2}{\omega^2}\delta(\omega-kv\mu-\Omega_e) \\ &\quad+\frac{\pi e^2}{m_e^2}\int dk\int d\omega\,\langle\delta E_\parallel\rangle_{k,\omega}\begin{pmatrix} \mu^2 \\ \mu(1-\mu^2) \\ (1-\mu^2)^2 \end{pmatrix}\delta(\omega-kv\mu).\end{aligned} \tag{16}$$

For a steady state, the formal solution (12) is still applicable, with the coefficient $A = \int_{-1}^{1} d\mu A_v$ and $D = \int_{-1}^{1} d\mu D_{vv}$ now containing the influence of whistler-mode fluctuations as well as the background turbulence. Making use of $\mathrm{Im}\,[\omega^2\epsilon_\perp(k,\omega)-c^2k^2]^{-1*} = \pi\delta(\omega-\omega_W)(\Omega_e/\omega_{pe}^2)$ and $\langle\delta E_\perp^2\rangle_{k,\omega} = I_W(k)\,\delta(\omega-\omega_W)$ and approximating the resonance delta function by $\delta(\omega_W-kv\mu-\Omega_e)\approx\delta(kv\mu+\Omega_e)$, we may proceed with the computation of generalized A and D coefficients. For the present purpose, we adopt the whistler-mode spectrum by considering the effects of thermal fluctuations and the background turbulence spectrum, that is, Equation (8), but in a simplified form. In particular, we are interested in the frequency range that is sufficiently higher than both the MHD scale and proton kinetic scale but is sufficiently below the electron cyclotron frequency. Thus, in such a low-frequency limit relative to the electron cyclotron frequency, $\omega^2 \ll \Omega_e^2$, the whistler-mode fluctuations can be approximated by $I_W(\omega) \approx [k_m^2 T_e/(4\pi)](\omega\Omega_e/\omega_{pe}^2)$ and $M_W(k\omega) \approx [k_m^2 T_e/(4\pi)]$, which, upon making use of the low-frequency version of the dispersion relation, $\omega = \Omega_e(ck/\omega_{pe})^2$, can be written as

$$I_W(k) \sim \frac{k_m^2 T_e}{4\pi}\frac{\Omega_e^2}{\omega_{pe}^2}\frac{c^2k^2}{\omega_{pe}^2}, \qquad M_W(k) \sim \frac{k_m^2 T_e}{4\pi}. \tag{17}$$

This result, together with the Langmuir fluctuation spectrum, $I_L(k) \sim k_m^2 T_e/(4\pi)$, will be inserted into the expressions for A and D.

We may also simplify the model of the turbulence given by Equation (8) in that we only focus on the portion of the background turbulence spectrum corresponding to the whistler-mode range inverse power law, which we simplify by $\propto k^{-2\nu}$. If we thus superpose this simplified background turbulence spectrum to the approximate form of the spontaneous emission spectrum corresponding to the low-frequency whistler-mode thermal emission, then we may adopt a simplified form of the combined spectrum,

$$I_W(k) = \frac{k_m^2 T_e}{4\pi}\frac{\Omega_e^2}{\omega_{pe}^2}\left[\frac{c^2k^2}{\omega_{pe}^2} + \left(\frac{k_W^2}{k^2}\right)^\nu\right]. \tag{18}$$

Here, k_W^2 is an appropriate parameter for correct dimensionality, which can be adjusted. This parameter effectively dictates the level of background turbulence as well. In applying the above model, we reiterate that the model spectrum (18) is meant for the whistler-mode frequency range satisfying $\Omega_i^2 < \omega^2 < \Omega_e^2$. As such, we confine the width of wave numbers, $c\Delta k/\omega_{pe}$, roughly corresponding to the above frequency limitation. In an earlier attempt to incorporate the solar wind turbulence effects into the model whistler-mode spectrum, Ref. [41] adopted a model where the thermal fluctuation spectrum was modified to reflect the inverse power-law feature, namely, $I_W(k) \to [k_m^2 T_e/(4\pi)](\Omega_e^2/\omega_{pe}^2)(c^2k^2/\omega_{pe}^2)^{1-\beta}$, where β is a control parameter that can be chosen as 0 in the case of purely spontaneous emission and as $\beta = 1+\nu$ if we wish to model the overall spectral profile to behave as an inverse power law, $I_W(k) \propto k^{-2\nu}$. However, we now realize that the more proper way to model the combined spontaneously emitted quasi-thermal whistler-mode spectrum and the background pre-existing turbulence is the linear superposition (8), which we simplify as shown in Equation (18). Thus, in the present section, we take the total whistler-mode spectral intensity to possess the proportionality dictated by the functional relationship, $I_W(k) \propto c^2k^2/\omega_{pe}^2 + (k_W^2/k^2)^\nu$.

For the Langmuir mode spectrum, however, we only consider the thermal fluctuation, which is distinct from the previous section. Recall that in Section 3 we included the steady-state Langmuir turbulence factor, $(k_L/k)^2$, in the Langmuir turbulence spectrum (9), which led to the electron kappa distribution. In the present section, we are concerned with an alternative theory of a non-thermal, generalized kappa distribution, which is based upon the notion of background whistler-mode turbulence. In short, the transverse and longitudinal electric field spectral intensities adopted in the present discussion are defined by

$$\begin{aligned}\frac{\langle\delta E_\perp^2\rangle_{k,\omega}}{4} &= \frac{k_m^2 T_e}{4\pi}\frac{\Omega_e^2}{\omega_{pe}^2}\left[\frac{c^2k^2}{\omega_{pe}^2} + \left(\frac{k_W^2}{k^2}\right)^\nu\right]\delta(\omega-\omega_W),\\ \langle\delta E_\parallel^2\rangle_{k,\omega} &= \frac{k_m^2 T_e}{4\pi}\delta(\omega-\omega_L).\end{aligned} \tag{19}$$

Inserting this into the generalized coefficients (16), we obtain the desired coefficients A and D, which are now given by

$$
\begin{aligned}
A &= \frac{e^2k_m^2}{2m_e}\left(\frac{\Omega_e^4}{\omega_{pe}^4}\frac{c^2}{v^2}\int_0^1 d\mu\,\frac{1-\mu^2}{\mu^3}+\int_0^1 d\mu\mu\right),\\
D &= \frac{T_e}{m_e v}\frac{e^2k_m^2}{2m_e}\frac{\Omega_e^2}{\omega_{pe}^2}\left[\frac{c^2}{v^2}\frac{\Omega_e^2}{\omega_{pe}^2}\int_0^1 d\mu\,\frac{1-\mu^2}{\mu^3}+\left(\frac{k_W^2}{\Omega_e^2}\right)^{\nu}v^{2\nu}\int_0^1 d\mu(1-\mu^2)\mu^{2\nu-1}\right]\\
&\quad+\frac{T_e}{m_e v}\frac{e^2k_m^2}{2m_e}\int_0^1 d\mu\mu.
\end{aligned}
\tag{20}
$$

The integral $\int_0^1 d\mu\,(1-\mu^2)\mu^{-3}$ is formally divergent. To regularize the divergence, we introduce the lower limit, $\int_0^1 d\mu\,(1-\mu^2)\mu^{-3} \to \int_{\mu_{\min}}^1 d\mu\,(1-\mu^2)\mu^{-3} = (1-\mu_{\min}^2)/(2\mu_{\min}^2) + \ln\mu_{\min}$. The other μ integral is evaluated in a straightforward manner: $\int_0^1 d\mu(1-\mu^2)\mu^{2\nu-1} = 1/[2\nu(\nu+1)]$. Making use of all this, we have

$$
\begin{aligned}
f &= C\exp\left(-\int^x dx'\,\frac{2x'(a+x'^2)}{a[1+(x'^2/\kappa_W)^{\nu+1}]+x'^2}\right), \qquad x=\frac{v}{\alpha_e},\\
a &= \frac{2\Lambda}{(\omega_{pe}/\Omega_e)^2\beta_e}, \qquad \kappa_W=\frac{1}{\beta_e}\left(\frac{2\nu(\nu+1)\Lambda}{(ck_W/\Omega_e)^{2\nu}}\right)^{\frac{1}{\nu+1}},\\
\Lambda &= \frac{1-\mu_{\min}^2}{2\mu_{\min}^2}+\ln\mu_{\min}.
\end{aligned}
\tag{21}
$$

Here, we have made use of $(c/\alpha_e)^2(\Omega_e/\omega_{pe})^2 = B_0^2/(8\pi n_0 T_e) = 1/\beta_e$. This is a three-parameter model distribution, with ν, a, and κ_W being the adjustable parameters. If we consider the limit of $a \to \infty$, then we have

$$
f_{W\text{ only}} = C\exp\left(-2\int^x dx'\,\frac{x'}{1+(x'^2/\kappa_W)^{\nu+1}}\right). \tag{22}
$$

In this limit, the contribution from electrostatic Langmuir-mode fluctuation, that is, the term x'^2 in both the numerator and denominator within the integrand, is ignored. This limiting form can be termed the W-only distribution. However, if we take the limit of $a \to 0$, then we simply have

$$
f_{L\text{ only}} = C\exp\left(-2\int^x x'\,dx'\right) = C\exp\left(-x^2\right), \tag{23}
$$

the Maxwell–Boltzmann (MB) distribution. In this limit, the contribution from the whistler-mode related terms are ignored, and, thus, this limit can be termed the L-only distribution. Another interesting limit is when $\kappa_W \to \infty$. In this limit, the contribution from the background turbulence disappears, and the resulting distribution is that of the MD distribution again.

The parameters a and κ_W, in turn, are determined by $\mu_{\min}$, ω_{pe}/Ω_e, β_e, ν, and ck_W/Ω_e. The parameter ω_{pe}^2/Ω_e^2 can be determined from the solar wind data. Also, β_e is known from the data. The fitting parameters ck_W/Ω_e and ν relate to the spectral profile of the solar wind turbulence in the whistler-mode frequency range. Thus, these parameters can also be determined from observational properties. The truly free parameter is Λ, which is determined from the choice of $\mu_{\min}$. Let us consider the resonance condition, $kv\mu + \Omega_e = 0$ or $\mu = -\Omega_e/(kv)$. We are interested in the minimum value for μ. In the formal μ integral, this is taken to be $\mu_{\min} = 0$, but this means either $k \to \infty$ or $v \to \infty$, neither of which are physical. For whistler turbulence and fluctuations in the low-frequency limit, we choose the maximum k by $ck_{\max}/\omega_{pe} \sim 1$ or so. For the velocity v, we generally determine the maximum value to be sufficiently higher than the thermal speed, $v_{\max} \gg \alpha_e$. From this, we may see that $\mu_{\min} \sim -\Omega_e/(k_{\max} v_{\max})$, which, while small, can have a substantial range of freedom. If, for instance, we choose $\mu_{\min} \sim 10^{-6}$ or so, then we obtain $\Lambda \sim 10^{10}$. However, if we choose $\mu_{\max}$ to be approximately 10^{-4} or so, then we have $\Lambda \sim 10^6$ and so on and so forth. With this information, let us consider the ratio a/κ_W. If we choose $\nu = 1$, which implies k^{-2} spectral behavior associated with the whistler frequency range turbulence, then we have

$$\frac{a}{\kappa_W} = \frac{(ck_W/\Omega_e)}{(\omega_{pe}/\Omega_e)^2 \beta_e} \Lambda^{1/2}. \tag{24}$$

Suppose we take $(\omega_{pe}/\Omega_e)^2 \beta_e = 10^2$ and $ck_W/\Omega_e = 0.2$. Then, by choosing $\Lambda = 2.25 \times 10^6$ or so, we arrive at $a/\kappa_W \sim 3$. If, however, $(\omega_{pe}/\Omega_e)^2 \beta_e = 10^4$, then the choice of $\Lambda = 2.25 \times 10^{10}$ leads to the similar value of $a/\kappa_W \sim 3$. In the solar wind, the ratio ω_{pe}/Ω_e can be quite high, ranging from $\mathcal{O}(10)$ to $\mathcal{O}(10^2)$. The electron beta value in the solar wind can range from $\beta \sim \mathcal{O}(10^{-2})$ to $\mathcal{O}(1)$ or so, hence the above two choices of parameters, $(\omega_{pe}/\Omega_e)^2 \beta_e = 10^2$ and $(\omega_{pe}/\Omega_e)^2 \beta_e = 10^4$. The choice of $ck_W/\Omega_e = 0.2$ relates to the turbulence property in that this number represents the maximum effective range of whistler-mode turbulence in the wave number space. Since the low-frequency whistler mode is characterized by $ck_W/\Omega_e < 1$, such a choice is eminently reasonable. The above estimation of the crucial dimensionless parameter a/κ_W, of course, is a rough exercise, and more precise attempts should be made by surveying the 1 au data. However, in view of the uncertainty associated with the lower limit of the cosine of the pitch angle, $\mu_{\min}$, we defer the more accurate attempts for future.

With these considerations, we construct the asymptotic electron velocity distribution function (21) by performing a numerical indefinite integration over the dimensionless velocity $x = v/\alpha_e$. The result is displayed in Figure 6, where we display on the left-hand panel the case for $a/\kappa_W = 3$ with $a = 30$ and $\kappa_W = 10$. For all the examples, we restrict ourselves to $\nu = 1$. As visual guides, we plot the so-called L-only and W-only limiting case distributions. We also plot the inverse power-law velocity slop $v^{-6.5}$. In the solar wind, such an asymptotic high-velocity tail distribution is often observed [29]. On the right-hand panel, we show the velocity distribution by varying the parameter a, which ranges from $a = 1$ to 10 to 20 to 30. Other parameters are fixed: $\kappa_W = 10$ and $\nu = 1$. Figure 6 thus demonstrates that the combined effects of background turbulence and finite spontaneously emitted fluctuations are capable of producing the electron velocity distribution function that remarkably resembles the observed distribution in the solar wind. We should note, however, that there exists a certain degree of freedom in our choice of parameters a and κ_W, in particular, their ratio, a/κ_W, which turns out to be important for determining the shape of the velocity distribution function, as the right-hand panel of Figure 6 indicates.

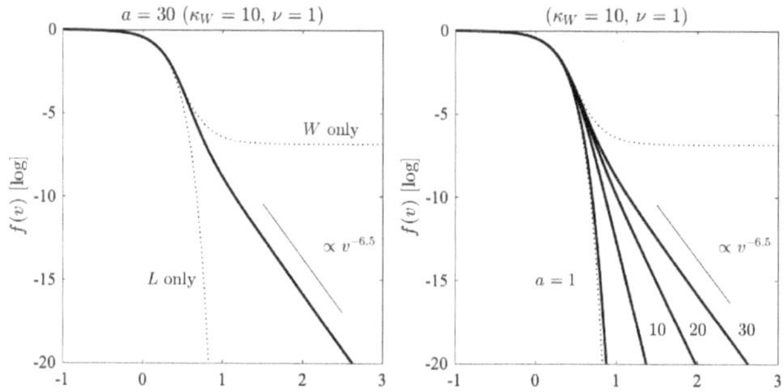

Figure 6. **[Left]** The three-parameter electron velocity distribution function f versus $x = v/\alpha_e$, for $a = 30$, $\kappa_W = 10$, and $\nu = 1$. **[Right]** The variation in the input parameter a, which ranges from $a = 1$ to 10 to 20 to 30.

5. Summary

The main purpose of the present paper was to put forth a first principle theory of the steady-state electron velocity distribution function with non-thermal characteristics, which resembles the quiet-time solar wind electron distribution detected in the near-Earth space environment. Unlike the previous model [27], which invoked the steady-state Langmuir turbulence and the accompanying kappa distribution, the present paper employed the combined influence of the background solar wind turbulence in the whistler frequency range, as well as the quasi-thermal electromagnetic and electrostatic fluctuations. The resulting model electron distribution function was given in terms of an exponential function of an indefinite velocity integral, which does not in general lend itself to further closed-form analytical manipulations—Equation (21)—but must, in general, be computed by numerical means. Under a reasonable set of assumptions and input conditions, we have found that the resulting numerical calculation leads to a velocity distribution function whose profile is reminiscent of the measured distribution in space.

The formal electron velocity distribution function in the steady-state was given by Equation (21), and this mathematical expression contains the effects of background fluctuations as well as the impact of the pre-existing whistler-mode turbulence. This contrasts to the formal solution (14), which reflects the influence of electrostatic thermal fluctuations and the enhanced Langmuir wave turbulence. It is possible to construct a more general formal distribution by combining the effects of both the electrostatic and electromagnetic thermal fluctuations on the electrons, as well as the influence of enhanced electrostatic (Langmuir) and electromagnetic (whistler) turbulence intensities. The result is

$$f(x) = C\exp\left(-\int^{x} dx' \, \frac{2x'(a+x'^2)}{a[1+(x'^2/\kappa_W)^{\nu+1}]+(1+x'^2/\kappa_L)x'^2}\right), \qquad x = \frac{v}{\alpha_e}. \tag{25}$$

Here, $\kappa_L = 2\omega_{pe}^2/(k_L\alpha)^2$, as defined in Equation (15). With this form of the electron distribution function, we now summarily discuss the various limits. Suppose that we ignore the influence of background turbulence altogether. This amounts to taking $\kappa_W \to \infty$ and $\kappa_L \to \infty$, which leads to

$$f_{\rm MB}(x) = C\exp(-x^2) \qquad (\kappa_W \to \infty,\ \kappa_L \to \infty). \tag{26}$$

Thus, in the absence of turbulence, we obtain the MB distribution, which is as expected. Ignoring the influence of electromagnetic whistler modes, both the thermal fluctuations and the enhanced pre-existing turbulence, is equivalent to taking the limit of $a \to 0$, which leads to the generalized form of the L-only distribution—see Equation (23)—which also happens to be the same kappa distribution discussed in Equation (14)

$$f_{L\ \rm only}(x) = f_\kappa(x) = C\left(1+\frac{x^2}{\kappa_L}\right)^{-\kappa_L} \qquad (a \to 0). \tag{27}$$

If, however, we are to ignore the influence of electrostatic modes, both the thermal fluctuations and enhanced Langmuir turbulence, then all we need to do is consider the limit of $a \gg 1$,

$$f_{W\ \rm only}(x) = C\exp\left(-\int^{x} dx' \, \frac{2x'}{1+(x'^2/\kappa_W)^{\nu+1}}\right) \qquad (a \gg 1). \tag{28}$$

This form of limiting solution was referred to as the W-only distribution in Equation (22), but this stand-alone solution is not a realistic model since the electrostatic fluctuations cannot simply be ignored. Nevertheless, at least as a mathematical exercise, one can certainly entertain such a limit. In our final solution (21), we have considered the limit of $\kappa_L \to \infty$, while other parameters, a and κ_W, are considered finite.

The overall concept of charged particles maintaining a steady-state wave–particle interaction with steady-state turbulence and fluctuations is an example of a stationary state far from equilibrium [79]. Such a state, in turn, may be considered as an example of the non-extensive statistical state [18,19]. It is in this regard that the present paper is relevant to the Special Issue "Nonadditive Entropies and Nonextensive Statistical Mechanics". The fact that the space plasma, which is governed by a long-range electromagnetic force, frequently exhibits a kappa-like non-thermal distribution function is in a way not too surprising in that, thanks to Tsallis's pioneering work, we now have a rather insightful understanding that any system with a long-range interaction is likely to be governed by a non-extensive, non-additive statistical principle. The present paper, as with the related earlier work [27], provides the physical "mechanism" that leads to a concrete example of a kappa-like non-thermal phase space distribution function.

Author Contributions: Conceptualization, P.H.Y., R.A.L. and S.K.; Methodology, P.H.Y., R.A.L., C.S.S. and S.K.; Software, P.H.Y., R.A.L. and C.S.S.; Validation, P.H.Y., R.A.L., C.S.S. and J.W.B.; Formal analysis, P.H.Y., R.A.L., C.S.S. and S.K.; Investigation, P.H.Y., R.A.L., C.S.S., J.W.B. and S.K.; Resources, P.H.Y.; Data curation, C.S.S. and J.W.B.; Writing—original draft, P.H.Y.; Writing—review & editing, P.H.Y., R.A.L., C.S.S., J.W.B. and S.K.; Visualization, P.H.Y., R.A.L., C.S.S. and J.W.B.; Funding acquisition, P.H.Y. All authors have read and agreed to the published version of the manuscript.

Funding: This material is based upon work funded by the Department of Energy (DE-SC0022963) through the NSF/DOE Partnership in Basic Plasma Science and Engineering. This research was also partially supported by NSF Grants 2203321 to the University of Maryland. S.K. was supported by the National Research Foundation (NRF) of Korea through grant no. 2022R1I1A1A01070881.

Data Availability Statement: Data are contained within the article.

Conflicts of Interest: The authors declare no conflicts of interest.

References

1. Feldman, W.C.; Asbridge, J.R.; Bame, S.J.; Montgomery, M.D.; Gary, S.P. Solar wind electrons. *J. Geophys. Res.* **1975**, *80*, 4181. [CrossRef]
2. Gosling, J.T.; Asbridge, J.R.; Bame, S.J.; Feldman, W.C.; Zwickl, R.D.; Paschmann, G.; Sckopke, N.; Hynds, R.J. Interplanetary ions during an energetic storm particle event: The distribution function from solar wind thermal energies to 1.6 MeV. *J. Geophys. Res.* **1981**, *86*, 547. [CrossRef]
3. Armstrong, T.P.; Paonessa, M.T.; Bell, E.V., II; Krimigis, S.M. Voyager observations of Saturnian ion and electron phase space densities. *J. Geophys. Res.* **1983**, *88*, 8893. [CrossRef]
4. Halekas, J.S.; Whittlesey, P.; Larson, D.E.; McGinnis, D.; Maksimovic, M.; Berthomier, M.; Kasper, J.C.; Case, A.W.; Korreck, K.E.; Stevens, M.L.; et al. Electrons in the young solar wind: First results from the *Parker Solar Probe*. *Astrophys. J. Suppl. Ser.* **2020**, *246*, 22. [CrossRef]
5. Berčič, L.; Larson, D.; Whittlesey, P.; Maksimović, M.; Badman, S.T.; Landi, S.; Matteini, L.; Bale, S.D.; Bonnell, J.W.; Case, A.W.; et al. Coronal electron temperature inferred from the strahl electrons in the inner heliosphere: *Parker Solar Probe* and *Helios* observations. *Astrophys. J.* **2020**, *892*, 88. [CrossRef]
6. Berčič, L.; Verscharen, D.; Owen, C.J.; Colomban, L.; Kretzschmar, M.; Chust, T.; Maksimovic, M.; Kataria, D.O.; Anekallu, C.; Behar, E.; et al. Whistler instability driven by the sunward electron deficit in the solar wind: High-cadence *Solar Orbiter* observations. *Astron. Astrophys. (A&A)* **2021**, *656*, A31.
7. Olbert, S. Summary of experimental results from M.I.T. detector on IMP-1. In *Physics of the Magnetosphere*; Carovillano, R.L., McClay, J.F., Radoski, H.R., Eds.; Springer: New York, NY, USA, 1968; pp. 641–659.
8. Binsack, J.H. Plasma Studies with the IMP-2 Satellite. Ph.D. Thesis, Massachusetts Institute of Technology, Cambridge, MA, USA, 1966.
9. Vasyliunas, V. M. A survey of low-energy electrons in the evening sector of the magnetosphere with OGO1 and OGO 3. *J. Geophys. Res.* **1968**, *73*, 2839. [CrossRef]
10. Livadiotis, G. *Kappa Distributions*; Elsevier: Amsterdam, The Netherlands, 2017.
11. Salem, C.S.; Pulupa, M.; Bale, S.D.; Verscharen, D. Precision electron measurements in the solar wind at 1 au from NASA's Wind spacecraft. *Astron. Astrophys. (A&A)* **2023**, *675*, A162.
12. Boltzmann, L. Weitere studien über das Wärmegleichgewicht unter gas molekülen (Further studies on thermal equilibrium between gas molecules). *Sitzungsberichte Akad. Wiss.* **1872**, *66*, 275–370.
13. Boltzmann, L. On the relation of a general mechanical theorem to the second law of thermodynamics. In *Kinetic Theory*; Brush, S., Ed.; Pergamon Press: Oxford, UK, 1966; Volume 2, *Irreversible Processes*, p. 188.
14. Gibbs, J.W. *Elementary Principles in Statistical Mechanics—Developed with Especial Reference to the Rational Foundation of Thermodynamics*; C. Scribner's Sons: New York, NY, USA, 1902; Yale University Press: New Haven, CT, USA, 1948.

15. Boltzmann, L. Vorlesungen über Gatheorie (Leipzig, 1896). In *[Lectures on Gas Theory]*; Brush, S., Transl.; Univ. California Press: Berkeley, CA, USA, 1964; Part II, Chapter I, Paragraph 1, p. 217.
16. Einstein, A. Theorie der opaleszenz von homogenen Flüssigkeiten und Flüssigkeitsgemischen in der Nähe des kritischen Zustandes. *Ann. Physik* **1910**, *33*, 1275. [CrossRef]
17. Fermi, E. *Thermodynamics*; Dover: New York, NY, USA, 1936; p. 53.
18. Tsallis, C. *Introduction to Nonextensive Statistical Mechanics*; Springer: New York, NY, USA, 2009.
19. Tsallis, C. Possible generalization of Boltzmann-Gibbs statistics. *J. Stat. Phys.* **1988**, *52*, 479. [CrossRef]
20. Lazar, M.; Fichtner, H. (Eds.) *Kappa Distributions*; Springer: New York, NY, USA, 2021.
21. Livadiotis, G. Kappa and q indices: Dependence on the degrees of freedom. *Entropy* **2015**, *17*, 2062. [CrossRef]
22. Leubner, M.P. Fundamental issues on kappa-distributions in space plasmas and interplanetary proton distributions. *Phys. Plasmas* **2004**, *11*, 1308. [CrossRef]
23. Livadiotis, G.; McComas, D.J. Beyond kappa distributions: Exploiting Tsallis statistical mechanics in space plasmas. *J. Geophys. Res.* **2009**, *114*, A11105. [CrossRef]
24. Livadiotis, G. On the simplification of statistical mechanics for space plasmas. *Entropy* **2017**, *19*, 285. [CrossRef]
25. Yoon, P.H.; Rhee, T.; Ryu, C.-M. Self-consistent generation of superthermal electrons by beam-plasma interaction. *Phys. Rev. Lett.* **2005**, *95*, 215003. [CrossRef] [PubMed]
26. Ryu, C.-M.; Rhee, T.; Umeda, T.; Yoon, P.H.; Omura, Y. Turbulent acceleration of superthermal electrons. *Phys. Plasmas* **2007**, *14*, 100701. [CrossRef]
27. Yoon, P.H. Electron kappa distribution and quasi-thermal noise. *J. Geophys. Res.* **2014**, *119*, 70774. [CrossRef]
28. Yoon, P.H.; Lazar, M.; Scherer, K.; Fichtner, H.; Schlickeiser, R. Modified κ-distribution of solar wind electrons and steady-state Langmuir turbulence. *Astrophys. J.* **2018**, *868*, 131. [CrossRef]
29. Wang, L.; Lin, R.; Salem, C.; Pulupa, M.; Larson, D.E.; Yoon, P.H.; Luhmann, J.G. Quiet-time interplanetary $\sim$ 2–20 keV superhalo electrons at solar minimum. *Astrophys. J.* **2012**, *753*, L23. [CrossRef]
30. Maksimovic, M.; Hoang, S.; Meyer-Vernet, N.; Moncuquet, M.; Bougeret, J.-L.; Phillips, J.L.; Canu, P. Solar wind electron parameters from quasi-thermal noise spectroscopy and comparison with other measurements on Ulysses. *J. Geophys. Res.* **1995**, *199*, 19881. [CrossRef]
31. Lin, R.P. WIND observations of suprathermal electrons in the interplanetary medium. *Space Sci. Rev.* **1998**, *86*, 61. [CrossRef]
32. Tong, Y.; Vasko, I.Y.; Pulupa, M.; Mozer, F.S.; Bale, S.D.; Artemyev, A.V.; Krasnoselskikh, V. Whistler wave generation by halo electrons in the solar wind. *Astrophys. J. Lett.* **2019**, *870*, L6. [CrossRef]
33. Tong, Y.; Vasko, I.Y.; Artemyev, A.V.; Bale, S.D.; Mozer, F.S. Statistical study of whistler waves in the solar wind at 1 au. *Astrophys. J.* **2019**, *878*, 41. [CrossRef]
34. Cattell, C.; Breneman, A.; Dombeck, J.; Short, B.; Wygant, J.; Halekas, J.; Case, T.; Kasper, J.C.; Larson, D.; Stevens, M.; et al. Parker Solar Probe evidence for scattering of electrons in the young solar wind by narrowband whistler-mode waves. *Astrophys. J. Lett.* **2021**, *911*, L29. [CrossRef]
35. Kretzschmar, M.; Chust, T.; Krasnoselskikh, V.; Graham, D.; Colomban, L.; Maksimovic, M.; Khotyaintsev, Y.V.; Soucek, J.; Steinvall, K.; Santolík, O.; et al. Whistler waves observed by *Solar Orbiter/RPW* between 0.5 AU and 1 AU. *Astron. Astrophys. (A&A)* **2021**, *656*, A24.
36. Sitenko, A.G. *Electromagnetic Fluctuations in Plasma*; Academic Press: New York, NY, USA, 1967.
37. Sitenko, A.G. *Fluctuations and Nonlinear Wave Interactions in Plasmas*; Pergamon: New York, NY, USA, 1982.
38. Meyer-Vernet, N. On natural noises detected by antennas in plasmas. *J. Geophys. Res.* **1979**, *84*, 5373. [CrossRef]
39. Kim, S.; Yoon, P.H.; Choe, G.S. Spontaneous emission of electromagnetic and electrostatic fluctuations in magnetized plasmas: Quasi-parallel modes. *Phys. Plasmas* **2016**, *23*, 022111. [CrossRef]
40. Gaelzer, R.; Yoon, P.H.; Kim, S.; Ziebell, L.F. On the dimensionally correct kinetic theory of turbulence for parallel propagation. *Phys. Plasmas* **2015**, *22*, 032310. [CrossRef]
41. Kim, S.; Yoon, P.H.; Choe, G.S.; Wang, L. Asymptotic theory of solar wind electrons. *Astrophys. J.* **2015**, *806*, 32. [CrossRef]
42. Astudillo, H.F. High-order modes of left-handed electromagnetic waves in a solar-wind-line plasma. *J. Geophys. Res.* **1996**, *101*, 24433. [CrossRef]
43. Valdivia, J.A.; Toledo, B.A.; Gallo, N.; Muñoz, V.; Rogan, J.; Stepanova, M.; Moya, P.S.; Navarro, R.E.; Viñas, A.F.; Araneda, J.; et al. Magnetic fluctuations in anisotropic space plasmas: The effect of the plasma environment. *Adv. Space Res.* **2016**, *58*, 2126. [CrossRef]
44. López, R.A.; Yoon, P.H. Simulation of electromagnetic fluctuations in thermal magnetized plasma. *Plasma Phys. Control. Fusion* **2017**, *59*, 115003. [CrossRef]
45. Vasquez, B.J.; Markovskii, S.A. Velocity power spectra from cross-field turbulence in the proton kinetic regime. *Astrophys. J.* **2012**, *747*, 19. [CrossRef]
46. Vasquez, B.J.; Markovskii, S.A.; Chandran, B.D.G. Three-dimensional hybrid simulation study of anisotropic turbulence in the proton kinetic regime. *Astrophys. J.* **2014**, *788*, 178. [CrossRef]
47. Franci, L.; Landi, S.; Matteini, L.; Verdini, A.; Hellinger, P. High-resolution hybrid simulations of kinetic plasma turbulence at proton scales. *Astrophys. J.* **2015**, *812*, 21. [CrossRef]

48. Markovskii, S.A.; Vasquez, B.J. Four-dimensional frequency-wavenumber power spectrum of a strong turbulence obtained from hybrid kinetic simulations. *Astrophys. J.* **2020**, *903*, 80. [CrossRef]
49. Bruno, R.; Carbone, V. *Turbulence in the Solar Wind*; Springer: Heidelberg, Germany, 2016.
50. von Kármán, T. Progress in the statistical theory of turbulence. *Proc. Natl. Acad. Sci. USA* **1948**, *34*, 530. [CrossRef] [PubMed]
51. Taylor, G.I. The spectrum of turbulence. *Proc. R. Soc. Lond.* **1938**, *164*, 476. [CrossRef]
52. Salem, C.S.; Howes, G.G.; Sundkvist, D.; Bale, S.D.; Chaston, C.C.; Chen, C.H.K.; Mozer, F.S. Identification of kinetic Alfvén wave turbulence in the solar wind. *Astrophys. J. Lett.* **2012**, *745*, L9. [CrossRef]
53. Yoon, P.H. *Classical Kinetic Theory of Weakly Turbulent Nonlinear Plasma Processes*; Cambridge University Press: Cambridge, UK, 2019.
54. Kadomtsev, B.B. *Plasma Turbulence*; Academic Press: New York, NY, USA, 1965.
55. Sagdeev, R.Z.; Galeev, A.A. *Nonlinear Plasma Theory*; Benjamin: New York, NY, USA, 1969.
56. Tsytovich, V.N. *Nonlinear Effects in a Plasma*; Plenum Press: New York, NY, USA, 1970.
57. Tsytovich, V.N. *An Introduction to the Theory of Plasma Turbulence*; Pergamon Press: New York, NY, USA, 1977.
58. Tsytovich, V.N. *Theory of Turbulent Plasma*; Consultants Bureau: New York, NY, USA, 1977.
59. Davidson, R.C. *Methods in Nonlinear Plasma Theory*; Academic Press: New York, NY, USA, 1972.
60. Ichimaru, S. *Basic Principles of Plasma Physics*; Benjamin: New York, NY, USA, 1973.
61. Akhiezer, A.I.; Akhiezer, I.A.; Polovin, R.V.; Sitenko, A.G.; Stepanov, K.N. *Plasma Electrodynamics*; Pergamon Press: New York, NY, USA, 1973.
62. Kaplan, S.A.; Tsytovich, V.N. *Plasma Astrophysics*; Pergamon Press: New York, NY, USA, 1973.
63. Melrose, D.B. *Plasma Astrophysics, Vol. 1 & 2*; Gordon and Breach: New York, NY, USA, 1980.
64. Melrose, D.B. *Quantum Plasmadynamics: Unmagnetized Plasmas*; Springer: New York, NY, USA, 2008.
65. Melrose, D.B. *Quantum Plasmadynamics: Magnetized Plasmas*; Springer: New York, NY, USA, 2013.
66. Hasegawa, A.; Mima, K.; Duong-van, M. Plasma distribution function in a superthermal radiation field. *Phys. Rev. Lett.* **1985**, *54*, 2608. [CrossRef] [PubMed]
67. Ma, C.; Summers, D. Formation of power-Law energy spectra in space plasmas by stochastic acceleration due to whistler-mode waves. *Geophys. Res. Lett.* **1998**, *25*, 4099. [CrossRef]
68. Shizgal, B.D. Kappa and other nonequilibrium distributions from the Fokker-Planck equation and the relationship to Tsallis entropy. *Phys. Rev. E.* **2018**, *97*, 052144. [CrossRef] [PubMed]
69. Sahraoui, F.; Goldstein, M.L.; Robert, P.; Khotyaintsev, Y.V. Evidence of a cascade and dissipation of solar-wind turbulence at the electron gyroscale. *Phys. Rev. Lett.* **2009**, *102*, 231102. [CrossRef] [PubMed]
70. Chen, C.H.K. Recent progress in astrophysical plasma turbulence from solar wind observations. *J. Plasma Phys.* **2016**, *82*, 535820602. [CrossRef]
71. Zhao, L.-L.; Zank, G.P.; Adhikari, L.; Nakanotani, M.; Telloni, D.; Carbone, F. Spectral features in field-aligned solar wind turbulence from Parker Solar Probe observations. *Astrophys. J.* **2020**, *898*, 113. [CrossRef]
72. Zank, G.P.; Zhao, L.-L.; Adhikari, L.; Telloni, D.; Kasper, J.C.; Bale, S.D. Turbulence transport in the solar corona: Theory, modeling, and Parker Solar Probe. *Phys. Plasmas* **2021**, *28*, 080501. [CrossRef]
73. Zhao, L.-L.; Zank, G.P.; Telloni, D.; Stevens, M.; Kasper, J.C.; Bale, S.D. The turbulent properties of the sub-Alfvénic solar wind measured by the Parker Solar Probe. *Astrophys. J. Lett.* **2022**, *928*, L15. [CrossRef]
74. Markovskii, S.A.; Vasquez, B.J. Observational analysis and numerical modeling of the solar wind fluctuation spectra during intervals of plasma instability. *Astrophys. J.* **2022**, *941*, 72. [CrossRef]
75. Vocks, C.; Mann, G. Generation of suprathermal electrons by resonant wave-particle interaction in the solar corona and wind. *Astrophys. J.* **2003**, *593*, 1134. [CrossRef]
76. Vocks, C.; Salem, C.; Lin, R.P.; Mann, G. Electron halo and strahl formation in the solar wind by resonant interaction with whistler waves. *Astrophys. J.* **2005**, *627*, 540. [CrossRef]
77. Vocks, C.; Mann, G. Scattering of solar energetic electrons in interplanetary space. *Astron. Astrophys. (A&A)* **2009**, *502*, 325.
78. Pierrard, V.; Lazar, M.; Schlickeiser, R. Evolution of the electron distribution function in the whistler wave turbulence of the solar wind. *Sol. Phys.* **2011**, *269*, 421. [CrossRef]
79. Treumann, R.A.; Jaroschek, C.H.; Scholer, M. Stationary plasma states far from equilibrium. *Phys. Plasmas* **2004**, *11*, 1317. [CrossRef]

entropy

MDPI

Article

Tsallis Distribution as a Λ-Deformation of the Maxwell–Jüttner Distribution

Jean-Pierre Gazeau

Centre National de la Recherche Scientifique (CNRS), Astroparticule et Cosmologie, Université Paris Cité, F-75013 Paris, France; gazeau@apc.in2p3.fr

Abstract: Currently, there is no widely accepted consensus regarding a consistent thermodynamic framework within the special relativity paradigm. However, by postulating that the inverse temperature 4-vector, denoted as $\boldsymbol{\beta}$, is future-directed and time-like, intriguing insights emerge. Specifically, it is demonstrated that the q-dependent Tsallis distribution can be conceptualized as a de Sitterian deformation of the relativistic Maxwell–Jüttner distribution. In this context, the curvature of the de Sitter space-time is characterized by $\sqrt{\Lambda/3}$, where Λ represents the cosmological constant within the ΛCDM standard model for cosmology. For a simple gas composed of particles with proper mass m, and within the framework of quantum statistical de Sitterian considerations, the Tsallis parameter q exhibits a dependence on the cosmological constant given by $q = 1 + \ell_c\sqrt{\Lambda}/\mathfrak{n}$, where $\ell_c = \hbar/mc$ is the Compton length of the particle and $\mathfrak{n}$ is a positive numerical factor, the determination of which awaits observational confirmation. This formulation establishes a novel connection between the Tsallis distribution, quantum statistics, and the cosmological constant, shedding light on the intricate interplay between relativistic thermodynamics and fundamental cosmological parameters.

Keywords: Maxwell–Jüttner distribution; Tsallis distribution; de Sitter quantum field; ΛCDM standard model

Citation: Gazeau, J.-P. Tsallis Distribution as a Λ-Deformation of the Maxwell–Jüttner Distribution. *Entropy* **2024**, *26*, 273. https://doi.org/10.3390/e26030273

Academic Editor: Yong Deng

Received: 28 February 2024
Revised: 17 March 2024
Accepted: 20 March 2024
Published: 21 March 2024

1. Preamble: Temperature, Heat, and Entropy, That Obscure Objects of Desire

It is opportune to start out this contribution by quoting what de Broglie wrote in Ref. [1] about the relation between entropy invariance and relativistic variance of temperature (translated from French):

> *It is well known that entropy, alongside the space-time interval, electric charge, and mechanical action, is one of the fundamental "invariants" of the theory of relativity. To convince oneself of this, it is enough to recall that, according to Boltzmann, the entropy of a macroscopic state is proportional to the logarithm of the number of microstates that realize that state. To strengthen this reasoning, one can argue that, on the one hand, the definition of entropy involves a integer number of microstates, and, on the other hand, the transformation of entropy during a Galilean reference frame change must be expressed as a continuous function of the relative velocity of the reference frames. Consequently, this continuous function is necessarily constant and equal to unity, which means that entropy is constant.*

Let us now give more insights about what "relativistic thermodynamics" could be. In relativistic thermodynamics (i.e., in accordance with special relativity), there exist three points of view [2], distinguished from the way heat ΔQ and temperature T transform under a Lorentz boost from frame $\mathcal{R}_0$ (e.g., laboratory) to comoving frame $\mathcal{R}$ with velocity $\mathbf{v} = v\hat{\mathbf{n}}$ relative to $\mathcal{R}_0$ and Lorentz factor

$$\gamma(v) = \frac{1}{\sqrt{1 - v^2/c^2}}. \tag{1}$$

(**a**) The covariant viewpoint (Einstein [3], Planck [4], de Broglie [1] ...),

$$\Delta Q = \Delta Q_0 \gamma^{-1}, \quad T = T_0 \gamma^{-1}. \tag{2}$$

(**b**) The anti-covariant one (Ott [5], Arzelies [6], ...),

$$\Delta Q = \Delta Q_0 \gamma, \quad T = T_0 \gamma. \tag{3}$$

(**c**) The invariant one, "nothing changes" (Landsberg [7,8], ...),

$$\Delta Q = \Delta Q_0, \quad T = T_0. \tag{4}$$

Also note that, for some authors (Landsberg [9], Sewell [10], ...), "there is no meaningful law of temperature under boosts".

Nevertheless, more recent approaches (e.g., Ref. [11]) show that there is a covariant relativistic thermodynamics with proper absolute temperature in full agreement with relativistic hydrodynamics.

In this paper, we adopt the viewpoint in Section 1 and review de Broglie's arguments in Section 2. In Section 3, we remind you of the construction of the so-called Maxwell–Jüttner distribution presented by Synge in Ref. [12]. In Section 4, we then present the de Sitter space-time, its geometric description as a hyperboloid embedded in the $1+4$ Minkowski space-time, and give some insights of the fully covariant quantum field theory of free scalar massive elementary systems propagating on this manifold. In Section 5, we then develop our arguments in favor of a novel connection between the Tsallis distribution, quantum statistics, and the cosmological constant, shedding light on the intricate interplay between relativistic thermodynamics and fundamental cosmological parameters. A few comments end our paper in Section 6.

2. Relativistic Covariance of Temperature According to de Broglie (1948)

Here, we give an account of the de Broglie arguments given in Ref. [1] in favor of the covariant viewpoint (a).

Let us consider a body $\mathcal{B}$ with proper frame $\mathcal{R}_0$, and total proper mass M_0. It is assumed to be in thermodynamical equilibrium with temperature T_0 and fixed volume V_0 (e.g., a gas enclosed with surrounding rigid wall). Let us then observe $\mathcal{B}$ from an inertial frame $\mathcal{R}$, in which $\mathcal{B}$ has constant velocity $\mathbf{v} = v\hat{\mathbf{n}}$ relative to $\mathcal{R}_0$. We suppose that a source in $\mathcal{R}$ provides $\mathcal{B}$ with heat ΔQ. In order to keep the velocity $\mathbf{v}$ of $\mathcal{B}$ constant, work W has to be performed on $\mathcal{B}$. Its proper mass is consequently modified $M_0 \to M_0'$. Then, from energy conservation,

$$(M_0' - M_0)\gamma c^2 = \Delta Q + W, \quad \gamma = \gamma(v) = \frac{1}{\sqrt{1 - v^2/c^2}}, \tag{5}$$

and the relativistic second Newton law,

$$\Delta P = M_0'\gamma v - M_0 \gamma v = \int \mathrm{F} dt = \frac{1}{v}\int F v dt = \frac{W}{v}, \tag{6}$$

we derive

$$\Delta Q = \frac{c^2}{v^2}\gamma^{-2} W = (M_0' - M_0)c^2\gamma^{-2}. \tag{7}$$

In frame $\mathcal{R}_0$, there is no work performed (the volume is constant), there is just transmitted heat $\Delta Q_0 = (M_0' - M_0)c^2$. By comparison with (7), one infers that heat transforms as

$$\Delta Q = \Delta Q_0 \gamma^{-1}. \tag{8}$$

Since the entropy $S = \int \frac{\mathrm{d}Q}{T}$ is relativistic invariant, $S = S_0$, temperature finally transforms as

$$T = T_0 \gamma^{-1} \tag{9}$$

3. Maxwell–Jüttner Distribution

We now present a relativistic version of the Maxwell–Boltzmann distribution for simple gases, namely the Maxwell–Jüttner distribution [13–15]. We follow the derivation given by Synge in Ref. [12]; see also Ref. [16], and the recent article [17] for a comprehensive list of references. Note that this distribution is defined on the mass hyperboloid, and not expressed in terms of velocities (see the recent [18] and references therein).

Our notations [19] for event four-vector $\underline{x}$ in the Minkowskian space-time $\mathbb{M}_{1,3}$ and for four-momentum $\underline{k}$ are the following:

$$\mathbb{M}_{1,3} \ni \underline{x} = (x^\mu) = (x^0 = x_0, x^i = -x_i, i = 1,2,3) \equiv (x^0, \mathbf{x}), \tag{10}$$

equipped with the metric $\mathrm{d}s^2 = (\mathrm{d}x^0)^2 - \mathrm{d}\mathbf{x} \cdot \mathbf{x} \equiv g_{\mu\nu} \mathrm{d}x^\mu \mathrm{d}x^\nu$, $g_{\mu\nu} = \mathrm{diag}(1, -1, -1, -1)$,

$$\underline{k} = (k^\mu) = (k^0, \mathbf{k}). \tag{11}$$

The Minkowskian inner product is noted by:

$$\underline{x} \cdot \underline{x'} = g_{\mu\nu} x^\mu x'^\nu = x^\mu x'_\mu = x^0 x'^0 - \mathbf{x} \cdot \mathbf{x}'. \tag{12}$$

Let $\underline{k}$ be four-momentum, pointing toward point A of the mass shell hyperboloid $\mathcal{V}_m^+ = \{\underline{k}, \underline{k} \cdot \underline{k} = m^2 c^2\}$, and an infinitesimal hyperbolic interval at A, with length

$$\mathrm{d}\sigma = mc\, \mathrm{d}\omega, \tag{13}$$

where $\mathrm{d}\omega = \dfrac{\mathrm{d}^3\mathbf{k}}{k_0}$ is the Lorentz-invariant element on $\mathcal{V}_m^+$. Given a time-like unit vector $\underline{n}$, and a straight line Δ passing through the origin and orthogonal (in the $\mathbb{M}_{1,3}$ metric sense) to $\underline{n}$, denote by $\mathrm{d}\Omega$ the length of the projection of $\mathrm{d}\sigma$ on Δ along $\underline{n}$. As is illustrated in Figure 1, one easily proves that

$$\mathrm{d}\Omega = |\underline{k} \cdot \underline{n}|\, \mathrm{d}\omega \quad (= \mathrm{d}^3\mathbf{k} \text{ if } \underline{n} = (1, \mathbf{0})). \tag{14}$$

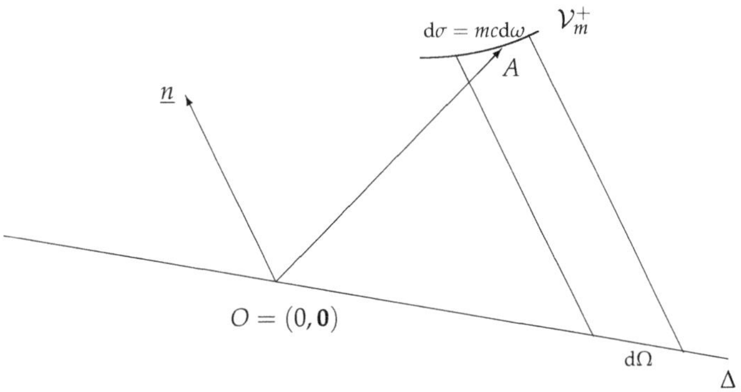

Figure 1. $\underline{n}$ is a time-like unit vector, Δ is a straight line passing through the origin and orthogonal (in the Minkowskian metric sense) to $\underline{n}$. The 4-momentum $\underline{k} = (k^\mu) = (k^0, \mathbf{k})$ points toward a point A of the mass shell hyperboloid $\mathcal{V}_m^+ = \{\underline{k}, \underline{k} \cdot \underline{k} = m^2c^2\}$. $\mathrm{d}\Omega$ is the length of the projection, along $\underline{n}$, of an infinitesimal hyperbolic interval at A of length $\mathrm{d}\sigma = mc\mathrm{d}\omega$.

The sample population consists of those particles with world lines cutting the infinitesimal space-like segment $\mathrm{d}\Sigma$ orthogonal to the time-like unit vector $\underline{n}$, as is shown in Figure 2.

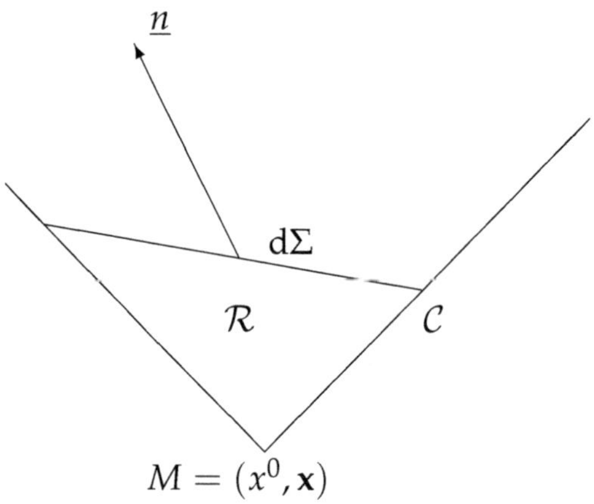

Figure 2. $\mathcal{C}$ is the portion of the null cone starting at the event $M = (x^0, \mathbf{x})$ and limited by the infinitesimal space-like segment $\mathrm{d}\Sigma$ orthogonal to the time-like unit vector $\underline{n}$. $\mathcal{R}$ is the region delimited by M, the portion of the light cone $\mathcal{C}$, and $\mathrm{d}\Sigma$.

Every particle that traverses the segment $\mathcal{C}$ of the null cone between M and $\mathrm{d}\Sigma$ must also traverse $\mathrm{d}\Sigma$ (causal cone). Consequently, regardless of the collisions that take place within the infinitesimal region $\mathcal{R}$ bounded by M, the segment of the light cone $\mathcal{C}$, and $\mathrm{d}\Sigma$, the number of particles crossing Σ, is predetermined as the number crossing $\mathcal{C}$:

$$\nu = \underline{N} \cdot \underline{n}\, \mathrm{d}\Sigma = \mathrm{d}\Sigma \int_{V_m^+} \mathcal{N}(\underline{x}, \underline{k})\, \mathrm{d}\Omega\,, \tag{15}$$

where $\underline{N}$ is the numerical-flux four-vector and $\mathcal{N}(\underline{x}, \underline{k})$ is the distribution function. By the conservation of four-momentum at each collision in a simple gas, the flux of four-momentum across $\mathrm{d}\Sigma$ is predetermined as the flux across $\mathcal{C}$,

$$T_\mu \cdot \underline{n}\, \mathrm{d}\Sigma = \mathrm{d}\Sigma \int_{V_m^+} \mathcal{N}(\underline{x}, \underline{k})\, ck_\mu \mathrm{d}\Omega\,, \tag{16}$$

where $\underline{\underline{T}} = (T_{\mu\nu})$ is the energy-momentum tensor.

The most probable distribution function $\mathcal{N}$ at M is that which maximizes the following entropy integral:

$$F = -\mathrm{d}\Sigma \int_{V_m^+} \mathcal{N}(\underline{x}, \underline{k})\, \log \mathcal{N}(\underline{x}, \underline{k})\, \mathrm{d}\Omega. \tag{17}$$

Variational calculus with five Lagrange $\underline{x}$-dependent multipliers α and η_μ associated with constraints on ν and $T_\mu \cdot \underline{n}$, respectively, leads to the solution

$$\mathcal{N}(\underline{x}, \underline{k}) = C(\underline{x})\, \exp(-\underline{\eta}(\underline{x}) \cdot \underline{k})\,, \quad C = e^{\alpha - 1}. \tag{18}$$

Scalar C and time-like four-vector $\underline{\eta}$ are determined by the constraints on $\nu = \underline{N} \cdot \underline{n}\, \mathrm{d}\Sigma$ and $T_\mu \cdot \underline{n}\, \mathrm{d}\Sigma$:

$$C \int_{V_m^+} k_\mu\, e^{-\underline{\eta} \cdot \underline{k}}\, \mathrm{d}\omega = N_\mu\,, \qquad C \int_{V_m^+} ck_\mu k_\nu\, e^{-\underline{\eta} \cdot \underline{k}}\, \mathrm{d}\omega = T_{\mu\nu}. \tag{19}$$

established by taking into account that $\underline{n}$ is arbitrary.

With the equations of conservation

$$\underline{\partial} \cdot \underline{N} = 0, \quad \underline{\partial} \cdot T_\mu = 0, \tag{20}$$

We finally obtain as many equations as the 19 functions of $\underline{x}$: $C, \underline{\eta}, \underline{N}, T$. The following partition function is essential for all relevant calculations.

$$Z(\eta) := \int_{\mathcal{V}_m^+} e^{-\underline{\eta}\cdot\underline{k}} \frac{\mathrm{d}^3\mathbf{k}}{k_0} = \frac{4\pi mc}{\sqrt{\underline{\eta}\cdot\underline{\eta}}} K_1\left(mc\sqrt{\underline{\eta}\cdot\underline{\eta}}\right) \tag{21}$$

where K_ν is the modified Bessel function [20]. Hence, the components of the numerical flux four-vector $\underline{N}$ and of the energy tensor $\underline{\underline{T}}$ in (19) are given in terms of derivatives of Z and, finally, in terms of Bessel functions by

$$N_\mu = -C\frac{\partial Z}{\partial \eta^\mu} = C\frac{4\pi m^2 c^2 \eta_\mu}{\underline{\eta}\cdot\underline{\eta}} K_2\left(mc\sqrt{\underline{\eta}\cdot\underline{\eta}}\right), \tag{22}$$

$$T_{\mu\nu} = Cc\frac{\partial^2 Z}{\partial \eta^\mu \partial \eta^\nu} = C4\pi m^2 c^3 \left[mc\frac{K_3\left(mc\sqrt{\underline{\eta}\cdot\underline{\eta}}\right)}{(\underline{\eta}\cdot\underline{\eta})^{3/2}} \eta_\mu \eta_\nu - \frac{K_2\left(mc\sqrt{\underline{\eta}\cdot\underline{\eta}}\right)}{\underline{\eta}\cdot\underline{\eta}} g_{\mu\nu} \right]. \tag{23}$$

For a simple gas consisting of material particles of proper mass m, the components of the energy–momentum tensor $\underline{\underline{T}}$ are given by

$$T_{\mu\nu} = (\rho + p) u_\mu u_\nu - p g_{\mu\nu}, \tag{24}$$

where ρ is the mean density, p is the pressure, and $\underline{u} = \left(u_\mu = \frac{\mathrm{d}x_\mu}{\mathrm{d}s}\right)$, $\underline{u}\cdot\underline{u} = 1$, is the mean four-velocity of the fluid. Hence, by identification with (23), Synge [12] proved that *a relativistic gas consisting of material particles of proper mass m is a perfect fluid* through the relations:

$$u_\mu = \frac{\eta_\mu}{\sqrt{\underline{\eta}\cdot\underline{\eta}}}, \tag{25}$$

$$\rho + p = C4\pi m^3 c^4 \frac{K_3\left(mc\sqrt{\underline{\eta}\cdot\underline{\eta}}\right)}{\sqrt{\underline{\eta}\cdot\underline{\eta}}}, \tag{26}$$

$$p = C4\pi m^2 c^3 \frac{K_2\left(mc\sqrt{\underline{\eta}\cdot\underline{\eta}}\right)}{\underline{\eta}\cdot\underline{\eta}}. \tag{27}$$

From (26) and (27), we derive the expression of the density:

$$\rho = C\frac{4\pi m^3 c^4}{\sqrt{\underline{\eta}\cdot\underline{\eta}}} \frac{K_1\left(mc\sqrt{\underline{\eta}\cdot\underline{\eta}}\right) + K_3\left(mc\sqrt{\underline{\eta}\cdot\underline{\eta}}\right)}{2} = -C\frac{4\pi m^3 c^4}{\sqrt{\underline{\eta}\cdot\underline{\eta}}} K_2'\left(mc\sqrt{\underline{\eta}\cdot\underline{\eta}}\right). \tag{28}$$

Let us define the invariant quantity, i.e., the projection of the numerical flux (57) along the four-velocity of the fluid,

$$\mathcal{N}_0 = \underline{N}\cdot\underline{u} = C\frac{4\pi m^2 c^2}{\sqrt{\underline{\eta}\cdot\underline{\eta}}} K_2\left(mc\sqrt{\underline{\eta}\cdot\underline{\eta}}\right). \tag{29}$$

This expression, which represents the number of particles per unit length ("numerical density") in the rest frame of the fluid ($u_0 = 1$), allows us to determine the function $C = C(\underline{x})$, and to eventually write Distribution (18) as:

$$\mathcal{N}(\underline{x},\underline{k}) = \frac{\mathcal{N}_0}{m^2 c k_B T_a K_2(mc^2/k_B T_a)} \exp\left(-\frac{c\underline{u}\cdot\underline{k}}{k_B T_a}\right). \tag{30}$$

The term $T_a := c/(k_B\sqrt{\underline{\eta}\cdot\underline{\eta}})$, where k_B is the Boltzmann constant, is a "relativistic" absolute temperature. It is precisely the relativistic invariant, which might fit pointview (**c**).

Note that, with this expression, (27) reads as the usual gas law:

$$p = \mathcal{N}_0 k_B T_a. \tag{31}$$

The Maxwell–Boltzmann non relativistic distribution (in the space of momenta) is recovered by considering the limit at $k_B T_a \ll mc^2$ in the rest frame of the fluid:

$$\begin{aligned} &K_2\left(\frac{mc^2}{k_B T_a}\right) \approx \sqrt{\frac{\pi k_B T_a}{2mc^2}} e^{-\frac{mc^2}{k_B T_a}} \\ &\Rightarrow \mathcal{N}(\underline{x},\underline{k}) \\ &\approx N_0 (2\pi m k_B T_a)^{-3/2} \exp\left(-\frac{k_0 c - mc^2}{k_B T_a}\right) \approx N_0 (2\pi m k_B T_a)^{-3/2} \exp\left(-\frac{\mathbf{k}^2}{2m k_B T_a}\right). \end{aligned} \tag{32}$$

Inverse Temperature Four-Vector

The found distribution (30) on the Minkowskian mass shell for a simple gas consisting of particles of proper mass m leads us to introduce the relativistic thermodynamic, future directed, time-like four-coldness vector $\underline{\beta}$, as the four-version of the reciprocal of the thermodynamic temperature (see also Ref. [2]):

$$\frac{c\underline{u}}{k_B T_a} \equiv \underline{\beta} = (\beta^0 = \beta_0 > 0, \beta^i = -\beta_i) = (\beta_0, \boldsymbol{\beta}), \tag{33}$$

with *absolute coldness* as relativistic invariant,

$$\sqrt{\underline{\beta}\cdot\underline{\beta}} = \frac{c}{k_B T_a} \equiv \beta_a\,. \tag{34}$$

It is precisely the way the component β_0 transforms under a Lorentz boost, $\beta_0' = \gamma(v)(\beta_0 - \mathbf{v}\cdot\boldsymbol{\beta}/c)$, which explains the way the temperature transforms à la de Broglie, $T \mapsto T' = T\gamma^{-1}$. So, in the follow-up, we call Maxwell–Jüttner distribution the following relativistic invariant:

$$\mathcal{N}(\underline{\beta},\underline{k}) = \frac{\mathcal{N}_0}{mcK_1(mc\beta_a)} \exp\left(-\underline{\beta}\cdot\underline{k}\right), \tag{35}$$

where the space-time dependence holds through the coldness four-vector coldness field $\underline{\beta} = \underline{\beta}(\underline{x})$.

4. de Sitter Material

We now turn our attention to the de Sitter (dS) space-time and some important features of a dS covariant quantum field theory.

4.1. de Sitter Geometry

The de Sitter space-time can be viewed as a hyperboloid embedded in a five-dimensiona Minkowski space $\mathbb{M}_{1,4}$ with metric $g_{\alpha\beta}$ =diag$(1,-1,-1,-1,-1)$ (see Figure 3). Of course, one should keep in mind that all choices of one point in the manifold as an origin are physically equivalent, as are the points of the Minkowski space-time $\mathbb{M}_{1,3}$.

$$\mathsf{M}_R \equiv \{x \in \mathbb{R}^5;\ x^2 = g_{\alpha\beta}\, x^\alpha x^\beta = -R^2\}, \quad \alpha,\beta = 0,1,2,3,4, \tag{36}$$

where the pseudo-radius R (or inverse of curvature) is given by $R = \sqrt{\frac{3}{\Lambda}}$ within the cosmological ΛCDM standard model. The de Sitter symmetry group is the group $SO_0(1,4)$ of proper (i.e., det. $= 1$) and orthochronous (to be precised later) transformations of the manifold (36). This group has ten (Killing) generators $K_{\alpha\beta} = x_\alpha \partial_\beta - x_\beta \partial_\alpha$.

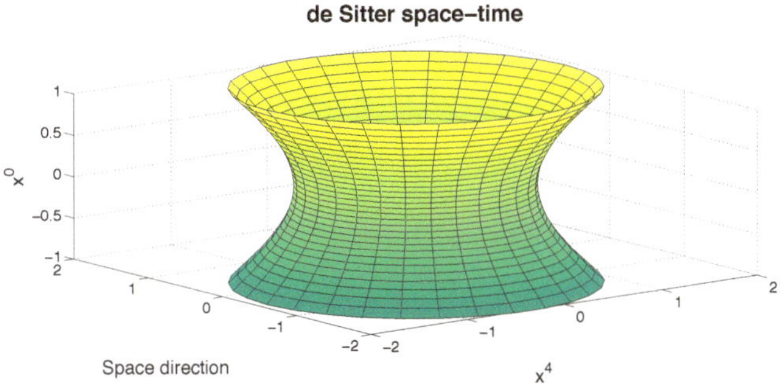

Figure 3. The de Sitter space-time as viewed as a one-sheet hyperboloid embedded in Minkowski space $\mathbb{M}_{1,4}$.

4.2. Flat Minkowskian Limit of de Sitter Geometry

Let us choose the global coordinates $ct \in \mathbb{R}, \mathbf{n} \in \mathbb{S}^2, r/R \in [0,\pi]$ for the dS manifold M_R. They are defined by:

$$\begin{aligned} \mathsf{M}_R \ni x &= (x^0, x^1, x^2, x^3, x^4) \equiv (x^0, \mathbf{x}, x^4) \\ &= (R\sinh(ct/R),\ R\cosh(ct/R)\sin(r/R)\mathbf{n}, R\cosh(ct/R)\cos(r/R)) \equiv x(t, \mathbf{x}). \end{aligned} \tag{37}$$

At the limit $R \to \infty$, and the manifold $\mathsf{M}_R \to \mathbb{M}_{1,3}$, the Minkowski space-time tangent to M_R at, say, the de Sitter point $O_{dS} = (0, \mathbf{0}, R)$, chosen as the origin, since

$$\mathsf{M}_R \ni x \underset{R\to\infty}{\approx} (ct, \mathbf{r} = r\,\mathbf{n}, R) \equiv (\underline{x}, R), \quad \underline{x} \in \mathbb{M}_{1,3}. \tag{38}$$

At this limit, the de Sitter group becomes the Poincaré group:

$$\lim_{R\to\infty} SO_0(1,4) = \mathcal{P}_+^\uparrow(1,3) = \mathbb{M}_{1,3} \rtimes SO_0(1,3). \tag{39}$$

Consistently, the ten de Sitter Killing generators contract (in the Wigner–Inönü sense) to their Poincaré counterparts $K_{\mu\nu}, \Pi_\mu, \mu = 0,1,2,3$, after rescaling the four $K_{4\mu} \longrightarrow \Pi_\mu = K_{4\mu}/R$.

4.3. de Sitter Plane Waves as Binomial Deformations of Minkowskian Plane Waves

The de Sitter (scalar) plane waves are defined in [21] as

$$\phi_{\tau,\xi}(x) = \left(\frac{x\cdot\xi}{R}\right)^\tau, \quad x \in \mathsf{M}_R, \quad \xi \in \mathcal{C}_{1,4}, \tag{40}$$

where $\mathcal{C}_{1,4} = \{\xi \in \mathbb{R}^5, \xi\cdot\xi = 0\}$ is the null cone in $\mathbb{M}_{1,4}$. They are solutions of the Klein–Gordon-like equation

$$\frac{1}{2} M_{\alpha\beta} M^{\alpha\beta} \phi_{\tau,\xi}(x) \equiv R^2 \Box_R \phi_{\tau,\xi}(x) = \tau(\tau+3)\phi_{\tau,\xi}(x),$$

where $M_{\alpha\beta} = -\mathrm{i}(x_\alpha \partial_\beta - x_\beta \partial_\alpha)$ is the quantum representation of the Killing vector $K_{\alpha\beta}$, and $\Box_R$ stands for the d'Alembertian operator on M_R. For the values

$$\tau = -\frac{3}{2} + \mathrm{i}\nu, \quad \nu \in \mathbb{R}, \tag{41}$$

they describe free quantum motions of "massive" scalar particles on M_R. The term "massive" is justified by the flat Minkowskian limit $R \to \infty$, i.e., $\Lambda \to 0$. This limit is understood as follows.

(i) First, one has the Garidi [22] relation between proper mass m (curvature independent) of the spinless particle and the parameter $\nu \geq 0$:

$$m = \frac{\hbar}{Rc}\left[\nu^2 + \frac{1}{4}\right]^{1/2} \Leftrightarrow \nu = \sqrt{\frac{R^2 m^2 c^2}{\hbar^2} - \frac{1}{4}} \underset{R\,\text{large}}{\approx} \frac{Rmc}{\hbar} = \frac{mc}{\hbar}\sqrt{\frac{3}{\Lambda}}. \tag{42}$$

The quantity $\dfrac{\hbar c \nu}{R}$ is a kind of *at rest de Sitterian energy*, which is distinct of the proper mass energy mc^2 if $\Lambda \neq 0$.

(ii) Then, with the mass shell parameterization $\xi = \left(\xi^0 = \frac{k_0}{mc}, \boldsymbol{\xi} = \frac{\mathbf{k}}{mc}, \xi^4 = 1\right) \in \mathcal{C}^+_{1,4}$, one obtains at the limit $R \to \infty$:

$$\phi_{\tau,\xi}(x) = (x \cdot \xi / R)^{-3/2+\mathrm{i}\nu} \underset{R\to\infty}{\to} e^{\mathrm{i}\underline{k}\cdot\underline{\ell}/\hbar}, \quad \underline{\ell} = (ct, \mathbf{r}). \tag{43}$$

This relation allows us to consider Function (40) as deformation of the plane waves propagating in the Minkowskian space-time $\mathbb{M}_{1,4}$. This pivotal property justifies the name "dS plane waves" granted to Function (40).

4.4. Analytic Extension of dS Plane Waves for dS QFT

The dS plane waves $\phi_{\tau,\xi}(x) = \left(\dfrac{x\cdot\xi}{R}\right)^\tau$, $\tau = -3/2 + \mathrm{i}\nu$, are not defined on all M_R, due to the possible change of sign of $x \cdot \xi$. A solution to this drawback is found through the extension to the tubular domains in the complexified hyperboloid $\mathrm{M}_R^{\mathbb{C}} = \{z = x + \mathrm{i}y \in \mathbb{C}^5, \, z^2 = g_{\alpha\beta}\, z^\alpha z^\beta = -R^2$ or, equivalently, $x^2 - y^2 = -R^2, \, x \cdot y = 0\}$:

$$\mathcal{T}^\pm := \mathrm{T}^\pm \cap \mathrm{M}_R^{\mathbb{C}}, \quad \mathrm{T}^\pm := \mathbb{M}_{1,4} + \mathrm{i}\mathrm{V}^\pm, \tag{44}$$

where the forward and backward light cones $\mathrm{V}^\pm := \left\{x \in \mathbb{M}_{1,4}, \, x^0 \gtrless \sqrt{\mathbf{x}^2 + (x^4)^2}\right\}$ allow for a causal ordering in $\mathbb{M}_{1,4}$.

Then, the extended plane waves $\phi_{\tau,\xi}(z) = \left(\dfrac{z\cdot\xi}{R}\right)^\tau$ are globally defined for $z \in \mathcal{T}^\pm$ and $\xi \in \mathcal{C}^+_{1,4}$.

These analytic extensions allow for a consistent QFT for free scalar fields on M_R: the two-point Wightman function $\mathcal{W}_\nu(x,x') = \langle \Omega, \phi(x)\phi(x')\Omega\rangle$ can be extended to the complex covariant, maximally analytic, two-point function having the spectral representation in terms of these extended plane waves:

$$W_\nu(z,z') = c_\nu \int_{\mathcal{V}_m^+ \cup \mathcal{V}_m^-} (z\cdot\xi)^{-3/2+\mathrm{i}\nu} (\xi \cdot z')^{-3/2-\mathrm{i}\nu} \frac{\mathrm{d}\mathbf{k}}{k_0}, \quad z \in \mathcal{T}^-, z' \in \mathcal{T}^+. \tag{45}$$

Details are found in Ref. [21] and in the recent volume [23].

4.5. KMS Interpretation of $W_\nu(z,z')$ Analyticity

From the analyticity of $W_\nu(z,z')$, we deduce that $\mathcal{W}_\nu(x,x')$ defines a $2\mathrm{i}\pi R/c$ periodic analytic function of t, whose domain is the periodic cut plane

$$\mathbb{C}^{\mathrm{cut}}_{x,x'} = \{t \in \mathbb{C}\,,\ \mathrm{Im}(t) \neq 2n\pi R/c\,,\ n \in \mathbb{Z}\} \cup \{t\,,\ t - 2\mathrm{i}n\pi R/c \in I_{x,x'}\,,\ n \in \mathbb{Z}\}\,, \tag{46}$$

where $I_{x,x'}$ is the real interval on which $(x - x')^2 < 0$. Hence, $W_\nu(z,z')$ is analytic in the strip

$$\{t \in \mathbb{C}\,,\ 0 < \mathrm{Im}(t) < 2\mathrm{i}\pi R/c\}\,, \tag{47}$$

and satisfies

$$\mathcal{W}_\nu(x'(t+t',\mathbf{x}),x) = \lim_{\epsilon\to 0^+} W_\nu\big((x, x'(t+t'+2\mathrm{i}\pi R/c - \mathrm{i}\epsilon,\mathbf{x})\big)\,,\quad t' \in \mathbb{R}\,. \tag{48}$$

This is a KMS relation at ($\sim$ Hawking) temperature

$$T_\Lambda = \frac{\hbar c}{2\pi k_B R} := \frac{\hbar c}{2\pi k_B}\sqrt{\frac{\Lambda}{3}}. \tag{49}$$

5. de Sitterian Tsallis Distribution

5.1. Tsallis Entropy and Distribution: A Short Reminder

Given a discrete (resp. continuous) set of probabilities $\{p_i\}$ (resp. continuous $x \mapsto p(x)$) with $\sum_i p_i = 1$ (resp. $\int p(x)\mathrm{d}x = 1$), and a real q, the Tsallis entropy [24] is defined as

$$S_q(p_i) = k\frac{1}{q-1}\left(1 - \sum_i p_i^q\right) \quad \text{resp.} \quad S_q[p] = \frac{1}{q-1}\left(1 - \int (p(x))^q \mathrm{d}x\right). \tag{50}$$

As $q \to 1$, $S_q(p_i) \to S_{\mathrm{BG}}(p) = -k\sum_i p_i \ln p_i$ (Boltzmann–Gibbs). The Tsallis entropy is non additive for two independent systems, A and B, for which $p(A \cup B) = p(A)\,p(B)$, $S_q(A \cup B) = S_q(A) + S_q(B) + (1-q)S_q(A)S_q(B)$. A *Tsallis distribution* is a probability distribution derived from the maximization of the Tsallis entropy under appropriate constraints. The so-called q-exponential Tsallis distribution has the probability density function

$$(2-q)\lambda[1-(1-q)\lambda x]^{1/(1-q)} \equiv (2-q)\lambda e_q(-\lambda x)\,, \tag{51}$$

where $q < 2$ and $\lambda > 0$ (rate) arise from the maximization of the Tsallis entropy under appropriate constraints, including constraining the domain to be positive. More details are given, for instance, in Ref. [25].

Let us now show how the Tsallis distribution can be viewed as a Λ-deformation of the Maxwell–Jüttner distribution.

5.2. Coldness in de Sitter

Analogous with the de Sitter plane waves, we introduce the following distributions on the subset $\sim \mathcal{V}_m^+$ of the null cone $\mathcal{C}^+_{1,4} = \{\xi \in \mathbb{M}_{1,4}\,,\ \xi\cdot\xi = 0\,,\ \xi^0 > 0\}$:

$$\phi_{\tau,\xi}(x) = \left(\frac{\mathfrak{b}\cdot\xi}{B}\right)^\tau\,,\quad \mathfrak{b} \in \mathsf{M}_B\,,\quad \xi = \left(\frac{k^0}{mc} > 0, \frac{\mathbf{k}}{mc}, -1\right), \tag{52}$$

where one should note the negative value -1 for ξ_4, and

$$\mathsf{M}_B \equiv \{\mathfrak{b} \in \mathbb{M}_{1,4}\,,\ \mathfrak{b}^2 = g_{\alpha\beta}\,\mathfrak{b}^\alpha\mathfrak{b}^\beta = -B^2\}, \quad \alpha,\beta = 0,1,2,3,4\,, \tag{53}$$

is the manifold of the "de Sitterian five-vector coldness fields" $\mathfrak{b} = \mathfrak{b}(x)$.

Like for M_R, we use global coordinates on M_B:

$$\beta^0 \in \mathbb{R}\,,\quad \boldsymbol{\beta} = \|\boldsymbol{\beta}\|\mathbf{n} \in \mathbb{R}^3\,,\quad \|\boldsymbol{\beta}\|/B \in [0,\pi]\,, \tag{54}$$

with

$$\begin{aligned} \mathsf{M}_B \ni \mathfrak{b} &\equiv \mathfrak{b}(\underline{\beta}) = (\mathfrak{b}^0, \mathfrak{b}^1, \mathfrak{b}^2, \mathfrak{b}^3, \mathfrak{b}^4) \equiv (\mathfrak{b}^0, \boldsymbol{\mathfrak{b}}, \mathfrak{b}^4) \\ &= \Big(B\sinh(\beta^0/B),\, B\cosh(\beta^0/B)\sin(\|\boldsymbol{\beta}\|/B)\mathbf{n}, -B\cosh(\beta^0/B)\cos(\|\boldsymbol{\beta}\|/B)\Big), \end{aligned} \tag{55}$$

in such a way that at large B we recover the Minkowskian coldness $\underline{\beta}$:

$$\mathsf{M}_B \ni \mathfrak{b} \underset{B\to\infty}{\sim} (\underline{\beta}, B).$$

We now need to connect the de Sitterian coldness scale B with Λ. Inspired by the relativistic invariant $\beta_a = \dfrac{c}{k_B T_a}$ and the KMS temperature $T_\Lambda = \frac{\hbar c}{2\pi k_B}\sqrt{\frac{\Lambda}{3}}$, we write

$$B \propto \frac{2\pi}{\hbar}\sqrt{\frac{3}{\Lambda}}, \quad \text{i.e.,} \quad B = \frac{\mathfrak{n}}{\hbar\sqrt{\Lambda}}, \tag{56}$$

where $\mathfrak{n}$ is a numerical factor. Note that, with the values

$$\Lambda_{\text{current}} = 1.1056 \times 10^{-52}\,\text{m}^{-2}, \quad \hbar = 1.054571817\ldots \times 10^{-34}\,\text{J s},$$

one obtains $B \approx 0.9 \times 10^{60}\,\mathfrak{n}$ SI (inverse of a momentum).

5.3. A de Sitterian Tsallis Distribution

We now consider the distribution on $\mathsf{M}_B \times \mathcal{V}_m^+$ with $B = \frac{\mathfrak{n}}{\hbar\sqrt{\Lambda}}$:

$$\mathcal{N}(\mathfrak{b}, \underline{k}) = C_B\left(\frac{\mathfrak{b}\cdot\xi}{B}\right)^{-mcB} = C_B\left(\frac{\mathfrak{b}^0}{B}\frac{k^0}{mc} - \frac{\boldsymbol{\mathfrak{b}}}{B}\cdot\frac{\mathbf{k}}{mc} + \frac{\mathfrak{b}^4}{B}\right)^{-mcB}. \tag{57}$$

$$\mathfrak{b} \in \mathsf{M}_B, \quad \xi = \left(\frac{k^0}{mc} > 0, \frac{\mathbf{k}}{mc}, -1\right),$$

where the constant C_B involves an associated Legendre function of the First Kind [26].

With the global coordinates (55), and with the constraint $\beta^0/B \in [0, \pi/2)$, the distribution $\mathcal{N}(\mathfrak{b}, \underline{k})$ reads

$$\begin{aligned} &\mathcal{N}(\mathfrak{b}, \underline{k}) \\ &= C_B\left(\cosh(\beta^0/B)\cos(\|\boldsymbol{\beta}\|/B) + \sinh(\beta^0/B)\,\frac{k^0}{mc} - \cosh(\beta^0/B)\sin(\|\boldsymbol{\beta}\|/B)\frac{\mathbf{n}\cdot\mathbf{k}}{mc}\right)^{-mcB} \\ &= C_B \exp\left[-mcB\log\Big(\cosh(\beta^0/B)\cos(\|\boldsymbol{\beta}\|/B)\Big)\right] \\ &\times \exp\left[-mcB\log\left(1 + \frac{\sinh(\beta^0/B)\frac{k^0}{mc} - \cosh(\beta^0/B)\sin(\|\boldsymbol{\beta}\|/B)\frac{\mathbf{n}\cdot\mathbf{k}}{mc}}{\cosh(\beta^0/B)\cos(\|\boldsymbol{\beta}\|/B)}\right)\right]. \end{aligned} \tag{58}$$

At large B this expression becomes the Maxwell–Jüttner distribution:

$$\mathcal{N}(\mathfrak{b}, \underline{k}) \underset{B\to\infty}{\sim} C_B e^{-\underline{\beta}\cdot\underline{k}}.$$

Hence, going back to the original expression

$$\begin{aligned} \mathcal{N}(\mathfrak{b}, \underline{k}) &= C_B\left(\frac{\mathfrak{b}\cdot\xi}{B}\right)^{-mcB} = C_B\left(\frac{\mathfrak{b}^0}{B}\frac{k^0}{mc} - \frac{\boldsymbol{\mathfrak{b}}}{B}\cdot\frac{\mathbf{k}}{mc} + \frac{\mathfrak{b}^4}{B}\right)^{-mcB} \\ &= C_B\left(\frac{\mathfrak{b}^4}{B}\right)^{-mcB}\left(1 + \frac{\underline{\mathfrak{b}}\cdot\underline{k}}{\mathfrak{b}^4 mc}\right)^{-mcB}, \quad \underline{\mathfrak{b}} := (\mathfrak{b}^0, \boldsymbol{\mathfrak{b}}), \end{aligned}$$

and introducing

$$q = 1 + \frac{1}{mcB} = 1 + \frac{\hbar\sqrt{\Lambda}}{mc\mathfrak{n}}, \tag{59}$$

We finally obtain the Tsallis-type distribution

$$\mathcal{N}(\mathfrak{b}, \underline{k}) = C_B \left(\frac{\mathfrak{b}^4}{B}\right)^{-mcB} \left(1 - (1-q)\frac{B}{\mathfrak{b}^4}\,\underline{\mathfrak{b}} \cdot \underline{k}\right)^{\frac{1}{1-q}}. \tag{60}$$

Analogously to (21) and all subsequent determinations of thermodynamical quantities, the following partition function is essential for their transcriptions to the de Sitter case:

$$Z_{\mathrm{dS}}(\mathfrak{b}, \underline{k}) = \left(\frac{\mathfrak{b}^4}{B}\right)^{-mcB} \int_{\mathcal{V}_m^+} \left(1 + \frac{\underline{\mathfrak{b}} \cdot \underline{k}}{\mathfrak{b}^4 mc}\right)^{-mcB} \frac{\mathrm{d}^3\mathbf{k}}{k_0} \tag{61}$$

$$= 4\pi m^2 c^2 \left(\frac{\mathfrak{b}^4}{B}\right)^{-mcB} \int_0^\infty \left(1 + \left(\frac{\mathfrak{b}_0}{\mathfrak{b}^4}\right)\cosh t\right)^{-mcB} \sinh^2 t\, \mathrm{d}t. \tag{62}$$

With the following integral representation of the associated Legendre function of the First Kind $P_\nu^\mu(z)$ [26],

$$P_\nu^\mu(z) = \frac{2^{-\nu}(z^2-1)^{-\mu/2}}{\Gamma(-\nu-\mu)\Gamma(\nu+1)} \int_0^\infty (z + \cosh t)^{-\nu-\mu-1} \sinh^{2\nu+1} t\, \mathrm{d}t, \tag{63}$$

valid for $z \notin (-\infty, -1]$ and $\mathrm{Re}(-\mu) > \mathrm{Re}(\nu) > -1$, the function (61) reads as

$$Z_{\mathrm{dS}}(\mathfrak{b}, \underline{k}) = (8\pi)^{3/2}\Gamma(1 - mcB)\left(\frac{B}{\mathfrak{b}_0}\right)^{mcB} \left(\frac{B^2 - \mathbf{b}\cdot\mathbf{b}}{\mathfrak{b}_0^2}\right)^{mcB/2-3/4} P_{1/2}^{mcB-3/2}\left(\frac{\mathfrak{b}^4}{\mathfrak{b}_0}\right). \tag{64}$$

6. Conclusions

In this contribution, we have forged a groundbreaking link between the Tsallis distribution, quantum statistics, and the cosmological constant, illuminating the complex interplay between relativistic thermodynamics and a fundamental cosmological parameter.

Our key findings are encapsulated in Equations (59) and (60). The intricate technical details of the associated thermodynamic features (flux number, energy-momentum tensor, etc.) in the de Sitter space-time, along with their physical (and astrophysical!) implications and determinations (e.g., numerical factor(s) $\mathfrak{n}$), are reserved for future exploration. In this endeavor, analogous studies, such as those found in Refs. [27,28], may provide useful insights and avenues for the advancement of this project.

Funding: This research received no external funding.

Institutional Review Board Statement: Not applicable.

Data Availability Statement: Data are contained within the article.

Conflicts of Interest: The author declares no conflicts of interest.

References

1. de Broglie, L. Sur la variance relativiste de la température. *Cah. Phys.* **1948**, *31*, 1–11.
2. Wu, Z.C. Inverse Temperature 4-vector in Special Relativity. *Eur. Phys. Lett.* **2009**, *88*, 20005. [CrossRef]
3. Einstein, A. Ueber das Relativitaetsprinzip und die aus demselben gezogenen Folgerungen. *Jahrb. Rad. Elektr.* **1907**, *4*, 411.
4. Planck, M. Zur Dynamik bewegter Systeme. *Ann. Phys.* **1908**, *26*, 1–35. [CrossRef]
5. Ott, H. Lorentz-Transformation der Wärme und der Temperatur. *Zeitschr. Phys.* **1963**, *175*, 70–104. [CrossRef]
6. Arzeliès, H. Transformation relativiste de la température et de quelques autres grandeurs thermodynamiques. *Nuov. Cim.* **1965**, *35*, 792–804. [CrossRef]
7. Landsberg, P.T. Does a Moving Body Appear Cool? *Nature* **1966**, *212*, 571–572. [CrossRef]
8. Landsberg, P.T. Does a Moving Body Appear Cool? *Nature* **1967**, *214*, 903–904. [CrossRef]

9. Landsberg, P.T.; Matsas, G.E.A. Laying the ghost of the relativistic temperature transformation. *Phys. Lett. A* **1996**, *223*, 401–403. [CrossRef]
10. Sewell, G.L. On the question of temperature transformations under Lorentz and Galilei boosts. *J. Phys. A Math. Theor.* **2008**, *41*, 382003. [CrossRef]
11. Bíró, T.S.; Ván, P. About the temperature of moving bodies. *EPL* **2010**, *89*, 30001. [CrossRef]
12. Synge, J.L. *The Relativistic Gas*; North-Holland Publishing Company: Amsterdam, The Netherlands, 1957.
13. Jüttner, F. Das maxwellsche gesetz der geschwindigkeitsverteilung in der relativtheorie. *Ann. Phys.* **1911**, *339*, 856–882. [CrossRef]
14. van Dantzig, D. On the phenomenological thermodynamics of moving matter. *Physica* **1939**, *6*, 673–704. [CrossRef]
15. Taub, A.H. Relativistic Ranirine-Hugoniot Equations. *Phys. Rev.* **1948**, *74*, 328–334. [CrossRef]
16. Gazeau, J.-P.; Graffi, S. Quantum Harmonic Oscillator: A Relativistic and Statistical Point of View. *Boll. Della Unione Mat. Ital. A* **1997**, *3*, 815–839.
17. Chacón-Acosta, G.; Dagdug Hugo, L.; Morales-Técotl, A. Manifestly covariant Jüttner distribution and equipartition theorem. *Phys. Rev. E* **2010**, *81*, 021126. [CrossRef] [PubMed]
18. Curado, E.M.F.; Cedeño, C.E.; Soares, I.D.; Tsallis, C. Relativistic gas: Lorentz-invariant distribution for the velocities. *Chaos* **2022**, *32*, 103110. [CrossRef]
19. Landau, L.D.; Lifshitz, E.M. *The Classical Theory of Fields*, 4th ed.; Butterworth-Heinemann: Oxford, UK, 1980; Volume 2.
20. Magnus, W.; Oberhettinger, F.; Soni, R.P. *Formulas and Theorems for the Special Functions of Mathematical Physics*, 3rd ed.; Springer: Berlin/Heidelberg, Germany, 1966.
21. Bros, J.; Gazeau, J.-P.; Moschella, U. Quantum Field Theory in the de Sitter Universe. *Phys. Rev. Lett.* **1994**, *73*, 1746–1749. [CrossRef] [PubMed]
22. Garidi, T. What is mass in desitterian physics? *arXiv* **2003**, arXiv:hep-th/0309104.
23. Enayati, M.; Gazeau, J.-P.; Pejhan, H.; Wang, A. *The de Sitter (dS) Group and Its Representations, an Introduction to Elementary Systems and Modeling the Dark Energy Universe*; Springer: Berlin/Heidelberg, Germany, 2022.
24. Tsallis, C. Possible generalization of Boltzmann-Gibbs statistics. *J. Stat. Phys.* **1988**, *52*, 479–487. [CrossRef]
25. Tsallis, C. Nonadditive entropy and nonextensive statistical mechanics-an overview after 20 years. *Braz. J. Phys.* **2009**, *39*, 337–356. [CrossRef]
26. Abramowitz, M.; Stegun, I.A. *Handbook of Mathematical Functions with Formulas, Graphs, and Mathematical Tables*; National Bureau of Standards: Gaithersburg, MD, USA, 1964.
27. Bíró, T.S. Gyulassy, M.; Schram, Z. Unruh gamma radiation at RHIC. *Phys. Lett. B* **2012**, *708*, 276–279. [CrossRef]
28. Bíró, T.S.; Czinner,V.G. A q-parameter bound for particle spectra based on black hole thermodynamics with Rényi entropy. *Phys. Lett. B* **2013**, *726*, 861–865. [CrossRef]

entropy MDPI

Article

Group Structure as a Foundation for Entropies

Henrik Jeldtoft Jensen [1,2,*] and Piergiulio Tempesta [3,4]

1 Centre for Complexity Science and Department of Mathematics, Imperial College London, South Kensington Campus, London SW7 2AZ, UK
2 Department of Computer Science, School of Computing, Tokyo Institute of Technology, 4259, Nagatsuta-cho, Yokohama 226-8502, Japan
3 Departamento de Fisica Teórica, Universidad Complutense de Madrid, 28040 Madrid, Spain; p.tempesta@fis.ucm.es
4 Instituto de Ciencias Matemáticas (ICMAT), 28049 Madrid, Spain
* Correspondence: h.jensen@imperial.ac.uk

Abstract: Entropy can signify different things. For instance, heat transfer in thermodynamics or a measure of information in data analysis. Many entropies have been introduced, and it can be difficult to ascertain their respective importance and merits. Here, we consider entropy in an abstract sense, as a functional on a probability space, and we review how being able to handle the trivial case of non-interacting systems, together with the subtle requirement of extensivity, allows for a systematic classification of the functional form.

Keywords: entropy; composability; extensivity; information theory; power laws; group theory

Citation: Jensen, H.J.; Tempesta, P. Group Structure as a Foundation for Entropies. *Entropy* **2024**, *26*, 266. https://doi.org/10.3390/e26030266

Academic Editors: Antony N. Beris and Wolfgang Muschik

Received: 24 January 2024
Revised: 6 March 2024
Accepted: 15 March 2024
Published: 18 March 2024

1. Introduction

The term "entropy" is used extensively in the modern scientific literature. Originating in the 19th-century theory of thermal dynamics [1], the concept is now, to a near bewildering extent, used widely in one form or another across many sciences. For example, entropy is at the foundation of information theory [2] and is of crucial use in computer science [3,4]. Also, neurosciences make use of entropy both as a tool to characterize and interpret data from brain scans [5] and, more fundamentally, in theories of the dynamics of the brain and mind [6]. Generally speaking, entropy is a fundamental notion in complexity science [7]. Here, we present a brief review of some recent mathematical developments in the theory of entropy.

In mathematical terms, an entropy is a functional $S[p]$ defined on a space of probability distributions $p = (p_1, p_2, \ldots, p_W)$ associated with a W-dimensional event space. Thus, we use the word "entropy" with the same meaning it assumes, for instance, in the case of Rényi's entropy, without direct reference to thermodynamics. From this perspective, the relevance of entropies is clear. They can be considered as analytic tools that can help in the analysis of the inter-dependencies within the system behind a given event space. Similarly, their use in information-theoretic analysis of time series is likewise natural. The connection between entropies as mathematical functionals and the thermodynamic entropy of Clausius defined in terms of heat transfer is much less immediate. Here, we will concentrate on the mathematical aspects of entropies as functionals and only make a few comments on the possible connection to thermodynamics.

The first question to tackle is which functional form of $S[p]$ yields useful entropies. i.e., how to limit the infinite number of choices for $S[p]$. It is well known that the Boltzmann–Gibbs–Shannon form

$$S_{\mathrm{BGS}}[p] = \sum_{i=1}^{W} p_i \log \frac{1}{p_i} \tag{1}$$

(we assume $k_B = 1$) is the unique possibility if one assumes that the entropy must satisfy the four Shannon–Kinchin (SK) axioms [8]:

(SK1) (Continuity). The function $S(p_1,\ldots,p_W)$ is continuous with respect to all its arguments.
(SK2) (Maximum principle). The function $S(p_1,\ldots,p_W)$ takes its maximum value over the uniform distribution $p_i = 1/W, i = 1,\ldots,W$.
(SK3) (Expansibility). Adding an event of zero probability to a probability distribution does not change its entropy: $S(p_1,\ldots,p_W,0) = S(p_1,\ldots,p_W)$.
(SK4) (Additivity). Given two subsystems A, B of a statistical system, $S(A \cup B) = S(A) + S(B|A)$.

Therefore, to derive entropies of a functional form different from the one in Equation (1), it is necessary to go beyond the four SK axioms. Various strategies in this respect have been adopted in the literature.

Let us start by recalling Constantino Tsallis's elegant observation [9] that the formula

$$S_q[p] = k\frac{1-\sum_{i=1}^{W} p_i^q}{q-1}, \quad p = (p_1, p_2, \ldots, p_W) \in [0,1]^W, \quad k \in \mathbb{R}_+ \tag{2}$$

provides a possible generalization of Boltzmann's entropy. This is the case in the sense that S_q is a functional on the space of probability distributions $p : \{1,2,\ldots,W\} \mapsto [0,1]^W$, and in the limit $q \to 1$, the entropy $S_q[p]$ becomes equal to the Boltzmann–Gibbs–Shannon entropy in Equation (1). Tsallis's 1988 article [9] has inspired a tremendous effort to generalize Boltzmann's entropy in different scenarios, including what we will review in this paper. Tsallis pointed out that the entropy S_q fulfills a specific procedure for combining independent systems which can be seen as a generalization of the additivity property (SK4) of the Boltzmann–Gibbs–Shannon entropy. In particular, Tsallis suggested that the free parameter q should be determined by requiring that S_q for a given system is extensive (for a recent reference to Tsallis's argument, see [10]), i.e., that in the uniform case where the probabilities are $p_i = 1/W$ for all $i = 1,2,\ldots,W$, the entropy $S_q \propto N$ for $n \to \infty$, where N denotes the number of components in the system under analysis. For clarity, we note that when considering physical systems, the entropy may become volume-dependent; for example, because the number of states available, W, depends on the volume. Volume dependence can also enter through the probabilities p_i^* determined by the maximum entropy principle.

Although the Tsallis entropy does not fulfill axiom SK4 in its original form and hence is *non-additive*, it does satisfy a composition relation different from addition.

Another set of non-Boltzmann–Gibbs–Shannon entropies was derived by Hanel and Thurner [11] by simply discarding axiom SK4 and then determining the functional form from the asymptotic behavior of the number of events, or states, W, as a function of the number of components in the system. However, in this approach, there is no systematic rule for handling the computation of the entropy of a system consisting of independent parts.

It is well known that in physics, the investigation of required symmetries has often been helpful. Think of Einstein's use of the symmetry between different reference frames to derive special and general relativity theory. Consider also the eightfold way and the derivation of QCD. Additionally, consider the application of symmetry and group theory to atomic spectra. Therefore, it seems natural to, rather than discarding the fourth SK axiom, replace it in a way informed by the symmetry properties (and related group-theoretic restrictions) that an entropy must necessarily satisfy. Consequently, the question is, which symmetry cannot be ignored when dealing with entropies?

The fourth SK axiom addresses how the entropy of a system AB, consisting of two independent parts A and B, can be expressed as a sum of the entropy of A and the entropy of B. Tsallis entropy also allows the entropy of AB to be expressed in terms of the entropy of the two parts, not as a sum but as a generalized combination of the entropies of the parts.

The notion of group entropy, introduced in [12,13], goes one step further and exploits the idea that the process of combining two independent systems can be seen as a group operation. The group entropies satisfy the three first SK axioms, as well as a fourth one, which consists of a generalized composition procedure making use of formal group theory [14,15].

This approach leads to axiomatically defined entropies, whose composition rule is defined in terms of the generator $G(t)$ of a suitable formal group law, namely

$$S[p] = \frac{G\left(\ln \sum_{i=1}^{W} p_i^{\alpha}\right)}{1-\alpha} \quad \text{with } \alpha > 0 \text{ and } \alpha \neq 1. \tag{3}$$

Although this restricts the allowed functional forms available for an entropy, it does not uniquely determine the entropy as the four SK axioms do. Below, we will discuss how the analysis of combining independent systems using formal group theory, together with requiring extensivity, allows for a systematic classification of entropies in "universality classes". These classes are defined by taking into account how fast the number of available states W grows with the number of components N. We accomplish this by starting with a more general functional non-trace form than the one given in Equation (2). For details, see [12].

By generalizing the Tsallis functional form and requiring composability together with extensivity, we are able to regard Tsallis entropy as the composable entropy associated with systems where interdependence between their components forces W to grow slowly, namely as a power of N. Below, we will discuss why composability on the entire probability space is an indispensable property of an entropy. We will also address the need for extensivity in a general sense. We will point out that extensivity can be very relevant even beyond the thermodynamic need for a well-defined limit as the number of components approaches infinity. For example, extensivity is essential for using an entropy as a measure of the complexity of a time series or for handling power-law probability distributions.

2. Why Composability

The need for composability does not arise because real systems can always be regarded as a simple combination of subsystems. The requirement is, in a sense, a logical necessity [16]. When we consider two independent systems with state spaces A and B, we should obtain the same result if we compute the entropy of the Cartesian combined system $A \times B$ as if we first compute the entropy of A and B separately and then afterward decide to consider them as one combined system. By Cartesian combination, we mean that the system $A \times B$ is given by the set of states $\{(a,b)|a \in A, b \in B\}$, with the probabilities for the individual states given by $p(a,b) = p(a)p(b)$. This Cartesian combination immediately suggests familiar properties from group theory. The composition is as follows:

Commutative: Since we have state spaces in mind, we consider $A \times B = B \times A$. The ordering is immaterial.

Associative: $A \times (B \times C) = (A \times B) \times C$.

"Neutral" element: $A \times B \sim A$ if $B = \{b\}$. In other words, $A \times B$ is essentially the same set as A if B consists of one element only. In terms of state spaces, all sets with one state only are considered to be identical, that is, indistinguishable. In this sense, a unique "neutral" element exists in our composition process. Accordingly, we want the entropy of a probability distribution on a set containing a single element to be zero: indeed, it would correspond to a certainty configuration. Moreover, we want the entropy of $A \times B$ to be equal to the entropy of A if the entropy of B is zero.

The group structure of the Cartesian combination of the event spaces for systems must also be satisfied by the entropy functional operating on the corresponding probability spaces. This can be ensured by employing formal group theory [16]. Define the entropy using the expression in Equation (3), where the function $G(t) = t + \sum_{k=2}^{\infty} \beta_k t^k$ is the "group generator". Here, the formal power series G(t) is said to be the group exponential in the formal group literature [15]. The combination of independent systems is now expressed as

$$S(A \times B) = \phi(S(A), S(B)), \tag{4}$$

where the function $\phi(x,y)$ is given by $\phi(x,y) = G(G^{-1}(x) + G^{-1}(y))$. Given a formal group law, namely when $\phi(x,y)$ is a formal power series in two variables, it is possible to prove that there exists a one-variable formal power series $\psi(x)$ such that $\phi(x,\psi(x)) = 0$. This series represents the formal inverse and completes the group structure.

3. Why Extensivity

Let us first recall the definitions of extensivity and additivity. We say that an entropy is extensive if the entropy per component is finite in the limit of infinitely many components, i.e.,

$$\lim_{N\to\infty} S(N)/N = \text{constant} < \infty \tag{5}$$

An entropy is additive if, for two statistically independent systems A and B, the entropy of the two systems considered as a combined system is equal to the sum of the entropies, i.e.,

$$S(A+B) = S(A) + S(B). \tag{6}$$

When considering the thermodynamics of macroscopic systems with the number of constituents, N, of the order of Avogadro's number, the usual procedure is to compute quantities such as the thermodynamic free energy F for an arbitrary value of N. The limit of large, essentially infinite systems is then handled by considering intensive quantities, e.g., the free energy per constituent. Hence, for an entropy to be thermodynamically useful, it needs to be extensive, given the fundamental thermodynamic relation $F = E - TS$. Since the temperature T is an intensive quantity, the entropy must be extensive. Thus, we need the limit $\lim_{N\to\infty} S(N)/N$ to be well defined.

Outside thermodynamics, entropy finds a significant application within information theory as a tool to characterize the complexity of a deterministic or random process generating a time series. More precisely, we can associate with a time series an ordinal representation formed by all ordinal patterns of length $L \in \mathbb{N}$ assigned [17]. Assuming that all different patterns are allowed for a process, we have $W(L) = L!$, and each pattern i will occur with a probability of $p_i = 1/L!$. The Boltzmann–Gibbs–Shannon entropy in Equation (1) is given by $S_{\text{Shan}}[p] = \ln L! \simeq L\ln L - L$. So, we obtain a diverging entropy rate $S[p]/L$ as the length of the time series increases. As we will see, this is a common situation since random processes exhibit super-exponential growth in the number of permitted patterns. Again, extensivity enters into play. Thus, we would need an entropy that grows proportionally to the number of allowed patterns in the considered time series.

The widespread occurrence of power-law probability distributions in nature, either exact or approximate, has long been the focus of self-organized criticality (for an overview, see [18,19]). It is now clear that power-law distributions with fat tails are common, and for this reason, it seems natural to consider the extent to which the workhorse of information theory, the Shannon entropy, can be used as a meaningful entropic measure for such distributions.

Consider a probability distribution of the following form:

$$P_S(s) = \frac{A}{s^a} \quad \text{for} \quad s = 1, 2, \ldots, s(N)_{\text{max}}. \tag{7}$$

Here, A is a normalization factor and a is a positive exponent. The variable s denotes the "size" of some process, e.g., an avalanche or a structure such as a spatial cluster. When $s(N)_{\text{max}}$ grows with N, the usual Boltzmann–Gibbs–Shannon entropy will, in general, not allow a well-defined limit $S[P_S](N)/N$ as $N \to \infty$.

4. The Structure of the Group Entropies

Here, we explain why the expression in Equation (3) is a good starting point for deriving generalized entropies. First, we address why we choose the argument of the generating function $G(t)$ to be $\ln\sum_i p_i^\alpha$. We also comment on the so-called trace form of the group entropies given by

$$S[p] = \sum_{i=1}^{W} p_i G(\ln \frac{1}{p_i}). \quad (8)$$

Finally, we briefly recapitulate how the functional form of $G(t)$ is determined by reference to formal group theory and the requirement that $S[p]$ is extensive on the uniform (also denoted as the microcanonical) ensemble, given by

$$p_i = \frac{1}{W(N)}, \quad \text{for } i = 1, 2 \ldots, W(N). \quad (9)$$

The structure of Equation (3) is used as the starting point because $G(t)$ being a group generator ensures composability for all distributions p_i, not only the uniform distributions. And, taking the argument to be $\ln\sum_i p_i^\alpha$ enables this functional form to generate a range of well-known entropies, including Boltzmann–Gibbs–Shannon, Rényi, and Tsallis [12]. More specifically, if one chooses

$$G(t) = \frac{e^{at} - e^{bt}}{(a-b)(\alpha - \beta)} \quad (10)$$

one recovers the Boltzmann–Gibbs–Shannon entropy in the limit $\alpha \to 1$; Rényi's entropy in the double limit $a \to 0, b \to 0$; and Tsallis's entropy in the double limit $a \to 1, b \to 0$.

4.1. *Extensivity and the Group Law $G(T)$*

Let us now briefly describe how the requirement of extensivity determines the group law $G(t)$ in Equation (3). Details can be found in [20,21]. For a given dependence of the number of available states $W(N)$, we want to ensure that the entropy given in Equation (3) is extensive, i.e., that on the uniform ensemble $p_i = 1/W(N)$ for $i = 1, \ldots, W(N)$ we have $\lim_{N\to\infty} S[p]/N = \text{constant}$.

We can express this as

$$S\left(p_i = \frac{1}{W}\right) = \lambda N. \quad (11)$$

Asymptotically, we have

$$S\left(\frac{1}{W}\right) = \frac{G(\ln(W^{1-\alpha})}{1-\alpha} \approx \lambda N. \quad (12)$$

Then, we invert the relation between S and G, which, by Equation (12), amounts to inverting the relation between G and N. For $G(t)$ to generate a group law, we must require $G(0) = 0$ [12,16], so we adjust the expression for $G(t)$ accordingly and conclude that

$$G(t) = \lambda(1-\alpha)\{W^{-1}[\exp(\frac{t}{1-\alpha})] - W^{-1}(1)\}. \quad (13)$$

Hence, given the asymptotic behavior of $W(N)$, we derive different corresponding entropies. In the expressions below, $\lambda \in \mathbb{R}_+$, $\alpha > 0$, and $\alpha \neq 1$ are free parameters.

Non-trace-form case:

(I) Algebraic, $W(N) = N^a$

$$S[p] = \lambda\left\{\exp\left[\frac{\ln(\sum_{i=1}^{W(N)} p_i^\alpha)}{a(1-\alpha)}\right] - 1\right\}. \quad (14)$$

(II) Exponential, $W(N) = k^N$

$$S[p] = \frac{\lambda}{\ln k}\frac{\ln(\sum_{i=1}^{W(N)} p_i^\alpha)}{1-\alpha}. \quad (15)$$

This is, of course, the Rényi entropy.

(III) Super-exponential, $W(N) = N^{\gamma N}$

$$S[p] = \lambda \left\{ \exp\left[L\left(\frac{\ln \sum_{i=1}^{W(N)} p_i^{\alpha}}{\gamma(1-\alpha)} \right) \right] - 1 \right\}. \tag{16}$$

This entropy was recently studied in relation to a simple model in which the components can form emergent paired states in addition to the combination of single-particle states [22].

So far, we have only considered the so-called non-trace form of the group entropies given in Equation (3). A set of entropies can be constructed in the same manner, starting with the trace-form ansatz in Equation (8).

4.2. Trace-Form Group Entropies

It is interesting to observe that the ansatz in Equation (8) directly leads to either the Boltzmann, the Tsallis, or an entirely new entropy, depending on the asymptotic behavior of $W(N)$. By applying the procedure described in Section 4.1, we obtain the following three classes corresponding to the ones considered for the non-trace case.
Trace-form case:

(I) Algebraic, $W(N) = N^a$

$$S[p] = \lambda \sum_{i=1}^{W(N)} p_i \left[\left(\tfrac{1}{p_i}\right)^{\frac{1}{a}} - 1 \right] \tag{17}$$

$$= \tfrac{1}{q-1}\left(1 - \sum_{i=1}^{W(N)} p_i^q\right). \tag{18}$$

To emphasize the relation with the Tsallis q-entropy, we have introduced $q = 1 - 1/a$ and $\lambda = 1/(1-q)$. Note that the parameter q is determined by the exponent a, so it is controlled entirely by $W(N)$.

(II) Exponential, $W(N) = k^N, k > 0$

$$S[p] = \frac{\lambda}{\ln k} \sum_{i=1}^{W(N)} p_i \ln \frac{1}{p_i}. \tag{19}$$

This is the Boltzmann–Gibbs–Shannon entropy.

(III) Super-exponential, $W(N) = N^{\gamma N}, \gamma > 0$

$$S[p] = \lambda \sum_{i=1}^{W(N)} p_i \left\{ \exp\left[L\left(-\frac{\ln p_i}{\gamma}\right) \right] - 1 \right\}. \tag{20}$$

4.3. Examples of Systems and Corresponding Group Entropies

To illustrate the classification of group entropies based on the asymptotic behavior of $W(N)$, we consider three Ising-type models:

(a) The Ising model on a random network [11].
(b) The usual Ising model, for example, with nearest-neighbor interaction on a hypercubical lattice.
(c) The so-called pairing model in which Ising spins can form paired states [22].

Let E denote the total energy of the system. We are interested in the asymptotic behavior of the number of possible states for the three models as a function of N for fixed energy per component $\epsilon = E/N$. First, consider (a). As explained in [11], $W(N) \sim N^a$ when the fraction of interaction links, the connectance, in the considered network, is kept constant as the number of nodes N is increased. The exponent a is given by the ratio between the energy density and the connectance. The entropy corresponding to this functional form of $W(N)$ is, for all values of the exponent a, given by the Tsallis entropy [21].

The entropy corresponding to the standard Ising model (case (b)) with $W(N) = 2^N$ is the Boltzmann–Gibbs–Shannon entropy. The pairing version of the Ising model (case (c)) admits a super-exponential growth in the number of states $W(N) \sim N^{\gamma N}$, leading us to a new functional form of the entropy [22]

$$S_{\gamma,\alpha}[p] = \exp\left[L\left(\frac{\ln \sum_{i=1}^{W} p_i^{\alpha}}{\gamma(1-\alpha)}\right)\right] - 1. \tag{21}$$

5. Group Entropies and the Ubiquity of the Q-Exponential Distribution

It is well known that the q-exponential form relating to the Tsallis q-entropy provides a very good fit to an impressively broad range of data sets (see, e.g., [10]). This may, at first, appear puzzling given that we saw in Section 4.1 that the Tsallis entropy corresponds to one of the three classes considered here, namely systems with strong interdependence between the components that $W(N) \sim N^a$. The reason that the q-exponential appears to be much more pervasive than one would expect, given that the q-entropy is restricted to the case $W(N) \sim N^a$, may be due to the following.

Consider the maximum entropy principle. For all the classes of entropies considered in Section 4, the probability distribution that maximizes the entropy is a q-exponential. The probability distribution for the specific case of $W(N) \sim k^N$ is the usual exponential Boltzmann distribution. But since the Boltzmann distribution is the limiting case of the q-exponential for $q \to 1$, we can say that, independently of the asymptotic behavior of $W(N)$, the maximum entropy principle always leads to q-exponential distributions [21].

How can this be? The reason is the functional form of the argument

$$x \equiv \ln \sum_{i=1}^{N} p_i^{\alpha}$$

of the ansatz in Equation (3). When one applies Lagrange multipliers and extremizes the entropy in Equation (3), the q-exponential functional form will arise from the derivative $\partial x / \partial p_i$. The remaining factors in the expression for the derivative of $S[p]$ will depend on the functional form of the group law $G(t)$ but will formally just be a constant if evaluated on the maximizing distribution p^* and do not depend explicitly on p_i.

6. An Entropic Measure of Complexity

Fully interacting complex systems possess a number of microstates $W(N)$ that may be different from the Cartesian exponential case $W(N) = \Pi_{i=1}^{N} k_i$, where k_i is the number of states available to component number i in isolation. When interactions freeze out states, $W(N)$ can grow slower than exponentially with increasing N. In contrast, when interactions allow for the creation of new states from the combination of components, $W(N)$ can grow faster than exponentially. As an example, think of hydrogen atoms that form hydrogen molecules $H + H \to H_2$. The states of H_2 are not just the Cartesian product of free single hydrogen atomic states.

The possible difference between the cardinality of the state space of the fully interacting system and the state space formed as a Cartesian product of the states available to the individual components can be used to construct a new measure of the degree of emergent interdependence among the components of a complex system. We can think of this as a quantitative measure of the degree of complexity in a given system. We imagine the entire system AB to be divided into two parts, A and B, and compare the entropy of the system $A \times B$, obtained by combining the micro-sates of the two parts as a Cartesian product, with the system AB, obtained by allowing full interaction between the components of A and those of B. We denote by AB this fully interacting system. The complexity measure is given by [20]

$$\Delta(AB) = S(A \times B) - S(AB) = \phi(S(A), S(B)) - S(AB). \tag{22}$$

From the dependence of $\Delta(AB)$ on the number of components in the separate systems A and B, one can, in principle, determine the kind of emergence generated by the interactions in a specific complex system. In [20], we conjectured that the number of available states for the brain grows faster than exponentially in the number of brain regions involved. It might, at first, appear impossible to check this conjecture. However, experiments like those conducted on rat brain tissue, such as the famous avalanche experiment by Beggs and Plentz [23], seem to open up the possibility for a study of $\Delta(AB)$ as a function of tissue size. We imagine it would be possible to study a piece of tissue of size N and one of size $2N$, allowing, at least in principle, to determine how $\Delta(AB)$ behaves for such a neuronal system. A different, although related, notion of complexity, the defect entropy, was proposed in [24].

7. Group Entropy Theory and Data Analysis

The theory of group entropies has recently proved to be relevant in data analysis. One important reason for this relevance is extensivity. When the number of patterns that may occur in a given time sequence depends, in a non-exponential way, on the length L of the sequence, the Shannon-based entropy of the sequence $S(L)$ will not permit a well-defined entropy rate $S(L)/L$ because the Shannon entropy will not be extensive in L. This may, for example, pose a problem for the widely used Lempel–Ziv [25] complexity measure. This is similar to the discussion above concerning how the Boltzmann-Gibbs-Shannon entropy fails to be extensive on state spaces that grow non-exponential in the number of constituents. We will see below that time series very often contain a number of patterns that grow super-exponentially in the length of the sequence.

To discuss this fundamental application of group entropies, we start with a brief review of the ordinal analysis of time-series data. We follow the discussion and notations in [17,26,27]. Consider the time series

$$(x_t)_{t\geq 0} = x_0, x_1, \ldots, x_t, \ldots$$

where t represents a discrete time and $x_t \in \mathbb{R}$. Let $L \geq 2$. We introduce the sequence of length L (or L-sequence)

$$x_t^L := x_t, x_{t+1}, \ldots, x_{t+L-1}$$

Let $\rho_0, \rho_1, \ldots, \rho_{L-1}$ be the permutation of $0, 1, \ldots, L-1$ such that

$$x_{t+\rho_0} < x_{t+\rho_1} < \ldots < x_{t+\rho_{L-1}} \,. \tag{23}$$

We denote the rank vector of the sequence x_t^L as follows:

$$\mathbf{r}_t := (\rho_0, \rho_1, \ldots, \rho_{L-1}), \tag{24}$$

The rank vectors

$\mathbf{r}_t$ are called *ordinal patterns* of length L (or L-ordinal patterns). The sequence x_t^L is said to be "of type" $\mathbf{r}_t$. In this way, given the original time series $(x_t)_{t\geq 0}$, we have constructed an *ordinal representation* associated with it: the family of all ordinal patterns $(\mathbf{r}_t)_{t\geq 0}$ of length L.

We denote by S_L the group of the $L!$ permutations of $0, 1, \ldots, L-1$, which represents the set of symbols (also called "alphabet") of the ordinal representation.

In the following, we consider discrete-time stationary processes $X = (X_t)_{t\geq 0}$, both deterministic and random, taking values in a closed interval $I \subset \mathbb{R}$. We define a "deterministic process" as a "one-dimensional dynamical system" $(I, \mathcal{B}, \mu, f)$, where I is the state space (a bounded interval of $\mathbb{R}$), $\mathcal{B}$ is the "Borel σ-algebra" of I, μ is a "measure" such that $\mu(I) = 1$, and $f : I \to I$ is a μ-invariant map. In this case, the image $(X_t)_{t\geq 0}$ of X is the orbit of X_0, i.e., $(X_t)_{t\geq 0} = (f^t(X_0))_{t\geq 0}$, where $f^0(X_0) = X_0 \in I$ and $f^t(X_0) = f(f^{t-1}(X_0))$.

First, we associate with an ordinal representation the probability $p(\mathbf{r})$ of finding an ordinal pattern of a given rank $\mathbf{r} \in \mathcal{S}_L$. To this aim, we assume the *stationary condition*: for $k \leq L-1$, the probability of $X_t < X_{t+k}$ cannot depend on t. This condition ensures that estimates of $p(\mathbf{r})$ converge as data increase. Non-stationary processes with stationary increments, such as the fractional Brownian motion and the fractional Gaussian noise, satisfy the condition above.

7.1. Metric and Topological Permutation Entropy

Let $\mathbf{X}$ be a deterministic or random process taking real values. Let $p(\mathbf{r})$ be the probability of a sequence X_t^L generated by $\mathbf{X}$ being of type $\mathbf{r}$, and let $p = p(\mathbf{r})$ be the corresponding probability distribution. We define the following:

(i) If $p(\mathbf{r}) > 0$, then $\mathbf{r}$ is a permitted pattern for X.
(ii) If $p(\mathbf{r}) = 0$, then $\mathbf{r}$ is a forbidden pattern.

The *permutation metric entropy of order* L of p is defined as

$$H^*(X_0^L) = -\sum_{\mathbf{r} \in \mathcal{S}_L} p(\mathbf{r}) \ln p(\mathbf{r}). \tag{25}$$

The topological entropy of order L of the finite process X_t^L, $H_0^*(X_t^L)$ is the upper limit of the values of the permutation metric entropy of order L. Formally, we obtain it by assuming that all allowed patterns of length L are equiprobable:

$$H_0^*(X_t^L) := \ln \mathcal{A}_L(\mathbf{X}), \tag{26}$$

where $\mathcal{A}_L(\mathbf{X})$ is the number of allowed patterns of length L for $\mathbf{X}$. It is evident that the following inequalities hold:

$$H^*(X_0^L) \leq \ln \mathcal{A}_L(\mathbf{X}) \leq \ln L!$$

We observe that $\mathcal{A}_L(\mathbf{X}) = L!$ if all L-ordinal patterns are allowed.

7.2. Bandt–Pompe Permutation Entropy

In their seminal paper [28], Bandt and Pompe introduced the following notions:

- Permutation metric entropy of $\mathbf{X}$:

$$h_M(\mathbf{X}) := \limsup_{L \to \infty} \frac{1}{L} H^*(X_0^L) = -\limsup_{L \to \infty} \frac{1}{L} \sum_{\mathbf{r} \in SL} p(\mathbf{r}) \ln p(\mathbf{r}),$$

  where $X_0^L = X_0, \ldots, X_{L-1}$.
- Topological permutation entropy of $\mathbf{X}$:

$$h_T(\mathbf{X}) := \limsup_{L \to \infty} \frac{1}{L} H_0^*(X_0^L) = \limsup_{L \to \infty} \frac{1}{L} \ln \mathcal{N}_L(\mathbf{X}).$$

An important question is, what is the relationship between the permutation metric entropy and the standard *Kolmogorov–Sinai (KS) entropy* of a map?

Let f be a strictly piecewise monotone map on a closed interval $I \subset \mathbb{R}$. The vast majority of, if not all, one-dimensional maps used in concrete applications belong to the class of piecewise monotone maps. In [29], it was proved that

$$h_M(f) = h_{\mathrm{KS}}(f).$$

The same relation holds for the topological versions of the two entropies. This is a fundamental result since it allows us to compute the KS entropy using the ordinal analysis approach. The above theorem and its generalizations imply that the number of permitted patterns of length L for a deterministic process grows exponentially as L increases.

$$|\text{L-permitted patterns for deterministic } \mathbf{X} = f| \sim e^{\tau(f)L},$$

where $\tau(f)$ is the topological KS entropy. In turn, this implies that the number of prohibited patterns grows super-exponentially.

At the other extreme, we have random processes without prohibited patterns. An elementary example is *white noise*. According to Stirling's formula,

$$|L\text{-possible patterns }| = L! \sim e^{L \ln L}.$$

It is also worth noting that noisy deterministic time series may not have prohibited patterns.

For example, in the case of dynamics on a non-trivial attractor where the orbits are dense, observational white noise will "destroy" all prohibited patterns, regardless of how little the noise is.

In general, *random processes exhibit super-exponential growth in permitted patterns*.

Random processes can also have prohibited patterns. In this case, the growth will be "intermediate," meaning it is still super-exponential but subfactorial.

7.3. A Fundamental Problem

For random processes without prohibited patterns, the permutation entropy diverges in the limit as $L \to \infty$:

$$h_T(\mathbf{X}) = \lim_{L\to\infty} \frac{1}{L} \ln|L\text{-possible permitted patterns}| = \lim_{L\to\infty} \frac{1}{L} \ln L! = \lim_{L\to\infty} \ln L = \infty$$

Also, in general, $h^M(\mathbf{X}) = \infty$. Therefore, it is natural to consider the problem of extending the notion of permutation entropy to make it an intrinsically finite quantity. We assume that for a random process $\mathbf{X}$,

$$|L\text{-possible permitted patterns for } \mathbf{X}| \sim e^{g(L)}.$$

where $g(L)$ is a certain function that depends on the type of process considered.

Can we find a suitable, generalized permutation entropy that converges as $L \to \infty$?

7.4. Group Entropies and Ordinal Analysis

We can obtain a new solution to this problem through the theory of group entropies.

Philosophy: Instead of using the Shannon-type permutation entropy introduced by Bandt and Pompe as a universal entropy valid for all random processes, we will adapt our entropic measure to the specific problem we wish to address:

- We will classify our processes into *complexity classes*, defined by complexity functions $g(t)$. These classes, in ordinal analysis, represent a notion entirely analogous to the *universality class* described earlier (inspired by statistical mechanics).
- Each complexity class will correspond to a *group permutation entropy*, i.e., a specific information measure designed for the class under consideration.
- This measure will be convergent as $L \to \infty$.

Functions and Complexity Classes

A process $\mathbf{X}$ is said to belong to the complexity class g if

$$\ln \underbrace{|\text{allowed } L\text{-patterns for } \mathbf{X}|}_{\mathcal{A}_L(\mathbf{X})} \sim g(L) \text{ for } L \to \infty.$$

The bi-continuous function $g(t)$ is called the *complexity function* of $\mathbf{X}$. The process $\mathbf{X}$ belongs to the *exponential class* if

$$g(L) = cL \quad (c > 0)$$

$\mathbf{X}$ belongs to the *factorial class* if

$$g(L) = L \ln L$$

Example 1. *A deterministic process* $\mathbf{X}$ *belongs to the exponential class. A random process* $\mathbf{X}$ *like white noise (*$\mathbf{X}$ *i.i.d.) belongs to the factorial class.*
A process $\mathbf{X}$ *belongs to the subfactorial class if one of the following conditions holds:*

(i)

$$g(L) = o(L \ln L)$$

(ii)

$$g(L) = cL \ln L; \; with \; ;0 < c < 1$$

Example 2. *Processes with*

$$g(L) = L \ln^{(k)} L;; (\ln^{(k)} L \equiv \underbrace{\ln \circ \ln \circ \cdots \circ \ln}_{k \; times}(L)) \; with \; k \geq 2$$

belong to subfactorial class (i). Processes with $g(L) = cL \ln L$, $0 < c < 1$ *can also be constructed explicitly.*

7.5. Group Permutation Entropy

Main Result: The conventional permutation entropy of Bandt–Pompe can be consistently generalized. According to our philosophy, *the complexity class g "dictates" its associated permutation entropy*, which becomes finite in the limit of large L.

Definition 1. *The group entropy of order L for a process* $\mathbf{X}$ *of class g is*

$$Z^*_{g,\alpha}(\mathrm{p}L) = g^{-1}(R\alpha(\mathrm{p}_L)) - g^{-1}(0)$$

where p_L *is the probability distribution of the L-ordinal patterns of* $X0^L = X_0, \ldots, X_{L-1}$ *and* $R_\alpha(\mathrm{p}_L)$ *is the Rényi entropy. The corresponding topological group entropy of order L is*

$$Z^*_{g,0}(\mathrm{p}L) = g^{-1}(\ln \mathcal{A}L(\mathbf{X})) - g^{-1}(0)$$

The group metric permutation entropy is

$$z^*_{g,\alpha}(\mathbf{X}) = \lim_{L \to \infty} \frac{1}{L} g^{-1}(R_\alpha(\mathrm{p}_L))$$

The topological group permutation entropy is

$$z^*_{g,0}(\mathbf{X}) = \lim_{L \to \infty} \frac{1}{L} g^{-1}(\ln \mathcal{A}_L(\mathbf{X}))$$

The functions defined in this manner are group entropies. Furthermore, they satisfy the inequalities

$$0 \leq z^*_{g,\alpha}(\mathbf{X}) \leq z^*_{g,0}(\mathbf{X}) = 1 \quad \forall \alpha > 0.$$

The following are various examples of group permutation entropies:

$$
\begin{array}{lll}
(a) & \text{For } g_{exp}(t) = ct: & Z^*_{g_{exp},\alpha}(\mathrm{p}L) = \frac{1}{c} R\alpha(\mathrm{p}_L) \\
(b) & \text{For } g_{fac}(t) = t \ln t: & Z^*_{g_{fac},\alpha}(\mathrm{p}L) = e^{\mathcal{L}[R\alpha(\mathrm{p}_L)]} - 1 \\
(c) & \text{For } g_{sub}(t) = ct \ln t \ \ (0 < c < 1): & Z^*_{g_{sub},\alpha}(\mathrm{p}L) = e^{\mathcal{L}[R\alpha(\mathrm{p}_L)/c]} - 1
\end{array} \tag{27}
$$

8. Thermodynamics

The application of non-Boltzmann–Gibbs–Shannon entropies to thermodynamics is subtle. We recall that in standard thermodynamics, it is possible to interpret the Lagrange multiplier corresponding to the constraint on the average energy as the inverse of the physical temperature. However, it is not clear if a similar procedure can be adopted for any generalized entropy.

One can certainly derive the probability weights p_i^* corresponding to the extrema of

$$J = S - \lambda_1(\sum p_i - \mathcal{N}) - \lambda_2(\sum_i E_i p_i - E) \tag{28}$$

and we can compute the entropy for these weights $S[p_i^*]$. However, given an arbitrary generalized entropy S, we do not know if, for some physical systems, there exists a relationship between $S[p_i^*]$ and Clausius's thermodynamic entropy defined in terms of heat flow. Hence, to us, the relationship between generalized entropies and thermodynamics in the sense of a theory of heat and energy of physical systems, apart from several interesting analogies, remains an open field of research. Detailed discussions concerning the construction of generalized thermostatistics for the case of the Tsallis entropy S_q are available, e.g., in the monographs in [30,31].

9. Discussion

The group entropy formalism described has the pleasant property that all group entropies arise systematically and transparently from a set of underlying axioms combined with the requirement of extensivity. This approach is in contrast to those adopted to define many of the existing entropies, which, sometimes, are intuitively proposed or justified by axioms that ignore the need for composability. Many of the most commonly used entropies are included and classified within the group theoretic framework.

The use of information measures adapted to the universality classes of systems, which are extensive by construction, looks promising in several application contexts, such as the study of neural interconnections in the human brain, classical and quantum information geometry, and data analysis in a broad sense. We plan to further investigate complex systems with super-exponentially growing state spaces as a paradigmatic class of examples where these new ideas can be fruitfully tested.

10. Conclusions

We have reviewed a group-theoretic approach to the classification and characterization of entropies, regarded as functionals on spaces of probability distributions. The theoretical framework proposed is axiomatic and generalizes the set of Shannon–Khinchin axioms by replacing the fourth additivity axiom with a more general composition axiom. Perhaps the most relevant achievement so far is the systematic classification of the multitude of existing entropies in terms of the rate at which the corresponding dimension of the state space grows with the number of components in the system. A related result is a constructive procedure for entropies, which exhibit extensivity on state spaces of any assigned growth rate. In turn, this property triggers the application of group entropies to information geometry and data analysis.

Author Contributions: H.J.J. and P.T. constructively collaborated in developing the proposed research and writing and reviewing this paper. All authors have read and agreed to the published version of the manuscript. All authors have read and agreed to the published version of the manuscript.

Funding: The research of P.T. was supported by the Severo Ochoa Programme for Centres of Excellence in R&D (CEX2019-000904-S), Ministerio de Ciencia, Innovación y Universidades y Agencia Estatal de Investigación, Spain.

Data Availability Statement: Data are contained within the article.

Acknowledgments: P.T. is a member of the Gruppo Nazionale di Fisica Matematica (GNFM) of the Istituto Nazionale di Alta Matematica (INdAM).

Conflicts of Interest: The authors declare no conflicts of interest.

References

1. Reif, F. *Fundamentals of Statistical and Thermal Physics*; Waveland Press: Long Grove, IL, USA, 2010.
2. Cover, T.M.; Thomas, J.A. *Elements of Information Theory*, 2nd ed.; JohnWiley & Sons Ltd.: Hoboken, NJ, USA, 2005.
3. Ziv, J.; Lempel, A. Compression of Individual sequences via Variable-Rate Coding. *IEEE Trans. Inform. Theory* **1978**, *24*, 530–536. [CrossRef]
4. Takaoka, T.; Nakagawa, Y. Entropy as computational complexity. *J. Inf. Process.* **2010**, *18*, 227–241. [CrossRef]
5. Carhart-Harris, R.L.; Leech, R.; Hellyer, P.J.; Shanahan, M.; Feilding, A.; Tagliazucchi, E.; Chialvo, D.R.; Nutt, D. The entropic brain: A theory of conscious states informed by neuroimaging research with psychedelic drugs. *Front. Hum. Neurosci.* **2014**, *8*, 20. [CrossRef]
6. Oizumi, M.; Albantakis, L.; Tononi, G. From the Phenomenology to the Mechanisms of Consciousness: Integrated Information Theory 3.0. *PLoS Comput. Biol.* **2014**, *10*, 316. [CrossRef]
7. Jensen, H.J. *Complexity Science: The Study of Emergence*; Cambridge University Press: Cambridge, UK, 2022.
8. Khinchin, A.I. *Mathematical Foundations of Information Theory*; Dover: New York, NY, USA, 1957.
9. Tsallis, C. Possible Generalization of Boltzmann-Gibbs Statistics. *J. Stat. Phys.* **1988**, *52*, 479–487. [CrossRef]
10. Tsallis, C. Entropy. *Encyclopedia* **2022**, *2*, 264–300. [CrossRef]
11. Hanel, R.; Thurner, S. When do generalized entropies apply? How phase space volume determines entropy. *Europhys. Lett.* **2011**, *96*, 50003. [CrossRef]
12. Tempesta, P. Formal Groups and Z-Entropies. *Proc. R. Soc. A* **2016**, *472*, 20160143. [CrossRef] [PubMed]
13. Tempesta, P. Group entropies, correlation laws and zeta functions. *Phys. Rev. E* **2011**, **84**, 021121. [CrossRef]
14. Bochner, S. Formal Lie groups. *Ann. Math.* **1946**, 47, 192–201. [CrossRef]
15. Hazewinkel, M. *Formal Groups and Applications*; Academic Press: Cambridge, MA, USA, 1978.
16. Tempesta, P. Beyond the Shannon-Khinchin formulation: The composability axiom and the universal-group entropy. *Ann. Phys.* **2016**, *365*, 180–197. [CrossRef]
17. Amigó, J.M.; Dale, R.; Tempesta, P. Permutation group entropy: A new route to complexity for real-valued processes. *Chaos* **2022**, *32*, 112101. [CrossRef] [PubMed]
18. Jensen, H.J. *Self-Oranized Criticality. Emergent Complex Behavior in Physical and Biological Systems*; Cambridge University Press: Cambridge, UK, 1998.
19. Pruessner, G. *Self-Organised Criticality: Theory, Models and Characterisation*; Cambridge University Press: Cambridge, UK, 2012.
20. Tempesta, P.; Jensen, H.J. Universality Classes and Information-Theoretic Measures of Complexity via Group Entropies. *Nat. Sci. Rep.* **2020**, *10*, 5952. [CrossRef] [PubMed]
21. Jensen, H.J.; Tempesta, P. Group Entropies: From Phase Space Geometry to Entropy Functionals via Group Theory. *Entropy* **2018**, *20*, 804. [CrossRef] [PubMed]
22. Jensen, H.J.; Pazuki, R.H.; Pruessner, G.; Tempesta, P. Statistical mechanics of exploding phase spaces: Ontic open systems. *J. Phys. A Math. Theor.* **2018**, 51, 375002. [CrossRef]
23. Beggs, J.M.; Plenz, D. Neuronal Avalanches in neocortical circuits. *J. Neurosci.* **2003**, *23*, 11167–11177. [CrossRef]
24. Livadiotis, G.; McComas, D.J. Entropy defect in thermodynamics. *Nat.-Sci. Rep.* **2023**, *13*, 9033. [CrossRef]
25. Ziv, J. Coding theorems for individual sequences. *IEEE Trans. Inf. Theory***1978**, *24*, 405–412. [CrossRef]
26. Amigo, J.M.; Dale, R.; Tempesta, P. Complexity-based permutation entropies: From deterministic time series to white noise. *Commun. Nonlinear Sci. Numer. Simul.* **2022**, *105*, 106077. [CrossRef]
27. Amigó, J.M.; Dale, R.; Tempesta, P. A generalized permutation entropy for noisy dynamics and random processes. *Chaos* **2021**, *31*, 0131115. [CrossRef]
28. Bandt, C.; Pompe, B. Permutation Entropy: A Natural Complexity Measure for Time Series. *Phys. Rev. Lett.* **2002**, *88*, 174102. [CrossRef] [PubMed]
29. Bandt, C.; Keller, K.; Pompe, B. Permutations and the Kolmogorov-Sinai entropy. *Nonlinearity* **2002**, *15*, 1595–1602. [CrossRef]
30. Tsallis, C. *Introduction to Nonextensive Statistical Mechanics: Approaching a Complex World*, 2nd ed.; Springer: Berlin/Heidelberg, Germany, 2023.
31. Naudts, J. *Generalised Thermostatistics*; Springer: Berlin/Heidelberg, Germany, 2011.

entropy

MDPI

Article

Analogies and Relations between Non-Additive Entropy Formulas and Gintropy

Tamás S. Biró [1,2,3,*], András Telcs [1] and Antal Jakovác [1]

1 HUN-REN Wigner Research Centre for Physics, 1121 Budapest, Hungary; telcs.andras@wigner.hun-ren.hu (A.T.); jakovac.antal@wigner.hun-ren.hu (A.J.)
2 Hungarian Physics Department, Physics Faculty, University Babeş-Bolyai, 400084 Cluj-Napoca, Romania
3 Complexity Science Hub, 1080 Vienna, Austria
* Correspondence: biro.tamas@wigner.hun-ren.hu

Abstract: We explore formal similarities and mathematical transformation formulas between general trace-form entropies and the Gini index, originally used in quantifying income and wealth inequalities. We utilize the notion of gintropy introduced in our earlier works as a certain property of the Lorenz curve drawn in the map of the tail-integrated cumulative population and wealth fractions. In particular, we rediscover Tsallis' q-entropy formula related to the Pareto distribution. As a novel result, we express the traditional entropy in terms of gintropy and reconstruct further non-additive formulas. A dynamical model calculation of the evolution of Gini index is also presented.

Keywords: entropy; Gini index; Lorenz curve; non-extensive

Citation: Biró, T.S.; Telcs, A.; Jakovác, A. Analogies and Relations between Non-Additive Entropy Formulas and Gintropy. *Entropy* **2024**, *26*, 185. https://doi.org/10.3390/e26030185

Academic Editor: Antonio M. Scarfone

Received: 6 January 2024
Revised: 9 February 2024
Accepted: 21 February 2024
Published: 22 February 2024

1. Motivation

This paper responds to a call by the journal *Entropy* to accompany various contributions in honor of Constantino Tsallis' 80th birthday. Professor Tsallis initiated the field of non-extensive statistical mechanics with his seminal paper in 1988 [1] and kept this field flourishing with his continuous activity since then. One of his recent books on Non-Extensive Statistical Mechanics [2], has the subtitle "Approaching a Complex World". It characterizes the range of research fields, beyond physics, where non-additive entropy formulas can be applied [3–7]. Adding a physicist's approach to the mathematical predecessor formulas, such as Rényi entropy [8], and further generalizations of the Boltzmannian log-formula proliferating in the field of informatics and mathematics [9–12], his work is acknowledged to date in a wide and strengthening community of researchers dealing with complexity [13–20].

Over the years, newcomers and opponents of non-extensive thermodynamics have often argued that using any formula between entropy and probability besides the classical Boltzmann–Gibbs–Shannon version can only then be generally applied, and it is advised to use it if it moves beyond merely being an alternative formal possibility—when it must be applied. Therefore, there is an ongoing challenge to find real-world data and applications that can only be described by a non-Boltzmannian entropy formula. Such cases are found with increasing frequency in complex systems. An interesting approach is presented in [21]: it shows how to analyze nuclear production data to reveal non-extensive thermodynamics. (Our earlier calculations of fluctuations and deviations from an exponential kinetic energy distribution due to the finiteness of a heat bath, presented in several publications, should not be cited here, because the Editors at MDPI consider self-citations, even one sixth of the total, to be biased and unnecessary.)

The Tsallis and Rényi entropy formulas are monotonic functions of one another; therefore, their respective canonical equilibrium distribution functions coincide, not accounting for constant factors related to the partition sum. Since the Rényi entropy is defined as

$$S_R = \frac{1}{1-q} \ln \sum_i p_i^q, \tag{1}$$

and the Tsallis entropy as

$$S_T = \frac{\sum_i (p_i^q - p_i)}{1-q} = \frac{e^{S_R(1-q)} - 1}{1-q}, \tag{2}$$

one obtains, in the canonical approach to the physical energy distribution,

$$\frac{\partial S_T}{\partial p_i} = e^{S_R(1-q)} \frac{\partial S_R}{\partial p_i} = \beta E_i + \alpha. \tag{3}$$

The actual energy level is denoted by E_i in this formula, while α and β are Lagrange multipliers. The former is related to the partition function and the latter to the absolute temperature (via the average value of the energy). The prefactor Equation (3) is independent of p_i; therefore, the functional forms of the canonical PDFs coincide, reconstructing the Pareto or Lomax distribution [22–25].

In a microcanonical approach, all trace-form entropies are maximal at the distribution uniform in x, provided that the non-trivial function in the formula satisfies the general properties of non-negativity and convexity. Constraining the expectation value of the base variable, $\langle x \rangle$, of which we intend to study the probability density function, $P(x)$, leads to an entropy depending on the constrained value, say $\alpha + \beta \langle E \rangle$ for an energy (E) distribution. These functions, of course, vary. The properties of entropy formulas also differ: while the Rényi entropy is additive for the factorization of probabilities and the Tsallis q-entropy is not, the q-entropy is formally an expectation value and the Rényi entropy is not.

In this paper, we first briefly review the Gini index and the Lorenz curve, spanning a map of the tail-cumulative fractions of a population and the wealth owned by this population. We furthermore review the definition and basic properties of gintropy, defined as the difference between the above two cumulatives. Following this, we introduce some gintropy formulas being formal doubles of well-known and used entropies. Finally, we explore the transformations from one (entropic) view to the other (gintropic view) and present a dynamical model calculation of the evolution of the Gini index based on a master equation.

2. About Gintropy

In our search for additional motivation for the use of non-Boltzmannian entropy formulas, we encounter the Gini index [26–28], classically used in income and wealth data analyses. It measures the expectation value of the absolute difference, $\langle |x-y| \rangle$, normalized by that of the sum, $\langle x+y \rangle = 2\langle x \rangle$, when taking both variables from the same distribution. It delivers values between zero and one (100%):

$$G = \frac{\langle |x-y| \rangle}{\langle x+y \rangle} = \frac{1}{2\langle x \rangle} \int_0^\infty dx \int_x^\infty dy |y-x| P(x)P(y). \tag{4}$$

Here, $P(x)$ is the underlying PDF. This formula can be transformed into several alternate forms, as has been shown in Ref. [29] in detail. We have also found that a function defined by tail-cumulative functions, gintropy, has properties very similar to those of an entropy–probability trace formula function.

Two basic tail-cumulative functions constitute the definition and usefulness of gintropy. The first is the cumulative population,

$$\overline{C}(x) \equiv \int_x^\infty dy\, P(y), \tag{5}$$

and the second is the cumulative wealth normalized by its average value (also called the scaled and (from below) truncated expectation value),

$$\overline{F}(x) \equiv \int_x^\infty dy\, \frac{y}{\langle x \rangle} P(y). \tag{6}$$

We note here that the notions "population" and "wealth" are used in a general sense: any type of real random variable x associated with a well-defined PDF, $P(x)$, has a tail-cumulative fraction (cf. Equation (5)) and a scaled fraction of the occurrence of the basic variable defined in Equation (6). For example, x may denote the number of citations that an individual author receives and $P(x)$ the distribution of this number in the analyzed population. Then, $\overline{C}(x)$ is the fraction of papers cited x times or more, and $\overline{F}(x)$ is the fraction of citations received for these relative to all citations [30]. The above definitions and the following analysis of gintropy can be used for any PDF defined on non-negative variables $x \geq 0$ and having a finite expectation value.

The Lorenz map [31] plots the essence of a PDF on a $\overline{C} - \overline{F}$ plane. Since always $\overline{F} \geq \overline{C}$, following from the positivity of the PDF, $P(x)$, the Lorenz curve always runs on this map above or on the diagonal. At $x = \infty$, both quantities are vanishing, $\overline{F}(\infty) = \overline{C}(\infty) = 0$, because the integration range shrinks to zero, and they also coincide at $x = 0$, following from their normalized definitions: $\overline{F}(0) = \overline{C}(0) = 1$. The Gini index can be described as the area fraction between the Lorenz curve and the diagonal to the whole upper triangle (with an area of $1/2$). The quantity of gintropy, introduced by us in an earlier work [29], is the difference

$$\sigma \equiv \overline{F} - \overline{C}. \tag{7}$$

This is a function of the fiducial variable x, and it vanishes as a function only for those PDFs that allow only a single value for x. The gintropy is non-negative and it shows a definite sign of curvature. On the Lorenz map, it is best viewed and expressed as a function of $\overline{C}$. The connection between these two variables, derived from Equation (5), is given by $d\overline{C}/dx = -P(x)$. Likewise, $d\overline{F}/dx = -xP(x)/\langle x \rangle$ follows from the definition in Equation (6). Then, it is easy to establish that it has a maximum exactly at the average case, $x = \langle x \rangle$:

$$\frac{\mathrm{d}\sigma}{\mathrm{d}\overline{C}} = \frac{\mathrm{d}\overline{F}}{\mathrm{d}\overline{C}} - 1 = \frac{x}{\langle x \rangle} - 1. \tag{8}$$

The second derivative of gintropy in the Lorenz map is always negative:

$$\frac{\mathrm{d}^2\sigma}{\mathrm{d}\overline{C}^2} = \frac{1}{\langle x \rangle} \frac{\mathrm{d}x}{\mathrm{d}\overline{C}} = -\frac{1}{\langle x \rangle P(x)} < 0. \tag{9}$$

As a consequence, the gintropy, $\sigma(\overline{C})$, has a single maximum (between two maxima, there would be a region with an opposite-sign second derivative for a continuous function). This maximum can be expressed as a function of the average value:

$$\sigma_{\max} = \overline{F}(\langle x \rangle) - \overline{C}(\langle x \rangle). \tag{10}$$

Finally, the Gini index itself is twice the area under the gintropy:

$$G = 2\int_0^1 d\overline{C}\,\sigma(\overline{C}). \tag{11}$$

3. Entropy from Gintropy

It is important to consider a few simple cases for gintropy. First of all, a PDF allowing only a singular value, such as $P(x) = \delta(x-a)$, leads to vanishing gintropy. Then, $\sigma = 0$ for all $\overline{C} \in [0,1]$. This case is degenerate; the second derivative is also zero across the whole interval and there is no definite maximum. A few examples have been discussed in Ref. [29]. Here, we use the Tsallis–Pareto distribution, as a limiting case, as it includes the Boltzmann–Gibbs exponential too. The tail-cumulative function is given as a two-parameter set with a power-law tail and the proper $\overline{C}(0) = 1$ normalization:

$$\overline{C}(x) = (1+ax)^{-b}. \tag{12}$$

Here, a and b are positive. It follows a PDF,

$$P(x) = ab(1+ax)^{-b-1}, \tag{13}$$

an expectation value of $\langle x\rangle = 1/a(b-1)$, and finally a gintropy formula:

$$\sigma = abx(1+ax)^{-b} = b\left(\overline{C}^{1-1/b} - \overline{C}\right). \tag{14}$$

Related to the more popular form, one uses $q = 1 - 1/b$ as a parameter and arrives at the q-gintropy formula:

$$\sigma_q(\overline{C}) = \frac{\overline{C}^q - \overline{C}}{1-q}. \tag{15}$$

The $q \to 1$ limit of this formula is the Boltzmann–Gibbs–Shannon relation:

$$\sigma_1(\overline{C}) = -\overline{C}\ln\overline{C}. \tag{16}$$

The Gini index in the Tsallis–Pareto case is easily obtained as being

$$G = \frac{2}{1-q}\int_0^1 (\overline{C}^q - \overline{C})d\overline{C} = \frac{1}{q+1}. \tag{17}$$

The formal analogy between the expressions of gintropy in terms of the tail-cumulative data population on the one hand and the entropy density in terms of the PDF on the other hand is obvious (cf. Equation (15)). Moreover, the general form of trace entropy is given as

$$S = \int_0^\infty dx\, P(x)\, \mathrm{s}(1/P(x)), \tag{18}$$

while the Gini index is obtained according to our previous discussion above as

$$G = \int_0^\infty dx\, P(x)\, 2\sigma(\overline{C}(x)). \tag{19}$$

Here, we utilize the fact that

$$\int_0^1 d\overline{C}\, f(\overline{C}) = \int_0^\infty dx\, P(x)\, f(\overline{C}(x)) \tag{20}$$

for an arbitrary integrand, $f(\overline{C}(x))$.

Despite the intriguing analogies, we do not have a quantity that would be equivalent to the total entropy in social and econophysics. On the other hand, the nontrivial identification, $2\sigma(\overline{C}(x)) = \mathrm{s}(P(x))$, would make the Gini index equal to the entropy, $G = S$. Since $P(x)$ is a negative derivative of the cumulative function $\overline{C}(x)$, the above $G = S$ correspondence is a complex differential equation for $\overline{C}$. It may therefore be valid only for a single PDF, $P(X)$, for the solution of the above implicit differential equation. In conclusion, gintropy cannot be replaced by entropy for a general PDF.

Let us review, briefly, how to obtain the general trace-form entropy once the gintropy, $\sigma(\overline{C})$, is known. To begin with, one uses a general function, $\mathrm{s}(1/P)$, in the definition of entropy with the required non-negativity and convexity properties. Due to its relation to the fiducial PDF, $P(x)$, and using Equation (18), we obtain

$$S = \int_0^\infty dx\; P(x)\, \mathrm{s}(1/P(x)) = \int_0^1 d\overline{C}\; \mathrm{s}(-\langle x\rangle\sigma'') \tag{21}$$

with the short-hand notation

$$\sigma'' \equiv \frac{\mathrm{d}^2\sigma}{\mathrm{d}\overline{C}^2}. \tag{22}$$

In particular, the Boltzmann entropy becomes

$$S_{\mathrm{BG}} = \ln\langle x\rangle + \int_0^1 d\overline{C}\; \ln(-\sigma''(\overline{C})). \tag{23}$$

4. Dynamics of the Gini Index

After the introduction of gintropy, the authors of [32] provided several examples for different socioeconomic systems and compared the inequality measure G for their wealth distribution. Here, we supplement this steady picture with a dynamic one. We demonstrate, based on the example of the linear growth with reset (LGGR) model [33,34], that the Gini index mostly (i.e., not accounting for a short overshoot period, probably of numerical origin) increases monotonically, as the wealth distribution tends towards the stationary Tsallis–Pareto distribution. This behavior of the Gini index is not yet proven for the general case, in contrast to the entropy, cf. [32].

As in [32], the society members may have $k \geq 0$ discrete units of wealth. We assume that these members of the society acquire another unit of wealth with a rate that is linear to their actual wealth value (the rich get richer effect). We also incorporate a constant reset rate as in [32].

The evolution equation for the probability density function of the wealth distribution in the LGGR model is applied here to a binned wealth representation. In this case, the evolution equation, denoting $\frac{\partial P}{\partial t}$ with an overdot, reads

$$\dot{P}(k,t) = \mu(k-1)P(k-1,t) - (\mu(k) + \gamma(k))P(k,t), \tag{24}$$

where $P(k,t)$ is the actual fraction of people in the wealth slot around k. In other words, one becomes richer with a state-dependent rate, $\mu(k)$, while there is a reset mechanism to zero wealth with the rate $\gamma(k)$. This means not only a ruin probability rate, but also includes any type of exit of people, receiving the income k, from the studied population (e.g., resorting to pensions or the decay of hadrons containing energy k). The boundary condition at $P(0,t)$ ensures that $\sum_{k=0}^{\infty} P(k,t) = 1$ remains constant in time. This requirement results in

$$\dot{P}(0,t) = \langle\gamma\rangle(t) - (\gamma(0) + \mu(0))P(0,t), \tag{25}$$

with $\langle\gamma\rangle(t) = \sum_k kP(k,t)$.

We solve Equation (24) as a time recursion problem, with the linear $\mu(k) = ak + b$ and the constant $\gamma(k) = \gamma$ parameter functions. In the numerical simulation, we discretize the possible values of k and use them as an integer index. Starting from a theoretical society where everybody has zero wealth, $P(k,0) = \delta(k)$ is represented by a Kronecker delta $\delta_{k,0}$, delivering a vanishing Gini index, $G = 0$. Moreover, the whole Lorenz curve shrinks in this case to the diagonal and correspondingly the gintropy vanishes everywhere as a function of either k or $\overline{C}(k)$.

The growth rate $\mu(k)$, which is linear in k, is a common choice when dealing with the distribution of network hubs' connection numbers and is called a preferential rate [35–38]. Obviously, the linear assumption is the mathematically simplest between all possible models. Nevertheless, further assumptions, such as a quadratic one, also can be made. The linear preference in the growth rate, utilized in the present discussion, together with a constant reset rate, has the Tsallis–Pareto distribution as the stationary PDF in the LGGR model.

We also observe in our numerical simulations that the Tsallis–Pareto power-law tailed wealth distribution develops, as was already anticipated in Ref. [32], cf. Figure 1. Furthermore, in Ref. [39], analytical expressions were given for the evolution of a general distribution for the cases with constant rates and for the presently discussed case of a linear growth rate with a constant reset rate.

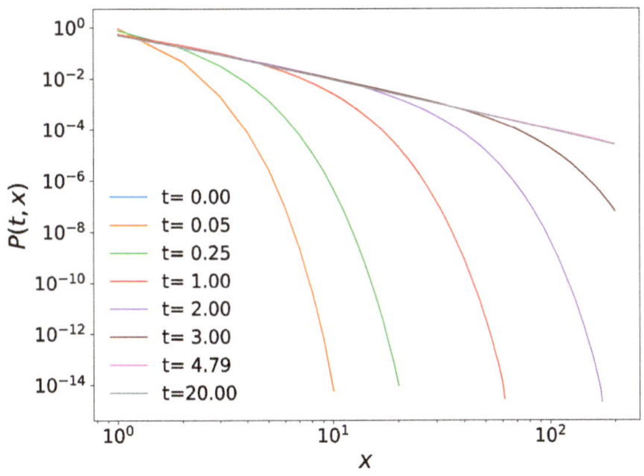

Figure 1. The time evolution of the wealth distribution starting from a society in which everybody has zero wealth.

We follow the time evolution of the Lorenz curve, $\overline{F}$ vs. $\overline{C}$, as well as the time-dependent Gini index. The results of the numerical calculation are shown in the upper and lower panels of Figure 2, respectively.

As can be observed, the wealth inequality grows in this theoretical example until it reaches its stationary position. The apparent slight overshoot at mid-time may be a numerical consequence of the time discretization. Recent, yet unpublished, analytical calculations of the time evolution of the Gini index in the very unique case studied numerically in the present paper indicate that $G(t)$ would monotonically increase from zero to its stationary value. These somewhat laborious calculations will be published in a separate paper. On the other hand, since the Gini index is not an entropy underlying the second law in thermodynamics, the issue of the monotonity of the Gini index's evolution in the general case calls for further investigations for a better understanding.

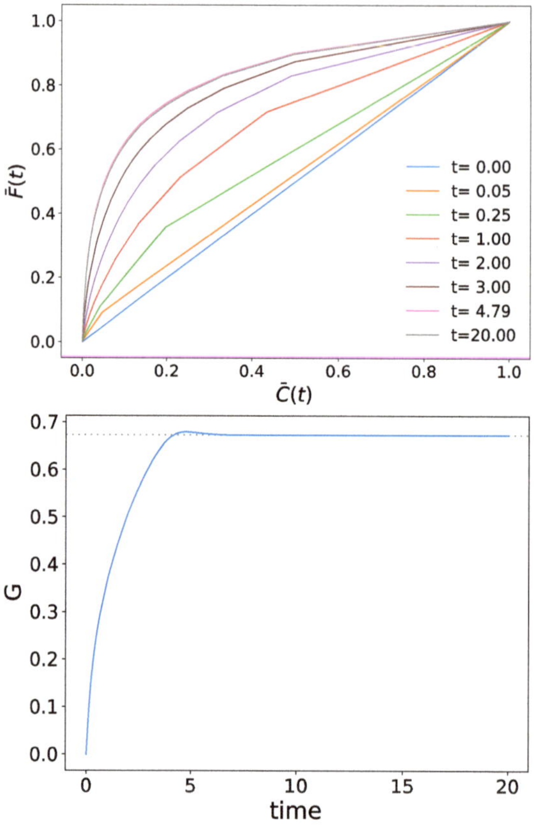

Figure 2. Time evolution of the Lorenz curve (**upper panel**) and the Gini index (**lower panel**). The steady dotted line in the lower panel corresponds to the final stationary Gini index.

5. Summary

In summary, the quantity of gintropy, the difference between two tail-cumulative integrals of any PDF defined on non-negative values, features a formal dependence on the cumulative data population fraction having the form of various entropy formulas in terms of the original PDF [32]. In this paper, the particular form of Tsallis entropy was discussed in some detail.

The Gini index, used in economic studies to describe income and wealth inequality in societies, is an integral of the gintropy-cumulative data population fraction function. However, the Gini index–total entropy correspondence cannot be generally held, but only for a special PDF, given the trace entropy formula specification. Without this, the gintropic view of known entropy formulas can be obtained by expressing the PDF with the help of the gintropy's second derivative with respect to the cumulative data population fraction and the average value of the base variable.

Time evolution in the particular but widespread case of a linear growth rate paired with a uniform reset rate was obtained numerically to demonstrate the evolution of the Gini index in time. A slight overshoot beyond its stationary value has been observed, so the Gini index does not appear to behave similarly to entropy in this particular case. However, to obtain a final conclusion, the scaling with the finite index space size should be studied.

Article

A Nonlinear Dynamical View of Kleiber's Law on the Metabolism of Plants and Animals

Luis Jovanny Camacho-Vidales * and Alberto Robledo *

Instituto de Física, Universidad Nacional Autónoma de México, Apartado Postal 20-364, Mexico City 01000, Mexico
* Correspondence: lj.camachovidales@ugto.mx (L.J.C.-V.); robledo@fisica.unam.mx (A.R.)

Abstract: Kleiber's empirical law, which describes that metabolism increases as the mass to the power 3/4, has arguably remained life sciences' enigma since its formal uncovering in 1930. Why is this behavior sustained over many orders of magnitude? There have been quantitative rationalizations put forward for both plants and animals based on realistic mechanisms. However, universality in scaling laws of this kind, like in critical phenomena, has not yet received substantiation. Here, we provide an account, with quantitative reproduction of the available data, of the metabolism for these two biology kingdoms by means of broad arguments based on statistical mechanics and nonlinear dynamics. We consider iterated renormalization group (RG) fixed-point maps that are associated with an extensive generalized (Tsallis) entropy. We find two unique universality classes that satisfy the 3/4 power law. One corresponds to preferential attachment processes—rich gets richer—and the other to critical processes that suppress the effort for motion. We discuss and generalize our findings to other empirical laws that exhibit similar situations, using data based on general but different concepts that form a conjugate pair that gives rise to the same power-law exponents.

Keywords: Kleiber's law; allometry; nonlinear dynamics; complex systems; statistical mechanics

1. Introduction

At least two of the kingdoms of biology on earth, plant and animal, seem to have found sustainable coexistence over an extended period of time. This is perhaps best quantified via the metabolic rates of organisms. When these rates are sorted out according to their mass, a robust scaling relation emerges, a power law with an exponent close to 3/4 spanning several orders of magnitude for both kingdoms. This is known as Kleiber's law [1–4] or, more generally, allometric scaling [5–15]. Since its discovery, this scaling law has attracted attention, and many attempts have been put forward towards its understanding [5–15]. One instance is to consider dissipation via a surface-to-volume ratio that indicates a slightly different value for the exponent, 2/3 [5,15,16]. Other more structured developments are (i) a branching scheme for plants with unassisted conveyance of raw materials and nutrients [6,7,14] and (ii) a set of scaling laws for animals that require a pump to propel raw materials and nutrients [6,9–11]. In our case, we look for a general principled conjugate pair of kingdom universality classes without reference to mechanisms but linked to a nonlinear dynamical approach that, in turn, can be couched in the language of statistical mechanics.

Over the last few years, we have developed a general theoretical procedure [17–19] to quantitatively reproduce the distributions of many real types of ranked data. The approach is based on dissipative nonlinear dynamics of low dimensionality. See also in [17–19] earlier references on how our approach developed. We specifically consider iterated maps at or near a tangent bifurcation [20,21]. A central role is played by the renormalization group (RG) fixed-point map $f^*(x)$ for the route out of chaos known as intermittency [21–23]. A

Citation: Camacho-Vidales, L.J.; Robledo, A. A Nonlinear Dynamical View of Kleiber's Law on the Metabolism of Plants and Animals. *Entropy* 2024, 26, 32. https://doi.org/10.3390/e26010032

Academic Editor: Antonio M. Scarfone

Received: 14 November 2023
Revised: 18 December 2023
Accepted: 25 December 2023
Published: 28 December 2023

Copyright: © 2023 by the authors. Licensee MDPI, Basel, Switzerland. This article is an open access article distributed under the terms and conditions of the Creative Commons Attribution (CC BY) license (https://creativecommons.org/licenses/by/4.0/).

brief recall [21–23] for the derivation of $f^*(x)$ is to consider that a generic (one-dimensional) map in the neighborhood of tangency at $x = 0$ with the identity function reads,

$$f(x) = x + u|x|^z, \tag{1}$$

where we omitted higher-order terms, u is a constant, and the power z defines the nonlinearity at tangency. The customarily applied [21,22] RG transformation for this nonlinear dynamical route to (or out of) chaos is the functional composition $f(f(x))$; the RG flow occurs in the space of functions tangent to the identity; and its RG fixed-point, the map $f^*(x)$, satisfies

$$f^*(f^*(x)) = \gamma^{-1} f^*(\gamma x), \tag{2}$$

where the scaling parameter γ is to be determined, while the first two terms of the expansion of $f^*(x)$ must reproduce $f(x)$ in Equation (1). The fixed-point map $f^*(x)$ was obtained in analytical closed form by Hu and Rudnick over 40 years ago [22]. This is

$$f^*(x) = x \exp_z(u x^{z-1}), \tag{3}$$

where $x^{z-1} \equiv \text{sign}(x) \mid x \mid^{z-1}$, and where $\exp_z$ is the q-deformed exponential function, $\exp_q(x) \equiv [1 + (1-q)x]^{1/(1-q)}$. The scaling parameter is $\gamma = 2^{1/(z-1)}$. All the trajectories $x_t, t = 0, 1, 2, \ldots,$ of $f^*(x)$ have the form [23]

$$x_t = x_0 \exp_z(x_0^{z-1} u t). \tag{4}$$

That is, for all z, u, and x_0, any pair of trajectories can be transformed into each other via appropriate rescaling of these parameters. Interestingly, as we describe here, the tangency feature of $f^*(x)$ present for $z \geq 2$ transforms below $z = 2$, first, into a cusp and then into a different map shape relevant to our description of Kleiber's law below.

It is worth mentioning that the fixed-point maps $f^*(x)$ for the other (and only) two routes to (or out of) chaos, period doubling and quasi-periodicity [24], were originally obtained numerically via approximations of their power series representation [21]. Their analytical closed-form expressions, also in terms of the q-exponential function $\exp_q(x)$, have become known only very recently [25]. The inverse function of the q-exponential, the q-logarithm, is given by $\ln_q(x) \equiv [x^{1-q} - 1/(1-q)]$. Both functions reduce, respectively, to the ordinary exponential and logarithmic functions when $q = 1$. The latter pair of functions plays a central role in ordinary statistical mechanics, while the q-deformed pair is correspondingly central for the Tsallis generalized statistical mechanics [26,27]. When the deformation parameter q (the nonlinearity z in $f^*(x)$) falls within $1 < q < \infty$, both $\exp_q(x)$ and $\ln_q(x)$ asymptotically approach power laws.

Actually, the origin of the rank distributions approach was expressed in a stochastic process language [28], but we provided a precise analogy [18] that converts the random variable description of the ranked data sample into a deterministic iterated map trajectory, $x_t, t = 0, 1, 2 \ldots,$ for the same data. The starting point in the stochastic approach is a parent (or source) probability distribution $P(N)$ for the data samples of magnitudes N. The parent distribution is assumed to take the form of a power law $P(N) = aN^{-\alpha}$, a being a constant factor, $\alpha > 1$, together with the limits $\alpha = 1$ and $\alpha \to \infty$, hyperbolic and exponential decay, respectively. The rank distributions are obtained from the parent distribution $P(N)$ via integration. First, obtain the complementary cumulative distribution $\Pi(N(k), N_{\text{max}})$ of $P(N)$,

$$\Pi(N(k), N_{\text{max}}) = a \int_{N(k)}^{N_{\text{max}}} N^{-\alpha} dN, \tag{5}$$

where the magnitudes in a sample with $\mathcal{N}$ items are sorted out starting with the largest, N_{max}, and continuing with decreasing magnitudes down to $N(k)$, and where $k = 0, 1, 2, \ldots,$ is the rank variable, with $k = 0$ for N_{max}. We call the function $N(k)$ the size-rank distribution, though technically, it is a quantile [29]. On the other hand, the rank k is equal to $\mathcal{N}\Pi$ so that Equation (5) becomes

$$\ln_\alpha N(k) = \ln_\alpha N_{\max} - (a\mathcal{N})^{-1}k, \tag{6}$$

where we used the q-deformed logarithm expression. The size-rank distribution $N(k)$ is explicitly obtained from Equation (6) by making use of the q-deformed inverse functions. This is

$$N(k) = N_{\max} \exp_\alpha[-N_{\max}^{\alpha-1} (a\mathcal{N})^{-1}k]. \tag{7}$$

The translation from the language of rank distributions into that for the trajectories of the RG fixed-point map $f^*(x)$ is obtained via $t = k$, $x_0 = -N_{\max}$, $x_t = -N(k)$, $u = 1/a\mathcal{N}$, and $z = \alpha$ [17–19]. Notice that the trajectory x_t that translates into $N(k)$ takes place at the left $x < 0$ of the point of tangency $x = 0$. Furthermore, the map that corresponds to the parent distribution $P(N)$, the starting point, is given by Equation (1), rewritten as [18]

$$f(x) = x + u/P(-x). \tag{8}$$

In the following Section 2, we succinctly present our approach to reproduce rank distributions of very diverse kinds with emphasis on the features that are prominent to our consideration of Kleiber's law. These are universality classes indicated by the values of the exponent α (also denoted as the deformation q or the nonlinearity z, $\alpha = q = z$). In particular, we focus on the location of the conjugate pairs (q, Q), values where the deformed exponential and its inverse function, the deformed logarithm, share the same power law decay. When referring to these pairs, we write q for $\exp_q$ and Q for $\ln_Q$. These pairs include a limit for validity of ordinary statistical mechanics ($q = 1, Q \to \infty$), the frequency and magnitude coincidence for Zipf's law [30] ($q = 2, Q = 2$), and other cases mentioned below. In the next Section 3, we extend the approach to incorporate rates of change of key quantities, as it is the case of metabolism in biology. As we shall see, this extension involves the consideration of the RG fixed-point map for the tangent bifurcation into a different regime (that for values of the nonlinearity $z < 2$). In Section 4, we present our results for Kleiber's law as derived from our formalism by specific choices of universality classes that represent the guiding principle of each biological kingdom. Finally, in Section 5, we discuss our results in connection with the Tsallis generalized entropy.

2. Rank Distributions and Their Universality Classes

Importantly, particularly for our purposes here, there is a well-defined conceptual distinction concerning rank distributions, on the one hand, those referring to magnitudes, sizes, and, on the other hand, those referring to frequencies, occurrences. According to our approach [17], the former, $N(k)$, $k = 0, 1, 2, \cdots$, is given by Equation (7), while the latter, denoted as $F(k')$, $k' = 0, 1, 2, \cdots$, is given by

$$F(k') = a\mathcal{N}[\ln_\alpha N_{\max} - \ln_\alpha k'], \tag{9}$$

where we have rewritten Equation (6) by introducing the changes of the variables $F = \mathcal{N}\Pi$ and $k' = N$. The non-normalized frequency-rank distribution $F(k')$ is often used as it is constructed directly from the numbers of occurrences in data samples. These functions are inverses of each other and asymptotically exhibit the same power-law exponent $\zeta = -1$ with $q = Q = 2$ for the Zipf class (city sizes or moon crater diameters obey the same power law as occurrences of words or earthquake frequencies) [19]. Interestingly, when $\alpha = q = Q = 2$, the asymptotic power-law rank interval for both the q-exponential and the Q-logarithm displays the same exponent $\zeta = 1/(1-q) = (1-Q) = -1$.

Typically, ranked finite data samples show power-law decay only through an intermediate rank interval with different conducts for small and large ranks. The prevailing focus of interest in this central power-law interval in real finite data rank distributions and not on the small and large rank deviations from the power law led to the same identification as Zipf's law for both magnitude and frequency ranked data samples. However, we can clearly distinguish between these two qualities in our formalism [17]. Additionally, we can choose a parent distribution from the start to represent 'frequency' instead of 'magnitude' and find that the values of q and Q appear interchanged [17]. Alternatively, we can use the precise analogy that exists between the trajectories of the RG fixed-point map $f^*(x)$ with the rank distributions derived from a parent distribution $P(N)$. As we have seen, our approach leads to rank distributions expressions in terms of q-exponential and q-logarithmic functions. These expressions reproduce real behavior for small rank, whereas the finite-size effect observed for large rank is also obtained quantitatively simply via the shift of the map $f^*(x)$ off tangency [18]. Ordinary exponential decay of rank distributions occurs for the pair of exponents $\alpha = 1$ and $\alpha \to \infty$ for both magnitudes and frequencies. All other values of $(1 < \alpha < \infty)$ lead to rank distributions of the form in Equations (7) and (9) [17–19].

We now assign some meaning, backed by real data examples, to natural numbered values of the exponent $\alpha = z = q$. In the limit when $\alpha = 1$, hyperbolic $P(N)$ and linear iterated map, we obtain exponential decay for $N(k)$ consistent with the ordinary statistical mechanics $q = 1$. See the comment at the end of this Section. Magnitudes and frequencies take values within real number intervals without restriction (a real data case we have analyzed is that of infant mortality [18]). We have also shown that this case applies to Benford's first digit law [17]. When $\alpha = 2$, we have a borderline case that corresponds to the classical Zipf's law [30]. There are many real data examples that illustrate this circumstance [18,19]. Magnitudes (or frequencies) do not fill real number intervals but much less, like an infinite numerable set (e.g., an infinite vocabulary). When $\alpha = 2$, the map $f(x)$ is tangent to the identity line with nonzero curvature and trajectories develop hyperbolic power-law behavior, $\zeta = -1$, near tangency. For an ample discussion of this borderline case, see Ref. [19]. For $\alpha = 3$, we have selective behavior that corresponds to rich-gets-richer processes that is analogous to preferential attachment network growth [31,32]. This is represented by a map $f(x)$ with cubic tangency with the identity line. We end this list with $\alpha = 4$, when $f(x)$ displays vanishing curvature at tangency with the identity line, a circumstance analogous to critical point behavior where displacements in the neighborhood of tangency (or criticality) have (thermodynamic potential) vanishing cost [33].

We have made a clear distinction between data that result from quantities related to the consideration of sizes or magnitudes and data produced by temporal behaviors that manifest as frequencies. We turn our attention now to the occurrence of conjugate universality classes (given by pairs of specific values of α) that asymptotically generate power-law scaling laws that have the same exponents. Here, we point out examples for rank distributions, but in the next section, we focus on dissipation or other rates such as in the case of Kleiber's law. These are shown in Figure 1, where the q-exponential (magnitudes) exhibits the same power-law exponent ζ as its inverse function, the Q-logarithm (frequencies). The (q, Q)-indexes for this condition satisfy the simple relation $\zeta = 1 - Q = 1/(1 - q)$. A prominent case we have already pointed out is $Q = q = 2$, the borderline case [19] for the empirical Zipf's law. Another example corresponds to the Boltzmann–Gibbs statistics. When $q = 1$, the q-exponential and q-logarithmic functions become the ordinary exponential and logarithmic functions, respectively. Likewise, when $q = 1$, Tsallis entropy reduces to the Boltzmann–Gibbs or Shannon expression. See Refs. [26,27] for an extended description. The value we have quoted for $\alpha = q = 1$, the Fibonacci number set [19] (illustrated by infant mortality [18]), is conjugate to $Q \to \infty$ displayed by the factorial number set [19] (illustrated by gun ownerships per capita [18]). Additionally, when $Q \to \infty$ the q-exponential and the q-logarithm become the ordinary exponential and logarithmic functions, but with the roles interchanged.

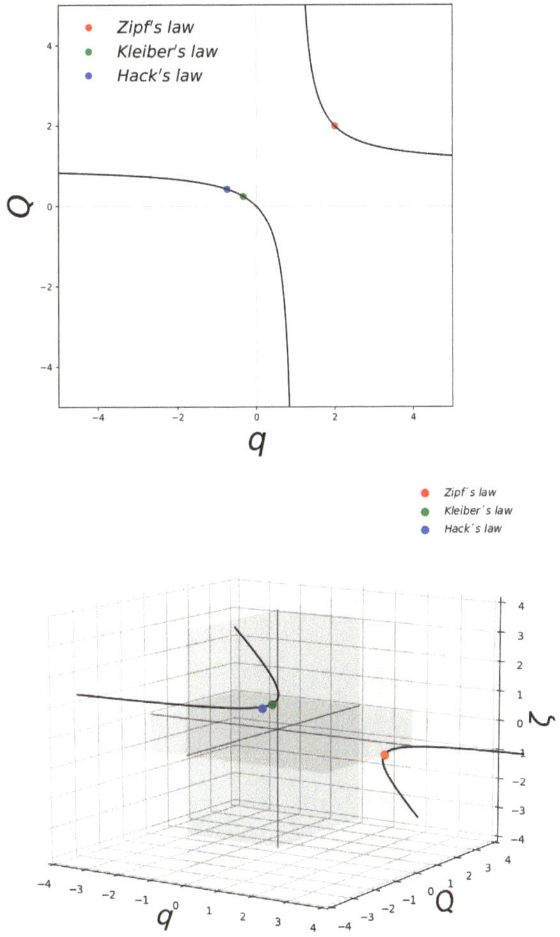

Figure 1. Upper panel shows the locus for identical power-law exponent ζ shown (within an interval of the independent variable) by the q-exponential function and its inverse function, the Q-logarithm. That is, $\zeta = 1/(1-q) = 1-Q$. There are two mirror branches. The dots show the values of the conjugate pairs (q, Q) relevant for Zipf's law $(2,2)$, Kleiber's law $(-1/3, 1/4)$, and Hack's law $(-1/2, 1/3)$. See text. Lower panel. The same as above but a three-dimensional rendering that shows the value of the power-law exponent ζ. See text.

3. Scaling of Rates and Characteristic Times and Their Universality Classes

We extend here our formalism for rank distributions to incorporate in it the determination of other important quantities. Specifically, we consider now the concept of rate, or equivalently, its reciprocal, the characteristic time, relevant, for instance, to Kleiber's law. The particular example of interest here is the metabolic M (or energy dissipation) rate of organisms as a function of the individual mass or volume N. We start with the parent or source probability distribution for the metabolism of a living organism $P(M)$, where M shall be considered to be a function of the organism size N. If metabolic rate values are to span real number intervals compatible with ordinary statistical mechanics, we have $P(M) = aM^{-1}$, a being a constant factor. Recall that $\alpha = 1$ returns the ordinary exponential and logarithmic functions to the rank distribution expressions Equations (7) and (9). This is similar to the exponential decay of configurational distributions, and access via the logarithm to thermodynamic potentials form partition functions in ordinary statistical mechanics.

We now particularize the parent distribution to a specific universality class $\alpha \geq 1$, e.g., a kingdom in biology. We consider then the parent distribution $P(R) = cR^{\alpha}$, c being a constant, for an energy dissipation rate, or metabolic rate, R. Here, the size or magnitude is the reciprocal, the characteristic time $T = R^{-1}$. As we pointed out, the value of α, which specifies the universality class, carries a general meaning. This choice determines not only the form of the rank distributions but also, as we see now, rates such as R. As a consequence of the two parent distributions, $P(M)$ and $P(R)$, we have introduced a new function, $R(M)$, that follows the power law $R(M) = bM^{-1/\alpha}$. We have the following differential equation:

$$\frac{dM}{dN} = R(M(N)) = bM^{-\frac{1}{\alpha}}\,, \tag{10}$$

with $b = a/c$. Considering that the use of data for metabolism to illustrate Kleiber's law is sorted out from small to large organism mass or volume N, we integrate the above to obtain the cumulative metabolic rate $\mu(M(N))$:

$$\mu(M(N)) = \int_{M_0}^{M(N)} R(M')dM' = b\int_{M_0}^{M(N)} M'^{-1/\alpha}dM'\,. \tag{11}$$

If $\mu(M(N))$ is normalized, this is equal to $N/b\mathcal{N}$, where $\mathcal{N}$ is the sum total of sizes in the data sample. After integration, we have

$$\frac{N}{b\mathcal{N}} = \frac{1}{1-\alpha^{-1}}M(N)^{1-\alpha^{-1}} - \frac{1}{1-\alpha^{-1}}M_0^{1-\alpha^{-1}} = \ln_{\alpha^{-1}} M(N) - \ln_{\alpha^{-1}} M_0 \tag{12}$$

and solving for $M(N)$, we have

$$M(N) = M_0 \exp_{\alpha^{-1}}\left[M_0^{\alpha^{-1}-1}\left(b\mathcal{N}\right)^{-1}N\right]. \tag{13}$$

Just as it is the case we have described above for rank distributions, here, we can also establish an exact analogy between the rate $M(N)$ and the trajectories of the RG fixed-point map. Equations (12) and (13) are equivalent to Equations (14) and (15), respectively,

$$\ln_z(x_t) = \ln_z(x_0) + ut \tag{14}$$

and

$$x_t = x_0 \exp_z(x_0{}^{z-1}ut) \tag{15}$$

provided that we adopt the following identifications: $N = t$, $M_0 = x_0$, $M(N) = x_t$, $\alpha^{-1} = z$, $(b\mathcal{N})^{-1} = u$, and $\mu(M) = \sum_{\tau=0}^{t} x_\tau$. Except for a sign in the trajectory positions, these are the same that exhibit the equivalence between the stochastic process led by the parent distribution $P(N)$ and the nonlinear iterated map $f(x)$ [17–19]. That is, the trajectories of the RG fixed-point map for the tangent bifurcation reproduce the metabolism data of our formalism. However, there is an important issue here: the RG fixed-point map

$$f^*(x) = x\exp_z(ux^{z-1}) \tag{16}$$

departs from the condition $\alpha = z = q \geq 2$ and enters a previously unexplored regime. In Figure 2, we show $f^*(x)$ for a range of positive and negative values of $\alpha = z = q$. In this figure, we observe in red/orange/yellow the known case $z \geq 2$ that consists of two branches, one that displays tangency with the identity function and the other at the bottom-right quadrant. Trajectories originated in this regime experience two different growth rates, slow growth at the left of the origin and superexponential growth at the right of the origin. If the RG fixed-point map is perturbed away from tangency, trajectories will exhibit intermittency, a nonlinear phenomenon we have employed in previous descriptions about complex systems from our nonlinear dynamical perspective. See Sections 2.3, 3.3, and 4.3 in Ref. [34]. When $z \leq 2$ tangency transforms into a cusp; the cusp is made of straight lines when the nonlinearity reaches $z = 1$, and consequently, the trajectories either decay exponentially ($x < 0$) or grow exponentially ($x > 0$). Below $z = 1$, the cusp separates from the identity line and becomes rounded as z distances from 1. The next limit case is $z = 0$, where the curvature of the map vanishes and trajectories grow linearly with time. As $z < 0$, a curvature develops opposite to the identity line, as is shown in Figure 2 in green-blue. Trajectories originated in this regime experience two different growth rates, fast growth near the origin and slower growth far from the origin, $x \gg 0$. See also Figure 3.

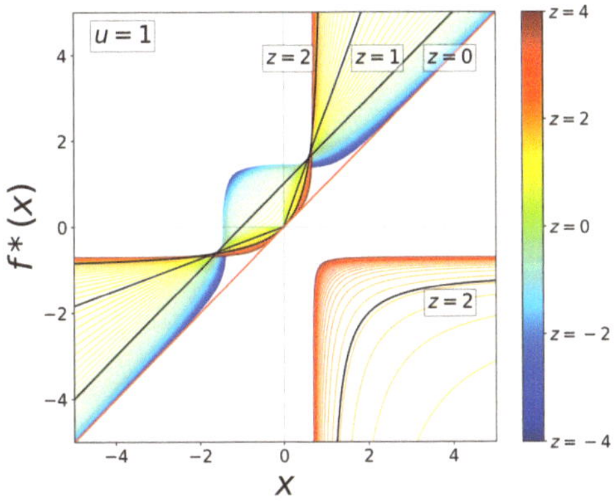

Figure 2. The RG fixed-point map $f^*(x)$ for the tangent bifurcation in Equation (3) shown for an extended range of values of the nonlinearity z. A two-branch map occurs for $z > 1$ with one branch tangent with the identity line. When $0 \leq z \leq 2$, the left branch shows a cusp touching the identity line up to $z \geq 1$. The branch at the right moves fast to infinity and dissapears at and below $z \leq 1$. The map separates from the identity line for $0 \leq z \leq 1$ and shows positive curvature around $x = 0$. When $0 \leq z$, the shape of the map is inverted, showing now negative curvature around $x = 0$. See text.

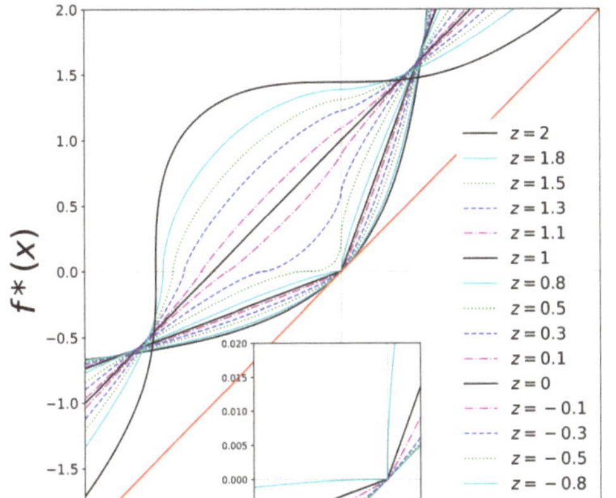

Figure 3. Similar to Figure 2, but showing more detail in the neighborhood of $x = 0$. The inset shows the cusp feature. See text.

4. Rich Gets Richer and Effortless Motion

We choose for the vegetable kingdom the universality class $\alpha = 3$ that we have identified to represent the rich-gets-richer principle or, in a network language, the preferential attachment processes [32]. In the preferential attachment network model [32], the connectivity (or degree) distribution is given by $P(L) = cL^{-3}$, where L is the degree, or number of links stemming out of a node. This is equivalent to the parent distribution with $\alpha = 3$ we have chosen for the vegetable kingdom. This implies the metabolic rate

$$R(M) = bM^{-1/3} \tag{17}$$

and the iterated map

$$f(x) = x + ux^{-1/3} \tag{18}$$

from which we obtain (see Equation (15)) the RG fixed-point map $f^*(x)$ trajectories

$$x_t = x_0 \exp_{-1/3}(x_0^{-1/3-1}ut) \to [4/3ut]^{3/4}, \; t \gg (3/4u)x_0^{4/3}. \tag{19}$$

That is, with $t = N$ and $x_t = M(N)$, we obtain, in accordance with Kleiber's law, the scaling law $M(N) \sim N^{3/4}$ for the metabolism $M(N)$. See Figure 4. Notice that we have considered for the vegetable kingdom the metabolic rate $R(M)$ to be associated with 'magnitude' in our formalism in the sense previously described above.

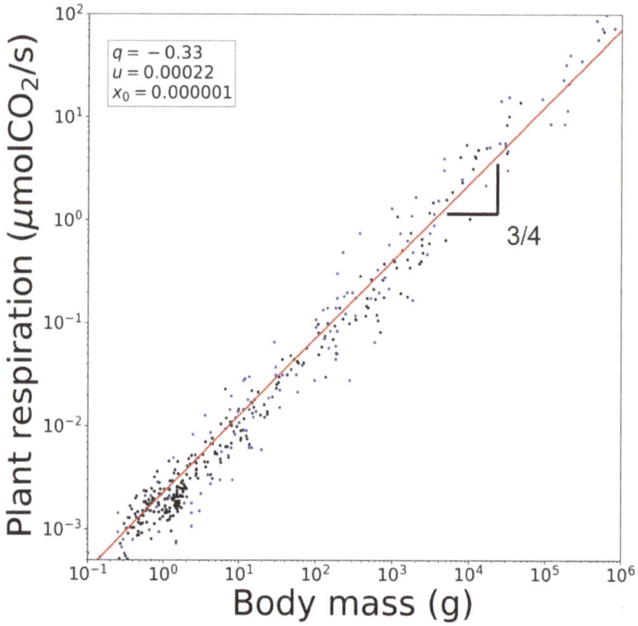

Figure 4. Reproduction of Kleiber's law for the vegetable kingdom using data for plant respiration rates. Blue dots are data taken from [14]. Black dots are data taken from [35]. The red line is from Equation (19). See text.

Next, we consider the animal kingdom and choose the universality class $\alpha = 4$ that represents criticality, e.g., the absence of a (quadratic) curvature term in a Landau free energy [33]. In the Landau theory, the free energy functional is assumed to be an analytic function of the order parameter η. A typical example is a magnet, for which the free energy is a function only of even powers of η, and where the first (quadratic) term is a function of temperature T. At the phase transition, $T = T_c$, a critical point, the quadratic term vanishes, making the next quartic term the dominant term. As a consequence, small displacements around the rest (or equilibrium) are costless.

However, as a difference with the above Equations (17)–(19), the metabolic rate $R(M)$ is now considered to be associated with 'frequency', not 'magnitude', in the sense described in the previous sections. We can start our analysis of this case with a parent distribution $P(F) \sim F^{-\beta}$, $\beta = 4$ and proceed to determine $M(N)$. However, as we know, this is equivalent to evaluating the functional inverse of the RG fixed-point map trajectories $x_{t+1} = f^*(x_t)$ that correspond to the map

$$f(x) = x + ux^{1/4}. \tag{20}$$

We have (see Equation (14))

$$t = u^{-1}[\ln_{1/4} x_t \; - \; \ln_{1/4} x_0] \rightarrow 4/3u^{-1}x_t^{3/4}, \;\; x_t \gg x_0. \tag{21}$$

Now $t = M(N)$ and $x_t = N$, as the conjugate pair of the trajectory in Equation (19) with $q = -1/3$, is the inverse function of the trajectory with $Q = 1/4$. That is, we obtain again, in accordance with Kleiber's law, the scaling law $M(N) \sim N^{3/4}$ for the metabolism $M(N)$ of the animal kingdom. See Figure 5.

The occurrence of the same power-law exponent $3/4$ for the metabolism of the two kingdoms involved in Kleiber's law, plants and animals, appears as one instance in the locus of conjugate values for the pairs of deformation exponents (q, Q) for the q-exponential and the Q-logarithmic functions shown in Figure 1.

Another possible example of a conjugate pair (q, Q) that involves a tight relationship between 'magnitudes' and 'frequencies' is that of river flow. In this case, we have Hack's law that relates river lengths with flow through transverse sections [36]. Hack's law shows the scaling of the largest upstream length $L_{\max}$ with its total cumulative area $A_{\max}$, $L_{\max} \sim A_{\max}^h$, where $h \sim 0.57$ [37]. This river structure can be theoretically approximated, among other possibilities [37], by the 'directed network model' [37] that complies with $(q = -1/2, Q = 1/3)$ and yields $\zeta = h = 2/3$ [37].

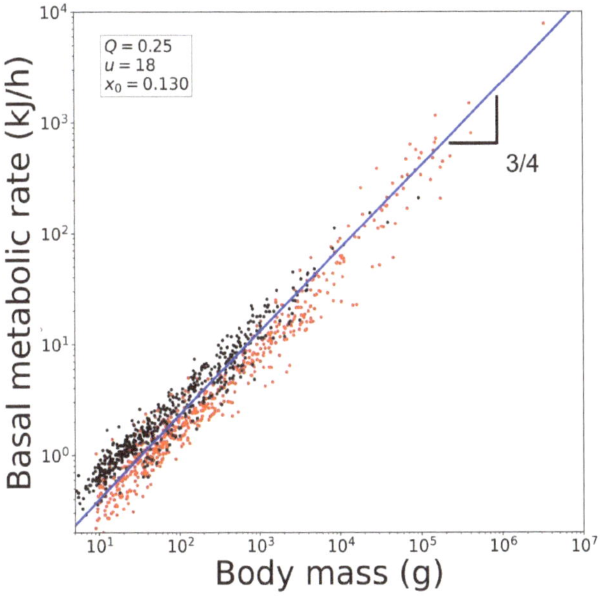

Figure 5. Reproduction of Kleiber's law for the animal kingdom using data for basal metabolic rates. Mammals (red) [38] and avians (black) [39]. The blue line is from Equation (21). See text.

5. Summary and Discussion

We have extended our nonlinear dynamical approach that reproduces real data for rank distributions [17–19], functions that decay either exponentially or as a power law (e.g., Zipf's law), to other measurable quantities, like dissipation rates as functions of mass or volume of organisms (geological, biological, urban), functions that increase exponentially or as power laws (e.g., Kleiber's law). We have emphasized the presence of universality classes (given by the exponent values α of the parent or source distributions $P(N) \sim N^{-\alpha}$). These exponent values coincide with the nonlinearity exponent z of the iterated map $f(x)$ equivalent to $P(N)$ and with values of the deformation parameter q of the deformed exponential in the RG fixed-point map $f^*(x)$ ruling in the background, $\alpha = z = q$. We have, in particular, focused on the occurrence of conjugate pairs of deformation values (q, Q) that display the same power-law exponent ζ (within appropriate intervals of the independent variable: rank k, iteration time t, mass or volume N) for the q-exponential function and its functional inverse, the Q-logarithm. See Figure 1. One important instance is that of Zipf's law $(q = 2, Q = 2)$, a situation in which our approach is capable of distinguishing between magnitude-rank and frequency-rank distributions [17]. Additionally, significantly, at these deformation values $(q = 2, Q = 2)$, the RG fixed-point map $f^*(x)$ is at a borderline (signaled, e.g., by the divergence of prime number reciprocals [19]), where the shape of $f^*(x)$ undergoes an important transformation (see Figures 2 and 3).

The transformation undergone by $f^*(x)$ at $z = 2$ is precisely the feature that we have taken advantage of to extend our approach from rank distributions to the description of scaling laws for quantities such as rates of dissipation as a function of system size (e.g., metabolic rates). Figure 2 shows $f^*(x)$ for a range of values of its nonlinearity z. When $z > 1$, the RG map has two branches, one of them tangent with the identity line. The map develops a cusp at $x = 0$ as $z \to 1$, while for $z \leq 1$, the second branch vanishes. The cusp becomes disconnected with the identity line just below $z = 1$ and from there shows an indentation (positive curvature) around $x = 0$. The shape of $f^*(x)$ transforms again at $z = 0$ when the curvature near $x = 0$ changes sign.

What we have done here is to show that the trajectories produced by the RG fixed-point map, in one case $0 < z < 1$ and in the other case $-1 < z < 0$, are capable of quantitatively reproducing the metabolism data involved in Kleiber's law. Our reasoning started by choosing two universality class exponent values: $\alpha = z = q = 3$ (for 'magnitudes', representing 'rich gets richer') and $\alpha = z = q = 4$ (for 'frequencies', representing null cost for small displacement motion). With these values, we formulated the RG fixed-point map and its trajectories that yield us the desired function $M(N)$, with metabolism being a function of individual mass or volume N. The chosen values $\alpha = 3$ and $\alpha = 4$ became, in our formalism, one pair of conjugate values $(q = -1/3, Q = 1/4)$ that have the property of producing the same value of the scaling exponent $3/4$ in $M(N) \sim N^{3/4}$, or Kleiber's law. See Figures 1, 4 and 5.

Recently [25], we have demonstrated that the trajectories of all RG fixed-point maps for the three known routes to chaos (intermittency, period doubling, and quasi-periodicity [24]) can be couched in the statistical–mechanical language of the (discrete time) Landau–Ginzburg (LG) equation. Additionally, the associated Lyapunov function [40] is precisely the expression for the Tsallis entropy [25]. Equation (10) is a particular case of the LG equation used to describe the most probable evolution of processes in statistical–mechanical systems. See [25] and references therein. The role of time t in the LG equation in Equation (10) is taken by the mass N, while M is a macroscopic variable relevant to the process described. For the plant kingdom, the differential equation's driving force is the power law $M^{-1/3}$. This driving force is the (functional) derivative of the Lyapunov function. This function represents a generalized thermodynamic potential and evolves monotonically as t, or N, increases along the solution of the LG equation [25]. In the case of Equations (10) and (17), it is given by

$$S_{\mathbf{q}} = \ln_{\mathbf{q}} M, \;\; \mathbf{q} = 1/3. \tag{22}$$

The Tsallis entropy above corresponds to a uniformly distributed set of events. It merely states that every time unit that makes up the characteristic time $T = R^{-1}$ for an organism of mass N equally contributes to its total value $T(N)$. Furthermore, for large N

$$S_{\mathbf{q}} \sim M(N)^{4/3} = [N^{3/4}]^{4/3} = N; \tag{23}$$

i.e., the Tsallis entropy in Equation (22) is extensive for the mass N. A parallel argument for the animal kingdom, which takes into account that the conjugate pair (q, Q) involves functions inverse to each other, leads too to an extensive Tsallis entropy. Moreover, considering that data for Kleiber's law consist of a list (or lists) of measured values of metabolic rates for a set (or sets) of species, we can write the rate equation in Equation (10) for discrete time. Clearly, this is the nonlinear iterated map in Equation (18) that, under the requirement that functional composition is equivalent to rescaling, leads to the RG fixed-point map $f^*(x)$ in Equations (3) or (16) with $z = -1/3$, and similarly with Equation (20).

It is important to emphasize that our approach leads to analytical closed-form expressions for the metabolic rate $R(M)$ in terms of the q-exponential and q-logarithmic functions in Equations (19) and (21). The power laws with the exponent $3/4$ correspond to the asymptotic, large N, behavior of these expressions. The full set of properties of $R(M)$ includes consideration of the entire positive real number interval, small and large N. The small N conduct of the q-deformed functions may explain the observed $2/3$ exponent in some data samples. Meanwhile, finite-size effects present for large N can be quantitatively reproduced via the shift of the maps involved away or towards the identity function, as it has been done for the rank distributions [17–19] . Therefore, the study presented here is yet another example of a complex system problem where the Tsallis generalized statistical mechanics provide pertinent results. Other issues addressed that involve Tsallis generalized entropy and related quantities are [34] within condensed matter physics: the formation of glasses, the transformation of a conductor into an insulator, and critical point fluctuations; concerning complex systems problems, the phenomenon of self-organization and the development of diversity (biological or social, like languages); and, as described here, the comprehension of empirical laws, like those relating to the universality of ranked data or the power-law scalings present in allometry. A common feature in all these cases is that access to their configurational space is severely hindered to a point where the allowed configurational space has a vanishing measure with respect to the initial setup [25]. This restriction is naturally provided by the attractors at the transitions to chaos present in the nonlinear dissipative maps employed to model these subjects [25].

As a finishing remark, we would like to bring attention to a set of curious circumstances where low-dimensional nonlinear dynamics have inadvertently been used to model complex systems. Such is the case of the "cobweb theorem" in economics [41,42], where successive iterations are employed to model actual price dependence on past offer. The next instance is in the study of biological rhythms [43], where cobweb plots are referred to as "zig-zag lines from cause to effect". These encounters with nonlinear dynamics occurred years before the subject was more formally advanced with the use of the RG technique as in the works of Feigenbaum [44] and Hu and Rudnick [22], but point towards its use in the modeling of complex phenomena. Ours is a quantitative attempt to establish a methodology based on nonlinear dynamics to study complex systems.

We wish a joyful 80th birthday to Constantino Tsallis.

Author Contributions: Conceptualization, A.R. and L.J.C.-V.; methodology, A.R. and L.J.C.-V.; software, L.J.C.-V.; validation, A.R. and L.J.C.-V.; formal analysis, A.R. and L.J.C.-V.; investigation, A.R. and L.J.C.-V.; resources, A.R.; data curation, L.J.C.-V.; writing—original draft preparation, A.R. and L.J.C.-V.; writing—review and editing, A.R. and L.J.C.-V.; visualization, L.J.C.-V.; supervision, A.R.; project administration, A.R.; funding acquisition, A.R. All authors have read and agreed to the published version of the manuscript.

Funding: This research was funded by IN106120-PAPIIT-DGAPA-UNAM and 39572-Ciencia-de-Frontera-CONACyT.

Data Availability Statement: Data are available upon request.

Acknowledgments: L.J.C.-V. is deeply thankful to A.R. for all the fruitful discussions.

Conflicts of Interest: The authors declare no conflicts of interest.

References

1. Kleibers's Law. Wikipedia. Available online: https://en.wikipedia.org/wiki/Kleiber%27s_law (accessed on 24 December 2023).
2. Kleiber, M. Body size and metabolism. *Hilgardia* **1932**, *6*, 315–353. [CrossRef]
3. Kleiber, M. Body size and metabolic rate. *Physiol. Rev.* **1947**, *27*, 511–541. [CrossRef] [PubMed]
4. Kleiber, M. *The Fire of Life. An Introduction to Animal Energetics*; John Wiley & Sons, Inc.: New York, NY, USA; London, UK, 1961.
5. Von Bertalanffy, L. Quantitative laws in metabolism and growth. *Q. Rev. Biol.* **1957**, *32*, 217–231. [CrossRef] [PubMed]
6. West, G.; Brown, J.; Enquist, B. A general model for the origin of allometric scaling laws in biology. *Science* **1997**, *276*, 122–126. [CrossRef] [PubMed]
7. West, G.; Brown, J.; Enquist, B. A general model for the structure and allometry of plant vascular systems. *Nature* **1999**, *400*, 664–667. [CrossRef]
8. West, G.; Brown, J.; Enquist, B. The fourth dimension of life: Fractal geometry and allometric scaling of organisms. *Science* **1999**, *284*, 1677–1679. [CrossRef]
9. West, G.; Woodruff, W.; Brown, J. Allometric scaling of metabolic rate from molecules and mitochondria to cells and mammals. *Proc. Natl. Acad. Sci. USA* **2002**, *99*, 2473–2478. [CrossRef]
10. Banavar, J.; Maritan, A.; Rinaldo, A. Size and form in efficient transportation networks. *Nature* **1999**, *399*, 130–132. [CrossRef]
11. Banavar, J.; Moses, M.; Brown, J.; Damuth, J.; Rinaldo, A.; Sibly, R.; Maritan, A. A general basis for quarter-power scaling in animals *Proc. Natl. Acad. Sci. USA* **2010**, *107*, 15816–15820. [CrossRef]
12. Banavar, J.; Cooke, T.; Rinaldo, A.; Maritan, A. Form, function, and evolution of living organisms. *Proc. Natl. Acad. Sci. USA* **2014**, *111*, 3332–3337. [CrossRef]
13. Reich, P.; Tjoelker, M.; Machado, J.; Oleksyn, J. Universal scaling of respiratory metabolism, size and nitrogen in plants. *Nature* **2006**, *439*, 457–461. [CrossRef] [PubMed]
14. Mori, S.; Yamaji, K.; Ishida, A.; Prokushkin, S.; Masyagina, O.; Hagihara, A.; Hoque, A.; Suwa, R.; Osawa, A.; Nishizono, T. Others Mixed-power scaling of whole-plant respiration from seedlings to giant trees. *Proc. Natl. Acad. Sci. USA* **2010**, *107*, 1447–1451. [CrossRef] [PubMed]
15. Ballesteros, F.; Martinez, V.; Luque, B.; Lacasa, L.; Valor, E.; Moya, A. On the thermodynamic origin of metabolic scaling. *Sci. Rep.* **2018**, *8*, 1448. [CrossRef] [PubMed]
16. Rameaux, S. Rapport sur un mémoire adressé a l'Académie royale de Médicine. *Bull. Acad. Nat. Roy.* **1838**, 3, 1094–1100.
17. Velarde, C.; Robledo, A. Rank distributions: Frequency vs. magnitude. *PLoS ONE* **2017**, *12*, e0186015. [CrossRef] [PubMed]
18. Velarde, C.; Robledo, A. Dynamical analogues of rank distributions. *PLoS ONE* **2019**, *14*, e0211226. [CrossRef] [PubMed]
19. Velarde, C.; Robledo, A. Number theory, borderline dimension and extensive entropy in distributions of ranked data. *PLoS ONE* **2022**, *17*, e0279448. [CrossRef]
20. Saddle-Node Bifurcation (Redirected from Tangent Bifurcation). Wikipedia. Available online: https://en.wikipedia.org/wiki/Saddle-node_bifurcation (accessed on 24 December 2023).
21. Schuster, H.; Just, W. *Deterministic Chaos: An Introduction*; John Wiley & Sons, Inc.: New York, NY, USA; London, UK, 2006.
22. Hu, B.; Rudnick, J. Exact solutions to the Feigenbaum renormalization-group equations for intermittency. *Phys. Rev. Lett.* **1982**, *48*, 1645. [CrossRef]
23. Baldovin, F.; Robledo, A. Sensitivity to initial conditions at bifurcations in one-dimensional nonlinear maps: Rigorous nonextensive solutions. *Europhys. Lett.* **2002**, *60*, 518. [CrossRef]
24. Routes to Chaos. Encyclopedia of Mathematics. Wikipedia. Available online: https://encyclopediaofmath.org/wiki/Routes_to_chaos (accessed on 24 December 2023).
25. Robledo, A.; Velarde, C. How, why and when Tsallis statistical mechanics provides precise descriptions of natural phenomena. *Entropy* **2022**, *24*, 1761. [CrossRef]
26. Tsallis, C. Possible generalization of Boltzmann-Gibbs statistics. *J. Stat. Phys.* **1988**, 52, 479–487. [CrossRef]
27. Tsallis, C. *Introduction to Nonextensive Statistical Mechanics: Approaching a Complex World*; Springer: Berlin/Heidelberg, Germany, 2009.
28. Pietronero, L.; Tosatti, E.; Tosatti, V.; Vespignani, A. Explaining the uneven distribution of numbers in nature: the laws of Benford and Zipf. *Phys. Stat. Mech. Appl.* **2001**, 293, 297–304. [CrossRef]
29. Quantile Function. Wikipedia. Available online: https://en.wikipedia.org/wiki/Quantile_function (accessed on 24 December 2023).
30. Zipf's Law. Wikipedia. Available online: https://en.wikipedia.org/wiki/Zipf%27s_law (accessed on 24 December 2023).
31. Barabási, A.; Albert, R. Emergence of scaling in random networks. *Science* **1999**, *286*, 509–512.
32. Barabási, A.-L. The Barabási-Albert Model. In *Network Science*; Cambridge University Press: Cambridge, UK, 2016. Available online: http://barabasi.com/networksciencebook/ (accessed on 24 December 2023). [CrossRef] [PubMed]
33. Landau Theory. Wikipedia. Available online: https://en.wikipedia.org/wiki/Landau_theory (accessed on 24 December 2023).

34. Robledo, A.; Camacho-Vidales, L.J. A zodiac of studies on complex systems. *Supl. Rev. Mex. Física* **2020**, *1*, 32–53.
35. Kurosawa, Y.; Mori, S.; Wang, M.; Pedro, Ferrio, J.; Nishizono, T.; Yamaji, K.; Koyama, K.; Haruma, T.; Doyama, K. Ontogenetic changes in root and shoot respiration, fresh mass and surface area of Fagus crenata. *Ann. Bot.* **2023**, *131*, 313–322. [CrossRef]
36. Hack's Law. Wikipedia. Available online: https://en.wikipedia.org/wiki/Hack%27s_law (accessed on 24 December 2023). [CrossRef] [PubMed]
37. Rinaldo, A.; Rigon, R.; Banavar, J.; Maritan, A.; Rodriguez-Iturbe, I. Evolution and selection of river networks: Statics, dynamics, and complexity. *Proc. Natl. Acad. Sci. USA* **2014**, *111*, 2417–2424.
38. McNab, B. An analysis of the factors that influence the level and scaling of mammalian BMR. *Comp. Biochem. Physiol. Part Mol. Integr. Physiol.* **2008**, *151*, 5–28. [CrossRef]
39. McNab, B. Ecological factors affect the level and scaling of avian BMR. *Comp. Biochem. Physiol. Part Mol. Integr. Physiol.* **2009**, 152, 22–45. [CrossRef]
40. Lyapunov Function. Wikipedia. Available online: https://en.wikipedia.org/wiki/Lyapunov_function (accessed on 24 December 2023). [CrossRef]
41. Ezekiel, M. The cobweb theorem. *Q. J. Econ.* **1938**, 52, 255–280.
42. Waugh, F. Cobweb models. *Am. J. Agric. Econ.* **1964**, 46, 732–750. [CrossRef]
43. Winfree, A. Biological rhythms and the behavior of populations of coupled oscillators. *J. Theor. Biol.* **1967**, 16, 15–42. [CrossRef]
44. Feigenbaum, M. Quantitative universality for a class of nonlinear transformations. *J. Stat. Phys.* **1978**, 19, 25–52. [CrossRef] [PubMed]

Article

First-Principle Validation of Fourier's Law: One-Dimensional Classical Inertial Heisenberg Model

Henrique Santos Lima [1,2,*], Constantino Tsallis [1,2,3,4] and Fernando Dantas Nobre [1,2]

1. Centro Brasileiro de Pesquisas Físicas, Rua Xavier Sigaud 150, Rio de Janeiro 22290-180, RJ, Brazil; tsallis@cbpf.br (C.T.); fdnobre@cbpf.br (F.D.N.)
2. National Institute of Science and Technology for Complex Systems, Rua Xavier Sigaud 150, Rio de Janeiro 22290-180, RJ, Brazil
3. Santa Fe Institute, 1399 Hyde Park Road, Santa Fe, NM 87501, USA
4. Complexity Science Hub Vienna, Josefstädter Strasse 39, 1080 Vienna, Austria
* Correspondence: hslima94@cbpf.br

Abstract: The thermal conductance of a one-dimensional classical inertial Heisenberg model of linear size L is computed, considering the first and last particles in thermal contact with heat baths at higher and lower temperatures, T_h and T_l ($T_h > T_l$), respectively. These particles at the extremities of the chain are subjected to standard Langevin dynamics, whereas all remaining rotators ($i = 2, \cdots, L-1$) interact by means of nearest-neighbor ferromagnetic couplings and evolve in time following their own equations of motion, being investigated numerically through molecular-dynamics numerical simulations. Fourier's law for the heat flux is verified numerically, with the thermal conductivity becoming independent of the lattice size in the limit $L \to \infty$, scaling with the temperature, as $\kappa(T) \sim T^{-2.25}$, where $T = (T_h + T_l)/2$. Moreover, the thermal conductance, $\sigma(L, T) \equiv \kappa(T)/L$, is well-fitted by a function, which is typical of nonextensive statistical mechanics, according to $\sigma(L, T) = A \exp_q(-Bx^\eta)$, where A and B are constants, $x = L^{0.475}T$, $q = 2.28 \pm 0.04$, and $\eta = 2.88 \pm 0.04$.

Keywords: Fourier's law; generalized entropies; non-equilibrium physics; stochastic processes

1. Introduction

Two centuries ago, Fourier proposed the law for heat conduction in a given macroscopic system, where the heat flux varies linearly with the temperature gradient, $\mathbf{J} \propto -\nabla T$ [1]. For a simple one-dimensional system (e.g., a metallic bar along the $\hat{x}$ axis, $\mathbf{J} = J\hat{x}$), the heat flux J (rate of heat per unit area) is given by

$$J = -\kappa \frac{dT}{dx}, \qquad (1)$$

where κ is known as thermal conductivity. In principle, κ may depend on the temperature, although most measurements are carried at room temperature, leading to values of κ for many materials (see, e.g., Ref. [2]). Usually, metals (like silver, copper, and gold) present large values of κ, and are considered good heat conductors, whereas poor heat conductors (such as air and glass fiber) are characterized by small thermal conductivities; typically, the ratio between the thermal conductivities of these two limiting cases may differ by a 10^4 factor. In most cases, good thermal conductors are also good electrical conductors, and obey the Wiedemann–Franz law, which states that the ratio of their thermal and electrical conductivities follows a simple formula, being directly proportional to the temperature [3].

In recent years, numerous studies have been conducted to validate Fourier's law in a wide variety of physical systems, both experimentally and theoretically. Particularly, investigations for which microscopic ingredients may be responsible for the property of heat conduction were carried out, and it has been verified that thermal conductivity may be generated by different types of particles (or quasi-particles). In the case of good electrical conductors, the most significant contribution to thermal conductivity comes from free

Citation: Lima, H.S.; Tsallis, C.; Nobre, F.D. First-Principle Validation of Fourier's Law: One-Dimensional Classical Inertial Heisenberg Model. *Entropy* **2024**, *26*, 25. https://doi.org/10.3390/e26010025

Academic Editor: Giuliano Benenti

Received: 21 November 2023
Revised: 17 December 2023
Accepted: 22 December 2023
Published: 25 December 2023

Copyright: © 2023 by the authors. Licensee MDPI, Basel, Switzerland. This article is an open access article distributed under the terms and conditions of the Creative Commons Attribution (CC BY) license (https://creativecommons.org/licenses/by/4.0/).

electrons, whereas in electrical insulators, such contributions may arise from quasi-particles, like phonons and magnons, or even from defects. For instance, for antiferromagnetic electrical insulators, such as Sr_2CuO_3 and $SrCuO_2$, which surprisingly behave as $S = 1/2$

Heisenberg chains, magnons yield the most relevant contribution for the thermal conductivity, which can be fitted by a $1/T^2$ law, at high temperatures [4]. In these materials, the low-temperature regime presents ballistic-like heat conduction, increasing as the size of the system increases, while the high-temperature regime presents normal heat conduction [5–7].

Being a classical result, there is, in principle, no reason why Fourier's law should generally apply to physical systems. This aspect has generated controversies in the literature, both in experimental and theoretical studies (for a comprehensive theoretical discussion, see, e.g., Ref. [8]). As a typical anomaly, the thermal conductivity κ (which should be an intensive quantity) appears, in many cases, to depend on the size of the system, e.g., on the total number of constituents, as it happens for chains of nonlinear oscillators, where κ increases with the total number of elements [9]. This anomaly is usually considered a failure of Fourier's law. In addition, non-Fourier heat conduction can also emerge from the Maxwell–Cattaneo–Vernotte hyperbolic heat equation, which represents the relativistic version of the heat equation [10]. Recent advances in non-Fourier heat conduction can be found in the work by Benenti et al. [11].

Several experimental investigations have verified Fourier's law in a diverse range of systems [4,12–15], including coal and rocks from coalfields [13], as well as two-dimensional materials [14,15]. On the other hand, some authors claim to have found anomalies [16], or even violations of this law for silicon nanowires [17], carbon nanotubes [18], and low-dimensional nanoscale systems [19]. Furthermore, a curious crossover, induced by disorder, was observed in quantum wires, where, by gradually increasing disorder, one goes from a low-disorder regime, where the law is apparently not valid, to another regime characterized by a uniform temperature gradient inside the wire, in agreement with Fourier's law [20,21].

From the theoretical point of view, many authors have investigated Fourier's law in a wide diversity of models [9,22–46], like a Lorentz gas [23], biological [30] and small quantum systems [29], chains of coupled harmonic [31] or anharmonic [9,28,34] oscillators, models characterized by long-range [38,46] or disordered [41] interactions, as well as systems of coupled classical rotators [42–45]. In the case of a coupled XY nearest-neighbor-interacting rotator chain [44], the temperature dependence of the thermal conductance was well-fitted by a q-Gaussian distribution,

$$P_q(u) = P_0 \exp_q(-\beta u^2) \,, \tag{2}$$

defined in terms of the q-exponential function,

$$\exp_q(u) = [1 + (1-q)u]_+^{1/(1-q)} \,; \quad (\exp_1(u) = \exp(u)) \,, \tag{3}$$

where $P_0 \equiv P_q(0)$ and $[y]_+ = y$, for $y > 0$ (zero otherwise). The distribution in Equation (2) is very common in the context of nonextensive statistical mechanics [47], since it appears from the extremization of the generalized entropy, known as S_q, characterized by a real index q [48],

$$S_q = k \sum_{i=1}^{W} p_i \left(\ln_q \frac{1}{p_i} \right) , \tag{4}$$

where we introduced the q-logarithm definition,

$$\ln_q u = \frac{u^{1-q} - 1}{1-q} \,; \qquad (\ln_1 u = \ln u) \,. \tag{5}$$

Therefore, one recovers Boltzmann–Gibbs (BG) entropy,

$$S_{BG} = -k \sum_{i=1}^{W} p_i \ln p_i \,, \tag{6}$$

as $\lim_{q\to 1} S_q = S_{\rm BG}$, whereas in the microcanonical ensemble, where all microstates present equal probability, $p_i = 1/W$, Equation (4) becomes,

$$S_q = k \ln_q W \,. \tag{7}$$

Above, the q-exponential function in Equation (3) appears precisely as the inverse function of the q-logarithm of Equation (5), i.e., $\exp_q(\ln_q u) = \ln_q(\exp_q(u)) = u$.

Since the introduction of the entropy S_q in Equation (4), a large amount of works appeared in the literature, defining generalized functions and distributions (see, e.g., Ref. [47]). In particular, a recent study based on superstatistics has found a stretched q-exponential probability distribution [49],

$$P_q(u) = P_0 \exp_q(-\beta|u|^\eta) \quad (0 < \eta \le 1), \tag{8}$$

as well as its associated entropic form.

As already mentioned, the latest advances in experimental techniques made it possible to investigate thermal and transport properties and, hence, Fourier's law, in low-dimensional (or even finite-size) systems, like two-dimensional materials [14,15], silicon nanowires [17], carbon nanotubes [18], and low-dimensional nanoscale systems [19]. These measurements motivate computational studies in finite-size systems of particles that present their own equations of motion, e.g., systems of interacting classical rotators, whose dynamics may be followed through the direct integration of their equations of motion. In this way, one may validate (or not) Fourier's law, by computing the temperature and size dependence of the thermal conductance. A recent analysis of a system of coupled nearest-neighbor-interacting classical XY rotators [45], on d-dimensional lattices ($d = 1, 2, 3$) of linear size L, has shown that, for a wider range of temperatures, the temperature dependence of the thermal conductance was better fitted by a more general ansatz than the q-Gaussian distribution of Equation (2). In fact, Fourier's law was validated in Ref. [45] by fitting the thermal conductance in terms of the functional form of Equation (8), with values of $\eta(d) > 2$.

In the present work, we analyze the thermal conductance of a one-dimensional classical inertial Heisenberg model of linear size L, considering the first and last particles in thermal contact with heat baths at temperatures T_h and T_l ($T_h > T_l$), respectively. All remaining rotators ($i = 2, \cdots, L-1$) interact by means of nearest-neighbor ferromagnetic couplings and evolve in time through molecular-dynamics numerical simulations. For this classical model, we specifically concentrate on the high-temperature limit, where there is no need for a spin wave approach, such as the Holstein–Primakoff quantum transformations. Our numerical data validate Fourier's law, and similar to those of Ref. [45], the thermal conductance is well-fitted by the functional form of Equation (8). The present results suggest that this form should apply in general for the thermal conductance of nearest-neighbor-interacting systems of classical rotators. In the Section 2, we define the model and the numerical procedure; in Section 3, we present and discuss our results; in Section 4, we present our conclusions.

2. Materials and Methods

The one-dimensional classical inertial Heisenberg model, for a system of L-interacting rotators, is defined by the Hamiltonian,

$$\mathcal{H} = \frac{1}{2}\sum_{i=1}^{L} \boldsymbol{\ell}_i^2 + \frac{1}{2}\sum_{\langle ij\rangle}\left(1 - \mathbf{S}_i \cdot \mathbf{S}_j\right), \tag{9}$$

where $\boldsymbol{\ell}_i \equiv (\ell_{ix}, \ell_{iy}, \ell_{iz})$ and $\mathbf{S}_i \equiv (S_{ix}, S_{iy}, S_{iz})$ represent, respectively, continuously varying angular momenta and spin variables at each site of the linear chain, whereas $\sum_{\langle ij\rangle}$ denote summations over pairs of nearest-neighbor spins; herein, we set, without loss of generality, $k_{\rm B}$, moments of inertia, and ferromagnetic couplings, all equal to the unit. Moreover, spins present the unit norm, $\mathbf{S}_i^2 = 1$, and at each site, angular momentum $\boldsymbol{\ell}_i$ must be perpendicular to $\mathbf{S}_i$, yielding $\boldsymbol{\ell}_i \cdot \mathbf{S}_i = 0$; these two constraints are imposed at the initial state and should be preserved throughout the whole time evolution.

One should notice that, in contrast to a system of coupled classical XY rotators, where canonical conjugate polar coordinates are commonly used [45], in the Heisenberg case, one often chooses Cartesian coordinates [50–52]. The reason for this is essentially technical, since in terms of spherical coordinates (more precisely, θ, ϕ, and their canonical conjugates ℓ_θ, ℓ_ϕ), a troublesome term $(1/\sin^2\theta)$ appears in the corresponding equations of motion, leading to numerical difficulties [53,54]. However, some of the analytical results to be derived next recover those of the classical inertial XY model for $\mathbf{S}_i = (\sin\theta_i, \cos\theta_i, 0)$ and $\boldsymbol{\ell}_i = \ell_i\hat{\mathbf{z}}$.

It is important to mention that previous research on the thermal conductivity has been carried out for a classical one-dimensional Heisenberg spin model, by using Monte Carlo and Langevin numerical simulations [55], as well as for a classical one-dimensional spin-phonon system, through linear-response theory and the Green–Kubo formula [56]. These investigations did not take into account the kinetic contribution in Equation (9), so that in order to obtain the thermal conductivity they assumed the validity of Fourier's law. The main advantage of the introduction of the kinetic term in Equation (9) concerns the possibility of deriving equations of motion, making it feasible to follow the time evolution of the system through molecular-dynamics simulations, by a numerical integration of such equations. This technique allows one to validate Fourier's law, as well as obtain its thermal conductivity directly.

In order to carry out this procedure, we consider an open chain of rotators with the first and last particles in thermal contact with heat baths at higher and lower temperatures, T_h and T_l ($T_h > T_l$), respectively (cf. Figure 1), whereas all remaining rotators ($i = 2, \cdots, L-1$) follow their usual equations of motion (see, e.g., Refs. [50–52]). In this way, one has for sites $i = 2, \ldots, L-1$,

$$\begin{aligned} \dot{\mathbf{S}}_i &= \boldsymbol{\ell}_i \times \mathbf{S}_i\,, \\ \dot{\boldsymbol{\ell}}_i &= \mathbf{S}_i \times (\mathbf{S}_{i+1} + \mathbf{S}_{i-1})\,, \end{aligned} \tag{10}$$

whereas the rotators at extremities follow standard Langevin dynamics,

$$\begin{aligned} \dot{\boldsymbol{\ell}}_1 &= -\gamma_h \boldsymbol{\ell}_1 + \mathbf{S}_1 \times \mathbf{S}_2 + \boldsymbol{\eta}_h\,, \\ \dot{\boldsymbol{\ell}}_L &= -\gamma_l \boldsymbol{\ell}_L + \mathbf{S}_L \times \mathbf{S}_{L-1} + \boldsymbol{\eta}_l\,. \end{aligned} \tag{11}$$

Above, γ_h and γ_l represent friction coefficients, whereas $\boldsymbol{\eta}_h$ and $\boldsymbol{\eta}_l$ denote independent three-dimensional vectors, $\boldsymbol{\eta}_h \equiv (\eta_{hx}, \eta_{hy}, \eta_{hz})$, $\boldsymbol{\eta}_l \equiv (\eta_{lx}, \eta_{ly}, \eta_{lz})$, where each Cartesian component stands for a Gaussian white noise with zero mean and correlated in time,

$$\begin{aligned} \langle \eta_{h\mu}(t) \rangle &= \langle \eta_{l\mu}(t) \rangle = 0\,, \\ \langle \eta_{h\mu}(t)\eta_{l\nu}(t') \rangle &= \langle \eta_{h\mu}(t')\eta_{l\nu}(t) \rangle = 0\,, \\ \langle \eta_{h\mu}(t)\eta_{h\nu}(t') \rangle &= 2\delta_{\mu\nu}\gamma_h T_h \delta(t-t')\,, \\ \langle \eta_{l\mu}(t)\eta_{l\nu}(t') \rangle &= 2\delta_{\mu\nu}\gamma_l T_l \delta(t-t')\,, \end{aligned} \tag{12}$$

with the indexes μ and ν denoting Cartesian components; from now on, we will set the friction coefficients γ_h and γ_l equal to the unit. One should mention that different types of thermostats have been used to investigate transport properties in systems out of equilibrium (see, e.g., Ref. [42] for an application of Nosé–Hoover thermostats to a system of interacting planar rotators); however, for the present Heisenberg chain, we found it more convenient to use standard Langevin thermostats, as defined above.

The condition of a constant norm for the spin variables yields

$$\frac{dS_i}{dt} = \frac{d(\mathbf{S}_i \cdot \mathbf{S}_i)^{1/2}}{dt} = 0 \quad \Rightarrow \quad \mathbf{S}_i \cdot \dot{\mathbf{S}}_i = 0\,, \tag{13}$$

which should be used together with $\boldsymbol{\ell}_i \cdot \mathbf{S}_i = 0$ in order to eliminate $\dot{\boldsymbol{\ell}}_i$ and calculate $\ddot{\mathbf{S}}_i$ from Equations (10) and (11). For rotators at sites $i = 2, \cdots, L-1$, one has

$$\ddot{\mathbf{S}}_i = (\mathbf{S}_{i+1} + \mathbf{S}_{i-1}) - \left[\mathbf{S}_i \cdot (\mathbf{S}_{i+1} + \mathbf{S}_{i-1}) + \dot{\mathbf{S}}_i^2\right]\mathbf{S}_i\,, \tag{14}$$

whereas, for those at extremities,

$$\begin{aligned}\ddot{\mathbf{S}}_1 &= -\dot{\mathbf{S}}_1 + \mathbf{S}_2 - \left[\mathbf{S}_1 \cdot \mathbf{S}_2 + \dot{\mathbf{S}}_1^2\right]\mathbf{S}_1 + \mathbf{S}_1 \times \boldsymbol{\eta}_h\,, \\ \ddot{\mathbf{S}}_L &= -\dot{\mathbf{S}}_L + \mathbf{S}_{L-1} - \left[\mathbf{S}_L \cdot \mathbf{S}_{L-1} + \dot{\mathbf{S}}_L^2\right]\mathbf{S}_L + \mathbf{S}_L \times \boldsymbol{\eta}_l\,.\end{aligned} \tag{15}$$

For the system illustrated in Figure 1, we will consider the temperatures of the heat baths differing by 2ε, with ε representing a positive dimensionless parameter; moreover, the temperature parameter $T = (T_h + T_l)/2$ will vary in a certain range of positive values. Equations (14) and (15) are transformed into first-order differential equations (e.g., by defining a new variable $\mathbf{V}_i \equiv \dot{\mathbf{S}}_i$) to be solved numerically through the velocity Verlet method [57,58], with a time step $dt = 0.005$, for different lattice sizes L (please, see the Appendix A). The rotators at the bulk (i= $2, \cdots, L-1$) follow a continuity equation,

$$\frac{dE_i}{dt} = -(J_i - J_{i-1})\,, \tag{16}$$

where

$$E_i = \frac{1}{2}\ell_i^2 + \frac{1}{2}\sum_{j=i\pm 1}\left(1 - \mathbf{S}_i \cdot \mathbf{S}_j\right), \tag{17}$$

so the stationary state is attained for $(dE_i/dt) = 0$, i.e., $J_i = J_{i-1}$. The derivation is simple, since from Equation (13) and $\ell_i \cdot \mathbf{S}_i = 0$, we have $\dot{\mathbf{S}}_i^2 = \ell_i^2$, hence,

$$\frac{d}{dt}E_i = \dot{\mathbf{S}}_i \cdot \ddot{\mathbf{S}}_i - \frac{1}{2}\left[\dot{\mathbf{S}}_i \cdot (\mathbf{S}_{i+1} + \mathbf{S}_{i-1}) + \mathbf{S}_i \cdot \left(\dot{\mathbf{S}}_{i+1} + \dot{\mathbf{S}}_{i-1}\right)\right]. \tag{18}$$

This equation, together with Equation (14), yields

$$\frac{d}{dt}E_i = \frac{1}{2}\left[\dot{\mathbf{S}}_i \cdot (\mathbf{S}_{i+1} + \mathbf{S}_{i-1}) - \mathbf{S}_i \cdot \left(\dot{\mathbf{S}}_{i+1} + \dot{\mathbf{S}}_{i-1}\right)\right] = 0 \tag{19}$$

at the stationary state. Data are obtained at stationary states, which, as usual, take longer to reach for increasing lattice sizes. For numerical reasons, to decrease fluctuations in the bulk due to the noise, we compute an average heat flux by discarding a certain number of particles p near the extremities (typically $p \simeq 0.15L$). In this way, we define an average heat flux as

$$J \equiv \frac{1}{L-2p}\sum_{i=p+1}^{L-p}\langle J_i\rangle\,, \tag{20}$$

$$J_i = \frac{1}{2}\left(\mathbf{S}_i \cdot \dot{\mathbf{S}}_{i+1} - \mathbf{S}_{i+1} \cdot \dot{\mathbf{S}}_i\right), \tag{21}$$

whereas $\langle .. \rangle$ denotes time and sample averages, which will be described next.

Let us emphasize that for $\mathbf{S}_i = (\sin\theta_i, \cos\theta_i, 0)$ and $\boldsymbol{\ell}_i = \ell_i\hat{\mathbf{z}}$, one recovers the expression for the heat flux of the classical inertial XY model, i.e., $J_i = \frac{1}{2}(\ell_i + \ell_{i+1})\sin(\theta_i - \theta_{i+1})$ [45,59], showing the appropriateness of the Cartesian-coordinate approach used herein for the classical inertial Heisenberg model.

Let us now describe the time evolution procedure; for a time step $dt = 0.005$, each unit of time corresponds to 200 integrations of the equations of motion. We considered a transient of 5×10^7 time units to compute the averages $\langle J_i \rangle$ in Equation (20), and checked that this transient time was sufficient to fulfill the condition $J_i = J_{i-1}$ (within, at least, a three-decimal digits accuracy), for all values of L analyzed. After that, simulations were carried out for an additional interval of 2×10^8 time units (leading to a total time of 2.5×10^8 for each simulation). The interval 2×10^8 was divided into 80 equally spaced windows of 2.5×10^6 time units, so that time averages were taken inside each window; then an additional sample average was taken over these 80 time windows, leading to the averages $\langle J_i \rangle$.

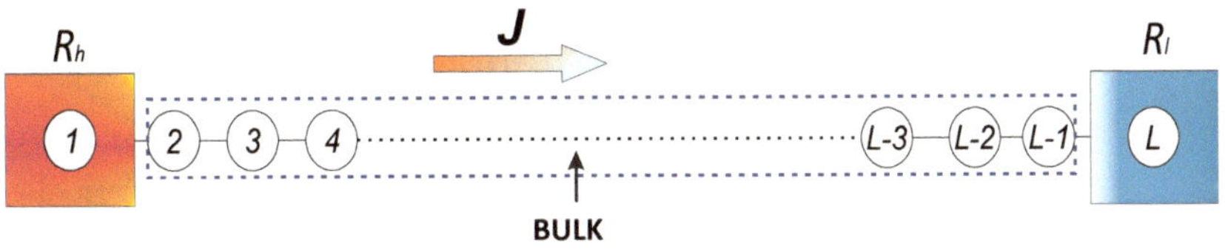

Figure 1. Illustration of the system defined in Equation (9), where the rotators at extremities of the chain are subjected to heat baths at different temperatures. The hot (R_h) and cold (R_l) reservoirs are at temperatures $T_h = T(1+\varepsilon)$ and $T_l = T(1-\varepsilon)$, respectively, leading to an average heat flux $\mathbf{J} = J\mathbf{x}$ throughout the bulk (see text). The rotators at sites $i = 2, \ldots, L-1$ interact with their respective nearest neighbors.

Using the results of Equation (20), one may calculate the thermal conductivity of Equation (1), and consequently, the thermal conductance,

$$\sigma = \frac{J}{T_h - T_l} = \frac{J}{2T\varepsilon} \equiv \frac{\kappa}{L}\,. \tag{22}$$

In the next section, we present the results of both quantities, obtained from the numerical procedure described above.

3. Results

We simulate the system of Figure 1 for different lattice sizes, namely, $L = 50, 70, 100, 140$, considering the heat-bath temperatures differing by 2ε, with $\varepsilon = 0.125$. The temperature parameter $T = (T_h + T_l)/2$ varied in the interval $0 < T \leq 3.5$, capturing both low- and high-temperature regimes. The values of L ($L \geq 50$) were chosen adequately to guarantee that the thermal conductivity κ did not present any dependence on the size L in the high-temperature regime, as expected.

In Figure 2, we present numerical data for the thermal conductivity Figure 2a and thermal conductance Figure 2b versus temperature (log–log representations) and different sizes L. The similar qualitative behaviors of the data displayed in both properties of Figure 2, for different values of L, evidence that the sizes considered in the present analysis ($L \geq 50$) are sufficiently large, in the sense that finite-size effects do not play a relevant role. In Figure 2a, we exhibit $\kappa(L,T)$ (the dependence of the thermal conductivity on the size L, used herein, will become clear below), showing a crossover between two distinct regimes (for $T \simeq 0.3$), as described next. (i) A low-temperature regime, where κ depends on the size L, decreasing smoothly for increasing temperatures (L fixed). The plots of Figure 2a show that, in the limit $T \to 0$, an extrapolated value, $\kappa(L,0) \equiv \lim_{T\to 0} \kappa(L,T)$, increases with L. Such a low-temperature increase with L has been observed in other one-dimensional models (see, e.g., Refs. [42–45]) and is reminiscent of the behavior expected for a chain of coupled classical harmonic oscillators. This anomaly is attributed to the classical approach used herein, indicating that for low temperatures, a quantum–mechanical procedure should be applied. (ii) A high-temperature regime, where κ essentially does not depend on L (in the limit $L \to \infty$), as expected from Fourier's law. Moreover, in this regime, one notices that κ decreases with the temperature as it generally occurs with liquids and solids. For increasing temperature, the thermal conductivity of most liquids usually decreases as the liquid expands and the molecules move apart; in the case of solids, due to lattice distortions, higher temperatures make it more difficult for electrons to flow, leading to a reduction in their thermal conductivity. The results of Figure 2a indicate that the thermal conductivity becomes independent of the lattice size in the limit $L \to \infty$, scaling with the temperature as $\kappa(T) \sim T^{-2.25}$ at high temperatures. Therefore, the system becomes a thermal insulator at high temperatures, approaching this state according to $\kappa(T) \sim T^{-2.25}$. Despite the simplicity of the one-dimensional classical inertial Heisenberg model of Figure 1, the present results are very close to experimental verifications in some antiferromagnetic electrical insulators, such as the Heisenberg chain cuprates Sr_2CuO_3

and $SrCuO_2$, for which the thermal conductivity is well-fitted by a $1/T^2$ law at high temperatures [4]. We should note that the one-dimensional Heisenberg model with nearest-neighbor ferromagnetic interactions, defined by the Hamiltonian of Equation (9), does not present an equilibrium phase transition, being characterized by a paramagnetic state for all temperatures $T > 0$. In this case, one may perform the following transformations in the Hamiltonian of Equation (9), leaving it unaltered: $1/2 \to -1/2$ (which incorporates the coupling constant), as well as $\mathbf{S}_j \to -\mathbf{S}_j$, keeping $\mathbf{S}_i$ unchanged. Consequently, the Hamiltonian of Equation (9) applies to antiferromagnetic systems at high temperatures, as well.

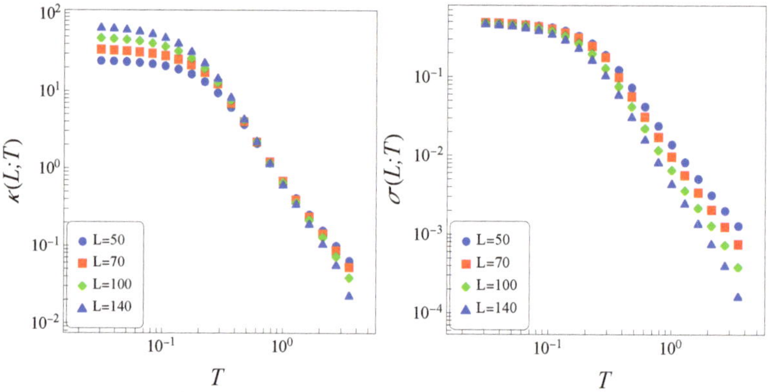

(**a**) (**b**)

Figure 2. (Color online) Numerical data for the thermal conductivity [panel (**a**)] and thermal conductance [panel (**b**)] are represented versus temperature (log–log plots) for different sizes ($L = 50, 70, 100, 140$) of the one-dimensional classical inertial Heisenberg model. One notices a crossover between the low- and high-temperature regimes for $T \simeq 0.3$. As expected, higher temperatures amplify the effects of the multiplicative noise, which is proportional to the square root of the corresponding temperatures (T_h, T_l), currently leading to larger fluctuations in numerical data, as shown in panel (**a**). All quantities shown are dimensionless.

The same data of Figure 2a are exhibited in Figure 2b where we plot the thermal conductance $\sigma(L,T) = \kappa(L,T)/L$ versus temperature, characterized by the two distinct temperature regimes described above. The low-temperature regime shows that the zero-temperature extrapolated value $\kappa(L,0)$ scales as $\kappa(L,0) \sim L$, leading to $\sigma(L,0) \equiv \lim_{T\to 0} \kappa(L,T)/L \simeq 0.5$. Such low-temperature results are in full agreement with those obtained in previous simulations of coupled classical XY rotators [42–45]. On the other hand, in the high-temperature regime, the thermal conductance presents a dependence on L, as expected.

In Figure 3, we exhibit the thermal-conductance data of Figure 2b in conveniently chosen variables, yielding a data collapse for all values of L considered. The full line essentially represents the form of Equation (8), so that one writes

$$\sigma(L,T) = A \exp_q(-Bx^{\eta}) , \tag{23}$$

where $x = L^{0.475}T$, $q = 2.28 \pm 0.04$, $\eta = 2.88 \pm 0.04$, $A = 0.492 \pm 0.002$, and $B = 0.33 \pm 0.04$. Notice that this value of η lies outside the range of what is commonly known as "stretched" [cf. Equation (8)], so that the form above should be considered rather as a "shrinked" q-exponential.

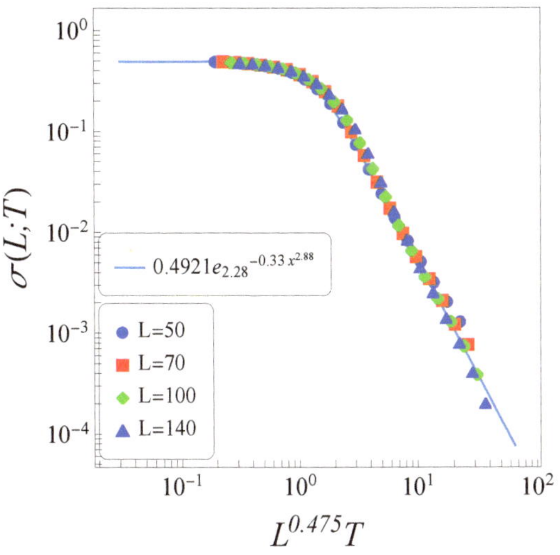

Figure 3. The plots for the thermal conductance of Figure 2b are shown in a log–log representation, for a conveniently chosen abscissa ($x = L^{0.475}T$), leading to a collapse of data for all values of L considered. The fitting (full line) is given by the function of Equation (23).

It should be mentioned that, in the case of coupled nearest-neighbor-interacting classical XY rotators on d-dimensional lattices ($d = 1, 2, 3$) [45], the thermal conductance was also fitted by the form of Equation (23), with values of $\eta(d) > 2$. In particular, in the one-dimensional case, such a fitting was attained for $x = L^{0.3}T$, $q = 1.7$, and $\eta = 2.335$, showing that these numbers present a dependence on the number of spin components ($n = 2$, for XY spins and $n = 3$, for Heisenberg spins), as well as on the lattice dimension d. It is important to mention that the generalized forms in Equations (8) and (23) have been used in the literature for an appropriate description of a wide variety of physical phenomena, like velocity measurements in a turbulent Couette–Taylor flow [60], relaxation curves of RKKY spin glasses, such as CuMn and AuFe [61], cumulative distribution for the magnitude of earthquakes [62], and more recently, for the thermal conductance of a system of interacting XY rotators [45]. Moreover, its associated entropic form has been studied in detail in Ref. [49].

By defining the abscissa variable of Figure 3 in the general form $x = L^{\gamma(n,d)}T$, and using the q-exponential definition of Equation (3), the slope of the high-temperature part of the thermal-conductance data scales with L, as

$$\sigma \sim L^{-[\eta(n,d)\gamma(n,d)]/[q(n,d)-1]}\,, \tag{24}$$

where we introduce the dependence (n, d) on all indices. Since the thermal conductivity ($\kappa = L\sigma$) should not depend on the size L (in the limit $L \to \infty$), Fourier's law becomes valid for

$$\frac{\eta(n,d)\gamma(n,d)}{q(n,d)-1} = 1\,. \tag{25}$$

The data of Figure 3 lead to $[\eta(3,1)\gamma(3,1)]/[q(3,1)-1] = 1.069 \pm 0.083$, whereas those for XY rotators on d-dimensional lattices yield 1.0007, 0.95, and 0.93, for $d = 1, 2$, and 3, respectively [45], indicating the validation of Fourier's law for systems of coupled nearest-neighbor-interacting classical n-vector rotators, through the thermal conductance form of Equation (23).

Recently, similar analyses were carried out for an XY Hamiltonian with anisotropies, in such a way to approach the Ising model in particular limits [63]. All the results for the quantity in Equation (25), computed up to the moment, are summarized in Table 1, where one notices that finite-size effects play an important role in increasing dimensions, as expected.

Table 1. Values of the ratio $\eta\gamma/(q-1)$ (highlighted in blue color) analyzed up to the moment: $n = 1$ ($d = 1$) [63], $n = 2$ (dimensions $d = 1,2,3$) [45], together with the present results for $n = 3$ ($d = 1$). In all cases studied, the limit of Equation (25) is numerically approached.

$\frac{\eta\gamma}{q-1}$	$d = 1$ (linear chain)	$d = 2$ (square lattice)	$d = 3$ (simple cubic lattice)
$n = 1$ (Ising ferromagnet)	1.0063 $q = 1.65$, $\eta = 1.94$, $\gamma = 0.336$	-	-
$n = 2$ (XY ferromagnet)	1.0007 $q = 1.7$, $\eta = 2.335$, $\gamma = 0.3$	0.95 $q = 3.2$, $\eta = 5.23$, $\gamma = 0.4$	0.93 $q = 3.5$, $\eta = 5.42$, $\gamma = 0.43$
$n = 3$ (Heisenberg ferromagnet)	1.069 $q = 2.28$, $\eta = 2.88$, $\gamma = 0.475$	-	-

4. Conclusions

We studied the heat flow along a one-dimensional classical inertial Heisenberg model of linear size L, by considering the first and last particles in thermal contact with heat baths at different temperatures, T_h and T_l ($T_h > T_l$), respectively. These particles at the extremities of the chain were subjected to standard Langevin dynamics, whereas all remaining rotators ($i = 2, \cdots, L-1$) interacted by means of nearest-neighbor ferromagnetic couplings and evolved in time following their own classical equations of motion, being investigated numerically through molecular-dynamics numerical simulations.

Fourier's law for the heat flux was verified numerically, and both thermal conductivity $\kappa(T)$ and thermal conductance $\sigma(L,T) = \kappa(T)/L$ were computed, by defining $T = (T_h + T_l)/2$. The slope of the high-temperature part of thermal-conductance data scales with the system size was $\sigma \sim L^{-1.069}$, indicating that in the limit $L \to \infty$, one should obtain a thermal conductivity independent of L. Indeed, in this limit, we found $\kappa(T) \sim T^{-2.25}$ for high temperatures. The thermal-conductance data were well-fitted by the function $\sigma(L,T) = A\exp_q(-Bx^{\eta})$, typical of nonextensive statistical mechanics, where A and B are constants, $x = L^{0.475}T$, $q = 2.28 \pm 0.04$, and $\eta = 2.88 \pm 0.04$. This fitting augments the applicability of such a function, which has been used for describing several physical phenomena in the literature, like velocity measurements in a turbulent Couette–Taylor flow [60], relaxation curves of RKKY spin glasses [61], cumulative distribution for the magnitude of earthquakes [62], and thermal conductance of a system of interacting XY rotators [45]. Since the value of η found herein lies outside the range of what is commonly known as "stretched" ($0 < \eta \leq 1$), herein, we refer to this fitting function of a "shrinked" q-exponential. The present results reinforce those obtained recently for XY rotators on d-dimensional lattices [45], indicating that Fourier's law should be generally valid for systems of coupled nearest-neighbor-interacting classical n-vector rotators, through the "shrinked" q-exponential function for the thermal conductance, with the indices $q(n,d)$ and $\eta(n,d)$ presenting a dependence on the number of spin components and lattice dimension.

Despite the simplicity of the model considered herein, the results for the thermal thermal conductivity at high temperatures ($\kappa(T) \sim T^{-2.25}$) are very close to experimental verifications in some antiferromagnetic electrical insulators, such as the Heisenberg chain cuprates Sr_2CuO_3 and $SrCuO_2$, for which thermal conductivity is well-fitted by a $1/T^2$ law at high temperatures [4]. At equilibrium, the present model exhibits a paramagnetic state for all temperatures, so that its Hamiltonian may be shown to cover both ferromagnetic and antiferromagnetic systems. The present results show that even for models exhibiting simple equilibrium properties, one may have out-of-equilibrium regimes characterized by transport properties typical of nonextensive statistical mechanics, like the ones found herein. Since nonextensive statistical mechanics have been used in the description of a wide variety of complex systems, one expects that the present results should be applicable to many of these systems in diverse, non-equilibrium regimes.

In summary, we demonstrated that (i) for the classical one-dimensional inertial ferromagnetic Heisenberg model, the (macroscopic) Fourier-law is validated from (microscopic) first principles, i.e., the temperature-dependent thermal conductivity is, in the high-temperature regime, finite and independent of the system size (the low-temperature regime is to be handled within a quantum grounding, which is out of the goal of the present paper); (ii) For all temperatures and sizes, the thermal conductivity appears to be consistent with q-statistics since it can be neatly collapsed within a shrunken q-exponential form; (iii) within this shrunken q-exponential form, a single universal condition, namely $\frac{\eta(n,d)\gamma(n,d)}{q(n,d)-1} = 1$, validates the Fourier law for the n-vector models for $n = 1, 2, 3$, which constitutes a numerical indication that this centennial macroscopic law is possibly valid for all values of (n, d), where $n \to \infty$ and $n \to 0$ correspond to the spherical model and 'self-avoiding walk', respectively. It is not our present aim to review the rich existing literature on the validity of the Fourier law within diverse classical and quantum approaches, but we rather restrict our focus to analytical and numerical first-principle approaches of classical systems that are similar to the present one.

Author Contributions: Conceptualization, H.S.L., C.T. and F.D.N.; methodology, H.S.L., C.T. and F.D.N.; formal analysis, H.S.L., C.T. and F.D.N.; writing—original draft, H.S.L., C.T. and F.D.N.; writing—review and editing, H.S.L., C.T. and F.D.N. All authors have read and agreed to the published version of the manuscript.

Funding: This research was funded by the National Council for Scientific and Technological Development grant number 465618/2014-6 and by Fundação Carlos Chagas Filho de Amparo à Pesquisa do Estadodo Rio de Janeiro grant number E-26/202.529/2019.

Institutional Review Board Statement: Not applicable.

Informed Consent Statement: Not applicable.

Data Availability Statement: All data will be available upon request.

Acknowledgments: We thank CNPq and Faperj (Brazilian agencies) for partial financial support.

Conflicts of Interest: The authors declare no conflicts of interest.

Appendix A. Numerical Procedures

Let us focus on the numerical integration of the equations of motion of the classical inertial Heisenberg chain. Considering the change of variable $\dot{\mathbf{S}}_i = \mathbf{V}_i$, we have the following equations of motion:

$$\begin{aligned}
\dot{\mathbf{S}}_i &= \mathbf{V}_i \text{ for all } i \\
\dot{\mathbf{V}}_i &= (\mathbf{S}_{i+1} + \mathbf{S}_{i-1}) - \left[\mathbf{S}_i \cdot (\mathbf{S}_{i+1} + \mathbf{S}_{i-1}) + \mathbf{V}_i^2\right]\mathbf{S}_i\,,\ i = 2, \ldots, L-1 \\
\dot{\mathbf{V}}_1 &= -\mathbf{V}_1 + \mathbf{S}_2 - \left[\mathbf{S}_1 \cdot \mathbf{S}_2 + \mathbf{V}_1^2\right]\mathbf{S}_1 + \mathbf{S}_1 \times \boldsymbol{\eta}_\mathrm{h}\,, \\
\dot{\mathbf{V}}_L &= -\mathbf{V}_\mathrm{L} + \mathbf{S}_{\mathrm{L}-1} - \left[\mathbf{S}_\mathrm{L} \cdot \mathbf{S}_{\mathrm{L}-1} + \mathbf{V}_\mathrm{L}^2\right]\mathbf{S}_\mathrm{L} + \mathbf{S}_\mathrm{L} \times \boldsymbol{\eta}_\mathrm{l}\,.
\end{aligned} \tag{A1}$$

which is a system of $6L$ first-order differential equations. To solve the set of equations entirely with the velocity Verlet method, we need to define $\boldsymbol{\eta}_{h/l} = \sqrt{2T_{h/l}/dt}\,\mathbf{w}_{h/l}$, where w is a vector of dimensionless Gaussian white noises and dt is the time-step of the integration. Therefore, we have the following discretized procedure:

$$\begin{aligned}
\mathbf{S}_i^{k+1} &= \mathbf{S}_i^k + \mathbf{V}_i\,dt + \frac{1}{2}\mathbf{F}_i^k\,(dt)^2 \\
\mathbf{V}_i^{k+1} &= \mathbf{V}_i^k + \frac{1}{2}(\mathbf{F}_i^k + \mathbf{F}_i^{k+1})dt
\end{aligned} \tag{A2}$$

where the generalized forces are as follows:

$$
\begin{aligned}
\mathbf{F}_i &= (\mathbf{S}_{i+1} + \mathbf{S}_{i-1}) - \left[\mathbf{S}_i \cdot (\mathbf{S}_{i+1} + \mathbf{S}_{i-1}) + \mathbf{V}_i^2\right]\mathbf{S}_i\,,\ i = 2,\ldots,L-1 \\
\mathbf{F}_1 &= -\mathbf{V}_1 + \mathbf{S}_2 - \left[\mathbf{S}_1 \cdot \mathbf{S}_2 + \mathbf{V}_1^2\right]\mathbf{S}_1 + \sqrt{\frac{2T_h}{dt}}(\mathbf{S}_1 \times \mathbf{w}_h)\,, \\
\mathbf{F}_L &= -\mathbf{V}_L + \mathbf{S}_{L-1} - \left[\mathbf{S}_L \cdot \mathbf{S}_{L-1} + \mathbf{V}_L^2\right]\mathbf{S}_L + \sqrt{\frac{2T_l}{dt}}(\mathbf{S}_L \times \mathbf{w}_l)\,.
\end{aligned}
\tag{A3}
$$

Notice that $(dt)^{-1/2}$ in the stochastic part of the forces is equivalent to $(dt)^{3/2}$ and $(dt)^{1/2}$ in $\mathbf{F}_i^k\,(dt)^2$ and $\mathbf{F}_i^k\,dt$ respectively; this equivalence contains weak order 1/2 and strong order 3/2 properties.

References

1. Fourier, J.B.J. *Théorie Analytique de La Chaleur*; Firmin Didot: Paris, France, 1822.
2. Çengel, Y.A.; Boles, M.A. *Thermodynamics—An Engineering Approach*, 9th ed.; McGraw-Hill: New York, NY, USA, 2018.
3. Kittel, C. *Introduction to Solid State Physics*, 5th ed.; John Wiley and Sons: New York, NY, USA, 1976.
4. Hlubek, N.; Zotos, X.; Singh, S.; Saint-Martin, R.; Revcolevschi, A.; Büchner, B.; Hess, C. Spinon heat transport and spin-phonon interaction in the spin-1/2 Heisenberg chain cuprates Sr_2CuO_3 and $SrCuO_2$. *J. Stat. Mech.* **2012**, *2012*, 03006. [CrossRef]
5. Kawamata, T.; Takahashi, N.; Adachi, T.; Noji, T.; Kudo, K.; Kobayashi, N.; Koike, Y. Evidence for Ballistic Thermal Conduction in the One-Dimensional S=1/2 Heisenberg Antiferromagnetic Spin System Sr_2CuO_3. *J. Phys. Soc. Jpn.* **2008**, *77*, 034607. [CrossRef]
6. Hlubek, N.; Ribeiro, P.; Saint-Martin, R.; Revcolevschi, A.; Roth, G.; Behr, G.; Büchner, B.; Hess, C. Ballistic heat transport of quantum spin excitations as seen in $SrCuO_2$. *Phys. Rev. B* **2010**, *81*, 020405. [CrossRef]
7. Hlubek, N.; Ribeiro, P.; Saint-Martin, R.; Nishimoto, S.; Revcolevschi, A.; Drechsler, S.-L.; Behr, G.; Trinckauf, J.; Hamann-Borrero, J.E.; Geck, J.; et al. Bond disorder and breakdown of ballistic heat transport in the spin-1/2 antiferromagnetic Heisenberg chain as seen in Ca-doped $SrCuO_2$. *Phys. Rev. B* **2011**, *84*, 214419. [CrossRef]
8. Prosen, T.; Campbell, D.K. Normal and anomalous heat transport in one-dimensional classical lattices. *Chaos* **2005**, *15*, 015117. [CrossRef] [PubMed]
9. Lepri, S.; Livi, R.; Politi, A. Heat Conduction in Chains of Nonlinear Oscillators. *Phys. Rev. Lett.* **1997**, *78*, 1896. [CrossRef]
10. Zhmakin, A.I. Heat Conduction Beyond the Fourier Law. *Tech. Phys.* **2021**, *66*, 1–22. [CrossRef]
11. Benenti, G.; Donadio, D.; Lepri, S.; Livi, R. Non-Fourier heat transport in nanosystems. *Riv. Nuovo Cim.* **2023**, *46*, 105–161. [CrossRef]
12. Flumerfelt, R.W.; Slattery, J.C. An experimental study of the validity of Fourier's law. *AIChE J.* **1969**, *15*, 291–292. [CrossRef]
13. Wen, H.; Lu, J.H.; Xiao, Y.; Deng, J. Temperature dependence of thermal conductivity, diffusion and specific heat capacity for coal and rocks from coalfield. *Thermochim. Acta* **2015**, *619*, 41–47. [CrossRef]
14. Xu, X.; Chen, J.; Li, B. Phonon thermal conduction in novel 2D materials. *J. Phys. Condens. Matter.* **2016**, *28*, 483001. [CrossRef]
15. Wu, X.; Varshney, V.; Lee, J.; Pang, Y.; Roy, A.K.; Luo, T. How to characterize thermal transport capability of 2D materials fairly? Sheet thermal conductance and the choice of thickness. *Chem. Phys. Lett.* **2017**, *669*, 233–237. [CrossRef]
16. Hurtado, P.I.; Garrido, P.L. A violation of universality in anomalous Fourier's law. *Sci. Rep.* **2016**, *6*, 38823. [CrossRef] [PubMed]
17. Yang, N.; Zhang, G.; Li, B. Violation of Fourier's law and anomalous heat diffusion in silicon nanowires. *Nano Today* **2010**, *5*, 85–90. [CrossRef]
18. Han, Z.; Fina, A. Thermal conductivity of carbon nanotubes and their polymer nanocomposites: A review. *Prog. Polym. Sci.* **2011**, *36*, 914–944. [CrossRef]
19. Liu, S.; Xu, X.F.; Xie, R.G.; Zhang, G.; Li, B.W. Anomalous heat conduction and anomalous diffusion in low dimensional nanoscale systems. *Eur. Phys. J. B* **2012**, *85*, 10. [CrossRef]
20. Dubi, Y.; Ventra, M.D. Fourier's law: Insight from a simple derivation. *Phys. Rev. E* **2009**, *79*, 042101. [CrossRef] [PubMed]
21. Dubi, Y.; Ventra, M.D. Reconstructing Fourier's law from disorder in quantum wires. *Phys. Rev. B* **2009**, *79*, 115415. [CrossRef]
22. Rieder, Z.; Lebowitz, J.L.; Lieb, E. Properties of a Harmonic Crystal in a Stationary Nonequilibrium State. *J. Math. Phys.* **1967**, *8*, 1073. [CrossRef]
23. Lebowitz, J.L.; Spohn, H. Transport properties of the Lorentz gas: Fourier's law. *J. Stat. Phys.* **1978**, *19*, 633–654. [CrossRef]
24. Büttner, H.; Mokross, F. Fourier's law and thermal conduction. *Nature* **1984**, *311*, 217–218. [CrossRef]
25. Maddox, J. Fourier's law obeyed—Official. *Nature* **1984**, *309*, 511. [CrossRef]
26. Wang, L. Generalized Fourier's law. *Int. J. Heat Mass Transf.* **1994**, *37*, 2627–2634. [CrossRef]
27. Laurençot, P. Weak Solutions to a Penrose-Fife Model with Fourier's Law for the Temperature. *J. Math. Anal. Appl.* **1998**, *219*, 331–343. [CrossRef]
28. Aoki, K.; Kusnezov, D. Bulk properties of anharmonic chains in strong thermal gradients: Non-equilibrium ϕ^4 theory. *Phys. Lett. A* **2000**, *265*, 250–256. [CrossRef]
29. Michel, M.; Hartmann, M.; Gemmer, J.; Mahler, G. Fourier's Law confirmed for a class of small quantum systems. *Eur. Phys. J. B* **2003**, *34*, 325–330. [CrossRef]

30. Kawaguchi, T.; Honda, H.; Hatori, K.; Imai, E.; Matsuno, K. Fourier's law of heat transfer and its implication to cell motility. *Biosystems* **2005**, *81*, 19–24. [CrossRef] [PubMed]
31. Landi, G.T.; de Oliveira, M.J. Fourier's law from a chain of coupled planar harmonic oscillators under energy-conserving noise. *Phys. Rev. E* **2014**, *89*, 022105. [CrossRef]
32. Gruber, C.; Lesne, A. Hamiltonian model of heat conductivity and Fourier's law. *Phys. AStat. Mech. Appl.* **2005**, *351*, 358–372. [CrossRef]
33. Bernardin, C.; Olla, S. Fourier's Law for a Microscopic Model of Heat Conduction. *J. Stat. Phys.* **2005**, *121*, 271–289. [CrossRef]
34. Bricmont, J.; Kupiainen, A. Towards a Derivation of Fourier's Law for Coupled Anharmonic Oscillators. *Commun. Math. Phys.* **2007**, *274*, 555–626. [CrossRef]
35. Bricmont, J.; Kupiainen, A. Fourier's Law from Closure Equations. *Phys. Rev. Lett.* **2007**, *98*, 214301. [CrossRef]
36. Wu, L.A.; Segal, D. Fourier's law of heat conduction: Quantum mechanical master equation analysis. *Phys. Rev. E* **2008**, *77*, 060101. [CrossRef]
37. Gaspard, P.; Gilbert, T. Heat Conduction and Fourier's Law by Consecutive Local Mixing and Thermalization. *Phys. Rev. Lett.* **2008**, *101*, 020601. [CrossRef] [PubMed]
38. Gerschenfeld, A.; Derrida, B.; Lebowitz, J.L. Anomalous Fourier's Law and Long Range Correlations in a 1D Non-momentum Conserving Mechanical Model. *J. Stat. Phys.* **2010**, *141*, 757–766. [CrossRef]
39. Ezzat, M.A. Thermoelectric MHD with modified Fourier's law. *Int. J. Therm. Sci.* **2011**, *50*, 449–455. [CrossRef]
40. De Masi, A.; Presutti, E.; Tsagkarogiannis, D. Fourier's Law, Phase Transitions and the Stationary Stefan Problem. *Arch. Ration. Mech. Anal.* **2011**, *201*, 681–725. [CrossRef]
41. Dhar, A.; Venkateshan, K.; Lebowitz, J.L. Heat conduction in disordered harmonic lattices with energy-conserving noise. *Phys. Rev. E* **2011**, *83*, 021108. [CrossRef] [PubMed]
42. Giardiná, C.; Livi, R.; Politi, A.; Vassalli, M. Finite Thermal Conductivity in 1D Lattices. *Phys. Rev. Lett.* **2000**, *84*, 2144. [CrossRef] [PubMed]
43. Li, Y.; Li, N.; Li, B. Temperature dependence of thermal conductivities of coupled rotator lattice and the momentum diffusion in standard map. *Eur. Phys. J. B* **2015**, *88*, 182. [CrossRef]
44. Li, Y.; Li, N.; Tirnakli, U.; Li, B.; Tsallis, C. Thermal conductance of the coupled-rotator chain: Influence of temperature and size. *Europhys. Lett.* **2017**, *117*, 60004. [CrossRef]
45. Tsallis, C.; Lima, H.S.; Tirnakli, U.; Eroglu, D. First-principle validation of Fourier's law in d = 1, 2, 3 classical systems. *Phys. D Nonlinear Phenom.* **2023**, *446*, 133681. [CrossRef]
46. Olivares, C.; Anteneodo, C. Role of the range of the interactions in thermal conduction. *Phys. Rev. E* **2016**, *94*, 042117. [CrossRef] [PubMed]
47. Tsallis, C. *Introduction to Nonextensive Statistical Mechanics: Approaching a Complex World*, 2nd ed.; Springer: New York, NY, USA, 2023.
48. Tsallis, C. Possible generalization of Boltzmann-Gibbs statistics. *J. Stat. Phys.* **1988**, *52*, 479–487. [CrossRef]
49. Dos Santos, M.A.F.; Nobre, F.D.; Curado, E.M.F. Entropic form emergent from superstatistics. *Phys. Rev. E* **2023**, *107*, 014132. [CrossRef] [PubMed]
50. Rapaport, D.C.; Landau, D.P. Critical dynamics of a dynamical version of the classical Heisenberg model. *Phys. Rev. E* **1996**, *53*, 4696–4702. [CrossRef] [PubMed]
51. Cirto, L.J.L.; Lima, L.S.; Nobre, F.D. Controlling the range of interactions in the classical inertial ferromagnetic Heisenberg model: Analysis of metastable states. *J. Stat. Mech.* **2015**, *2015*, P04012. [CrossRef]
52. Rodríguez, A.; Nobre, F.D.; Tsallis, C. d-Dimensional Classical Heisenberg Model with Arbitrarily-Ranged Interactions: Lyapunov Exponents and Distributions of Momenta and Energies. *Entropy* **2019**, *21*, 31. [CrossRef]
53. Evans, D.J. On the Representation of Orientation Space. *Mol. Phys.* **1977**, *34*, 317–325. [CrossRef]
54. Evans, D.J.; Murad, S. Singularity free algorithm for molecular dynamics simulation of rigid polyatomics. *Mol. Phys.* **1977**, *34*, 327–331. [CrossRef]
55. Savin, A.V.; Tsironis, G.P.; Zotos, X. Thermal conductivity of a classical one-dimensional Heisenberg spin model. *Phys. Rev. B* **2005**, *72*, 140402. [CrossRef]
56. Savin, A.V.; Tsironis, G.P.; Zotos, X. Thermal conductivity of a classical one-dimensional spin-phonon system. *Phys. Rev. B* **2007**, *75*, 214305. [CrossRef]
57. Verlet, L. Computer Experiments on Classical Fluids. I. Thermodynamical Properties of Lennard-Jones Molecules. *Phys. Rev.* **1967**, *159*, 98–103. [CrossRef]
58. Paterlini, M.G.; Ferguson, D.M. Constant temperature simulations using the Langevin equation with velocity Verlet integration. *Chem. Phys.* **1998**, *236*, 243–252. [CrossRef]
59. Mejía-Monasterio, C.; Politi, A.; Rondoni, L. Heat flux in one-dimensional systems. *Phys. Rev. E* **2019**, *100*, 032139. [CrossRef] [PubMed]
60. Beck, C.; Lewis, G.S.; Swinney, H.L. Measuring nonextensitivity parameters in a turbulent Couette-Taylor flow. *Phys. Rev. E* **2001**, *63*, 035303. [CrossRef] [PubMed]
61. Pickup, R.M.; Cywinski, R.; Pappas, C.; Farago, B.; Fouquet, P. Generalized Spin-Glass Relaxation. *Phys. Rev. Lett.* **2009**, *102*, 097202. [CrossRef] [PubMed]

62. Darooneh, A.H.; Mehri, A. A nonextensive modification of the Gutenberg-Richter law: q-stretched exponential form. *Phys. A* **2010**, *389*, 509. [CrossRef]
63. Lima, H.S.; Tsallis, C. Ising chain: Thermal conductivity and first-principle validation of Fourier's law. *Phys. A Stat. Mech. Appl.* **2023**, *628*, 129161. [CrossRef]

entropy

MDPI

Article

Results for Nonlinear Diffusion Equations with Stochastic Resetting

Ervin K. Lenzi [1,2,*], Rafael S. Zola [3], Michely P. Rosseto [1], Renio S. Mendes [4], Haroldo V. Ribeiro [4], Luciano R. da Silva [2,5] and Luiz R. Evangelista [4,6]

1 Departamento de Física, Universidade Estadual de Ponta Grossa, Ponta Grossa 84030-900, PR, Brazil; michelyrosseto@gmail.com
2 National Institute of Science and Technology for Complex Systems, Centro Brasileiro de Pesquisas Físicas, Rio de Janeiro 22290-180, RJ, Brazil; luciano@fisica.ufrn.br
3 Departamento de Física, Universidade Tecnológica Federal do Paraná, Apucarana 86812-460, PR, Brazil; rzola1@kent.edu
4 Departamento de Física, Universidade Estadual de Maringá, Maringa 87020-900, PR, Brazil; rsmendes@dfi.uem.br (R.S.M.); hvr@dfi.uem.br (H.V.R.); lre@dfi.uem.br (L.R.E.)
5 Departamento de Física, Universidade Federal do Rio Grande do Norte, Natal 59078-900, RN, Brazil
6 Istituto dei Sistemi Complessi (ISC–CNR), Via dei Taurini, 19, 00185 Rome, Italy
* Correspondence: eklenzi@uepg.br (E.K.L.)

Abstract: In this study, we investigate a nonlinear diffusion process in which particles stochastically reset to their initial positions at a constant rate. The nonlinear diffusion process is modeled using the porous media equation and its extensions, which are nonlinear diffusion equations. We use analytical and numerical calculations to obtain and interpret the probability distribution of the position of the particles and the mean square displacement. These results are further compared and shown to agree with the results of numerical simulations. Our findings show that a system of this kind exhibits non-Gaussian distributions, transient anomalous diffusion (subdiffusion and superdiffusion), and stationary states that simultaneously depend on the nonlinearity and resetting rate.

Keywords: Tsallis entropy; q-exponentials; anomalous diffusion; Lévy distributions

Citation: Lenzi, E.K.; Zola, R.S.; Rosseto, M.P.; Mendes, R.S.; Ribeiro, H.V.; Silva, L.R.d.; Evangelista, L.R. Results for Nonlinear Diffusion Equations with Stochastic Resetting. *Entropy* **2023**, *25*, 1647. https://doi.org/10.3390/e25121647

Academic Editors: Ugur Tirnakli, Christian Beck, Hans J. Herrmann, Airton Deppman, Henrik Jeldtoft Jensen, Evaldo M. F. Curado, Fernando D. Nobre, Angelo Plastino, Astero Provata and Andrea Rapisarda

Received: 6 November 2023
Revised: 3 December 2023
Accepted: 8 December 2023
Published: 12 December 2023

1. Introduction

Stochastic processes are one of the most captivating occurrences in the natural world and significantly impact various contexts. Diffusion completely depends on these processes, determining the type of diffusion the system manifests. For example, Markovian processes are typical of the Brownian motion characterized by a linear dependence on the mean square displacement, i.e., $\langle(\Delta x)^2\rangle \sim t$, and can be connected with the Gaussian distribution. On the other hand, the non-Markovian processes can be connected to extensions of the Brownian motion where the sub- or super-diffusion is present. In these cases, we have a nonlinear time dependence on the mean-square displacement, e.g., $\langle(\Delta x)^2\rangle \sim t^\sigma$, where $\sigma < 1$ and $\sigma > 1$ correspond to sub- and superdiffusion, respectively. Other behaviors for the mean-square displacement are also possible, such as $\langle(\Delta x)^2\rangle \sim \ln^\sigma t$, which characterize an ultraslow diffusion. Behind each of these processes, we have a density of probability, which is the solution of the differential equation related to the type of stochastic process present in the system. The usual diffusion is connected to Markovian processes, which have the Gaussian distribution as a solution. Several kinds of differential equations can emerge in the context of non-Markovian processes. The porous media equation is one of them, as a consequence of a Langevin equation with multiplicative noise [1,2] with implications in different contexts [3,4]. It is given by

$$\frac{\partial}{\partial t}\rho(x,t) = D\frac{\partial^2}{\partial x^2}\rho^\nu(x,t)\,, \tag{1}$$

where D is the diffusion coefficient and $\rho(x,t)$ represents the probability distribution of finding a particle around position x at time t. Equation (1) can be obtained by using different approaches, such as the ones present in Refs. [1,5,6]. This equation has been successfully applied in many situations such as heavy-ion collisions [7], climate modeling, particles with repulsive power-law interactions [8], life sciences [9], and hydrological setting [10]. Further, it can be related to the Tsallis formalism [11] and connected to the thermostatistic aspects [12], similar to the standard diffusion equation and the Boltzmann–Gibbs statistics. These scenarios and others related to stochastic processes are part of the diffusion phenomena, which can be found in different contexts and are essential mechanisms in nature. The diffusion can often appear combined with different phenomena such as stochastic resetting [13,14], a process in which particles are stochastically repositioned to their initial positions at a constant rate (see, for example, Figure 1).

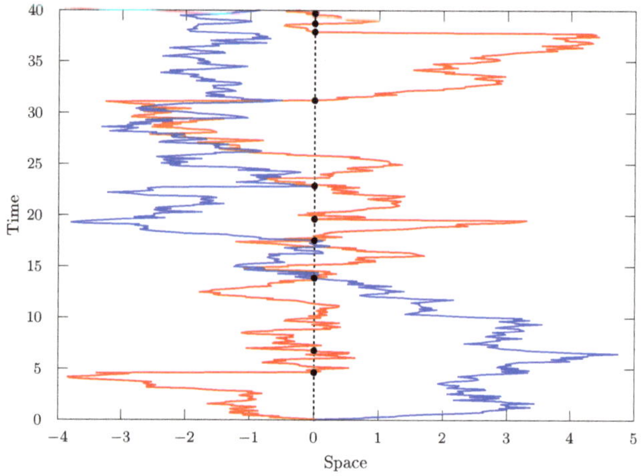

Figure 1. This figure illustrates the stochastic resetting process. The red and blue lines represent the stochastic motion of two particles, which after some time restart the motion (black points) with some rate.

Examples of systems with stochastic reset include the production of proteins by ribosomes [15], visual working memory in humans [16], protein identification in DNA [17], and animal foraging [18]. Motivated by this myriad of possible applications, several works have systematically investigated the combination of diffusion with stochastic resetting [19–26]. Other phenomena that are often combined with diffusion are the reaction–diffusion processes, which play an essential role in different contexts such as physics [4,27,28] and biology [29,30]. Despite this increasing interest in studying diffusion with stochastic resetting and reaction processes, much less attention has been paid to considering nonlinear diffusion processes.

Here, we help to fill this gap by investigating a diffusive process governed by a nonlinear diffusion equation with stochastic resetting and linear reaction processes, both irreversible and reversible. We consider the diffusion governed by Equation (1), a nonlinear equation whose solutions are distributions asymptotically characterized by a compact or a long-tailed behavior. In the last case, we can relate them with the Lévy distributions [31,32], characterized asymptotically by power laws. The results that emerge from this context combine different processes, i.e., the nonlinear diffusion, which may exhibit compact or long-tailed solutions, reaction terms, and stochastic resetting. It is also worth mentioning that the nonlinear diffusion equation considered here can be connected to unusual characteristics such as fractal and multifractal properties, e.g., present in a porous media. The reaction terms can be used to simulate different situations. One of them is the case where the substrate can immobilize the particles. Another can result in an intermittent motion, where the terms are related to the motion and pause while the diffusion proceeds [27]. We perform analytical and numerical analysis for this nonlinear diffusion process with stochastic resetting and reaction terms. In particular, we found an analytical solution for the stationary state when reaction terms are absent, in terms of the q-exponential, which has a power-law behavior. The analytical solution for the stationary state is also obtained when a reversible reaction process is considered. These solutions, given in terms of the q-exponentials [33], are different from the standard cases discussed in Refs. [19,34]. This feature can be connected to the diffusion process, which is governed by a nonlinear diffusion equation instead of the usual one and results in a correlated anomalous diffusion [35,36].

The remainder of this manuscript is organized as follows. Section 2 defines the diffusion equation, presents the approach to finding its solution, and describes the probability distribution of the positions of particles and the mean square displacement for stochastic resetting for different scenarios. This section also considers the first passage-time distribution and reaction terms for the nonlinear diffusion process with resetting. Finally, Section 3 concludes this work with an overview of our main findings.

2. Nonlinear Diffusion Equation with Stochastic Resetting

Let us start our analysis by considering a system subjected to the following diffusion equation:

$$\frac{\partial}{\partial t}\rho(x,t) = D\frac{\partial^2}{\partial x^2}[\rho(x,t)]^{\nu} - r\big[\rho(x,t) - \delta(x-x')\big]\,, \tag{2}$$

where $\rho(x,t)$ represents the probability distribution of finding a particle around position x at time t, r is the rate under which particles stochastically reset their positions to x', ν is a parameter associated with the properties of the media, and D is a constant corresponding to the usual diffusion coefficient. It is worth mentioning that we will also consider some extensions of Equation (2) and implications for the reset process. The solution of this equation in the absence of the resetting term, that is, for $r = 0$, can be found in terms of the q-exponential present in the Tsallis formalism [11], which is based on the following entropy:

$$S_q = \frac{k}{q-1}\left\{1 - \int dx[\rho(x,t)]^q\right\}, \tag{3}$$

where q represents a degree of nonextensivity and k is a constant. Equation (3) recovers the Boltzmann–Gibbs entropy in the limit of $q \to 1$. In particular, it is possible to show that the solution is given by

$$\rho(x,t) = \frac{1}{\Phi(t)}\exp_q\left[-\frac{k'x^2}{2(2-q)D\Phi^2(t)}\right], \tag{4}$$

where $q = 2 - \nu$ and the q-exponential is defined as follows:

$$\exp_q[x] = \begin{cases} [1+(1-q)x]^{\frac{1}{1-q}} & ,x \geq 1/(q-1) \\ 0 & ,x < 1/(q-1) \end{cases}, \tag{5}$$

and $\Phi(t) = [(1+\nu)k't]^{\frac{1}{1+\nu}}$, with

$$k' = 2\nu D\pi\begin{cases} \frac{1}{1-\nu}\left[\frac{\Gamma\left(\frac{1}{1-\nu}-\frac{1}{2}\right)}{\Gamma\left(\frac{1}{1-\nu}\right)}\right]^2 & ,\nu < 1 \\ \frac{1}{\nu-1}\left[\frac{\Gamma\left(\frac{1}{\nu-1}-1\right)}{\Gamma\left(\frac{1}{\nu-1}+\frac{3}{2}\right)}\right]^2 & ,\nu > 1 \end{cases}. \tag{6}$$

The mean square displacement for this case is given by $\sigma_x^2(t) = \langle(x-\langle x\rangle)^2\rangle \propto t^{2/(1+\nu)}$, which implies that depending on the values of ν, sub, normal, or superdiffusion can be obtained. Another interesting point about these solutions is their connection with the Lévy distributions for $q > 1$ or $\nu < 1$ as discussed in Refs. [31,32].

Equation (2) may be obtained from a random walk approach for $r \neq 0$, similar to the standard case [37,38]; however, with a nonlinear dependence to obtain the nonlinearity present in the diffusive term. To proceed this way, we follow the approach of Ref. [39], yielding

$$\begin{aligned}\rho(x,t+\tau) &= \int_{-\infty}^{\infty} e^{-r\tau}\Psi[x-x',t;\rho(x-x',t)]\rho(x-x',t)\Phi(x')dx' \\ &+ \{1-\Psi[x,t;\rho(x,t)]\}e^{-r\tau}\rho(x,t) + \left(1-e^{-r\tau}\right)\{\rho(x,t)-\mathcal{R}[\rho(x,t)]\}\,. \end{aligned} \tag{7}$$

By taking the limits $\tau \to 0$ and $x' \to 0$ as discussed in Ref. [39], it is possible to simplify Equation (7) and obtain

$$\frac{\partial}{\partial t}\rho(x,t) = \frac{\partial^2}{\partial x^2}\left\{\Psi[x,t;\rho(x,t)]\rho(x,t)\right\} - r\mathcal{R}[\rho(x,t)]\,, \tag{8}$$

which for $\Psi[x,t;\rho(x,t)] = D[\rho(x,t)]^{\nu-1}$ and $\mathcal{R}[\rho(x,t)] = (\rho(x,t)-\delta(x-x'))$ recovers Equation (2). In fact, replacing the previous expressions for $\Psi[x,t;\rho(x,t)]$ and $\mathcal{R}[\rho(x,t)]$ in Equation (8), we obtain the following:

$$\frac{\partial}{\partial t}\rho(x,t) = D\frac{\partial^2}{\partial x^2}[\rho(x,t)]^{\nu} - r\left[\rho(x,t)-\delta(x-x')\right]. \tag{9}$$

We notice that $\Psi[x,t;\rho(x,t)]$ directly influences the behavior exhibited by the particles during the diffusion process, which can lead us to normal or anomalous diffusion. It is also possible to consider situations with different regimes of diffusion depending on the expressions used for $\Psi[x,t;\rho(x,t)]$. Later, we examine a case characterized by two different regimes, i.e., $\Psi[x,t;\rho(x,t)] = D_1 + D_\nu[\rho(x,t)]^{\nu-1}$, where one of the processes is normal and another is anomalous. Formulating the stochastic resetting in terms of a Langevin equation is also possible using the procedure employed in Ref. [21]. To do this, we need to consider the following equation $\dot{x} = \sqrt{\Psi[x,t;\rho(x,t)]}\xi(t)$, where $\xi(t)$ is a stochastic variable, i.e., a Gaussian white noise [39] with $\langle\xi(t)\rangle = 0$ and $\langle\xi(t)\xi(t')\rangle \propto \delta(t-t')$. In this manner, Equation (2) (or Equation (8)) can be obtained from a random walk approach with a nonlinear dependence on the probability density function connected to the dynamics of the walkers or employing a stochastic equation with a nonlinear term that is coupled with a nonlinear diffusion equation.

By performing some numerical calculations, it is possible to find the solution for Equation (2) as shown in Figure 2a,b for $\nu > 1$ and $\nu < 1$ at three different moments in time. To do this, the system was defined in the interval $[-5000, 5000]$ and discretized in increments of $dx = 2\times10^{-2}$, with $dt = 10^{-6}$, to numerically explore the evolution of time and obtain the results exhibited in these figures. These values for dx and dt verify the condition $Ddt/\left(dx^2\right) < 1/2$ required for the stability of the solutions during the time evolution of the initial condition to satisfy the boundary conditions [28,40].

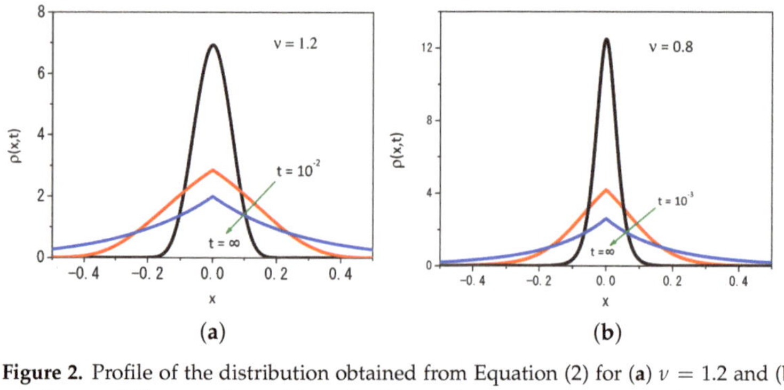

Figure 2. Profile of the distribution obtained from Equation (2) for (**a**) $\nu = 1.2$ and (**b**) $\nu = 0.8$ by considering different values of time. For illustrative purposes, we consider $D = 1$, $\rho(x,0) = \delta(x)$, $x' = 0$, and $r = 20$.

Figure 3 exhibits the time-dependence of the mean square displacement for the cases shown in Figure 2a,b. The system reaches a stationary state for long times as in the standard case, i.e., for $\nu = 1$, when the resetting is considered. We have an anomalous diffusion for short times in both cases, as shown in Figure 3. We have a superdiffusion for $\nu < 1$, whereas the subdiffusion behavior is verified for $\nu > 1$.

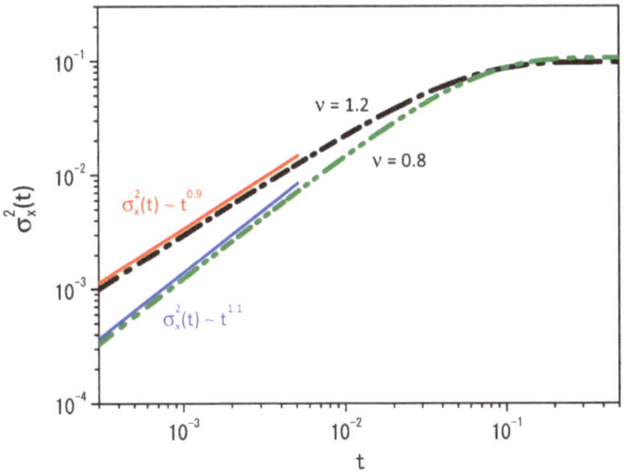

Figure 3. Time-dependence of the mean square displacement, i.e., $\sigma_x^2(t) = \langle (x - \langle x \rangle)^2 \rangle$, obtained from Equation (2) when $\nu = 0.8$ (green line) and $\nu = 1.2$ (black line). The red and blue lines were incorporated to evidence the behavior of the mean square displacement for short times. Again, for illustrative purposes, we consider $D = 1, \rho(x,0) = \delta(x), x' = 0$, and $r = 20$.

The result shown in Figure 3 for the stationary state allows us to consider, in the asymptotic limit of $t \to \infty$, the following equation:

$$D\frac{\partial^2}{\partial x^2}[\rho_{st}(x)]^\nu - r[\rho_{st}(x) - \delta(x - x')] = 0\,, \tag{10}$$

where $\rho_{st}(x) = \lim_{t\to\infty} \rho(x,t)$. It is possible to verify that the solution of Equation (10) is given by

$$\rho_{st}(x) = \frac{1}{\mathcal{Z}} \exp_q\left[-\beta|x - x'|\right], \tag{11}$$

with $\mathcal{Z}\beta = 2/(2-q)$, $\nu = 3 - 2q$, and

$$\beta = \left[\frac{r}{2D\nu}\left(\frac{2}{2-q}\right)^{3-2q}\right]^{\frac{1}{4-2q}}. \tag{12}$$

Equation (11), for the particular case $q = 1$ (or $\nu = 1$), leads to the result obtained in Ref. [14] for the normal case. Figure 4 illustrates the numerical result obtained from Equation (2) for long times, i.e., in the stationary scenario, and the previous analytical result, obtained for Equation (11). It reveals a strong agreement between the numerical and analytical results when we examine two different values of the ν parameter: the analytical result depicted for $\nu = 0.8$, with a solid black line and $\nu = 1.2$, with a solid green line, while the dotted red line represents the numerical result. In both cases, we employ a stochastic resetting rate of $r = 20$.

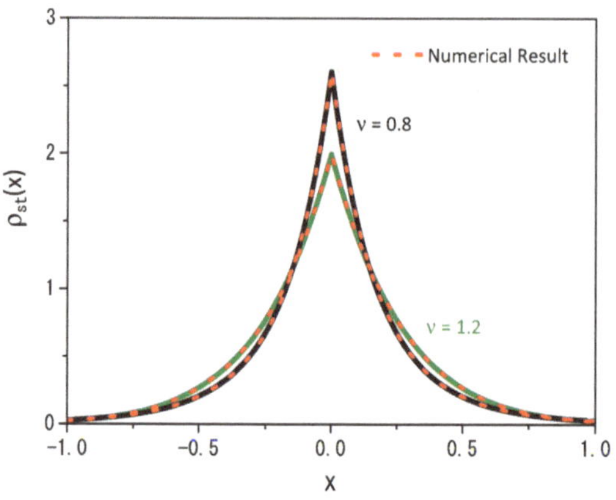

Figure 4. Comparison of the trends of the analytical results (black and green solid lines), given by Equation (11), with the numerical results (red dotted lines), obtained for Equation (2) when $\nu = 0.8$ and $\nu = 1.2$. As before, the calculations consider $D = 1$, $\rho(x,0) = \delta(x)$, $x' = 0$, and $r = 20$.

We may also consider the survival probability and the first passage time distribution for the situation we are analyzing. To proceed further, we consider the following boundary condition: $\rho(0,t) = \rho(\infty,t) = 0$, which implies assuming the presence of an absorbent surface at $x = 0$, and fix, as an initial condition, $\rho(x,0) = \delta(x - x_0)$. In this framework, Equation (8) becomes

$$\frac{\partial}{\partial t}\rho(x,t) = D\frac{\partial^2}{\partial x^2}\rho^{\nu}(x,t) - r\left[\rho(x,t) - S(t)\delta(x-x')\right] , \tag{13}$$

where $S(t) = \int_0^\infty dx\rho(x,t)$ is the survival probability. The first passage time distribution can be found by using Equation [41]

$$F(t) = -\frac{\partial}{\partial t}\int_0^\infty dx\rho(x,t) = -\frac{\partial}{\partial t}S(t) . \tag{14}$$

Figures 5–7, for the boundary conditions $\rho(0,t) = 0$ and $\rho(\infty,t) = 0$, depict some cases with fixed values of the diffusion coefficient $D = 1$ and position $x' = x_0$, for $\nu = 1.2$ and $\rho(x,0) = \delta(x - x_0)$.

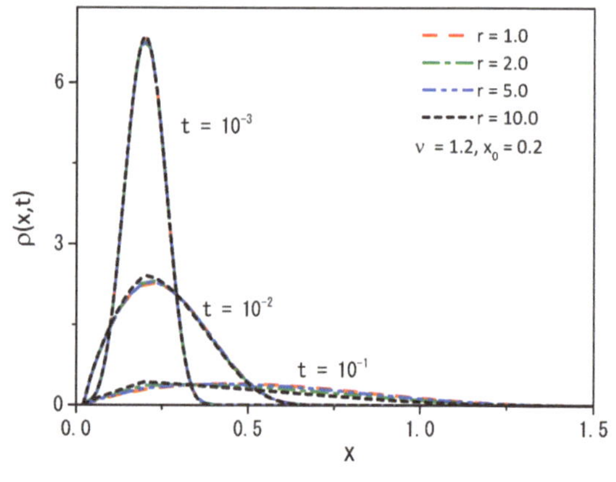

Figure 5. The probability distribution function obtained from Equation (13) when $\nu = 1.2$ for the boundary conditions $\rho(0,t) = 0$ and $\rho(\infty,t) = 0$. We consider, for simplicity, $D = 1$, $\rho(x,0) = \delta(x - x_0)$, and $x' = x_0$.

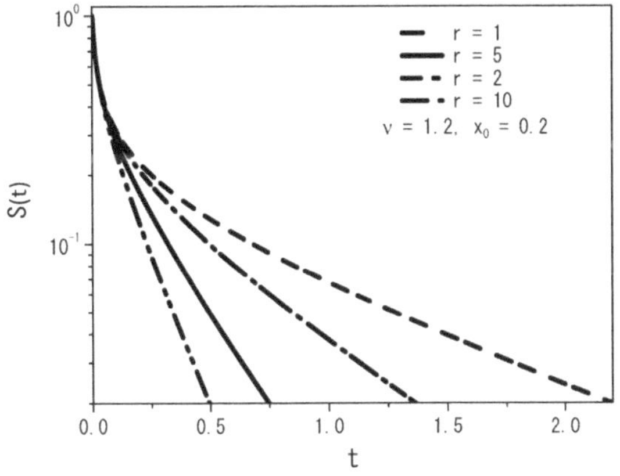

Figure 6. Time-dependence of the survival probability using Equation (13) for various values of the resetting rate r, with $\nu = 1.2$ for the boundary conditions $\rho(0,t) = 0$ and $\rho(\infty,t) = 0$. We consider, again, $D = 1$, $\rho(x,0) = \delta(x - x_0)$, and $x' = x_0$.

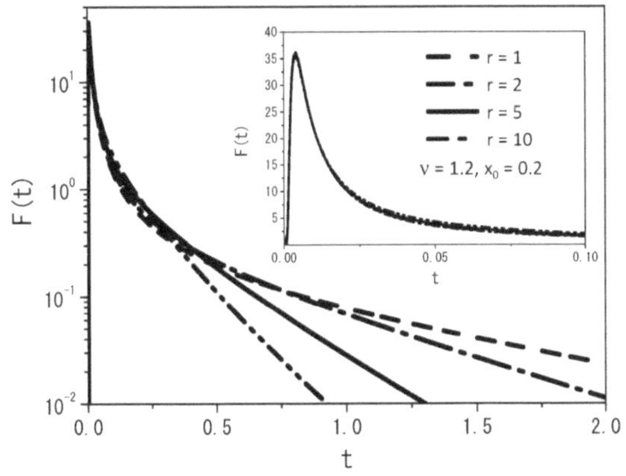

Figure 7. The first passage time distribution obtained from Equation (14) for $\nu = 1.2$ and the boundary conditions $\rho(0,t) = 0$ and $\rho(\infty,t) = 0$. Again, for simplicity, we consider $D = 1$, $\rho(x,0) = \delta(x - x_0)$, and $x' = x_0$.

From Figure 5, we may conclude that the quantity of particles decreases with increasing rate r, demonstrating that the particles can find the absorbent surface more easily for large values of the stochastic resetting rate. A similar behavior is illustrated in Figure 6, where we observe the changing dynamics of particle survival probability over time. An increase in the rate parameter r corresponds to faster adsorption of the particles at the surface. Figure 7 presents a graph illustrating the first passage time distribution over time, with the curves representing the analytical results obtained from Equation (14).

Another challenging scenario, which emerges when the system is subjected to the resetting process, is represented by the presence of a subtract that immobilizes the particles while the diffusion proceeds. To face this case, we can consider the following equation:

$$\rho(x,t+\tau) = \int_{-\infty}^{\infty} e^{-\alpha\tau}\Psi[x-x',t;\rho(x-x',t)]\rho(x-x',t)\Phi(x')dx' + \{1-\Psi[x,t;\rho(x,t)]\}e^{-\alpha\tau}\rho(x,t) + \left(1-e^{-\alpha\tau}\right)\{\rho(x,t) - \mathcal{R}[\rho(x,t)]\}\,. \quad (15)$$

From this equation, it is possible to obtain the following diffusion equation:

$$\frac{\partial}{\partial t}\rho(x,t) = \frac{\partial^2}{\partial x^2}\left\{\Psi[x,t;\rho(x,t)]\rho(x,t)\right\} - r\left[\rho(x,t) - e^{-\alpha t}\delta(x-x')\right] - \alpha\rho(x,t)\,, \tag{16}$$

in which $\Psi[x,t;\rho(x,t)] = D[\rho(x,t)]^{\nu-1}$ and $\mathcal{R}[\rho(x,t)] = \rho(x,t) + (r/\alpha)\left[\rho(x,t) - e^{-\alpha t}\delta(x-x')\right]$. This equation differs from Equation (2) by the presence of a reaction term that immobilizes particles with the rate α. Note that the resetting term considers the exponential $e^{-\alpha t}$ multiplied by the delta function. This factor corresponds to the time behavior of the survival probability in this case. In the absence of the resetting term, it is possible to find the solution in terms of the q-exponential as in the previous case, and it is given by

$$\rho(x,t) = e^{-\alpha t}\frac{1}{\Phi_\alpha(t)}\exp_q\left[-\frac{k'x^2}{2(2-q)D\Phi_\alpha^2(t)}\right], \tag{17}$$

with

$$\Phi_\alpha(t) = \left\{\frac{1+\nu}{(1-\nu)\alpha}\left[e^{(1-\nu)\alpha t} - 1\right]\right\}^{\frac{1}{1+\nu}}. \tag{18}$$

In the case of an intermittent motion, we have to consider the following time behavior for $S_1(t) = (\alpha_2/\alpha_t)\left(1 - \alpha_2 e^{-\alpha_t t}/\alpha_t\right)$, where $\alpha_t = \alpha_1 + \alpha_2$. In this scenario, the process of resetting and motion is governed by the constants α_1 and α_2, and the equations are given by

$$\frac{\partial}{\partial t}\rho_1(x,t) = D\frac{\partial^2}{\partial x^2}\rho_1^\nu(x,t) - r\left[\rho_1(x,t) - S_1(t)\delta(x-x')\right] - \alpha_1\rho_1(x,t) + \alpha_2\rho_2(x,t) \tag{19}$$

and

$$\frac{\partial}{\partial t}\rho_2(x,t) = \alpha_1\rho_1(x,t) - \alpha_2\rho_2(x,t)\,. \tag{20}$$

From an analytical point of view, it is possible to find the solution of the linear case, i.e., $\nu = 1$. It is

$$\begin{aligned}\rho_1(x,t) &= \rho_0(x,t) + \sum_{n=1}^{\infty}(-\alpha_1)^n\int_{-\infty}^{\infty}dx_n\int_0^t dt_n\mathcal{G}_2(x-x_n,t-t_n)\\ &\times \int_{-\infty}^{\infty}dx_{n-1}\int_0^{t_n}dt_{n-1}\mathcal{G}_2(x_n-x_{n-1},t_n-t_{n-1})\cdots\\ &\times \int_{-\infty}^{\infty}dx_1\int_0^{t_2}dt_1\mathcal{G}_2(x_2-x_1,t_2-t_1)\rho_0(x_1,t_1)\end{aligned} \tag{21}$$

and

$$\rho_2(x,t) = \alpha_1\int_0^t dt' e^{-\alpha_2(t-t')}\rho_1(x,t')\,, \tag{22}$$

where

$$\rho_0(x,t) = \mathcal{G}_1(x,t) + r\int_0^t dt' S_1(t')\mathcal{G}_1(x,t-t')\,, \tag{23}$$

$$\mathcal{G}_2(x,t) = \mathcal{G}_1(x,t) + \int_0^t dt' e^{\alpha_2 t'}\mathcal{G}_1(x,t-t')\,, \tag{24}$$

and

$$\mathcal{G}_1(x,t) = e^{-rt-x^2/(4Dt)}/\sqrt{4\pi Dt}\,. \tag{25}$$

Figures 8 and 9 illustrate the behavior of the mean square displacement and the distributions obtained from Equations (19) and (20) for different values of ν. For Equations (19) and (20), it is also possible to find the stationary solution, i.e., the one in the limit $t \to \infty$. We consider that in this limit, $\alpha_1\rho_1(x,t)$ is nearly equivalent to $\alpha_2\rho_2(x,t)$, and thus we solve the equation

$$D\frac{\partial^2}{\partial x^2}\Big[\rho_{1(2),st}(x)\Big]^{\nu} - r\Big[\rho_{1(2),st}(x) - S_{1(2),st}\delta(x-x')\Big] = 0\,, \tag{26}$$

where $\rho_{1(2),st}(x) = \lim_{t\to\infty}\rho_{1(2)}(x,t)$ and $S_{1(2),st} = \lim_{t\to\infty}S_{1(2)}(t)$. It is possible to verify that the solution of Equation (26) is given by

$$\rho_{1(2),st}(x) = \frac{1}{\mathcal{Z}_{1(2)}}\exp_q\Big[-\beta_1|x-x'|\Big], \tag{27}$$

with $\mathcal{Z}_{1(2)}\beta_{1(2)}S_{1(2),st} = 2/(2-q)$, $\nu = 3-2q$, and

$$\beta_{1(2)} = \left[\frac{r}{2D\nu S_{1(2),st}^{2-2q}}\left(\frac{2}{2-q}\right)^{3-2q}\right]^{\frac{1}{4-2q}}. \tag{28}$$

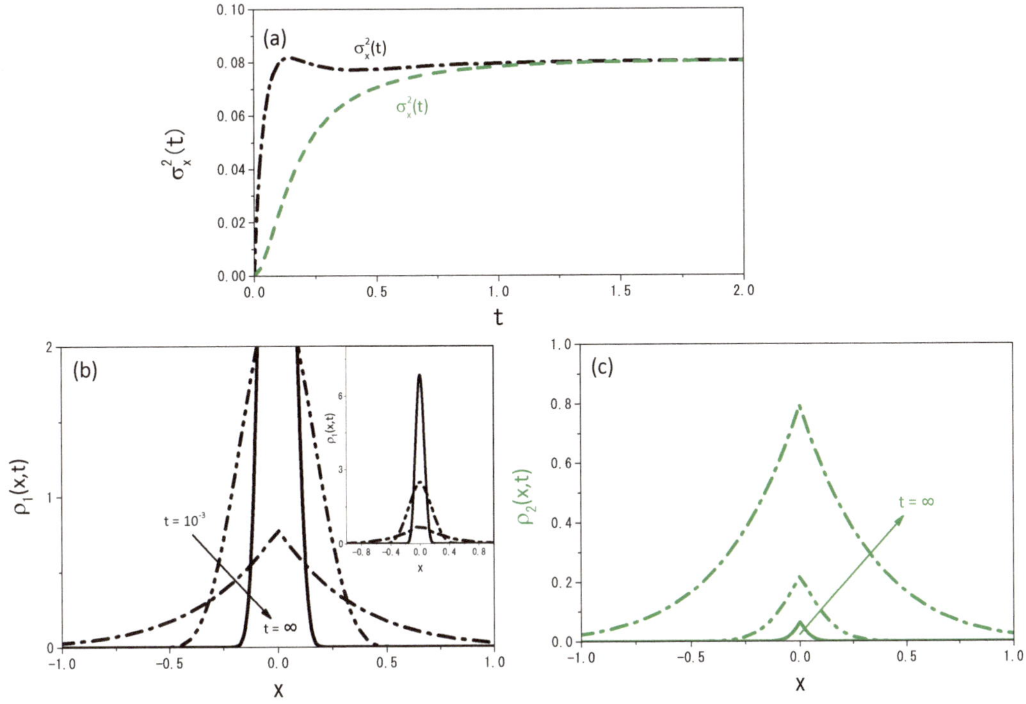

Figure 8. Profiles of the probability distributions obtained from Equations (19) and (20), when $\nu = 1.2$. (a) exhibits the time-dependence of the mean square displacement for the distributions $\rho_1(x,t)$ and $\rho_2(x,t)$; (b) and (c) show the spatial profiles of $\rho_1(x,t)$ and $\rho_2(x,t)$. The curves were drawn for $D = 1$, $r = 20$, $\rho_1(x,0) = \delta(x)$, $\rho_2(x,0) = 0$, and $\alpha_1 = \alpha_2 = 5$, for illustrative purposes.

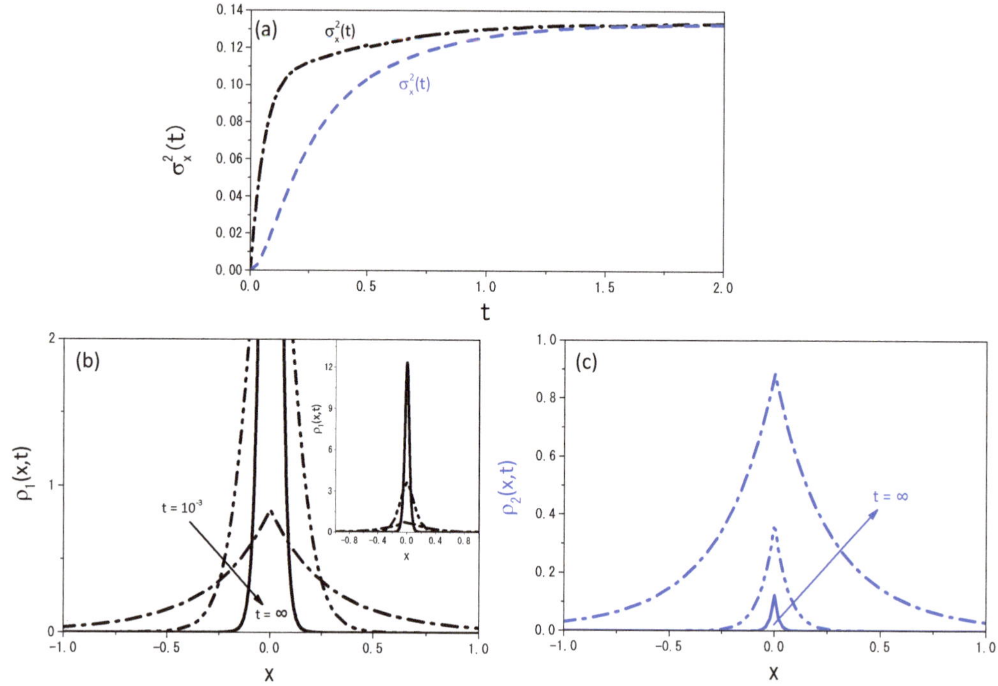

Figure 9. The same as in Figure 8 for $\nu = 0.8$.

Figures 10 and 11 exhibit the stationary solution for $\rho_1(x,t)$ and $\rho_2(x,t)$ from the numerical and the analytical point of view.

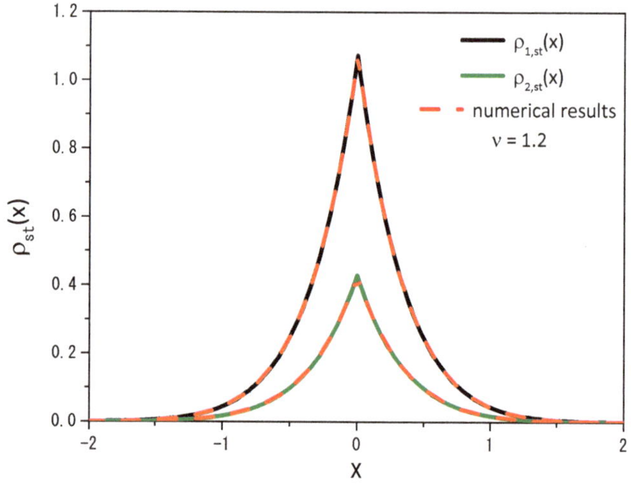

Figure 10. Comparison of the analytical results (black and green solid lines), given by Equation (27), $\rho_{2,st}(x) = (\alpha_1/\alpha_2)\rho_{1,st}(x)$, with the numerical results (red dotted lines) obtained from Equation (2) for $\nu = 1.2$. The curves were drawn for $D = 1$, $r = 10$, $\rho_1(x,0) = \delta(x)$, $\rho_2(x,0) = 0$, $\alpha_1 = 2$, and $\alpha_2 = 5$.

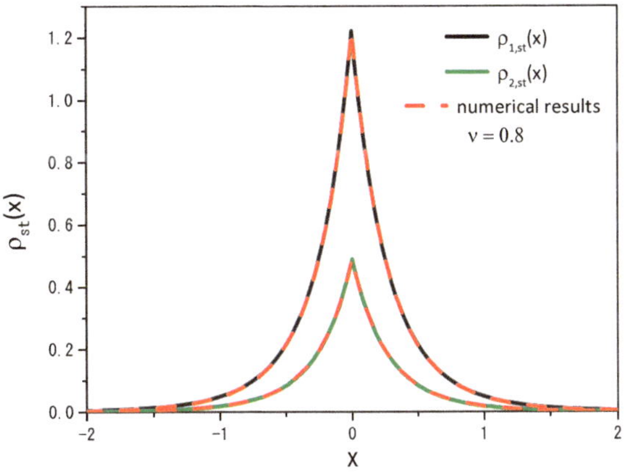

Figure 11. The same as in Figure 10 for the case $\nu = 0.8$.

Let us reconsider the random walk approach for $r \neq 0$, i.e., Equation (7), given by

$$\begin{aligned} \rho(x,t+\tau) &= \int_{-\infty}^{\infty} e^{-r\tau}\Psi[x-x',t;\rho(x-x',t)]\rho(x-x',t)\Phi(x')dx' \\ &+ \{1-\Psi[x,t;\rho(x,t)]\}e^{-r\tau}\rho(x,t) + \left(1-e^{-r\tau}\right)\{\rho(x,t)-\mathcal{R}[\rho(x,t)]\} \end{aligned} \quad (29)$$

which for $\Psi[x,t;\rho(x,t)] = D_1 + D_\nu[\rho(x,t)]^{\nu-1}$ implies that the diffusion is governed by the following equation

$$\frac{\partial}{\partial t}\rho(x,t) = D_1\frac{\partial^2}{\partial x^2}\rho(x,t) + D_\nu\frac{\partial^2}{\partial x^2}[\rho(x,t)]^\nu - r\mathcal{R}[\rho(x,t)]\,, \quad (30)$$

with $\mathcal{R}[\rho(x,t)] = \rho(x,t) - \delta(x-x')$ in connection with the stochastic resetting. Equation (30) has two different diffusive terms, which allows us to obtain two different regimes, where one of the processes is normal and the other is anomalous. Figure 12 illustrates the behavior of the mean square displacement and stationary distributions obtained from Equation (30) for different values of the diffusion coefficients for $\nu = 1.2$. The first regime, which is shown in Figure 12 for the mean square displacement, is anomalous, and the second is normal before reaching the stationary state.

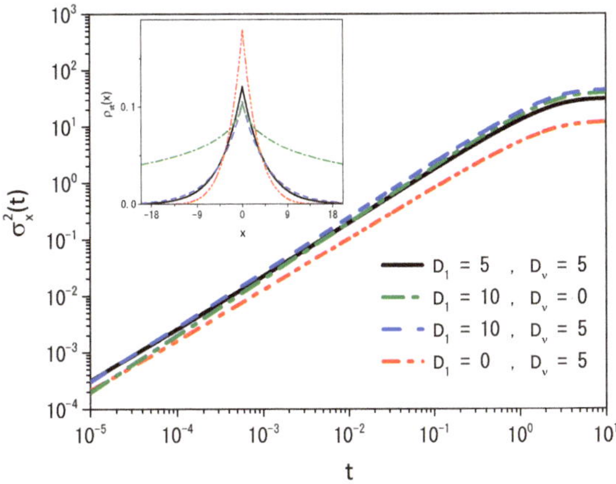

Figure 12. Time-dependence of the mean square displacement obtained from Equation (30) for different values of diffusion coefficients. The inset corresponds to the stationary distribution for different diffusion coefficients. We consider, for illustrative purposes, $\nu = 1.2$, $x' = 0$, and the initial condition $\rho(x,0) = \delta(x)$, for $r = 0.5$.

3. Discussion and Conclusions

We have investigated the diffusion process governed by a nonlinear diffusion equation when stochastic resetting and linear reaction terms are present. The nonlinear diffusion equation analyzed is the porous media equation with the diffusive part characterized by a single nonlinear term or a combination of different terms, resulting in different diffusion regimes. One of the solutions of Equation (2), in the absence of stochastic resetting and reaction terms, is given in terms of the q-Gaussian, as discussed in Section 2. It is different from the normal one expressed in terms of the Gaussian distribution as a consequence of the stochastic processes related to the motion of the particles [1]. It presents an anomalous behavior evidenced by the time dependence of the mean square displacement, which can be connected with sub- and superdiffusion. Under the influence of stochastic resetting, these processes exhibit a stationary state that differs from the expected exponential, characterized by a power-law behavior, as illustrated in Figure 4. This feature is a consequence of the nature of the diffusion process promoted by the nonlinear term, which can be connected to the correlated anomalous diffusion [35,36]. These general results extend the ones obtained in Refs. [19,34]. Subsequently, we analyzed the reaction process in this context by considering an irreversible and reversible scenario. The first case can be related to a substrate that immobilizes the particles while diffusion proceeds. The stationary solution is absent in a different way from the other scenarios. The second case can be considered an intermittent process between the resting and the motion with some rates. For this case, we also obtained a stationary solution in terms of the q-exponential, evidencing the influence of the nature of the diffusion on the stochastic resetting. The diffusion process represented by Equation (1) is described by power-law distributions, which promote a different behavior from the normal one for the stochastic resetting and, consequently, a stationary solution expressed in terms of a power-law.

We also analyzed a situation characterized by different diffusion regimes, such that the first regime is slower than the normal one, while the second is faster before the stationary state is reached. We verified that these changes in the diffusion equation directly influence the resetting process, leading the system to exhibit anomalous behavior. These features also open the possibility of considering mixing between different cases, such as the fractional diffusion equations [42–44] and nonlinear diffusion equations, which results in fractional nonlinear diffusion equations [45]. Combining different equations will produce a wide class of behaviors to describe a variety of scenarios. Finally, we hope that the results found here can be useful in discussing the processes related to the nonlinear diffusion equation when the stochastic process is present.

Author Contributions: Conceptualization, E.K.L., R.S.Z., M.P.R., R.S.M., H.V.R., L.R.d.S. and L.R.E.; methodology, E.K.L., R.S.Z., M.P.R., R.S.M., H.V.R., L.R.d.S. and L.R.E.; formal analysis, E.K.L., R.S.Z., M.P.R., R.S.M., H.V.R., L.R.d.S. and L.R.E.; investigation, E.K.L., R.S.Z., M.P.R., R.S.M., H.V.R., L.R.d.S. and L.R.E.; writing—original draft preparation, E.K.L., R.S.Z., M.P.R., R.S.M., H.V.R., L.R.d.S. and L.R.E.; writing—review and editing, E.K.L., R.S.Z., M.P.R., R.S.M., H.V.R., L.R.d.S. and L.R.E. All authors have read and agreed to the published version of the manuscript.

Funding: This study was financed in part by the Coordenação de Aperfeiçoamento de Pessoal de Nível Superior, Brasil (CAPES), Finance Code 001 (M.P.R.), and by the Program of Visiting Professor of Politecnico di Torino (L.R.E.). E.K.L. thanks the partial financial support of the CNPq under Grant No. 301715/2022–0. H.V.R. thanks the partial financial support of the CNPq under Grant No. 303533/2021-8. R.S.Z. thanks to the National Council for Scientific and Technological Development, CNPq, process number 304634/2020–4 and 465259/2014–6, the National Institute of Science and Technology Complex Fluids (INCT-FCx), and the São Paulo Research Foundation (FAPESP—2014/50983-3).

Institutional Review Board Statement: Not applicable.

Data Availability Statement: Data sharing not applicable.

Acknowledgments: We thank the CNPq for partial financial support.

Conflicts of Interest: The authors declare no conflict of interest.

References

1. Borland, L. Microscopic dynamics of the nonlinear Fokker-Planck equation: A phenomenological model. *Phys. Rev. E* **1998**, *57*, 6634–6642. [CrossRef]
2. Borland, L. Ito-Langevin equations within generalized thermostatistics. *Phys. Lett. A* **1998**, *245*, 67–72. [CrossRef]
3. Vázquez, J.L. *The Porous Medium Equation: Mathematical Theory*; Oxford University Press: Oxford, UK, 2007.
4. Frank, T.D. *Nonlinear Fokker-Planck Equations: Fundamentals and Applications*; Springer: Berlin/Heidelberg, Germany, 2005.
5. Curado, E.M.; Nobre, F.D. Derivation of nonlinear Fokker-Planck equations by means of approximations to the master equation. *Phys. Rev. E* **2003**, *67*, 021107. [CrossRef] [PubMed]
6. Muskat, M. The flow of homogeneous fluids through porous media. *Soil Sci.* **1938**, *46*, 169. [CrossRef]
7. Simon, A.; Wolschin, G. Examining nonextensive statistics in relativistic heavy-ion collisions. *Phys. Rev. C* **2018**, *97*, 044913. [CrossRef]
8. Moreira, A.A.; Vieira, C.M.; Carmona, H.A.; Andrade, J.S.; Tsallis, C. Overdamped dynamics of particles with repulsive power-law interactions. *Phys. Rev. E* **2018**, *98*, 032138. [CrossRef]
9. Frank, T. Strongly nonlinear stochastic processes in physics and the life sciences. *Int. Sch. Res. Not.* **2013**, *2013*, 149169 . [CrossRef]
10. Płociniczak, Ł. Derivation of the nonlocal pressure form of the fractional porous medium equation in the hydrological setting. *Commun. Nonlinear Sci. Numer. Simul.* **2019**, *76*, 66–70. [CrossRef]
11. Umarov, S.; Constantino, T. *Mathematical Foundations of Nonextensive Statistical Mechanics*; World Scientific: Singapore, 2022.
12. Abe, S.; Okamoto, Y. *Nonextensive Statistical Mechanics and Its Applications*; Springer: Berlin/Heidelberg, Germany, 2001; Volume 560,
13. Evans, M.R.; Majumdar, S.N. Diffusion with stochastic resetting. *Phys. Rev. Lett.* **2011**, *106*, 160601. [CrossRef]
14. Evans, M.R.; Majumdar, S.N. Diffusion with resetting in arbitrary spatial dimension. *J. Phys. A-Math. Theor.* **2014**, *47*, 285001. [CrossRef]
15. Nagar, A.; Valleriani, A.; Lipowsky, R. Translation by ribosomes with mRNA degradation: Exclusion processes on aging tracks. *J. Stat. Phys.* **2011**, *145*, 1385–1404. [CrossRef]
16. Balaban, H.; Luria, R. Neural and behavioral evidence for an online resetting process in visual working memory. *J. Neurosci.* **2017**, *37*, 1225–1239. [CrossRef] [PubMed]
17. Reuveni, S.; Urbakh, M.; Klafter, J. Role of substrate unbinding in Michaelis–Menten enzymatic reactions. *Proc. Natl. Acad. Sci. USA* **2014**, *111*, 4391–4396. [CrossRef] [PubMed]
18. Bartumeus, F.; Catalan, J. Optimal search behavior and classic foraging theory. *J. Phys. A* **2009**, *42*, 434002. [CrossRef]
19. Evans, M.R.; Majumdar, S.N.; Mallick, K. Optimal diffusive search: Nonequilibrium resetting versus equilibrium dynamics. *J. Phys. A* **2013**, *46*, 185001. [CrossRef]
20. Sandev, T.; Domazetoski, V.; Iomin, A.; Kocarev, L. Diffusion–Advection Equations on a Comb: Resetting and Random Search. *Mathematics* **2021**, *9*, 221. [CrossRef]
21. Evans, M.R.; Majumdar, S.N.; Schehr, G. Stochastic resetting and applications. *J. Phys. A* **2020**, *53*, 193001. [CrossRef]
22. Ray, S.; Reuveni, S. Diffusion with resetting in a logarithmic potential. *J. Chem. Phys.* **2020**, *152*, 234110. [CrossRef]
23. Ray, S.; Reuveni, S. Resetting transition is governed by an interplay between thermal and potential energy. *J. Chem. Phys.* **2021**, *154*, 171103. [CrossRef]
24. Shkilev, V. Continuous-time random walk under time-dependent resetting. *Phys. Rev. E* **2017**, *96*, 012126. [CrossRef]
25. Dos Santos, M.A. Fractional Prabhakar derivative in diffusion equation with non-static stochastic resetting. *Physics* **2019**, *1*, 40–58. [CrossRef]
26. Kuśmierz, Ł.; Gudowska-Nowak, E. Subdiffusive continuous-time random walks with stochastic resetting. *Phys. Rev. E* **2019**, *99*, 052116. [CrossRef] [PubMed]
27. Méndez, V.; Campos, D.; Bartumeus, F. *Stochastic Foundations in Movement Ecology*; Springer: Berlin/Heidelberg, Germany, 2016.
28. Crank, J. *The Mathematics of Diffusion*; Oxford University Press: Oxford, UK, 1979.
29. Murray, J.D. Mathematical biology: I. An introduction. Interdisciplinary applied mathematics. In *Mathematical Biology*; Springer: New York, NY, USA, 2002; Volume 17.
30. Murray, J.D.; Murray, J.D. *Mathematical Biology: II: Spatial Models and Biomedical Applications*; Springer: New York, USA, 2003; Volume 3.
31. Tsallis, C.; Levy, S.V.F.; Souza, A.M.C.; Maynard, R. Statistical-Mechanical Foundation of the Ubiquity of Lévy Distributions in Nature. *Phys. Rev. Lett.* **1995**, *75*, 3589–3593. [CrossRef] [PubMed]
32. Prato, D.; Tsallis, C. Nonextensive foundation of Lévy distributions. *Phys. Rev. E* **1999**, *60*, 2398–2401. [CrossRef]
33. Tsallis, C. *Introduction to Nonextensive Statistical Mechanics: Approaching a Complex World*; Springer: New York, NY, USA, 2009; Volume 1.
34. Chełminiak, P. Non-linear diffusion with stochastic resetting. *J. Phys. A Math. Theor.* **2022**, *55*, 384004. [CrossRef]
35. Upadhyaya, A.; Rieu, J.P.; Glazier, J.A.; Sawada, Y. Anomalous diffusion and non-Gaussian velocity distribution of Hydra cells in cellular aggregates. *Phys. A Stat. Mech. Its Appl.* **2001**, *293*, 549–558. [CrossRef]
36. Sogo, K.; Kishikawa, Y.; Ohnishi, S.; Yamamoto, T.; Fujiwara, S.; Aoki, K.M. Correlated anomalous diffusion: Random walk and Langevin equation. *J. Math. Phys.* **2010**, *51*, 033302. [CrossRef]
37. Gupta, S.; Jayannavar, A.M. Stochastic resetting: A (very) brief review. *Front. Phys.* **2022**, *10*, 789097. [CrossRef]

38. Méndez, V.; Campos, D. Characterization of stationary states in random walks with stochastic resetting. *Phys. Rev. E* **2016**, *93*, 022106. [CrossRef]
39. Lenzi, E.; Lenzi, M.; Ribeiro, H.; Evangelista, L. Extensions and solutions for nonlinear diffusion equations and random walks. *Proc. R. Soc. A* **2019**, *475*, 20190432. [CrossRef]
40. Burden, R.L.; Faires, J.D. *Numerical Analysis*, 9th ed.; PWS Publishing Co.: Boston, MA, USA, 2011.
41. Gardiner, C.W. *Handbook of Stochastic Methods for Physics, Chemistry and the Natural Sciences*; Springer: Berlin/Heidelberg, Germany, 1985; Volume 3.
42. Kang, Y.M. Simulating transient dynamics of the time-dependent time fractional Fokker–Planck systems. *Phys. Lett. A* **2016**, *380*, 3160–3166. [CrossRef]
43. Singh, R.; Górska, K.; Sandev, T. General approach to stochastic resetting. *Phys. Rev. E* **2022**, *105*, 064133. [CrossRef]
44. da Rocha, G.G.; Lenzi, E.K. Stochastic resetting and linear reaction processes: A continuous time random walk approach. *Commun. Nonlinear Sci. Numer. Simul.* **2023**, *126*, 107423. [CrossRef]
45. Tsallis, C.; Lenzi, E. Anomalous diffusion: Nonlinear fractional Fokker–Planck equation. *Chem. Phys.* **2002**, *284*, 341–347. [CrossRef]

entropy

MDPI

Article

Centrality and System Size Dependence among Freezeout Parameters and the Implications for EOS and QGP in High-Energy Collisions

Muhammad Waqas [1,*], Abd Haj Ismail [2,*], Haifa I. Alrebdi [3,*] and Muhammad Ajaz [4,*]

1 School of Mathematics, Physics and Optoelectronic Engineering, Hubei University of Automotive Technology, Shiyan 442002, China
2 College of Humanities and Sciences, Ajman University, Ajman P.O. Box 346, United Arab Emirates
3 Department of Physics, College of Science, Prince Nourah Bint Abdulrahman Univeristy, P.O.Box 84428, Riyadh 11671, Saudi Arabia
4 Department of Physics, Abdul Wali Khan University Mardan, Mardan 23200, Pakistan
* Correspondence: 20220073@huat.edu.cn (M.W.); a.hajismail@ajman.ac.ae (A.H.I.); hialrebdi@pnu.edu.sa (H.I.A.); ajaz@awkum.edu.pk (M.A.)

Abstract: Utilizing the Modified Hagedorn function with embedded flow, we analyze the transverse momenta (p_T) and transverse mass (m_T) spectra of π^+ in Au–Au, Cu–Cu, and d–Au collisions at $\sqrt{s_{NN}}$ = 200 GeV across various centrality bins. Our study reveals the centrality and system size dependence of key freezeout parameters, including kinetic freezeout temperature (T_0), transverse flow velocity (β_T), entropy-related parameter (n), and kinetic freezeout volume (V). Specifically, T_0 and n increase from central to peripheral collisions, while β_T and V show the opposite trend. These parameters also exhibit system size dependence; T_0 and β_T are smaller in larger collision systems, whereas V is larger. Importantly, central collisions correspond to a stiffer Equation of State (EOS), characterized by larger β_T and smaller T_0, while peripheral collisions indicate a softer EOS. These insights are crucial for understanding the properties of Quark–Gluon Plasma (QGP) and offer valuable constraints for Quantum Chromodynamics (QCD) models at high temperatures and densities.

Keywords: freezeout parameters; non-extensivity; qauntum chromodynamics; EOS; QGP

Citation: Waqas, M.; Haj Ismail, A.; Alrebdi, H.I.; Ajaz, M. Centrality and System Size Dependence among Freezeout Parameters and the Implications for EOS and QGP in High-Energy Collisions. *Entropy* **2023**, *25*, 1586. https://doi.org/10.3390/e25121586

Academic Editor: Edward Sarkisyan-Grinbaum

Received: 19 October 2023
Revised: 22 November 2023
Accepted: 24 November 2023
Published: 26 November 2023

1. Introduction

The collisions of heavy ions at relativistic energies in the laboratory allow the creation as well as the investigation of the hot and dense QCD matter [1–3]. The QCD phase diagram can be probed by tuning of collision energy, which enables the possibility of producing nuclear matter at various temperatures and baryon densities. The Relativistic Heavy Ion Collider (RHIC) [4,5] and Large Hadron Collider (LHC) [6–8] provide the opportunity to produce a medium that has the thermodynamic conditions of high temperatures and negligible baryon chemical potentials. This medium can be studied with high precision using the first-principle QCD calculations [9–13] within the Lattice QCD (lQCD) framework. The moderate temperature and finite net baryon densities in QCD can be created by lowering the beam energies. The application of lQCD to the study of such a matter is limited due to the so-called sign problem. However, there are current and future accelerator facilities, such as RHIC [14], Super Proton Synchrotron (SPS) [15,16], Nuclotron-based Ion Collider (NICA) [17], and the Facility for Anti-proton Ion Research (FAIR) [18,19], which have carried out or plan to conduct diverse experimental programs to explore this part of the QCD phase diagram. The sequence of events in relativistic heavy ion collisions involving the generation of hot and dense matter can be outlined as follows: a pre-equilibrium phase, the attainment of thermal (or chemical) equilibrium among partons, the potential formation of Quark–Gluon Plasma (QGP) or a mixed state of QGP and hadron gas, the emergence of a gas comprising hot interacting hadrons, and, ultimately, a freezeout state where the produced hadrons cease strong interactions. As the produced hadrons encapsulate information pertaining to the collision dynamics and the comprehensive spacetime evolution of the system from its initial to final stages, a precise assessment of transverse momentum (p_T) distributions and yields of identified hadrons in relation to collision geometry becomes crucial for comprehending the dynamics and properties of the generated matter.

The freezeout conditions of the fireball have great importance and have been one of the compelling topics in the study of heavy ion collisions at various energies and in different centrality intervals. From the analysis of two-particle correlations [20,21] and hadron yields, the freezeout is claimed to occur in two stages: (1) chemical freezeout, where the particle ratio stabilizes as the inelastic scattering stops; and (2) kinetic freezeout, where the momentum distribution of the particles is frozen.

The kinetic freezeout stage is very important in the evolution of heavy ion collisions because it provides information about the properties of nuclear matter and the underlying dynamics of the strong interactions. Different hydrodynamic models [22–26] can be used to investigate the hot and dense matter in terms of various parameters to be extracted. In the present work, the (p_T) spectra of pions in Au–Au, Cu–Cu, and d–Au interactions at 200 GeV in several centrality intervals are analyzed by the Modified Hagedorn function with the embedded flow to extract T_0, β_T, n, and V. All these parameters are discussed in our previous works in detail [27–30]. The T_0 is the temperature at which the QGP is already transformed into a gas of hadrons and the interactions between the particles cease. The β_T is the collective motion of the particles in the transverse direction, perpendicular to the beam axis, due to the pressure gradients within the QGP. It should be noted that we took pions because they are the most abundant particles that are produced in collisions.

The subsequent sections of the paper follow this structure: Section 2 outlines the methodology and formal framework, Section 3 delves into the discussion of results, and Section 4 provides the concluding remarks.

2. The Method and Formalism

The p_T parameters of the final state particles have great importance in high-energy physics and are distributed among several components. These components include the soft, hard, very soft, and very hard components, which are discussed in detail in our previous work [31]. Let us bind our discussion to the soft and hard components. Several functions and distributions may be used to describe the p_T spectra. Some distributions may describe soft components, while some of them may be used to describe both the soft and hard components. The p_T range of 0–2 or 2.5 GeV/c can be referred to as the soft component, while the range above that is considered the hard component.

Various versions of the Tsallis distribution function , rooted in non-extensive Tsallis statistics, have become widely used models for describing the p_T distributions of hadrons in high-energy collisions [32–35]. Unlike others, the Tsallis function offers a distinct advantage: it is directly linked to thermodynamics through entropy [35]. The Tsallis function includes a crucial parameter, the non-extensivity index q, which indicates how much the particle p_T distribution deviates from the Boltzmann–Gibbs exponential distribution. Additionally, the parameter q serves as a measure of the system's departure from equilibrium or thermal equilibrium [36]. The significance of q and its profound physical implications, directly related to thermodynamics, have been reaffirmed in recent research by Tsallis [33].

The Tsallis function at mid-rapidity in its most basic form is provided as [37,38]

$$f(p_T) = C\left(1 + (q-1)\frac{m_T}{T}\right)^{-1/(q-1)}, \tag{1}$$

C denotes the normalized constant, while T represents the effective temperature. This temperature, encompassing the flow effect, is defined as $T = \sqrt{\frac{T_0(1+\beta_T)}{(1-\beta_T)}}$. As cited in [38–40], the Tsallis distribution, expressed in the following form, aligns with thermodynamic principles:

$$f(p_T) = C\left(1 + (q-1)\frac{m_T}{T}\right)^{-q/(q-1)}, \tag{2}$$

The β_T is incorporated into a QCD-inspired (power law) Hagedorn function using a straightforward Lorentz transformation [41,42]. This approach effectively replicated the observed extended ranges of momentum spectra for final particles in both heavy-ion and pp collisions at high energies.

For the description of the hard component of the p_T spectra, one may use the Hagedorn function [43], which is described by the inverse power law [44–46]

$$\frac{1}{N}\frac{d^2N}{2\pi p_T dp_T dy} = C\left(1 + \frac{m_T}{p_0}\right)^{-n}, \tag{3}$$

and

$$m_T = \sqrt{(m_0)^2 + (p_T)^2}, \tag{4}$$

In the given context, N denotes the number of particles, and p_T (m_T) represents the transverse momentum (mass) of these particles. The parameters p_0 and n are variables allowed to vary freely during the fitting process, with the latter expressed as $n = (q-1)^{-1}$. The value m_0 corresponds to the rest mass of the pion, which is 0.139 GeV$/c^2$ [47].

Equations (1) and (3) are mathematically identical when one sets $p_0 = nT_0$ and $n = (q-1)^{-1}$. So, Equation (3) becomes

$$\frac{1}{N}\frac{d^2N}{2\pi p_T dp_T dy} = C\left(1 + \frac{m_T}{nT_0}\right)^{-n}. \tag{5}$$

In the current work, the simplest transformation is used to incorporate the collective transverse (radial) flow into Equation (5) $m_T \longrightarrow < \gamma_t > (m_T - p_T/\beta_T)^{-n}$, such that Equation (5) becomes

$$f(p_T) = C\left(1 + \frac{< \gamma_T > (m_T - p_T < \beta_T >)}{nT_0}\right)^{-n}, \tag{6}$$

This is the Hagedorn function with embedded flow, where $C = gV/(2\pi)^2$ is the normalization constant and V is the kinetic freezeout volume. T_0 and β_T represent the kinetic freezeout temperature and transverse flow velocity, respectively. n is a parameter that is related to non-extensivity, and $\gamma_t = 1/\sqrt{1- < \beta_T >^2}$. One can further read about the Hagedorn model with the embedded flow in Refs. [41,48]. Before proceeding to the next section, we would like to clarify that, if the hard component is included, we can apply the superposition principle to combine Equations (3) and (6), as indicated by references [27,31].

3. Results and Discussion

The p_T (m_T) spectra of π^+ in Au–Au, Cu–Cu, and d–Au collisions at $\sqrt{s_{NN}}$ = 200 GeV are presented in Figure 1. We have analyzed p_T spectra in various centrality bins. The data are taken from [49–51], denoted by different symbols for different centrality intervals. One can see that the model provides a good fit to the experimental data. The values of the extracted parameters and χ^2 are presented in Table 1. The data/fit in the lower segment of each panel, and the values of χ^2 show the quality of the fit. The normalization constant C is integrated into the equations to normalize them to unity, while N_0 is used to compare the experimental data with the model fit and is considered as the multiplicity parameter.

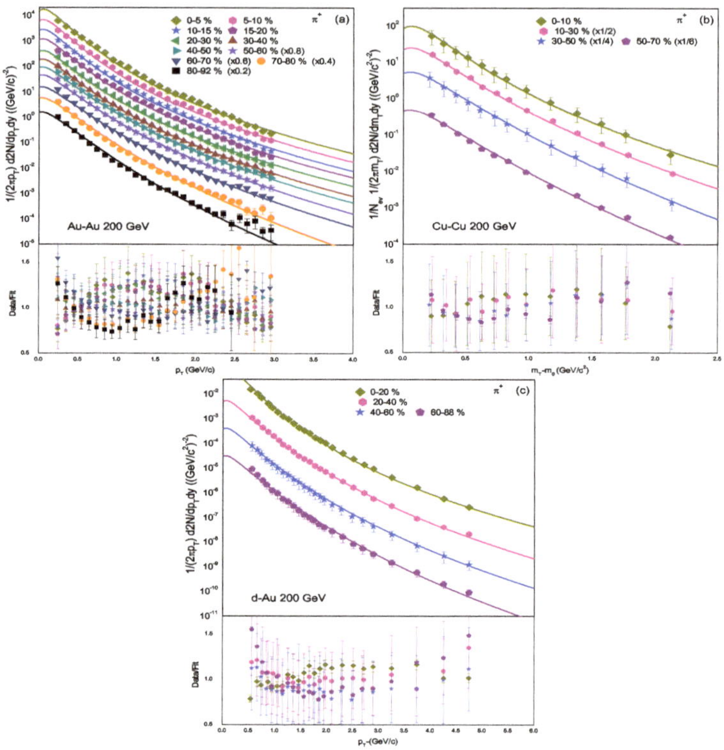

Figure 1. p_T spectra of π^+ produced in (**a**) Au–Au, (**b**) Cu–Cu, and (**c**) d–Au collisions in various centrality intervals at $\sqrt{s_{NN}}$ = 200 GeV. The experimental data from the PHENIX and BRAHMS collaborations are taken from [49–51], while the solid lines represent the fit results of the model. The lower segment in each panel provides the data/fit.

Table 1. Collision, centrality, the extracted parameters (T_0, β_T, and n), fitting constant (N_0), χ^2, and degrees of freedom (dof) corresponding to the graphs in Figure 1.

Collision	Centrality	T_0 (GeV)	β_T	n	$V(fm^3)$	N_0	χ^2/dof
Au–Au	0–5%	0.065 ± 0.004	0.380 ± 0.008	8.4 ± 0.5	5568 ± 131	680 ± 37	31/25
	5–10%	0.070 ± 0.004	0.365 ± 0.005	8.5 ± 0.3	5400 ± 113	280 ± 28	28/25
	10–15%	0.075 ± 0.005	0.345 ± 0.007	8.7 ± 1.1	5357 ± 108	120 ± 19	76/25
	15–20%	0.081 ± 0.005	0.331 ± 0.009	8.75 ± 0.5	5224 ± 111	55 ± 9.2	15.8/25
	20–30%	0.087 ± 0.004	0.320 ± 0.010	8.8 ± 0.4	5102 ± 102	21 ± 4	11/25
	30–40%	0.095 ± 0.006	0.304 ± 0.008	9.5 ± 0.5	5000 ± 106	10 ± 0.6	3.3/21
	40–50%	0.104 ± 0.005	0.288 ± 0.008	10 ± 1.1	4800 ± 90	5.5 ± 0.4	13.4/25
	50–60%	0.111 ± 0.006	0.270 ± 0.009	11 ± 1.1	4670 ± 100	3.5 ± 0.3	5.8/25
	60–70%	0.120 ± 0.004	0.255 ± 0.009	12 ± 1.2	4535 ± 109	1.7 ± 0.22	2/25
	70–80%	0.126 ± 0.004	0.241 ± 0.007	16 ± 1.2	4404 ± 102	0.95 ± 0.08	159/25
	80–92%	0.130 ± 0.004	0.220 ± 0.007	19 ± 1.2	4300 ± 102	0.5 ± 0.04	57/25
Cu–Cu	0–10%	0.074 ± 0.005	0.421 ± 0.011	8.1 ± 0.6	5307 ± 127	5.2 ± 0.3	1/10
	10–30%	0.093 ± 0.006	0.400 ± 0.008	10.3 ± 1.4	5183 ± 141	0.25 ± 0.04	0.4/10
	30–50%	0.111 ± 0.006	0.370 ± 0.011	14.7 ± 1.3	5007 ± 136	0.02 ± 0.004	1/10
	50–70%	0.120 ± 0.004	0.342 ± 0.010	17 ± 2	4800 ± 139	0.0035 ± 0.0005	1.3/10
d–Au	0–20%	0.082 ± 0.007	0.445 ± 0.009	10.9 ± 1	4529 ± 135	0.01 ± 0.003	4/21
	20–40%	0.118 ± 0.005	0.409 ± 0.009	14.5 ± 1.5	4400 ± 152	$5 \times 10^{-4} \pm 4 \times 10^{-5}$	7/23
	40–60%	0.129 ± 0.004	0.381 ± 0.010	13.1 ± 1.4	4346 ± 147	$4 \times 10^{-6} \pm 6 \times 10^{-7}$	3/21
	60–88%	0.142 ± 0.006	0.352 ± 0.012	15.3 ± 2.1	4231 ± 163	$1.6 \times 10^{-7} \pm 5 \times 10^{-8}$	7.2/21

The extracted parameters, T_0, β_T, n, and V, as a function of centrality and system size, are shown in Figure 2. Figure 2a shows that T_0 increases toward peripheral collisions, indicating that the fireball lifetime decreases towards the peripheral collisions. On the other hand, β_T decreases as we move to non-central collisions as the pressure gradient decreases toward peripheral collisions. We know that T_0 in heavy ion collisions is sensitive to the thermal and dynamical properties of the created system and β_T characterizes the collective motion of the particles in the transverse direction. The fluctuations in these quantities are determined by the interplay between the preliminary conditions, the expansion dynamics, and the freezeout process. Basically, in peripheral collisions, the weak pressure gradients result in a more gradual cooling of the system and, hence, lower β_T, and the particle density decreases more slowly, which results in larger T_0 in peripheral collisions compared to central collisions. Therefore, larger T_0 corresponds to smaller β_T in peripheral collisions, indicating a short-lived fireball with a steady expansion of the system. Our results agree with the STAR results at 200 GeV [52], but the specific parameter values differ. The parameters obtained by BRAHMS [50] are relatively larger than ours. The variation in parameter values is attributed to different models. These findings are also consistent with those obtained from the blast wave model [52], accurately reflecting the physical reality of the collisions. Our model includes the non-extensive parameter, which offers a more suitable description of particle spectra in extreme conditions and accounts for deviations from equilibrium in non-extensive systems. The disparity between the T_0 values in our work and the chemical freezeout temperature extracted from the statistical and thermal models [49] is substantial. This difference may be due to the complex dynamics and non-equilibrium effects in high-energy systems, such as 200 GeV, which encompass processes like hadronization and hadronic rescattering. Precisely measuring chemical and kinetic freezeout temperatures in experiments is challenging, and the discrepancy in these temperatures underscores the difficulty in extracting these values from experimental data.

We also see (Figure 2a) that T_0 depends on the colliding system's size. For a larger system, the T_0 is smaller. Similarly, in Figure 2b, β_T has the same behavior as the system size. Large colliding nuclei can provide a larger volume of the system, which results in a longer expansion time and a lower energy density at the time of kinetic freezeout. This leads the particles to have less time to interact and thermalize with each other, leading to a lower T_0. On the other hand, we know that β_T refers to the collective motion of the particles in the transverse direction, perpendicular to the beam axis. This velocity can be generated by the pressure gradients created by the initial collision and subsequent expansion of the system. Therefore, a larger β_T can also correspond to a smaller system size as the particles will be more spread out in the transverse direction due to their collective motion. The smaller β_T for large systems in the current work can be explained in terms of, in larger collision systems, there is typically a higher initial energy density, which can lead to a longer duration of the early dense stage of the collision. Additionally, because of the longer interaction time and larger system size, the expansion can be more gradual and less violent. As a result, the transverse flow velocity may increase more slowly.

Figure 2c provides the result of the dependence of n on centrality. Basically, $n = (q-1)^{-1}$, and q is the non-extensive parameter [36,53]. The parameter q is used to explain the deviation from thermal equilibrium and can be used for quantification of the fluctuations in temperature around the equilibrated value of temperature. The parameter q and temperature can be interconnected as

$$q - 1 = \frac{Var(T_0)}{< T_0 >} \tag{7}$$

Larger (small) q refers to a large (small) deviation in the system from thermal equilibrium, where larger q corresponds to smaller n. In the present work, the central collisions are far from thermal equilibrium because the value of n is smaller in central collisions, and it increases toward peripheral collisions, which means that the peripheral collisions are closer to equilibrium. The above statement seems unusual but it is not. It is possible that the peripheral collisions may have a closer approach to equilibrium than the central collision systems, which can be explained in terms of higher energy densities and more violent interactions being experienced by the system in central collisions, where there is a greater overlap between the colliding nuclei. This may cause the system to expand and cool quickly, which could shorten the amount of time it takes for the particles to reach thermal equilibrium. Central collisions may therefore show non-equilibrium features. Peripheral collisions, on the other hand, involve lower energy densities and less overlap. The system can evolve more slowly in peripheral collisions due to the longer interaction times, even though the overall energy deposited is lower. The system may become more "equilibrated" in terms of conventional thermodynamic properties as a result of this prolonged evolution, which may give the particles more chances to achieve a state of thermal equilibrium.

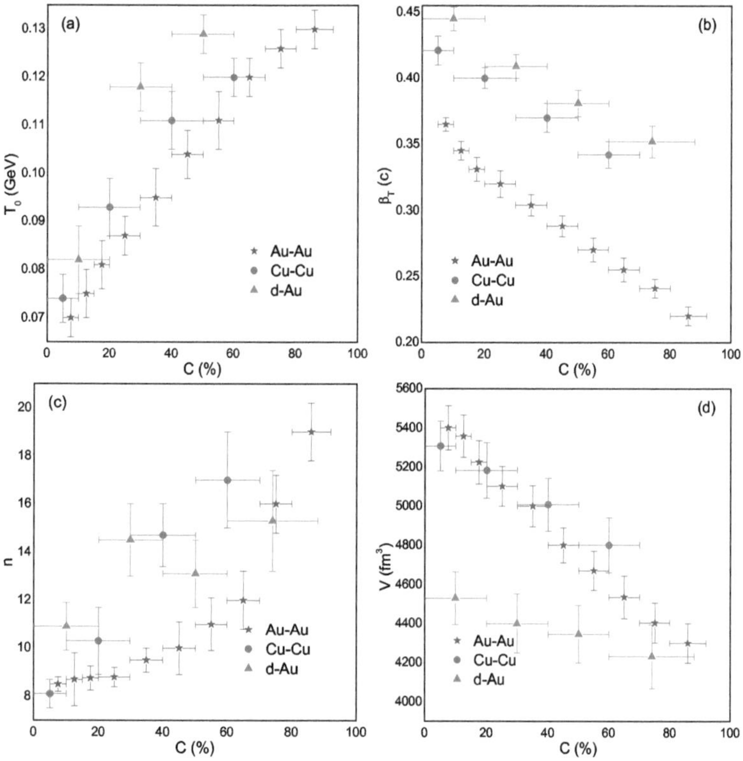

Figure 2. T_0, β_T, n, and V are shown in centrality classes in panels (**a**), (**b**), (**c**), and (**d**), respectively. Different symbols with different colors in all four panels of Figure 2 demonstrate different collision systems. The change in these symbols towards the right shows their dependence on centrality.

The dependence of (V) is shown in Figure 2d. One can see that V depends on both the system size and collision centrality. This occurs because central collisions are associated with larger initial bulk systems at higher energies. This, in turn, results in longer evolution times and the formation of larger partonic systems. Naturally, a larger partonic system corresponds to a larger V. Meanwhile, the scenario is the opposite regarding the periphery, where V becomes smaller. V is also dependent on the system size. The larger the system, the larger the V. The fact behind this is that a large number of particles are produced in larger systems; as a result, larger volume is required to accommodate these particles at the time of kinetic freezeout.

Figure 3 shows the multiplicity parameter (N_0) as a function of centrality and the size of the collision system. Central collisions correspond to large multiplicity because the overlapping region contains huge energy during the collision. At the time of ion collision, a high-temperature and high-density medium of quarks and gluons known as the QGP is produced. This plasma quickly expands and cools, eventually breaking up into a large number of particles. In other words, the multiplicity of particles produced in the central collisions is related to the energy density of the QGP. High energy density means that there are more particles per unit volume, leading to a larger number of particles. This is why central collisions, which have the highest energy densities, are more likely to produce a large number of particles. When the centrality decreases, the energy densities in the system also decrease, which results in smaller multiplicity.

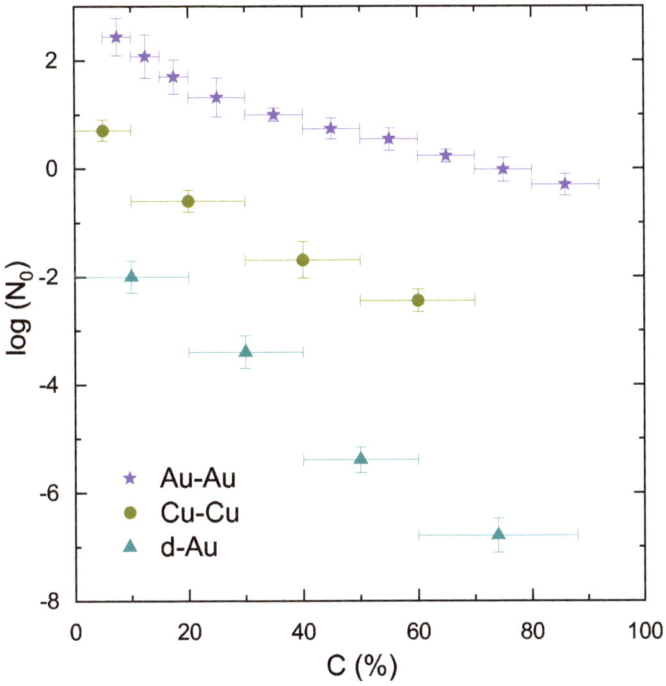

Figure 3. The variation in N_0 with centrality and size of the interacting system.

Before advancing to the conclusion, we would like to emphasize that the present work is very important because, in heavy ion collisions, the T_0 and β_T are two important observables that are related to the EOS of the QGP. The EOS describes the relationship between the thermodynamic variables of the QGP, such as temperature, pressure, and energy density.

The relationship between the T_0 and the β_T can be used to constrain the EOS of the QGP. In this work, the higher values of β_T and smaller values of T_0 in the highest centrality correspond to a stiffer EOS, showing large pressure. The stiffer EOS is due to a large pressure gradient and lower T_0, which will lead to a faster expansion of the QGP and a larger pressure gradient, resulting in greater collective motion of the particles. Conversely, peripheral collisions correspond to a softer EOS, which shows a slower expansion. The softer EOS corresponds to lower pressure for a given energy density, which will result in a smaller β_T and a higher T_0. This is because a softer EOS will lead to a slower expansion of the QGP and a smaller pressure gradient, resulting in lesser collective motion of the particles. A stiffer EOS indicates a stronger interaction between the quarks and gluons in QGP, whereas a softer EOS indicates a weaker interaction. This information is important for understanding the properties of the QGP and for constraining theoretical models of QCD at high temperatures and densities.

4. Conclusions

The transverse momentum (mass) spectra of π^+ at $\sqrt{s_{NN}}$ = 200 GeV in different centrality bins of Au–Au, Cu–Cu, and d–Au collisions are analyzed, and the freezeout parameters are extracted. The extracted parameters are the T_0, β_T, kinetic freezeout, and the non-extensive parameter.

We presented the dependence of the extracted parameters on centrality as well as on the size of the interacting system. The T_0 shows a declining trend from peripheral to central collisions, which shows a short-lived fireball in central collisions. On the other hand, the β_T shows an opposite trend from peripheral to central to peripheral collisions, which suggests a large pressure gradient in a central collision that results in a quicker expansion of the system. The T_0 and β_T have a negative correlation. The larger the T_0, the smaller the β_T. Furthermore, the V follows the trend of the β_T, which indicates that a greater number of participant nucleons take part in central collisions. The parameter n follows the trend of the T_0, showing that the peripheral collisions come to an equilibrium state easily. The above parameters also depend on the size of the colliding system. Large colliding systems have smaller T_0 and β_T, and larger V.

Author Contributions: Conceptualization, M.W. and M.A.; methodology, A.H.I.; software, H.I.A. and M.A.; validation, M.W., H.I.A. and M.A.; formal analysis, M.W.; investigation, A.H.I.; resources, H.I.A.; data curation, M.W.; writing—original draft preparation, M.W., H.I.A. and M.A; writing—review and editing, A.H.I.; visualization, M.A.; supervision, M.A.; project administration, M.W.; funding acquisition, M.W. and H.I.A. All authors have read and agreed to the published version of the manuscript.

Funding: This work is supported by the Hubei University of Automotive Technology Doctoral Research Fund under Grant Number BK202313 and and Princess Nourah bint Abdulrahman University Researchers Supporting Project number (PNURSP2023R106), Princess Nourah bint Abdulrahman University, Riyadh, Saudi Arabia. We also acknowledge Ajman University, Internal Research Grant No. [DRGS Ref. 2023-IRG-HBS-13] for supporting the research project.

Institutional Review Board Statement: The authors declare that they comply with ethical standards regarding the content of this paper.

Informed Consent Statement: Not applicable.

Data Availability Statement: All data generated or analyzed during this study are included and cited in this article.

Conflicts of Interest: The authors declare no conflict of interest.

References

1. Heinz, U.W. Concepts of Heavy-Ion Physics. *arXiv* **2004**, arXiv:hep-ph/0407360. [CrossRef]
2. Florkowski, W. Basic phenomenology for relativistic heavy-ion collisions. *Acta Phys. Polon. B* **2014**, *45*, 2329–2354. [CrossRef]
3. Braun-Munzinger, P.; Wambach, J. The Phase Diagram of Strongly-Interacting Matter. *Rev. Mod. Phys.* **2009**, *81*, 1031–1050. [CrossRef]
4. Adams, J.; Aggarwal, M.M.; Ahammed, Z.; Amonett, J.; Anderson, B.D.; Arkhipkin, D.; Averichev, G.S.; Badyal, S.K.; Bai, Y.; Balewski, J.; et al. Experimental and theoretical challenges in the search for the quark gluon plasma: The STAR Collaboration's critical assessment of the evidence from RHIC collisions. *Nucl. Phys. A* **2005**, *757*, 102–183. [CrossRef]
5. Adcox, K.; Adler, S.S.; Afanasiev, S.; Aidala, C.; Ajitan, N.N.; Akiba, Y.; Al-Jamel, A.; Alexander, J.; Amirikas, R.; Aoki, K.; et al. Formation of dense partonic matter in relativistic nucleus-nucleus collisions at RHIC: Experimental evaluation by the PHENIX collaboration. *Nucl. Phys. A* **2005**, *757*, 184–283. [CrossRef]
6. Chatrchyan, S.; Khachatryan, V.; Sirunyan, A.M.; Tumasyan, A.; Adam, W.; Bergauer, T.; Dragicevic, M.; Eroe, J.; Fabjan, C.; Friedl, M.; et al. Measurement of Higher-Order Harmonic Azimuthal Anisotropy in PbPb Collisions at $\sqrt{s_{NN}}$ = 2.76 TeV. *Phys. Rev. C* **2014**, *89*, 044906. [CrossRef]
7. Aamodt, K.; Abelev, B.; Quintana, A.A.; Adamova, D.; Adare, A.M.; Aggarwal, M.M.; Rinella, G.A.; Agocs, A.G.; Agostinelli, A.; Salazar, S.A.; et al. Higher harmonic anisotropic flow measurements of charged particles in Pb-Pb collisions at $\sqrt{s_{NN}}$=2.76 TeV. *Phys. Rev. Lett.* **2011**, *107*, 032301. [CrossRef] [PubMed]

8. Aad, G.; Abbott, B.; Abdallah, J.; Khalek, S.A.; Abdelalim, A.A.; Abdesselam, A.; Abi, B.; Abolins, M.; AbouZeid, O.S.; Abramowicz, H.; et al. Measurement of the azimuthal anisotropy for charged particle production in $\sqrt{s_{NN}} = 2.76$ TeV lead-lead collisions with the ATLAS detector. *Phys. Rev. C* **2012**, *86*, 014907. [CrossRef]
9. Borsanyi, S.; Fodor, Z.; Hoelbling, C.; Katz, S.D.; Krieg, S.; Szabo, K.K. Full result for the QCD equation of state with 2 + 1 flavors. *Phys. Lett. B* **2014**, *730*, 99–104. [CrossRef]
10. Bazavov, A.; Bhattacharya, T.; Cheng, M.; Christ, N.H.; DeTar, C.; Ejiri, S.; Gottlieb, S.; Gupta, R.; Heller, U.M.; Huebner, K.; et al. Equation of state and QCD transition at finite temperature. *Phys. Rev. D* **2009**, *80*, 014504. [CrossRef]
11. Bazavov, A.; Bhattacharya, T.; DeTar, C.; Ding, H.T.; Gottlieb, S.; Gupta, R.; Hegde, P.; Heller, U.M.; Karsch, F.; Laermann, E.; et al. Equation of state in (2 + 1)-flavor QCD. *Phys. Rev. D* **2014**, *90*, 094503. [CrossRef]
12. Borsanyi, S.; Endrodi, G.; Fodor, Z.; Jakovac, A.; Katz, S.D.; Krieg, S.; Ratti, C.; Szabo, K.K. The QCD equation of state with dynamical quarks. *J. High Energy Phys.* **2010**, *1011*, 077. [CrossRef]
13. Fodor, Z.; Katz, S.D. Available online: https://ui.adsabs.harvard.edu/abs/2009arXiv0908.3341F (accessed on 28 September 2023).
14. Bzdak, A.; Esumi, S.; Koch, V.; Liao, J.; Stephanov, M.; Xu, N. Mapping the Phases of Quantum Chromodynamics with Beam Energy Scan. *Phys. Rept.* **2020**, *853*, 1–87. [CrossRef]
15. Agnello, M.; Antinori, F.; Appelshäuser, H.; Arnaldi, R.; Bailhache, R.; Barioglio, L.; Beole, S.; Beraudo, A.; Bianchi, A.; Bianchi, L.; et al. Study of hard and electromagnetic processes at CERN-SPS energies: An investigation of the high-μ_B region of the QCD phase diagram with NA60+. *JPS Conf. Proc.* **2021**, *33*, 011113. [CrossRef]
16. Lewicki, M.P.; Turko, L. NA61/SHINE shining more light on the onset of deconfinement. *arXiv* **2020**, arXiv:2002.00631.
17. Geraksiev, N.S.; theNICA/MPD Collaboration. The physics programme for the multi-purpose detector. *J. Phys. Conf. Ser.* **2019**, *1390*, 012121. [CrossRef]
18. Senger, P. Exploring Cosmic Matter in the Laboratory—The Compressed Baryonic Matter Experiment at FAIR. *Particles* **2019**, *2*, 499–510. [CrossRef]
19. Ablyazimov, T.; Abuhoza, A.; Adak, R.P.; Adamczyk, M.; Agarwal, K.; Aggarwal, M.M.; Ahammed, Z.; Ahmad, F.; Ahmad, N.; Ahmad, S.; et al. Challenges in QCD matter physics –The scientific programme of the Compressed Baryonic Matter experiment at FAIR. *Eur. Phys. J. A* **2017**, *53*, 60. [CrossRef]
20. Karsch, F. Lattice results on QCD thermodynamics. In *Proceedings of the 15th International Conference on Ultrarelativistic Nucleus Nucleus Collisions, Quark Matter 2001, Stony Brook, NY, USA, 15–20 January 2001*; Hallman, T.J., Kharzeev, D.E., Mitchell, J.T., Ullrich, T.S., Eds.; Elsevier: Amsterdam, The Netherlands, 2001; Volume 698, pp. 199–208.
21. Heinz, U. The little bang: Searching for quark-gluon matter in relativistic heavy-ion collisions. *Nucl. Phys. A* **2001**, *685*, 414. [CrossRef]
22. Urmossy, K.; Jakovac, A. Scale dependence of the q and T parameters of the Tsallis distribution in the process of jet fragmentation. *Eur. Phys. J. A* **2023**, *59*, 122. [CrossRef]
23. Singh, A.K.; Akhil, A.; Tiwari, S.K.; Pareek, P. Nuclear Modification Factor in Pb-Pb and p-Pb collisions at $\sqrt{s_{NN}}$=5.02 TeV at LHC energies using Boltzmann Transport Equation with Tsallis Blast Wave Description. *arXiv* **2023**, arXiv:2309.17071.
24. Wang, R.Q.; Li, Y.H.; Song, J.; Shao, F.L. Production properties of deuterons, helions and tritons via an analytical nucleon coalescence method in Pb-Pb collisions at $\sqrt{s_{NN}} = 2.76$ TeV. *arXiv* **2023**, arXiv:2309.16296.
25. Geng, Y.F.; Li, B.C. Properties of the particle distribution in Pb–Pb collisions at $\sqrt{s_{NN}}$=5.02 TeV and $\sqrt{s_{NN}}$=2.76 TeV. *Front. Phys.* **2023**, *11*, 1257937. [CrossRef]
26. Wang, Q.; Liu, F.H. Excitation function of initial temperature of heavy flavor quarkonium emission source in high energy collisions. *Adv. High Energy Phys.* **2020**, *2020*, 5031494. [CrossRef]
27. Waqas, M.; Peng, G.X.; Ajaz, M.; Haj, A.A.K.I.; Wazir, Z.; Li, L.L. Extraction of different temperatures and kinetic freeze-out volume in high energy collisions. *J. Phys. G* **2022**, *49*, 095102. [CrossRef]
28. Badshah, M.; Waqas, M.; Khubrani, A.M.; Ajaz, M. Systematic analysis of the pp collisions at LHC energies with Tsallis function. *EPL* **2023**, *141*, 64002. [CrossRef]
29. Waqas, M.; Ismail, A.A.K.H.; Ajaz, M.; AbdelKader, A. Excitation Function of Kinetic Freeze-Out Parameters at 6.3, 17.3, 31, 900 and 7000 GeV. *Universe* **2022**, *8*, 138. [CrossRef]
30. Li, L.L.; Waqas, M.; Ajaz, M.; Khubrani, A.M.; Yao, H.; Khan, M.A. Analyses of pp, Cu–Cu, Au–Au and Pb–Pb Collisions by Tsallis-Pareto Type Function at RHIC and LHC Energies. *Entropy* **2022**, *24*, 1219. [CrossRef]
31. Waqas, M.; Liu, F.H. Centrality dependence of kinetic freeze-out temperature and transverse flow velocity in high energy nuclear collisions. *Indian J. Phys.* **2022**, *96*, 1217–1235. [CrossRef]
32. Tsallis, C. Possible generalization of Boltzmann-Gibbs statistics. *J. Statist. Phys.* **1988**, *52*, 479. [CrossRef]
33. Tsallis, C. Enthusiasm and Skepticism: Two Pillars of Science—A Nonextensive Statistics Case. *Physics* **2022**, *4*, 609. [CrossRef]
34. Tsallis, C. Nonadditive entropy: The concept and its use. *Eur. Phys. J. A* **2009**, *40*, 257. [CrossRef]
35. Cleymans, J.; Lykasov, G.I.; Parvan, A.S.; Sorin, A.S.; Teryaev, O.V.; Worku, D. Systematic properties of the Tsallis Distribution: Energy Dependence of Parameters in High-Energy p p Collisions. *Phys. Lett. B* **2013**, *723*, 351. [CrossRef]
36. Wilk, G.; Wlodarczyk, Z. Interpretation of the Nonextensivity Parameter q in Some Applications of Tsallis Statistics and Lévy Distributions. *Phys. Rev. Lett.* **2000**, *84*, 2770. [CrossRef] [PubMed]
37. Khandai, P.K.; Sett, P.; Shukla, P.; Singh, V. System size dependence of hadron p_T spectra in p+p and Au+Au collisions at $\sqrt{s_{NN}}$ = 200 GeV. *J. Phys. G* **2014**, *41*, 025105. [CrossRef]

38. Zheng, H.; Zhu, L. Comparing the Tsallis Distribution with and without Thermodynamical Description in $p+p$ Collisions. *Adv. High Energy Phys.* **2016**, *2016*, 9632126. [CrossRef]
39. Cleymans, J.; Worku, D. The Tsallis Distribution in Proton-Proton Collisions at $\sqrt{s}$ = 0.9 TeV at the LHC. *J. Phys. G* **2012**, *39*, 025006. [CrossRef]
40. Cleymans, J. On the Use of the Tsallis Distribution at LHC Energies. *J. Phys. Conf. Ser.* **2017**, *779*, 012079. [CrossRef]
41. Olimov, K.K.; Liu, F.H.; Musaev, K.A.; Olimov, K.; Tukhtaev, B.J.; Yuldashev, B.S.; Saidkhanov, N.S.; Umarov, K.I.; Gulamov, K.G. Multiplicity dependencies of midrapidity transverse momentum spectra of identified charged particles in $p+p$ collisions at $(s)^{1/2}$ = 13 TeV at LHC. *Int. J. Mod. Phys. A* **2021**, *36*, 2150149. [CrossRef]
42. Ajaz, M.; Haj Ismail, A.A.K.; Waqas, M.; Suleymanov, M.; AbdelKader, A.; Suleymanov, R. Pseudorapidity dependence of the bulk properties of hadronic medium in pp collisions at 7 TeV. *Sci. Rep.* **2022**, *12*, 8142. [CrossRef]
43. Hagedorn, R. Multiplicities, p_T Distributions and the Expected Hadron $\rightarrow$ Quark - Gluon Phase Transition. *Riv. Nuovo Cim.* **1983**, *6N10*, 1–50. [CrossRef]
44. Odorico, R. Does a transverse energy trigger actually trigger on large p(t) jets? *Phys. Lett. B* **1982**, *118*, 151–154. [CrossRef]
45. Biyajima, M.; Mizoguchi, T.; Suzuki, N. Analyses of whole transverse momentum distributions in $p\bar{p}$ and pp collisions by using a modified version of Hagedorn's formula. *Int. J. Mod. Phys. A* **2017**, *32*, 1750057. [CrossRef]
46. Arnison, G.; Astbury, A.; Aubert, B.; Bacci, C.; Bernabei, R.; Bezaguet, A.; Böck, R.; Bowcock, T.J.V.; Calvetti, M.; Carroll, T.; et al. Transverse Momentum Spectra for Charged Particles at the CERN Proton anti-Proton Collider. *Phys. Lett. B* **1982**, *118*, 167–172. [CrossRef]
47. Particle Data Group; Workman, R.L. Review of Particle Physics. *Prog. Theor. Exp. Phys.* **2022**, *8*, 083C01. [CrossRef]
48. Olimov, K.K.; Lebedev, I.A.; Fedosimova, A.I.; Liu, F.H.; Dmitriyeva, E.; Musaev, K.A.; Olimov, K.; Yuldashev, B.S. Correlations among parameters of the Tsallis distribution and Hagedorn function with embedded transverse flow in proton–proton collisions at $(s)^{1/2}$ = 7 and 13 TeV. *Eur. Phys. J. Plus* **2023**, *138*, 414. [CrossRef]
49. Adler, S.S.; Afanasiev, S.; Aidala, C.; Ajitan, N.N.; Akiba, Y.; Alex, E.J.; Amirikas, R.; Aphecetche, L.; Aronson, S.H.; Averbeck, R.; et al. Identified charged particle spectra and yields in Au+Au collisions at S(NN)**1/2 = 200-GeV. *Phys. Rev. C* **2004**, *69*, 034909. [CrossRef]
50. Arsene, I.C.; Bearden, I.G.; Beavis, D.; Bekele, S.; Besliu, C.; Budick, B.; Bøggild, H.; Chasman, C.; Christensen, C.H.; Christiansen, P.; et al. Rapidity and centrality dependence of particle production for identified hadrons in Cu+Cu collisions at $\sqrt{s_{NN}} = 200$ GeV. *Phys. Rev. C* **2016**, *94*, 014907. [CrossRef]
51. Adare, A.; Afanasiev, S.; Aidala, C.; Ajitan, N.N.; Akiba, Y.; Al-Bataineh, H.; Alex, E.J.; Angerami, A.; Aoki, K.; Apadula, N.; et al. Spectra and ratios of identified particles in Au+Au and *d*+Au collisions at $\sqrt{s_{NN}} = 200$ GeV. *Phys. Rev. C* **2013**, *88*, 024906. [CrossRef]
52. Adamczyk, L.; Adkins, J.K.; Agakishiev, G.; Aggarwal, M.M.; Ahammed, Z.; Ajitan, N.N.; Alekseev, I.; Anderson, D.M.; Aoyama, R.; Aparin, A.; et al. Bulk Properties of the Medium Produced in Relativistic Heavy-Ion Collisions from the Beam Energy Scan Program. *Phys. Rev. C* **2017**, *96*, 044904. [CrossRef]
53. Wilk, G.; Wlodarczyk, Z. Consequences of temperature fluctuations in observables measured in high energy collisions. *Eur. Phys. J. A* **2012**, *48*, 161. [CrossRef]

entropy

Article

Some New Results Involving Past Tsallis Entropy of Order Statistics

Mansour Shrahili and Mohamed Kayid *

Department of Statistics and Operations Research, College of Science, King Saud University, P.O. Box 2455, Riyadh 11451, Saudi Arabia; msharahili@ksu.edu.sa
* Correspondence: drkayid@ksu.edu.sa

Abstract: This work focuses on exploring the properties of past Tsallis entropy as it applies to order statistics. The relationship between the past Tsallis entropy of an ordered variable in the context of any continuous probability law and the past Tsallis entropy of the ordered variable resulting from a uniform continuous probability law is worked out. For order statistics, this method offers important insights into the characteristics and behavior of the dynamic Tsallis entropy, which is associated with past events. In addition, we investigate how to find a bound for the new dynamic information measure related to the lifetime unit under various conditions and whether it is monotonic with respect to the time when the device is idle. By exploring these properties and also investigating the monotonic behavior of the new dynamic information measure, we contribute to a broader understanding of order statistics and related entropy quantities.

Keywords: order statistics; past Tsallis entropy; Shannon entropy; past lifetime; $(n-i+1)$-out-of-n structure

Citation: Shrahili, M.; Kayid, M. Some New Results Involving Past Tsallis Entropy of Order Statistics. *Entropy* **2023**, *25*, 1581. https://doi.org/10.3390/e25121581

Academic Editor: Yong Deng

Received: 11 October 2023
Revised: 22 November 2023
Accepted: 23 November 2023
Published: 24 November 2023

1. Introduction

The mathematical study of the storage, transmission, and quantification of information is known as information theory. The field of applied mathematics lies at the intersection of statistical mechanics, computer science, electrical engineering, probability theory, and statistics. A foundational method for determining the level of uncertainty in random events is provided by information theory. Its applications are many and are outlined in Shannon's influential work [1]. Entropy is an important parameter in information theory. The degree of uncertainty regarding the value of a random variable or the outcome of a random process is measured by entropy. For example, determining the outcome of a fair coin toss provides less information (lower entropy and lower uncertainty) than determining the outcome of a dice roll where six equally likely outcomes are obtained. Relative entropy, the error exponent, mutual information, and channel capacity are some other important metrics in information theory. Source coding, algorithmic complexity theory, algorithmic information theory, and information-theoretic security are important subfields of information theory.

Applications of the basic concepts of information theory include channel coding/error detection and correction and source coding/data compression. The development of the Internet, the compact disk, the viability of cell phones, and the Voyager space missions have all benefited greatly from its influence. Statistical inference, cryptography, neurobiology, perception, linguistics, thermophysics, molecular dynamics, quantum computing, black holes, information retrieval, intelligence, plagiarism detection, pattern recognition, anomaly detection, and even the creation of art are other areas where the theory has found application.

Probability theory and statistics form the basis of information theory, in which quantifiable data is usually expressed in the form of bits. Information measures of distributions associated with random variables are a frequent topic of discussion in information theory. Entropy is a crucial metric that serves as the basis for numerous other measurements. The information measure of a single random variable can be quantified thanks to entropy.

Mutual information, which is defined as a measure of the joint information of two random variables and can be used to characterize their correlation, is another helpful idea. The first number sets a limit on the rate at which the data generated from independent samples with the given distribution can be successfully compressed. It is a property of the probability distribution of a random variable. The second number, which represents the maximum rate of reliable communication over a noisy channel in the limiting case of long block lengths, is a property of the joint distribution of two random variables when the joint distribution determines the channel statistics.

When analyzing a random variable (rv) X that is non-negative and has a cumulative distribution function (cdf) $F(x)$, which is continuous, and a probability density function (pdf) $f(x)$, the Tsallis entropy of order α is an important measure, which is elucidated in [2] as follows:

$$H_\alpha(X) = k_\alpha\left[\int_0^\infty (f(x))^\alpha dx - 1\right], \tag{1}$$

where $k_\alpha = 1/(1-\alpha)$ with $\alpha > 0, \alpha \neq 1$. Note that $H_\alpha(X) = k_\alpha[E(f^{\alpha-1}(F^{-1}(U))) - 1]$ in which $F^{-1}(u)$ represents the right-continuous inverse of F and U is a random number (according to the uniform distribution) from the unit interval. The Tsallis entropy can yield nonpositive values in general, but appropriate choices of α can ensure non-negativity. It is worth noting that as α approaches one, $H(X)$ converges to the Shannon differential entropy as $\mathbb{E}(-\ln f(X))$, thereby signifying an important relationship.

In situations involving the analysis of the random lifetime X of a newly introduced system, $H_\alpha(X)$ is commonly used to quantify the unsureness inherent in a fresh unit. Despite this, there are cases where operators know the age of the system. To be more specific, assume that they are aware that the system has been in use during an interval time with a length t. Then, they can calculate the amount of uncertainty in the residual lifetime after t, i.e., $X^t = [X - t \mid X > t]$, so that X stands for the original lifetime of the system. In such cases, the conventional Tsallis entropy $H_\alpha(X)$ does not provide the desired insight. Therefore, a novel quantity, the Tsallis entropy for the residual lifetime of the device of the lifetime unit under consideration, is introduced to address this limitation as follows:

$$\begin{aligned} H_\alpha(X;t) &= k_\alpha\left[\int_0^\infty f_t^\alpha(x)dx - 1\right] \\ &= k_\alpha\left[\int_t^\infty \left(\frac{f(x)}{S(t)}\right)^\alpha dx - 1\right], \end{aligned} \tag{2}$$

in which $f_t(x) = \frac{f(x+t)}{S(t)}$ represents the pdf of X_t. The term $S(t)$ corresponds to the reliability function (rf) of X. The new dynamic information quantity takes into account the system's age and provides a more accurate measure of uncertainty in scenarios where this temporal information is available. Several recent studies have contributed to the generalization of the new measure, as discussed in Nanda and Paul [3], Rajesh and Sunoj [4], Toomaj and Agh Atabay [5], and the references therein.

Uncertainty is a pervasive feature found in various systems in nature, which is influenced by future events and even past events. This has led to the development of an interdependent concept of entropy that encapsulates the amount of uncertainty induced by incidents in the past. The past entropy is different from the residual entropy, in which the quantification of uncertainty is regarded to be influenced by events in the future. The study of entropy for past events and the relevant applications that have arisen have been accomplished by many researchers. The works carried out by Di Crescenzo and Longobardi [6] and Nair and Sunoj [7] have shed light on this topic. The research carried out by Gupta et al. [8] on the aspects and use of past entropy for order statistics was helpful in this area. In particular, they studied and performed stochastic comparisons between the entropy of the remaining lifetime of a lifespan and the entropy of the past lifetime of the lifespan, where the lifespan was quantified with respect to an ordered random variable.

Consider an rv X and assume it signifies the system's lifetime. The pdf of $X_t = [t - X|X < t]$ is $f_t(x) = f(t-x)/F(t)$, in which $x \in (0,t)$. Now, the past Tsallis entropy (PTE) as a function of t, the time of an observation of past failure of the system, is recognized by (see, e.g., Kayid and Alshehri [9])

$$\overline{H}_\alpha(X;t) = k_\alpha \left[\int_0^t f_t^\alpha(x)dx - 1 \right], \tag{3}$$

for every $t \in (0, +\infty)$. We emphasize that $\overline{H}_\alpha(X;t)$ has a wide range of possible values, from negative infinity to positive infinity. In the context of system failures, $\overline{H}_\alpha(X;t)$ serves as a metric to quantify the uncertainty related to the inactivity time of a system, especially if it has experienced a failure at time t.

Extensive research has been conducted in the literature to explore Tsallis entropy's numerous characteristics and statistical uses. For detailed insights, we recommend the work of Asadi et al. [10], Nanda and Paul [3], Zhang [11], Maasoumi [12], Abe [13], Asadi et al. [14], and the sources provided in these works. These sources provide comprehensive discussions on the topic and offer a deeper understanding of Tsallis entropy in various contexts.

In this paper, our main goal is to scrutinize the traits of PTE in terms of ordered variables. We focus on $X_1, \ldots, X_n$, as n identical random variables, which are independent and follow F. The order statistic refers to the ordering of these sample values in ascending order so that $X_{i:n}$ represents the ith ordered variable. These statistics have important roles in various areas of probability and statistics, as they allow for the description of probability distributions, the evaluation of the fit of data to certain models, the quality control of products or processes, the analysis of the reliability of systems or components, and numerous other applications. For a thorough understanding of the theory and applications of order statistics, we recommend the comprehensive review by David and Nagaraja [15]. The degree of predictability of an ordered random variable is usually related to its distribution; the entropy of this random variable can actually access this property. It is worth exploring the quantification of information for ordered random variables, including order statistics as a general class of statistics relevant to survival analysis and systems engineering. Aspects of information for order statistics have garnered significant attention from researchers in the literature. Several studies have explored various information properties associated with order statistics. For instance, Wong and Chen [16] demonstrated that the discrepancy among the mean entropy of ordered variables and the empirical entropy remains unchanged. They further established that, for distributions which are symmetric, the entropy of ordered variables exhibits symmetry around the median. Park [17] established some relations to acquire the entropy of ordered variables. Ebrahimi et al. [18] studied the information features of ordered random variables using Shannon entropy and the Kullback–Leibler distance. Similarly, Abbasnejad and Arghami [19] and Baratpour and Khammar [20] obtained similar results for the Renyi and Tsallis entropy of ordered random variables, respectively. Despite these efforts, the Tsallis entropy of the past lifetime of ordered variables has not been considered in literature thus far. It is commonly known that the past Tsallis entropy can be used to measure the amount of information that can be gleaned from historical observations in order to improve the forecasts of future events. This motivates us to investigate aspects of the Tsallis entropy of the past lifetime distribution of order statistics. By building upon existing research, our study aims to contribute significantly to this area by examining the behaviors of past Tsallis entropy examples for ordered variables. By highlighting previous studies and emphasizing the gap in the literature regarding the investigation of past Tsallis entropy examples in order statistics, we establish the significance and novelty of our research.

The current work's outcomes are organized as follows: In Section 2, we derive the representation of PTE for order statistics denoted as $X_{i:n}$, which is arisen from a sample taken from an arbitrary distribution recognized by cdf F. We express this PTE on the basis of the PTE for ordered variables from a sample selected according to the law of uniform probability. We derive upper and lower bounds to approximate the PTE, since equations with exact solutions for the PTE of order statistics are frequently unavailable for many statistical models. We provide several illustrative examples to demonstrate the practicality and usefulness of these bounds. In addition, we scrutinize the monotonicity of the PTE for the extremum of a sample provided that some convenient conditions are satisfied. We find that the PTEs of the extremum of a random sample exhibit monotonic behavior as the sample's number of individuals rises. However, we counter this observation by presenting a counterexample that demonstrates the nonmonotonic behavior of PTE for $X_{i:n}$ based on n. To further analyze the monotonic behavior, we examine the PTE of order statistics $X_{i:n}$ with respect to the index of order statistics i. Our results show that the PTE of $X_{i:n}$ does not change monotonically with i.

In what follows in the paper, the notations "$\leq_{st}$" and "$\leq_{lr}$" will be used to indicate the usual stochastic order and the likelihood ratio order, respectively. For a more detailed discussion on definitions and properties of these stochastic orders, the reader can refer to Shaked and Shanthikumar [21].

2. Past Tsallis Entropy of Order Statistics

Here, we acquire an expression that relates the PTE of the ordinal statistic to the PTE of an ordered random variable based on a set of values that are randomly generated according to the law of uniform probability. Let us consider the pdf and the rf of $X_{i:n}$ denoted as $f_{i:n}(x)$ and $F_{i:n}(x)$, respectively, where $i = 1, \ldots, n$. We have the following relationships:

$$f_{i:n}(x) = \frac{1}{B(i, n-i+1)}(F(x))^{i-1}(S(x))^{n-i}f(x), x > 0, \tag{4}$$

$$F_{i:n}(x) = \sum_{k=i}^{n} \binom{n}{k} (F(x))^{k}(S(x))^{n-k}, x > 0, \tag{5}$$

in which $B(a, b)$ represents the complete beta function (see [15] for more details). Additionally, the cdf of $X_{i:n}$, i.e., the function $F_{i:n}$, is derived as

$$F_{i:n}(x) = \frac{B_{F(x)}(i, n-i+1)}{B(i, n-i+1)}, \tag{6}$$

where $B_x(a, b)$ represents the lower incomplete beta function. Hereafter, we shall write $Y \sim B_t(a, b)$ to specifiy that the rv Y follows a beta distribution truncated on $[0, t]$, which has density

$$f_Y(y) = \frac{1}{B_t(a, b)} y^{a-1}(1-y)^{b-1}, \ 0 \leq y \leq t. \tag{7}$$

In our context, we are concerned with the analysis of Tsallis entropy, which is measured by the cdf or pdf of the rv $X_{i:n}$. In this way, one quantifies the strength of the uncertainty induced by $[t - X_{i:n} | X_{i:n} \leq t]$ in terms of how predictable the elapsed time since the failure time of a system is. In the reliability literature, $(n-i+1)$-out-of-n structures have proven to be very useful for modeling the life lengths of typical systems. In such systems, the functionality is guaranteed only if at least $(n-i+1)$ of the n units or constituents in the system are operational. A system with separate component lifetimes is headed in this way. Furthermore, a consistent distribution of the component lifetimes is assumed. The lifetime of the components in the system is denoted by $X_1, X_2, \ldots, X_n$. The lifetime of the system is determined by the ordered rv $X_{i:n}$, where the value of i is the position of the order statistic. When $i = 1$, this corresponds to a serial system, while $i = n$ represents a parallel system. In the context of $(n-i+1)$-out-of-n structures that have experienced failures before time t, the PTE of $X_{i:n}$ serves as a measure of entropy associated with the past lifetimes of the system. This dynamic entropy measure provides system designers with valuable insights into the entropy of the lifetime of systems with $(n-i+1)$-out-of-n structures operating at a given time t.

To increase the computational efficiency, we introduce a lemma that establishes the relationship the PTE of ordered uniformly distributed rvs has with the beta function in its imperfect form. From a practical perspective, this link is essential, since it makes the computation of PTE easier. Since it only requires a few simple computations, the demonstration of this lemma—which flows immediately from the definition of PTE—is not included here.

Lemma 1. *Suppose we have drawn a random sample of size n from* $(0,1)$ *according to the law of uniform probability. Let we arrange the sample values in ascending order, where* $U_{i:n}$ *is the ith order statistic. Then,*

$$\overline{H}_{\alpha}(U_{i:n};t)=\frac{1}{\bar{\alpha}}\left[\frac{B_t(\alpha i\bar{\alpha},1+n\alpha-i\alpha)}{B_t^{\alpha}(i,1+n-i)}-1\right],\ 0<t<1,$$

for all $\alpha>0,\ \alpha\neq 1$, *with* $\bar{\alpha}=1-\alpha$.

This lemma provides researchers and practitioners with a useful tool to work out the PTE of the ordered variables of a sample adopted from uniform distribution. The computation can be conveniently performed via the imperfect beta function. In Figure 1, the plot of $\overline{H}_{\alpha}(Ui:n;t)$ is exhibited for various amounts of α, where i takes the values $1,2,\cdots,5$, and the total number of observations is $n=5$. The figure illustrates that there is no inherent monotonic relationship between the order statistics. The next theorem shows how the PTE of the order statistic $X_{i:n}$ is related to the PTE of the order statistic calculated for a uniform distribution.

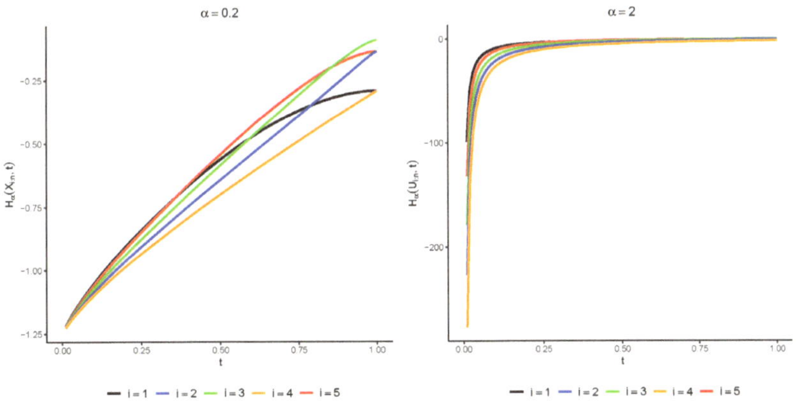

Figure 1. Amounts of $\overline{H}_{\alpha}(U_{i:n};t)$ for $\alpha=0.2$ (left console) and $\alpha=2$ (right console) for various choices of $0<t<1$.

Theorem 1. *The past Tsallis entropy of* $X_{i:n}$, *for all* $\alpha\in(0,+\infty)$, $\alpha\neq 1$, *can be expressed as follows:*

$$\overline{H}_{\alpha}(X_{i:n};t)=\frac{1}{\bar{\alpha}}\left[(\bar{\alpha}\overline{H}_{\alpha}(U_{i:n};F(t))+1)\mathbb{E}[f^{\alpha-1}(F^{-1}(Y_i))]-1\right],\ t\in(0,+\infty), \tag{8}$$

so that $Y_i\sim B_{F(x)}(\alpha i+\bar{\alpha},1+\alpha(n-i))$.

Proof. Remember that $k_{\alpha}=1/(1-\alpha)$. By making the change in variables as $u=F(x)$, based on the formulas given in (2), (4), and (6), we obtain:

$$\begin{aligned}
\overline{H}_\alpha(X_{i:n};t) &= k_\alpha\left[\int_0^t\left(\frac{f_{i:n}(x)}{S_{i:n}(t)}\right)^\alpha dx-1\right]\\
&= k_\alpha\left[\int_0^t\left(\frac{F^{i-1}(x)S^{n-i}(x)f(x)}{B_{F(t)}(i,1+n-i)}\right)^\alpha dx-1\right]\\
&= k_\alpha\left[\frac{B_{F(t)}(\alpha i+\bar{\alpha},1+\alpha(n-i))}{B^\alpha_{F(t)}(i,n-i+1)}\int_0^t\frac{F^{\alpha(i-1)}(x)S^{\alpha(n-i)}(x)f^\alpha(x)}{B_{F(t)}(\alpha i+\bar{\alpha},1+\alpha(n-i))}dx-1\right]\\
&= k_\alpha\left[\frac{B_{F(t)}(\alpha i+\bar{\alpha},1+\alpha(n-i))}{B^\alpha_{F(t)}(i,1+n-i)}\int_0^{F(t)}\frac{u^{\alpha(i-1)}(1-u)^{\alpha(n-i)}f^{\alpha-1}(F^{-1}(u))}{B_{F(t)}(\alpha i+\bar{\alpha},1+\alpha(n-i))}du-1\right]\\
&= k_\alpha\left[(\bar{\alpha}\overline{H}_\alpha(U_{i:n};F(t))+1)\mathbb{E}[f^{\alpha-1}(F^{-1}(Y_i))]-1\right],\ t>0. \qquad (9)
\end{aligned}$$

The recent equality above is due to Lemma 1. This finalizes the proof. □

$$\frac{1}{\bar{\alpha}}\left[\frac{\int_0^{\exp(-1/t)}x^{\alpha(i-1)}(1-x)^{\alpha(n-i)}(-\log(x))^{\alpha-1}dx}{\left(\int_0^{\exp(-1/t)}x^{i-1}(1-x)^{n-i}dx\right)^\alpha}dx-1\right]$$

Upon further calculation, it can be deduced that when the order α approaches unity in Equation (8), the Shannon entropy of the ith ordered variable from a set of random variables adopted from F can be expressed as follows:

$$\overline{H}(X_{i:n};t)=\overline{H}(U_{i:n};F(t))-\mathbb{E}[f(F^{-1}(Y_i))],$$

in which $Y_i\sim B_{F(t)}(i,n-i+1)$. This specific result for $t=\infty$ has previously been derived by Ebrahimi et al. [18]. Next, we establish a fundamental result concerning the problem of monotonicity of the PTE of an rv X, provided that X fulfills the decreasing reversed hazard rate (DRHR) trait. More precisely, we say that X possesses the DRHR if the reversed hazard rate (rhr) function it has, i.e., the function $\tau(x)=\frac{d}{dx}\ln(F(x))$, decreases monotonically for all $x>0$.

Lemma 2. *If $X_{i:n}$ denotes the ith order statistic obtained from a sample following a DRHR distribution, then $X_{i:n}$ is also a DRHR.*

Proof. We can express the rhr function of $X_{i:n}$ as follows:

$$\tau_{i:n}(t)=\frac{f_{i:n}(t)}{F_{i:n}(t)}=h\left(\frac{F(t)}{S(t)}\right)\tau(t),\ t>0, \qquad (10)$$

where

$$h(x)=\frac{x^i}{B(i,1+n-i)\sum_{k=i}^n\binom{n}{k}x^k},\ x>0.$$

Under the assumption that X is a DRHR, according to Equation (10), the distribution of $X_{i:n}$ is a DRHR if, and only if, $h(x)$ decreases in $x>0$. Evidently, $h(x)$ indeed decreases in x, thus completing the proof. □

We now demonstrate how the behavior of the new information measure is influenced by the DRHR feature of X.

Theorem 2. *If X induces the DRHR feature, then the Tsallis entropy $\overline{H}_\alpha(X_{i:n};t)$ increases in t for every $\alpha\in(0,+\infty)$.*

Proof. The DRHR trait of the distribution of X further induces that the distribution of $X_{i:n}$ also has the DRHR trait, as stated in Lemma 2. The proof is obtained directly using Theorem 2 of the paper by Kayid et al. [9]. □

Using an example, we illustrate the application of Theorems 1 and 2.

Example 1. We contemplate a distribution with the cdf $F(x) = x^2$ for $x \in (0,1)$ to be the distribution of the components' lifetimes. It is evident that $f(F^{-1}(u)) = 2\sqrt{u}$ for $0 < u < 1$. Using this information, we can derive the expression:

$$\mathbb{E}[f^{\alpha-1}(F^{-1}(Y_i))] = \frac{2^{\alpha-1}B_{t^2}(\alpha(i-\frac{1}{2})+\frac{1}{2}, 1+\alpha(n-i))}{B_{t^2}(\alpha i+\bar{\alpha}, 1+\alpha(n-i))},$$

Furthermore, we can obtain:

$$\overline{H}_\alpha(U_{i:n}; F(t)) = \frac{1}{\bar{\alpha}}\left[\frac{B_{t^2}(\alpha i+\bar{\alpha}, 1+\alpha(n-i))}{B^{\alpha}_{t^2}(i, 1+n-i)} - 1\right].$$

Using Equation (8), we deduce that

$$\overline{H}_\alpha(X_{i:n}; t) = \frac{1}{\bar{\alpha}}\left[\frac{2^{\alpha-1}B_{t^2}(\alpha(i-\frac{1}{2})+\frac{1}{2}, 1+\alpha(n-i))}{B^{\alpha}_{t^2}(i, 1+n-i)} - 1\right], \; i = 1, 2, \cdots, n. \quad (11)$$

In Figure 2, we have plotted $\overline{H}_\alpha(X_{i:n}; t)$ for various amounts of α with $i = 1, \cdots, 5$ and $n = 5$. It can be observed that the PTR increases with t, which aligns with the expectation from Theorem 2.

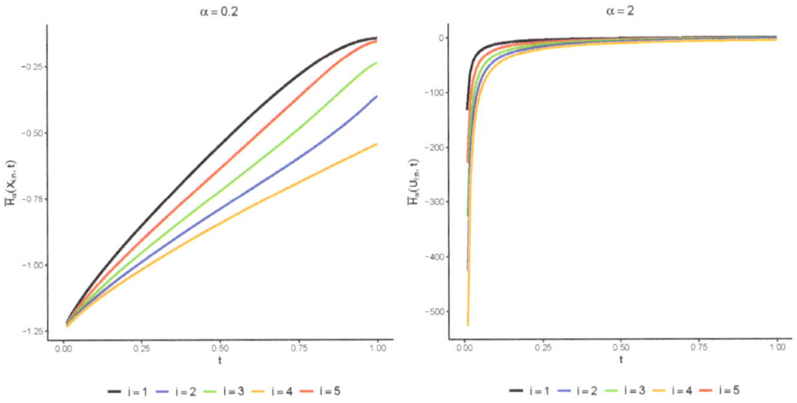

Figure 2. The amounts of $\overline{H}_\alpha(X_{i:n}; t)$ for $\alpha = 0.2$ (left console) and $\alpha = 2$ (right console) with regard to t.

Unfortunately, convenient statements for the PTE of ordered rvs are not available in some situations for many distributions. Given this limitation, we are motivated to explore alternative approaches to characterizing the PTE of order statistics. We therefore propose to establish thresholds for the PTE of order statistics. To this end, we present the following theorem as a conclusive proof that provides valuable insight into the nature of these bounds and their applicability in practical scenarios.

Theorem 3. *Consider a nonnegative rv X, which is continuous having pdf f and cdf F. Suppose we have $\mathcal{M} = f(m) < +\infty$, in which m plays the role of the mode of the underlying distribution with density F such that $f(x) \leq \mathcal{M}$. Then, for every $\alpha \in (0, +\infty)$, we obtain*

$$\overline{H}_\alpha(X_{i:n};t) \geq \frac{1}{\bar{\alpha}}\Big[((\bar{\alpha})\overline{H}_\alpha(U_{i:n};F(t))+1)\mathcal{M}^{\alpha-1}-1\Big].$$

Proof. Because for every $\alpha \in (1, +\infty)(\alpha \in (0,1)))$, one has

$$f^{\alpha-1}(F^{-1}(u)) \leq (\geq)\mathcal{M}^{\alpha-1},$$

one can write

$$\mathbb{E}[f^{\alpha-1}(F^{-1}(Y_i))] \leq (\geq)\mathcal{M}^{\alpha-1}.$$

The desired conclusion now clearly follows from the use of (8). This concludes the proof of the theorem. □

The recent result introduces a boundary on the PTE of $X_{i:n}$, i.e., the function which is signified by $\overline{H}_\alpha(X_{i:n};t)$. This limiting value is expressed via the PTE of the ordered variable of a set of random variables selected according to the uniform probability law and, further, the mode of the distribution under consideration, which is represented by m. This result yields a quantitative measure of the lower bound of the PTE with regard to the distribution mode and offers intriguing insights into the uncertainty features of $X_{i:n}$. Based on Theorem 4, we show the bound of the PTE on the ordered rvs for a few standard and reputable distributions in Table 1.

Table 1. Lower bound on $\overline{H}_\alpha(X_{i:n};t)$ derived from Theorem 4.

pdf	**Bounds**
$f(x) = \frac{2}{\pi(1+x^2)},\ x > 0,$	$\geq \frac{1}{\bar{\alpha}}\Big[(1+\bar{\alpha}\overline{H}_\alpha(U_{i:n};F(t)))\Big(\frac{2}{\pi}\Big)^{-\bar{\alpha}}-1\Big]$
$f(x) = \frac{2}{\sigma\sqrt{2\pi}}e^{-(x-\mu)^2/2\sigma^2},\ x \in (\mu, +\infty), \mu > 0,$	$\geq \frac{1}{\bar{\alpha}}\Big[(1+\bar{\alpha}\overline{H}_\alpha(U_{i:n};F(t)))\Big(\frac{2}{\sigma\sqrt{2\pi}}\Big)^{-\bar{\alpha}}-1\Big]$
$f(x) = \frac{\lambda}{\beta}e^{-\frac{(x-\mu)}{\beta}}(1-e^{-\frac{(x-\mu)}{\beta}})^{\lambda-1},\ x \in (\mu, +\infty), \mu > 0,$	$\geq \frac{1}{\bar{\alpha}}\Big[(1+\bar{\alpha}\overline{H}_\alpha(U_{i:n};F(t)))(\beta(1-\frac{1}{\lambda})^{1-\lambda})^{\bar{\alpha}}-1\Big]$
$f(x) = \frac{b^c}{\Gamma(c)}x^{c-1}e^{-bx},\ x > 0,$	$\geq \frac{1}{1-\alpha}\Big[(1+\bar{\alpha}\overline{H}_\alpha(U_{i:n};F(t)))(\frac{b(c-1)^{c-1}e^{1-c}}{\Gamma(c)})^{-\bar{\alpha}}-1\Big]$

The following result establishes an upper boundary condition for the new information measure of the system with parallel structure with regard to the rhr of the distribution under consideration.

Theorem 4. *Let the distribution of X fulfill the DRHR trait. For $\alpha > 1$, we have the inequality*

$$\overline{H}_\alpha(X_{n:n};t) \leq \frac{\alpha - \tau^{\alpha-1}(t)}{\alpha(\alpha-1)},$$

in which $\tau(t)$ is the rhr of X, which is a decreasing function by assumption.

Proof. Since the distribution of X has a decreasing rhr function, thus Theorem 2 provides that $\overline{H}_\alpha(X_{n:n};t)$ increases as t increases. Therefore, based on Theorem 3 of Kayid and Alshehri [9], we have

$$\overline{H}_\alpha(X_{n:n};t) \leq k_\alpha\frac{\alpha - \tau_{n:n}^{\alpha-1}(t)}{\alpha} \leq k_\alpha\frac{\alpha - \tau^{\alpha-1}(t)}{\alpha}, \quad t > 0,$$

in which $k_\alpha = 1/(1-\alpha)$. Since $\tau_{n:n}(t) = n\tau(t) \geq \tau(t)$, the last inequality is easily obtained for $\alpha > 1$, and the proof is now complete. □

Next, we delve into the monotone behavior of the PTE of extreme order statistics with components whose lifetimes are uniformly distributed.

Lemma 3. *In a system with parallel (series) structure in which components have random lifetimes following a uniform probability law, the PTE of the lifetime of the device is decreasing with respect to the components' number.*

Proof. We give the proof when the system operates in parallel. Analogous reasoning can be applied to a series system. Let us set two rvs Z_1 and Z_α with densities $f_1(z)$ and $f_\alpha(z)$, respectively, which are given by the following:

$$f_1(z) = \frac{z^{n-1}}{\int_0^t x^{n-1}dx} \text{ and } f_\alpha(z) = \frac{z^{\alpha(n-1)}}{\int_0^t x^{\alpha(n-1)}dx}, \; z \in (0,t).$$

Next, one obtains

$$\xi_n = \overline{H}_\alpha(U_{n:n};t) = \frac{1}{\bar{\alpha}}\left[\frac{\int_0^t x^{\alpha(n-1)}dx}{\left(\int_0^t x^{n-1}dx\right)^\alpha} - 1\right], \; 0 < t < 1. \tag{12}$$

Let us assume that $n \in [1, +\infty)$. Then, we suppose that the derivative of ξ_n with regard to n is well defined. We have the following:

$$\frac{\partial \xi_n}{\partial n} = \frac{1}{\bar{\alpha}}\frac{\partial \varsigma_n}{\partial n},$$

where

$$\varsigma_n = \frac{\int_0^t x^{\alpha(n-1)}dx}{\left(\int_0^t x^{n-1}dx\right)^\alpha}.$$

It is evident that for $\alpha \in (1, +\infty)(\alpha \in (0,1))$:

$$\frac{\partial \varsigma_n}{\partial n} = \frac{\alpha A(t)}{B^\alpha(t)}\Big(\mathbb{E}[\ln(Z_\alpha)] - \mathbb{E}[\ln(Z_1)]\Big) \geq (\leq) 0, \tag{13}$$

where

$$A(t) = \int_0^t x^{\alpha(n-1)}dx, \text{ and also } B(t) = \int_0^t x^{n-1}dx.$$

It is readily seen that for $\alpha \in (1, +\infty)(\alpha \in (0,1))$, it holds that Z_α is greater (less) than Z_1 in usual stochastic order. Consequently, $\ln(z)$ increases as z grows; as an application of Theorem 1.A.3. of [21], one has $\mathbb{E}[\ln(Z_\alpha)] \geq (\leq)\mathbb{E}[\ln(Z_1)]$. Hence, (13) is positive (negative), and as a result, ξ_n decreases as n grows. Consequently, it is deduced that the PTE of the life length of a system with parallel units decreases as the number of components increases. □

A large class of distributions consists of those that have density functions that decrease as the value increases. Some examples of these distributions are exponential, Pareto, and mixtures of distributions, among others. There are also distributions that have density functions that increase as the value increases like the power distribution. We will use the result from the previous lemma to establish the next theorem by which distributions that have density functions that are either increasing or decreasing are involved.

Theorem 5. *Suppose that f is the pdf of the component's lifetime in a parallel (series) system, and let f be an increasing (a decreasing) function. Then, the PTE of the system's lifetime decreases as n grows.*

Proof. Assuming that $Y_n \sim B_{F(t)}(\alpha(n-1)+1,1)$, then $f_{Y_n}(y)$ indicates the density of Y_n. It is evident that

$$\frac{f_{Y_{n+1}}(y)}{f_{Y_n}(y)} = \frac{B_{F(t)}(\alpha(n-1)+1,1)}{B_{F(t)}(\alpha n+1,1)} y^{\alpha},\ 0<y<F(t),$$

increases as y grows. This in turn concludes that Y_n is less than or equal to Y_{n+1} in likelihood ratio order and, therefore, Y_n is less than or equal to Y_{n+1} in usual stochastic order also. In addition, $\alpha \in (1,+\infty)(\alpha \in (0,1))$, $f^{-\bar{\alpha}}(F^{-1}(x))$ increases (decreases)as x grows. Therefore,

$$\mathbb{E}[f^{\alpha-1}(F^{-1}(Y_n))] \leq (\geq)\mathbb{E}[f^{\alpha-1}(F^{-1}(Y_{n+1}))]. \tag{14}$$

From Theorem 3, for $\alpha \in (1,+\infty)(\alpha \in (0,1))$, one obtains

$$\begin{aligned} 1+\bar{\alpha}\overline{H}_{\alpha}(X_{n:n};t) &= [1+\bar{\alpha}\overline{H}_{\alpha}(U_{n:n};F(t))]\mathbb{E}[f^{-\bar{\alpha}}(F^{-1}(Y_n))] \\ &\leq (\geq)\ [1+\bar{\alpha}\overline{H}_{\alpha}(U_{n:n};F(t))]\mathbb{E}[f^{-\bar{\alpha}}(F^{-1}(Y_{n+1}))] \\ &\leq (\geq)\ [1+\bar{\alpha}\overline{H}_{\alpha}(U_{n+1:n+1};F(t))]\mathbb{E}[f^{-\bar{\alpha}}(F^{-1}(Y_{n+1}))] \\ &= 1+\bar{\alpha}\overline{H}_{\alpha}(X_{n+1:n+1};t). \end{aligned}$$

The initial inequality is obtained by noting that $1+\bar{\alpha}\overline{H}_{\alpha}(U_{n:n};F(t))$ is nonnegative, whereas the last one is due to Lemma 3(i). Thus, we deduce that $\overline{H}_{\alpha}(X_{n:n};t) \geq \overline{H}_{\alpha}(X_{n+1:n+1};t)$ for all $t \in (0,+\infty)$. □

The following example shows that this Theorem does not work for all kinds of systems with an $(n-i+1)$-out-of-n structure.

Example 2. We presume a system is operational when more than or equal to $(n-1)$ of the n components in the system are in operation. It is then not difficult to observe that the system's random lifetime is $X_{2:n}$. The components are assumed to have an identical distribution, which is uniform on $(0,1)$. In Figure 3, we see how the PTE of $X_{2:n}$ changes with n when $\alpha=2$ and $t=0.2$. In fact, it is observed in the graph that the PTE of the system does not always decrease as n increases. For example, it reveals that $\overline{H}_{\alpha}(X_{2:2};0.2)$ is less than that of $\overline{H}_{\alpha}(X_{2:n};0.2)$ for $n=3,4,\ldots,23$.

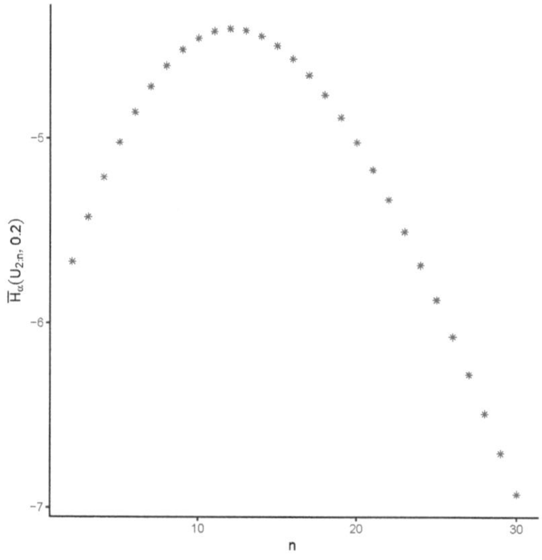

Figure 3. The amounts of the PTE for several choices of n in a system with an $(n-1)$-out-of-n structure with an underlying uniform distribution and where $\alpha=2$ when $t=0.2$.

3. Conclusions

We investigated the idea of PTE for order statistics in this paper. A novel method has been suggested by us to merge the PTE of ordered random variables belonging to a continuous distribution set with the PTE of the ordered random variables belonging to a set of random numbers selected from a uniform distribution. This relationship aids in our comprehension of PTE's characteristics and behavior for various distributions. Additionally, because it is challenging to derive precise formulas for the PTE of order statistics, we have discovered constraints that offer helpful approximations and enable a deeper comprehension of their characteristics. The derived limits and bounds can be applied to evaluate the PTE and compare its values in different situations from different perspectives. In addition, we have investigated how the index of ordered random variables, denoted by i, and the number of observations, denoted by n, affect PTE. In order to corroborate our findings and show how our method is applicable, we included examples. These illustrations showed the usefulness of PTE for ordered random variables and the adaptability of our approach to various distributions. In short, the current work improves the perception of PTE for ordered random variables by providing the connections this quantity has with other measures, by obtaining bounds and exploring the effects of the position of the ordered variable, and by determining the impact of the size of the sample under consideration. The findings reported in this paper provide useful and profitable intuitions for professionals engaged in the analysis of information measures and statistical inferential procedures.

Author Contributions: Methodology, M.S.; Software, M.S.; Validation, M.S.; Formal analysis, M.S.; Investigation, M.K.; Resources, M.S.; Writing—original draft, M.K.; Writing—review and editing, M.K. and M.S.; Visualization, M.K.; Supervision, M.K.; Project administration, M.S. All authors have read and agreed to the published version of the manuscript.

Funding: The authors acknowledge financial support from the Researchers Supporting Project number (RSP2023R464) through King Saud University in Riyadh, Saudi Arabia.

Institutional Review Board Statement: Not applicable.

Data Availability Statement: No new data were created or analyzed in this study. Data sharing is not applicable to this article.

Conflicts of Interest: The authors declare no conflict of interest.

References

1. Shannon, C.E. A mathematical theory of communication. *Bell Syst. Tech. J.* **1948**, *27*, 379–423. [CrossRef]
2. Tsallis, C. Possible generalization of Boltzmann-Gibbs statistics. *J. Stat. Phys.* **1988**, *52*, 479–487. [CrossRef]
3. Nanda, A.K.; Paul, P. Some results on generalized residual entropy. *Inf. Sci.* **2006**, *176*, 27–47. [CrossRef]
4. Rajesh, G.; Sunoj, S. Some properties of cumulative Tsallis entropy of order α. *Stat. Pap.* **2019**, *60*, 583–593. [CrossRef]
5. Toomaj, A.; Atabay, H.A. Some new findings on the cumulative residual Tsallis entropy. *J. Comput. Appl. Math.* **2022**, *400*, 113669. [CrossRef]
6. Di Crescenzo, A.; Longobardi, M. Entropy-based measure of uncertainty in past lifetime distributions. *J. Appl. Probab.* **2002**, *39*, 434–440. [CrossRef]
7. Nair, N.U.; Sunoj, S. Some aspects of reversed hazard rate and past entropy. *Commun. Stat. Theory Methods* **2021**, *32*, 2106–2116. [CrossRef]
8. Gupta, R.C.; Taneja, H.; Thapliyal, R. Stochastic comparisons of residual entropy of order statistics and some characterization results. *J. Stat. Theory Appl.* **2014**, *13*, 27–37. [CrossRef]
9. Kayid, M.; Alshehri, M.A. Tsallis entropy for the past lifetime distribution with application. *Axioms* **2023**, *12*, 731. [CrossRef]
10. Asadi, M.; Ebrahimi, N.; Soofi, E.S. Dynamic generalized information measures. *Stat. Probab. Lett.* **2005**, *71*, 85–98. [CrossRef]
11. Zhang, Z. Uniform estimates on the Tsallis entropies. *Lett. Math. Phys.* **2007**, *80*, 171–181. [CrossRef]
12. Maasoumi, E. The measurement and decomposition of multi-dimensional inequality. *Econ. J. Econ. Soc.* **1986**, *54*, 991–997. [CrossRef]
13. Abe, S. Axioms and uniqueness theorem for Tsallis entropy. *Phys. Lett. A* **2000**, *271*, 74–79. [CrossRef]
14. Asadi, M.; Ebrahimi, N.; Soofi, E.S. Connections of Gini, Fisher, and Shannon by Bayes risk under proportional hazards. *J. Appl. Probab.* **2017**, *54*, 1027–1050. [CrossRef]
15. David, H.A.; Nagaraja, H.N. *Order Statistics*; John Wiley & Sons: Hoboken, NJ, USA, 2004.

16. Wong, K.M.; Chen, S. The entropy of ordered sequences and order statistics. *IEEE Trans. Inf. Theory* **1990**, *36*, 276–284. [CrossRef]
17. Park, S. The entropy of consecutive order statistics. *IEEE Trans. Inf. Theory* **1995**, *41*, 2003–2007. [CrossRef]
18. Ebrahimi, N.; Soofi, E.S.; Soyer, R. Information measures in perspective. *Int. Stat. Rev.* **2010**, *78*, 383–412. [CrossRef]
19. Abbasnejad, M.; Arghami, N.R. Renyi entropy properties of order statistics. *Commun. Stat. Methods* **2010**, *40*, 40–52. [CrossRef]
20. Baratpour, S.; Khammar, A. Tsallis entropy properties of order statistics and some stochastic comparisons. *J. Stat. Res. Iran JSRI* **2016**, *13*, 25–41. [CrossRef]
21. Shaked, M.; Shanthikumar, J.G. *Stochastic Orders*; Springer: Berlin/Heidelberg, Germany, 2007.

entropy

MDPI

Article

Rapidity and Energy Dependencies of Temperatures and Volume Extracted from Identified Charged Hadron Spectra in Proton–Proton Collisions at a Super Proton Synchrotron (SPS)

Pei-Pin Yang [1], Fu-Hu Liu [2,*] and Khusniddin K. Olimov [3,4,*]

1 Department of Physics, Xinzhou Normal University, Xinzhou 034000, China; peipinyang@xztu.edu.cn
2 State Key Laboratory of Quantum Optics and Quantum Optics Devices, Institute of Theoretical Physics, Shanxi University, Taiyuan 030006, China
3 Laboratory of High Energy Physics, Physical-Technical Institute of Uzbekistan Academy of Sciences, Chingiz Aytmatov Str. 2b, Tashkent 100084, Uzbekistan
4 Department of Natural Sciences, National University of Science and Technology MISIS (NUST MISIS), Almalyk Branch, Almalyk 110105, Uzbekistan
* Correspondence: fuhuliu@163.com (F.-H.L.); khkolimov@gmail.com (K.K.O.)

Abstract: The standard (Bose–Einstein/Fermi–Dirac, or Maxwell–Boltzmann) distribution from the relativistic ideal gas model is used to study the transverse momentum (p_T) spectra of identified charged hadrons (π^-, π^+, K^-, K^+, $\bar{p}$, and p) with different rapidities produced in inelastic proton–proton (pp) collisions at a Super Proton Synchrotron (SPS). The experimental data measured using the NA61/SHINE Collaboration at the center-of-mass (c.m.) energies $\sqrt{s} = 6.3$, 7.7, 8.8, 12.3, and 17.3 GeV are fitted well with the distribution. It is shown that the effective temperature (T_{eff} or T), kinetic freeze-out temperature (T_0), and initial temperature (T_i) decrease with the increase in rapidity and increase with the increase in c.m. energy. The kinetic freeze-out volume (V) extracted from the π^-, π^+, K^-, K^+, and $\bar{p}$ spectra decreases with the rapidity and increase with the c.m. energy. The opposite tendency of V, extracted from the p spectra, is observed to be increasing with the rapidity and decreasing with the c.m. energy due to the effect of leading protons.

Keywords: transverse momentum spectra; identified charged hadrons; effective temperature; kinetic freeze-out temperature; initial temperature; kinetic free-out volume

PACS: 12.40.Ee; 13.85.Hd; 24.10.Pa

Citation: Yang, P.-P.; Liu, F.-H.; Olimov, K.K. Rapidity and Energy Dependencies of Temperatures and Volume Extracted from Identified Charged Hadron Spectra in Proton–Proton Collisions at a Super Proton Synchrotron (SPS). *Entropy* **2023**, *25*, 1571. https://doi.org/10.3390/e25121571

Academic Editors: Lino Miramonti and Lawrence Horwitz

Received: 11 October 2023
Revised: 16 November 2023
Accepted: 20 November 2023
Published: 22 November 2023

1. Introduction

The existence of confinement and asymptotic freedom in Quantum Chromodynamics (QCD) has led to many conjectures about the thermodynamic and transport properties of hot and dense matter. Because of confinement, nuclear matter should be composed of low-energy hadrons, and it is considered a weakly interacting gas of hadrons. On the other hand, at very high energies, asymptotic freedom means that the interactions between quarks and gluons are very weak, and the nuclear matter is considered as a weakly coupling gas of quarks and gluons. There should be a phase transition between these two configurations, in which the degrees of freedom of hadrons disappear and Quark–Gluon Plasma (QGP) is formed, which is generated at a sufficiently high temperature or density [1–6]. QGP existed in the very early universe (a few microseconds after the Big Bang), and some forms of this matter may still exist in the core of neutron stars. Ultra-relativistic heavy-ion collisions have provided opportunities to systematically create and study different phases of bulk nuclear matter.

Several experiments performed at the Super Proton Synchrotron (SPS) [7,8], Relativistic Heavy Ion Collider (RHIC) [2,3,9–15], and Large Hadron Collider (LHC) [16–19] have reported abundant experimental data. The system of proton–proton (pp) collisions is usually used as a reference measurement for heavy ion collisions, as it has several valence quarks involved in the collisions. Collective flow is one of the characteristics of the thermal dense medium of this strongly interacting matter. The generated medium expands collectively such that the flow effect is expected to be distinguished from the thermal motion, which reflects the temperature. The heavy ion physics community has been fascinated by observing unexpected collective behavior in high-multiplicity pp collision events. It is therefore necessary and important to study pp collisions.

The transverse momentum (p_T) spectra of identified charged hadrons produced in relativistic or high-energy collisions contain abundant information on the collision dynamics and the evolution properties of the system from the initial stage to the end of freeze-out phase [20]. Traditionally, it is believed that the flattening of the p_T spectra with high multiplicity is a signal for the formation of a mixed phase of de-confined partons and hadrons. In the hydrodynamical model, the slopes of p_T spectra are co-determined by the kinetic freeze-out temperature and the transverse expansion flow of the collision system [21]. The study of p_T spectra can reveal information related to the effective temperature (T_{eff} or T) of the system. A plateau-like region observed in the excitation function of T is considered a possible signal for the formation of mixed-phases, similar to the temperature dependence of entropy observed in the first-order phase transition. In addition, in order to understand the phase transition from QGP to hadronic matter, the transverse momentum density is often studied.

In the physical process of high-energy heavy ion collisions, at least four temperatures are often used, namely initial temperature (T_i), chemical freeze-out temperature (T_{ch}), kinetic (or thermal) freeze-out temperature (T_0), and T. These temperatures correspond to different stages of collisions. The excitation degree of the interaction system at the initial stage is described by T_i, at which hadrons undergo elastic and inelastic interactions in the hadronic medium. Due to the shortage of research methods, there is limited research on T_i in the community, which should be based on the p_T. With the decrease in temperature, the system begins to form hadronic matter and enters the chemical freeze-out stage. Under the condition of maintaining a certain degree of local dynamic equilibrium through quasi-elastic resonance scattering, the final stable hadronic yield has almost no change [22–25]. The T_{ch}, and baryon chemical potential (μ_B) at this stage can be obtained by using various thermodynamic models [3,26–28]. After the chemical freeze-out stage, the system further expands as the interactions become weak. Finally, the system enters the kinetic freeze-out stage as the elastic collisions between hadrons disappear.

In this paper, the p_T spectra of identified charged hadrons (π^-, π^+, K^-, K^+, $\bar{p}$, and p) with different rapidities produced in inelastic pp collisions at the center-of-mass (c.m.) energies $\sqrt{s}$ = 6.3, 7.7, 8.8, 12.3, and 17.3 GeV at the SPS [29] are studied, where the c.m. energy is also referred to as collision energy. Although the nonextensive distribution of the Tsallis statistics [30–35] has been widely used in recent years, the standard (Bose–Einstein/Fermi–Dirac, or Maxwell–Boltzmann) distribution from the relativistic ideal gas model is still used to extract T directly and then to obtain the average transverse momentum ($\langle p_T \rangle$), root-mean-square transverse momentum ($\sqrt{\langle p_T^2 \rangle}$), T_0, and T_i indirectly.

The remainder of this paper is structured as follows. The formalism and method are described in Section 2. Results and discussion are provided in Section 3. In Section 4, we summarize our main observations and conclusions.

2. Formalism and Method

The particles produced in inelastic pp collisions are thought to be controlled by two main mechanisms or excitation degrees. The low-p_T region, which is less than 1–2 GeV/c is dominated by the soft excitation process [36,37]. The high-p_T region that is more than 1–2 GeV/c is governed by the hard scattering process [36,37]. The soft process corresponds to a low excitation degree, and the hard process implies a high excitation degree. The two-mechanism scheme is only one possible choice in understanding particle production. If the particles are distributed in a very wide p_T region, one should consider the multiple mechanisms or excitation degrees. If the particles are distributed in a relatively narrow p_T region, one may choose the single mechanism or excitation degree. In the two-mechanism scenario, it is currently believed that most light-flavor particles are produced in the soft process. The spectrum in the low-p_T region shows exponential behavior, which can be fitted by the thermal distribution [38–40]. Heavy-flavor particles and some light-flavor particles are produced in the hard process. The spectrum in high-p_T region shows inverse power-law behavior and can be fitted using the Hagedorn [41,42], Tsallis–Levy [31,32], or Tsallis–Pareto-type functions [32–35].

In this investigation, the light particle spectra in the low-p_T region in inelastic pp collisions at the SPS are studied by using the most basic thermal distribution, the standard distribution, which comes from the relativistic ideal gas model. The invariant particle momentum (p) distribution described by the standard distribution can be given by [30]

$$E\frac{d^3N}{d^3p} = \frac{1}{2\pi p_T}\frac{d^2N}{dydp_T} = \frac{gV}{(2\pi)^3}E\left[\exp\left(\frac{E-\mu}{T}\right)+S\right]^{-1}, \tag{1}$$

where N is the particle number, g is the degeneracy factor, V is the volume, μ is the chemical potential,

$$E = \sqrt{p^2+m_0^2} = m_T\cosh y \tag{2}$$

is the energy,

$$m_T = \sqrt{p_T^2+m_0^2} \tag{3}$$

is the transverse mass,

$$y = \frac{1}{2}\ln\left(\frac{1+\beta_z}{1-\beta_z}\right) = \tanh^{-1}(\beta_z) \tag{4}$$

is the rapidity, β_z is the longitudinal velocity, and $S = -1$, 1, and 0 correspond to the Bose–Einstein, Fermi–Dirac, and Maxwell–Boltzmann statistics, respectively.

For the wide p_T spectra, if a multi-component standard distribution

$$\begin{aligned} E\frac{d^3N}{d^3p} &= \frac{1}{2\pi p_T}\frac{d^2N}{dydp_T} \\ &= \sum_{i=1}^{n}\frac{gV_i}{(2\pi)^3}E\left[\exp\left(\frac{E-\mu}{T_i}\right)+S\right]^{-1} \end{aligned} \tag{5}$$

can be used in the fit, one may obtain multiple temperatures, that is, the temperature fluctuation. Here, n denotes the number of components. Let k_i ($i = 1, 2, \ldots, n$) denote the relative fraction of the i-th component, and V_i and T_i are the volume and temperature corresponding to the i-th component, respectively. Naturally, one has

$$V = \sum_{i=1}^{n}V_i, \quad T = \sum_{i=1}^{n}k_iT_i, \quad \sum_{i=1}^{n}k_i = 1. \tag{6}$$

Here, $k_i = V_i/V$.

Because of the temperature fluctuation, there are interactions among different subsystems or local sources due to the exchange of heat energy. This causes the couplings of entropy functions of various subsystems. The total entropy is then the sum of the entropies of subsystems plus the entropies of the couplings. The temperature fluctuation in the multi-component standard distribution is a way to explain the origin of the Tsallis distribution. Generally, the p_T spectra, which can be fitted using the multi-component standard distribution, can also be fitted using the Tsallis distribution. Because of the influence of the entropy index (q), the temperature value extracted from the Tsallis distribution is smaller than that from the multi-component standard distribution. In fact, in the fit using the Tsallis distribution, increasing T and/or q can increase the particle yield in the high-p_T region conveniently.

The data sample analyzed in the present work is in the low-p_T region. This implies that the standard distribution can be used. In the standard distribution, the unit-density function of y and p_T is written as

$$\frac{d^2N}{dydp_T} = \frac{gV}{(2\pi)^2} p_T m_T \cosh y \times \left[\exp\left(\frac{m_T \cosh y - \mu}{T}\right) + S\right]^{-1}. \tag{7}$$

Then, the density function of p_T is

$$\frac{dN}{dp_T} = \frac{gV}{(2\pi)^2} p_T m_T \int_{y_{\min}}^{y_{\max}} \cosh y \times \left[\exp\left(\frac{m_T \cosh y - \mu}{T}\right) + S\right]^{-1} dy, \tag{8}$$

where $y_{\min}$ and $y_{\max}$ are the minimum and maximum rapidities in the rapidity interval, respectively. The density function of y is

$$\frac{dN}{dy} = \frac{gV}{(2\pi)^2} \cosh y \int_0^{p_{T\max}} p_T m_T \times \left[\exp\left(\frac{m_T \cosh y - \mu}{T}\right) + S\right]^{-1} dp_T, \tag{9}$$

where $p_{T\max}$ is the maximum p_T in the considered rapidity interval. Although $p_{T\max}$ can be mathematically infinite, it is only large enough in physics due to the limitations of the conservation of energy and momentum.

No matter what the specific form of particle momentum distribution is used, the probability density function of p_T is written in general as

$$f(p_T) = \frac{1}{N}\frac{dN}{dp_T}. \tag{10}$$

Naturally, $f(p_T)$ is normalized to 1. That is,

$$\int_0^\infty f(p_T)dp_T = 1. \tag{11}$$

One has the average transverse momentum,

$$\langle p_T \rangle = \frac{\int_0^\infty p_T f(p_T)dp_T}{\int_0^\infty f(p_T)dp_T} = \int_0^\infty p_T f(p_T)dp_T, \tag{12}$$

and the root-mean-square p_T,

$$\sqrt{\langle p_T^2 \rangle} = \sqrt{\frac{\int_0^\infty p_T^2 f(p_T)dp_T}{\int_0^\infty f(p_T)dp_T}} = \sqrt{\int_0^\infty p_T^2 f(p_T)dp_T}. \tag{13}$$

In principle, there are three independent chemical potentials, baryon (μ_B), electric charge or isospin (μ_I), and strangeness (μ_S), which are related to the three conserved charges. Although the chemical potential, μ_π (μ_K or μ_p), of the pion (kaon or proton) can be written in terms of the above three chemical potentials [43–49], we obtained them by using an alternative method in the present work for more convenience.

Considering the yield ratio [k_j ($j = \pi$, K, and p)] of negatively to positively charged hadrons (j^- to j^+), the corresponding chemical potentials (μ_{j^-} and μ_{j^+}), and the corresponding source temperature (T_{j^-} and T_{j^+}), one has that the relationship between k_j and μ_j is [20,50–53]

$$k_j \equiv \frac{j^-}{j^+} = \exp\left(\frac{\mu_{j^-}}{T_{j^-}} - \frac{\mu_{j^+}}{T_{j^+}}\right) = \exp\left(-\frac{2\mu_j}{T_j}\right) \tag{14}$$

if the conditions

$$T_{j^-} = T_{j^+} = T_j, \quad \mu_{j^-} = -\mu_{j^+} = -\mu_j \tag{15}$$

are satisfied. Here, j^- and j^+ also denote the yields of negative and positive hadrons respectively. k_j can be obtained simply from the experimental data, and T_j should be the chemical kinetic-freezing temperature T_{ch}, which is slightly larger than or equal to the effective temperature T due to the short lifetime of the system formed in pp collisions. One has $T_j \approx T$ in this work.

Further, one has

$$\mu_j = -\frac{1}{2} T_j \ln k_j. \tag{16}$$

Obviously, μ_j is energy-dependent due to T_j and k_j being energy-dependent. Based on a collection of large amounts of experimental data, our previous work [52,53] presents the excitation functions of μ_j in pp and central heavy ion collisions, which can be used for a direct extraction for this study. In particular, μ_j decreases quickly with the increase in energy in pp collisions in the concerned SPS energy range. However, the tendency of μ_π in central heavy ion collisions is opposite to that in pp collisions, though the tendency of μ_K is similar, and that of μ_p is also similar in the two collisions. The three μ_j in both the collisions are close to 0 at around 100 GeV and above.

The chemical freeze-out temperature T_{ch} in central heavy ion collisions is also energy-dependent [43–49], which shows a tendency for a rapid increase at a few GeV and then saturation at dozens of GeV and above. In view of the fact that the tendency of T_{ch} has a parameterized excitation function with unanimity in the community, the present work does not study T_{ch} parameter.

Generally, the kinetic freeze-out temperature T_0 has a tendency of a rapid increase at a few GeV, and then an ambiguous tendency (increase, decrease, or saturation) appears at dozens of GeV and above. It is worth studying the tendency of T_0 further. A thermal-related method shows that [54]

$$T_0 = \frac{\langle p_T \rangle}{2\kappa_0}, \tag{17}$$

where $\kappa_0 = 3.07$ is a coefficient, and a value 2 is introduced by us because two participant partons (one from the projectile and the other from the target) are assumed to contribute to $\langle p_T \rangle$. This formula gives an approximate consistent tendency of T_0 as another thermal-related method [55], which shows T_0 to be proportional to $\langle p_T \rangle$ and the coefficient to be energy-related, though the results from the two methods are not the same.

The initial temperature T_i, which is comparable to the experimental data, is less studied in the community. According to the string percolation model [56–58], T_i is expressed as

$$T_i = \sqrt{\frac{\langle p_T^2 \rangle}{2F(\xi)}}, \tag{18}$$

where

$$F(\xi) = \sqrt{\frac{1 - \exp(-\xi)}{\xi}} \quad (19)$$

is the color-suppression factor related to the dimensionless percolation density parameter ξ. In pp collisions, $F(\xi) \sim 1$ due to the low string overlap probability. As an initial quantity, T_i should reflect the excitation degree of the system at the parton level. Correspondingly, the final quantity T_0 should also be extracted at the parton level. This is also the reason that the value of 2 is introduced by us in the denominator of the T_0 expression if one assumes that two participant partons are the energy sources in the formation of a particle.

The kinetic energy of a particle's directional movement should not be reflected in the temperature parameters. The experimental data used in this paper were all measured in the forward-rapidity region. In order to remove the influence of directional motion, one can directly shift the forward rapidity and its interval to the mid-rapidity with the same interval width during the fitting process. In this paper, we integrate y from $y_{\rm min} = -0.1$ to $y_{\rm max} = 0.1$ in the fit to give a more accurate result, though $y \approx 0$ and $\cosh y \approx 1$ near the mid-rapidity. The small difference (<1%) between the accurate and approximate calculations appears mainly in the normalization but not in the temperature parameter.

The method of least squares based on obtaining the minimum χ^2 is adopted to obtain the best parameters and their uncertainties. The treatment method is given in Appendix A.

3. Results and Discussion

Figures 1 and 2 show the rapidity-dependent double differential p_T spectra, $d^2N/dydp_T$, of π^- and π^+ respectively, produced in inelastic pp collisions at the SPS. Panels (a)–(e) correspond to the results of $\sqrt{s} = 6.3, 7.7, 8.8, 12.3$, and 17.3 GeV, respectively. The symbols represent the experimental data at different y, with an interval width of 0.2 units, measured using the NA61/SHINE Collaboration [29], and the curves are our results fitted from the Bose–Einstein distribution. In order to see the fitting effect more clearly, the experimental data and fitting results at different rapidities are multiplied by different factors labeled in the panel for scaling. The values of related free parameters (T), the normalization constant (V), χ^2, and the number of degrees of freedom (ndof) for the curves in Figures 1 and 2 are listed in Table A1 in Appendix B. One can see that the fitting results with the Bose–Einstein distribution are in good agreement with the experimental data of π^- and π^+ spectra, measured using the NA61/SHINE Collaboration in pp collisions at different $\sqrt{s}$ and in different y intervals.

Similarly, Figures 1–4 show the rapidity-dependent $d^2N/dydp_T$ of K^- and K^+, respectively, produced in inelastic pp collisions at different $\sqrt{s}$. The values of T, V, and χ^2/ndof for the curves in Figures 3 and 4 are listed in Table A2 in Appendix B. One can see that the fitting results from the Bose–Einstein distribution are in agreement with the experimental data of K^- and K^+, measured by the NA61/SHINE Collaboration in pp collisions at different $\sqrt{s}$ and in different y intervals.

Similar to Figures 1–4, Figures 5 and 6 show the rapidity-dependent $d^2N/dydp_T$ of $\bar{p}$ and p, respectively, produced in inelastic pp collisions at different $\sqrt{s}$. The experimental data of $\bar{p}$ at $\sqrt{s} = 6.3$ GeV in Figure 5 are not available. The values of T, V, and χ^2/ndof for the curves in Figures 5 and 6 are listed in Table A3 in Appendix B. One can see that the p_T spectra of $\bar{p}$ and p in pp collisions are shown to obey approximately the Fermi–Dirac distribution.

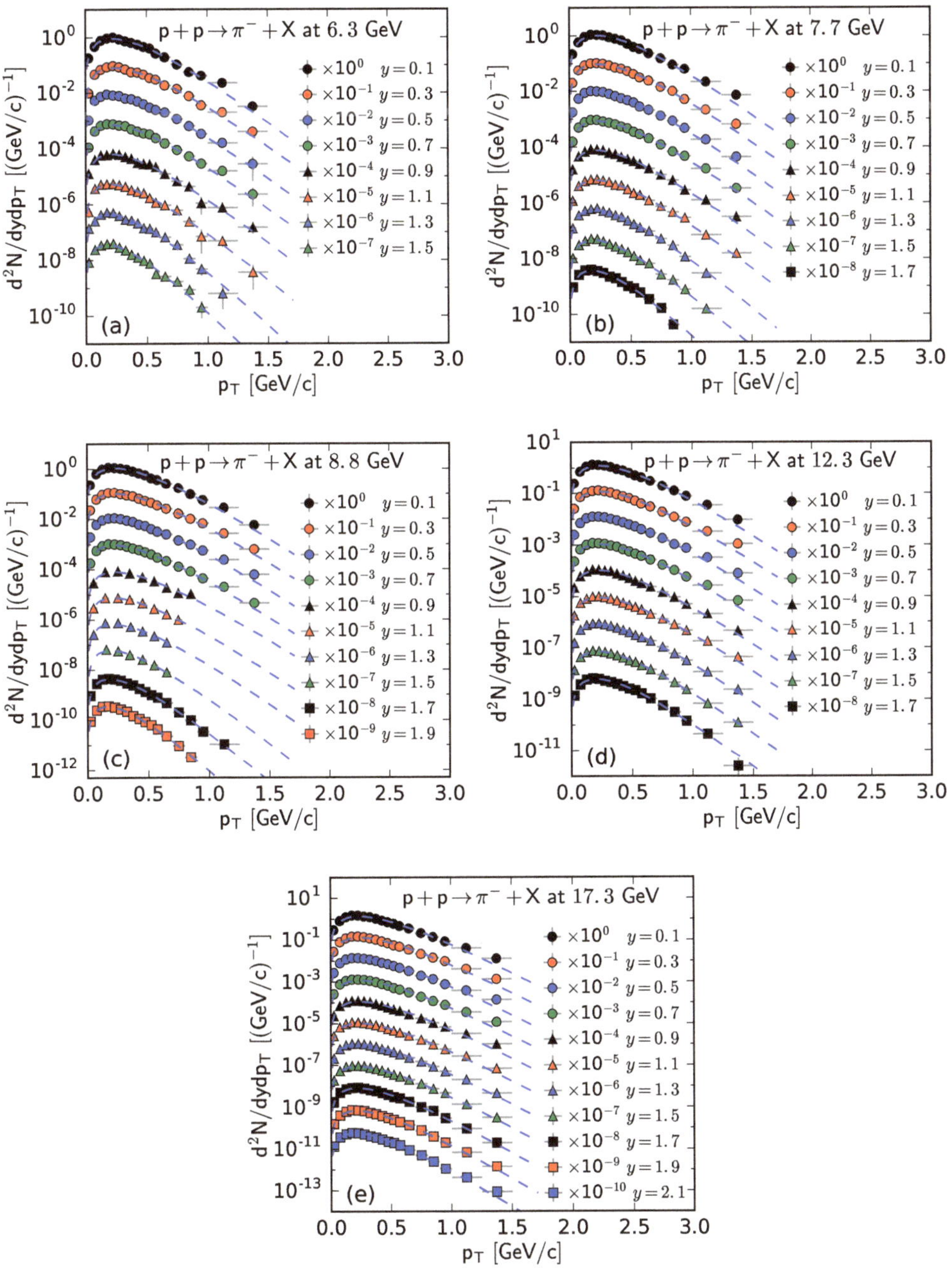

Figure 1. The spectra of π^- produced in pp collisions at $\sqrt{s}$ = (**a**) 6.3, (**b**) 7.7, (**c**) 8.8, (**d**) 12.3, and (**e**) 17.3 GeV at different y with an interval width of 0.2. The symbols represent the experimental data measured by the NA61/SHINE Collaboration [29] and the curves are the fitting results from the Bose–Einstein distribution.

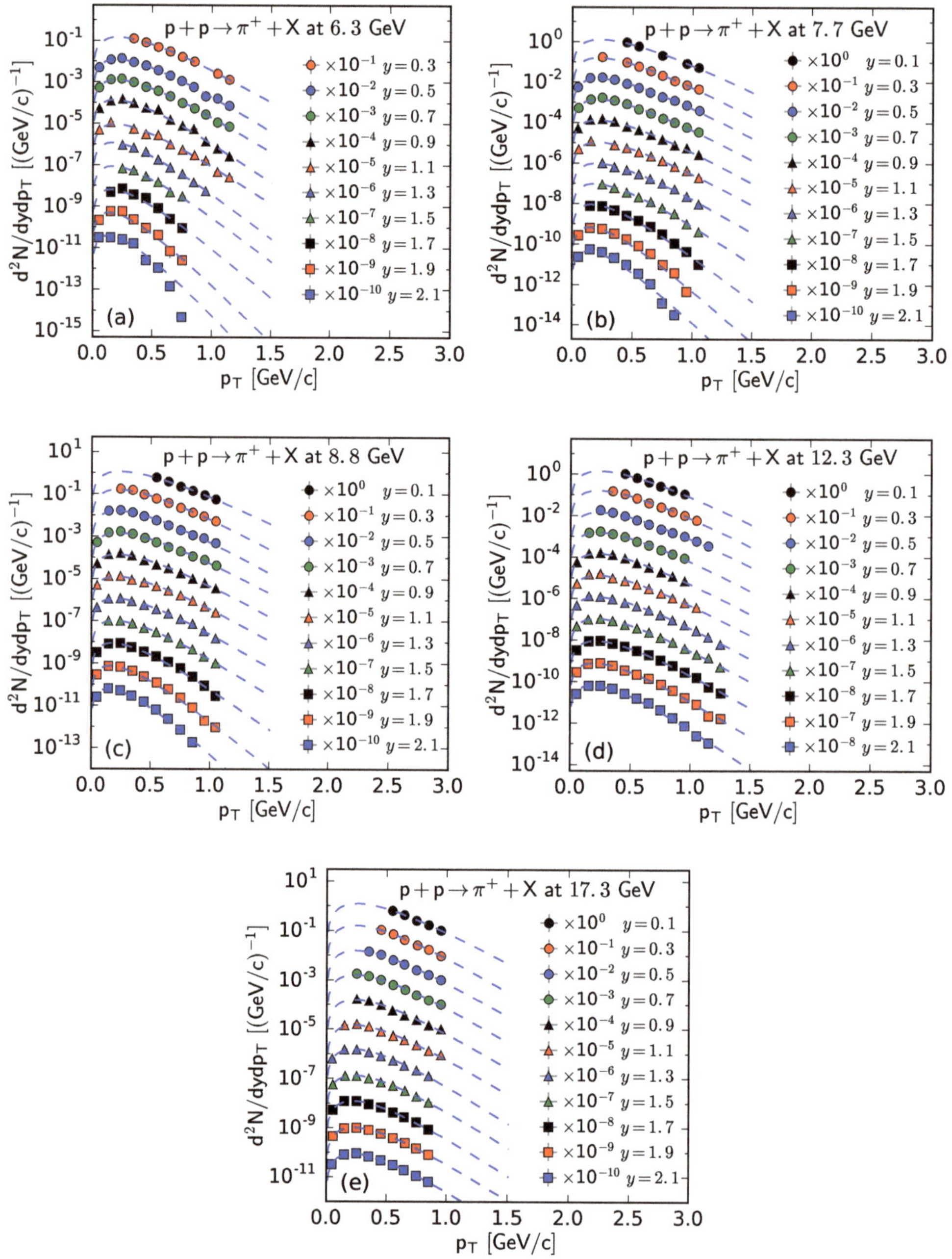

Figure 2. The spectra of π^+ produced in pp collisions at $\sqrt{s}$ = (**a**) 6.3, (**b**) 7.7, (**c**) 8.8, (**d**) 12.3, and (**e**) 17.3 GeV at different y. The symbols represent the experimental data measured by the NA61/SHINE Collaboration [29] and the curves are the fitting results from the Bose–Einstein distribution.

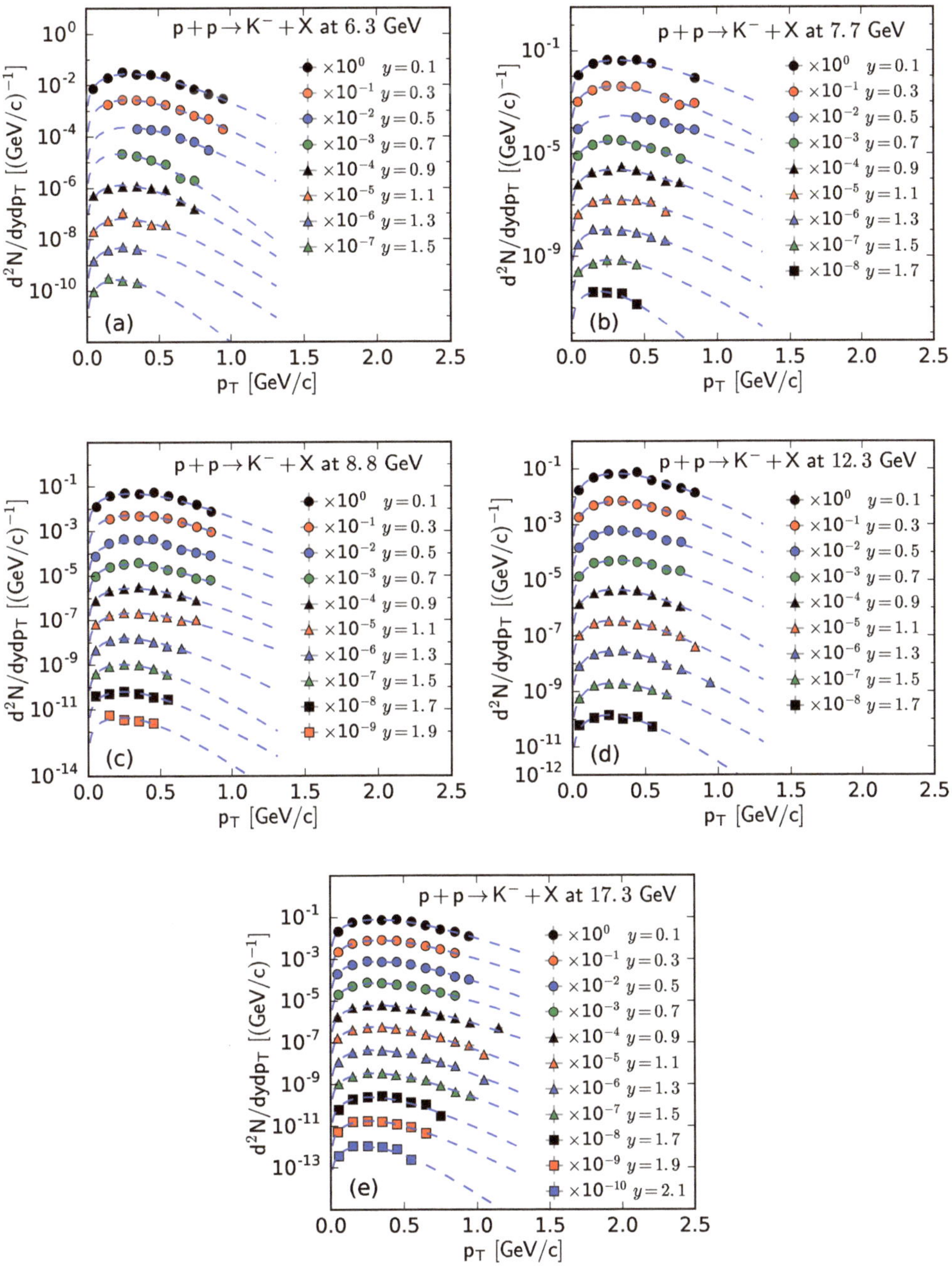

Figure 3. The spectra of K^- produced in pp collisions at $\sqrt{s}$ = (**a**) 6.3, (**b**) 7.7, (**c**) 8.8, (**d**) 12.3, and (**e**) 17.3 GeV at different y. The symbols represent the experimental data measured by the NA61/SHINE Collaboration [29] and the curves are the fitting results from the Bose–Einstein distribution.

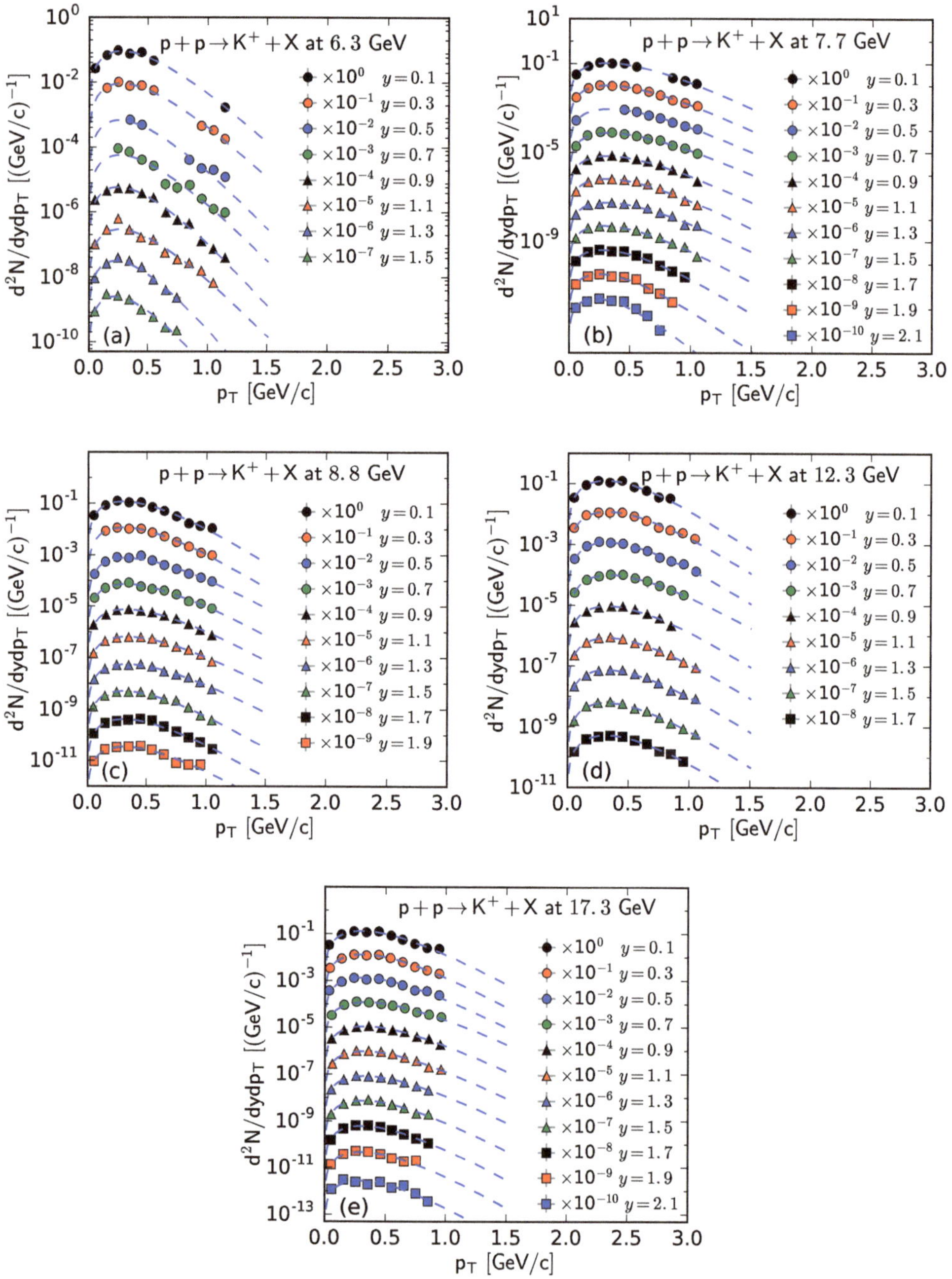

Figure 4. The spectra of K^+ produced in pp collisions at $\sqrt{s}$ = (**a**) 6.3, (**b**) 7.7, (**c**) 8.8, (**d**) 12.3, and (**e**) 17.3 GeV at different y. The symbols represent the experimental data measured by the NA61/SHINE Collaboration [29] and the curves are the fitting results from the Bose–Einstein distribution.

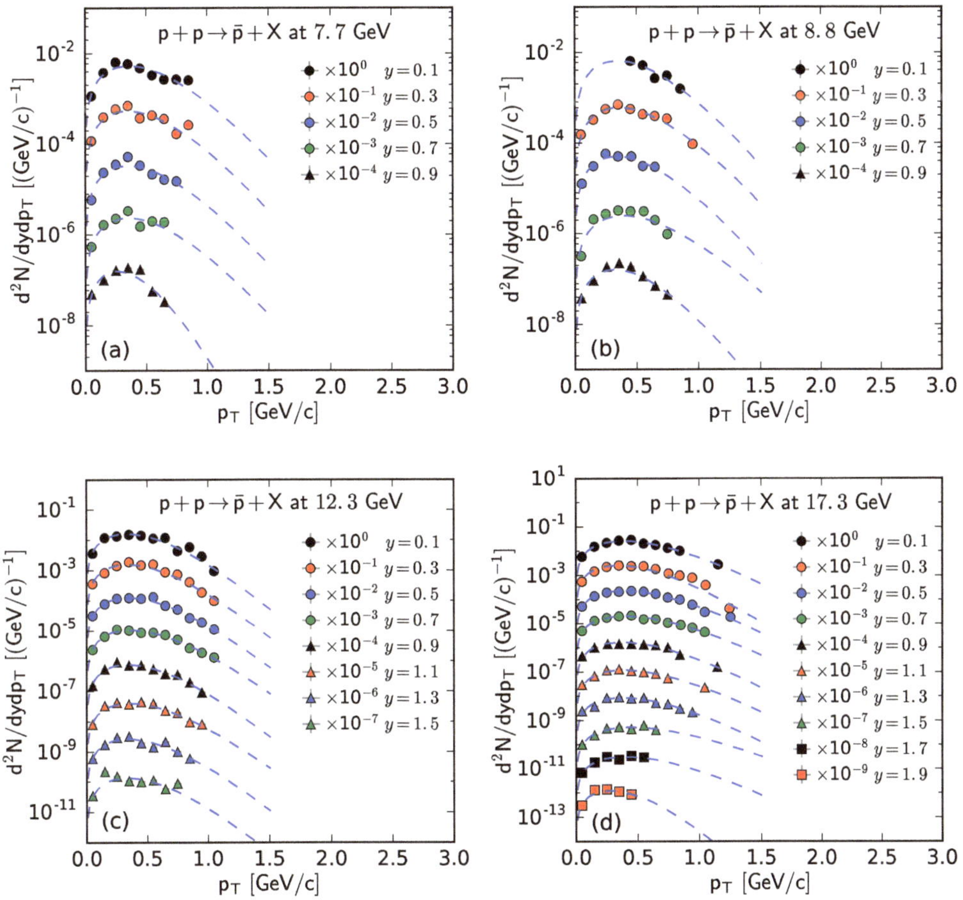

Figure 5. The spectra of $\bar{p}$ produced in pp collisions at $\sqrt{s}$ = (**a**) 7.7, (**b**) 8.8, (**c**) 12.3, and (**d**) 17.3 at different y. The symbols represent the experimental data measured by the NA61/SHINE Collaboration [29] and the curves are the fitting results from the Fermi–Dirac distribution.

To show more intuitively the dependence of the free parameter T and derived quantities (the kinetic freeze-out temperature T_0 and initial temperature T_i) on rapidity, y, and c.m. energy, $\sqrt{s}$, Figures 7–10 show the relations of T–y, T_0–y, T_i–y, and V–y at different $\sqrt{s}$, respectively, and Figures 11–14 show the relations of T–$\sqrt{s}$, T_0–$\sqrt{s}$, T_i–$\sqrt{s}$, and V–$\sqrt{s}$ at different y, respectively. Panels (a)–(f) correspond to the results from π^-, π^+, K^-, K^+, $\bar{p}$, and p spectra, respectively. These figures show some changing trends of parameters.

In most cases, one can generally see that T, T_0, and T_i decrease (increase) with the increase in y ($\sqrt{s}$). There is a tendency of saturation for the three temperatures at $\sqrt{s}$ = 7.7 GeV and above. Being the initial energy of a saturation effect, 7.7 GeV is a special energy at which the reaction products are proton-dominated and above which the products are meson-dominated. For π^-, π^+, K^-, K^+, and $\bar{p}$ spectra, the extracted V also decreases (increases) with the increase in y ($\sqrt{s}$). However, for p spectra, the extracted V shows an opposite tendency, increasing (decreasing) with the increase in y ($\sqrt{s}$).

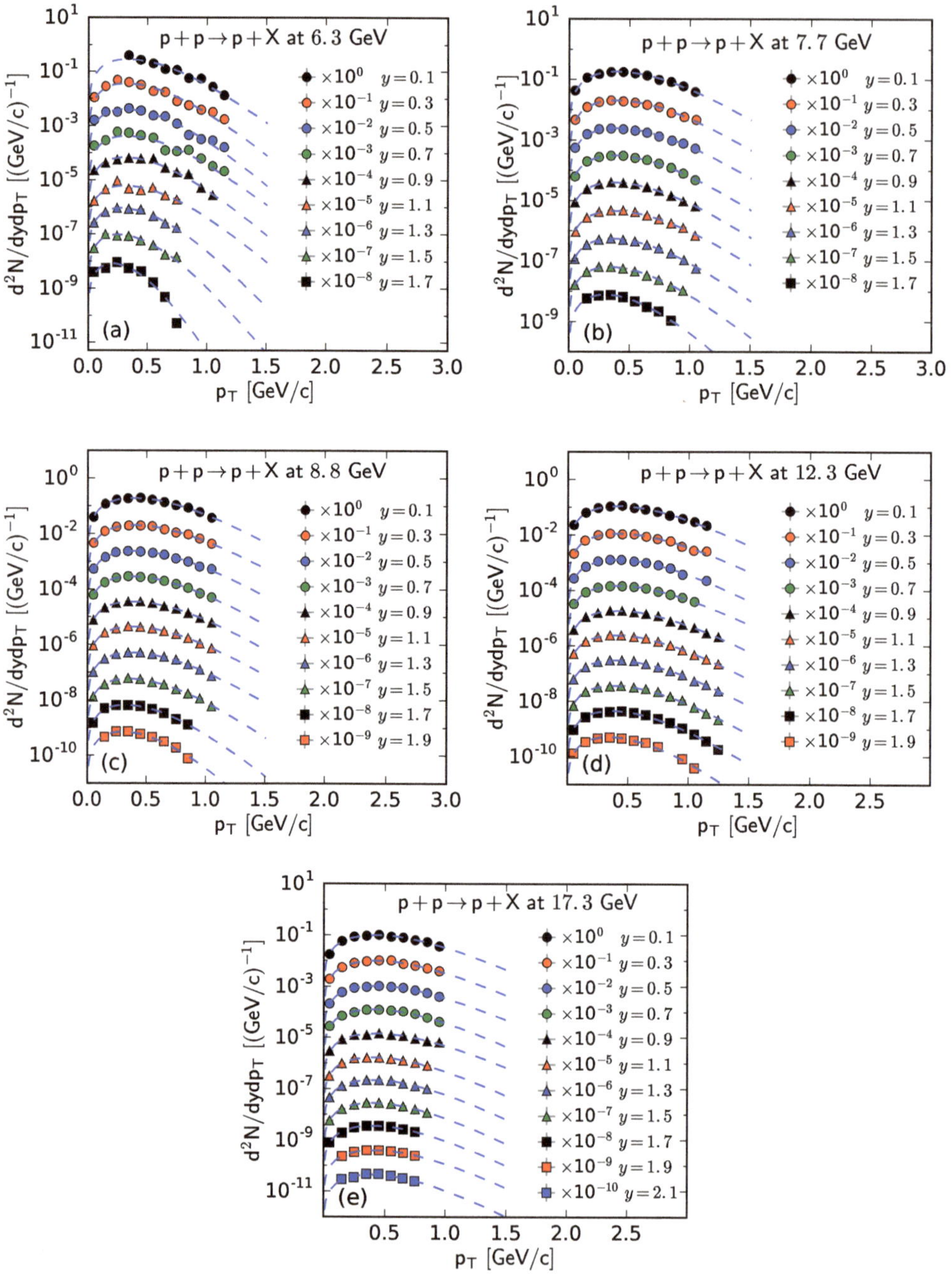

Figure 6. The spectra of p produced in pp collisions at $\sqrt{s}$ = (**a**) 6.3, (**b**) 7.7, (**c**) 8.8, (**d**) 12.3, and (**e**) 17.3 GeV at different y. The symbols represent the experimental data measured by the NA61/SHINE Collaboration [29] and the curves are the fitting results from the Fermi–Dirac distribution.

There is an isospin and mass independence of T. This property is exactly that of T_{ch}, which implies a single scenario of chemical freeze-out. However, although T_0 and T_i are isospin-independent, they increase with the increase in mass. The mass dependence of T_0 is a reflection of a mass-dependent differential kinetic freeze-out scenario or multiple kinetic freeze-out scenarios. The mass dependence of T_i means that the formation moments of different particles are different. With the increase in T_0 (T_i), massive particles are emitted (formed) earlier. On average, this work shows that $\bar{p}(p)$ are emitted (formed) earlier than $K^{\mp}$, and $K^{\mp}$ are emitted (formed) earlier than $\pi^{\mp}$, though the relaxation times for the emissions (formations) of different particles can overlap.

Except for V from the p spectra, the tendencies of other parameters from the p spectra, and the tendencies of parameters from the spectra of other particles are easy to understand. It is expected that the local system in the mid-rapidity region has more deposited energy than that in the forward region. Meanwhile, the collision system at a higher energy has more deposited energy than that at lower energy. This results in a higher excitation degree (then higher temperature) at the mid-rapidity and more produced particles (then larger volume) at a higher energy.

The V tendency from the p spectra is opposite to that from the spectra of other particles. The reason is that the pre-existing leading protons affect the p spectra. Because of the leading protons appearing in the forward region, the number of protons and then the volume of a proton source in the fixed interval are small at the mid-rapidity. At a higher energy, the leading protons appear in the more forward region, which leads to a smaller V in the fixed interval in the rapidity space. In the present work, the fixed interval is that $\Delta y = y_{\max} - y_{\min} = 0.2$.

The values of V depend on particle mass and charge. Excluding the case of p, which contains pre-existing leading protons in the pp system, V decreases significantly with the increase in mass, and positive hadrons correspond to the larger V of the emission source. This is because the larger the mass, the more difficult it is to produce this particle. Meanwhile, there is an electromagnetic exclusion (attraction) between positive (negative) hadrons and pre-existing protons. This causes larger (smaller) V with an emission source of positive (negative) hadrons.

Generally, the effective temperature T is proportional to the mean transverse momentum $\langle p_T \rangle$. The present work shows that $T_{\pi^-} \approx 0.351\langle p_T \rangle_{\pi^-}$, $T_{\pi^+} \approx 0.348\langle p_T \rangle_{\pi^+}$, $T_{K^-} \approx 0.284\langle p_T \rangle_{K^-}$, $T_{K^+} \approx 0.293\langle p_T \rangle_{K^+}$, $T_{\bar{p}} \approx 0.234\langle p_T \rangle_{\bar{p}}$, and $T_p \approx 0.240\langle p_T \rangle_p$. Here, the type of a particle appears as the subscript label of the related quantity. The ratio of $T/\langle p_T \rangle$ is approximately independent of a particle mass. This is consistent with the ratios of $T_0/\langle p_T \rangle$ and $T_i/\sqrt{\langle p_T^2 \rangle}$, which are independent of particle mass according to Equations (17) and (18).

As only a free parameter, T does not show an obvious dependence on particle type or mass. However, it is hard to extract exact information from T because it is not a real temperature, because it also contains the contribution of transverse flow. T_0 is smaller than T_i due to the fact that T_0 is "measured" at the kinetic freeze-out stage (the final one), and T_i is "measured" at the initial stage. From the initial stage to the final one, the system becomes colder and colder. This is indeed observed in the present work.

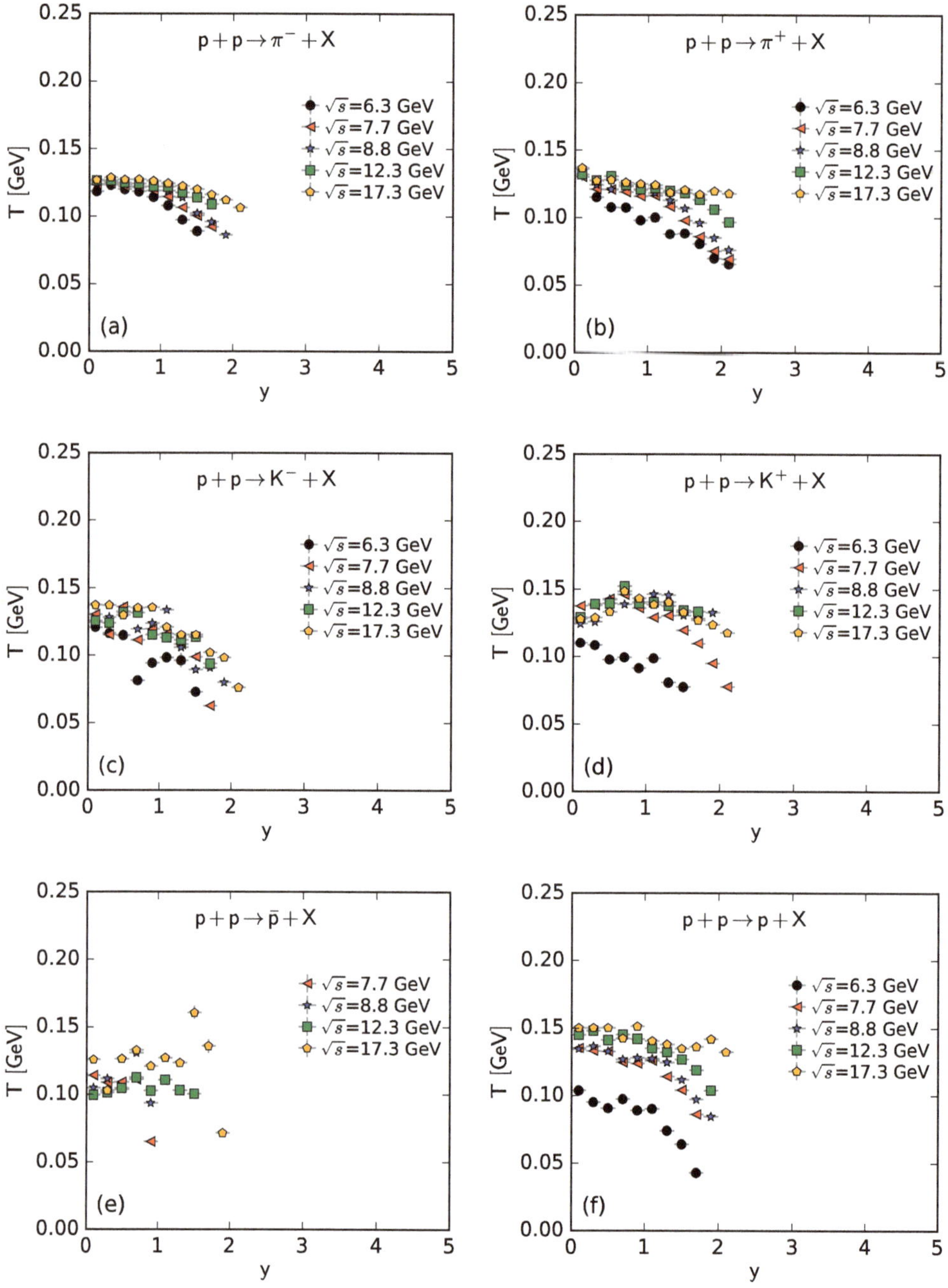

Figure 7. Dependence of T on y at different $\sqrt{s}$ from the spectra of (**a**) π^-, (**b**) π^+, (**c**) K^-, (**d**) K^+, (**e**) $\bar{p}$, and (**f**) p.

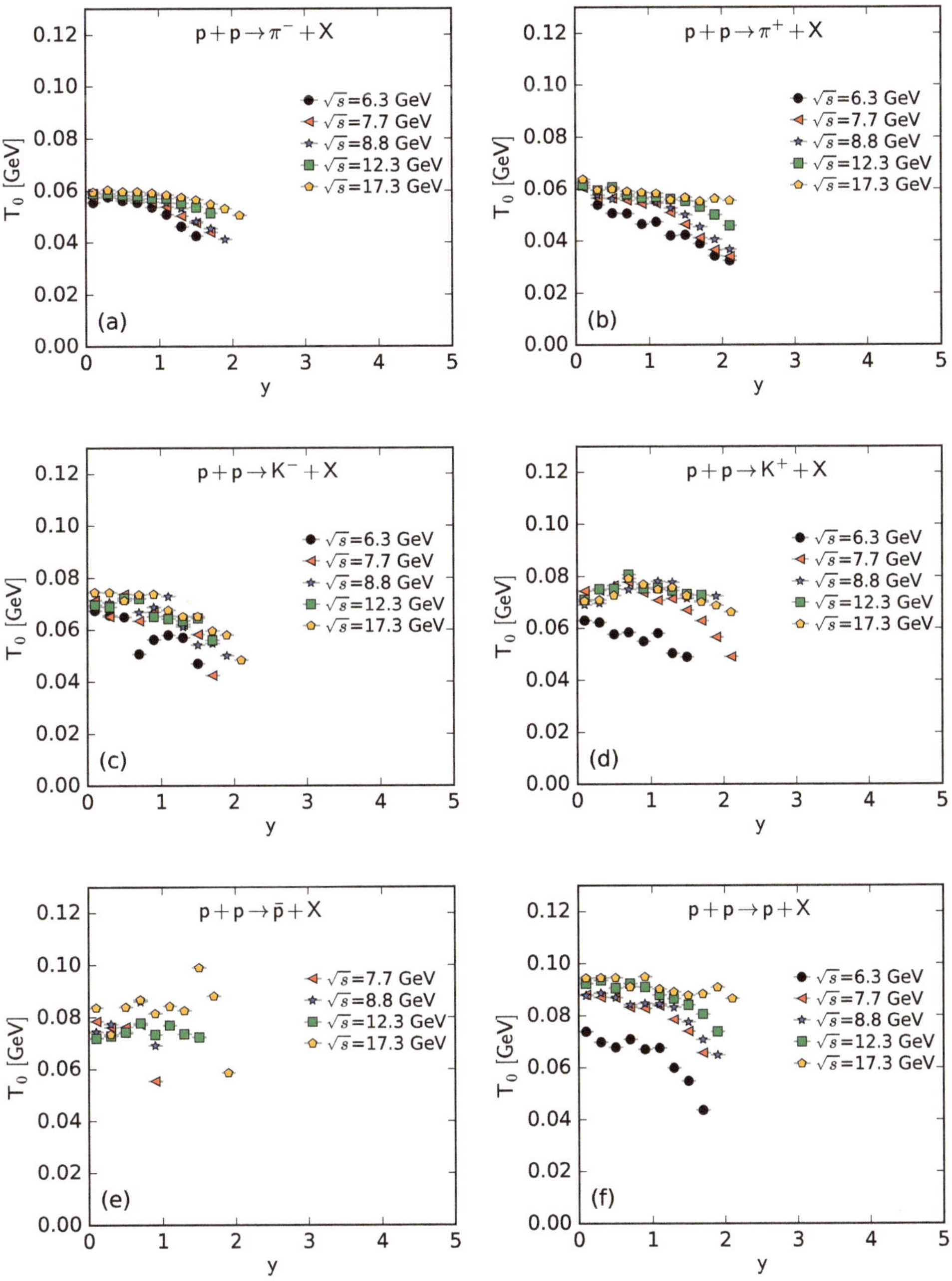

Figure 8. Dependence of T_0 on y at different $\sqrt{s}$ from the spectra of (**a**) π^-, (**b**) π^+, (**c**) K^-, (**d**) K^+, (**e**) $\bar{p}$, and (**f**) p.

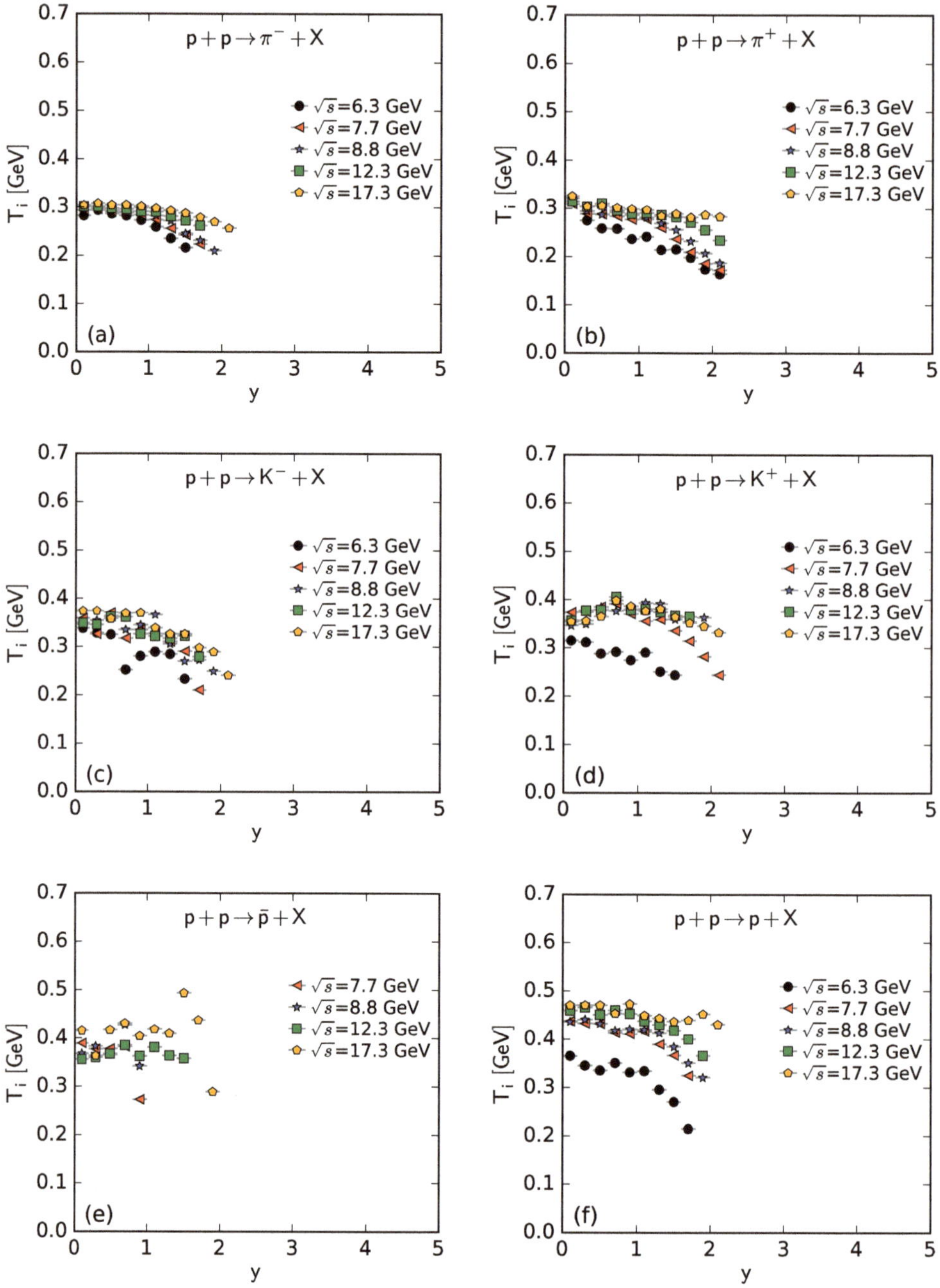

Figure 9. Dependence of T_i on y at different $\sqrt{s}$ from the spectra of (**a**) π^-, (**b**) π^+, (**c**) K^-, (**d**) K^+, (**e**) $\bar{p}$, and (**f**) p.

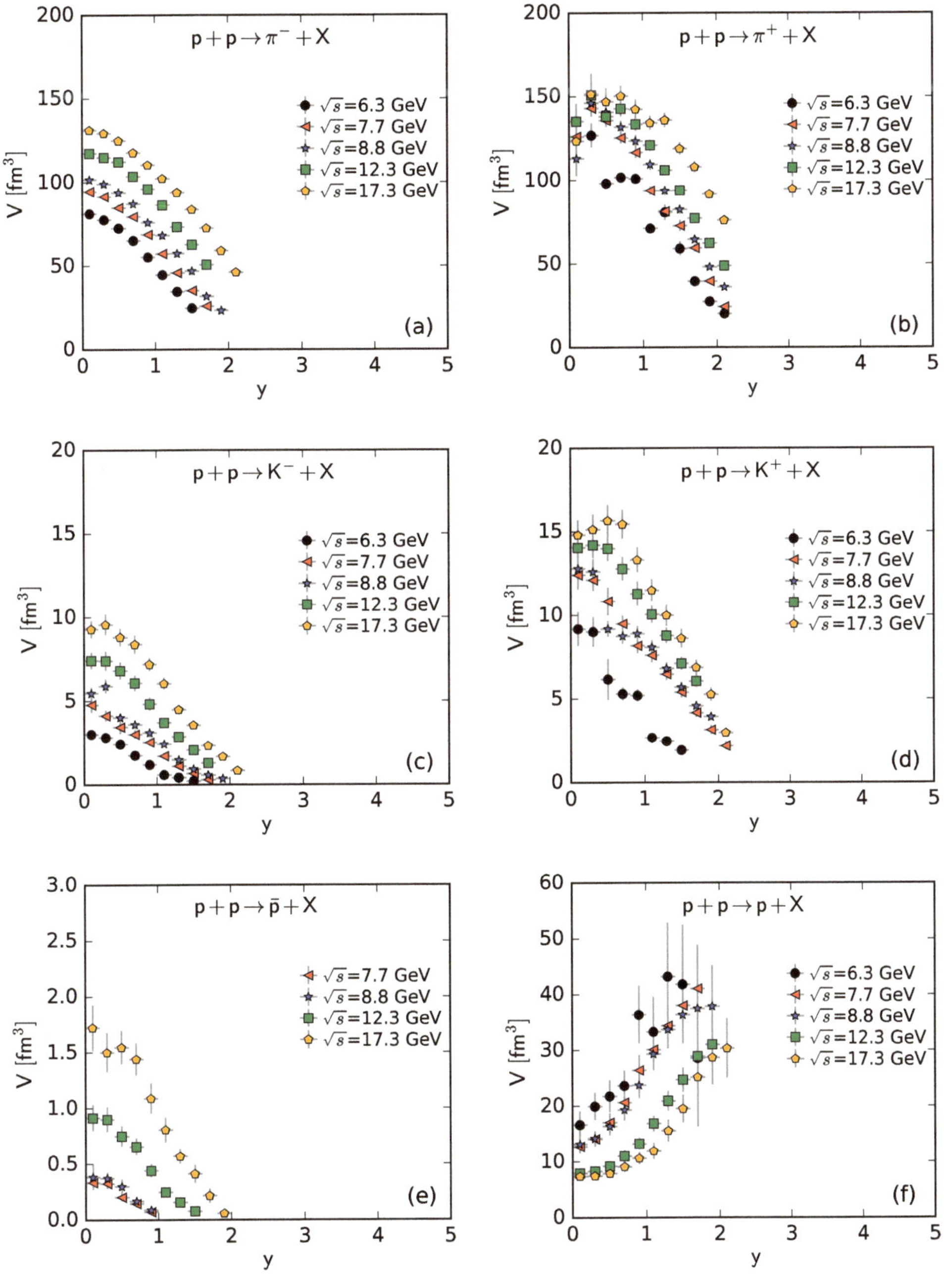

Figure 10. Dependence of V on y at different $\sqrt{s}$ from the spectra of (**a**) π^-, (**b**) π^+, (**c**) K^-, (**d**) K^+, (**e**) $\bar{p}$, and (**f**) p.

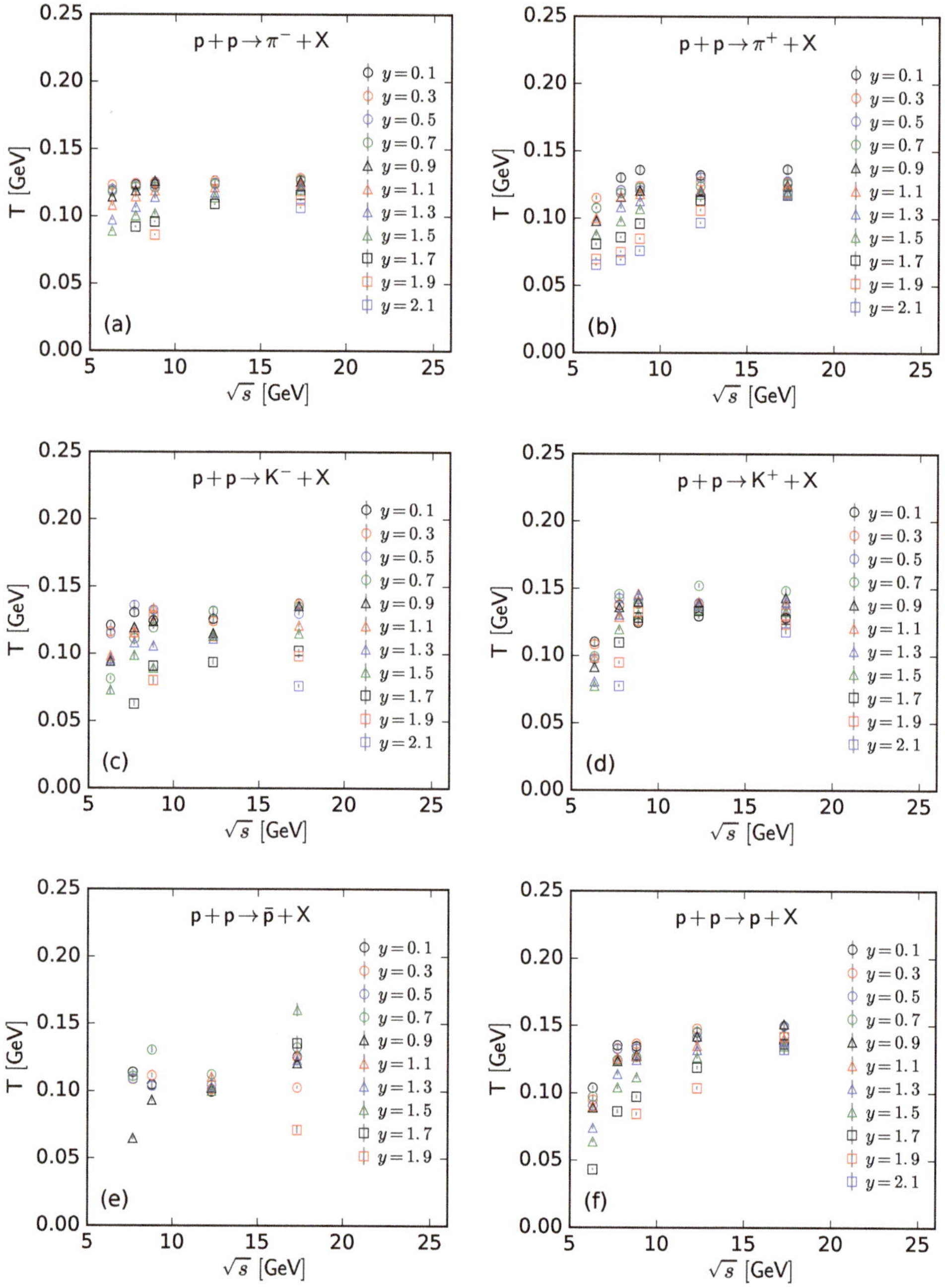

Figure 11. Dependence of T on $\sqrt{s}$ at different y from the spectra of (**a**) π^-, (**b**) π^+, (**c**) K^-, (**d**) K^+, (**e**) $\bar{p}$, and (**f**) p.

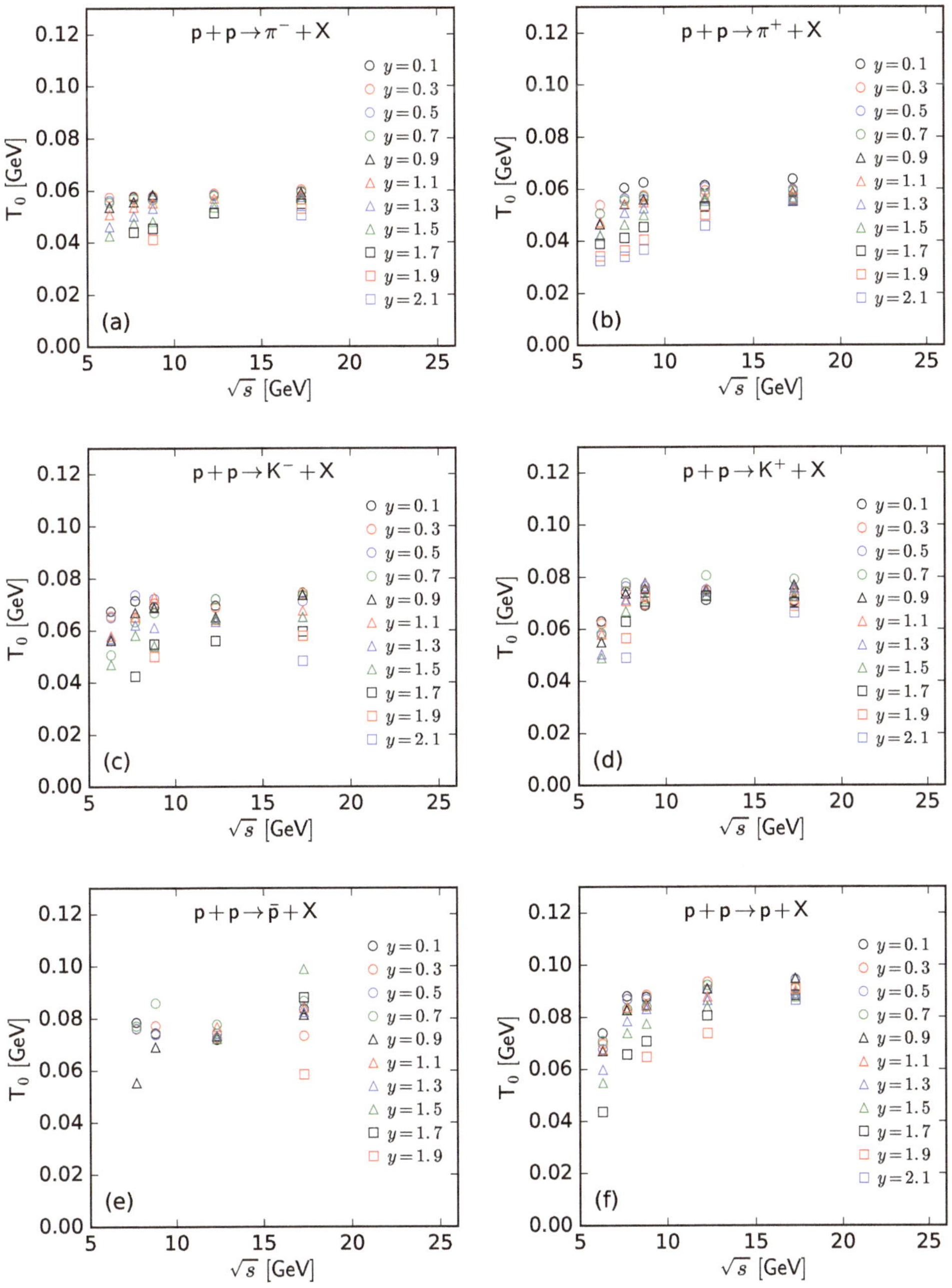

Figure 12. Dependence of T_0 on $\sqrt{s}$ at different y from the spectra of (**a**) π^-, (**b**) π^+, (**c**) K^-, (**d**) K^+, (**e**) $\bar{p}$, and (**f**) p.

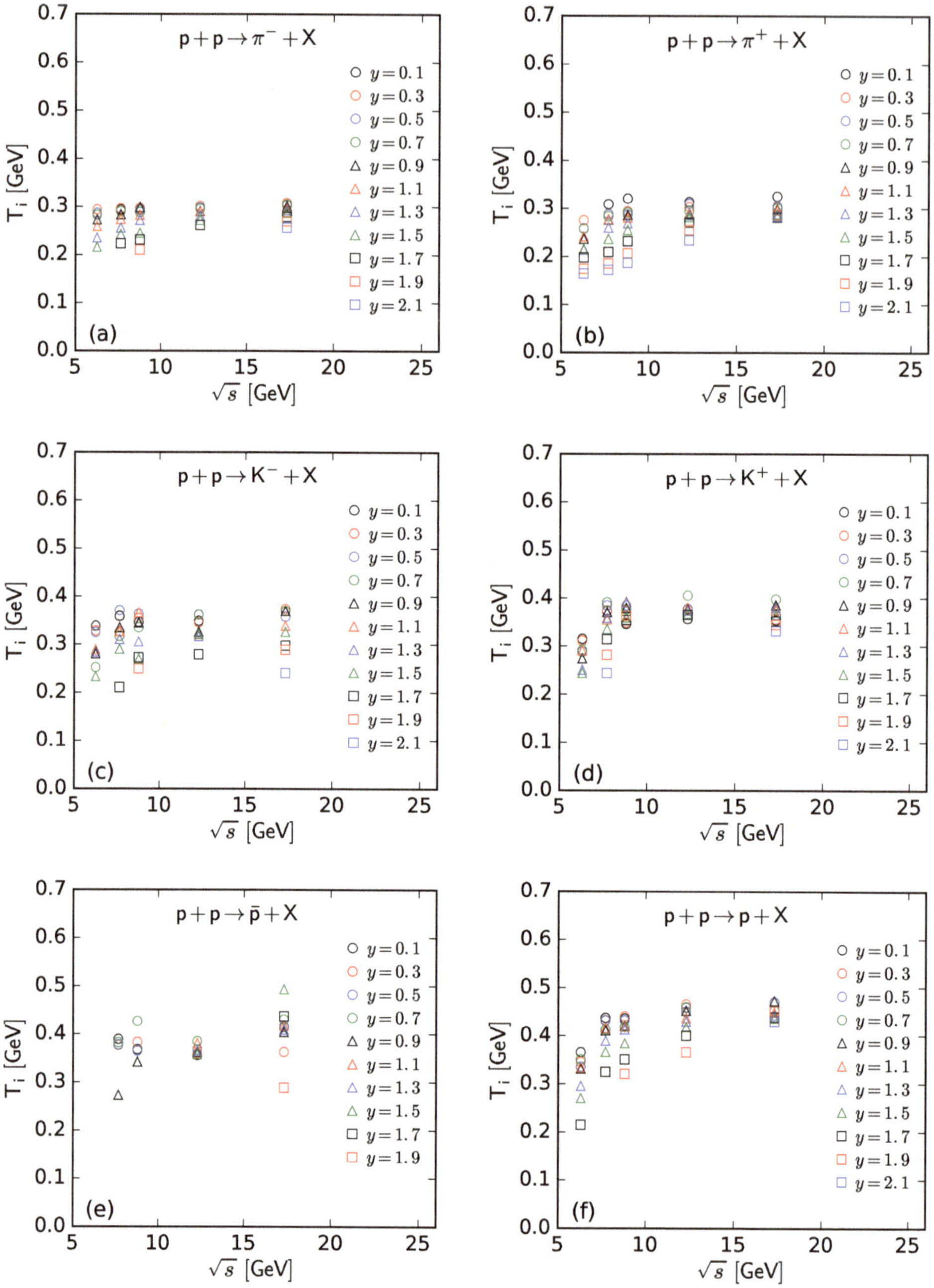

Figure 13. Dependence of T_i on $\sqrt{s}$ at different y from the spectra of (**a**) π^-, (**b**) π^+, (**c**) K^-, (**d**) K^+, (**e**) $\bar{p}$, and (**f**) p.

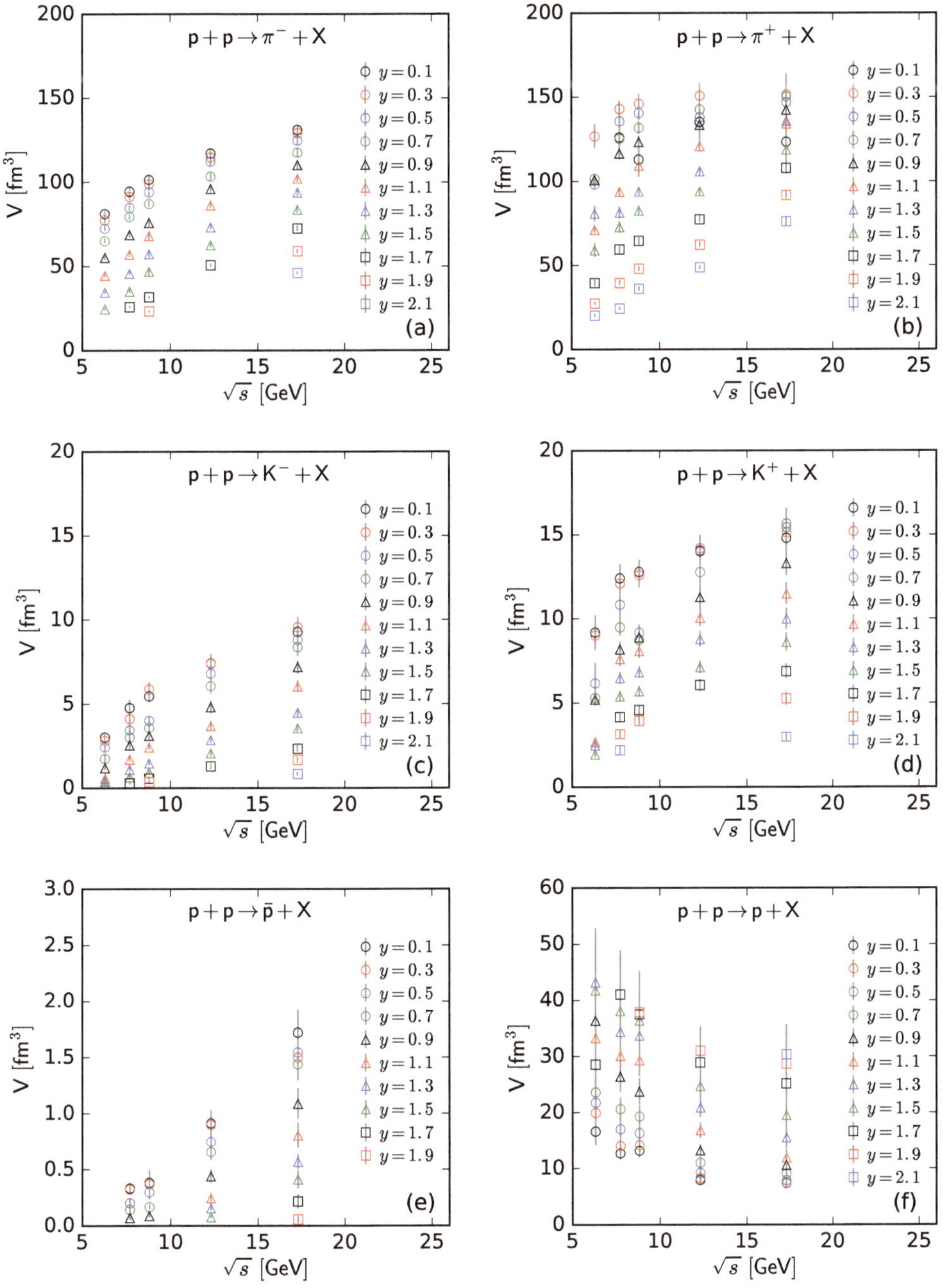

Figure 14. Dependence of V on $\sqrt{s}$ at different y from the spectra of (**a**) π^-, (**b**) π^+, (**c**) K^-, (**d**) K^+, (**e**) $\bar{p}$, and (**f**) p.

In the above discussions, although chemical potential μ runs through the entire process, it is an insensitive quantity in the fit and not a free parameter due to the fact that it depends on T_{ch} and k_j. Our previous work [52,53] shows that, from 6.3 to 17.3 GeV, μ_{π^+}, μ_{K^+}, and μ_p are around 0.041–0.017, 0.110–0.042, and 0.510–0.180 GeV, respectively, which are directly used in this work. These results have excluded the contributions from resonance decays [59]. Although the resonance decays contribute considerably to the yields of negative and positive hadrons, they contribute to the yield ratios, and then, the chemical potentials are small [52,53].

Before the summary and conclusions, it should be pointed out that the data sets analyzed by us are in a narrow and low-p_T range and obey the standard distribution. We believe that even if the narrow spectra are in a high-p_T range, the standard distribution can be used, and a high temperature can be obtained. The success of this work reflects that the classical concept and distribution can still play a great role in the field of high-energy collisions, though the application is in a local region. In our opinion, when researchers search for novel theoretical models, they first need to take into account classical theories.

Although the topic has been extensively studied in many papers for the SPS, RHIC, and LHC heavy-ion collisions and outline the validity of a nonextensive statistical distribution [60–66], those investigations used the spectra in a wide p_T range. It is unanimous that for the wide p_T spectra, a two-, three-, or multi-component standard distribution is needed in the fit. Then, a temperature fluctuation can be observed from the multi-component standard distribution. At this point, the Tsallis distribution is needed. This is the relationship between the standard distribution and the Tsallis distribution in the fit process.

In addition, in comparison with Hanbury–Brown–Twiss (HBT) results [67], large values of volume are obtained in the present work. The reason is that different volumes are studied. Generally, the former describes the system size in the initial state of collisions, and the latter is a reflection of the size of an expanded fireball in the final state (at the kinetic freeze-out) of collisions. Obviously, the latter is much larger than the former. The values of the three temperatures obtained in the present work seem reasonable.

4. Summary and Conclusions

The main observations and conclusions are summarized here.

(a) The transverse momentum spectra of the identified charged hadrons (π^-, π^+, K^-, K^+, $\bar{p}$, and p) with different rapidities produced in proton–proton collisions at center-of-mass energies $\sqrt{s} = 6.3, 7.7, 8.8, 12.3$, and 17.3 GeV have been studied using the standard distribution. The fitted results are in agreement with the experimental data measured by the NA61/SHINE Collaboration at the SPS. The effective temperature T, kinetic freeze-out temperature T_0, initial temperature T_i, and kinetic freeze-out volume V are extracted. The present work shows that the standard distribution coming from the relativistic ideal gas model works well in some cases.

(b) In most cases, T, T_0, and T_i decrease with the increase in rapidity y and increase with the increase in $\sqrt{s}$. There is a tendency of saturation for the three temperatures at $\sqrt{s} = 7.7$ GeV and above. From a quick increase to a slow saturation in the three temperatures, the transition energy 7.7 GeV is the boundary for proton-dominated and meson-dominated final states. For the spectra of produced hadrons (π^-, π^+, K^-, K^+, and $\bar{p}$), the extracted V also decreases with the increase in y and increases with the increase in $\sqrt{s}$. For the spectra of p, the extracted V increases with the increase in y and decreases with the increase in $\sqrt{s}$. This is opposite to other hadrons because p contains the pre-existing leading protons, which affect the result.

(c) The three temperatures do not show an obvious isospin dependence. However, V shows a significant isospin dependence. The reason for the isospin dependence of V is the electromagnetic interactions between positive (negative) hadrons and pre-existing protons. The exclusion (attraction) between positive (negative) hadrons and pre-existing protons causes larger (smaller) V of an emission source of positive (negative) hadrons. Compared with the three temperature types, V shows a larger mass dependence. The mass dependence of V is also a reflection of a mass-dependent differential kinetic freeze-out scenario or multiple kinetic freeze-out scenario.

Author Contributions: Conceptualization, F.-H.L. and K.K.O.; Methodology, F.-H.L. and K.K.O.; Software, P.-P.Y.; Validation, F.-H.L. and K.K.O.; Formal analysis, P.-P.Y.; Investigation, P.-P.Y.; Resources, P.-P.Y.; Data curation, P.-P.Y.; Writing—original draft, P.-P.Y.; Writing—review and editing, F.-H.L. and K.K.O.; Visualization, P.-P.Y.; Supervision, F.-H.L. and K.K.O.; Project administration, P.-P.Y. and F.-H.L.; Funding acquisition, P.-P.Y., F.-H.L. and K.K.O. All authors have read and agreed to the published version of the manuscript.

Funding: The work of P.-P.Y. was supported by the Shanxi Provincial Natural Science Foundation under Grant No. 202203021222308 and the Doctoral Scientific Research Foundations of Shanxi Province and Xinzhou Normal University. The work of F.-H.L. was supported by the National Natural Science Foundation of China under Grant No. 12147215, the Shanxi Provincial Natural Science Foundation under Grant No. 202103021224036, and the Fund for Shanxi "1331 Project" Key Subjects Construction. The work of K.K.O. was supported by the Agency of Innovative Development under the Ministry of Higher Education, Science and Innovations of the Republic of Uzbekistan within the fundamental project No. F3-20200929146 on the analysis of open data on heavy-ion collisions at RHIC and LHC.

Institutional Review Board Statement: Not applicable.

Informed Consent Statement: Not applicable.

Data Availability Statement: The data used to support the findings of this study are included within the article and are cited at relevant places within the text as references.

Conflicts of Interest: The authors declare no conflict of interest. The funding agencies have no role in the design of the study; in the collection, analysis, or interpretation of the data; in the writing of the manuscript; or in the decision to publish the results.

Appendix A. The Method to Obtain the Parameter and its Uncertainty

Let

$$y_i = f(x_i), \quad i = 1, 2, \ldots, n \tag{A1}$$

be the model value of the i-th fitting point. The physical quantities or parameters, λ $(\lambda_1, \lambda_2, \ldots, \lambda_j)$, can be obtained by fitting the experimental data, where j is the number of parameters, which includes the normalization constant. One has

$$\chi^2 = \sum_{i=1}^{n} \frac{[f(x_i) - Y_i]^2}{(\delta Y_i)^2}, \tag{A2}$$

where n is the number of fitting points, Y_i represents the experimental value, and δY_i represents the uncertainty of the experimental value, usually including statistical and systematic uncertainties.

Due to the small particle number of p_T samples being studied in this paper, the parameter uncertainty is assumed to follow the Student's distribution (shortened to the t-distribution) [68],

$$f(\lambda \mid \nu) = \frac{\left(\frac{\nu}{\nu+\lambda^2}\right)^{\frac{\nu+1}{2}} \Gamma\left(\frac{\nu+1}{2}\right)}{\sqrt{\mu\pi}\,\Gamma\left(\frac{\nu}{2}\right)}, \tag{A3}$$

where ν represents the ndof and $\Gamma(x)$ represents the Gamma function. With the increase in ν, the t-distribution gradually approaches the normal or Gaussian distribution $N(0,1)$. When ν approaches 1, the t-distribution approaches the Cauchy distribution.

In the present fitting, a 0.5% confidence interval is used to describe the parameter uncertainty. This means that there is a 0.5% probability that the parameter will fall within

$(\lambda_j - t\sigma, \lambda_j + t\sigma)$, where σ is the standard deviation of each parameter and t satisfies the equation

$$P = \int_{-t\sigma}^{t\sigma} f(\lambda) d\lambda = 0.005. \tag{A4}$$

The standard deviation of each parameter can be calculated using

$$\sigma = \sqrt{(J_\lambda^T J_\lambda)^{-1} \frac{s^2}{v}}, \tag{A5}$$

where

$$(J_\lambda)_{ij} = \frac{\partial [f(x_i) - Y_i]}{\partial \lambda_j} \tag{A6}$$

is the Jacobian matrix and determinant of the model, J_λ^T is the transpose of the Jacobian matrix, the superscript -1 represents matrix inversion, and

$$s^2 = \sum_{i=1}^{n} [f(x_i) - Y_i]^2 \tag{A7}$$

is the variance. Then, the corresponding best parameter is given by

$$\lambda_j \in [\lambda_j - t\sigma_{j,j}, \lambda_j + t\sigma_{j,j}] \tag{A8}$$

with an uncertainty of $t\sigma_{j,j}$.

Appendix B. Parameter Tables Obtained in the Fitting Process

Table A1. Values of T, V, χ^2, and ndof corresponding to the curves in Figures 1 and 2 for π^- and π^+ produced in pp collisions, respectively, where the values of $\sqrt{s}$ are given together. The values of χ^2 are reserved as an integer or the first non-zero decimal (if less than 1). The symbol "−" indicates that the data are not available.

$\sqrt{s}$ (GeV)	y	π^- T (GeV)	π^- V (fm^3)	π^- χ^2/ndof	π^+ T (GeV)	π^+ V (fm^3)	π^+ χ^2/ndof
6.3	0.1	0.118 ± 0.001	$(8.119 \pm 0.177) \times 10^1$	13/16	−	−	−
	0.3	0.123 ± 0.001	$(7.755 \pm 0.167) \times 10^1$	17/16	0.115 ± 0.002	$(1.268 \pm 0.072) \times 10^2$	0.09/6
	0.5	0.119 ± 0.001	$(7.247 \pm 0.157) \times 10^1$	15/16	0.108 ± 0.001	$(9.805 \pm 0.269) \times 10^1$	2/10
	0.7	0.118 ± 0.001	$(6.514 \pm 0.141) \times 10^1$	11/16	0.107 ± 0.001	$(1.017 \pm 0.028) \times 10^2$	1/10
	0.9	0.114 ± 0.001	$(5.516 \pm 0.121) \times 10^1$	11/16	0.098 ± 0.001	$(1.007 \pm 0.029) \times 10^2$	3/10
	1.1	0.108 ± 0.001	$(4.464 \pm 0.098) \times 10^1$	16/16	0.100 ± 0.001	$(7.106 \pm 0.179) \times 10^1$	2/9
	1.3	0.097 ± 0.001	$(3.466 \pm 0.081) \times 10^1$	14/15	0.087 ± 0.001	$(8.072 \pm 0.468) \times 10^1$	1/6
	1.5	0.088 ± 0.001	$(2.472 \pm 0.061) \times 10^1$	9/14	0.088 ± 0.001	$(5.903 \pm 0.423) \times 10^1$	1/4
	1.7	−	−	−	0.081 ± 0.001	$(3.957 \pm 0.196) \times 10^1$	4/5
	1.9	−	−	−	0.070 ± 0.001	$(2.736 \pm 0.112) \times 10^1$	4/6
	2.1	−	−	−	0.066 ± 0.001	$(2.036 \pm 0.099) \times 10^1$	0.1/5
7.7	0.1	0.123 ± 0.001	$(9.450 \pm 0.204) \times 10^1$	43/16	0.130 ± 0.003	$(1.261 \pm 0.137) \times 10^2$	0.5/3
	0.3	0.124 ± 0.001	$(9.141 \pm 0.197) \times 10^1$	33/16	0.121 ± 0.001	$(1.423 \pm 0.052) \times 10^2$	0.5/6
	0.5	0.122 ± 0.001	$(8.475 \pm 0.183) \times 10^1$	32/16	0.121 ± 0.001	$(1.356 \pm 0.037) \times 10^2$	2/9
	0.7	0.122 ± 0.001	$(7.944 \pm 0.172) \times 10^1$	19/16	0.119 ± 0.001	$(1.253 \pm 0.035) \times 10^2$	1/9
	0.9	0.119 ± 0.001	$(6.865 \pm 0.149) \times 10^1$	20/16	0.116 ± 0.001	$(1.165 \pm 0.032) \times 10^2$	2/9
	1.1	0.115 ± 0.001	$(5.715 \pm 0.124) \times 10^1$	17/16	0.116 ± 0.001	$(9.373 \pm 0.251) \times 10^1$	0.5/8
	1.3	0.107 ± 0.001	$(4.585 \pm 0.104) \times 10^1$	14/15	0.108 ± 0.001	$(8.131 \pm 0.354) \times 10^1$	1/7
	1.5	0.101 ± 0.001	$(3.526 \pm 0.081) \times 10^1$	12/15	0.098 ± 0.001	$(7.273 \pm 0.343) \times 10^1$	1/7
	1.7	0.092 ± 0.001	$(2.600 \pm 0.066) \times 10^1$	12/13	0.086 ± 0.001	$(5.933 \pm 0.223) \times 10^1$	4/8
	1.9	−	−	−	0.075 ± 0.001	$(3.963 \pm 0.141) \times 10^1$	12/8
	2.1	−	−	−	0.069 ± 0.001	$(2.440 \pm 0.115) \times 10^1$	35/9
8.8	0.1	0.124 ± 0.001	$(1.015 \pm 0.025) \times 10^2$	53/16	0.136 ± 0.003	$(1.130 \pm 0.104) \times 10^2$	0.2/4
	0.3	0.125 ± 0.001	$(9.894 \pm 0.219) \times 10^1$	70/16	0.124 ± 0.001	$(1.460 \pm 0.057) \times 10^2$	1/7
	0.5	0.124 ± 0.001	$(9.394 \pm 0.208) \times 10^1$	69/16	0.121 ± 0.001	$(1.405 \pm 0.044) \times 10^2$	1/8
	0.7	0.122 ± 0.001	$(8.704 \pm 0.193) \times 10^1$	43/16	0.123 ± 0.001	$(1.318 \pm 0.036) \times 10^2$	1/9
	0.9	0.126 ± 0.001	$(7.596 \pm 0.245) \times 10^1$	2/7	0.121 ± 0.001	$(1.235 \pm 0.035) \times 10^2$	1/9
	1.1	0.119 ± 0.001	$(6.808 \pm 0.245) \times 10^1$	0.2/6	0.118 ± 0.001	$(1.093 \pm 0.031) \times 10^2$	0.4/9
	1.3	0.114 ± 0.001	$(5.736 \pm 0.229) \times 10^1$	1/5	0.113 ± 0.001	$(9.364 \pm 0.273) \times 10^1$	1/9
	1.5	0.102 ± 0.001	$(4.687 \pm 0.238) \times 10^1$	0.2/4	0.107 ± 0.001	$(8.245 \pm 0.270) \times 10^1$	0.2/8
	1.7	0.096 ± 0.001	$(3.175 \pm 0.076) \times 10^1$	11/15	0.096 ± 0.001	$(6.446 \pm 0.198) \times 10^1$	4/9
	1.9	0.086 ± 0.001	$(2.337 \pm 0.062) \times 10^1$	8/13	0.084 ± 0.001	$(4.803 \pm 0.152) \times 10^1$	4/9
	2.1	−	−	−	0.076 ± 0.001	$(3.612 \pm 0.137) \times 10^1$	3/7

Table A1. *Cont.*

$\sqrt{s}$ (GeV)	y	π^- T (GeV)	π^- V (fm^3)	π^- χ^2/ndof	π^+ T (GeV)	π^+ V (fm^3)	π^+ χ^2/ndof
12.3	0.1	0.126 ± 0.001	$(1.172 \pm 0.025) \times 10^2$	88/16	0.132 ± 0.002	$(1.351 \pm 0.106) \times 10^2$	0.3/4
	0.3	0.126 ± 0.001	$(1.149 \pm 0.025) \times 10^2$	91/16	0.128 ± 0.002	$(1.507 \pm 0.076) \times 10^2$	0.4/6
	0.5	0.125 ± 0.001	$(1.123 \pm 0.024) \times 10^2$	69/16	0.131 ± 0.001	$(1.379 \pm 0.046) \times 10^2$	2/8
	0.7	0.124 ± 0.001	$(1.034 \pm 0.022) \times 10^2$	60/16	0.124 ± 0.001	$(1.426 \pm 0.046) \times 10^2$	0.4/7
	0.9	0.122 ± 0.001	$(9.590 \pm 0.206) \times 10^1$	51/16	0.121 ± 0.001	$(1.334 \pm 0.039) \times 10^2$	1/8
	1.1	0.122 ± 0.001	$(8.621 \pm 0.185) \times 10^1$	43/16	0.122 ± 0.001	$(1.208 \pm 0.033) \times 10^2$	1/9
	1.3	0.118 ± 0.001	$(7.327 \pm 0.158) \times 10^1$	27/16	0.120 ± 0.001	$(1.060 \pm 0.026) \times 10^2$	1/11
	1.5	0.114 ± 0.001	$(6.270 \pm 0.136) \times 10^1$	19/16	0.118 ± 0.001	$(9.376 \pm 0.233) \times 10^1$	1/11
	1.7	0.109 ± 0.001	$(5.063 \pm 0.112) \times 10^1$	20/16	0.113 ± 0.001	$(7.718 \pm 0.020) \times 10^1$	2/11
	1.9	–	–	–	0.106 ± 0.001	$(6.229 \pm 0.016) \times 10^1$	3/11
	2.1	–	–	–	0.097 ± 0.001	$(4.876 \pm 0.014) \times 10^1$	4/10
17.3	0.1	0.127 ± 0.001	$(1.312 \pm 0.028) \times 10^2$	89/16	0.137 ± 0.003	$(1.234 \pm 0.145) \times 10^2$	0.05/3
	0.3	0.129 ± 0.001	$(1.293 \pm 0.027) \times 10^2$	99/16	0.127 ± 0.002	$(1.514 \pm 0.127) \times 10^2$	0.1/4
	0.5	0.127 ± 0.001	$(1.248 \pm 0.026) \times 10^2$	93/16	0.128 ± 0.002	$(1.469 \pm 0.087) \times 10^2$	0.4/5
	0.7	0.127 ± 0.001	$(1.176 \pm 0.025) \times 10^2$	92/16	0.126 ± 0.002	$(1.502 \pm 0.064) \times 10^2$	1/6
	0.9	0.126 ± 0.001	$(1.104 \pm 0.023) \times 10^2$	87/16	0.125 ± 0.002	$(1.442 \pm 0.061) \times 10^2$	2/6
	1.1	0.124 ± 0.001	$(1.022 \pm 0.021) \times 10^2$	66/16	0.125 ± 0.001	$(1.342 \pm 0.045) \times 10^2$	1/7
	1.3	0.122 ± 0.001	$(9.378 \pm 0.971) \times 10^1$	37/16	0.120 ± 0.001	$(1.358 \pm 0.045) \times 10^2$	1/7
	1.5	0.120 ± 0.001	$(8.359 \pm 0.177) \times 10^1$	27/16	0.120 ± 0.001	$(1.189 \pm 0.039) \times 10^2$	0.2/7
	1.7	0.116 ± 0.001	$(7.247 \pm 0.154) \times 10^1$	20/16	0.117 ± 0.001	$(1.079 \pm 0.035) \times 10^2$	0.4/7
	1.9	0.112 ± 0.001	$(5.898 \pm 0.126) \times 10^1$	16/16	0.120 ± 0.001	$(9.162 \pm 0.030) \times 10^1$	0.1/7
	2.1	0.106 ± 0.001	$(4.619 \pm 0.100) \times 10^1$	20/16	0.118 ± 0.001	$(7.601 \pm 0.024) \times 10^1$	0.2/7

Table A2. Values of T, V, χ^2, and ndof corresponding to the curves in Figures 3 and 4 for K^- and K^+ produced in pp collisions, respectively.

$\sqrt{s}$ (GeV)	y	K^- T (GeV)	K^- V (fm^3)	K^- χ^2/ndof	K^+ T (GeV)	K^+ V (fm^3)	K^+ χ^2/ndof
6.3	0.1	0.121 ± 0.001	$(3.013 \pm 0.186) \times 10^0$	2/8	0.110 ± 0.002	$(9.184 \pm 0.990) \times 10^0$	1/5
	0.3	0.116 ± 0.001	$(2.824 \pm 0.195) \times 10^0$	1/7	0.108 ± 0.002	$(9.001 \pm 0.863) \times 10^0$	3/6
	0.5	0.115 ± 0.002	$(2.422 \pm 0.284) \times 10^0$	2/4	0.098 ± 0.003	$(6.165 \pm 1.215) \times 10^0$	6/4
	0.7	0.081 ± 0.001	$(1.748 \pm 0.247) \times 10^0$	3/4	0.100 ± 0.001	$(5.302 \pm 0.461) \times 10^0$	18/10
	0.9	0.094 ± 0.001	$(1.190 \pm 0.108) \times 10^0$	4/6	0.091 ± 0.001	$(5.201 \pm 0.359) \times 10^0$	5/10
	1.1	0.098 ± 0.002	$(5.859 \pm 0.722) \times 10^{-1}$	4/4	0.099 ± 0.001	$(2.675 \pm 0.166) \times 10^0$	10/9
	1.3	0.096 ± 0.005	$(4.229 \pm 1.372) \times 10^{-1}$	0.09/2	0.081 ± 0.001	$(2.467 \pm 0.243) \times 10^0$	3/6
	1.5	0.073 ± 0.003	$(2.041 \pm 0.654) \times 10^{-1}$	0.7/2	0.078 ± 0.001	$(1.935 \pm 0.200) \times 10^0$	5/6

Table A2. *Cont.*

$\sqrt{s}$ (GeV)	y	K^- T (GeV)	K^- V (fm^3)	K^- χ^2/ndof	K^+ T (GeV)	K^+ V (fm^3)	K^+ χ^2/ndof
7.7	0.1	0.130 ± 0.002	$(4.775 \pm 0.457) \times 10^0$	0.5/5	0.137 ± 0.002	$(1.240 \pm 0.087) \times 10^1$	1/7
	0.3	0.115 ± 0.002	$(4.123 \pm 0.335) \times 10^0$	2/6	0.138 ± 0.002	$(1.211 \pm 0.065) \times 10^1$	1/9
	0.5	0.136 ± 0.003	$(3.434 \pm 0.386) \times 10^0$	1/4	0.142 ± 0.001	$(1.083 \pm 0.084) \times 10^1$	1/6
	0.7	0.111 ± 0.002	$(3.004 \pm 0.244) \times 10^0$	1/6	0.146 ± 0.001	$(9.481 \pm 0.497) \times 10^0$	1/9
	0.9	0.120 ± 0.002	$(2.526 \pm 0.197) \times 10^0$	1/6	0.136 ± 0.001	$(8.165 \pm 0.439) \times 10^0$	1/9
	1.1	0.116 ± 0.002	$(1.703 \pm 0.162) \times 10^0$	1/5	0.129 ± 0.001	$(7.598 \pm 0.423) \times 10^0$	1/9
	1.3	0.108 ± 0.002	$(1.097 \pm 0.108) \times 10^0$	1/5	0.130 ± 0.001	$(6.466 \pm 0.358) \times 10^0$	4/9
	1.5	0.099 ± 0.003	$(6.563 \pm 1.121) \times 10^{-1}$	0.3/3	0.120 ± 0.001	$(5.394 \pm 0.317) \times 10^0$	2/9
	1.7	0.063 ± 0.002	$(2.875 \pm 0.807) \times 10^{-1}$	0.4/2	0.110 ± 0.001	$(4.168 \pm 0.277) \times 10^0$	1/8
	1.9	–	–	–	0.095 ± 0.001	$(3.140 \pm 0.256) \times 10^0$	2/7
	2.1	–	–	–	0.078 ± 0.001	$(2.172 \pm 0.229) \times 10^0$	7/6
8.8	0.1	0.124 ± 0.002	$(5.460 \pm 0.357) \times 10^0$	3/7	0.124 ± 0.001	$(1.278 \pm 0.072) \times 10^1$	3/9
	0.3	0.128 ± 0.002	$(5.890 \pm 0.431) \times 10^0$	0.4/6	0.126 ± 0.001	$(1.259 \pm 0.076) \times 10^1$	1/8
	0.5	0.133 ± 0.002	$(4.015 \pm 0.250) \times 10^0$	3/7	0.142 ± 0.001	$(9.172 \pm 0.468) \times 10^0$	2/9
	0.7	0.119 ± 0.002	$(3.591 \pm 0.245) \times 10^0$	1/7	0.139 ± 0.001	$(8.748 \pm 0.463) \times 10^0$	1/9
	0.9	0.124 ± 0.002	$(3.099 \pm 0.239) \times 10^0$	0.4/6	0.140 ± 0.001	$(8.885 \pm 0.470) \times 10^0$	0.5/9
	1.1	0.134 ± 0.002	$(2.426 \pm 0.185) \times 10^0$	1/6	0.146 ± 0.002	$(8.079 \pm 0.418) \times 10^0$	1/9
	1.3	0.106 ± 0.002	$(1.478 \pm 0.144) \times 10^0$	1/5	0.146 ± 0.001	$(6.816 \pm 0.352) \times 10^0$	1/9
	1.5	0.089 ± 0.002	$(9.181 \pm 1.199) \times 10^{-1}$	0.2/4	0.131 ± 0.001	$(5.690 \pm 0.313) \times 10^0$	1/9
	1.7	0.091 ± 0.002	$(5.613 \pm 0.733) \times 10^{-1}$	2/4	0.128 ± 0.001	$(4.577 \pm 0.252) \times 10^0$	2/9
	1.9	0.080 ± 0.003	$(3.513 \pm 0.860) \times 10^{-1}$	1/2	0.132 ± 0.001	$(3.929 \pm 0.228) \times 10^0$	5/8
12.3	0.1	0.125 ± 0.002	$(7.420 \pm 0.487) \times 10^0$	1/7	0.129 ± 0.002	$(1.404 \pm 0.093) \times 10^1$	1/7
	0.3	0.124 ± 0.002	$(7.399 \pm 0.563) \times 10^0$	0.3/6	0.139 ± 0.002	$(1.419 \pm 0.075) \times 10^1$	2/9
	0.5	0.132 ± 0.002	$(6.808 \pm 0.504) \times 10^0$	0.4/6	0.139 ± 0.001	$(1.398 \pm 0.073) \times 10^1$	1/9
	0.7	0.132 ± 0.002	$(6.064 \pm 0.452) \times 10^0$	0.4/6	0.152 ± 0.002	$(1.278 \pm 0.070) \times 10^1$	0.1/8
	0.9	0.115 ± 0.001	$(4.823 \pm 0.380) \times 10^0$	0.5/6	0.139 ± 0.002	$(1.128 \pm 0.072) \times 10^1$	1/7
	1.1	0.113 ± 0.001	$(3.704 \pm 0.262) \times 10^0$	1/7	0.140 ± 0.002	$(1.005 \pm 0.523) \times 10^1$	0.4/9
	1.3	0.111 ± 0.001	$(2.861 \pm 0.207) \times 10^0$	0.4/7	0.137 ± 0.001	$(8.783 \pm 0.463) \times 10^0$	1/9
	1.5	0.113 ± 0.002	$(2.064 \pm 0.196) \times 10^0$	0.08/5	0.134 ± 0.001	$(7.117 \pm 0.375) \times 10^0$	0.4/9
	1.7	0.094 ± 0.002	$(1.293 \pm 0.169) \times 10^0$	2/4	0.133 ± 0.001	$(6.053 \pm 0.354) \times 10^0$	0.3/8

Table A2. *Cont.*

$\sqrt{s}$ (GeV)	y	K^- T (GeV)	K^- V (fm^3)	K^- χ^2/ndof	K^+ T (GeV)	K^+ V (fm^3)	K^+ χ^2/ndof
17.3	0.1	0.137 ± 0.002	$(9.281 \pm 0.516) \times 10^0$	0.4/8	0.128 ± 0.001	$(1.480 \pm 0.088) \times 10^1$	2/8
	0.3	0.137 ± 0.002	$(9.562 \pm 0.601) \times 10^0$	0.05/7	0.129 ± 0.002	$(1.512 \pm 0.090) \times 10^1$	1/8
	0.5	0.130 ± 0.002	$(8.807 \pm 0.511) \times 10^0$	0.3/8	0.133 ± 0.002	$(1.566 \pm 0.092) \times 10^1$	3/8
	0.7	0.135 ± 0.002	$(8.375 \pm 0.527) \times 10^0$	0.1/7	0.149 ± 0.002	$(1.543 \pm 0.086) \times 10^1$	1/8
	0.9	0.136 ± 0.001	$(7.181 \pm 0.381) \times 10^0$	1/9	0.143 ± 0.002	$(1.331 \pm 0.075) \times 10^1$	0.2/8
	1.1	0.121 ± 0.001	$(6.036 \pm 0.346) \times 10^0$	1/44	0.139 ± 0.002	$(1.149 \pm 0.065) \times 10^1$	0.4/8
	1.3	0.115 ± 0.001	$(4.485 \pm 0.283) \times 10^0$	2/8	0.140 ± 0.002	$(9.986 \pm 0.633) \times 10^0$	0.1/7
	1.5	0.115 ± 0.001	$(3.557 \pm 0.225) \times 10^0$	0.5/8	0.133 ± 0.002	$(8.618 \pm 0.554) \times 10^0$	1/7
	1.7	0.102 ± 0.001	$(2.318 \pm 0.189) \times 10^0$	4/6	0.127 ± 0.002	$(6.873 \pm 0.449) \times 10^0$	0.4/7
	1.9	0.098 ± 0.002	$(1.667 \pm 0.167) \times 10^0$	0.1/5	0.124 ± 0.002	$(5.261 \pm 0.401) \times 10^0$	1/6
	2.1	0.076 ± 0.001	$(0.833 \pm 0.115) \times 10^0$	2/4	0.118 ± 0.002	$(2.968 \pm 0.205) \times 10^0$	6/7

Table A3. Values of T, V, χ^2, and ndof corresponding to the curves in Figures 5 and 6 for $\bar{p}$ and p produced in pp collisions, respectively.

$\sqrt{s}$ (GeV)	y	$\bar{p}$ T (GeV)	$\bar{p}$ V (fm^3)	$\bar{p}$ χ^2/ndof	p T (GeV)	p V (fm^3)	p χ^2/ndof
6.3	0.1	–	–	–	0.104 ± 0.001	$(1.662 \pm 0.245) \times 10^1$	4/7
	0.3	–	–	–	0.095 ± 0.001	$(1.993 \pm 0.244) \times 10^1$	9/10
	0.5	–	–	–	0.091 ± 0.001	$(2.176 \pm 0.286) \times 10^1$	8/10
	0.7	–	–	–	0.097 ± 0.001	$(2.359 \pm 0.273) \times 10^1$	17/10
	0.9	–	–	–	0.089 ± 0.001	$(3.633 \pm 0.520) \times 10^1$	4/9
	1.1	–	–	–	0.090 ± 0.001	$(3.326 \pm 0.630) \times 10^1$	3/6
	1.3	–	–	–	0.074 ± 0.001	$(4.321 \pm 0.963) \times 10^1$	1/6
	1.5	–	–	–	0.064 ± 0.001	$(4.180 \pm 1.066) \times 10^1$	2/6
	1.7	–	–	–	0.043 ± 0.001	$(2.855 \pm 1.225) \times 10^1$	0.3/6
7.7	0.1	0.114 ± 0.002	$(3.326 \pm 0.458) \times 10^{-1}$	9/7	0.135 ± 0.002	$(1.270 \pm 0.121) \times 10^1$	1/9
	0.3	0.109 ± 0.002	$(3.236 \pm 0.457) \times 10^{-1}$	14/7	0.133 ± 0.002	$(1.405 \pm 0.136) \times 10^1$	1/9
	0.5	0.109 ± 0.002	$(2.025 \pm 0.332) \times 10^{-1}$	10/6	0.133 ± 0.002	$(1.704 \pm 0.165) \times 10^1$	1/9
	0.7	0.111 ± 0.003	$(1.433 \pm 0.301) \times 10^{-1}$	10/5	0.125 ± 0.002	$(2.061 \pm 0.211) \times 10^1$	0.3/9
	0.9	0.065 ± 0.001	$(6.943 \pm 1.945) \times 10^{-2}$	12/5	0.124 ± 0.002	$(2.637 \pm 0.272) \times 10^1$	0.2/9
	1.1	–	–	–	0.126 ± 0.002	$(3.075 \pm 0.302) \times 10^1$	2/9
	1.3	–	–	–	0.114 ± 0.001	$(3.436 \pm 0.384) \times 10^1$	1/9
	1.5	–	–	–	0.104 ± 0.001	$(3.801 \pm 0.505) \times 10^1$	1/8
	1.7	–	–	–	0.086 ± 0.001	$(4.103 \pm 0.783) \times 10^1$	1/6

Table A3. *Cont.*

$\sqrt{s}$ (GeV)	y	T (GeV)	$\bar{p}$ V (fm^3)	χ^2/ndof	T (GeV)	p V (fm^3)	χ^2/ndof
8.8	0.1	0.105 ± 0.003	$(3.835 \pm 1.138) \times 10^{-1}$	6/3	0.135 ± 0.002	$(1.318 \pm 0.125) \times 10^1$	0.2/9
	0.3	0.112 ± 0.002	$(3.713 \pm 0.535) \times 10^{-1}$	4/7	0.137 ± 0.002	$(1.417 \pm 0.134) \times 10^1$	0.3/9
	0.5	0.104 ± 0.002	$(2.982 \pm 0.647) \times 10^{-1}$	4/5	0.133 ± 0.002	$(1.632 \pm 0.156) \times 10^1$	1/9
	0.7	0.131 ± 0.002	$(1.682 \pm 0.241) \times 10^{-1}$	29/6	0.127 ± 0.002	$(1.928 \pm 0.194) \times 10^1$	0.1/9
	0.9	0.094 ± 0.002	$(8.812 \pm 1.583) \times 10^{-2}$	11/6	0.128 ± 0.002	$(2.374 \pm 0.236) \times 10^1$	0.08/9
	1.1	–	–	–	0.127 ± 0.002	$(2.931 \pm 0.293) \times 10^1$	0.08/9
	1.3	–	–	–	0.125 ± 0.002	$(3.365 \pm 0.342) \times 10^1$	1/9
	1.5	–	–	–	0.112 ± 0.001	$(3.630 \pm 0.411) \times 10^1$	0.2/9
	1.7	–	–	–	0.097 ± 0.001	$(3.748 \pm 0.584) \times 10^1$	1/7
	1.9	–	–	–	0.085 ± 0.001	$(3.785 \pm 0.730) \times 10^1$	1/6
12.3	0.1	0.100 ± 0.001	$(9.128 \pm 1.170) \times 10^{-1}$	11/9	0.145 ± 0.002	$(7.934 \pm 0.667) \times 10^0$	1/10
	0.3	0.101 ± 0.001	$(9.005 \pm 1.106) \times 10^{-1}$	5/9	0.148 ± 0.002	$(8.276 \pm 0.678) \times 10^0$	1/10
	0.5	0.104 ± 0.002	$(7.481 \pm 0.905) \times 10^{-1}$	2/9	0.141 ± 0.002	$(9.202 \pm 0.872) \times 10^0$	1/9
	0.7	0.112 ± 0.001	$(6.565 \pm 0.747) \times 10^{-1}$	2/9	0.145 ± 0.002	$(1.100 \pm 0.101) \times 10^1$	0.2/9
	0.9	0.103 ± 0.001	$(4.409 \pm 0.586) \times 10^{-1}$	5/8	0.142 ± 0.002	$(1.324 \pm 0.105) \times 10^1$	1/11
	1.1	0.111 ± 0.001	$(2.464 \pm 0.303) \times 10^{-1}$	4/8	0.135 ± 0.001	$(1.683 \pm 0.139) \times 10^1$	0.1/11
	1.3	0.103 ± 0.002	$(1.558 \pm 0.232) \times 10^{-1}$	8/7	0.132 ± 0.001	$(2.091 \pm 0.177) \times 10^1$	0.3/11
	1.5	0.100 ± 0.002	$(7.733 \pm 1.344) \times 10^{-2}$	11/6	0.127 ± 0.001	$(2.468 \pm 0.218) \times 10^1$	1/11
	1.7	–	–	–	0.119 ± 0.001	$(2.891 \pm 0.274) \times 10^1$	2/11
	1.9	–	–	–	0.104 ± 0.001	$(3.098 \pm 0.434) \times 10^1$	1/8
17.3	0.1	0.126 ± 0.002	$(1.719 \pm 0.206) \times 10^0$	0.4/8	0.150 ± 0.002	$(7.374 \pm 0.755) \times 10^0$	0.2/8
	0.3	0.102 ± 0.001	$(1.499 \pm 0.174) \times 10^0$	11/10	0.150 ± 0.002	$(7.430 \pm 0.760) \times 10^0$	0.2/8
	0.5	0.126 ± 0.001	$(1.544 \pm 0.149) \times 10^0$	3/10	0.150 ± 0.002	$(7.882 \pm 0.810) \times 10^0$	0.08/8
	0.7	0.133 ± 0.002	$(1.438 \pm 0.144) \times 10^0$	1/9	0.143 ± 0.002	$(9.096 \pm 0.964) \times 10^0$	0.2/8
	0.9	0.121 ± 0.002	$(1.086 \pm 0.136) \times 10^0$	2/8	0.151 ± 0.002	$(1.061 \pm 0.109) \times 10^1$	0.5/8
	1.1	0.127 ± 0.002	$(0.805 \pm 0.111) \times 10^0$	1/7	0.141 ± 0.002	$(1.191 \pm 0.149) \times 10^1$	0.09/7
	1.3	0.123 ± 0.002	$(0.568 \pm 0.066) \times 10^0$	4/8	0.138 ± 0.002	$(1.555 \pm 0.196) \times 10^1$	0.04/7
	1.5	0.161 ± 0.005	$(0.410 \pm 0.081) \times 10^0$	1/5	0.135 ± 0.002	$(1.950 \pm 0.248) \times 10^1$	0.02/7
	1.7	0.136 ± 0.005	$(0.214 \pm 0.064) \times 10^0$	2/4	0.136 ± 0.002	$(2.515 \pm 0.392) \times 10^1$	0.2/6
	1.9	0.071 ± 0.003	$(0.057 \pm 0.029) \times 10^0$	1/3	0.142 ± 0.003	$(2.868 \pm 0.491) \times 10^1$	0.001/5
	2.1	–	–	–	0.132 ± 0.003	$(3.033 \pm 0.531) \times 10^1$	0.4/5

References

1. Arsene, I.; Bearden, I.G.; Beavis, D.; Besliu, C.; Budick, B.; Bggild, H.; Chasman, C.; Chasman, C.; Christensen, C.H.; Christiansen, P.; et al. Quark gluon plasma and color glass condensate at RHIC? The perspective from the BRAHMS experiment. *Nucl. Phys. A* **2005**, *757*, 1–27. [CrossRef]
2. Adcox, K.; Adler, S.S.; Afanasiev, S.; Aidala, C.; Ajitanand, N.N.; Akiba, Y.; Al-Jamel, A.; Alexander, J.; Amirikas, R.; Aoki, K.; et al. Formation of dense partonic matter in relativistic nucleus-nucleus collisions at RHIC: Experimental evaluation by the PHENIX collaboration. *Nucl. Phys. A* **2005**, *757*, 184–283. [CrossRef]
3. Adams, J.; Aggarwal, M.M.; Ahammed, Z.; Amonett, J.; Anderson, B.D.; Arkhipkin, D.; Averichev, G.S.; Badyal, S.K.; Bai, Y.; Balewski, J.; et al. Experimental and theoretical challenges in the search for the quark gluon plasma: The STAR collaboration's critical assessment of the evidence from RHIC collisions. *Nucl. Phys. A* **2005**, *757*, 102–183. [CrossRef]
4. Schukraft, J. Heavy ion physics with the ALICE experiment at the CERN LHC. *Phil. Trans. R. Soc. Lond. A* **2012**, *370*, 917–932.
5. Braun-Munzinger, P.; Stachel, J. The quest for the quark-gluon plasma. *Nature* **2007**, *448*, 302–309. [CrossRef] [PubMed]
6. Harris, J.W.; Müller, B. The search for the quark-gluon plasma. *Ann. Rev. Nucl. Part. Sci.* **1996**, *46*, 71–107. [CrossRef]
7. Heinz, U.W.; Jacob, M. Evidence for a new state of matter: An assessment of the results from the CERN lead beam programme. *arXiv* **2000**, arXiv:nucl-th/0002042v1.
8. Podlaski, P. Results on system size dependence of strangeness production in the CERN SPS energy range from NA61/SHINE. *EPJ Web Conf.* **2023**, *276*, 03008. [CrossRef]
9. Tannenbaum, M.J. Recent results in relativistic heavy ion collisions: From 'a new state of matter' to 'the perfect fluid'. *Rept. Prog. Phys.* **2006**, *69*, 2005–2060. [CrossRef]
10. Abdulhamid, M.I.; Aboona, B.E.; Adam, J.; Adamczyk, L.; Adams, J.R.; Aggarwal, I.; Aggarwal, M.M.; Ahammed, Z.; Anderson, D.M.; Aschenauer, E.C.; et al. Energy dependence of intermittency for charged hadrons in Au+Au collisions at RHIC. *Phys. Lett. B* **2023**, *845*, 138165. [CrossRef]
11. Abdulhamid, M.I.; Aboona, B.E.; Adam, J.; Adamczyk, L.; Adams, J.R.; Agakishiev, G.; Aggarwal, I.; Aggarwal, M.M.; Ahammed, Z.; Aitbaev, A. Beam energy dependence of triton production and yield ratio ($N_t \times N_p/N_d^2$) in Au+Au collisions at RHIC. *Phys. Rev. Lett.* **2023**, *130*, 202301. [CrossRef] [PubMed]
12. Aboona, B.E.; Adam, J.; Adamczyk, L.; Adams, J.R.; Aggarwal, I.; Aggarwal, M.M.; Ahammed, Z.; Anderson, D.M.; Aschenauer, E.C.; Atchison, J. Search for the chiral magnetic effect in Au+Au collisions at $\sqrt{s_{NN}} = 27$ GeV with the STAR forward event plane detectors. *Phys. Lett. B* **2023**, *839*, 137779. [CrossRef]
13. Adam, J.; Adamczyk, L.; Adams, J.R.; Adkins, J.K.; Agakishiev, G.; Aggarwal, M.M.; Ahammed, Z.; Alekseev, I.; Anderson, D.M.; Aoyama, R.; et al. Bulk properties of the system formed in $Au + Au$ collisions at $\sqrt{s_{NN}} = 14.5$ GeV at the BNL STAR detector. *Phys. Rev. C* **2020**, *101*, 024905. [CrossRef]
14. Helmut, S. Limits of confinement: The first 15 years of ultra-relativistic heavy ion studies. *Nucl. Phys. A* **2003**, *715*, 3c–19c.
15. Back, B.B.; Baker, M.D.; Ballintijn, M.; Barton, D.S.; Becker, B.; Betts, R.R.; Bickley, A.A.; Bindel, R.; Budzanowski, A.; Busza, W.; et al. The PHOBOS perspective on discoveries at RHIC. *Nucl. Phys. A* **2005**, *757*, 28–101. [CrossRef]
16. Aamodt, K.; Abelev, B.; Quintana, A.A.; Adamová, D.; Adare, A.M.; Aggarwal, M.M.; Rinella, G.A.; Agocs, A.G.; Salazar, S.A.; Ahammed, Z.; et al. Elliptic flow of charged particles in Pb-Pb collisions at 2.76 TeV. *Phys. Rev. Lett.* **2010**, *105*, 252302. [CrossRef] [PubMed]
17. Aamodt, K.; Abelev, B.; Quintana, A.A.; Adamová, D.; Adare, A.M.; Aggarwal, M.M.; Rinella, G.A.; Agocs, A.G.; Salazar, S.A.; Ahammed, Z.; et al. Charged-particle multiplicity density at mid-rapidity in central Pb-Pb collisions at $\sqrt{s_{NN}} = 2.76$ TeV. *Phys. Rev. Lett.* **2010**, *105*, 252301. [CrossRef]
18. Aamodt, K.; Quintana, A.A.; Adamová, D.; Adare, A.M.; Aggarwal, M.M.; Rinella, G.A.; Agocs, A.G.; Salazar, S.A.; Ahammed, Z.; Ahmad, N.; et al. Centrality dependence of the charged-particle multiplicity density at mid-rapidity in Pb-Pb collisions at $\sqrt{s_{NN}} = 2.76$ TeV. *Phys. Rev. Lett.* **2011**, *106*, 032301. [CrossRef]
19. Aamodt, K.; Abelev, B.; Quintana, A.A.; Adamová, D.; Adare, A.M.; Aggarwal, M.M.; Rinella, G.A.; Agocs, A.G.; Agostinelli, A.; Salazar, S.A.; et al. Higher harmonic anisotropic flow measurements of charged particles in Pb-Pb collisions at $\sqrt{s_{NN}} = 2.76$ TeV. *Phys. Rev. Lett.* **2011**, *107*, 032301. [CrossRef]
20. Adler, S.S.; Afanasiev, S.; Aidala, C.; Ajitanand, N.N.; Akiba, Y.; Alexander, J.; Amirikas, R.; Aphecetche, L.; Aronson, S.H.; Averbeck, R.; et al. Identified charged particle spectra and yields in Au+Au collisions at $\sqrt{s_{NN}} = 200$ GeV. *Phys. Rev. C* **2004**, *69*, 034909. [CrossRef]
21. Van Hove, L. Multiplicity dependence of p_t spectrum as a possible signal for a phase transition in hadronic collisions. *Phys. Lett. B* **1982**, *118*, 138–140. [CrossRef]
22. Andronic, A.; Braun-Munzinger, P.; Stachel, J. Hadron production in central nucleus-nucleus collisions at chemical freeze-out. *Nucl. Phys. A* **2006**, *772*, 167–199. [CrossRef]
23. Cleymans, J.; Oeschler, H.; Redlich, K.; Wheaton, S. Comparison of chemical freeze-out criteria in heavy-ion collisions. *Phys. Rev. C* **2006**, *73*, 034905. [CrossRef]
24. Andronic, A.; Braun-Munzinger, P.; Stachel, J. Thermal hadron production in relativistic nuclear collisions. *Acta Phys. Pol. B* **2009**, *40*, 1005–1012.

25. Andronic, A.; Braun-Munzinger, P.; Stachel, J. The horn, the hadron mass spectrum and the QCD phase diagram: The statistical model of hadron production in central nucleus-nucleus collisions. *Nucl. Phys. A* **2010**, *834*, 237c–240c. [CrossRef]
26. Redlich, K.; Cleymans, J.; Oeschler, H.; Tounsi, A. Particle production and equilibration in heavy ion collisions. *Acta Phys. Polon. B* **2002**, *33*, 1609–1628.
27. Wheaton, S.; Cleymans, J.; Hauer, M. THERMUS: A thermal model package for ROOT. *Comput. Phys. Commun.* **2009**, *180*, 84–106. [CrossRef]
28. Andronic, A.; Beutler, F.; Braun-Munzinger, P.; Redlich, K.; Stachel, J. Statistical hadronization of heavy flavor quarks in elementary collisions: Successes and failures. *Phys. Lett. B* **2009**, *678*, 350–354. [CrossRef]
29. Aduszkiewicz, A.; Ali, Y.; Andronov, E.; Antićić, T.; Baatar, B.; Baszczyk, M.; Bhosale, S.; Blondel, A.; Bogomilov, M.; Brandin, A.; et al. Measurements of $\pi^{\pm}$, $K^{\pm}$, p and $\bar{p}$ spectra in proton–proton interactions at 20, 31, 40, 80 and 158 GeV/c with the NA61/SHINE spectrometer at the CERN SPS. *Eur. Phys. J. C* **2017**, *77*, 671. [CrossRef]
30. Cleymans, J.; Worku, D. Relativistic thermodynamics: Transverse momentum distributions in high-energy physics. *Eur. Phys. J. A* **2012**, *48*, 160. [CrossRef]
31. Abelev, B.I.; Adams, J.; Aggarwal, M.M.; Ahammed, Z.; Amonett, J.; Anderson, B.D.; Anderson, M.; Arkhipkin, D.; Averichev, G.S.; Bai, Y.; et al. Strange particle production in $p+p$ collisions at $\sqrt{s}=200$ GeV. *Phys. Rev. C* **2007**, *75*, 064901. [CrossRef]
32. Tsallis, C. Possible generalization of Boltzmann-Gibbs statistics. *J. Stat. Phys.* **1988**, *52*, 479–487. [CrossRef]
33. Biro, T.S.; Purcsel, G.; Urmossy, K. Non-extensive approach to quark matter. *Eur. Phys. J. A* **2009**, *40*, 325–340. [CrossRef]
34. Zheng, H.; Zhu, L.L.; Bonasera, A. Systematic analysis of hadron spectra in $p+p$ collisions using Tsallis distributions. *Phys. Rev. D* **2015**, *92*, 074009. [CrossRef]
35. Zheng, H.; Zhu, L.L. Can Tsallis distribution fit all the particle spectra produced at RHIC and LHC? *Adv. High Energy Phys.* **2015**, *2015*, 180491. [CrossRef]
36. Wang, X.N.; Hwa, R.C. The effect of jet production on the multiplicity dependence of average transverse momentum. *Phys. Rev. D* **1989**, *39*, 187–194. [CrossRef] [PubMed]
37. Sjöstrand, T.; van Zijl, M. A multiple-interaction model for the event structure in hadron collisions. *Phys. Rev. D* **1987**, *36*, 2019–2041. [CrossRef]
38. Parvan, A.S. Non-extensive statistics effects in transverse momentum spectra of hadrons. *arXiv* **2015**, arXiv:1502.01581.
39. Rath, R.; Khuntia, A.; Sahoo, R.; Cleymans, J. Event multiplicity, transverse momentum and energy dependence of charged particle production, and system thermodynamics in *pp* collisions at the Large Hadron Collider. *J. Phys. G* **2020**, *47*, 055111. [CrossRef]
40. Schnedermann, E.; Sollfrank, J.; Heinz, U. Thermal phenomenology of hadrons from 200A GeV S+S collisions. *Phys. Rev. C* **1993**, *48*, 2462–2475. [CrossRef]
41. Hagedorn, R. Multiplicities, p_T distributions and the expected hadron $\longrightarrow$ quark-gluon phase transition. *Riv. Nuovo Cimento* **1983**, *6*, 1–50. [CrossRef]
42. Adamczyk, L.; Adkins, J.K.; Agakishiev, G.; Aggarwal, M.M.; Ahammed, Z.; Ajitanand, N.N.; Alekseev, I.; Anderson, D.M.; Aoyama, R.; Aparin, A.; et al. Bulk properties of the medium produced in relativistic heavy-ion collisions from the beam energy scan program. *Phys. Rev. C* **2017**, *96*, 044904. [CrossRef]
43. Braun-Munzinger, P.; Stachel, J.; Wessels, J.P.; Xu, N. Thermal equilibration and expansion in nucleus-nucleus collisions at the AGS. *Phys. Lett. B* **1995**, *344*, 43–48. [CrossRef]
44. Andronic, A.; Braun-Munzinger, P.; Stachel, J. Thermal hadron production in relativistic nuclear collisions: The hadron mass spectrum, the horn, and the QCD phase transition. *Phys. Lett. B* **2009**, *673*, 142–145. [CrossRef]
45. Abelev, B.I.; Aggarwal, M.M.; Ahammed, Z.; Anderson, B.D.; Arkhipkin, D.; Averichev, G.S.; Bai, Y.; Balewski, J.; Barannikova, O.; Barnby, L.S.; et al. Systematic measurements of identified particle spectra in *pp*, *d*+Au and Au+Au collisions from STAR. *Phys. Rev. C* **2009**, *79*, 034909. [CrossRef]
46. Cleymans, J.; Oeschler, H.; Redlich, K. Influence of impact parameter on thermal description of relativistic heavy ion collisions at (1–2)A GeV. *Phys. Rev. C* **1999**, *59*, 1663–1673. [CrossRef]
47. Braun-Munzinger, P.; Heppe, I.; Stachel, J. Chemical equilibration in Pb+Pb collisions at the SPS. *Phys. Lett. B* **1999**, *465*, 15–20. [CrossRef]
48. Manninen, J.; Becattini, F. Chemical freeze-out in ultra-relativistic heavy ion collisions at $\sqrt{s_{NN}}=130$ and 200 GeV. *Phys. Rev. C* **2008**, *78*, 054901. [CrossRef]
49. Andronic, A.; Braun-Munzinger, P.; Redlich, K. Decoding the phase structure of QCD via particle production at high energy. *Nature* **2018**, *561*, 321–330. [CrossRef]
50. Koch, P.; Rafelski, J.; Greiner, W. Strange hadron in hot nuclear matter. *Phys. Lett. B* **1983**, *123*, 321–330. [CrossRef]
51. Braun-Munzinger, P.; Magestro, D.; Redlich, K.; Stachel, J. Hadron production in Au-Au collisions at RHIC. *Phys. Lett. B* **2001**, *518*, 41–46. [CrossRef]
52. Lao, H.-L.; Gao, Y.-Q.; Liu, F.-H. Energy dependent chemical potentials of light particles and quarks from yield ratios of antiparticles to particles in high energy collisions. *Universe* **2019**, *5*, 152. [CrossRef]
53. Lao, H.-L.; Gao, Y.-Q.; Liu, F.-H. Light particle and quark chemical potentials from negatively to positively charged particle yield ratios corrected by removing strong and weak decays. *Adv. High Energy Phys.* **2020**, *2020*, 5064737. [CrossRef]
54. Gardim, F.G.; Giacalone, G.; Luzum, M.; Ollitrault, J.Y. Thermodynamics of hot strong-interaction matter from ultrarelativistic nuclear collisions. *Nat. Phys.* **2020**, *16*, 615–619 [CrossRef]

55. Waqas, M.; Peng, G.-X.; Ajaz, M.; Haj Ismail, A.; Wazir, Z.; Li, L.-L. Extraction of different temperatures and kinetic freeze-out volume in high energy collisions. *J. Phys. G* **2022**, *49*, 095102. [CrossRef]
56. Gutay, L.J.; Hirsch, A.S.; Pajares, C.; Scharenberg, R.P.; Srivastava, B.K. De-confinement in small systems: Clustering of color sources in high multiplicity $\bar{p}p$ collisions at $\sqrt{s} = 1.8$ TeV. *Int. J. Mod. Phys. E* **2015**, *24*, 1550101. [CrossRef]
57. Scharenberg, R.P.; Srivastava, B.K.; Pajares, C. Exploring the initial stage of high multiplicity proton–proton collisions by determining the initial temperature of the quark-gluon plasma. *Phys. Rev. D* **2019**, *100*, 114040. [CrossRef]
58. Sahoo, P.; De, S.; Tiwari, S.K.; Sahoo, R. Energy and centrality dependent study of deconfinement phase transition in a color string percolation approach at RHIC energies. *Eur. Phys. J. A* **2018**, *54*, 136. [CrossRef]
59. Yu, N.; Luo, X.F. Particle decay from statistical thermal model in high-energy nucleus-nucleus collisions. *Eur. Phys. J. A* **2019**, *55*, 26. [CrossRef]
60. Biyajima, M.; Kaneyama, M.; Mizoguchi, T.; Wilk, G. Analyses of k_t distributions at RHIC by means of some selected statistical and stochastic models. *Eur. Phys. J. C* **2005**, *40*, 243–250. [CrossRef]
61. Cleymans, J.; Hamar, G.; Levai, P.; Wheaton, S. Near-thermal equilibrium with Tsallis distributions in heavy-ion collisions. *J. Phys. G* **2009**, *36*, 064018. [CrossRef]
62. Shao, M.; Yi, L.; Tang, Z.B.; Chen, H.F.; Li, C.; Xu, Z.B. Examination of the species and beam energy dependence of particle spectra using Tsallis statistics. *J. Phys. G* **2010**, *37*, 085104. [CrossRef]
63. Wong, C.-Y.; Wilk, G.; Cirto, L.J.L.; Tsallis, C. From QCD-based hard-scattering to nonextensive statistical mechanical descriptions of transverse momentum spectra in high-energy pp and $p\bar{p}$ collisions. *Phys. Rev. D* **2015**, *91*, 114027. [CrossRef]
64. Hui, J.-Q.; Jiang, Z.-J.; Xu, D.-F. A description of the transverse momentum distributions of charged particles produced in heavy ion collisions at RHIC and LHC energies. *Adv. High Energy Phys.* **2018**, *2018*, 7682325. [CrossRef]
65. Tripathy, S.; Tiwari, S.K.; Younus, M.; Sahoo, R. Elliptic flow in Pb+Pb collisions at $\sqrt{s_{NN}} = 2.76$ TeV at the LHC using Boltzmann transport equation with non-extensive statistics. *Eur. Phys. J. A* **2018**, *54*, 38. [CrossRef]
66. Rybczyński, M.; Włodarczyk, Z. Tsallis statistics approach to the transverse momentum distributions in p-p collisions. *Eur. Phys. J. C* **2014**, *74*, 2785. [CrossRef]
67. Zhang, S.; Ma, Y.G.; Chen, J.H.; Zhong, C. Beam energy dependence of Hanbury-Brown-Twiss radii from a blast-wave model. *Adv. High Energy Phys.* **2016**, *2016*, 9414239. [CrossRef]
68. Hogg, R.V.; McKean, J.W.; Craig, A.T. *Introduction to Mathematical Statistics*, 8th ed.; Pearson: Boston, MA, USA, 2018.

entropy

Article

On Complex Matrix-Variate Dirichlet Averages and Its Applications in Various Sub-Domains

Princy Thankamani [1], Nicy Sebastian [2] and Hans J. Haubold [3,*]

1 Department of Statistics, Cochin University of Science and Technology, Cochin 682 022, India; princyt@cusat.ac.in
2 Department of Statistics, St. Thomas College Thrissur, Calicut University, Thenhipalam 680 001, India; nicycms@gmail.com
3 Office for Outer Space Affairs, United Nations, Vienna International Center, A-1400 Vienna, Austria
* Correspondence: hans.haubold@gmail.com

Abstract: This paper is about Dirichlet averages in the matrix-variate case or averages of functions over the Dirichlet measure in the complex domain. The classical power mean contains the harmonic mean, arithmetic mean and geometric mean (Hardy, Littlewood and Polya), which is generalized to the y-mean by de Finetti and hypergeometric mean by Carlson; see the references herein. Carlson's hypergeometric mean averages a scalar function over a real scalar variable type-1 Dirichlet measure, which is known in the current literature as the Dirichlet average of that function. The idea is examined when there is a type-1 or type-2 Dirichlet density in the complex domain. Averages of several functions are computed in such Dirichlet densities in the complex domain. Dirichlet measures are defined when the matrices are Hermitian positive definite. Some applications are also discussed.

Keywords: Dirichlet average; generalized type-1; type-2 Dirichlet measures; functions of matrix argument; Dirichlet measures in the complex domain

MSC: 15B52; 15B48; 26B10; 33C60; 33C65; 60E05; 62E15; 62H10; 62H05

Citation: Thankamani, P.; Sebastian, N.; Haubold, H.J. On Complex Matrix-Variate Dirichlet Averages and Its Applications in Various Sub-Domains. *Entropy* **2023**, *25*, 1534. https://doi.org/10.3390/e25111534

Received: 27 September 2023
Revised: 1 November 2023
Accepted: 7 November 2023
Published: 10 November 2023

1. Introduction

Dirichlet averages are a type of weighted average used in mathematics and statistics. Given a function $f(x)$ and a probability distribution $p(x)$ defined over a domain D, the Dirichlet average of $f(x)$ over D with respect to $p(x)$ is defined as:

$$\langle f\rangle_p = \frac{1}{|D|}\int_D f(x)p(x)dx,$$

where $|D|$ is the measure of the domain D. Intuitively, the Dirichlet average is the average value of $f(x)$ weighted by the probability distribution $p(x)$ over the domain D. The name "Dirichlet average" comes from the fact that the formula for the average involves an integral that is similar to the Dirichlet integral, which is an important integral in the theory of functions of a complex variable. Dirichlet averages have connections to many other important mathematical concepts, such as harmonic analysis, the Fourier series, and the theory of functions of a complex variable. Dirichlet averages play an important role in various problems in number theory, including the study of prime numbers and the distribution of arithmetic functions; see [1,2], etc. [3] used Dirichlet averages in the study of random matrices. Dirichlet averages are used in the study of option pricing and risk management in finance; see [4,5] used it in the study of Bayesian inference and probabilistic modeling in machine learning. Dirichlet averages are used in the study of natural language processing and text analysis; see [6]. Overall, Dirichlet averages are an important mathematical tool that have many applications in various disciplines. They provide a way to compute the average value of a function over a probability distribution and have connections to many other important mathematical concepts.

In [7], there is a discussion of the classical power mean, which contains the harmonic, arithmetic and geometric means. The classical weighted average is of the following form:

$$f(b) = [w_1 z_1^b + \ldots + w_n z_n^b]^{\frac{1}{b}}.$$

where all the quantities are real scalar and where $w' = (w_1, \ldots, w_n), z' = (z_1, \ldots, z_n)$, $z_j > 0$, $w_j > 0, j = 1, \ldots, n$, and $\sum_{j=1}^n w_j = 1$ with a prime denoting the transpose. For $b = 1$, $f(1)$ gives $\sum_{j=1}^n w_j z_j$ or the arithmetic mean; when $b = -1$, $f(-1)$ provides $[\sum_j (\frac{w_j}{z_j})]^{-1}$ = the harmonic mean and when $b \to 0_+$, then $f(0_+)$ yields $\prod_{j=1}^n z_j^{w_j}$ = the geometric mean. This weighted mean $f(b)$ is generalized to the y-mean by de Finetti [8] and to the hypergeometric mean by Carlson [9]. A real scalar variable type-1 Dirichlet measure is involved for the weights $(w_1, \ldots, w_{n-1})$ in Carlson's generalization, and then average of a given function is taken over this Dirichlet measure. In the current literature this is known as Dirichlet average of that function, the function need not reduce to the classical arithmetic, harmonic, and geometric means. Additionally, Carlson offered a comprehensive and in-depth examination of the many types of Dirichlet averages Carlson developed the notion of the Dirichlet average in his work, see also [9–14]. The integral mean of a function with respect to the Dirichlet measure is known as its "Drichlet average".

The paper is organized as follows: Section 1 gives the basic concepts for developing the theory of the matrix-variate Dirichlet measure in complex domain. Dirichlet averages for a function of matrix argument in the complex domain are developed in Section 2. In Section 3, we discuss the complex matrix-variate type-2 Dirichlet measure and averages over some useful matrix-variate functions. The rectangular matrix-variate Dirichlet measure is presented in Section 4. In Section 5, we establish the connection between Dirichlet averages and Tsallis entropy. Section 6 provides an elaborate account of the diverse sub-domains in which the technology finds valuable applications.

Complex Domain

In the present paper, we consider Dirichlet averages of various functions over Dirichlet measures in the complex domain in the matrix-variate cases. All matrices appearing in this paper are Hermitian positive definite and $p \times p$ unless stated otherwise. In order to distinguish, matrices in the complex domain will be denoted by a tilde as $\tilde{X}$ and real matrices will be written without the tilde as X. We consider real-valued scalar functions of the complex matrix argument and such functions will be averaged over a complex matrix-variate Dirichlet measure. The following standard notations will be used: $\det(\tilde{X})$ will mean the determinant of the complex matrix variable $\tilde{X}$. The absolute value of the determinant will be denoted by $|\det(\cdot)|$. This means that if $\det(\tilde{X}) = a + ib, i = \sqrt{-1}$ then $\sqrt{(a+ib)(a-ib)} = (a^2 + b^2)^{\frac{1}{2}} = |\det(\tilde{X})|$. $tr(\cdot)$ will denote the trace of $(\cdot)$. $\int_{\tilde{X}}$ is integral over all $\tilde{X}$, where $\tilde{X}$ may be rectangular, square or positive definite. $\tilde{X} > O$ means that the $p \times p$ matrix $\tilde{X}$ is Hermitian positive definite. Constant matrices, whether real or in the complex domain, will be written without the tilde unless the fact is to be stressed, and in that case, we use a tilde. $O < A < \tilde{X} < B$ means $A > O, \tilde{X} - A > O, B - \tilde{X} > O$, where A and B are $p \times p$ constant positive definite matrices. Then,

$$\int_{O<A<\tilde{X}<B} f(\tilde{X}) \mathrm{d}\tilde{X} = \int_A^B f(\tilde{X}) \mathrm{d}\tilde{X},$$

means the integral over the Hermitian positive definite matrix $\tilde{X} > O$. When $O < A < \tilde{X} < B$ and $f(\tilde{X})$ is a real-valued scalar function of matrix argument, $\tilde{X}$ and $\mathrm{d}\tilde{X}$ stand for the wedge product of differentials. Hence, for $\tilde{Z} = (\tilde{z}_{jk}) = X + iY$, a $m \times n$ matrix of distinct variables $\tilde{z}_{jk}$'s, where X and Y are real matrices, $i = +\sqrt{-1}$. Then, the differential element $\mathrm{d}\tilde{Z} = \mathrm{d}X \wedge \mathrm{d}Y$, with $\mathrm{d}X$ and $\mathrm{d}Y$ being the wedge products of differentials in X

and Y, respectively. For example, $\mathrm{d}X = \wedge_{j=1}^{m} \wedge_{k=1}^{n} \mathrm{d}x_{jk}$ if $X = (x_{jk})$ and $m \times n$. When $\tilde{Z}$ is Hermitian, then $X = X'$(symmetric) and $Y = -Y'$(skew symmetric), where prime denotes the transpose. In this case, $\mathrm{d}X = \wedge_{j\geq k=1}^{p}\mathrm{d}x_{jk} = \wedge_{j\leq k=1}^{p}\mathrm{d}x_{jk}$ and $\mathrm{d}Y = \wedge_{j<k=1}^{p}\mathrm{d}y_{jk} = \wedge_{j>k=1}^{p}\mathrm{d}y_{jk}$. $\int_{\tilde{X}>O} f(\tilde{X})\mathrm{d}\tilde{X}$ means the integral over the Hermitian positive definite matrix $\tilde{X} > O$. It is a multivariate integral over all $\tilde{x}_{jk}$'s where $\tilde{X} = (\tilde{x}_{jk})$, $\tilde{x}_{jk}$'s are in the complex domain. The complex matrix-variate gamma function will be denoted by $\tilde{\Gamma}_p(\alpha)$, which has the following expression and integral representation:

$$\tilde{\Gamma}_p(\alpha) = \pi^{\frac{p(p-1)}{2}}\Gamma(\alpha)\Gamma(\alpha-1)\ldots\Gamma(\alpha-(p-1)), \Re(\alpha) > p-1 \tag{1}$$

and

$$\tilde{\Gamma}_p(\alpha) = \int_{\tilde{X}>O} |\det(\tilde{X})|^{\alpha-p}\mathrm{e}^{-\mathrm{tr}(\tilde{X})}\mathrm{d}\tilde{X}, \Re(\alpha) > p-1 \tag{2}$$

where $\Re(\cdot)$ means the real part of $(\cdot)$ and the integration is over all Hermitian positive definite matrix $\tilde{X}$. For our computations to follow, we will need some Jacobians of transformations in the complex domain. These will be listed here without proofs. For the proofs and for other such Jacobians, see [15].

Lemma 1. *Let $\tilde{X}$ and $\tilde{Y}$ be $m \times n$ with mn distinct complex variables as elements. Let A be $m \times m$ and B be $n \times n$ nonsingular constant matrices. Then*

$$\tilde{Y} = A\tilde{X}B, \det(A) \neq 0, \det(B) \neq 0 \Rightarrow \mathrm{d}\tilde{Y} = [\det(A^*A)]^n[\det(B^*B)]^m\mathrm{d}\tilde{X} \tag{3}$$

where A^* and B^* denote the conjugate transposes of A and B, respectively; if X, Y, A, B are real then

$$Y = AXB \Rightarrow \mathrm{d}Y = [\det(A)]^n[\det(B)]^m\mathrm{d}X \tag{3a}$$

and if a is a scalar quantity then

$$\tilde{Y} = a\tilde{X} \Rightarrow \mathrm{d}\tilde{Y} = |a|^{2mn}\mathrm{d}\tilde{X}. \tag{3b}$$

Lemma 2. *Let $\tilde{X}$ be $p \times p$ and Hermitian matrix of distinct complex variables as elements, except for Hermitianness. Let A be a nonsingular constant matrix. Then*

$$\tilde{Y} = A\tilde{X}A^* \Rightarrow \mathrm{d}\tilde{Y} = |\det(A)|^{-2p}\mathrm{d}\tilde{X}. \tag{4}$$

If $A, X, Y, X = X'$ are real then

$$Y = AXA' \Rightarrow \mathrm{d}Y = [\det(A)]^{p+1}\mathrm{d}X. \tag{4a}$$

If $Y, X, a, X = X'$ and a scalar, then

$$Y = aX \rightarrow dY = a^{\frac{p(p+1)}{2}}\mathrm{d}X \tag{4b}$$

Lemma 3. *Let $\tilde{X}$ be $p \times p$ and nonsingular with the regular inverse $\tilde{X}^{-1}$. Then*

$$\tilde{Y} = \tilde{X}^{-1} \Rightarrow \mathrm{d}\tilde{Y} = \begin{cases} |\det(\tilde{X}^*\tilde{X})|^{-2p}\mathrm{d}\tilde{X} \text{ for a general } \tilde{X} \\ |\det(\tilde{X}^*\tilde{X})|^{-p}\mathrm{d}\tilde{X} \text{ for } \tilde{X} = \tilde{X}^* \text{ or } \tilde{X} = -\tilde{X}^* \end{cases} \tag{5}$$

Lemma 4. *Let $\tilde{X}$ be $p \times p$ Hermitian positive definite of distinct elements, except for Hermitian positive definiteness. Let $\tilde{T}$ be a lower triangular matrix where $\tilde{T} = (\tilde{t}_{jk}), \tilde{t}_{jk} = 0, j < k, \tilde{t}_{jk}, j \geq k$ are distinct, $\tilde{t}_{kk} = t_{kk} > 0, k = 1, \ldots, p$, that is, the diagonal elements are real and positive. Then*

$$\tilde{X} = \tilde{T}\tilde{T}^* \Rightarrow \mathrm{d}\tilde{X} = 2^p\{\prod_{k=1}^{p} t_{kk}^{2(p-k)+1}\}\mathrm{d}\tilde{T}. \tag{6}$$

With the help of Lemma 4, we can evaluate the complex matrix-variate gamma integral in (2) and show that it is equal to the expression in (1). When Lemma 4 is applied to the integral in (2), the integral splits into p integrals of the form

$$\prod_{k=1}^{p} 2\int_0^\infty (t_{kk}^2)^{(\alpha-p)+\frac{1}{2}(2(p-k)+1)} e^{-t_{kk}^2} dt_{kk} = \prod_{k=1}^{p} \Gamma(\alpha-(k-1)), \Re(\alpha) > k-1, k=1,\ldots,p$$

which results in the final condition as $\Re(\alpha) > p-1$, and $p(p-1)/2$ integrals of the form

$$\begin{aligned}\prod_{j>k}\int_{-\infty}^{\infty} e^{-|\tilde{t}_{jk}|^2} d\tilde{t}_{jk} &= \prod_{j>k}\int_{-\infty}^{\infty}\int_{-\infty}^{\infty} e^{-(t_{jk1}^2+t_{jk2}^2)} dt_{jk1}\wedge dt_{jk2} \\ &= \prod_{j>k}\sqrt{\pi}\sqrt{\pi} = \pi^{\frac{p(p-1)}{2}}, |\tilde{t}_{jk}|^2 = t_{jk1}^2 + t_{jk2}^2.\end{aligned}$$

Thus, the integral in (2) reduces to the expression in (1).

Lemma 5. *Let $\tilde{X}$ be $n \times p, n \geq p$ matrix of full rank p. Let $\tilde{S} = \tilde{X}^*\tilde{X}$, a $p \times p$ Hermitian positive definite matrix. Let $d\tilde{X}$ and $d\tilde{S}$ denote the wedge product of the differentials in $\tilde{X}$ and $\tilde{S}$, respectively. Then*

$$d\tilde{X} = |\det(\tilde{S})|^{n-p}\frac{\pi^{np}}{\tilde{\Gamma}_p(n)} d\tilde{S}. \tag{7}$$

This is a very important result because $\tilde{X}$ is a rectangular matrix with mn distinct elements, whereas $\tilde{S}$ is Hermitian positive definite and $p \times p$. With the help of the above lemmas, we will average a few functions over the Dirichlet measures in the complex domain.

2. Dirichlet Averages for Functions of Matrix Argument in the Complex Domain

The Dirichlet distributions of real types 1 and 2 are generalized to standard distributions of beta and type-2. The literature contains these distributions, their characteristics, and a few generalizations in the form of Liouville distributions. Dirichlet type-1 and type-2 matrix-variate analogues can be found in the literature; [15] is one example. Generalizations of matrix variables to the Liouville family can be observed in [16]. Matrix-variate distributions, not generalized Dirichlet, may be seen from [17–19] provides examples of the use of scalar variable Dirichlet models in random division and other geometrical possibilities.

All the matrices appearing in this section are $p \times p$ Hermitian positive definite unless stated otherwise. Consider the following complex matrix-variate type-1 Dirichlet measure:

$$\begin{aligned} f_1(\tilde{X}_1,\ldots,\tilde{X}_k) &= \tilde{D}_k|\det(\tilde{X}_1)|^{\alpha_1-p}\ldots|\det(\tilde{X}_k)|^{\alpha_k-p} \\ &\times |\det(I-\tilde{X}_1-\ldots-\tilde{X}_k)|^{\alpha_{k+1}-p} \end{aligned} \tag{8}$$

where $\tilde{X}_1,\ldots\tilde{X}_k$ are $p \times p$ Hermitian positive definite, that is, $\tilde{X}_j > O, j=1,\ldots,k$, such that $I-\tilde{X}_j > O, j=1,\ldots,k, I-(\tilde{X}_1+\ldots+\tilde{X}_k) > O$. The normalizing constant $\tilde{D}_k$ can be evaluated by integrating out matrices one at a time and the individual integrals are evaluated by using a complex matrix-variate type-1 beta integral of the form

$$\int_O^I |\det(\tilde{X})|^{\alpha-p}|\det(I-\tilde{X})|^{\beta-p} d\tilde{X} = \frac{\tilde{\Gamma}_p(\alpha)\tilde{\Gamma}_p(\beta)}{\tilde{\Gamma}_p(\alpha+\beta)}, \Re(\alpha) > p-1, \Re(\beta) > p-1 \tag{9}$$

where $\tilde{\Gamma}_p(\alpha)$ is given in (1). It can be shown that the normalizing constant is the following:

$$\tilde{D}_k = \frac{\tilde{\Gamma}_p(\alpha_1+\ldots+\alpha_{k+1})}{\tilde{\Gamma}_p(\alpha_1)\ldots\tilde{\Gamma}_p(\alpha_{k+1})} \tag{10}$$

for $\Re(\alpha_j) > p-1, j=1,\ldots,k+1$. Since (10) is a probability measure, $f(\tilde{X}_1,\ldots,\tilde{X}_k)$ is non-negative for all $\tilde{X}_j, j=1,\cdots,k$ and the total integral is one. It is a Dirichlet measure associated with a Dirichlet density, and it is also a statistical density; hence, we can denote the averages of given functions as the expected values of those functions, denoted by $E(\cdot)$. Let us consider a few functions and take their averages over the complex matrix-variate Dirichlet measure in (8). Let

$$\phi_1(\tilde{X}_1,\ldots,\tilde{X}_k) = |\det(\tilde{X}_1)|^{\gamma_1}\ldots|\det(\tilde{X}_k)|^{\gamma_k}. \tag{11}$$

Then, the average of (11) over the measure in (8) is given by

$$E[\phi_1] = \tilde{D}_k\int_{\tilde{X}_1,\ldots,\tilde{X}_k}|\det(\tilde{X}_1)|^{\alpha_1+\gamma_1-p}\ldots|\det(\tilde{X}_k)|^{\alpha_k+\gamma_k-p}$$
$$\times|\det(I-\tilde{X}_1-\ldots-\tilde{X}_k)|^{\alpha_{k+1}-p}\mathrm{d}\tilde{X}_1\wedge\ldots.\wedge\mathrm{d}\tilde{X}_k.$$

Note that the only change is that α_j is changed to $\alpha_j+\gamma_j$ for $j=1,\ldots,k$; hence, the result is available from the normalizing constant. That is,

$$E[\phi_1] = \{\prod_{j=1}^{k}\frac{\tilde{\Gamma}_p(\alpha_j+\gamma_j)}{\tilde{\Gamma}_p(\alpha_j)}\}\frac{\tilde{\Gamma}_p(\alpha_1+\ldots+\alpha_k)}{\tilde{\Gamma}_p(\alpha_1+\gamma_1+\ldots+\alpha_k+\gamma_k+\alpha_{k+1})}, \tag{12}$$

for $\Re(\alpha_j+\gamma_j)>p-1, j=1,\ldots,k, \Re(\alpha_{k+1})>p-1$. Let

$$\phi_2(\tilde{X}_1,\ldots,\tilde{X}_k) = |\det(I-\tilde{X}_1-\ldots-\tilde{X}_k)|^{\delta}. \tag{13}$$

Then, in the integral for $E[\phi_2]$ the only change is that the parameter α_{k+1} is changed to $\alpha_{k+1}+\delta$. Hence, the result is available from the normalizing constant $\tilde{D}_k$. That is,

$$E[\phi_2] = \frac{\tilde{\Gamma}_p(\alpha_{k+1}+\delta)}{\tilde{\Gamma}_p(\alpha_{k+1})}\frac{\tilde{\Gamma}_p(\alpha_1+\ldots+\alpha_{k+1})}{\tilde{\Gamma}_p(\alpha_1+\ldots+\alpha_{k+1}+\delta)} \tag{14}$$

for $\Re(\alpha_{k+1}+\delta)>p-1, \Re(\alpha_j)>p-1, j=1,\ldots,k$. The structure in (14) is also the structure of the δ-th moment of the determinant of the matrix with a complex matrix-variate type-1 beta distribution. Hence, this ϕ_2 has an equivalent representation in terms of the determinant of a matrix with a complex matrix-variate type-1 beta distribution. Let

$$\phi_3(\tilde{X}_1,\ldots,\tilde{X}_k) = \mathrm{e}^{\mathrm{tr}(\tilde{X}_1)}. \tag{15}$$

Let us evaluate the Dirichlet average for $k=2$. Then

$$E[\phi_3] = \tilde{D}_2\int_{\tilde{X}_1,\tilde{X}_2}\mathrm{e}^{\mathrm{tr}(\tilde{X}_1)}|\det(\tilde{X}_1)|^{\alpha_1-p}|\det(\tilde{X}_2)|^{\alpha_2-p}$$
$$\times|\det(I-\tilde{X}_1-\tilde{X}_2)|^{\alpha_3-p}\mathrm{d}\tilde{X}_1\wedge\ldots\wedge\mathrm{d}\tilde{X}_3.$$

Take out $I-\tilde{X}_1$ from $|\det(I-\tilde{X}_1-\tilde{X}_2)|$ and make the transformation

$$\tilde{U}_2 = (I-\tilde{X}_1)^{-\frac{1}{2}}\tilde{X}_2(I-\tilde{X}_1)^{-\frac{1}{2}}.$$

Then, from Lemma 2, $\mathrm{d}\tilde{U}_2 = |\det(I-\tilde{X}_1)|^{-p}\mathrm{d}\tilde{X}_2$. Now, $\tilde{U}_2$ can be integrated out by using a complex matrix-variate type-1 beta integral given in (9). That is,

$$\int_{O<\tilde{U}_2<I}|\det(\tilde{U}_2)|^{\alpha_2-p}|\det(I-\tilde{U}_2)|^{\alpha_3-p}\mathrm{d}\tilde{U}_2 = \frac{\tilde{\Gamma}_p(\alpha_2)\tilde{\Gamma}_p(\alpha_3)}{\tilde{\Gamma}_p(\alpha_2+\alpha_3)} \tag{16}$$

for $\Re(\alpha_2)>p-1, \Re(\alpha_3)>p-1$. The $\tilde{X}_1$ integral to be evaluated is the following:

$$\int_{\tilde{X}_1}\mathrm{e}^{\mathrm{tr}(\tilde{X}_1)}|\det(\tilde{X}_1)|^{\alpha_1-p}|\det(I-\tilde{X}_1)|^{\alpha_2+\alpha_3-p}\mathrm{d}\tilde{X}_1. \tag{17}$$

In order to evaluate the integral in (17), we can expand the exponential part by using zonal polynomials for complex argument; see [15,20]. We need a few notations and results from zonal polynomial expansions of determinants. The generalized Pochhammer symbol is the following:

$$[a]_M = \prod_{j=1}^{p}(a-j+1)_{k_j} = \frac{\tilde{\Gamma}_p(a,M)}{\tilde{\Gamma}_p(a)}, \tilde{\Gamma}_p(a,M) = \tilde{\Gamma}_p(a)[a]_M \tag{18}$$

where the usual Pochhmmer symbol is

$$(a)_m = a(a+1)\dots(a+m-1), a \neq 0, (a)_0 = 1 \tag{19}$$

and M represents the partition, $M = (m_1, \dots, m_p), m_1 \geq m_2 \geq \dots \geq m_p, m_1 + \dots + m_p = m$ and the zonal polynomial expansion for the exponential function is the following:

$$\mathrm{e}^{\mathrm{tr}(\tilde{X})} = \sum_{m=0}^{\infty}\sum_{M}\frac{\tilde{C}_M(\tilde{X})}{m!} \tag{20}$$

where $\tilde{C}_M(\tilde{X})$ is zonal polynomial of order m in the complex matrix argument $\tilde{X}$; see (6.1.18) of [15]. One result on zonal polynomial that we require will be stated here as a lemma.

Lemma 6.

$$\begin{aligned}\int_{O<\tilde{Z}<I}&|\det(\tilde{Z})|^{\alpha-p}|\det(I-\tilde{Z})|^{\beta-p}\tilde{C}_M(\tilde{Z}\tilde{A})\mathrm{d}\tilde{Z}\\ &= \frac{\tilde{\Gamma}_p(\alpha,M)\tilde{\Gamma}_p(\beta)}{\tilde{\Gamma}_p(\alpha+\beta,M)}\tilde{C}_M(\tilde{A})\\ &= \frac{\tilde{\Gamma}_p(\alpha)\tilde{\Gamma}_p(\beta)}{\tilde{\Gamma}_p(\alpha+\beta)}\frac{(\alpha)_M}{(\alpha+\beta)_M}\tilde{C}_M(\tilde{A}),\end{aligned} \tag{21}$$

see also (6.1.21) of [15], for $\Re(\alpha) > p-1, \Re(\beta) > p-1, \tilde{A} > O$. *By using (21), we can evaluate the* $\tilde{X}_1$*-integral in* $E[\phi_3]$. *That is,*

$$\begin{aligned}\int_{O<\tilde{X}_1<I}&\mathrm{e}^{\mathrm{tr}(A\tilde{X}_1)}|\det(\tilde{X}_1)|^{\alpha_1-p}|\det(I-\tilde{X}_1)|^{\alpha_2+\alpha_3-p}\mathrm{d}\tilde{X}_1\\ &= \sum_{m=0}^{\infty}\sum_{M}\int_{O<\tilde{X}_1<I}\frac{\tilde{C}_M(\tilde{A}\tilde{X}_1)}{m!}|\det(\tilde{X}_1)|^{\alpha_1-p}|\det(I-\tilde{X}_1)|^{\alpha_2+\alpha_3-p}\mathrm{d}\tilde{X}_1\\ &= \sum_{m=0}^{\infty}\sum_{M}\frac{\tilde{C}_M(\tilde{A})}{m!}\frac{\tilde{\Gamma}_p(\alpha_1,M)\tilde{\Gamma}_p(\alpha_2+\alpha_3)}{\tilde{\Gamma}_p(\alpha_1+\alpha_2+\alpha_3,M)}.\end{aligned}$$

Now, with the result on $\tilde{X}_2$*-integral,* $\tilde{D}_2$ *and the above result will result in all the gamma products being canceled and the final result is the following:*

$$E[\phi_3] = \sum_{m=0}^{\infty}\sum_{M}\frac{\tilde{C}_M(\tilde{A})}{m!}\frac{(\alpha_1)_M}{(\alpha_1+\alpha_2+\alpha_3)_M} = {}_1F_1(\alpha_1;\alpha_1+\alpha_2+\alpha_3;\tilde{A}) \tag{22}$$

for $\Re(\alpha_j) > p-1, j = 1,2,3$ *and* ${}_1F_1$ *is a confluent hypergeometric function of complex matrix argument* $\tilde{A}$.

3. Dirichlet Averages in Complex Matrix-Variate Type-2 Dirichlet Measure

Consider the type-2 Dirichlet measure

$$\begin{aligned}f_2(\tilde{X}_1,\dots,\tilde{X}_k) &= \tilde{D}_k|\det(\tilde{X}_1)|^{\alpha_1-p}\dots|\det(\tilde{X}_k)|^{\alpha_k-p}\\ &\times|\det(I+\tilde{X}_1+\dots+\tilde{X}_k)|^{-(\alpha_1+\dots+\alpha_{k+1})}\end{aligned} \tag{23}$$

for $\Re(\alpha_j) > p-1, j=1,\ldots,k+1$ and it can be seen that the normalizing constant is the same as that in the type-1 Dirichlet measure. Let us evaluate some Dirichlet averages in the measure (23). Let

$$\phi_4(\tilde{X}_1,\ldots,\tilde{X}_k) = |\det(\tilde{X}_1)|^{\gamma_1}\ldots|\det(\tilde{X}_k)|^{\gamma_k}. \quad (24)$$

Then, when the average is taken, the change is that α_j changes to $\alpha_j+\gamma_j, j=1,\ldots,k$; hence, one should be able to find the value from the normalizing constant by adjusting for α_{k+1}. Write $(\alpha_1+\ldots+\alpha_{k+1}) = (\alpha_1+\gamma_1+\ldots+\alpha_k+\gamma_k)+(\alpha_{k+1}-\gamma_1-\ldots-\gamma_k)$. That is, replace α_j by $\alpha_j+\gamma_j, j=1,\ldots,k$ and replace α_{k+1} by $\alpha_{k+1}-\gamma_1-\ldots-\gamma_k$ to obtain the result from the normalizing constant. Therefore,

$$E[\phi_4] = \{\prod_{j=1}^{k}\frac{\tilde{\Gamma}_p(\alpha_j+\gamma_j)}{\tilde{\Gamma}_p(\alpha_j)}\}\frac{\tilde{\Gamma}_p(\alpha_{k+1}-\gamma_1-\ldots-\gamma_k)}{\tilde{\Gamma}_p(\alpha_{k+1})} \quad (25)$$

for $\Re(\alpha_j+\gamma_j) > p-1, j=1,\ldots,k$ and $\Re(\alpha_{k+1}-\gamma_1-\ldots-\gamma_k) > p-1, \Re(\alpha_{k+1}) > p-1$. Thus, only a few moments will exist, interpreting $E[\phi_4]$ as the product moment of the determinants of $\tilde{X}_1,\ldots\tilde{X}_k$. Let

$$\phi_5(\tilde{X}_1,\ldots,\tilde{X}_k) = |\det(I+\tilde{X}_1+\ldots+\tilde{X}_k)|^{-\delta}. \quad (26)$$

Then, when the average is taken the only change in the integral is that α_{k+1} is changed to $\alpha_{k+1}+\delta$; hence, from the normalizing constant the result is the following:

$$E[\phi_5] = \frac{\tilde{\Gamma}_p(\alpha_{k+1}+\delta)}{\tilde{\Gamma}_p(\alpha_{k+1})}\frac{\tilde{\Gamma}_p(\alpha_1+\ldots+\alpha_{k+1})}{\tilde{\Gamma}_p(\alpha_1+\ldots+\alpha_{k+1}+\delta)}, \quad (27)$$

for $\Re(\alpha_{k+1}+\delta) > p-1$, the other conditions on the parameters for $\tilde{D}_k$ remain the same. Observe that if $\Re(\delta) > 0$, then the structure in (27) is that of the δ-th moment of the determinant of a complex matrix-variate type-1 beta matrix. Thus, this type-2 form gives a type-1 form result. Let

$$\phi_6(\tilde{X}_1,\tilde{X}_2) = \mathrm{e}^{-\mathrm{tr}(A\tilde{X}_1)}|\det(I+\tilde{X}_1)|^{\alpha_1+\alpha_3}. \quad (28)$$

Then, the Dirichlet average of ϕ_6 in the complex matrix-variate type-2 Dirichlet measure in (23) for $k=2$ is the following:

$$E[\phi_6] = \tilde{D}_2\int_{\tilde{X}_1,\tilde{X}_2}\mathrm{e}^{-\mathrm{tr}(\tilde{X}_1)}|\det(I+\tilde{X}_1)|^{\alpha_2+\alpha_3}|\det(\tilde{X}_1)|^{\alpha_1-p}|\det(\tilde{X}_2)|^{\alpha_2-p}$$
$$\times|\det(I+\tilde{X}_1+\tilde{X}_2)|^{-(\alpha_1+\alpha_2+\alpha_3)}\mathrm{d}\tilde{X}_1\wedge\ldots\mathrm{d}\tilde{X}_3.$$

Take out $(I+\tilde{X}_1)$ from $I+\tilde{X}_1+\tilde{X}_2$ and make the transformation

$$\tilde{U}_2 = (I+\tilde{X}_1)^{-\frac{1}{2}}\tilde{X}_2(I+\tilde{X}_1)^{-\frac{1}{2}} \Rightarrow \mathrm{d}\tilde{U}_2 = |\det(I+\tilde{X}_1)|^{-p}\mathrm{d}\tilde{X}_2.$$

The $\tilde{U}_2$-integral gives

$$\int_{\tilde{U}_2>O}|\det(\tilde{U}_2)|^{\alpha_2-p}|\det(I+\tilde{U}_2)|^{-(\alpha_1+\alpha_2+\alpha_3)}\mathrm{d}\tilde{U}_2 = \frac{\tilde{\Gamma}_p(\alpha_2)\tilde{\Gamma}_p(\alpha_1+\alpha_3)}{\tilde{\Gamma}_p(\alpha_1+\alpha_2+\alpha_3)}. \quad (29)$$

Observe that the exponent becomes zero and the factor containing $|\det(I+\tilde{X}_1)|$ disappears. Then, the $\tilde{X}_1$-integral is

$$\int_{\tilde{X}_1>O}|\det(\tilde{X}_1)|^{\alpha_1-p}\mathrm{e}^{-\mathrm{tr}(A\tilde{X}_1)}\mathrm{d}\tilde{X}_1 = \tilde{\Gamma}_p(\alpha_1)|\det(A)|^{-\alpha_1}. \quad (30)$$

The results from (29), (30) and $\tilde{D}_2$ gives the final result as follows:

$$E[\phi_6] = \frac{\tilde{\Gamma}_p(\alpha_1+\alpha_3)}{\tilde{\Gamma}_p(\alpha_3)}|\det(A)|^{-\alpha_1} \tag{31}$$

and the original conditions on the parameters remain the same and no further conditions are needed, where $A > O$. Note that if ϕ_6 did not have the factor $|\det(I+\tilde{X}_1)|^{\alpha_1+\alpha_3}$, a factor containing $|\det(I+\tilde{X}_1)|$ would also have been present, then the $\tilde{X}_1$-integral would have gone in terms of a Whittaker function of matrix argument; see [15].

4. Dirichlet Averages in Complex Rectangular Matrix-Variate Dirichlet Measure

Let B_j be $n_j \times n_j$ a Hermitian positive definite constant matrix and let $B_j^{\frac{1}{2}}$ denote the Hermitian positive definite square root of B_j. Let $\tilde{X}_j$ be a $n_j \times p$, $n_j \geq p$ matrix of full rank p so that $\tilde{X}_j^*\tilde{X}_j = \tilde{S}_j > O$ or $\tilde{S}_j$ is a Hermitian positive definite. Observe that for $p = 1$, $\tilde{X}_j^* B_j \tilde{X}_j$ is a positive definite Hermitian form. Hence, our results to follow will also cover results on Hermitian forms. Consider the model

$$\begin{aligned} f_3(\tilde{X}_1,\ldots,\tilde{X}_k) &= \tilde{G}_k|\det(\tilde{X}_1^*B_1\tilde{X}_1)|^{\alpha_1}\ldots|\det(\tilde{X}_k^*B_k\tilde{X}_k)|^{\alpha_k} \\ &\quad\times|\det(I-\tilde{X}_1^*B_1\tilde{X}_1-\ldots-\tilde{X}_k^*B_k\tilde{X}_k)|^{\alpha_{k+1}-p} \end{aligned} \tag{32}$$

where $\tilde{G}_k$ is the normalizing constant and $O < \tilde{X}_j^*B_j\tilde{X}_j < I, j = 1,\ldots,k, O < \tilde{X}_1^*B_1\tilde{X}_1+\ldots+\tilde{X}_k^*B_k\tilde{X}_k < I, j = 1,\ldots,k$. The normalizing constant is evaluated by using the following procedure. Let $\tilde{Y}_j = B_j^{\frac{1}{2}}\tilde{X}_j \Rightarrow \mathrm{d}\tilde{Y}_j = |\det(B_j)|^p\mathrm{d}\tilde{X}_j$ from Lemma 1. Let $\tilde{Y}_j^*\tilde{Y}_j = \tilde{S}_j$. Then, from Lemma 5 we have

$$\mathrm{d}\tilde{Y}_j = \frac{\pi^{n_jp}}{\tilde{\Gamma}_p(n_j)}|\det(\tilde{S}_j)|^{n_j-p}\mathrm{d}\tilde{X}_j. \tag{33}$$

Then,

$$\mathrm{d}\tilde{X}_1\wedge\ldots\wedge\mathrm{d}\tilde{X}_k = \{\prod_{j=1}^{k}\frac{\pi^{n_jp}}{\tilde{\Gamma}_p(n_j)}|\det(\tilde{B}_j)|^{-p}|\det(\tilde{S}_j)|^{n_j-p}\}\mathrm{d}\tilde{S}_1\wedge\ldots\wedge\mathrm{d}\tilde{S}_k. \tag{34}$$

Since the total integral is 1, we have

$$\begin{aligned} 1 &= \int_{\tilde{X}_1,\ldots\tilde{X}_k} f_3(\tilde{X}_1,\ldots,\tilde{X}_k)\mathrm{d}\tilde{X}_1\wedge\ldots\wedge\mathrm{d}\tilde{X}_k \\ &= \tilde{G}_k\{\prod_{j=1}^{k}\frac{\pi^{n_jp}}{\tilde{\Gamma}_p(n_j)}\}\int_{\tilde{S}_1,\ldots,\tilde{S}_k}|\det(\tilde{S}_1)|^{\alpha_1+n_1-p}\ldots \\ &\times|\det(\tilde{S}_k)|^{\alpha_k+n_k-p}|\det(I-\tilde{S}_1-\ldots-\tilde{S}_k)|^{\alpha_{k+1}-p}\mathrm{d}\tilde{S}_1\wedge\ldots\wedge\mathrm{d}\tilde{S}_k. \end{aligned}$$

Now, evaluating the type-1 Dirichlet integrals over the $\tilde{S}_j$'s, one obtains the following result:

$$\begin{aligned} \tilde{G}_k &= \{\prod_{j=1}^{k}|\det(B_j)|^p\frac{\tilde{\Gamma}_p(n_j)}{\pi^{n_jp}}\frac{1}{\tilde{\Gamma}_p(\alpha_j+n_j)}\} \\ &\times\frac{\tilde{\Gamma}_p(\alpha_1+\ldots+\alpha_{k+1}+n_1+\ldots+n_k)}{\tilde{\Gamma}_p(\alpha_{k+1})} \end{aligned} \tag{35}$$

for $B_j > O, \Re(\alpha_j + n_j) > p-1, j = 1, \ldots, k, \Re(\alpha_{k+1}) > p-1$. Thus, (32) with (35) defines a rectangular complex matrix-variate type-1 Dirichlet measure. There is a corresponding type-2 Dirichlet measure, given by the following:

$$\begin{aligned} f_4(\tilde{X}_1, \ldots, \tilde{X}_k) &= \tilde{G}_k |\det(\tilde{X}_1)|^{\alpha_1} \ldots |\det(\tilde{X}_k)|^{\alpha_k} \\ &\quad \times |\det(I + \tilde{X}_1 + \ldots + \tilde{X}_k)|^{-(\alpha_1 + \ldots + \alpha_{k+1} + n_1 + \ldots + n_k)} \end{aligned} \tag{36}$$

for $B_j > O, \Re(\alpha_j + n_j) > p-1, j = 1, \ldots, k, \Re(\alpha_{k+1}) > p-1$ and $\tilde{G}_k$ is the same as the one appearing in (35). Let us compute the Dirichlet averages of some functions in the type-2 rectangular complex matrix-variate Dirichlet measure in (36). Let

$$\phi_7(\tilde{X}_1, \ldots, \tilde{X}_k) = |\det(\tilde{X}_1)|^{\gamma_1} \ldots |\det(\tilde{X}_k)|^{\gamma_k}. \tag{37}$$

Then, when we take the expected value of ϕ_7 in (36) the only change is that α_j changes to $\alpha_j + \gamma_j, j = 1, \ldots, k$; hence, the final result is available from the normalizing constant. Therefore

$$E[\phi_7] = \{\prod_{j=1}^{k} \frac{\tilde{\Gamma}_p(\alpha_j + n_j + \gamma_j)}{\tilde{\Gamma}_p(\alpha_j + n_j)}\} \frac{\tilde{\Gamma}_p(\alpha_{k+1} - \gamma_1 - \ldots - \gamma_k)}{\tilde{\Gamma}_p(\alpha_{k+1})} \tag{38}$$

for $\Re(\alpha_j + n_j + \gamma_j) > p-1, j = 1, \ldots, k, \Re(\alpha_{k+1} - \gamma_1 - \ldots - \gamma_k) > p-1, \Re(\alpha_{k+1}) > p-1$. Let

$$\phi_8(\tilde{X}_1, \ldots, \tilde{X}_k) = |\det(I + \tilde{X}_1 + \ldots + \tilde{X}_k)|^{-\delta}. \tag{39}$$

Then, the only change is that α_{k+1} goes to $\alpha_{k+1} + \delta$ in the integral and no other change is there ; hence, the average is available from the normalizing constant. That is,

$$E[\phi_8] = \frac{\tilde{\Gamma}_p(\alpha_{k+1} + \delta)}{\tilde{\Gamma}_p(\alpha_{k+1})} \frac{\tilde{\Gamma}_p(\alpha_1 + \ldots + \alpha_{k+1} + n_1 + \ldots + n_k)}{\tilde{\Gamma}_p(\alpha_1 + \ldots + \alpha_{k+1} + n_1 + \ldots + n_k + \delta)} \tag{40}$$

for $\Re(\alpha_j + n_j) > p-1, j = 1, \ldots, k, \Re(\alpha_{k+1} + \delta) > p-1, \Re(\alpha_{k+1}) > p-1$.

The case $p = 1$ in the complex rectangular matrix-variate type-1 Dirichlet measure is very interesting. We have a set of Hermitian positive definite quadratic forms here having a joint density of the following form:

$$\begin{aligned} f_5(\tilde{X}_1, \ldots, \tilde{X}_k) &= \tilde{G}_k [\tilde{X}_1^* B_1 \tilde{X}_1]^{\alpha_1} \ldots [\tilde{X}_k^* B_k \tilde{X}_k]^{\alpha_k} \\ &\quad \times |\det(I - [\tilde{X}_1^* B_1 \tilde{X}_1] - \ldots - [\tilde{X}_k^* B_k \tilde{X}_k])|^{\alpha_{k+1} - p} \end{aligned} \tag{41}$$

where $B_j > O$, and $\tilde{X}_j^* B_j \tilde{X}_j$ is a scalar quantity, $j = 1, \ldots, k$. Consider the same types of transformations as before. $\tilde{Y}_j = B_j^{\frac{1}{2}} \tilde{X}_j$. Then, $\tilde{Y}_j^* \tilde{Y}_j = |\tilde{y}_{j1}|^2 + \ldots + |\tilde{y}_{jn_j}|^2$ or the sum or squares of the absolute values of $\tilde{y}_{jr}$ where $\tilde{Y}_j^* = (\tilde{y}_{j1}^*, \ldots, \tilde{y}_{jn_j}^*)$. This is an isotropic point in in the $2n_j$-dimensional Euclidean space. From here, one can establish various connections to geometrical probability problems; see [19]. Also, (41) is associated with the theory of generalized Hermitian forms in pathway models; see [21]. Let us evaluate the h-th moment of

$$\phi_9(\tilde{X}_1, \ldots, \tilde{X}_k) = [\tilde{X}_1^* B_1 \tilde{X}_1 + \ldots + \tilde{X}_k^* B_k \tilde{X}_k]^h \tag{42}$$

for $p = 1$. For $p > 1$ we have seen that this is not available directly but moments of $|\det(I - \tilde{X}_1^* B_1 \tilde{X}_1 - \ldots - \tilde{X}_k^* B_k \tilde{X}_k)|$ was available. But for $p = 1$, one can obtain the h-th moment of both for an arbitrary h. By computing the h-th moment of $[1 - \tilde{X}_1^* B_1 \tilde{X}_1 - \ldots - \tilde{X}_k^* B_k \tilde{X}_k]$, for $p = 1$, we note that for arbitrary h, this quantity and its complementary part $[\tilde{X}_1^* B_1 \tilde{X}_1 + \ldots + \tilde{X}_k^* B_k \tilde{X}_k]$ are both scalar variable type-1 beta distributed with the parameters $(\alpha_{k+1}, \sum_{j=1}^k (\alpha_j + n_j))$ and $(\sum_{j=1}^k (\alpha_j + n_j), \alpha_{k+1})$, respectively. Then,

$$E[\phi_9] = \frac{\tilde{\Gamma}_p(\sum_{j=1}^k (\alpha_j + n_j) + h)}{\tilde{\Gamma}_p(\sum_{j=1}^k (\alpha_j + n_j))} \frac{\tilde{\Gamma}_p(\sum_{j=1}^k (\alpha_j + n_j) + \alpha_{k+1})}{\tilde{\Gamma}_p(\sum_{j=1}^k (\alpha_j + n_j) + \alpha_{k+1} + h)} \quad (43)$$

for $\Re(\alpha_j) > p - 1, j = 1, \ldots, k+1, \Re(\sum_{j=1}^k (\alpha_j + n_j) + h) > p - 1$. Consider ϕ_9 in the complex matrix-variate type-2 Dirichlet measure for $p = 1$. Then, the h-th moment will reduce to the following:

$$E[\phi_9] = \frac{\tilde{\Gamma}_p(\sum_{j=1}^k (\alpha_j + n_j) + h)}{\tilde{\Gamma}_p(\sum_{j=1}^k (\alpha_j + n_j))} \frac{\tilde{\Gamma}_p(\alpha_{k+1} - h)}{\tilde{\Gamma}_p(\alpha_{k+1})} \quad (44)$$

for $\Re(\alpha_{k+1} - h) > p - 1, \Re(\alpha_j) > p - 1, j = 1, \ldots, k+1, \Re(\sum_{j=1}^k (\alpha_j + n_j) + h) > p - 1$.

Many such results can be obtained for the type-1 and type-2 Dirichlet measures in Hermitian positive definite Dirichlet measures or in rectangular matrix-variate Dirichlet measures.

5. A Connection to Tsallis Statistics of Non-Extensive Statistical Mechanics

Ref. [22] introduced an entropy measure and, by optimizing this entropy in an escort density, and under the constraint that the first moment in the escort density is prefixed which will correspond to a physical law of conservation of energy, obtained the famous Tsallis statistics of non-extensive statistical mechanics. Tsallis entropy is a variant of Havrda–Charvát entropy; see [23]. Havrda–Charvát entropy is an α-generalized Shannon entropy and Shannon entropy in the discrete distribution is the following:

$$S(f) = -C \sum_{j=1}^k p_j \ln p_j, p_j > 0, j = 1, \ldots, k, p_1 + \ldots + p_k = 1 \quad (45)$$

and its continuous version is the following:

$$S(f) = -C \int_x f(x) \ln f(x) \mathrm{d}x, f(x) \geq 0 \text{ for all x } and \int_x f(x) \mathrm{d}x = 1 \quad (46)$$

where C is a constant. A generalized entropy, introduced by Mathai, is a variant of Havrda–Charvát entropy and Tsallis entropy in the real scalar variable case, but Mathai's entropy is set in a very general framework. It is the following:

$$M_\alpha(f) = \frac{\int_X [f(X)]^{1+\frac{a-\alpha}{\eta}} \mathrm{d}X - 1}{\alpha - a}, \alpha \neq a, \eta > 0 \quad (47)$$

where a is a fixed anchoring point, α is the parameter of interest, $\eta > 0$ is a fixed scaling factor or unit of measurement, $f(X)$ is a real-valued scalar function of X such that $f(X) \geq 0$ for all X, $\int_X f(X)\mathrm{d}X = 1$ or $f(X)$ is a statistical density where X can be a scalar or vector or matrix or a collection of matrices in the real or complex domain and $\mathrm{d}X$ is the wedge product of all distinct real scalar variables in X. For example, if $X' = [x_1, \ldots, x_p]$, where $x_j, j = 1, \ldots, p$ are distinct real scalar variables and a prime denoting the transpose, then $\mathrm{d}X = \mathrm{d}x_1 \wedge \ldots \wedge \mathrm{d}x_p = \mathrm{d}X'$. For two real scalar variables x and y, the wedge product of differentials is defined as $\mathrm{d}x \wedge \mathrm{d}y = -\mathrm{d}y \wedge \mathrm{d}x$, so that $\mathrm{d}x \wedge \mathrm{d}x = 0, \mathrm{d}y \wedge \mathrm{d}y = 0$. If $X = (x_{ij})$ is a $p \times q$ matrix of distinct real scalar variables x_{ij}'s, then $\mathrm{d}X = \wedge_{i=1}^p \wedge_{j=1}^q \mathrm{d}x_{ij}$. If $\tilde{X} = X_1 + iX_2, i = \sqrt{(-1)}, X_1, X_2$ is real, then $\mathrm{d}\tilde{X} = \mathrm{d}X_1 \wedge \mathrm{d}X_2$. If $X = [X_1, \ldots, X_k]$, a collection of matrices in the real domain, then $\mathrm{d}X = \mathrm{d}X_1 \wedge \ldots \wedge \mathrm{d}X_k$. If $\tilde{X} = [\tilde{X}_1, \ldots, \tilde{X}_k]$, then $\mathrm{d}\tilde{X} = \mathrm{d}\tilde{X}_1 \wedge \ldots \wedge \mathrm{d}\tilde{X}_k$. Thus, (47) is the expected value of $[f(X)]^{\frac{a-\alpha}{\eta}}$, where the deviation of α from the anchoring point a is measured in terms of η units.

When $\alpha \to a$ in the real scalar case, we can see that (47) goes to Shannon's entropy of (46). But (47) is set up in a very general framework. Let us consider (47) when X is a $p \times 1$ vector of distinct real scalar positive variables, $x_j > 0, j = 1, \ldots, p$ and let $x_1 + \ldots + x_p < 1$ so that the x_j's are in a unit ball. Let us optimize (47) under two product moment type constraints. Let

$$A = E[x_1^{\alpha_1 - 1} \ldots x_p^{\alpha_p - 1}]^{\frac{a-\alpha}{\eta}} \text{ and } B = E[(x_1^{\alpha_1 - 1} \ldots x_p^{\alpha_p - 1})^{\frac{a-\alpha}{\eta}}(\sum_{j=1}^{p} x_j)]$$

for $\Re(\alpha_j) > 0, j = 1, \ldots, p$, where $\Re(\cdot)$ denotes the real part of $(\cdot)$. Let the constraints be A is prefixed and B is prefixed. If we use calculus of variation to optimize (47) under the above constraints, then the Euler equation is the following, where λ_1 and λ_2 are Lagrangian multipliers:

$$\frac{\partial}{\partial f}\{f^{1+\frac{a-\alpha}{\eta}} - \lambda_1(x_1^{\alpha_1-1} \ldots x_p^{\alpha_p-1})^{\frac{a-\alpha}{\eta}} f - \lambda_2(x_1^{\alpha_1-1} \ldots x_p^{\alpha_p-1})^{\frac{a-\alpha}{\eta}}(\sum_{j=1}^{p} x_j) f\} = 0 \Rightarrow$$

$$(1 + \frac{a-\alpha}{\eta}) f^{\frac{a-\alpha}{\eta}} = \lambda_1(x_1^{\alpha_1-1} \ldots x_p^{\alpha_p-1})^{\frac{a-\alpha}{\eta}} + \lambda_2(x_1^{\alpha_1-1} \ldots x_p^{\alpha_p-1})^{\frac{a-\alpha}{\eta}}(\sum_{j=1}^{p} x_j) \Rightarrow$$

$$f = \lambda_3 x_1^{\alpha_1-1} \ldots x_p^{\alpha_p-1}[1 + \lambda_4 \sum_{j=1}^{p} x_j]^{\frac{\eta}{a-\alpha}}$$

for some λ_3 and λ_4. Let $\alpha < a$. Then, let us take $\lambda_4 = -b(a-\alpha), b > 0$ so that the right side of the above equation for f can form a density with λ_3 being the normalizing constant there. If $\lambda_4 = b(a-\alpha)$ with $b > 0, \alpha < a$, then the right side of f will be a positive exponential function and will not produce a density. Then,

$$f = \lambda_3 x_1^{\alpha_1-1} \ldots x_p^{\alpha_p-1}[1 - b(a-\alpha)(x_1 + \ldots + x_p)]^{\frac{\eta}{a-\alpha}}, \eta > 0, b > 0, \alpha < a \quad (48)$$

is a Mathai's pathway form of real scalar type-1 Dirichlet density. When $\alpha > a$, then (48) switches into a real scalar type-2 Dirichlet density with the corresponding normalizing constant.

Note that for $q = 1$, a $q \times q$ Hermitian positive definite matrix is a real scalar positive variable. Hence, (48) holds in the real and complex cases for $q = 1$ of $q \times q$ real positive definite or Hermitian positive definite matrices $X_1, \ldots, X_p$ or $\tilde{X}_1, \ldots, \tilde{X}_p$. The above is an example of the connection of type-1 and type-2 Dirichlet models to Tsallis entropy.

6. Applications

For our applications in the theory of special functions, fractional calculus, mechanics, biology, probability, and stochastic processes, Dirichlet averages and their diverse approaches are used. In this section, the main areas where the applications of Dirichlet averages are presented:

6.1. Special Functions

Dirichlet averages were introduced by Carlson in his 1977 work. Carlson [10–13] observed that the straightforward idea of this kind of averaging generalizes and unifies a wide range of special functions, including various orthogonal polynomials and generalized hyper-geometric functions. The relationship between Dirichlet splines and an important class of hypergeometric functions of several variables is given in [14,24]. Numerous investigations of B-splines, including those by [14,25,26], used Dirichlet averages.

6.2. Fractional Calculus

The Dirichlet average of elementary functions like power function, exponential function, etc. is given by many notable mathematicians. There are many results available in the literature converting the elementary function into the summation form after taking the Dirichlet average of those functions, using the fractional integral, and obtaining new results; see [27–32]. Those results will be used in the future by mathematicians and scientists in a variety of fields.

6.3. Statistical Mechanics

Statistical mechanics is a branch of physics that studies the behaviour of large systems of particles, such as gases, liquids, and solids. In statistical mechanics, entropy is a measure of the degree of disorder or randomness in a system; for more details, see [33,34]. The greater the entropy, the more disordered the system. Dirichlet averages and statistical mechanics are connected through the concept of entropy. Dirichlet averages are a type of mathematical average that weighs a set of values according to a given probability distribution. For example, given a set of values $x_1, x_2, \dots, x_n$ and a probability distribution $p_1, p_2, \dots, p_n$, the Dirichlet average is defined as:

$$D(p, x) = \sum_{i=1}^{n} p_i x_i.$$

Statistical mechanics is a branch of physics that studies the behavior of large systems of particles, such as gases, liquids, and solids. The connection between Dirichlet averages and statistical mechanics comes from the fact that the Dirichlet average can be seen as a type of average energy of a system weighted by a probability distribution. In statistical mechanics, the average energy of a system is also weighted by a probability distribution, and the entropy of the system is related to the probability distribution of the energy states. In particular, the Boltzmann entropy of a system is given by:

$$S = -k \sum_{i=1}^{n} p_i \ln p_i,$$

where k is the Boltzmann constant. This formula shows that the entropy of a system is proportional to the negative logarithm of the probability distribution of the energy states. Thus, Dirichlet averages and statistical mechanics are connected through the concept of entropy, which relates the average energy of a system to the probability distribution of its energy states. Dirichlet forms and their applications to quantum mechanics and statistical mechanics were established by [35]. Connections between Dirichlet distributions and a scale-invariant probabilistic model based on Leibniz-like pyramids are introduced by [36]. Ref. [37] showed that marginalizing the joint distribution of individual energies is a symmetric Dirichlet distribution.

6.4. Gene Expression Modeling

Clustering is a key data processing technique for interpreting microarray data and determining genetic networks. Hierarchical Dirichlet processes (HDP) clustering is able to capture the hierarchical elements that are common in biological data, such as gene expression data, by including a hierarchical structure into the statistical model. [38] presented a hierarchical Dirichlet process model for gene expression clustering.

6.5. Geometrical Probability

Thomas and Mathai [39] propose a generalized Dirichlet model application to geometrical probability problems. When the linearly independent random points in Euclidean n space have highly general real rectangle matrix-variate beta density, the volumes of random parallelotopes are explored. In order to evaluate statistical hypotheses, structural decomposition is provided, and random volumes are linked to generalized Dirichlet models and likelihood ratio criteria. This makes it possible to calculate percentage points of random volumes using the generalized Dirichlet marginal's p-values.

6.6. Bayesian Analysis

Carlson's original definition of Dirichlet averages is expressed as mixed multinomial distributions' probability-generating functions. They also significantly contribute to the solution of elliptic integrals and have several connections to statistical applications. Ref. [40] found that several nested families are built for Bayesian inference in multinomial sampling and contingency tables that generalize the Dirichlet distributions. These distributions can be used to model populations of personal probabilities evolving under the process of inference from statistical data.

7. Conclusions

In this study, the fundamental ideas for the theory development of the matrix-variate Dirichlet measure in the complex domain are presented. The complex matrix-variate type-2 Dirichlet measure and averages over some useful matrix-variate functions are discussed. We establish the Dirichlet measure of the rectangular matrix-variate and the relationship between Tsallis entropy and Dirichlet averages and identify a few applications in various domains. Additionally, a few applications are covered.

Author Contributions: Conceptualization, H.J.H.; Writing—original draft, P.T. and N.S.; Writing—review & editing, P.T., N.S. and H.J.H.; Supervision, H.J.H. All authors have read and agreed to the published version of the manuscript.

Funding: This research received no external funding.

Institutional Review Board Statement: Not applicable.

Data Availability Statement: No new data were created or analyzed in this study. Data sharing is not applicable to this article.

Acknowledgments: The authors would like to thank the referees for their valuable comments, which enabled the authors to improve the presentation of the material in the paper.

Conflicts of Interest: The authors declare no conflict of interest.

References

1. Hardy, G.H. On Dirichlet us Divisor Problem. *Proc. Lond. Math. Soc.* **1917**, *2*, 1–25. [CrossRef]
2. Hardy, G.H.; Littlewood, J.E. Some Problems of "Partitio Numerorum". III. On the Expression of a Number as a Sum of Primes. *Acta Math.* **1923**, *44*, 1–70. [CrossRef]
3. Erdős, L.; Yau, H. *A Dynamical Approach to Random Matrix Theory*; New York University: New York, NY, USA, 2017.
4. Mai, J.-F.; Schenk, S.; Scherer, M. Analyzing model robustness via a distortion of the stochastic root: A Dirichlet prior approach. *Stat. Risk Model.* **2015**, *32*, 177–195. [CrossRef]
5. Blei, D.M.; Ng, A.Y.; Jordan, M.I. Latent Dirichlet Allocation. *J. Mach. Learn. Res.* **2003**, *3*, 993–1022.
6. Griffiths, T.L.; Steyvers, M. Finding Scientific Topics. *Proc. Natl. Acad. Sci. USA* **2004**, *101*, 5228–5235. [CrossRef] [PubMed]
7. Hardy, G.H.; Littlewood, J.E.; Polya, G. *Inequalities*; Cambridge University Press: Cambridge, UK, 1952.
8. de Finetti, B. *Theory of Probability*; Wiley: New York, NY, USA, 1974; Volume I.
9. Carlson, B.C. *Special Functions of Applied Mathematics*; Academic Press: New York, NY, USA, 1977.
10. Carlson, B.C. Lauricella's hypergeometric function F_D. *J. Math. Anal. Appl.* **1963**, *7*, 452–470. [CrossRef]
11. Carlson, B.C. A connection between elementary and higher transcendental functions. *SIAM J. Appl. Math.* **1969**, *17*, 116–148. [CrossRef]
12. Carlson, B.C. Invariance of an integral average of a logarithm. *Amer. Math. Mon.* **1975**, *82*, 379–382. [CrossRef]
13. Carlson, B.C. Dirichlet Averages of $x^t logx$. *SIAM J. Math. Anal.* **1987**, *18*, 550–565. [CrossRef]
14. Carlson, B.C. $B-$splines, hypergeometric functions and Dirichlet average. *J. Approx. Theory* **1991**, *67*, 311–325. [CrossRef]
15. Mathai, A.M. *Jacobians of Matrix Transformations and Functions of Matrix Argument*; World Scientific Publishing: New York, NY, USA, 1997.
16. Gupta, R.D.; Richards, D.S.P. Multivariate Liouville distribution. *J. Multivariate Anal.* **1987**, *23*, 233–256. [CrossRef]
17. Hayakawa, T. On the distribution of the latent roots of a complex Wishart matrix (non-central case). *Ann. Inst. Statist. Math.* **1972**, *24*, 1–17 [CrossRef]
18. Fujikoshi, Y. Asymptotic expansions of the non-null distributions of two criteria for the linear hypothesis concerning complex multivariate normal populations. *Ann. Inst. Statist. Math.* **1971**, *23*, 477–490. [CrossRef]
19. Mathai, A.M. *An Introduction to Geometrical Probability: Distributional Aspects with Applications*; Gordon and Breach: Amsterdam, The Netherlands, 1999.

20. Mathai, A.M.; Provost, S.B.; Hayakawa, T. *Bilinear Forms and Zonal Polynomials*; Lecture Notes Series; Springer: New York, NY, USA, 1995.
21. Mathai, A.M. Random volumes under a general matrix-variate model. *Linear Algebra Its Appl.* **2007**, *425*, 162–170. [CrossRef]
22. Tsallis, C. Possible generalization of Boltzmann-Gibbs statistics. *J. Stat. Phys.* **1988**, *52*, 479—487. [CrossRef]
23. Mathai, A.M.; Rathie, P.N. *Basic Concepts in Information Theory and Statistics: Axiomatic Foundations and Applications*; Wiley Eastern: Mumbai, India, 1975.
24. Neuman, E.; Fleet, P.J.V. Moments of Dirichlet splines and their applications to hypergeometric functions. *J. Comput. Appl. Math.* **1994**, *53*, 225–241. [CrossRef]
25. Massopust, P.; Forster, B. Multivariate complex $B-$splines and Dirichlet averages. *J. Approx. Theory* **2010**, *162*, 252–269. [CrossRef]
26. Simić, S.; Bin-Mohsin, B. Stolarsky means in many variables. *Mathematics* **2020**, *8*, 1320. [CrossRef]
27. Kilbas, A.A.; Kattuveettill, A. Representations of Dirichlet averages of generalized Mittag–Leffler function via fractional integrals and special functions. *Frac. Calc. Appl. Anal.* **2008**, *11*, 471–492.
28. Saxena, R.K.; Pogány, T.K.; Ram, J.; Daiya, J. Dirichlet averages of generalized multi-index Mittag–Leffler functions. *Armen. J. Math.* **2010**, *3*, 174–187.
29. Uthayakumar, R.; Gowrisankar, A. Generalized Fractal Dimensions in Image Thresholding Technique, *Inf. Sci. Lett.* **2014**, *3*, 125–134. [CrossRef]
30. Noor, M.A.; Noor, K.I.; Iftikhar, S.; Awan, M.U. Fractal Integral Inequalities for Harmonic Convex Functions. *Appl. Math. Inf. Sci. Vol.* **2018**, **12**, 831–839. [CrossRef]
31. Dinesh, V.; Murugesan, G. A CPW-Fed Hexagonal Antenna With Fractal Elements For UWB Applications, *Appl. Math. Inf. Sci.* **2019**, *13*, 73–79. [CrossRef]
32. Kumar, D.; Ram, J.; Choi, J. Dirichlet Averages of Generalized Mittag–Leffler Type Function. *Fractal Fract.* **2022**, *6*, 297. [CrossRef]
33. Liu, Y. Extended Bayesian Framework for Multicategory Support Vector Machine. *J. Stat. Appl. Prob.* **2020**, *9*, 1–11.
34. Kumar, M.; Awasthi, A.A.; Kumar, A.; Patel, K.K. Sequential Testing Procedure for the Parameter of Left Truncated Exponential Distribution. *J. Stat. Appl. Prob.* **2020**, *9*, 119–125.
35. Albeverio, S.; Høegh-Krohn, R. Some remarks on Dirichlet forms and their applications to quantum mechanics and statistical mechanics. *Funct. Anal. Markov Process.* **1982**, *923*, 120–132.
36. Rodriguez, A.; Tsallis, C. Connection between Dirichlet distributions and a scale-invariant probabilistic model based on Leibniz-like pyramids. *J. Stat. Mech. Theory Exp.* **2014**, *12*, P12027. [CrossRef]
37. Scalas, E.; Gabriel, A.T.; Martin, E.; Germano, G. Velocity and energy distributions in microcanonical ensembles of hard spheres *Phys. Rev. E* **2015**, *92*, 022140.
38. Wang, L.; Wang, X. Hierarchical Dirichlet process model for gene expression clustering. *EURASIP J. Bioinform. Syst. Biol.* **2013**, *5*, 1–14. [CrossRef]
39. Thomas, S.; Mathai, A.M. p-Content of a p-Parallelotope and Its Connection to Lilkelihood Ratio Statistic. *Sankhyā Indian J. Stat. Ser.* **2009**, *71*, 49–63.
40. Dickey, J.M. Multiple hypergeometric functions: Probabilistic interpretations and statistical uses. *J. Amer. Statist. Assoc.* **1983**, *78*, 628–637. [CrossRef]

Article

Tsallis Entropy and Mutability to Characterize Seismic Sequences: The Case of 2007–2014 Northern Chile Earthquakes

Denisse Pasten [1,*], Eugenio E. Vogel [2,3,*], Gonzalo Saravia [4], Antonio Posadas [5,6] and Oscar Sotolongo [7]

1. Department of Physics, Universidad de Chile, Santiago Las Palmeras 3425, Santiago 8330111, Chile
2. Department of Physics, Universidad de La Frontera, Temuco Casilla 54-D, Temuco 4780000, Chile
3. Center for the Development of Nanoscience and Nanotechnology, Universidad de Santiago de Chile, Santiago 9170022, Chile
4. Los Eucaliptus 1189, Temuco 4812537, Chile; gonzalo.saravia@gmail.com
5. Departamento de Química y Física, Universidad de Almería, 04120 Almeria, Spain; aposadas@ual.es
6. Instituto Andaluz de Geofísica, Universidad de Granada, Campus Universitario de Cartuja, 18071 Granada, Spain
7. Cátedra de Sistemas Complejos "Henri Poincaré", Universidad de La Habana, Habana 10400, Cuba; osotolongo@gmail.com
* Correspondence: denisse.pasten.g@gmail.com (D.P.); eugenio.vogel@ufrontera.cl (E.E.V.)

Citation: Pasten, D.; Vogel, E.E.; Saravia, G.; Posadas, A.; Sotolongo, O. Tsallis Entropy and Mutability to Characterize Seismic Sequences: The Case of 2007–2014 Northern Chile Earthquakes. *Entropy* **2023**, *25*, 1417. https://doi.org/10.3390/e25101417

Academic Editors: Andrea Rapisarda, Airton Deppman, Astero Provata, Evaldo M. F. Curado, Christian Beck, Hans J. Herrmann, Henrik Jeldtoft Jensen, Ugur Tirnakli, Fernando D. Nobre and Angelo Plastino

Received: 29 August 2023
Revised: 25 September 2023
Accepted: 27 September 2023
Published: 5 October 2023

Copyright: © 2023 by the authors. Licensee MDPI, Basel, Switzerland. This article is an open access article distributed under the terms and conditions of the Creative Commons Attribution (CC BY) license (https://creativecommons.org/licenses/by/4.0/).

Abstract: Seismic data have improved in quality and quantity over the past few decades, enabling better statistical analysis. Statistical physics has proposed new ways to deal with these data to focus the attention on specific matters. The present paper combines these two progressions to find indicators that can help in the definition of areas where seismic risk is developing. Our data comes from the IPOC catalog for 2007 to 2014. It covers the intense seismic activity near Iquique in Northern Chile during March/April 2014. Centered in these hypocenters we concentrate on the rectangle Lat_{-22}^{-18} and Lon_{-68}^{-72} and deepness between 5 and 70 km, where the major earthquakes originate. The analysis was performed using two complementary techniques: Tsallis entropy and mutability (dynamical entropy). Two possible forecasting indicators emerge: (1) Tsallis entropy (mutability) increases (decreases) broadly about two years before the main $M_W 8.1$ earthquake. (2) Tsallis entropy (mutability) sharply decreases (increases) a few weeks before the $M_W 8.1$ earthquake. The first one is about energy accumulation, and the second one is because of energy relaxation in the parallelepiped of interest. We discuss the implications of these behaviors and project them for possible future studies.

Keywords: Tsallis entropy; information theory; subduction seismicity

1. Introduction

We can approach a variety of problems in physics through statistical mechanics. Some examples include real magnetization systems [1,2], spin models [3,4], molecular interactions [5], fluids [6], space plasmas [7,8] among others. However, statistical mechanics can be also useful in more complex systems such as social interactions [9], traffic [10], wind energy [11], and earthquakes [12–17]. A common key element in this variety of applications is entropy, which directly points to the accessible states under given conditions. Magnetic systems and rocks under tension could both alter their configuration spaces making some external manifestations more probable/improbable. When we speak about probability of states we are reaching the domain of entropy, that "lives" in the configuration space. Entropy can be defined in different ways. This paper focuses on two forms: Tsallis entropy and mutability (or dynamical entropy).

In recent years, studies of entropy in earthquakes have been used to show the evolution of the seismic systems in time. These studies have relied on datasets coming from different zones of the Earth. In a quick summary, we can mention the following recent developments: (i) Shannon entropy has been found useful in identifying earthquake risk areas [18]; (ii) a study established the way both the Shannon entropy and mutability reflect the seismic activity [19]; (iii) researchers have recently tested Tsallis entropy in different seismic zones of the world [20,21].

In addition, in all the studies previously mentioned we can use the concept of natural time. This concept has proven to be very useful in the study of earthquakes. The natural time allows one to follow a time series step-by-step through a scaling of the time such as $\chi_k = k/N$ where k follows the occurrence of a seismic event in time [22,23]. In the present paper, we will use it for comparison only so a simpler form is enough: the enumeration of events.

In the present article, we revisit the same seismic area of our recent articles [19,24] with the purpose of completing the study with the following recent developments: (a) for the first time we report mutability on the sequence of magnitudes (before we investigated it on intervals); (b) for the first time we compare and discuss Tsallis entropy and mutability on the same footage: this allows us to call the later "dynamical entropy"; (c) we perform a tuning process to detect the importance of the size of the time window to analyze the dynamical process; (d) we conduct a progressive approximation to days and hours prior to the large earthquake to detect premonitory signs and we believe we can report a couple of them; (e) we conclude that the aftershock regime closed quickly in this area and energy continues to accumulate at levels similar to those before the 2014 earthquakes.

2. Methodology

2.1. Data Source

Chile is placed close and almost parallel to the border of the subduction zone between the Nazca Plate and the South American Plate. This is a source of seismicity in a wide range of magnitudes along different geographical conditions. In recent years, scientists have concentrated their attention on the seismicity of the northern zone of Chile. IPOC is an outcome of this effort, which is a network of institutions from Europe and South America. Its networks have measured earthquakes on the Peru-Chile coastal margin for decades. This network's seismic data is helpful to understand the seismic dynamics in northern Chile and to identify potential risks.

Scientists are interested in the Northern zone of Chile because of its frequent earthquakes and the fact that there have been no major earthquakes in the recent past. The last historical mega-thrust earthquake in the northern zone of Chile was in 1877 [25–27]. A partial list of important recent earthquakes is: Antofagasta (1991) M_w8.0 [28], Tarapaca (2005) M_w7.7 [29], Tocopilla (2007) M_w7.7 [30], and Iquique (2014) M_w6.6, M_w8.1, M_w7.6 [31,32]. Each one of the previous large seisms generated a powerful chain of aftershocks. This seismicity is mainly shallow at intermediate depths (less than 80 km). The quality of the data has improved with time due to better stations, more stations, and more coordination among seismological institutions. This is the main reason to consider only a few years before 2014, up to 2007 considering the Tocopilla seism as the last previous event.

The Iquique earthquake has a complex structure that deserves a dedicated investigation. In its simplest form, it can be viewed as a triple earthquake in 2014: M_w6.6 on 03.16, M_w8.1 on 04.01 and M_w7.6 on 04.03. Each of the previous earthquakes generated aftershock activity. Even the first one (the weakest of the three) had two important aftershocks M_w6.4 on 03.17 and on 03.23, and several others over M_w6.0. Alternatively, one can consider that the M_w8.1 seism is the important one here, declaring all previous activity in the area as pre-shock and what came afterwards as aftershock activity; the M_w7.6 earthquake is absorbed within the aftershock of the larger one. However, one can also choose to consider this last seism on its own, with its aftershock regime and rupture area. This is an anticipation of the results and discussions to be represented below.

It is also important to consider some previous discussions concerning the aftershock activity in this region [31–33], and a zone with a low coupling [27]. Socquet et al. in 2017 [34] showed that the major shock was led by an acceleration that started aproximately eigth months before the large earthquake. Jara et al. 2017 [35] found a strong link between shallow and intermediate depth seismic activity, showing that it may have caused the Iquique earthquake. All this evidence points to the understanding of the physical process behind the occurrence of a great earthquake and it is to this understanding that this work also contributes.

2.2. Handling of Data

We center our attention on the large Iquique earthquake (1 April 2014) with M_w 8.1 located at 19.589° South Latitude and 70.940° West Longitude; its depth was 19.91 km (data from IPOC catalogue [36]), its preshock activity and the aftershock activity recorded in the IOPC catalogue. The epicenter was situated 95 km Northwest of Iquique city and a tsunami alert was issued for Chile, Peru and Ecuador, which was later extended to Colombia and Panama. Viewed in this way, the major shock is preceded by an intense foreshock sequence and followed by a large M_w7.6 [37] as is shown in Figure 1.

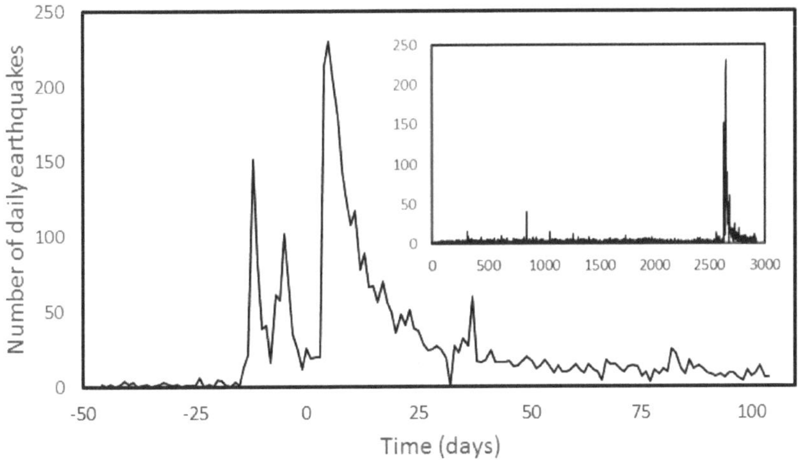

Figure 1. Number of daily earthquakes in the selected IPOC catalogue from years 2007 to 2014, fully displayed in the inset. On the abscissa axis in the main body, day 0 corresponds to 1 April 2014, coinciding with the M_w8.1 earthquake. It can be noticed that the pre−shock activity appears about 17 days before. The aftershock response extended months afterwards.

Preparing the initial dataset comprises three steps. First, we chose the epicentral area according to the main event coordinates. We drew a "rectangle" with Lat_{-22}^{-18} and Lon_{-68}^{-72} based on the main event coordinates, and found 65,050 seisms in the IPOC catalogue. We considered all these seisms to calculate the Gutenberg-Richter relationship to define the threshold magnitude M_0 (we used the MAXC technique [38] because it is a simple method for the goals we pursue). The second step involved setting up a $M_0$2.2 that is shown in the peak of the red triangles in Figure 2.

We consider all the seisms within the parallelepiped defined by Lat_{-22}^{-18} and Lon_{-68}^{-72} and 200 km depth. Longitude and depth are used as coordinates to make a map of all earthquakes, regardless of latitude. Dots represent the location of seisms in Figure 3. A careful look at this figure unveils the two plates, with the subduction front defining a downward diagonal from West to East.

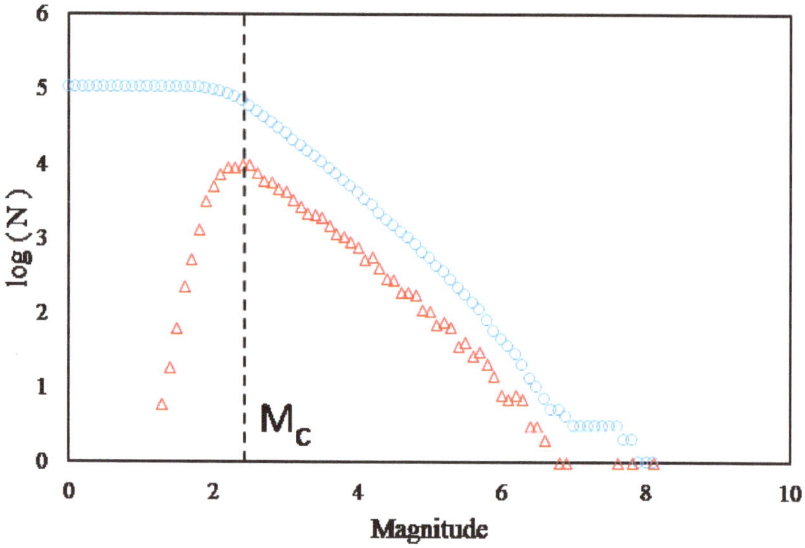

Figure 2. We analyzed the data from the IPOC catalog using the Gutenberg-Richter law, including earthquakes from 2007 to 2014 with epicenters within 18 °S–22 °S and 68 °W–72 °W. Circles denote the cumulative number of earthquakes; triangles denote the abundance of earthquakes for a magnitude. Based on the maximum curvature (MAXC) technique (Wiemer and Wyss, 2000), $M_0 = 2.2$.

The third step is the right panel of Figure 3 where now depth is the only variable while seisms result in a histogram giving the abundance of seisms as a function of depth. A bimodal is clearly appreciated, where the lower component receives most of its contributions from a mixture of tectonic (Continental Plate) and intra-plate earthquakes. The large deep distribution is originated within the Nazca plate. The first group of earthquakes deserves our full attention, as those earthquakes caused the most damage and could trigger deadly tsunamis. For this reason, we set the deepness filter at 70 km, corresponding to the minimum of the distribution in the right panel of Figure 3.

Moreover, we left out the shallower first 5 km to avoid contamination coming from the mining work conducted in the area. Earthquakes from 5 to 70 km will be handled in the rest of this paper. We make this cut in the dataset to focus this analysis in the zone close to the hypocenter. The number of earthquakes left for study after previous filtering is 10,640.

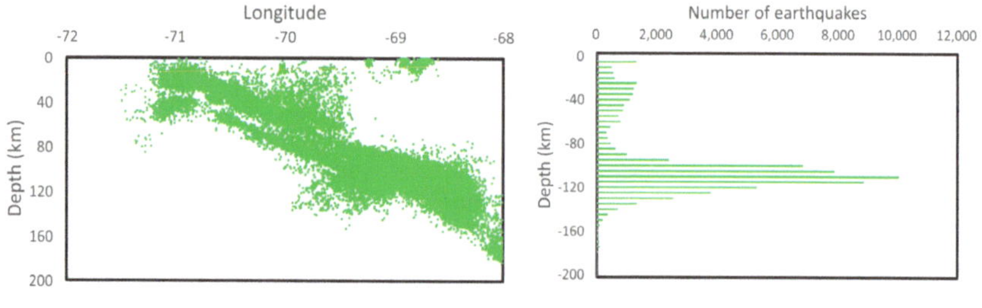

Figure 3. Depth distribution of earthquakes at different longitudes. Seisms at different latitudes are accumulated on this two−dimensional view. A histogram with respect to depth is presented on the right panel.

Finally, Figure 4 presents the epicentral zone with the selected earthquakes.

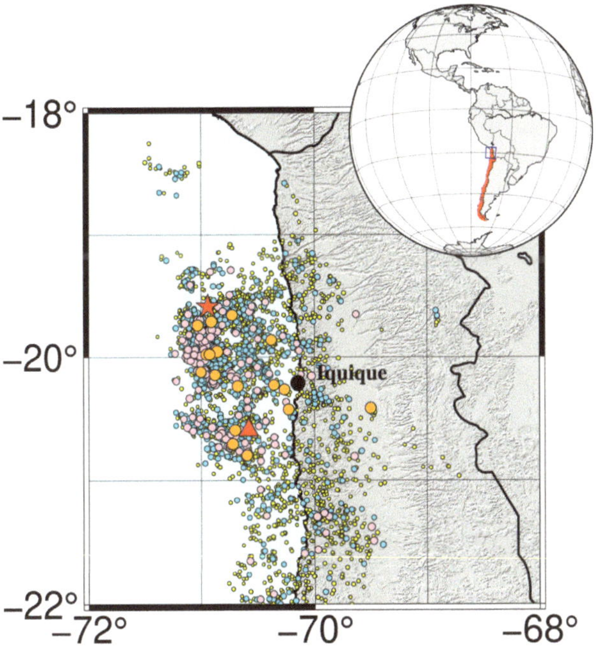

Figure 4. Epicentral map of the area under study: the black circle marks the city of Iquique, 95 km from the epicenter. Magnitude of the seisms are illustrated by both a proportional diameter and the color of the circles: yellow $3.0 \leq M_w \leq 3.9$, cyan $4.0 \leq M_w \leq 4.9$, pink $5.0 \leq M_w \leq 5.9$, orange $6.0 \leq M_w \leq 6.9$. The red star positions the great earthquake of Iquique with $M_w 8.1$, while the red triangle shows the epicenter of its main aftershock with $M_w 7.6$.

2.3. Tsallis Entropy

Let start by considering an earthquake as a critical phenomenon in a complex system (fracture zone) that experiences a phase transition from a non-equilibrium state (where stresses and strain in crust lead to fault slip) to another state (where stresses and strain have become to relax); several physical models have been developed to describe their essential properties [13,15,23,39–42]. Thereby, the maximum entropy principle has widely been applied in many out-of-equilibrium systems in physics (and other sciences), providing novel insights into their macroscopic states [43]. Sotolongo-Costa and Posadas (2004) [20] introduced the fragment-asperity interaction model for earthquake dynamics (SCP model) based on the non-extensive statistical formalism; in this model, the released seismic energy is related to the size of the fragments that fill the space between fault blocks. According to the SCP model, if $N\,(>M)$ is the cumulative distribution of the number of earthquakes N with magnitude greater than M, then:

$$\log(N(>M)) = \log(N) + \frac{2-q}{1-q}\log\left(1 + a(q-1)(2-q)^{\frac{1-q}{q-2}}10^{2M}\right). \tag{1}$$

where a is a real number expressing the proportionality between the released seismic energy and the size of the fragments, and q is the entropic index from Tsallis entropy. Equation (1) appropriately generalizes the Gutenberg–Richter relationship over a broad range of magnitudes [43] and exhibits an excellent fit to earthquake datasets [14,20,44,45]. In fact, the Gutenberg–Richter law can be easily deduced as [12,46]:

$$b = 2\frac{2-q}{q-1}. \tag{2}$$

Moreover, q values obtained from different regions of the world [12] are all $q \approx 1.5 - 1.7$, suggesting the universality of this constant.

Recently, Posadas and Sotolongo-Costa (2023) [24] established the entropy of fragments and asperities within fault fractures (i.e., within gouge fault zones) and determine their behavior during an earthquake. Authors assume the hypothesis that prior to an earthquake, the state of the system, characterized by a range of fragment sizes and stress distribution forms many "microstates" compatible with fragment distribution; such entropy can be assumed to be (relatively) large. During an earthquake, fragments are broken, while asperities and barriers are overcome. Furthermore, fragment sizes become homogenized and this decreases the number of possible "microstates", as such, entropy decreases. As this process is abrupt and rapid, the entropy decreases suddenly; it subsequently recovers as stress starts to re-accumulate. From a statistical mechanics perspective, the higher the number of microstates, the higher the entropy and vice versa.

Tsallis entropy (Equation (1)) for a continuous distribution $p(\sigma)$ of fragments of sizes σ is given by (for simplicity we set $k = 1$):

$$S = \frac{1 - \int_0^\infty p^q(\sigma)d\sigma}{q-1}, \tag{3}$$

subject to two restrictions:

$$\int_0^\infty p(\sigma)d\sigma = 1 \tag{4}$$

and

$$\int_0^\infty \sigma p^q(\sigma)d\sigma = \langle\langle\sigma\rangle\rangle_q, \tag{5}$$

where $\langle\langle\sigma\rangle\rangle_q$ is the mean of the distribution. Therefore, the maximum entropy principle allows us to form the following Lagrangian:

$$L(p) = \frac{1 - \int_0^\infty p^q(\sigma)d\sigma}{q-1} - \alpha\int_0^\infty p(\sigma)d\sigma - \beta\int_0^\infty \sigma p^q(\sigma)d\sigma. \tag{6}$$

where α and β are the Lagrange multipliers. Imposing the Lagrangian to be extreme:

$$\frac{\partial L}{\partial p} = 0 \tag{7}$$

after some algebra it is possible to find that:

$$p(\sigma) = \frac{\left[\frac{1-q}{q}\alpha\right]^{\frac{1}{q-1}}}{[1 + \beta\sigma(q-1)]^{\frac{1}{q-1}}}, \tag{8}$$

where, implicitly, a cut-off condition has been used for the denominator [47]. Finally, by substituting Equation (8) into that of non-extensive entropy (Equation (3)) and solving the integral in the numerator [21], we can obtain:

$$S = \frac{1 - \int_0^\infty p^q(\sigma)d\sigma}{q-1} = \frac{1 - (2-q)^{\frac{1}{2-q}}}{q-1}. \tag{9}$$

This equation allows us to find the value of the entropy for a dataset and to study its behavior as a function of the non-extensive q parameter; therefore, if a windowing process is carried out (i.e., choosing a certain number of earthquakes and sliding the window in time), it is possible to visualize the dynamic evolution of the seismic series in terms of non-extensive entropy. The process is as follows:

1. First, the time window W is determined for the calculation of entropy; in other words, the minimum number of earthquakes used to calculate S from Equation (9). In

general, the final window size is a reasonable compromise between the required resolution and smoothing results.

2. Second, parameter b from the Gutenberg–Richter relationship for the chosen window W is determined; this can be calculated from the classical expression of Aki (1965) [48] and the subsequent correction by Utsu (1965) [49]:

$$b = \frac{\log(e)}{\bar{M} - \left(M_0 - \frac{\Delta M}{2}\right)}, \tag{10}$$

where M_0 is the threshold magnitude; ΔM is the resolution of the magnitude (usually $\Delta M = 0.1$); and $\bar{M}$ is the average value of all possible magnitudes, which is given by:

$$\bar{M} = \int_{M_0}^{\infty} Mp(M)dM. \tag{11}$$

The estimation of M_0 is performed, as we noted before, using the maximum curvature (MAXC) technique [38].

3. Finally, approximation according to Sarlis et al. (2010) [12] Equation (2) is used to determine q; then, the non-extensive entropy is computed for each time t following Equation (9). By convention, the time attributed to each point of the analyses is the time of the last seismic event considered in each window.

2.4. Mutability

Information content is valuable information leading to entropy in different ways [50–52]. During the last decade or so a dynamical entropy called mutability has been introduced in an empirical way to characterize information content in a data sequence [53].

To obtain the value of mutability, we first create a vector file with the sequence or time series to be recognized (Monte Carlo simulation of the magnetization of a system, magnitude of consecutive earthquakes in a given region, variations in the value of a given economical asset, and similar sequences of measurable evolving quantities). All registers have the same number of digits filling with zeroes the empty positions. The number of bytes occupied by this vector file is w. This file is then compressed and the compressed file occupies w^* bytes. Then, the value of the mutability for this sequence is defined as the ratio:

$$\mu(\alpha) = \frac{w^*}{w}, \tag{12}$$

where α represents the set of parameters that characterize the system (size, temperature, etc.).

In principle any data compressor can accomplish this task and blzip2 was used previously [54]. However, data compressors are based on search for repetitive chains of characters, which can accidentally occur without a physical meaning. To cope with this inaccuracy, a data compressor based on exact matching of physically meaningful information was developed under the name "world length zipper" (wlzip for short) which will be summarized next [54].

2.5. Algorithm of the Data Recognizer

The compressed or recognized file is a map constructed from the original, according to an algorithm that obeys the following rules:

(a) Navigate to the first register of the original file, copy it onto the compressed file as a first register followed by a space and then the digit 0 to indicate the beginning or origin of the new file.

(b) Select the following register in the original file and compare it to the already stored register(s) in the compressed file.

- If this register already exists then navigate to its row, leave a space and write to the right the "distance" or number of registers since it was previously found in the original file.
- If the register repeats itself immediately after, place a comma and the number of consecutive repetitions.
- If this register is new, then write it at a new row followed a space and then the distance to the first register.

(c) Navigate to next register and repeat the procedure given in (b) until the last register in the file.

So now we have the original file with weight w and the compressed file with weight w^*. According to Equation (12) the mutability of the original file measured in this way is w^*/w.

We illustrate the concept of mutability and the use of wlzip by two sequences of 50 seisms each, both obtained from the filtered catalog defined above.

The first sequence, called "Before", lists the magnitudes of the 50 seisms beginning on 1 February 2014, covering a few days before the 6.6 earthquake. Their sequential magnitudes are: 2.4, 4.0, 3.8, 4.0, 2,2, 4.6, 3.5, 2.9, 2.2, 3.0, 4.1, 3.1, 3.1, 4.3, 4.3, 3.6, 5.5, 3.5, 2.4, 3.5, 2.7, 2.5, 2.2, 2.5, 2.3, 2.5, 2.6, 3.3, 2.4, 2.9, 2.6, 2.8, 2.3, 2.2, 2.2, 2.4, 3.8, 4.1, 2.8, 2.4, 2.5, 2.2, 2.5, 2.8, 2.3, 2.5, 3.4, 4.0, 4.0, 2.9.

The second one, called "After", gathers the sequence of magnitudes of the 50 seisms beginning with the 6.6 earthquake of March 16, 2014 and obtains the 49 following seisms. The list is the following: 6.6, 4.5, 4.8, 4.1, 3.1, 5.2, 4.8, 4.2, 3.8, 3.5 3.1, 4.8, 3.7, 3.1, 3.6, 3.3, 3.1, 4.0, 2.7, 3.5 3.2, 4.8, 2.8, 3.5, 2.4, 4.7, 3.0, 2.9, 3.2, 4.1 4.3, 4.0, 5.1, 3.3, 4.3, 3.4, 3.8, 4.7, 3.1, 3.1 2.6, 4.7, 3.4, 3.3, 3.7, 4.7, 3.0, 3.1, 3.7, 3.4.

The procedure is illustrated in Table 1. The left-hand-side is the compressed file of "Before" called "BeforeC" and the right-hand-side is the compressed file of "After", namely, "AfterC".

Let us begin with "Before". We obtain its first register in the first row of "BeforeC" followed by its position 0 at the origin. The following register is 4.0 (new) and just one position from the first one. The next register is 3.8 (new), two positions from the origin. The next one is 4.0, which is already listed so we navigate to its row in BeforeC and write a 2 to the right, meaning that its new position is two rows below its previous appearance. The next register is 2.2 which is new and four positions from the origin. Similarly, we continue with the new ones 4.6, 3.5 and 2.9. However, then we find 2.2 which we found found positions before so we add a 4 to its row. We continue to the magnitude 3.0 found nine positions from the origin. Next is also a new one: 4.1, ten positions distant from the origin. The following one is 3.1, also new, but repeats itself immediately so we write its coordinate 11 then a comma and then the number of repetitions which is two. Something similar happens with magnitude 4.3 coming next. In this way we can continue applying the rules above to complete the file "Before". We perform a similar procedure to the file "After".

One first results is obvious: The length of "After" is larger than the one of "Before" and so it is its span of values. When the mutability is measured for these two files the result is 0.94 for "Before" and 1.00 for "After". It is clear that the aftershock regime brings in a larger variety of magnitudes so the information content increases and so does the mutability (dynamical entropy).

Columns identified by f_B and f_A give the abundance or frequency of this value in the sequence. So these columns give the histograms for the sequences Before and After, respectively. However, columns marked as MapB and MapA also represent a histogram, but with an internal structure related to the dynamics of the sequence. This is the basis of the difference between the mutability and other forms of entropy where it is only the distribution of values that matters, regardless of the way the sequence was produced.

Table 1. Illustration of the generation of the compressed files. The first column is just an enumeration of lines. The second, third and fourth (sixth, seventh and eighth) columns refer to the rules applied to file "Before" ("After"), giving the magnitude M, the relative coordinates to construct the map and the corresponding frequencies of the magnitudes of that row. Details are given in the text.

	Before			After		
n	**M**	MapB	f_B	**M**	MapA	f_A
1	**2.4**	0 18 10 7 4	5	**6.6**	0	1
2	**4.0**	1 2 44,2	4	**4.5**	1	1
3	**3.8**	2 34	2	**4.8**	2 4 5 10	4
4	**2.2**	4 4 14 11,2 8	6	**4.1**	3 26	2
5	**4.6**	5	1	**3.1**	4 6 3 3 22,2 9	7
6	**3.5**	6 11 2	3	**5.2**	5	1
7	**2.9**	7 22 20	3	**4.2**	7	1
8	**3.0**	9	1	**3.8**	8 28	2
9	**4.1**	10 27	2	**3.5**	9 10 4	3
10	**3.1**	11,2	2	**3.7**	12 32 4	3
11	**4.3**	13,2	2	**3.6**	14	1
12	**3.6**	15	1	**3.3**	15 18 10	3
13	**5.5**	16	1	**4.0**	17 14	2
14	**2.7**	20	1	**2.7**	18	1
15	**2.5**	21 2 2 15 2 3	6	**3.2**	20 8	2
16	**2.3**	24 8 12	3	**2.8**	22	1
17	**2.6**	26 4	2	**2.4**	24	1
18	**3.3**	27	1	**4.7**	25 12 4 4	4
19	**2.8**	31 7 5	3	**3.0**	26 20	2
20	**3.4**	46	1	**2.9**	27	1
21				**4.3**	30 4	2
22				**5.1**	32	1
23				**3.4**	35 7 7	3
24				**2.6**	40	1

2.6. Tuning the Information Recognizer

The algorithm is now a powerful program that we offer for free—email ee.vogel@ufrontera.cl to download it. This allows us to distinguish and process different data according to what is appropriate for each system. The following adjustments need to be made:

(i) Is this a static calculation (entire file, just once) or a dynamical calculation through time windows? Answer: it is dynamic through windows with W registers.

(ii) Are these successive independent or overlapping windows? Answer: we use overlapping successive windows.

(iii) If they overlap, what is the size of the overlap? We consider here a displacement of just one register between consecutive windows so the overlap is $W-1$ events.

(iv) In step (b) of the algorithm described above, a numeric comparison is performed between two registers. How many digits and which digits bear the most sensitive information to perform this comparison? An estimation is possible after inspecting the data, but we let wlzip itself find the digits that lead to a better precision. The comparison is restricted to the r digits from position i and the following $r-1$ digits; this is denoted (i,r). In the examples of Table 1, all comparisons were for i = 1, r = 3 (the dot needs to be compared as well).

(v) If precision is needed, wlzip has the feature of handling different numeric bases (quaternary, binary, ...) which can help to discriminate intermediate positions.

WLZIP applies to any parameter $P(t)$ stored in a vector file and indeed it has been used to recognize phase transitions or criticality in different fields: magnetism [54,55], econophysics [56], polymer deposition on surfaces [57,58], wind energy optimization [59].

The first application of wlzip to seismology came recently using data from a Chilean catalogue measured by CSN [60] finding the variations in wlzip results years and months prior to large earthquakes [61]. Then the study was extended to four zones along the subduction trench, comparing their dynamics by means of Shannon entropy and mutability [19]. More recently, a deepness analysis of the same "rectangle" near Iquique was performed by means of Tsallis entropy [24].

3. Results

The earthquakes of 2014 have raised several questions concerning their dynamics. Here, we addressed their study computing the Tsallis entropy for the first time focusing on the magnitude of the quakes, complemented by the mutability on the same data. For the first time, we will compare these two entropies based on an analysis over time.

Figure 5 plots the Tsallis entropy for successive overlapping time windows defined by the last W seisms. (A) W = 256; (B) W = 512; (C) W = 1024; (D) W = 2048. Abscissas reflect real time in days with major ticks close to a year mark. Let us examine plot (A) where, apart from oscillations, we see a broad valley around day 800, a maximum or "swelling" around day 1600, and stronger oscillations with a sharp decrease near day 2600, which roughly coincides with the big earthquake. Then, Tsallis entropy partially recovers in an oscillatory way during the aftershock regime. In Figure 5B–D we can observe similar behaviors, except that oscillations are damped due to a larger statistics upon increasing the window spans. The larger W values also displaces the texture of the curves a bit to the right. The three main earthquakes that mark these complex seismic behaviors are shown by stars with the magnitudes displaced in the inset. They were vertically split since otherwise they would overlap at this scale.

It is interesting to notice how these four figures show a consistent increment in the Tsallis entropy before an abrupt decay. We believe this is a manifestation of the subduction process where the large fragments in between the Nazca plate and the South American plate prevent sliding. However, possibilities in which the dynamics can change increase with time leading to an increase in Tsallis entropy [21]. This effect begins about two years before the large earthquake which is in agreement with Socquet et al. in 2017 [34], who detected an increase in the acceleration in the displacement of the plates several months before the large earthquake.

When the fragments fracture, smaller pieces tend to fill in the interspace, thus lubricating the sliding of one plate with respect to the other. This leads to a sudden decrease in the Tsallis entropy to denote the time of the major seism and the beginning of the aftershock regime.

In addition, we should mention that prior to the large earthquakes events are mostly independent: their epicenters are at different locations, no time correlation is observed, and magnitudes are moderate. Thus, during the apparent calm period, mostly uncorrelated seisms are produced. The large $M_w 8.1$ earthquake fractures the fragments, unleashing a variety of correlated seismic chains in little time, causing an abrupt decrease in Tsallis entropy. As the underground layers settle, the near equilibrium goes back to the situation months or years before the violent earthquake.

In Figure 6A–D we present the mutability results for the same seisms, using the same time windows of previous figure. In all cases the plots sharply increase when the moving windows reach the time of three main earthquakes; for more clarity their times are marked using particular symbols as given in the inset. The main feature of these figures is the abrupt growth of mutability during the earthquake period. Larger time windows moderate the oscillations, but the sharp peak near day 2600 prevails in all of them. A more subtle feature becomes more pronounced as the time window increases: for years before the activity of 2010, the mutability goes through a maximum then it decreases reaching a minimum. It then quickly recovers, maximizing during the great seismic activity.

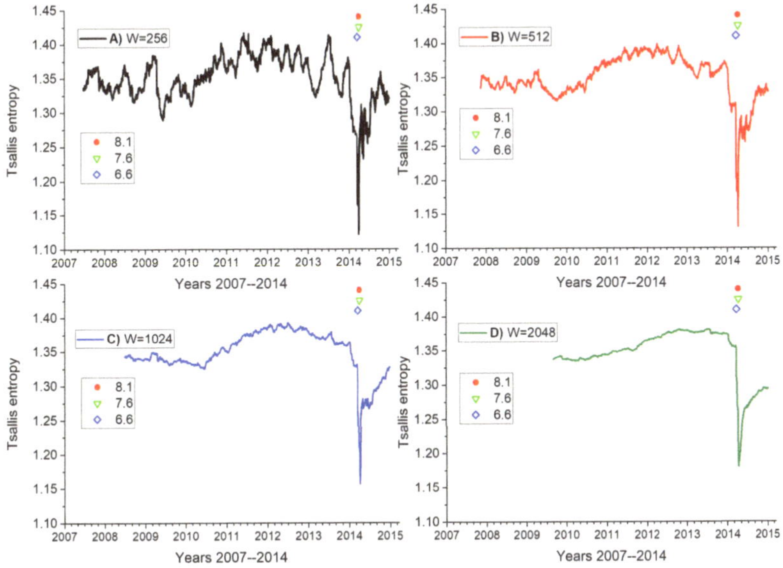

Figure 5. Tsallis entropy on magnitude sequence in terms of real time, using four different dynamic windows *W* as indicated in the code on top. (**A**) With 256 seismic events, (**B**) with 512 seismic events, (**C**) with 1024 seismic events and (**D**) with 2048 seismic events. Stars give the time of the most important earthquakes of the series whose magnitude is given in the inset.

Figures 5 and 6 show an inverse behavior. To understand the behavior of the mutability we must remember that it is essentially based on the special kind of histogram constructed in the way shown in Table 1. Just before the main seisms, the series are comparable to the case of BeforeC in Table 1: lower mutability. During and after the large seisms, the mutability is closer to the situation represented by the column AfterC in Table 1, namely, larger mutability values. So the mutability decreases during the calm periods before an earthquake at the same time the Tsallis entropy grows. During the large seisms and their immediate aftershock activity the mutability sharply grows at the same time Tsallis entropy sharply decreases. Turning to the aftershock period, Tsallis entropy gradually increases while the mutability gradually decreases, both in oscillatory ways.

In Figure 7 we use a window of 512 seismic events and we compute the Tsallis entropy and the mutability before the large earthquake of magnitude $M_w 8.1$, stopping short before including the main earthquake. Thus this series presents the instant picture 80, 40, 20 and 2 days before the major earthquake. Several features are of interest here. First, Tsallis entropy and mutability progress in complementary ways; this is probably due to the fact that Tsallis entropy is based on the real space, while mutability looks at the states in the configuration space. Second, a rather pronounced change in the dynamics of both Tsallis entropy and mutability is already noticeable 80 days before April 1, where no important seism has been reported. Third, this is confirmed 40 days prior the large earthquake, where both curves present a slight turn back. This picture remained frozen until 20 days before. Then, in the picture taken 2 days before, we have a pronounced change in both curves—a product of the 6.6 seism of March 16 and the subsequent aftershock activity. Fourth, this premonitory behavior is additional and shorter in time than the previously mentioned maximization (minimization) of the Tsallis entropy (mutability) around the years 2011 and 2012, namely, two years in advance.

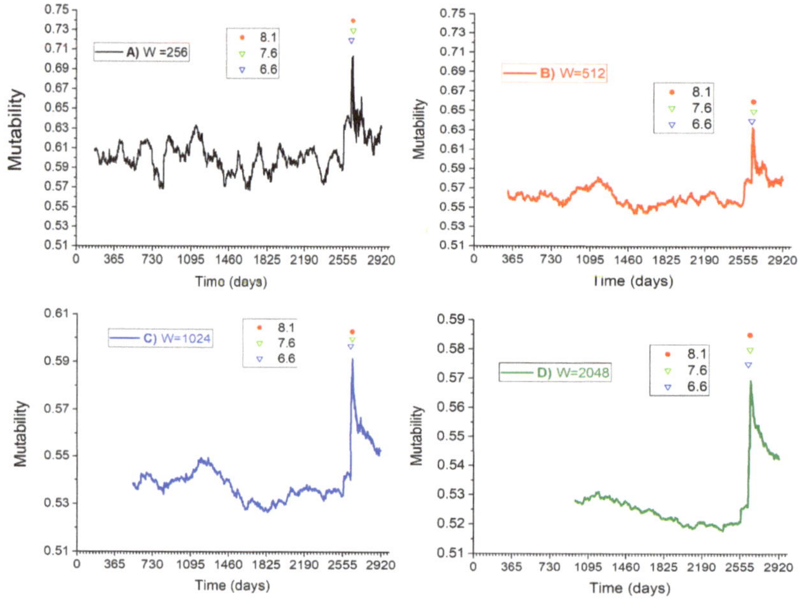

Figure 6. Mutability on magnitude sequence in real time using four different dynamic windows W as indicated in the insets. Construction is similar to previous figure but this time we choose to report the time in days, grouped in years. Stars report the three major earthquakes as given in the inset.

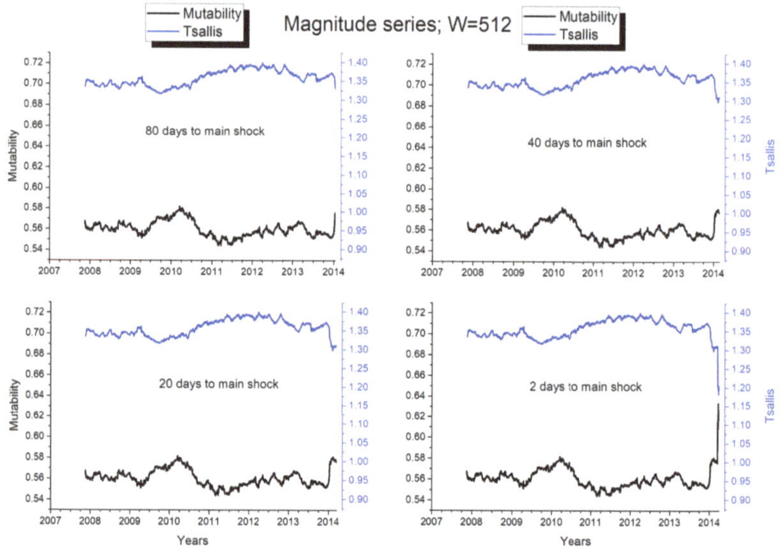

Figure 7. Approximation to the main shock by a dynamical window of W = 512 events. The data is the same in the four plots but time is stopped at 80, 40, 20 or 2 days before the strongest M_w8.1 quake. Eventually, a video could be a more appropriate way to represent this evolution, but the most relevant information is obtained from these four pictures. The black curve represents mutability and the blue curve Tsallis entropy.

These results show how the Tsallis entropy and the dynamic entropy could notify a change in the configuration of the seismic system days before the occurrence of a large earthquake being a contribution to the evaluation of seismic hazards in this zone. Eventually, this way of introducing the approach to the critical moment could be presented in video formto further stress the anticipation signals the system emitted before the breakdown.

Finally, Figure 8 is a remake of Figure 6 but now using the 10,640 seismic events as natural time along the abscissa axis. In this way the sequence is better appreciated. Thus, for instance, the symbols marking the three main earthquakes indicated in the inset open up, allowing to appreciate the role of each seism in each plot. The decrease in mutability before the leading earthquake is clearly manifested, especially for W = 512 and over.

More work has to be performed before claiming this could evolve into a method to diagnose seismic risk, but at the moment we leave it as a proposal or hypothesis. To delve deeper into this matter, catalogues of quality similar to IPOC are necessary, validated over many years or decades in different regions of the world. We shall attempt to conduct this with time whenever is possible.

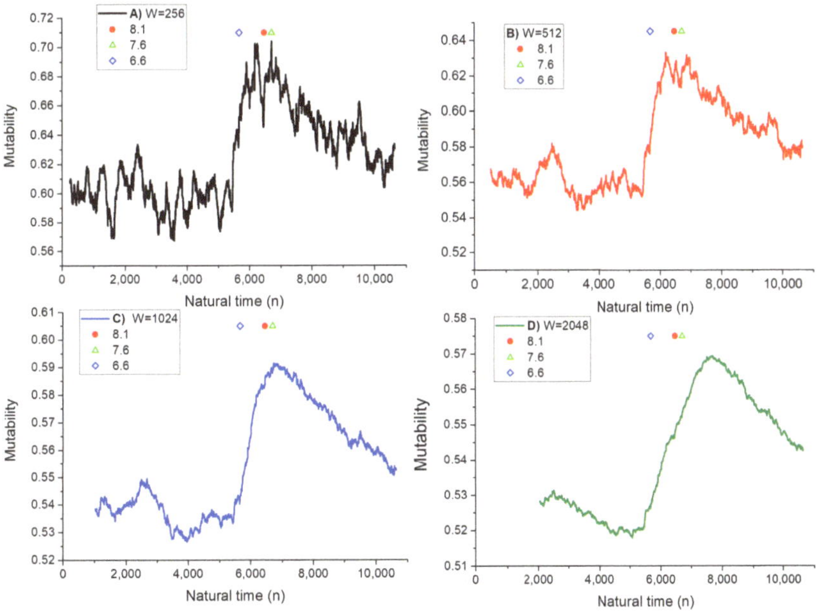

Figure 8. Mutability on magnitude sequence in natural time using four different dynamic windows W as indicated in the insets. Despite that the data is the same as in Figure 6, the texture of the curve looks different. In particular, the stars denoting the main seisms now open up.

4. Conclusions

The accommodation of the ground layers under the Earth's surface is accompanied by a variation in the energy of the system which is at times released in sudden ruptures and slides with catastrophic consequences in the events known as earthquakes. However, this transit from states prior and after the seism mean also a change in the entropy of the system ("cube" formed by the rectangle on the globe and the defined deepness).

This is an out-of-equilibrium system, since external fields act on it to provoke changes. In our case, the Nazca plate is coming from the West submerging under the Continental plate. Asperities make this process a discontinuous one. For many years, large rocks can prevent the flow of the plates until they fracture. The number of possible states for the system is not constant and varies with time according to the hidden physics under the planet's surface. However, we can have an indication of the way they change looking at the sequence of seismic data they produce.

The simultaneous application of both Tsallis entropy and mutability (dynamical entropy) to the magnitude series for the first time proved to render valuable information. Despite that magnitudes span no more than about 50 different values between 2.2 to about 7, they can recognize meaningful states on which a statistical analysis can be performed. In the past, mutability was applied to interval series [61], where meaningful values span about three orders of magnitude with intervals expressed in minutes as the time unit.

Tsallis entropy of magnitudes grows during the time the system accumulates tension and energy. Mutability on the same magnitude series decreases during that period. This behavior can be highlighted by choosing appropriate observation windows to analyse the dynamics. Thus, Tsallis entropy responds to the conditions in the real space, while mutability is driven by the accessible states in the configuration space.

We can perform the analysis of the seismic sequence either in real time or in natural time. Therefore, the combination of both pictures is very useful for a detailed understanding of the dynamical process. The most recent results within the data provided by the IPOC catalogue show that this zone recovered rather quickly to the conditions before the major earthquakes, which is a clear sign that energy accumulation resumed.

Author Contributions: Conceptualization, D.P., E.E.V. and O.S.; Methodology, E.E.V., G.S., A.P. and O.S.; Software, G.S. and A.P.; Formal analysis, D.P., E.E.V., G.S. and A.P.; Investigation, D.P., E.E.V. and A.P.; Data curation, A.P.; Writing—original draft, D.P., E.E.V. and A.P.; Writing—review & editing, E.E.V.; Visualization, A.P. All authors have read and agreed to the published version of the manuscript.

Funding: Partial support from the following two Chilean sources is acknowledged: Fondecyt under contract 1230055, Financiamiento Basal para Centros Científicos y Tecnológicos de Excelencia (Chile) through the Center for Development of Nanoscience and Nanotechnology (CEDENNA) under contract AFB220001. This research has been partially supported by the Agencia Estatal de Investigación (grant no. PID2021-124701NBC21 y C22); the Universidad de Almería (grant no. FEDER/UAL Project UAL2020-RNM-B1980); the Consejería de Universidad, Investigación e Innovación, Junta de Andalucía (grant no. RNM104). PPITUAL, Junta de Andalucía-FEDER 2021–2027. Programa: 54.A. A.P., D.P. and E.E.V. have been partially funded by the Spanish Project LEARNIG PID2022-143083NB-I00 by the Agencia Estatal de Investigación.

Data Availability Statement: The data set used in this article is free and can be downloaded from https://www.ipoc-network.org/welcome-to-ipoc/.

Conflicts of Interest: The authors declare no conflict of interest.

References

1. Zhang, Y.; Zuo, T.; Cheng, Y.; Liaw, P. High-entropy Alloys with High Saturation Magnetization, Electrical Resistivity and Malleability. *Sci. Rep.* **2013**, *3*, 1455. [CrossRef] [PubMed]
2. Oumezzine, M.; Peña, O.; Kallel, S.; Zemni, S. Critical phenomena and estimation of the spontaneous magnetization through magnetic entropy change in La0.67Ba0.33Mn0.98Ti0.02O3. *Solid State Sci.* **2011**, *13*, 1829–1834. [CrossRef]
3. Sauerwein, R.A.; de Oliveira, M.J. Entropy of spin models by the Monte Carlo method. *Phys. Rev. B* **1995**, *52*, 3060–3062. [CrossRef]
4. Zhang, Y.; Grover, T.; Vishwanath, A. Entanglement Entropy of Critical Spin Liquids. *Phys. Rev. Lett.* **2011**, *107*, 067202. [CrossRef] [PubMed]
5. Wand, A.J.; Sharp, K.A. Measuring Entropy in Molecular Recognition by Proteins. *Annu. Rev. Biophys.* **2018**, *47*, 41–61. [CrossRef]
6. Nezhad, S.Y.; Deiters, U.K. Estimation of the entropy of fluids with Monte Carlo computer simulation. *Mol. Phys.* **2017**, *115*, 1074–1085. [CrossRef]
7. Johnson, J.R.; Wing, S.; Camporeale, E. Transfer entropy and cumulant-based cost as measures of nonlinear causal relationships in space plasmas: Applications to D_{st}. *Ann. Geophys.* **2018**, *36*, 945–952. [CrossRef]
8. Du, S.; Zank, G.P.; Li, X.; Guo, F. Energy dissipation and entropy in collisionless plasma. *Phys. Rev. E* **2020**, *101*, 033208. [CrossRef]
9. Bailey, K. Social Entropy Theory: An overview. *Syst. Pract.* **1990**, *3*, 365–382. [CrossRef]
10. Liu, Z.; Wang, Y.; Cheng, Q.; Yang, H. Analysis of the Information Entropy on Traffic Flows. *IEEE Trans. Intell. Transp. Syst.* **2022**, *23*, 18012–18023. [CrossRef]

11. Liu, F.J.; Chang, T.P. Validity analysis of maximum entropy distribution based on different moment constraints for wind energy assessment. *Energy* **2011**, *36*, 1820–1826. [CrossRef]
12. Sarlis, N.; Skordas, E.; Varotsos, P. Nonextensivity and natural time: The case of seismicity. *Phys. Rev. E* **2010**, *82*, 021110. [CrossRef]
13. Telesca, L. Maximum likelihood estimation of the nonextensive parameters of the earthquake cumulative magnitude distribution. *Bull. Seismol. Soc. Am.* **2012**, *102*, 886–891. [CrossRef]
14. Varotsos, P.; Sarlis, N.; Skordas, E. Tsallis Entropy Index q and the Complexity Measure of Seismicity in Natural Time under Time Reversal before the M9 Tohoku Earthquake in 2011. *Entropy* **2018**, *20*, 757. [CrossRef] [PubMed]
15. Posadas, A.; Morales, J.; Ibáñez, J.; Posadas, A. Shaking earth: Non-linear seismic processes and the second law of thermodynamics: A case study from Canterbury (New Zealand) earthquakes. *Chaos Solitons Fractals Nonlinear Sci. Nonequilibrium Complex Phenom.* **2022**, *151*, 111243. [CrossRef]
16. Skordas, E.; Sarlis, N.; Varotsos, P. Precursory variations of Tsallis non-extensive statistical mechanics entropic index associated with the M9 Tohoku earthquake in 2011. *Eur. Phys. J. Spec. Top.* **2020**, *229*, 851–859. [CrossRef]
17. Sigalotti, L.; Ramírez-Rojas, A.; Vargas, C. Tsallis q-Statistics in Seismology. *Entropy* **2023**, *25*, 408. [CrossRef]
18. Santis, A.D.; Cianchini, G.; Favali, P.; Beranzoli, L.; Boschi, E. The Gutenberg-Richter Law and Entropy of Earthquakes: Two Case Studies in Central Italy. *Bull. Seismol. Soc. Am.* **2011**, *101*, 1386–1395. [CrossRef]
19. Vogel, E.E.; Brevis, F.G.; Pastén, D.; Muñoz, V.; Miranda, R.A.; Chian, A.C.-L. Measuring the sismic risk along the Nazca-South American subduction front: Shannon entropy and mutability. *Nat. Hazards Earth Syst. Sci.* **2020**, *20*, 2943 – 2960. [CrossRef]
20. Sotolongo-Costa, O.; Posadas, A. Fragment-asperity interaction model for earthquakes. *Phys. Rev. Lett.* **2004**, *92*, 048501. [CrossRef]
21. Posadas, A.; Sotolongo-Costa, O. Non-extensive entropy and fragment–asperity interaction model for earthquakes. *Commun. Nonlinear Sci. Numer. Simul.* **2023**, *117*, 106906. [CrossRef]
22. Varotsos, P.A.; Sarlis, N.; Skordas, E.S.; Uyeda, S.; Kamogawa, M. Natural time analysis of critical phenomena. *Proc. Natl. Acad. Sci. USA* **2011**, *108*, 11361–11364. [CrossRef]
23. Varotsos, P.A.; Sarlis, N.V.; Skordas, E.S. Phenomena preceding major earthquakes interconnected through a physical model. *Ann. Geophys.* **2019**, *37*, 315–324. [CrossRef]
24. Posadas, A.; Pasten, D.; Vogel, E.E.; Saravia, G. Earthquake hazard characterization by using entropy: Application to northern Chilean earthquakes. *Nat. Hazards Earth Syst. Sci.* **2023**, *23*, 1911–1920. [CrossRef]
25. Béjar-Pizarro, M.; Socquet, A.; Armijo, R.; Carrizo, D.; Genrich, J.; Simons, M. Andean structural control on interseismic coupling in the North Chile subduction zone. *Nat. Geosci.* **2013**, *6*, 462–467. [CrossRef]
26. Comte, D.; Pardo, M. Reappraisal of great historical earthquakes in the Northern Chile and Southern Peru seismic gaps. *Nat. Hazards* **1991**, *4*, 23–44. [CrossRef]
27. Métois, M.; Vigny, C.; Socquet, A. Interseismic Coupling, Megathrust Earthquakes and Seismic Swarms Along the Chilean Subduction Zone 38 °S–18 °S. *Pure Appl. Geophys.* **2016**, *173*, 1431–1449. [CrossRef]
28. Delouis, B.; Monfret, T.; Dorbath, L.; Pardo, M.; Rivera, L.; Comte, D.; Haessler, H.; Caminade, J.; Ponce, L.; Kausel, E.; et al. The Mw 8.0 Antofagasta (northern Chile) earthquake of 30 July 1995: A precursor to the end of the large 1877 gap. *Bull. Seismol. Soc. Am.* **1997**, *87*, 427–445. [CrossRef]
29. Peyrat, S.; Campos, J.; de Chabalier, J.B.; Bonvalot, S.; Bouin, M.P.; Legrand, D.; Nercessian, A.; Charade, O.; Patau, G.; Clévédé, E.; et al. Tarapacá intermediate-depth earthquake (Mw 7.7, 2005, northern Chile): A slab-pull event with horizontal fault plane constrained from seismologic and geodetic observations. *Geophys. Res. Lett.* **2006**, *33*, L22308. [CrossRef]
30. Schurr, B.; Asch, G.; Rosenau, M.; Wang, R.; Oncken, O.; Barrientos, S.; Salazar, P.; Vilotte, J.P. The 2007 Mw7.7 Tocopilla northern Chile earthquake sequence: Implications for along-strike and downdip rupture segmentationand megathrust frictional behavior. *J. Geophys. Res.* **2012**, *117*, 1–19.
31. Leon-Rios, S.; Ruiz, S.; Maksymowicz, A.; Leyton, F.; Fuenzalida, A.; Madariaga, R. Diversity of the 2014 Iquique's foreshocks and aftershocks: Clues about the complex rupture process of a Mw8.1 earthquake. *J. Seismol.* **2016**, *20*, 1059–1073. [CrossRef]
32. Ruiz, S.; Métois, M.; Fuenzalida, A.; Ruiz, J.; Leyton, F.; Grandin, R.; Vigny, C.; Madariaga, R.; Campos, J. Intense foreshocks and a slow slip event preceded the 2014 Iquique Mw 8.1 earthquake. *Science* **2014**, *345*, 1165–1169. [CrossRef] [PubMed]
33. Ruiz, S.; Madariaga, R. Historical and recent large megathrust earthquakes in Chile. *Tectonophysics* **2018**, *733*, 37–56. [CrossRef]
34. Socquet, A.; Valdes, J.P.; Jara, J.; Cotton, F.; Walpersdorf, A.; Cotte, N.; Specht, S.; Ortega-Culaciati, F.; Carrizo, D.; Norabuena, E. An 8 month slow slip event triggers progressive nucleation of the 2014 Chile megathrust. *Geophys. Res. Lett.* **2017**, *44*, 4046–4053. [CrossRef]
35. Jara, J.; Socquet, A.; Marsan, D.; Bouchon, M. Long-Term Interactions Between Intermediate Depth and Shallow Seismicity in North Chile Subduction Zone. *Geophys. Res. Lett.* **2017**, *44*, 9283–9292. [CrossRef]
36. IPOC. Available online: https://www.ipoc-network.org/welcome-to-ipoc/ (accessed on 25 August 2023).
37. Brodsky, E.E.; Lay, T. Recognizing foreshocks from the 1 April 2014 Chile earthquake. *Science* **2014**, *344*, 700–702. [CrossRef]
38. Wiemer, S.; Wyss, M. Minimum magnitude of complete reporting in earthquake catalogs: Examples from Alaska, the Western United States, and Japan. *Bull. Seismol. Soc. Am.* **2000**, *90*, 859–869. [CrossRef]
39. Telesca, L. Tsallis-based nonextensive analysis of the southern California seismicity. *Entropy* **2011**, *13*, 1267–1280. [CrossRef]

40. Papadakis, G.; Vallianatos, F.; Sammonds, P. A nonextensive statistical physics analysis of the 1995 Kobe, Japan earthquake. *Pure Appl. Geophys.* **2015**, *172*, 1923–1931. [CrossRef]
41. Varotsos, P.; Sarlis, N.; Skordas, E. Identifying the occurrence time of an impending major earthquake: A review. *Earthq. Sci.* **2017**, *30*, 209–218. [CrossRef]
42. Santis, A.D.; Abbattista, C.; Alfonsi, L.; Amoruso, L.; Campuzano, S.; Carbone, M.; Cesaroni, C.; Cianchini, G.; Franceschi, G.D.; Santis, A.D.; et al. Geosystemics View of Earthquakes. *Entropy* **2019**, *21*, 412. [CrossRef]
43. Vallianatos, F.; Michas, G.; Papadakis, G. A description of seismicity based on non-extensive statistical physics: A review. In *Earthquakes and Their Impact on Society*; D'Amico, S., Ed.; Springer Natural Hazards: Cham, Switzerland, 2015; pp. 1–41.
44. Vilar, C.; Franca, G.; Silva, R.; Alcaniz, J. Nonextensivity in geological faults? *Phys. A* **2007**, *377*, 285–290. [CrossRef]
45. Michas G. Generalized Statistical Mechanics Description of Fault and Earthquake Populations in Corinth Rift (Greece). PhD. Thesis, University College London, London, UK, 2016.
46. Telesca, L. Analysis of Italian seismicity by using a nonextensive approach. *Tectonophysics* **2010**, *494*, 155–162. [CrossRef]
47. Khordad, R.; Rastegar Sedehi, H.; Sharifzadeh, M. Susceptibility, entropy and specific heat of quantum rings in monolayer graphene: Comparison between different entropy formalisms. *J. Comput. Electron.* **2022**, *21*, 422–430. [CrossRef]
48. Aki, K. Maximum likelihood estimate of b in the formula log (N) = a – bm and its confidence limits. *Bull. Earthq. Res. Inst. Tokyo Univ.* **1965**, *43*, 237–239.
49. Utsu, T. A method for determining the value of b in a formula log n = a – bm showing the magnitude-frequency relation for earthquakes. *Geophys. Bull. Hokkaido* **1965**, *13*, 99–103.
50. Luenberg, D.G. *Information Science*, 2nd ed.; Princeton University Press: Princeton, NJ, USA, 2006.
51. Cover, T.M.; Thomas, J.A. *Elements of Information Theory*, 2nd ed.; John Wiley and Sons: New York, NY, USA, 2006.
52. Roederer, J.G. *Information and Its Role in Nature*, 2nd ed.; Springer: Heidelberg, Germany, 2005.
53. Vogel, E.; Saravia, G.; Bachmann, F.; Fierro, B.; Fischer, J. Phase transitions in Edwards-Anderson model by means of information theory. *Phys. A* **2009**, *388*, 4075–4082. [CrossRef]
54. Vogel, E.; Saravia, G.; Cortez, L. Data compressor designed to improve recognition of magnetic phases. *Phys. A* **2012**, *391*, 1591–1601. [CrossRef]
55. Negrete, O.A.; Vargas, P.; Peña, F.J.; Saravia, G.; Vogel, E.E. Entropy and mutability for the q-State Clock Model in Small Systems. *Renew. Energy* **2018**, *20*, 933. [CrossRef]
56. Vogel, E.; Saravia, G. Information Theory Applied to Econophysics: Stock Market Behaviors. *Eur. J. Phys. B* **2014**, *87*, 177. [CrossRef]
57. Vogel, E.; Saravia, G.; Ramirez-Pastor, A. Phase transitions in a system of long rods on two-dimensional lattices by means of information theory. *Phys. Rev. E* **2017**, *96*, 062133. [CrossRef] [PubMed]
58. Dos Santos, G.; Cisternas, E.; Vogel, E.E.; Ramirez-Pastor, A.J. Orientational phase transition in monolayers of multipolar straight ridid rods: The case of 2-thiophene molecule adsorption on the Au (111) surface. *Phys. Rev. E* **2023**, *107*, 014133. [CrossRef] [PubMed]
59. Vogel, E.E.; Saravia, G.; Kobe, S.; Schumann, R.; Schuster, R. A Novel Method to Optimize Electricity Generation from Wind Energy. *Renew. Energy* **2018**, *126*, 724–735. [CrossRef]
60. Universidad de Chile (2013): Red Sismologica Nacional. International Federation of Digital Seismograph Networks. Other/Seismic Network. 10.7914/SN/C1. Available online: https://www.fdsn.org/networks/detail/C1/ (accessed on 12 April 2022).
61. Vogel, E.; Saravia, G.; Pastén, D.; Muñoz, V. Time-series analysis of earthquake sequences by means of information recognizer. *Tectonophysics* **2017**, *712–713*, 723–728. [CrossRef]

entropy

MDPI

Article

Nonadditive Entropy Application to Detrended Force Sensor Data to Indicate Balance Disorder of Patients with Vestibular System Dysfunction

Harun Yaşar Köse [1] and Serhat İkizoğlu [2,*]

[1] Department of Mechatronics Engineering, Faculty of Electric and Electronics, Istanbul Technical University (ITU), 34469 Istanbul, Türkiye; kose21@itu.edu.tr
[2] Department of Control and Automation Engineering, Faculty of Electric and Electronics, Istanbul Technical University (ITU), 34469 Istanbul, Türkiye
* Correspondence: ikizoglus@itu.edu.tr; Tel.: +90-212-2853571

Abstract: The healthy function of the vestibular system (VS) is of vital importance for individuals to carry out their daily activities independently and safely. This study carries out Tsallis entropy (TE)-based analysis on insole force sensor data in order to extract features to differentiate between healthy and VS-diseased individuals. Using a specifically developed algorithm, we detrend the acquired data to examine the fluctuation around the trend curve in order to consider the individual's walking habit and thus increase the accuracy in diagnosis. It is observed that the TE value increases for diseased people as an indicator of the problem of maintaining balance. As one of the main contributions of this study, in contrast to studies in the literature that focus on gait dynamics requiring extensive walking time, we directly process the instantaneous pressure values, enabling a significant reduction in the data acquisition period. The extracted feature set is then inputted into fundamental classification algorithms, with support vector machine (SVM) demonstrating the highest performance, achieving an average accuracy of 95%. This study constitutes a significant step in a larger project aiming to identify the specific VS disease together with its stage. The performance achieved in this study provides a strong motivation to further explore this topic.

Keywords: vestibular disorders; insole force sensors; gait analysis; Tsallis entropy; detrending; feature extraction; classification

Citation: Köse, H.Y.; İkizoğlu, S. Nonadditive Entropy Application to Detrended Force Sensor Data to Indicate Balance Disorder of Patients with Vestibular System Dysfunction. *Entropy* **2023**, *25*, 1385. https://doi.org/10.3390/e25101385

Academic Editor: Carlos M. Travieso-González

Received: 14 August 2023
Revised: 22 September 2023
Accepted: 25 September 2023
Published: 27 September 2023

1. Introduction

The vestibular system (VS) is a perceptual system responsible for providing the brain with information regarding spatial orientation, head position, and motion. Additionally, it plays a crucial role in maintaining balance and stability [1]. Despite numerous studies in various medical fields, the detection of vestibular disorders is an area that has not received sufficient attention yet. This study aims to fill this gap by utilizing Tsallis entropy (TE) as a tool to identify VS-related diseases.

Various methods are employed in the literature to identify the specific VS problem but the most popular clinical method is still computerized dynamic posturography (CDP) [2]. The state-of-the-art methods are based on utilizing classification techniques following a machine learning step where the features are extracted from gait data. Gait data refer to the collection of information about an individual's walking patterns and habits. They capture various aspects of walking, such as force, rhythm, speed, and variability in different components of the gait cycle. The gait cycle is a complex activity consisting of two main phases: the stance phase, in which the foot remains on the ground, and the swing phase, in which the foot moves forward. By analyzing gait data, we can detect irregularities and deviations that differ from what is considered a 'normal' gait. These deviations can be indicative of a variety of health conditions, from musculoskeletal problems to neurological disorders.

The gait data are especially used to give information about balance disorders related to different diseases. Within this context, gait analysis has emerged as a valuable tool in the diagnosis and monitoring of neurodegenerative diseases, providing objective measures to assess motor impairments associated with these conditions. It has been extensively utilized in the evaluation of diseases such as Parkinson's disease (PD), Huntington's disease (HD), amyotrophic lateral sclerosis (ALS), and other related disorders. Numerous studies have demonstrated the effectiveness of gait analysis in identifying disease-specific gait abnormalities and distinguishing between different neurodegenerative conditions. As an example, Nir Giladi et al. proposed a new clinical classification scheme for gait and posture and discussed the use of gait analysis in identifying disease-specific gait abnormalities [3]. Bovonsunthonchai et al. investigated the use of spatiotemporal gait variables in distinguishing between three cognitive status groups and discussed the potential of gait analysis as a tool for early detection of neurodegenerative conditions [4]. Guo Yao et al. summarized the research on the effectiveness and accuracy of different gait analysis systems and machine learning algorithms in detecting Parkinson's disease based on gait analysis [5].

As an example of the use of gait data to evaluate balance disorders associated with dysfunction in the VS, A. R. Wagner et al. discussed how gait analysis can be used to assess vestibular-related impairments in older adults, and how these impairments can impact balance control [6]. In [7], Ikizoğlu and Heyderov search for significant features from IMU-sensor-based data to diagnose VS disorders. In [8], Agrawal et al. utilize wireless pressure sensors embedded in insoles along with machine learning models to predict fall risks, achieving promising results. In [9], Schmidheiny et al. focus on the discriminant validity and test–retest reproducibility of a gait assessment in patients with vestibular dysfunction.

In this study, our aim was to utilize contemporary classification methods to extract pertinent characteristics from gait data for the purpose of diagnosing VS-dysfunction-based balance disorders. To accomplish this objective, we employed an innovative approach that involved TE values as the feature. TE offers a framework for characterizing the statistical properties of complex systems and thus it is capable of defining non-extensive systems. TE has proven to be effective in diverse domains such as physics, information theory, and economics, enabling a more comprehensive analysis and understanding of systems with long-range correlations and heavy-tailed distributions [10]. As an example of the application of TE in the field of biomedical engineering, Zhang et al. investigated the dependency of the TE of EEG data on the burst signals after cardiac arrest [11]. Similarly, Tong et al. used the TE of EEG signals as a measure of brain injury in their study [12]. Considering the human gait to exhibit non-extensive behavior with long range correlations [13–16], we expected TE to be rather helpful in analyzing the balance performance of individuals. Thus, by applying TE to gait data, our objective was to capture vital information concerning the behavior and dynamics of the VS, which can contribute to the identification of related diseases.

This study is an important step within a larger project which we are conducting together with the audiologists at The Medical School Cerrahpaşa-Istanbul. We aim to develop a diagnosing system to identify the specific disease that is the source of the VS dysfunction causing imbalance. We also aim to determine the stage of the problem. The first step in this process is the classification of the individual as healthy or suffering. For this classification, we are searching for primary discriminative features. We collect various features which will then enter a feature reduction/selection process. According to the experience of the audiologists, these primary features are expected to be obtained from relatively short data acquisition periods, in order to not put the patient in stress, and thus increase the accuracy of the whole system. In [7], we discussed the effectiveness of features obtained from IMU sensor data, such as average step length, average speed, step symmetry, knee bending angle, lateral/posterior waist swing, etc., where we achieved an accuracy around 90%. In [17], we presented a feature based on insole pressure sensor data called fractal spectrum width that had an accuracy around 98% in distinguishing between the classes in the first step of the entire process. This study is also based on the same data as that one, but it looks for new features based on Tsallis entropy that would be effective in the feature selection/reduction process. We set our accuracy threshold as 90% for any individual feature to advance to the reduction stage.

We can briefly summarize the contributions we have brought with this study as follows: Most studies have focused on features related to gait analysis, such as stride time, stance time, etc., which require a relatively long walking time. This study aims to shorten the data acquisition period by capturing features from short walks. Pressure data collected from wearable insole sensors are used for feature extraction. This approach allows data to be obtained in daily life, helping the patient avoid the stress of the clinical environment and potentially improving the accuracy of the diagnosis [18,19]. We detrend the normalized raw data, allowing the identification of individual specific fluctuations around the trend, thereby increasing the accuracy. As one of our basic contributions, we propose a specific algorithm to determine the trend curve in each walking step. This process leads to a better ability to distinguish temporary imbalance from unusual walking habits.

After feature extraction, the extracted features were used to train models using classification methods. The main classification categories included decision trees (DT), discriminant analysis, logistic regression, naïve Bayes, support vector machine (SVM), k-nearest neighbors (KNN), kernel approximation, ensemble, and neural networks.

Considering the flow of the study, the rest of this article is structured as follows: The Materials and Methods section provides comprehensive details on TE. Subsequently, in the Data Acquisition Process section, a thorough explanation is given regarding the data collection process. In the Data Processing section, the step-by-step procedures for transforming the raw data into distinct features are elaborated upon. The outcomes of the subsequent experiments are presented comparatively within the Results section. Lastly, in the Discussion section, the results are analyzed, inferences are drawn, and future prospects regarding the utilization of the outcomes within the broader project are mentioned.

2. Materials and Methods

2.1. Entropy, Tsallis Entropy—Brief Background

Entropy is a property that is mostly used as a measure to describe the chaotic level of a dynamic system. The well-known Shannon entropy (SE) based on Boltzmann–Gibbs statistical mechanics and formulated as

$$\text{SE} = -\sum_{i=1}^{N} p_i ln(p_i), \tag{1}$$

is capable of describing the structure of extensive systems with short-term microscopic correlations [20,21]. In (1), the Boltzmann constant is taken as $k = 1$, N is the number of microstates, and p_i stands for the probability of the i-th microstate.

For systems with long-term interactions, however, or systems presenting long-term memory effect, the effectiveness of applying SE for the abovementioned purpose decreases [22]. At this point, forming the generalized structure of Boltzmann–Gibbs statistics, the Tsallis entropy (TE) within the non-extensive statistics contributes significantly to finding the hidden information in the time series [23].

TE has found applications in various fields, including biomedical research. In the context of biomedicine, TE has proven to be a valuable tool for analyzing complex systems and understanding the dynamics of biological processes, with its main advantage being the ability to capture the non-linear and long-range dependencies present in biological systems [12,17].

The Tsallis entropy with $k = 1$ is defined as

$$\text{TE} = \frac{1}{q-1}\left(1 - \sum_{i=1}^{N} p_i^q\right), \tag{2}$$

where q ($q \epsilon \mathcal{R}$) is a parameter to indicate the degree of non-additivity [24]. This is because, for two independent systems X and Y, we have

$$\mathrm{TE}(\mathrm{X}+\mathrm{Y}) = \mathrm{TE}(\mathrm{X}) + \mathrm{TE}(\mathrm{Y}) + (1-q)\mathrm{TE}(\mathrm{X})\mathrm{TE}(\mathrm{Y}), \tag{3}$$

where $(1 - q)$ is a measure of deviation from additivity. $q > 1$ and $q < 1$ correspond to sub-extensive and super-extensive statistics, respectively [12,25]. For $q = 1$ we have TE = SE, corresponding to extensive statistics. In (2), N is the number of possible states and p_i represents the probability of the i-th state. The determination of the value of the parameter q does not have specific criteria, but rather depends on the specific characteristics of the analyzed dataset [26]. By adjusting the value of q, the entropy metric can be tailored to capture particular features inherent in the analyzed dataset.

2.2. Data Collection

We recall that the data used in this study are the same as in our previous study [17].

When the gait analysis studies in the literature are examined, it is seen that the distribution of weight is concentrated especially at four main points on the soles of the feet, as depicted in Figure 1a [27–31]. Also in this study, these four points were chosen for the placement of the sensors in line with the opinions of several academics in the field of audiology, who are acknowledged in the Acknowledgments section.

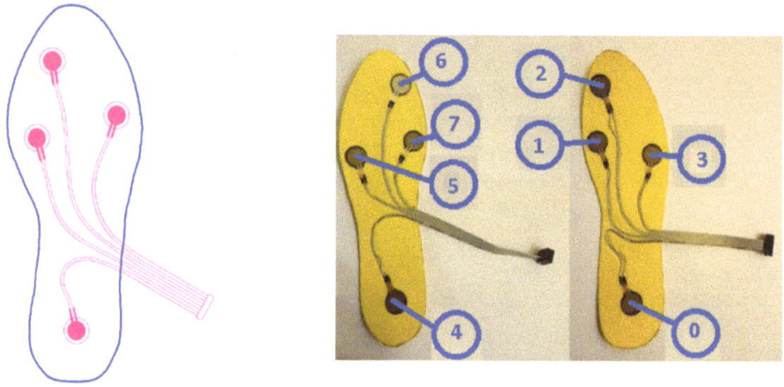

(a) (b)

Figure 1. (**a**) Sensor placement on the insole; (**b**) numbering of the sensors S0 to S7 (top view) [17].

To ensure data collection without disturbing the natural walking patterns of the participants, 5 pairs of insoles with different sizes (36, 38, 40, 42, 44—according to European standards) were manufactured. Prior to the commencement of the experiment, the correctly sized insoles were inserted into the subjects' shoes. For the production of the insoles, a durable and soft plastic material commonly employed in the manufacturing of orthopedic products was utilized.

Force-sensitive resistors (FSR) were chosen as pressure sensors, as they are widely used in gait analysis applications and offer several advantages [32]. Considering the physical dimensions and the acceptable repeatability feature, the FSR402-short tail model from Interlink was selected [33]. The characteristics of the sensor can be found in Table 1. The sensors on the insoles were numbered S0 to S7, as seen in Figure 1b.

Some explanatory information about the characteristics in Table 1 can be given as follows: Repeatability is a measure of the scattering of results for multiple measurements under the same conditions. For our sensor, the maximum deviation of the results of successive measurements of the same measurand from the mean is given as ±2%. Idle resistance is the resistance of the resistive force sensor when no force is applied to it. Hysteresis is a measure of how far the system output is different depending on whether a specific input value was reached by increasing vs. decreasing the input. Rise time is the time it takes for the system/sensor output to change from 10% to 90% of its final value. This time, given in Table 1 as less than 3 microseconds, shows that the sensor responds rapidly to the force/change in force applied to it.

Table 1. Characteristics of the FSR402-short tail sensors.

Parameter	Value
operation range	0.2 N–20 N
physical dimensions	ϕ_{pad} 18.3 mm, ϕ_{sens} 12.7 mm
thickness	0.46 mm
repeatability	±2%
idle resistance	>10 MΩ
hysteresis	10% max.
rising time	<3 μs

Data collection was carried out in the clinical setting of the Audiology Department at Cerrahpaşa Medical School, Istanbul University—Istanbul, Türkiye. The process was conducted in compliance with the principles outlined in the Helsinki Declaration. Before starting the process, approval was obtained from the Istanbul University Ethics Committee (Approval number: A-57/07.07.2015). In addition, informed consent was obtained from all subjects before participation in the study. For individuals with VS problems, their conditions had already been diagnosed by the audiologists using conventional systems (computerized dynamic posturography-CDP).

Data were collected on weekends to minimize the subjects' stress and avoid interference from other nearby devices. The subjects were asked to walk the 12 m long path twice. The first walk aimed to help them become familiar with the environment and reduce any possible stress, while the data from the second walk were used for analysis in general. In some cases, subjects walked a third time when needed as a result of the audiologists' observations.

The pressure sensor data collected with the Arduino Mega device placed on the subjects were transferred to the laptop wirelessly via an HC-06 Bluetooth unit. Sampling was performed from all sensors simultaneously at a rate of 20 samples per second. In order to convert the force to voltage, a 1 kΩ resistor in series with the FSR served as a voltage divider. As the next step, we calibrated this structure in the lab since the FSR has a highly non-linear characteristic curve. Supplying the structure with 5 V DC voltage presented an average function as

$$w = e^{\frac{v_o+0.2245}{0.9265}}, \tag{4}$$

where w (N) is the weight applied onto the sensor and v_o (V) is the output voltage. A 10% deviation from the values obtained by Equation (4) was taken as the criterion that would disqualify the relevant sensor from being used in the experiments.

Informative data about the participants are listed in Table 2.

Table 2. Information about the subjects.

	Healthy (30)		Diseased (30)	
	Male (15)	Female (15)	Male (13)	Female (17)
age	54.3 ± 8.5	55.1 ± 7.9	54.5 ± 8.5	56.8 ± 7.2
mass (kg)	66.6 ± 9.8	65.1 ± 8.8	65.9 ± 10.2	64.9 ± 7.9
height (cm)	169.2 ± 10.0	164.0 ± 6.2	170.3 ± 8.8	163.4 ± 5.7

The distribution of the subjects whose specific disease was detected by CDP by audiologists is given in Table 3.

Table 3. The distribution of diseased subjects.

	Male	Female
BPPV *	6	8
UVW *	3	4
Meniere	3	3
Vestibular Neuritis	1	2

(*) BPPV—benign paroxysmal positional vertigo, UVW—unilateral vestibular weakness.

To ensure the confidentiality and privacy of all participants, their identities have been anonymized for publication of this article.

2.3. Data Processing

In order to interpret the results more accurately on the basis of the subject, the obtained data were preprocessed before feature extraction. Thus, the feature extraction process was carried out in six stages.

Stage 1—Framing useful data

We framed the useful part of the whole walk, and data corresponding to the first and last steps were extracted from the overall data. Thus, data on steps with missing dynamic behavior were excluded from the evaluation.

Stage 2—Determining the intervals when the foot is actively touching the ground

Of all the gait data, only those corresponding to the time intervals during which the foot is actively touching the ground provide useful information. These intervals were determined for each foot as follows:

- All the sensor data were normalized to the range 0–1 as

$$X_{norm} = \frac{X - X_{min}}{X_{max} - X_{min}}, \tag{5}$$

where X is the original/raw data and X_{min} and X_{max} represent the minimum and maximum values, respectively.

- The maximum of all sensor data (S_{max}) was determined. As an example, for the right foot, these data were obtained as $S_{Rmax} = \max(S_0, S_1, S_2, S_3)$.
- A threshold was set so that the foot was interpreted as being in the air for the time interval where S_{max} remained below this threshold value.

The process is visualized for a sample subject in Figure 2; there, the individual sensor data are marked in different colors, their maximum in black, and the foot-in-the-air position is shown as zero amplitude.

Stage 3—Interpolation

As mentioned in the 'Data Collection' section, the sampling frequency for data acquisition was 20 Hz. On the other hand, for meaningful entropy calculation, we need a significant number of bins in the histogram of the relevant data, as well as a sufficient number of samples in each bin. Therefore, we applied 20-fold interpolation to all the sensor data. Prior to the interpolation process, the segments where the feet were not in contact with the ground were removed from the data sequences. The process is illustrated in Figure 3 for a sample subject. Linear interpolation was not preferred in order to maintain accuracy without compromising the representation of the data. Instead, the cubic Hermite interpolation method was chosen as the interpolation technique. This method provides a smoother and more accurate representation of the data while preserving its integrity [34].

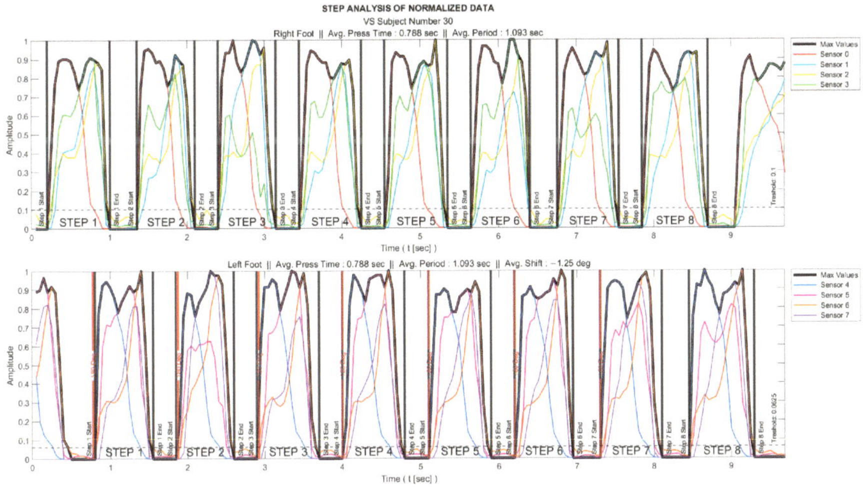

Figure 2. Normalizing the data followed by determining the intervals when the foot is actively touching the ground.

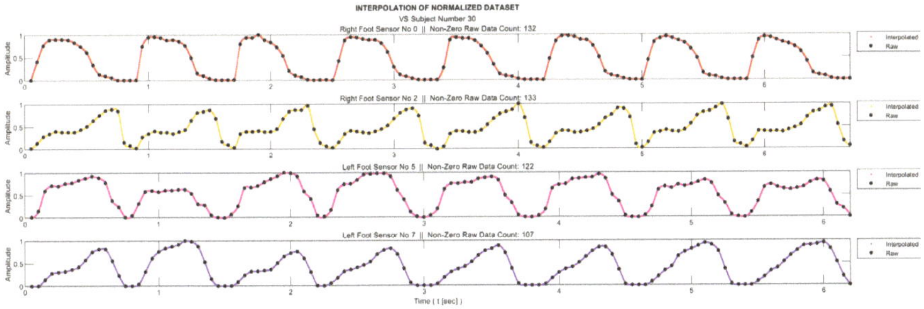

Figure 3. Twenty-fold interpolated data of some sensors after removal of segments where the foot does not actively touch the floor.

Stage 4—Detrending

To classify an individual as healthy or diseased, we are concerned with the deviation of the data from those corresponding to the person's walking habit. Therefore, we first determined the trend data related to the walking habit. The process illustrated in Figure 4 can be briefly explained as follows: For each step, the trend curve of the previous step is scaled in the time axis using the 'nearest-neighbor interpolation' method based on the length of the current step data; thus, we equate both the current and previous step data lengths. A trend dataset is then generated for the current step i using Equation (6).

$$\begin{aligned} T_i &= F_i \qquad\qquad for \qquad i = 1 \\ T_i &= \alpha F_i + (1-\alpha)\check{T}_{i-1} \qquad for \qquad i = 2, 3, \ldots, n. \end{aligned} \tag{6}$$

Here, T_i is the current-step trend data, and F_i stands for the current step data. $\check{T}$ denotes the trend data whose length is scaled, and α is a coefficient indicating the degree to which the previous trend curve is approximated to the current step data set. α_{max} represents the maximum rate of change that each data point of the trend curve can exhibit from one step to the next, for which the value 0.23 was statistically determined, considering data from healthy subjects. We note that α_{max} serves as a parameter to achieve a balance between flexibility in trend curve adaptation and avoiding overfitting, and although it has a role in shaping the trend curve, the key features of our analysis remain relatively insensitive to its exact value. The process is terminated when the α value reaches α_{max} or the error defined as $\varepsilon = mean\ \{|T_i - F_i|\}$ falls below a threshold so that it is considered negligible. The threshold level is set as 10^{-6}.

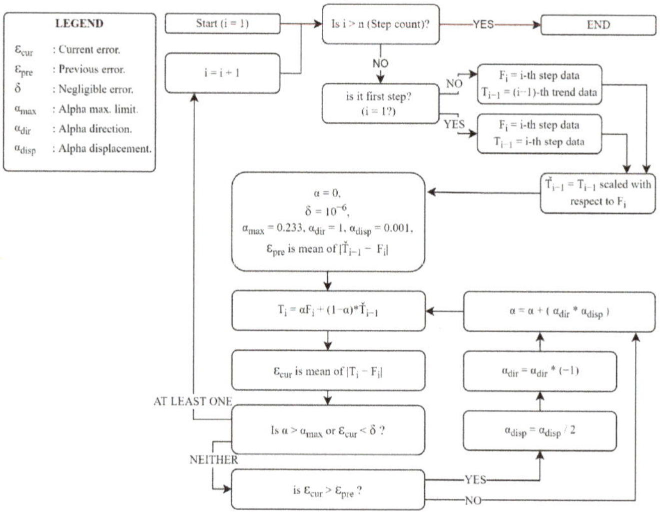

Figure 4. Flowchart of the algorithm developed to generate the stepwise trend curves.

Figure 5 presents the trend curves and the detrended dataset for a sample VS-diseased subject.

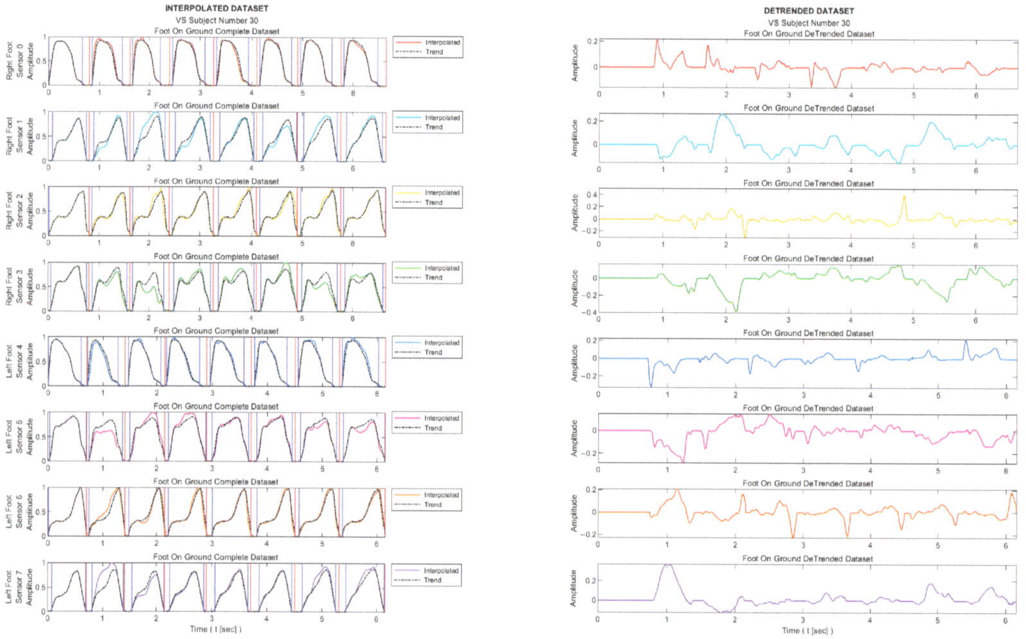

(**a**) (**b**)

Figure 5. (**a**) Trend curves and (**b**) curves of detrended dataset for a sample VS-diseased subject. Red vertical lines indicate the active stepping intervals of the foot; blue vertical lines indicate the active usage intervals of the relevant sensor.

Stage 5—Tsallis Entropy Calculations

At this stage, the TE calculation was performed with the help of the histograms generated from the detrended data. The process was performed for both the data for the entire gait from each sensor and for all the step data within the gait cycle. For each sensor, the data corresponding to the intervals in which the relevant sensor was not actively used were extracted from the data set. These intervals are marked as black bars in Figure 6a for a sample data set. Histograms were obtained from the absolute values of the detrended dataset, where the maximum number of bins was determined as 25 in order to achieve an acceptable granularity. Figure 6b illustrates the corresponding histograms for the data set in Figure 6a.

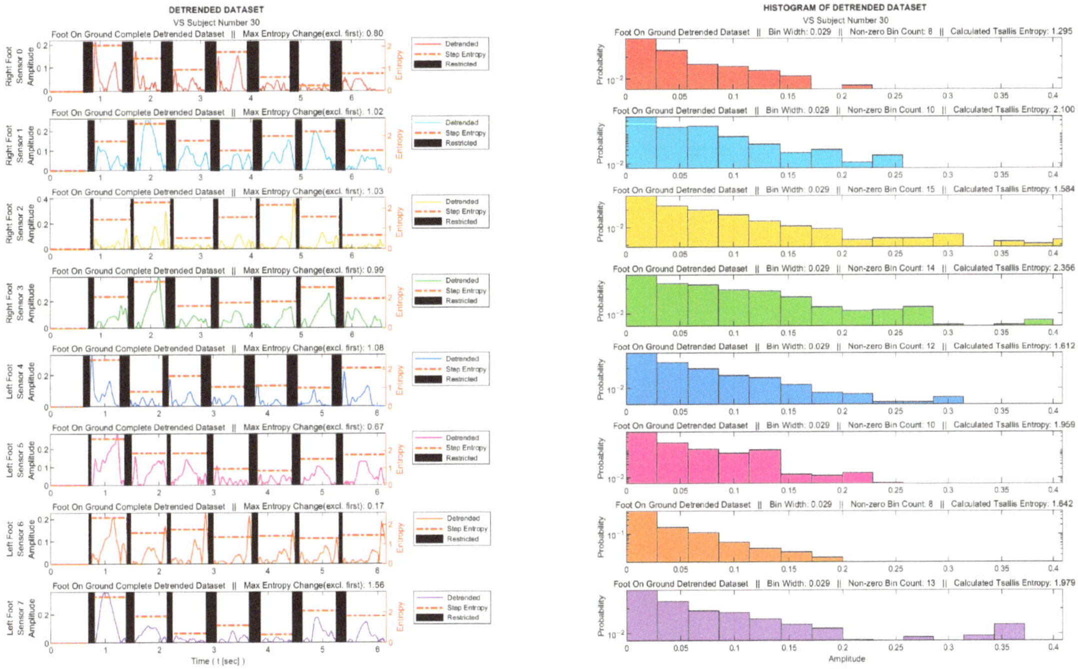

(a) (b)

Figure 6. For a sample diseased subject (no. 30): (**a**) absolute values of the detrended data in Figure 5b and the step-by-step TE values (black bars indicate ranges in which the corresponding sensor is inactive); (**b**) histograms derived from the data for the entire gait (sensor-inactive intervals removed).

As mentioned in Section 2.1, the selection of the q parameter value in TE calculation does not have a predefined criterion, it rather depends on the specific characteristics of the analyzed data set. The best q value that would achieve the highest accuracy for our data sets and therefore maximize the discriminatory power of TE was determined to be 0.82 by an iterative process. In the process of determining the q value, nine classification algorithms of the learning models outlined in Stage 6 took part with a 10-fold cross-validation technique. The ratios of the models attaining the highest success were employed as the benchmark. The learning success rates vs. q values are depicted in Figure 7.

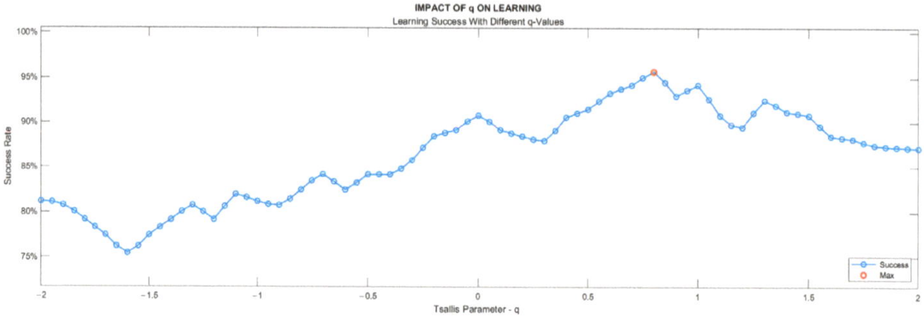

Figure 7. Dependency of the learning success on Tsallis parameter (q) value.

Stage 6—Feature Extraction

As stated in the introduction, although human gait seems to have a regular pattern, a literature review reveals that fluctuations are observed in this pattern. For healthy people, these fluctuations are long-range correlated. However, this correlation weakens for people with balance problems. Thus, the TE value could be a significant measure to classify individuals as healthy or diseased. In this study, we leveraged two TE-based possibilities to identify VS-dysfunction-based problems. One was to consider the TE value of the entire gait cycle, and the other was to examine the change in TE value from step to step. For the second case, we decided to examine the deviation of the TE value from zero, because in the ideal case it is clear that the step-to-step change of entropy for a healthy person would be zero. Thus, for this case, the data set containing the step-by-step entropy values was expanded by adding the negatives of all data values, and the standard deviation of the newly created data set ($\sigma(E')$) was calculated as given by Equation (7).

$$\begin{gathered} E = \{e_1, e_2, \ldots, e_n\} \ \ where \ e_k \in \mathbb{R} for \ \ k \in \mathbb{Z}^+, \\ E' = \{e_1, e_2, \ldots, e_n, -e_1, -e_2, \ldots, -e_n\} = \{x_1, x_2, \ldots, x_n, x_{n+1}, x_{n+2}, \ldots, x_{2n}\} \\ \sigma(E') = \sqrt{\frac{1}{2n} * \sum_{i=1}^{2n} (x_i - \mu)^2} \end{gathered} \quad (7)$$

In Equation (7), e_k is the TE value of the k-th step data, E denotes the set of step-by-step TE values, and E' represents the expanded set.

We had four sensors under each foot, so, eight sensors in total. Using both the TE value of the entire gait cycle for each sensor as well as the stepwise variation in the TEs, we had a total of 16 features that served for machine learning. For the classification process, we used the Matlab R2021b Classification Learner Tool (on MSI GE75 Raider 10875H). A 10-fold cross-validation technique was applied, where approximately 25% of the total data (from 15 subjects) was used for testing and the remainder (from 45 subjects) for training.

The process of classification training involved utilizing nine different model categories: decision trees (DT), discriminant analysis, logistic regression, naïve Bayes, support vector machine (SVM), k-nearest neighbors (KNN), kernel approximation, ensemble, and neural networks. Considering the sub-models of these categories that were used, such as 'Course: 4, Medium: 20, Fine: 100' for the maximum number of splits in the decision tree category, a total of thirty-two models were involved in the process.

Among all the classifiers examined, SVM (Gaussian), KNN (cosine, k = 10), and logistic regression showed the three best performances. Regarding these classifiers, the KNN algorithm determines the class membership of an object/vector by examining its k nearest neighbors [35]. In this study, the k value yielding the best result was determined to be 10. Logistic regression is a statistical model used to predict the probability of a dependent variable belonging to two or more classes in a dataset [36]. SVM seeks to find an optimal hyperplane to separate data clusters [37]. These three algorithms are among the most widely used in studies on biomedical signals in the literature [38–43].

3. Results

In this section, a comparative analysis is made based on data collected from both healthy and VS-diseased individuals. The comparison commences from the detrending stage of processing the sensor data, as described in the Data Processing section.

Figure 8 facilitates observation of discernible variations in the data from sensor S3 during walking for sample healthy and diseased individuals. Additionally, it visualizes the detrended data, i.e., the difference between the step data and the trend curve.

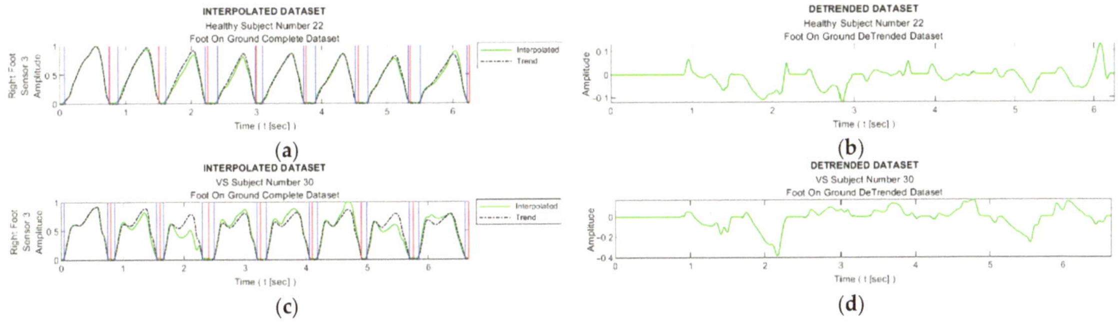

Figure 8. Sample interpolated S3 sensory data and the stepwise trend curves of (**a**) a healthy subject and (**c**) a VS-diseased subject; detrended data from (**b**) a healthy subject and (**d**) a VS-diseased subject.

To see the effect of the proposed trending algorithm, trend curves were created using 2nd-, 3rd-, and 4th-degree curve-fitting polynomials and the results were compared. The classification accuracies obtained with the different trending methods are listed in Table 4.

Table 4. Classification accuracies with different trend generation methods.

Classification Model	Proposed Algorithm	Second-Degree Polynomial	Third-Degree Polynomial	Fourth-Degree Polynomial
SVM-Gaussian	95.0%	71.7%	76.3%	81.7%
Logistic regression (LR)	95.0%	63.3%	78.3%	76.3%
KNN-cosine	93.3%	66.7%	70.0%	78.3%
Model with highest accuracy	95.0% (with SVM-G and LR)	83.3% (with Ensemble-Bagged Trees)	83.3% (with Decision Trees-Fine/Med.)	86.7% (with Ensemble Subsp. Discr.)

Figure 9 shows graphs of the detrended data with absolute values taken from Figure 8b,d and the histograms produced from these graphs. In Figure 9a,c, the black bars indicate the inactive periods of the related sensor. For these sample subjects and sensor data, the maximum step-by-step change in the TE value for the healthy subject was calculated as 0.63, whereas it was 0.99 for the VS-diseased person. The TE value for the entire gait cycle was calculated as 1.243 for the healthy individual and 2.356 for the suffering subject. In Table 5, the TE values are listed for these sample subjects for all sensor data. Figure 10 summarizes the entire-gait TE values for all participants.

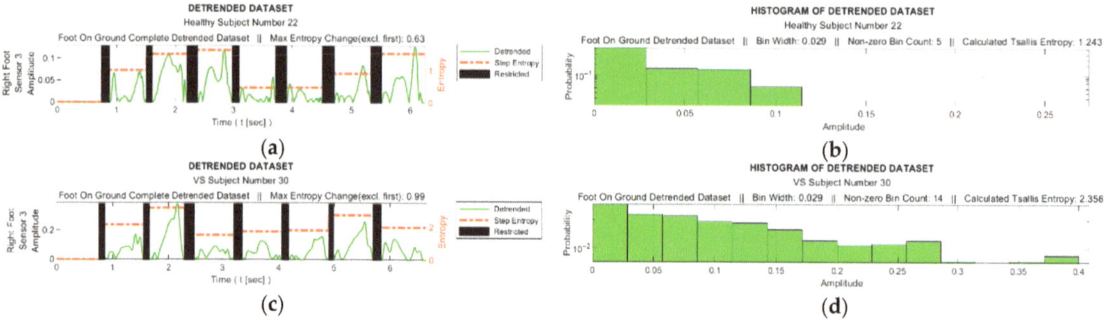

Figure 9. (**a**,**c**) Detrended data with absolute values taken from Figure 8b,d; (**b**,**d**) histograms produced from these graphs.

Table 5. TE values calculated from each sensor's data for sample subjects.

Sensor	Healthy Subject (no. 22) Entire Gait	Healthy Subject (no. 22) Stepwise Max	VS Subject (no. 30) Entire Gait	VS Subject (no. 30) Stepwise Max
S0	1.39	0.98	1.29	0.80
S1	2.15	0.83	2.10	1.02
S2	1.38	0.72	1.58	1.03
S3	1.24	0.63	2.36	0.99
S4	1.08	0.87	1.61	1.08
S5	1.38	0.79	1.96	0.67
S6	1.36	0.82	1.64	0.17
S7	1.54	0.86	1.98	1.56

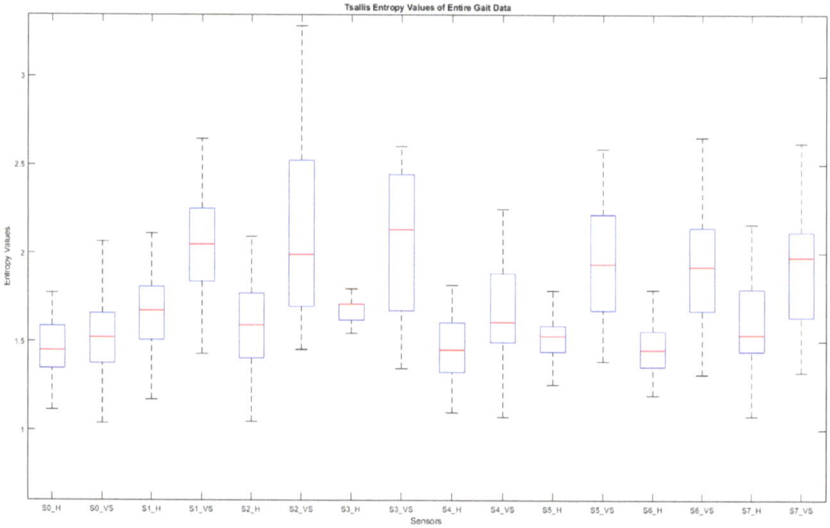

Figure 10. Box plot of the entire-gait TE values for all participants. S: sensor, H: healthy, VS: diseased.

As described in Data Processing section, thirty-two classifiers provided by the Classification Learner Tool in Matlab were trained using sixteen features with ten-fold cross-validation. The average accuracies of the major classification algorithms are listed in Tables 6 and 7 and Figure 11 display the confusion matrices and corresponding receiver operating characteristic (ROC) curves for one of the ten training test set pairs of the top three classifiers.

Table 6. Accuracy of major classification algorithms.

Algorithm	Accuracy (%)
SVM (Gaussian)	95.0
Logistic regression	95.0
KNN (cosine)	93.3
Neural network (wide)	93.3
Kernel (SVM)	91.7
Ensemble (bagged tree)	88.3
Naïve Bayes (kernel)	86.7
Quadratic discriminant	78.3
Decision tree (fine)	73.3

Table 7. Confusion matrices for one of the ten training test set pairs.

Predicted Class	SVM (Gaussian)		Logistic Regression		KNN (Cosine)	
	H	D	H	D	H	D
H	30	0	29	1	28	2
D	3	27	2	27	2	28

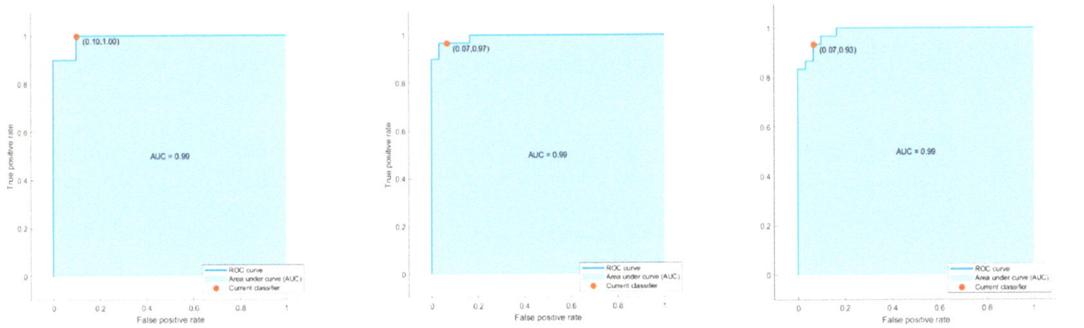

(**a**) (**b**) (**c**)

Figure 11. ROC curves associated with (**a**) the support vector machine (SVM) model with Gaussian kernel, (**b**) logistic regression, and (**c**) the k-nearest neighbors (KNN) algorithm using cosine similarity in Table 7.

4. Discussion

This study was carried out in conjunction with a project where our ultimate goal is to identify the specific diseases of individuals suffering from VS dysfunction, along with the level of the problem. In the full version of the project, a machine learning process will be conducted using distinctive features as input. For this purpose, features that will be effective in defining the problem are being sought and all of them will be placed in the candidate features basket, that is, they will be selected to take part in the feature reduction stage. According to the experience of the audiologists with whom we conducted the experiments, some important points need to be considered when collecting data from patients in order to achieve a high level of accuracy in diagnosis. These are particularly obtaining the data in a short time and collecting it under stress-free conditions. Having taken these guidelines into account, and thus aiming to capture the features from a short walk, we performed multifractal detrended fluctuation analysis (MFDFA) in our previous study [17]. Our current study also used these same data as our previous work but it provided additional features for the feature selection/reduction step.

In this study, we utilized TE-based methods for feature extraction from gait data collected from insole pressure/force sensors. The reason for considering the TE was its ability to capture the level of the fluctuations in the detrended data, providing insight into the complexity and irregularity of the gait pattern. Unlike other entropies, TE enables a parameterized analysis, offering flexibility in quantifying uncertainty and capturing certain characteristics of the data distribution.

Data from eight insole sensors, four under each foot, were first normalized and then detrended to provide information about fluctuation around the trend curve of the individual. With this process, we aimed to consider the gait habit of the person in order not to misinterpret an unusual gait habit as identifying a balance disorder. As one of the effective innovations brought by this study, we developed an algorithm that determines the trend curve at each step. The efficiency of this algorithm can be seen when the results are compared with other curve fitting methods. Using our algorithm, we achieved an average accuracy of 95% in distinguishing VS patients from healthy subjects, while the best rate was 86.7% even with a fourth-order curve-fitting polynomial. A total of sixteen features were involved in the classification process, eight of which were derived from the TEs of the entire gait cycle and the other eight from the step-by-step TE change for each sensor. The TE value for the entire gait cycle and the step-by-step variation in the TE value were observed to be greater in VS patients than in healthy individuals, which we explained by the high data deviation around the trend curve for these individuals. The TE parameter q was determined experimentally as 0.82. As we can see from Figure 10, of all the sensor data, those from the under-the-heel sensors (S0 and S4) contributed the least to the classification process, such that the differences in TE values for these data were the smallest. This is easy to explain, as the sensors in question were placed at points where even a diseased person does not show a significant fluctuation.

Regarding the data collection time, the subjects had to walk for around 10–15 s. As we described in detail in [17], this time period is much shorter than most experiments in the literature, meeting the expectations of the respected audiologists we consulted with throughout the project. Despite such a short test time, high accuracy was achieved by processing the instantaneous values of the gait data using appropriate methods rather than dealing with step-based features such as stride time, stance time, etc.

The SVM with Gaussian kernel and logistic regression performed best in the classification process with 95%, followed by KNN (cosine) and neural network (wide) with 93.3%. At this point, we would like to emphasize that we had defined our criterion for categorizing any feature as distinctive and labeling it as a candidate for feature reduction as an individual accuracy level threshold of 90% [17]; thus, the TE-based features passed this evaluation stage successfully. On the other hand, we believe that a more reliable result will be achieved with an increase in the number of participants.

In addition to the numerical values presented in the Results section, we provide further statistical data in Table 8, in order to provide a fuller picture of the results.

Table 8. Some statistical data about the top two classification algorithms.

Statistical Property	SVM (Gaussian)	Logistic Regression
accuracy (%)	95.0	95.0
sensitivity (%)	91.6	94.0
specificity (%)	97.9	95.1
F1 Score	0.945	0.943
MCC	0.899	0.891

Currently, we are conducting experiments for the binary classification phase of the larger project so that an individual can be described as 'suffering' or 'healthy'. As we stated in [17], features that take into account the trends specific to an individual are expected to be quite effective in determining the stage of the problem. So, we look forward to using these features also for this future step of the whole project.

Author Contributions: Conceptualization, S.İ.; methodology, S.İ.; software, H.Y.K.; validation, H.Y.K.; data acquisition, S.İ.; formal analysis, S.İ.; investigation, H.Y.K.; data curation, H.Y.K.; writing—original draft preparation, H.Y.K.; writing—review and editing, S.İ.; visualization, H.Y.K.; supervision, S.İ.; project administration, S.İ.; funding acquisition, S.İ. All authors have read and agreed to the published version of the manuscript.

Funding: This research constitutes a significant component of a project entitled "Development of an Algorithm for Dynamic Vestibular System Analysis and Design of a Balance Detector," which received funding from the Scientific and Technological Research Council of Türkiye (TÜBİTAK) for conducting the experiments (Project no: 115E258).

Institutional Review Board Statement: The research was conducted following the guidelines outlined in the Declaration of Helsinki. The experiments were carried out with the approval of the Ethics Committee of Istanbul University, as evidenced by the granted approval number A-57/07.07.2015.

Informed Consent Statement: Informed consent was obtained from all subjects and/or their legal guardian to participate in experiments before starting the process.

Data Availability Statement: The data are not publicly available due to confidentiality agreements and privacy concerns of the participants, as stated in the consent form.

Acknowledgments: The authors express their sincere gratitude to Ahmet Ataş and Eyyup Kara from the Audiology Department of Cerrahpaşa Medical School-Istanbul for their invaluable encouragement in initiating this research project and their unwavering support in data collection. Additionally, the authors extend their deep appreciation to Tunay Çakar and Saddam Heydarov for their assistance during the sensor calibration process.

Conflicts of Interest: The authors declare that they have no known competing financial interest or personal relationships that could have appeared to influence the work reported in this paper.

References

1. Khan, S.; Chang, R. Anatomy of the vestibular system: A review. *NeuroRehabilitation* **2013**, *32*, 437–443. [CrossRef] [PubMed]
2. Vanicek, N.; King, S.A.; Gohil, R.; Chetter, I.C.; Coughlin, P.A. Computerized dynamic posturography for postural control assessment in patients with intermittent claudication. *JoVE* **2013**, *82*, e51077.
3. Giladi, N.; Horak, F.B.; Hausdorff, J.M. Classification of gait disturbances: Distinguishing between continuous and episodic changes. *Mov. Disord.* **2013**, *28*, 1469–1473. [CrossRef] [PubMed]
4. Bovonsunthonchai, S.; Vachalathiti, R.; Hiengkaew, V.; Bryant, M.S.; Richards, J.; Senanarong, V. Quantitative gait analysis in mild cognitive impairment, dementia, and cognitively intact individuals: A cross-sectional case–control study. *BMC Geriatr.* **2022**, *22*, 767. [CrossRef]
5. Guo, Y.; Yang, J.; Liu, Y.; Chen, X.; Yang, G.-Z. Detection and assessment of Parkinson's disease based on gait analysis. *Front. Aging Neurosci.* **2022**, *14*, 916971. [CrossRef]
6. Wagner, A.R.; Reschke, M.F. Aging, vestibular function, and balance control: Physiological and behavioral considerations. *Curr. Opin. Physiol.* **2021**, *19*, 67–74.
7. Ikizoglu, S.; Heydarov, S. Accuracy comparison of dimensionality reduction techniques to determine significant features from IMU sensor-based data to diagnose vestibular system disorders. *Biomed. Signal Process. Control.* **2020**, *61*, 101963. [CrossRef]
8. Agrawal, D.K.; Usaha, W.; Pojprapai, S.; Wattanapan, P. Fall Risk Prediction Using Wireless Sensor Insoles with Machine Learning. *IEEE Access* **2023**, *11*, 23119–23126. [CrossRef]
9. Schmidheiny, A.; Swanenburg, J.; Straumann, D.; de Bruin, E.D.; Knols, R.H. Discriminant validity and test re-test reproducibility of a gait assessment in patients with vestibular dysfunction. *BMC Ear Nose Throat Disord.* **2015**, *15*, 6. [CrossRef]
10. Tsallis, C. Introduction to Nonextensive Statistical Mechanics: Approaching a Complex World. *Contemp. Phys.* **2009**, 431–438. [CrossRef]
11. Zhang, D.; Jia, X.; Ding, H.; Ye, D.; Thakor, N.V. Application of Tsallis entropy to EEG: Quantifying the presence of burst suppression after asphyxial cardiac arrest in rats. *IEEE Trans. Biomed. Eng.* **2010**, *57*, 867–874. [CrossRef] [PubMed]
12. Tong, S.; Bezerianos, A.; Paul, J.; Zhu, Y.; Thakor, N. Nonextensive entropy measure of EEG following brain injury from cardiac arrest. *Phys. A Stat. Mech. Appl.* **2002**, *305*, 619–628. [CrossRef]
13. Dutta, S.; Ghosh, D.; Chatterjee, S. Multifractal detrended fluctuation analysis of human gait diseases. *Front. Physiol.* **2013**, *4*, 274. [CrossRef] [PubMed]
14. Phinyomark, A.; Larracy, R.; Scheme, E. Fractal analysis of human gait variability via stride interval time series. *Front. Physiol.* **2020**, *11*, 333. [CrossRef]
15. Hausdorff, J.M.; Ashkenazy, Y.; Peng, C.; Ivanov, P.C.; Stanley, H.; Goldberger, A.L. When human walking becomes random walking: Fractal analysis and modeling of gait rhythm fluctuations. *Phys. A Stat. Mech. Appl.* **2001**, *302*, 138–147. [CrossRef]
16. Muñoz-Diosdado, A. Fractal and multifractal analysis of human gait. *AIP Conf. Proc.* **2003**, *682*, 243–250.

17. Günaydın, B.; İkizoğlu, S. Multifractal detrended fluctuation analysis of insole pressure sensor data to diagnose vestibular system disorders. *Biomed. Eng. Lett.* **2023**. [CrossRef]
18. Higuma, M.; Sanjo, N.; Mitoma, H.; Yoneyama, M.; Yokota, T. Wholeday gait monitoring in patients with Alzheimer's disease: A relationship between attention and gait cycle. *J. Alzheimer's Dis. Rep.* **2017**, *1*, 1–8. [CrossRef]
19. Nieto-Hidalgo, M.; Ferrández-Pastor, F.J.; Valdivieso-Sarabia, R.J.; Mora-Pascual, J.; García-Chamizo, J.M. Gait analysis using computer vision based on cloud platform and mobile device. *Mobile Inf. Syst.* **2018**, *2018*, 7381264. [CrossRef]
20. Schwaemmle, V.; Tsallis, C. Two-parameter generalization of the logarithm and exponential functions and Boltzmann-Gibbs-Shannon entropy. *J. Math. Phys.* **2007**, *48*, 113301. [CrossRef]
21. Liang, Z.; Wang, Y.; Sun, X.; Li, D.; Voss, L.J.; Sleigh, J.W.; Hagihira, S.; Li, X. Entropy Measures in Anesthesia. *Front. Comput. Neurosci.* **2015**, *9*, 16. [CrossRef] [PubMed]
22. Xiong, W.; Faes, L.; Ivanov, P.C. Entropy measures, entropy estimators, and their performance in quantifying complex dynamics: Effects of artifacts, nonstationarity, and long-range correlations. *Phys. Rev. E* **2017**, *95*, 062114. [CrossRef] [PubMed]
23. Li, C.; Pengjian, S. Multiscale Tsallis permutation entropy analysis for complex physiological time series. *Phys. A Stat. Mech. Appl.* **2019**, *529*, 10–20. [CrossRef]
24. Tsallis, C.; Tirnakli, U. Nonadditive entropy and nonextensive statistical mechanics Some central concepts and recent applications. *J. Phys. Conf. Ser.* **2009**, *201*, 012001. [CrossRef]
25. Sigalotti, L.D.G.; Ramírez-Rojas, A.; Vargas, C.A. Tsallis q-Statistics in Seismology. *Entropy* **2023**, *25*, 408. [CrossRef]
26. Wilk, G.; Włodarczyk, Z. Some Non-Obvious Consequences of Non-Extensiveness of Entropy. *Entropy* **2023**, *25*, 474. [CrossRef]
27. Healy, A.; Burgess-Walker, P.; Naemi, R.; Chockalingam, N. Repeatability of WalkinSense®in shoe pressure measurement system: A preliminary study. *Foot* **2012**, *22*, 35–39. [CrossRef]
28. Holleczek, T.; Ruegg, A.; Harms, H.; Tro, G. Textile pressure sensors for sports applications. In Proceedings of the 2010 IEEE Sensors, Waikoloa, HI, USA, 1–4 November 2010; pp. 732–737.
29. Saito, M.; Nakajima, K.; Takano, C.; Ohta, Y.; Sugimoto, C.; Ezoe, R.; Sasaki, K.; Hosaka, H.; Ifukube, T.; Ino, S.; et al. An in -shoe device to measure plantar pressure during daily human activity. *Med. Eng. Phys.* **2011**, *33*, 638–645. [CrossRef]
30. Salpavaara, T.; Verho, J.; Lekkala, J.; Halttunen, J. Wireless insole sensor system for plantar force measurements during sport events. In Proceedings of the IMEKO XIX World Congress on Fundamental and Applied Metrology, Lisbon, Portugal, 6–11 September 2009; pp. 2118–2123.
31. Shu, L.; Hua, T.; Wang, Y.; Li, Q.; Feng, D.D.; Tao, X. In-shoe plantar pressure measurement and analysis system based on fabric pressure sensing array. *IEEE Trans. Inf. Technol. Biomed.* **2010**, *14*, 767–775.
32. Tahir, A.M.; Chowdhury, M.E.; Khandakar, A.; Al-Hamouz, S.; Abdalla, M.; Awadallah, S.; Reaz, M.B.I.; Al-Emadi, N. A Systematic Approach to the Design and Characterization of a Smart Insole for Detecting Vertical Ground Reaction Force (vGRF) in Gait Analysis. *Sensors* **2020**, *20*, 957. [CrossRef]
33. FSR Technical Paper. Available online: https://cdn2.hubspot.net/hubfs/3899023/Interlinkelectronics%20November2017/Docs/Datasheet_FSR.pdf (accessed on 1 March 2023).
34. Burden, R.L.; Faires, J.D. *Numerical Analysis*; Cengage Learning: Boston, MA, USA, 2019; pp. 144–172.
35. Peterson, L. K-nearest neighbor. *Scholarpedia* **2009**, *4*, 1883. [CrossRef]
36. Schober, P.; Vetter, T.R. Logistic Regression in Medical Research. *Anesth. Analg.* **2021**, *132*, 365–366. [CrossRef] [PubMed]
37. Geron, A. Chapter 5: Support Vector Machines. In *Hands-On Machine Learning with Scikit-Learn, Keras, and TensorFlow: Concepts, Tools, and Techniques to Build Intelligent Systems*; O'Reilly Media, Inc.: Sebastopol, CA, USA, 2019.
38. Lin, Y.; Wang, C.; Wu, T.; Jeng, S.; Chen, J. Support vector machine for EEG signal classification during listening to emotional music. In Proceedings of the 2008 IEEE 10th Workshop on Multimedia Signal Processing, Cairns, QLD, Australia, 8–10 October 2008; pp. 127–130.
39. Saccà, V.; Campolo, M.; Mirarchi, D.; Gambardella, A.; Veltri, P.; Morabito, F.C. *On the Classification of EEG Signal by Using an SVM Based Algorithm*; Springer: Cham, Switzerland, 2018; pp. 271–278.
40. Saini, I.; Singh, D.; Khosla, A. QRS detection using K-Nearest Neighbor algorithm (KNN) and evaluation on standard ECG databases. *J. Adv. Res.* **2013**, *4*, 331–344. [CrossRef] [PubMed]
41. Yean, C.W.; Khairunizam, W.; Omar, M.I.; Murugappan, M.; Zheng, B.S.; Bakar, S.A.; Razlan, Z.M.; Ibrahim, Z. Analysis of the distance metrics of KNN classifier for EEG signal in stroke patients. In Proceedings of the 2018 International Conference on Computational Approach in Smart Systems Design and Applications (ICASSDA), Kuching, Malaysia, 15–17 August 2018.
42. Erguzel, T.T.; Noyan, C.O.; Eryilmaz, G.; Ünsalver, B.; Cebi, M.; Tas, C.; Dilbaz, N.; Tarhan, N. Binomial Logistic Regression and Artificial Neural Network Methods to Classify Opioid-Dependent Subjects and Control Group Using Quantitative EEG Power Measures. *Clin. EEG Neurosci.* **2019**, *50*, 303–310. [CrossRef] [PubMed]
43. Maria, G.; Juan, S.; Helbert, E. EEG signal analysis using classification techniques: Logistic regression, artificial neural networks, support vector machines, and convolutional neural networks. *Heliyon* **2021**, *7*, e07258.

Article

Effects of Nonextensive Electrons on Dust–Ion Acoustic Waves in a Collisional Dusty Plasma with Negative Ions

Zhipeng Liu

School of Science, Tianjin Chengjian University, Tianjin 300384, China; zhipengliu@tcu.edu.cn;
Tel.: +86-22-23085304

Abstract: The effects of nonextensive electrons on nonlinear ion acoustic waves in dusty negative ion plasmas with ion–dust collisions are investigated. Analytical results show that both solitary and shock waves are supported in this system. The wave propagation is governed by a Korteweg–de Vries Burgers-type equation. The coefficients of this equation are modified by the nonextensive parameter q. Numerical calculations indicate that the amplitude of solitary wave and oscillatory shock can be obviously modified by the nonextensive electrons, but the monotonic shock is little affected.

Keywords: ion acoustic waves; nonextensive statistics; kappa distribution; Korteweg–de Vries Burgers equation

Citation: Liu, Z. Effects of Nonextensive Electrons on Dust–Ion Acoustic Waves in a Collisional Dusty Plasma with Negative Ions. *Entropy* **2023**, *25*, 1363. https://doi.org/10.3390/e25091363

Academic Editor: Antonio M. Scarfone

Received: 16 August 2023
Revised: 31 August 2023
Accepted: 11 September 2023
Published: 21 September 2023

Copyright: © 2023 by the author. Licensee MDPI, Basel, Switzerland. This article is an open access article distributed under the terms and conditions of the Creative Commons Attribution (CC BY) license (https://creativecommons.org/licenses/by/4.0/).

1. Introduction

Ion acoustic wave (IAW) is a low-frequency electrostatic wave that can be commonly observed in space and experimental plasmas. Its linear or nonlinear properties have long been studied in the past decades. Examples include Landau damping [1,2], IAW instabilities [3,4], solitary wave propagation [5,6], etc. Among the above wave phenomena, ion acoustic solitary and shock wave problems occupy an important place in studies of plasmas. Early research on IAW can be traced back to the 1960s. Biscamp et al. theoretically investigated the shock structure and formation of IAW in a collisionless plasma [7]. They found that the wave can be described by a Korteweg–de Vries Burgers (KdVB) equation. For the first time, Ikezi et al. observed the shock wave structure in a novel double-plasma device [8]. Das gave systematic studies on IA solitary and shock waves in plasmas with negative ions [9]. Since then, explorations of IAW in muti-components plasmas have attracted much attention. The pioneering works by Shukla and Silin showed that IAW could also be supported in dusty plasma, namely dust–ion acoustic wave (DIAW) [10]. The dust grains, which have micrometer or sub-micrometer sizes, are ubiquitous in space and laboratory environments, such as solar wind [11], planetary rings [12], the interstellar medium [13], the Earth's lower ionosphere [14], semiconductor processing devices [15] and fusion plasmas [16]. A number of authors have shown that the existence of charged dust grains could modify the dynamical behavior of electrostatic waves in plasmas. These modifications may be due to the charge variation [17,18], dust size distribution [19], dust density waves [20], temperature [1,21], etc. Therefore, the wave properties in dusty plasmas would be quite complicated but interesting, especially for the coherent structure of IAW. Meanwhile, numerical simulation have shown that particle distributions of fluid systems, such as multiphase flows [22] and high-speed compressible flow [23–25], usually deviate from Maxwellin distribution. As a typical fluid system, plasma usually exhibits a power-law form distribution and cannot be modeled by Maxwellian distribution [26–28]. For instance, data from spacecraft or laboratory plasmas observations often reveal that plasmas often process a number of superthermal electrons (energetic particles). These high-energy particles make the plasmas obviously deviate from the Maxwellian. Vasyliunas was the first to give an empirical power-law form expression called generalized Lorentzian (kappa) distribution to model these superthermal particles [29]. They found that the plasmas can be well fitted by kappa distribution. Recently, Leubner [30], Livadiotis and McComas [31–33] have theoretically proven that the kappa-type distributions are a consequence of Tsallis distribution in nonextensive statistics [34]. Nonextensive statistics was first introduced by Tsallis [34] and further developed by many others. In nonextensive statistics, the nonadditive q-entropy has the form,

$$S_q = k_B \frac{\int (f^q - f) dx^3 dv^3}{1-q}, \tag{1}$$

where f is the probabilistic distribution function, and q is a real parameter different from unity, specifying the degree of nonextensivity. It was proven that q is related to the temperature gradient and the gravitational potential [35]. The physical meaning of q is connected to the non-isothermal (nonequilibrium stationary state) nature of the systems with long-range interactions.

Nowadays, nonextensive statistics have successfully been applied to a number of systems [36,37] and become a powerful tool to analyze complex systems with Coulomb long-range [38], self-gravitating interactions [39,40], astrophysics [41] and plasma physics phenomena such as ion acoustic instability [26], dust acoustic instability [27], permeating plasmas [42,43], transport [44], diffusion [45], viscosity [46], and statistical uncertainty [47] effects. For plasma waves, examples could be numerous. For instance, Lima et al. discussed the dispersion relations and Landau damping for electrostatic plane–wave propagation in a collisionless thermal plasma in the context of nonextensive statistics [48]. Tribeche et al. explored arbitrary amplitude ion acoustic solitary waves in a two-component plasma with a nonextensive electron velocity distribution. Their results showed that the ion acoustic solitary wave amplitude was sensitive to the nonextensive parameter q [49]. EI-Awady and Moslem studied the generation of nonlinear ionacoustic rogue and solitary waves in a plasma with nonextensive electrons and positrons [50]. The results from their work show a dependence of both solitary and rogue wave profiles on the nonextensive parameter. Recently, Yasmin et al. analyzed the modification of DIA shock waves in an unmagnetized, collisionless, dissipative dusty plasma containing nonextensive electrons [51]. They found that shock compression and rarefaction are sensitive to the degree of the nonextensivity of electrons.

Former studies on wave properties in nonextensive plasmas usually assume the plasmas are collisionless. This is reasonable for dustless plasmas, as collisions between ions and electrons are rare. However, when dust grains are encountered in plasmas, due to the large size of dust grains, the collisional effects of ions/electrons with dust grains may not be neglected. Recently, Misra et al. proved that, in a Maxwellian dusty plasma with negative ions, ion–dust collisions play a crucial role in the dissipation of ion acoustic solitary wave and shocks (IASWS) propagation [52]. Therefore, the nonlinear wave structure of non-Maxwellian plasmas, which have not been investigated before, would be very interesting and worth exploring. The aim of the present paper is to investigate the nonextensivity of electrons on IASWS in multi-ion plasma with ion–dust collisions. The paper is arranged as follows: In Section 2, basic equations for describing the system are given. In Section 3, following the standard reductive perturbation method, a KdV Burgers type equation are obtained. In Section 4, numerical calculations with related parameters and the nonextensive index q are carried out to check the nonextensivity of electrons on IASWS. Finally in Section 5, the summary and conclusive remarks are given.

2. Governing Equations

In this paper, we consider a fully ionized one-dimensional, unmagnetized collisional dusty plasma consisting of nonextensive electrons, positive and negative cold fluid ions, and immobile dust grains. The charge neutrality condition gives:

$$n_{p0} - n_{i0} - n_{e0} \pm Z_d n_{d0} = 0, \tag{2}$$

where n_{j0} is the unperturbed number density of species j (j stands for the electrons, dust grains, and positive and negative ions respectively), Z_d is the charge number of dust particles, the sign $\pm$ before Z_d represents the positively (negatively) charged dust. If we let $\mu_e = n_{e0}/n_{n0}$, $\mu_d = Z_{d0}n_{d0}/n_{n0}$ and $\mu_i = n_{p0}/n_{n0}$, then Equation (2) can be written as,

$$\mu_i - \mu_e \pm \mu_d - 1 = 0. \tag{3}$$

The basic equations for describing the dynamics of one-dimensional plasma systems are the following:

$$\frac{\partial n_j}{\partial t} + \frac{\partial}{\partial x}(n_j V_j) = 0, \tag{4}$$

$$\left(\frac{d}{dt} + \nu_{jd}\right)V_j = -\frac{Q_j}{m_j}\frac{\partial \phi}{\partial x} - \frac{3k_B T_j}{m_j n_{j0}^2}\cdot\frac{\partial n_j^2}{\partial x} + \eta_j \frac{\partial^2 V_j}{\partial x^2}, \tag{5}$$

$$\frac{\partial^2 \phi}{\partial x^2} = 4\pi e(n_e - n_p + n_n \mp Z_d n_d), \tag{6}$$

where n_j,V_j, Q_j, m_j and T_j are the number density, velocity, mass, charge and temperature of j-species ions, respectively; ϕ is the electrostatic potential; ν_{jd} is the collision rate of j-species ions with dust particles; η_i is the viscosity coefficient due to ion–dust collisions; and k_B is the Boltzmann constant. For simplicity, let us introduce the following dimensionless physical quantities:

$$\bar{\eta}_j \to \eta_j/\lambda_D^2\omega_{pd}, \bar{\nu}_{jd} \to \nu_{jd}/\omega_{pd}, \phi \to e\phi/k_B T_e,$$
$$n_j \to n_j/n_{j0}, V_j \to V_j/c_s, x \to x/\lambda_D, t \to t\cdot\omega_{pd}$$

where $\lambda_D = \sqrt{k_B/4\pi Z_d n_{d0} e^2}$ is the Debye length, $\omega_{pj} = \sqrt{4\pi n_{n0}e^2/m_j}$ is the plasma frequency, $c_s = \sqrt{Z_d k_B T_e/m_d}$ is the thermal speed, $\sigma_j = T_j/T_e$ and $\beta_j = m_n/m_j$. The nondimensional form of Equations (4)–(6) become,

$$\frac{\partial n_j}{\partial t} + \frac{\partial}{\partial x}(n_j V_j) = 0, \tag{7}$$

$$\left(\frac{d}{dt} + \bar{\nu}_{jd}\right)V_j = -\beta_j\left(\frac{\partial \phi}{\partial x} + \frac{3}{2}\sigma_j\frac{\partial n_j^2}{\partial x}\right) + \bar{\eta}_j\frac{\partial^2 V_j}{\partial x^2}, \tag{8}$$

$$\frac{\partial^2 \phi}{\partial x^2} = Z_d n_d + \mu_e n_e - \mu_i n_p + n_n. \tag{9}$$

We assume that the electrons in the plasma obey the normalized nonextensive electron distribution:

$$n_e = [1 + (q-1)\phi]^{(q+1)/2(q-1)}, \tag{10}$$

where q is the nonextensive parameter that describes the nonextensivity of the electrons.

3. Derivation of the KdV Burgers Type Equation

Following the routing procedure, we employ the standard reductive perturbation technique to derive the evolution equation for DIAW. First, let us introduce the new variables of space and time:

$$\xi = \varepsilon^{1/2}(x - U_0 t), \tau = \varepsilon^{3/2}t, \tag{11}$$

where ε is a small parameter characterizing the strength of the nonlinearity, U_0 is the wave speed in the moving frame of reference. We also introduce $\bar{\nu}_{jd} = \varepsilon^{3/2}\bar{\nu}_{j0}$ and $\eta_{jd} = \varepsilon^{1/2}\eta_{j0}$, where $\bar{\nu}_{j0}$ and η_{j0} are of the order of unity or less. Next, we expand the dynamical variables as

$$n_j = 1 + \varepsilon n_j^{(1)} + \varepsilon^2 n_j^{(2)} + \cdots, \tag{12}$$

$$V_j = \varepsilon V_j^{(1)} + \varepsilon^2 V_j^{(1)} + \cdots, \tag{13}$$

$$\phi = \varepsilon \phi^{(1)} + \varepsilon^2 \phi^{(2)} + \cdots. \tag{14}$$

Then we substitute Equations (12)–(14) into Equations (7)–(9) and equate the terms of the same powers of ε. From the $\varepsilon^{3/2}$ terms, we have,

$$n_j^{(1)} = \alpha_j \phi^{(1)}, V_j^{(1)} = \alpha_j U_0 \phi^{(1)}, \tag{15}$$

where $\alpha_j = \pm\beta_j / \left(U_0^2 - 3\beta_j\sigma_j\right)$. Here, the sign $\pm$ corresponds to the positive and negative ions, respectively. U_0 has the form of

$$U_0^2 = \frac{1}{2(q+1)\mu_e}\left\{s \pm \sqrt{s^2 - 12(1+q)\beta\mu_e\left[2\sigma_p + 3(1+q)\mu_e\sigma_p\sigma_n + 2\mu_i\sigma_n\right]}\right\}, \tag{16}$$

where

$$s = 2 + 2\beta\mu_i + 3(1+q)(\sigma_n + \beta\sigma_p)\mu_e. \tag{17}$$

The $\pm$ sign in Equation (16) indicates that there are two values. This means that the plasmas contain two types of ion acoustic waves, the fast mode (+) and the slow one (−). Detailed discussions related to these two modes are given in Section 4. Now, we proceed to the next order of ε, and the following equations for the second order perturbed quantities are obtained:

$$\alpha_j \frac{\partial \phi^{(1)}}{\partial \tau} - U_0 \frac{\partial n_j^{(2)}}{\partial \xi} + \alpha_j^2 U_0 \frac{\partial \left[\phi^{(1)}\right]^2}{\partial \xi} + \frac{\partial V_j^{(2)}}{\partial \xi} = 0, \tag{18}$$

$$\left(\frac{\partial}{\partial \tau} + \bar{\nu}_{j0}\right)\alpha_j U_0 \phi^{(1)} + \frac{1}{2}\alpha_j^2\left(U_0^2 + 3\beta_j\sigma_j\right)\frac{\partial \left[\phi^{(1)}\right]^2}{\partial \xi} = U_0\left[\frac{\partial V_j^{(2)}}{\partial \xi} + \bar{\eta}_{j0}\alpha_j\right]\frac{\partial^2 \phi^{(1)}}{\partial \xi^2} - \beta_j\left[3\sigma_j \frac{\partial n_j^{(2)}}{\partial \xi} \pm \frac{\partial \phi^{(2)}}{\partial \xi}\right], \tag{19}$$

$$\frac{\partial^3 \phi^{(1)}}{\partial \xi^3} = \frac{\partial n_n^{(2)}}{\partial \xi} - \mu_i \frac{\partial n_p^{(2)}}{\partial \xi} + \mu_e\left(\frac{1+q}{2}\right)\left[\frac{\partial \phi^{(2)}}{\partial \xi} + \frac{3-q}{4}\cdot\frac{\partial \left(\phi^{(1)}\right)^2}{\partial \xi}\right]. \tag{20}$$

Putting Equation (14) into Equations (18)–(20) and eliminating the second-order quantities, we obtain the following KdVB-type equation:

$$\frac{\partial \Phi}{\partial \tau} + A\Phi\frac{\partial \Phi}{\partial \xi} + B\frac{\partial^3 \Phi}{\partial \xi^3} - \eta\frac{\partial^2 \Phi}{\partial \xi^2} + \nu\Phi = 0, \tag{21}$$

where we set $\Phi = \phi^{(1)}$. The coefficients A, B, η and ν, which represent the nonlinearity, dispersion, dissipation due to ion kinematic viscosities and ion–dust collisions, respectively, can be written as,

$$A = \frac{3\alpha_p^3\mu_i(U_0^2+\beta\sigma_p) + 3\alpha_n^3\beta(U_0^2+\sigma_n) + \beta\left(\frac{3-q}{2}\right)(\alpha_n - \mu_i\alpha_p)}{2U_0\left(\beta\alpha_n^2 + \alpha_p^2\mu_i\right)}, \tag{22}$$

$$B = \frac{\beta}{2U_0\left(\beta\alpha_n^2 + \alpha_p^2\mu_i\right)}, \tag{23}$$

$$\eta = \frac{\bar{\eta}_{n0}\alpha_n^2\beta + \bar{\eta}_{p0}\alpha_p^2\mu_i}{2\left(\beta\alpha_n^2 + \alpha_p^2\mu_i\right)}, \tag{24}$$

$$\nu = \frac{\bar{\nu}_{n0}\alpha_n^2\beta + \bar{\nu}_{p0}\alpha_p^2\mu_i}{2\left(\beta\alpha_n^2 + \alpha_p^2\mu_i\right)}. \tag{25}$$

One may see that the evolution of Equation (21) has the same form as obtained by Misra et al. [52]. However, the coefficients A, B, η and ν, which determine the formation and evolution of ion acoustic wave structures, are modified by the nonextensive parameter q. It can be verified that in the limit $q \to 1$, the Maxwellian counterparts of these coefficients will be recovered [52]. The effects of these modifications due to nonextensivity will be analyzed in Section 4.

4. Numerical Results and Discussion

Equation (21) is a modified KdV Burgers equation that describes the DIAW in a collisional dusty plasma. The effects of the coefficients A, B, η and ν on the wave evolution for Maxweillian plasmas were discussed by Misra et al. in detail [52]. Therefore, here we just investigate the effects of the nonextensivity of the system. Since the exact solution of Equation (21) is still unknown, in order to obtain the effects of the nonextensivity of the wave evolution, we numerically investigate the influences of the nonextensive parameter q on the coefficients A, B, η and ν, respectively. During our calculation, the following space and laboratory observed parameters are employed (see Reference [52] for more details) for negatively charged dust, $m_n = 146m_{proton}$, $m_n = 39m_{proton}$, $T_e \sim T_p \sim 0.2$ eV, $T_n \sim T_e/8$, $n_{n0} \sim 2\times10^9$, $\eta_{p0} = 0.3$, $\eta_{n0} = 0.5$, $\nu_{p0} = 0.01$, $\nu_{p0} = 0.01$, where m_{proton} is the mass of protons. For positively charged dust, $m_n = 146m_{proton}$, $m_n = 39m_{proton}$, $T_e \sim T_p \sim 0.2$ eV, $T_n \sim T_e/2$, $n_{n0} \sim 2\times10^9$, $\eta_{p0} = 0.5$, $\eta_{n0} = 0.3$, $\nu_{p0} = 0.5$, and $\nu_{p0} = 0.3$.

Figure 1 shows that the nonlinearity coefficient A varies with μ_i for positively and negatively charged dust, respectively. As shown in Figure 1, with increasing μ_i, the strength of A will increase in subplots (a)–(c) but decrease in subplot (d). We can also obtain that if A has a growing trend, with fixed μ_i, the sub-extensive case $(q > 1)$ has the largest value, while the super-extensive case $(q < 1)$ has the smallest one. If A has a decreasing trend [subplot (d)], the nonextensive effects are opposite to those of (a)–(c), then the subextensive case $(q < 1)$ has the largest value. Therefore, the nonextensivity of the system has an enhancement on the growth or decrease in A.

Figure 2 gives that the dispersion coefficient B varies with the ion density ratio μ_i. From the figure, it is found that B will monotonically decrease with the growth in μ_i. The left panels (subplots (a) and (c)) indicate that the nonextensive effects on B are obvious. In the right panels (subplots (b) and (d)), it is found that the three lines are nearly overlapped. In this case, the effect of nonextensivity is quite weak. Amplification of the curves shows that with the growth of μ_i, the system nonextensivity has enhancement on the growth/decrease in the dispersion coefficient B. Therefore, the effects of nonextensivity are the same as those of A.

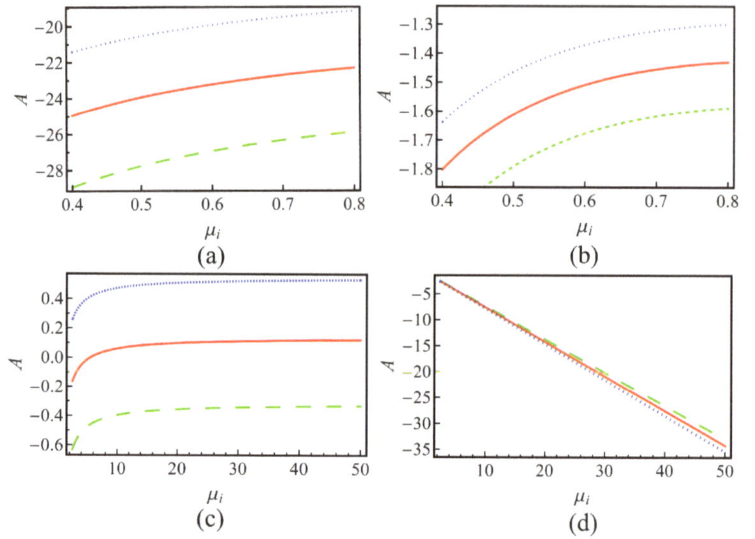

Figure 1. The nonlinearity coefficient A versus the positive-to-negative ion density ratio μ_i for plasmas with positive (subplots (**a**,**b**)) and negative (subplots (**c**,**d**)) charged dusts. The left panels (subplots (**a**,**c**)) corresponding to the positive sign in ${U_0}^2$ (in Equation (16)) and the right ones (subplots (**b**,**d**)) are negative. Lines in each subplot represent different nonextensive q values, where the blue dotted lines represent $q = 1.2$, the red solid lines represent $q = 1.0$ and the green dashed lines represent $q = 0.8$, respectively.

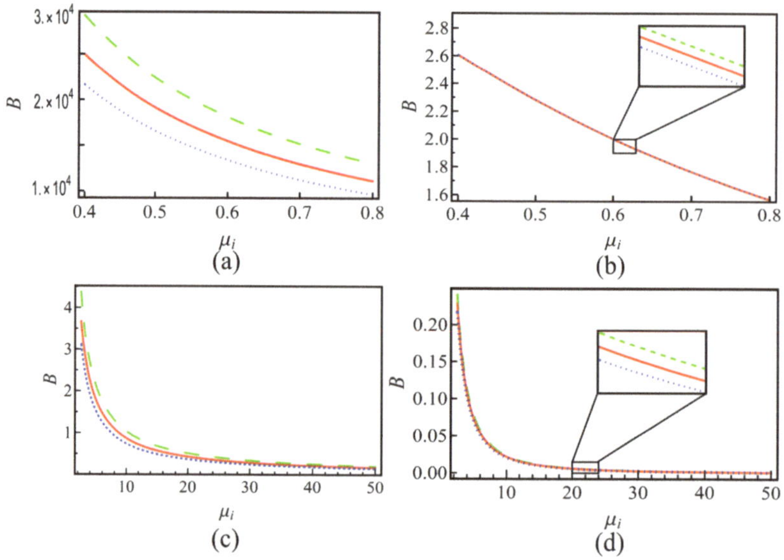

Figure 2. The nonlinearity coefficient B versus the positive-to-negative ion density ratio μ_i for plasmas with positive (subplots (**a**,**b**)) and negative (subplots (**c**,**d**)) charged dusts. The left panels (subplots (**a**,**c**)) corresponding to the positive sign in ${U_0}^2$ (in Equation (16)) and the right ones (subplots (**b**,**d**)) are negative. Lines in each subplot represent different nonextensive q values that are the same as that in Figure 1.

In Figure 3, we depict that the variation of η varies with the ion density ratio μ_i. As we can see, for the left panels (subplots (a) and (c)), which correspond to the sign in U_0^2

is positive, η will increase with the growing of μ_i. On the other hand, when the sign in U_0^2 is negative (subplots (b) and (d)), η will decrease as μ_i is increasing. When the dust is positively charged [the above panels (subplots (a) and (b))], η will have a decreasing trend. It is also seen that if the dust charge is positive, for different q, the changing of η is not significant. It means that the nonextensivity of the system on η is quite weak. However, when the dust is negatively charged, (subplots (c) and (d)), the nonextensivity will have a significant effect on η. When η has a growing trend, the larger the nonextensive parameter q is, the higher the value of η. It is the opposite when η has a decreasing trend, the larger the nonextensive parameter q, the lower the value of η. Therefore, the system's nonextensivity will enhance the growing/decreasing of η. The nonextensive parameter q has the same effects as that of A or B.

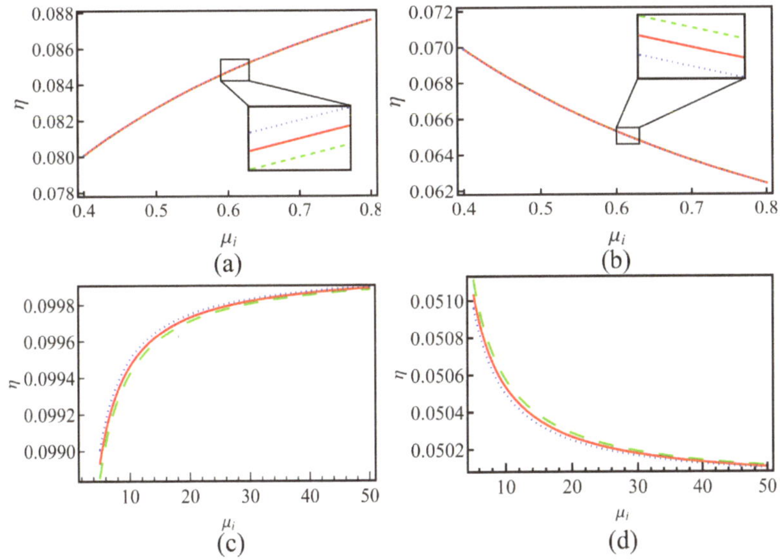

Figure 3. The nonlinearity coefficient B versus the positive-to-negative ion density ratio μ_i for plasmas with positive (subplots (**a**,**b**)) and negative (subplots (**c**,**d**)) charged dusts. The left panels (subplots (**a**,**c**)) corresponding to the positive sign in ${U_0}^2$ (in Equation (16)) and the right ones (subplots (**b**,**d**)) are negative. Lines in each subplot represent different nonextensive q values, where the blue dotted lines represent $q = 1.2$, the red solid lines represent $q = 1.0$ and the green dashed lines represent $q = 0.8$, respectively.

Figure 4 gives the ion–dust collisions coefficient ν versus the positive-to-negative ion density ratio u_i. As is shown, when the sign in U_0^2 is positive (subplots (a) and (c)), ν will decrease with the increasing of μ_i. When the sign in U_0^2 is negative (subplots (b) and (d)), the trend is the opposite and ν will increase as μ_i is increasing. It can be also seen that for different q, the changing of ν is not significant except the case of negative charged dust with the sign in U_0^2 being negative. The enlarged view of the curves shows that the sub-extensive electrons $(q > 1)$ can enhance the growing/decreasing of ν, while the super-extensive ones $(q < 1)$ will weaken it. Equation (21) is a KdV Burgers-type equation with a damping term; it has no analytical solution. In order to investigate the effects of nonextensive electrons on the evolution of the wave, we numerically calculate Equation (21) under different conditions. The results are shown in Figures 5–8.

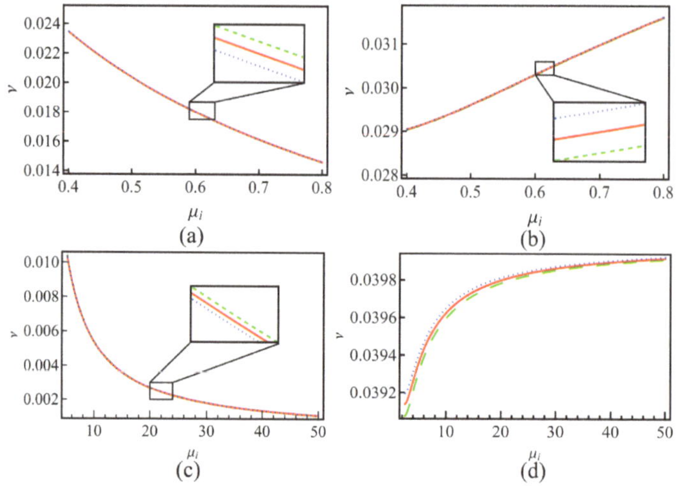

Figure 4. The ion–dust collisions coefficient ν versus the positive-to-negative ion density ratio u_i for plasmas with positive (subplots (**a**,**b**)) and negative (subplots (**c**,**d**)) charged dust. Lines in each subplot represent different nonextensive q values that are the same as that in Figure 1. Other parameters are the same as Figure 1.

Figure 5 corresponds to the case of negative charged dust and positive sign in U_0^2. Here, we let $u_i = 1.5$. In this case, the value $A > B \gg \eta \sim \nu$. Approximately, Equation (21), can be taken as a KdV equation. Therefore, we use a solitary wave solution as the initial condition $\Phi(\xi) = 3v_0/A * sech^2[\xi/(2\sqrt{B/v_0})]$, where $v_0 = 0.6$ is the wave speed. The wave evolutions for super-extensive ($q < 1$), Maxwellian ($q = 1.0$) and sub-extensive ($q > 1$) electrons are shown in Figure 5a–c, respectively. Figure 5d gives the wave profiles of the three cases at $\tau = 50$. As shown in Figure 5, all three cases have damping effects due to ion–dust collisions and the amplitudes of Φ will decrease with τ. From Figure 5d, it is obvious that $q = 1.6$ has the largest amplitude, while $q = 0.4$ has the smallest one. Therefore, the nonextensivity will suppress the damping effect induced by ion–dust collisions.

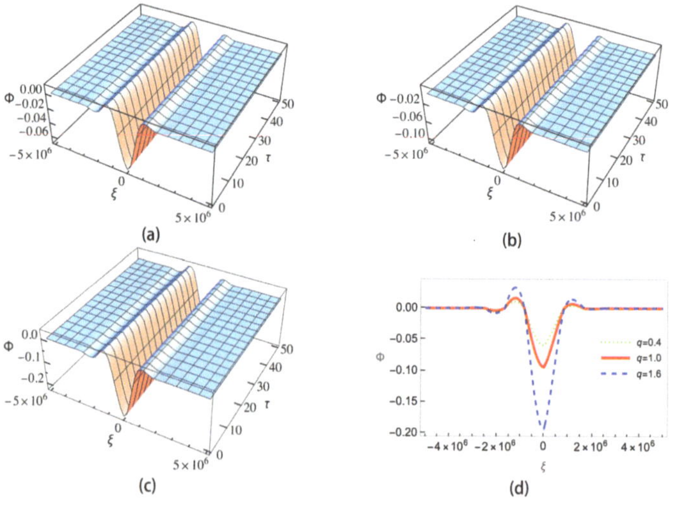

Figure 5. Wave evolutions with negative charged dust and positive sign in U_0^2 for (**a**) super-extensive ($q = 0.4$), (**b**) Maxwellian ($q = 1.0$), (**c**) sub-extensive electrons ($q = 1.6$) and (**d**) wave amplitudes of the three cases at $\tau = 50$.

Figure 6 depicts the wave evolutions of negatively charged dust and a negative sign in U_0^2. We let $u_i = 1.5$ and the initial condition is set as $-(2v_0/B)Exp[(-\eta/2B)\xi]Cos(\sqrt{v_0/B}\xi)$, where $v_0 = 0.1$ is the wave speed. The numerical results of Equation (21) show that monotonic shock waves will be formed. Compared with the negative sign in the U_0^2 case, the three curves in Figure 6d almost coincide with each other. Therefore in this case, the nonextensive effects on wave evolution are quite weak.

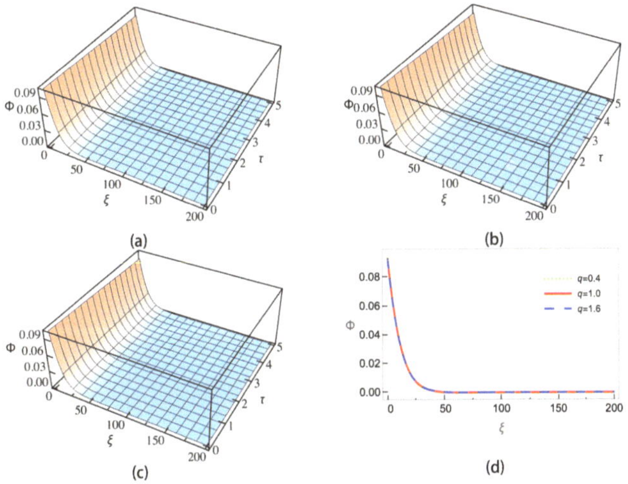

Figure 6. Wave profiles with negative charged dust and negative sign in U_0^2 for (**a**) super-extensive ($q = 0.4$), (**b**) Maxwellian ($q = 1.0$), (**c**) sub-extensive electrons ($q = 1.6$) and (**d**) wave amplitudes of the three cases at $\tau = 5$.

Figure 7 gives the wave evolution profiles of positive charged dust and positive sign in U_0^2. Here we let $u_i = 5/7$. The initial condition is set as $\Phi(\xi) = 3v_0/A * sech^2[\xi/(2\sqrt{B/v_0})]$, where $v_0 = 0.6$ is the wave speed. Similar to that of Figure 5, ion acoustic solitary waves will be formed. The sub-extensive case has the largest amplitude, and the super-extensive has the smallest one.

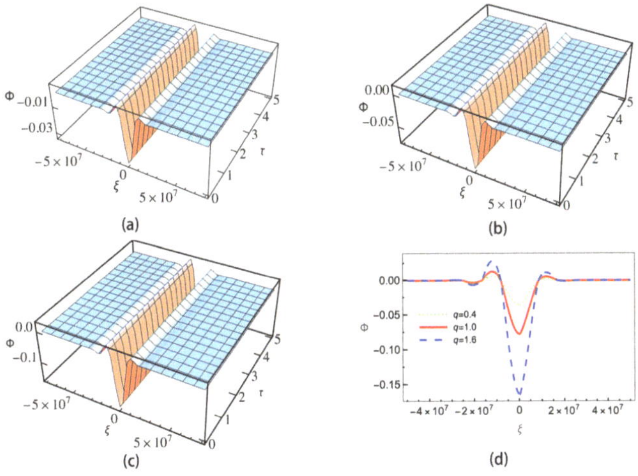

Figure 7. Wave evolution profiles with positive charged dust and positive sign in U_0^2 for (**a**) super-extensive ($q = 0.4$), (**b**) Maxwellian ($q = 1.0$), (**c**) sub-extensive electrons ($q = 1.6$) and (**d**) wave amplitudes of the three cases at $\tau = 5$.

Figure 8 gives the wave evolution profiles of positive charged dust and negative sign in U_0^2. Here, as that in Figure 7, we let $u_i = 5/7$. The initial condition is set as $-(2v_0/B)Exp[(-\eta/2B)\xi]Cos(\sqrt{v_0/B}\xi)$, where $v_0 = 0.1$ is the wave speed. Other parameters are the same as those of Figure 6. The numerical results show that oscillatory shock waves will be formed, and the system's nonextensivity mainly affects the wave oscillatory amplitude. Compare with Figure 6, we can find that the wave speed v_0 will determine whether it is a oscillatory shock wave or monotonic one. When the speed is small, it is more likely to form a monotonic shock wave, while if the speed is large, a oscillatory shock wave will be formed [53].

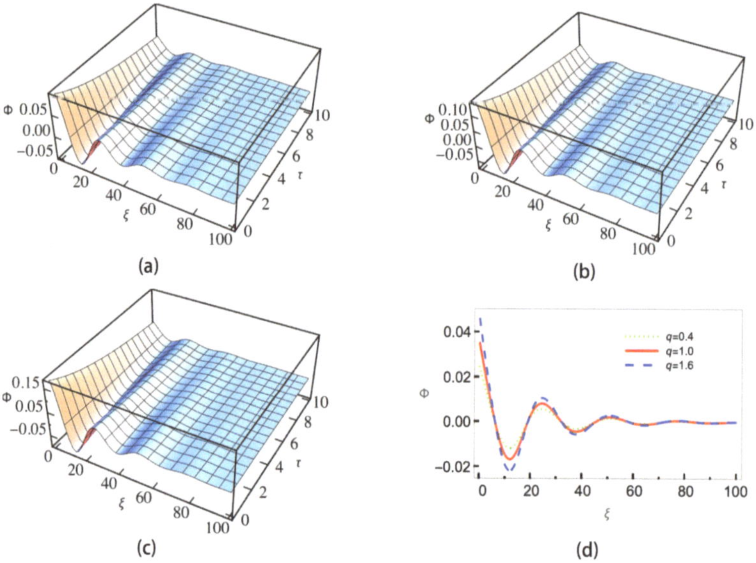

Figure 8. Wave evolution profiles with positive charged dust and negative sign in U_0^2 for (**a**) super-extensive ($q = 0.4$), (**b**) Maxwellian ($q = 1$), (**c**) sub-extensive electrons ($q = 1.6$) and (**d**) wave amplitudes of the three cases at $\tau = 10$.

5. Summary and Conclusions

In this paper, we studied the dust–ion acoustic waves in a collisional dusty plasma with negative ions. With the help of the reductive perturbation technique, we found that the wave evolution can be modeled by the KdV Burgers type equation with a damping term that is related to the ion–dust collisions. This plasma system has four types of ion acoustic waves, fast/slow mode with positive/negative ions, respectively. We analyze the effects of nonextensive electrons on wave evolution through numerical methods. Our results show that the nonextensive electrons will affect the wave amplitude. If the wave has a growing trend, the sub-extensive electrons ($q > 1$) will enhance the wave amplitude, while the super-extensive ones ($q < 1$) will weaken it. If the wave has a decreasing trend, the sub-extensive electrons will enhance the wave's decreasing trend, while the super-extensive ones will weaken it. Furthermore, we expect that our investigation will be helpful for future investigations on dust–ion acoustic solitary and shock waves.

Funding: This project is supported by the National Natural Science Foundation of China (Grant Nos. 11602162, 11775156).

Institutional Review Board Statement: Not applicable.

Data Availability Statement: The data that support the findings of this study are available from the corresponding author upon reasonable request.

Conflicts of Interest: The author declare no conflict of interest.

Abbreviations

The following abbreviations are used in this manuscript:

IAW	Ion Acoustic Wave
DIAW	Dust–Ion Acoustic Wave
IASWS	Ion Acoustic Solitary Wave and Shocks
KdVB	Korteweg–de Vries Burgers

Reference

1. Lee, M.J.; Jung, Y.D. Temperature effects on the propagation and Landau damping of the dust surface waves. *Phys. Plasmas* **2019**, *26*, 032103. [CrossRef]
2. Bilal, M.; Rehman, A.U.; Mahmood, S.; Shahzad, M.A.; Sarfraz, M. Landau damping of ion-acoustic waves with simultaneous effects of non-extensivity and non-thermality in the presence of hybrid Cairns-Tsallis distributed electrons. *Contrib. Plasma Phys.* **2023**, *63*, e202200102. [CrossRef]
3. Beving, L.P.; Hopkins, M.M.; Baalrud, S.D. Simulations of ion heating due to ion-acoustic instabilities in presheaths. *Phys. Plasmas* **2021**, *28*, 123516. [CrossRef]
4. Hellinger, P.; Trávníček, P.; Menietti, J.D. Effective collision frequency due to ion-acoustic instability: Theory and simulations. *Geophys. Res. Lett.* **2004**, *31*. [CrossRef]
5. Khalid, M. Oblique ion-acoustic solitary waves in anisotropic plasma with Tsallis distribution. *Europhys. Lett.* **2022**, *138*, 53003. [CrossRef]
6. Madhukalya, B.; Das, R.; Hosseini, K.; Baleanu, D.; Salahshour, S. Small amplitude ion-acoustic solitary waves in a magnetized ion-beam plasma under the effect of ion and beam temperatures. *Euro. Phys. J. Plus* **2023**, *138*, 315. [CrossRef]
7. Biskamp, D.; Parkinson, D. Ion Acoustic Shock Waves. *Phys. Fluids* **1970**, *13*, 2295–2299. [CrossRef]
8. Ikezi, H.; Taylor, R.; Baker, D. Formation and interaction of ion-acoustic solitions. *Phys. Rev. Lett.* **1970**, *25*, 11. [CrossRef]
9. Das, G.C. Ion-acoustic solutions and shock waves in multicomponent plasmas. *Plasma Phys.* **1979**, *21*, 257. [CrossRef]
10. Shukla, P.K.; Silin, V.P. Dust ion-acoustic wave. *Phys. Scr.* **1992**, *45*, 508. [CrossRef]
11. Saleem, H.; Shan, S.A. Solar wind interaction with dusty plasma produces electrostatic instabilities and solitons. *Astrophys. Space Sci.* **2021**, *366*, 41. [CrossRef]
12. Bansal, S.; Aggarwal, M.; Gill, T.S. Nonplanar ion acoustic waves in dusty plasma with two temperature electrons: Application to Saturn's E ring. *Phys. Plasmas* **2020**, *27*, 083704. [CrossRef]
13. Hirashita, H. Dust growth in the interstellar medium: how do accretion and coagulation interplay? *Mon. Not. R. Astron. Soc.* **2012**, *422*, 1263–1271. [CrossRef]
14. Mann, I.; Gunnarsdottir, T.; Häggström, I.; Eren, S.; Tjulin, A.; Myrvang, M.; Rietveld, M.; Dalin, P.; Jozwicki, D.; Trollvik, H. Radar studies of ionospheric dusty plasma phenomena. *Contrib. Plasma Phys.* **2019**, *59*, e201900005. [CrossRef]
15. Merlino, R. Dusty plasmas: from Saturn's rings to semiconductor processing devices. *Adv. Phys. X* **2021**, *6*, 1873859. [CrossRef]
16. Long, J.M.; Ou, J. Dust particle surface potential in fusion plasma with supra-thermal electrons. *Phys. Plasmas* **2022**, *29*. [CrossRef]
17. El-Labany, S.; Moslem, W.M.; Mowafy, A. Effects of trapped electron temperature, dust charge variations, and grain radius on the existence of the dust-ion-acoustic waves. *Phys. Plasmas* **2003**, *10*, 4217–4223. [CrossRef]
18. Vranješ, J.; Pandey, B.; Poedts, S. Ion–acoustic waves in dusty plasma with charge fluctuations. *Phys. Plasmas* **2002**, *9*, 1464–1467. [CrossRef]
19. El-Labany, S.; El-Siragy, N.; El-Taibany, W.; El-Shamy, E.; Behery, E. Linear and nonlinear quantum dust ion acoustic wave with dust size distribution effect. *Phys. Plasmas* **2010**, *17*, 053705. [CrossRef]
20. Chutia, B.; Deka, T.; Bailung, Y.; Sharma, D.; Sharma, S.; Bailung, H. Spatiotemporal evolution of a self-excited dust density wave in a nanodusty plasma under strong Havnes effect. *Phys. Plasmas* **2021**, *28*, 123702. [CrossRef]
21. Sharma, R.; Bhardwaj, S.; Dhiman, J.S. Effects of dust temperature and radiative heat-loss functions on the magnetogravitational instability of viscoelastic dusty plasma. *Astrophys. Space Sci.* **2020**, *365*, 106. [CrossRef]
22. Gan, Y.; Xu, A.; Zhang, G.; Succi, S. Discrete Boltzmann modeling of multiphase flows: Hydrodynamic and thermodynamic non-equilibrium effects. *Soft Matter* **2015**, *11*, 5336–5345. [CrossRef] [PubMed]
23. Gan, Y.; Xu, A.; Zhang, G.; Zhang, Y.; Succi, S. Discrete Boltzmann trans-scale modeling of high-speed compressible flows. *Phys. Rev. E* **2018**, *97*, 053312. [CrossRef] [PubMed]
24. Gan, Y.B.; Xu, A.G.; Zhang, G.C.; Lin, C.D.; Lai, H.L.; Liu, Z.P. Nonequilibrium and morphological characterizations of Kelvin–Helmholtz instability in compressible flows. *Front. Phys.* **2019**, *14*, 43602. [CrossRef]
25. Gan, Y.; Xu, A.; Lai, H.; Li, W.; Sun, G.; Succi, S. Discrete Boltzmann multi-scale modelling of non-equilibrium multiphase flows. *J. Fluid Mech.* **2022**, *951*, A8. [CrossRef]
26. Liu, Z.; Liu, L.; Du, J. A nonextensive approach for the instability of current-driven ion-acoustic waves in space plasmas. *Phys. Plasmas* **2009**, *16*, 072111. [CrossRef]

27. Liu, Z.; Du, J. Dust acoustic instability driven by drifting ions and electrons in the dust plasma with Lorentzian kappa distribution. *Phys. Plasmas* **2009**, *16*, 123707. [CrossRef]
28. Liu, Z.; Song, J.; Xu, A.; Zhang, Y.; Xie, K. Discrete Boltzmann modeling of plasma shock wave. *Proc. IMechE Part C J. Mech. Eng. Sci.* **2023**, *237*, 2532–2548. [CrossRef]
29. Vasyliunas, V.M. A survey of low-energy electrons in the evening sector of the magnetosphere with OGO 1 and OGO 3. *J. Geophys. Res.* **1968**, *73*, 2839–2884. [CrossRef]
30. Leubner, M.P. A Nonextensive Entropy Approach to Kappa-Distributions. *Astrophys. Space Sci.* **2002**, *282*, 573–579. [CrossRef]
31. Livadiotis, G.; McComas, D.J. Beyond kappa distributions: Exploiting Tsallis statistical mechanics in space plasmas. *J. Geophys. Res. Space Phys.* **2009**, *114*. [CrossRef]
32. Livadiotis, G.; McComas, D. Exploring transitions of space plasmas out of equilibrium. *Astrophys. J.* **2010**, *714*, 971. [CrossRef]
33. Livadiotis, G.; McComas, D. Invariant kappa distribution in space plasmas out of equilibrium. *Astrophys. J.* **2011**, *741*, 88. [CrossRef]
34. Tsallis, C. Possible generalization of Boltzmann-Gibbs statistics. *J. Stat. Phys.* **1988**, *52*, 479–487. [CrossRef]
35. Du, J. What does the nonextensive parameter stand for in self-gravitating systems? *Astrophys. Space Sci.* **2006**, *305*, 247–251. [CrossRef]
36. Deppman, A.; Megías, E.P.; Menezes, D. Fractal Structures of Yang–Mills Fields and Non-Extensive Statistics: Applications to High Energy Physics. *Physics* **2020**, *2*, 455–480. [CrossRef]
37. Megías, E.; Timóteo, V.; Gammal, A.; Deppman, A. Bose–Einstein condensation and non-extensive statistics for finite systems. *Phys. A* **2022**, *585*, 126440. [CrossRef]
38. Du, J. Nonextensivity in nonequilibrium plasma systems with Coulombian long-range interactions. *Phys. Lett. A* **2004**, *329*, 262–267. [CrossRef]
39. Du, J. The nonextensive parameter and Tsallis distribution for self-gravitating systems. *Europhys. Lett.* **2004**, *67*, 893. [CrossRef]
40. Du, J. Nonextensivity and the power-law distributions for the systems with self-gravitating long-range interactions. *Astrophys. Space Sci.* **2007**, *312*, 47–55. [CrossRef]
41. Yu, H.; Du, J. The nonextensive parameter for the rotating astrophysical systems with power-law distributions. *Europhys. Lett.* **2017**, *116*, 60005. [CrossRef]
42. Gong, J.; Du, J. Dust charging processes in the nonequilibrium dusty plasma with nonextensive power-law distribution. *Phys. Plasmas* **2012**, *19*, 023704. [CrossRef]
43. Gong, J.; Liu, Z.; Du, J. Dust-acoustic waves and stability in the permeating dusty plasma. II. Power-law distributions. *Phys. Plasmas* **2012**, *19*, 083706. [CrossRef]
44. Du, J. Transport coefficients in Lorentz plasmas with the power-law kappa-distribution. *Phys. Plasmas* **2013**, *20*, 092901. [CrossRef]
45. Wang, L.; Du, J. The diffusion of charged particles in the weakly ionized plasma with power-law kappa-distributions. *Phys. Plasmas* **2017**, *24*, 102305. [CrossRef]
46. Wang, Y.; Du, J. The viscosity of charged particles in the weakly ionized plasma with power-law distributions. *Phys. Plasmas* **2018**, *25*, 062309. [CrossRef]
47. Nicolaou, G.; Livadiotis, G. Statistical Uncertainties of Space Plasma Properties Described by Kappa Distributions. *Entropy* **2020**, *22*, 541. [CrossRef]
48. Lima, J.A.S.; Silva, R.; Santos, J. Plasma oscillations and nonextensive statistics. *Phys. Rev. E* **2000**, *61*, 3260–3263. [CrossRef]
49. Younsi, S.; Tribeche, M. Arbitrary amplitude electron-acoustic solitary waves in the presence of excess superthermal electrons. *Astrophys. Space Sci.* **2010**, *330*, 295–300. [CrossRef]
50. El-Awady, E.; Moslem, W. On a plasma having nonextensive electrons and positrons: Rogue and solitary wave propagation. *Phys. Plasmas* **2011**, *18*, 082306. [CrossRef]
51. Yasmin, S.; Asaduzzaman, M.; Mamun, A. Dust ion-acoustic shock waves in nonextensive dusty plasma. *Astrophys. Space Sci.* **2013**, *343*, 245–250. [CrossRef]
52. Misra, A.P.; Adhikary, N.C.; Shukla, P.K. Ion-acoustic solitary waves and shocks in a collisional dusty negative-ion plasma. *Phys. Rev. E* **2012**, *86*, 056406. [CrossRef] [PubMed]
53. Pakzad, H.R.; Javidan, K. Dust acoustic solitary and shock waves in strongly coupled dusty plasmas with nonthermal ions. *Pramana* **2009**, *73*, 913–926. [CrossRef]

entropy

Article

Magic Numbers and Mixing Degree in Many-Fermion Systems

D. Monteoliva [1], A. Plastino [2,*] and A. R. Plastino [3]

1 UNLP-Comisión de Investigaciones Científicas Provincia de Buenos Aires La Plata, La Plata 1900, Argentina; monteoli@fisica.unlp.edu.ar
2 Instituto de Física La Plata—CCT-CONICET, Universidad Nacional de La Plata, La Plata 1900, Argentina
3 CeBio-Departamento de Ciencias Básicas, Universidad Nacional del Noroeste, Prov. de Buenos Aires (UNNOBA), CONICET, Junin 6000, Argentina; arplastino@unnoba.edu.ar
* Correspondence: plastino@fisica.unlp.edu.ar

Abstract: We consider an N fermion system at low temperature T in which we encounter special particle number values N_m exhibiting special traits. These values arise when focusing attention upon the degree of mixture (DM) of the pertinent quantum states. Given the coupling constant of the Hamiltonian, the DMs stay constant for all N-values but experience sudden jumps at the N_m. For a quantum state described by the matrix ρ, its purity is expressed by $Tr\rho^2$ and then the degree of mixture is given by $1 - Tr\rho^2$, a quantity that coincides with the entropy S_q for $q = 2$. Thus, Tsallis entropy of index two faithfully represents the degree of mixing of a state, that is, it measures the extent to which the state departs from maximal purity. Macroscopic manifestations of the degree of mixing can be observed through various physical quantities. Our present study is closely related to properties of many-fermion systems that are usually manipulated at zero temperature. Here, we wish to study the subject at finite temperature. The Gibbs ensemble is appealed to. Some interesting insights are thereby gained.

Keywords: Tsallis entropy; many-fermion systems; mixture degree; finite temperature; magic numbers

1. Introduction

Tsallis q-entropy, also known as non-extensive entropy, is an alternative entropy measure introduced by Constantino Tsallis in 1988. Unlike the traditional Shannon entropy or Boltzmann–Gibbs entropy, which are based on logarithmic functions, Tsallis entropy incorporates a power-law function to capture certain characteristics of diverse physical scenarios, in particular, those involving complex systems. For instance, Tsallis entropy has been used to describe physical systems that exhibit long-range interactions, such as self-gravitating systems, turbulent flows, and systems with power-law distributions [1–14]. It provides a framework to characterize the statistical properties of these systems and has connections to generalized statistical mechanics and information theory. It is worth noting that Tsallis entropy has its own set of mathematical properties and implications, and its interpretation and applicability depend on the context and field of study [1–7].

Tsallis entropy has also been used to investigate a various range of quantum phenomena (see, for example, [8–14] and references therein). Some of these studies deal with the explicit application of Tsallis thermostatistics to describe particular quantum systems. It is worth noting, however, that Tsallis entropy also proved to be valuable for the analysis of quantum phenomena not related to Tsallis thermostatistics. In this sense, Tsallis entropy is already an important member of the general tool-kit employed by quantum scientists. Indeed, *Tsallis entropy* can nowadays be found mentioned in monographs devoted to aspects of quantum science, such as quantum entanglement [15] or quantum information [16], which are not necessarily linked to the Tsallis statistical theory. In particular, the entropy S_q, associated with the value $q = 2$ of the Tsallis parameter, which is sometimes referred to as *linear entropy*, is a widely used measure of the degree of mixedness exhibited by a quantum state.

Citation: Monteoliva, D.; Plastino, A.; Plastino, A.R. Magic Numbers and Mixing Degree in Many-Fermion Systems. *Entropy* **2023**, *25*, 1206. https://doi.org/10.3390/e25081206

Academic Editor: Yong Deng

Received: 5 July 2023
Revised: 8 August 2023
Accepted: 10 August 2023
Published: 14 August 2023

Present Goal

The aim of the present effort is to employ the S_2 entropy to characterize some features of many-fermion systems at low temperature, which constitute finite-temperature remnants of basic properties, related to quantum phase transitions, exhibited by these systems at zero temperature.

In particular, this work is devoted to studying properties of the quantum mixing-degree quantifier and of its manifestations at finite, but very low, temperatures.

2. Preliminaries

2.1. *Quantum Mixing-Degree Quantifier*

In quantum mechanics, quantum states can exist in two fundamental forms: pure states and mixed states. A pure state is a state that can be described by a single, normalized wave function, and it exhibits maximal coherence and well-defined quantum properties. On the other hand, a mixed state is a statistical ensemble of pure states, each with its associated probability. It exhibits less coherence and may have probabilistic uncertainties. The degree of mixing or superposition in a quantum state is measured here by the mixing quantifier C_f.

C_f is equal to unity less than the quantum purity P_y. The purity of a quantum state quantifies its coherence and is a measure of how close the state is to being pure. It is defined as the trace of the square of the state's density matrix ρ as $P_y = Tr(\rho^2)$. For a pure state, the purity is equal to 1, while for a mixed state, the purity is less than 1.

2.2. *Usefulness of Exactly Solvable Many-Body Systems*

In this work, we employ an exactly solvable model. Exactly solvable many-body systems are of great importance and usefulness in various areas of physics and related disciplines. These systems are analytically solvable, meaning their quantum states, dynamics, and properties can be described using closed-form mathematical expressions. Their usefulness stems from the deep insights they provide into the behavior of complex quantum systems, as well as their role in serving as benchmarks for testing and developing theoretical methods. Here are some key advantages and applications of exactly solvable many-body systems:

- Insight into quantum phenomena: Exactly solvable many-body systems often serve as simple and tractable models that exhibit essential quantum phenomena, such as quantum phase transitions, entanglement, and quantum correlations. They provide valuable intuition and understanding of fundamental quantum concepts.
- Testing quantum theories: Because these systems are analytically solvable, they are ideal for testing and validating theoretical methods and approximations used in more complicated systems. They allow researchers to check the accuracy and efficiency of numerical algorithms and analytical techniques.
- Educational tools: Exactly solvable many-body systems are commonly used as educational tools in teaching quantum mechanics and statistical physics. They provide students with concrete examples to illustrate abstract concepts and principles.
- Foundation for approximations: Many-body systems that are exactly solvable often serve as the foundation for developing approximate methods applicable to more complex systems. These methods include mean-field theory, perturbation theory, and variational approaches.
- Condensed matter physics: Exactly solvable models play a crucial role in understanding phase transitions and critical phenomena in condensed matter physics. They shed light on the emergence of collective behaviors in large systems.
- Quantum information theory: Solvable models are essential in quantum information theory, particularly in studies related to quantum computing, quantum error correction, and quantum communication protocols.

- Benchmarking numerical techniques: Exactly solvable models provide precise results that can be used as benchmarks to assess the accuracy and efficiency of numerical techniques, such as Monte Carlo simulations, tensor network methods, and a density-matrix renormalization group (DMRG).

In summary, exactly solvable many-body systems are indispensable tools in understanding and exploring quantum phenomena, testing theoretical methods, and providing insights into the behavior of complex quantum systems. Their importance extends beyond theoretical physics and has applications in condensed matter physics, quantum information, and related fields. In nuclear physics, a model of this type that has enjoyed considerable attention is the so-called Lipkin one [17,18]. We discuss here a variant of such a model.

2.3. Using Very Low Temperature Statistical Mechanics Techniques to Approximate Ground-State Properties

Using very low temperature statistical mechanics techniques is a powerful and common approach to approximate ground-state properties of quantum systems. Ground-state properties are of fundamental importance as they represent the system's lowest energy state, and understanding them is crucial for gaining insights into the system's behavior and properties. At very low temperatures (close to absolute zero), thermal fluctuations become negligible, and the system tends to occupy its ground state more predominantly. This allows for various low-temperature approximations that simplify the analysis and computation of ground-state properties.

This procedure, **which we use in this work**, is an essential tool for studying ground-state properties in various physical systems, including condensed matter physics, quantum chemistry, and quantum information theory. They allow researchers to gain insights into the behavior of complex quantum systems and provide a foundation for understanding and engineering quantum materials and technologies. Concomitant references are given below.

2.4. Magic Numbers in Many-Fermion Systems

In the context of nuclear physics, "magic numbers" refer to specific numbers of protons or neutrons in atomic nuclei that correspond to particularly stable and strongly bound configurations. These magic numbers are associated with closed-shell configurations, which have special quantum properties resulting in enhanced stability and distinct nuclear properties. For protons, the magic numbers are 2, 8, 20, 28, 50, 82, and 126, representing the number of protons needed to fill complete shells in the nuclear potential. For example, the nuclei with proton numbers 2, 8, 20, 28, 50, 82, and 126 (helium-4, oxygen-16, calcium-40, nickel-48, tin-100, and lead-208, respectively) are particularly stable and are known as "doubly magic" nuclei. Similarly, for neutrons, the magic numbers are 2, 8, 20, 28, 50, 82, and 126, representing the number of neutrons needed to fill complete shells in the nuclear potential. Nuclei with both proton and neutron magic numbers are especially stable and have unique nuclear properties.

Magic numbers play a crucial role in the nuclear structure and have significant implications in various nuclear processes, such as nuclear reactions and nuclear astrophysics. They also form the basis for understanding the behavior of nucleons (protons and neutrons) in the nuclear potential and are essential for interpreting nuclear data and predicting nuclear properties.

The concept of magic numbers extends beyond nuclear physics to other many-fermion systems, such as atomic and molecular clusters, where similar patterns of enhanced stability due to closed-shell configurations can be observed. Magic numbers in these systems have important consequences for their chemical and physical properties. Overall, magic numbers are fundamental in understanding the structure and stability of many-fermion systems and have far-reaching implications in various areas of physics and chemistry.

We will find them here, in an abstract many-fermions system.

2.5. Expanding on Our Present Objectives

The quantum N-fermion system exhibits various properties, some of them indeed intricate [10,19–31]. We will study manifestations of quantum properties at a very low finite temperature. How? As described by statistical mechanics and with reference to an exactly solvable model. This model is able to illuminate some interesting theoretical effects. We speak of a many-fermion model of the Hubbard model kind [28].

As stated above, thermal statistical manipulation of many-fermion body behavior at finite temperature can yield interesting insights [29]. Accordingly, we appeal here to an exactly solvable Lipkin-like model (LLM) [17,18] at finite temperature and consider the pertinent structural traits in the framework of Gibbs' canonical ensemble formalism. LLMs are nontrivial, finite, easily solvable fermion systems [17,18]. Indeed, they are quite useful testing grounds for envisaging new many-body approaches and using them, as we always have, for an exact solution with which to compare our approximations. In this effort, we work with one of the Lipkin model variants, called the AFP (Abecasis–Faessler–Plastino) model [26,32–34].

3. The AFP Model Structure

The AFP model can be regarded as a very simplified atomic nucleus containing N nucleons in just two levels. It is exactly solvable. The model considers a quite simple fermion–fermion interaction of strength v. In nature, of course, the coupling constants are fixed. In the model, of course, we vary it so as to observe how much the ground-state traits are affected by v changes. We also study the model behavior for different N, as we have in nature nuclei with quite distinct nucleon numbers, whose ground states display quite different traits.

Our model possesses $N = 2\,\Omega$ fermions that occupy two different N-fold degenerate single-particle (sp) energy levels. They are characterized by an sp energy gap ϵ. This entails 4Ω sp microstates. Two quantum numbers ($\mu = \pm 1$ and $p = 1, 2, \ldots, N$) are associated with a given microstate $p, \mu >$. The first one, called μ, adopts the values $\mu = -1$ (lower level) and $\mu = +1$ (upper level). The second runs from unity to N. This remaining quantum number, called p, is baptized as a quasi-spin or pseudo-spin, which singles out a specific microstate pertaining to the $2N$-fold degeneracy. In the pair p, μ is viewed as a "site" that can be occupied (by a fermion) or empty. Lipkin fixes

$$N = 2J. \tag{1}$$

Here, J is a sort of angular momentum. Lipkin [17,29] uses special operators called quasi-spin ones. Below, we use the usual creation operators $C^{+}_{p,\mu}$ and the associated destruction ones $C_{p,\mu}$ for creating or destroying a fermion at a site $|p, \mu>$.

3.1. Quasi-Spin Operators

Quasi-spin operators J are mathematical constructs used to describe certain collective properties of a many-body system. These operators arise in various areas of physics, such as nuclear physics, condensed matter physics, and quantum optics, where systems can exhibit collective behavior due to interactions between constituent particles. Quasi-spin operators are particularly useful in cases where the collective behavior resembles the behavior of spin systems, hence the name "quasi-spin". The concept of quasi-spin originates from the analogy between the properties of many-body systems and those of spin systems, which are well-understood and widely used in quantum mechanics. In a spin system, the angular momentum operators (spin operators) obey the commutation relations of the SU2 algebra, and they play a fundamental role in characterizing the system's angular momentum and magnetic properties. In many-body systems, the quasi-spin operators are introduced to represent collective excitations or modes that behave similarly to angular momentum. These operators often have algebraic properties resembling the SU2 algebra, making them suitable for describing the collective dynamics of the system. Overall, quasi-spin operators offer a valuable tool in theoretical physics for investigating collective behavior in complex many-body systems, facilitating the understanding of emergent phenomena, and enabling the development of analytical and numerical techniques to study these systems in different physical contexts.

In nuclear physics, for example, in the AFP model considered here, one utilizes quasi-spin operators to describe the collective behavior of nucleons in a nucleus. The specific form and properties of the quasi-spin operators depend on the nature of the many-body system being studied and the interactions between its constituents. They are introduced to simplify the description of collective phenomena and, as stated above, provide a powerful mathematical framework for treating many interacting fermions. One has for these operators the definitions

$$J_z = \sum_{p,\mu} \mu \, C^+_{p,\mu} C_{p,\mu}, \tag{2}$$

$$J_+ = \sum_{p} C^+_{p,+} C_{p,-}, \tag{3}$$

$$J_- = \sum_{p} C^+_{p,-} C_{p,+}, \tag{4}$$

and the Casimir operator

$$J^2 = J_z^2 + \frac{1}{2}(J_+J_- + J_-J_+). \tag{5}$$

The eigenvalues of J^2 take the form $J(J+1)$ and the Lipkin Hamiltonian reads (v is a coupling constant)

$$H = \epsilon J_z + \frac{v}{4}(J_+^2 + J_-^2). \tag{6}$$

3.2. The AFP Model

It displays [26,32,33,35] a similar quasi-spin structure. One uses the operators

$$G_{ij} = \sum_{p=1}^{2\Omega} C^+_{pi,} C_{p,j} \tag{7}$$

Also, v is the two-body-interaction coupling constant. Our Hamiltonian is

$$H_{AFP} = \epsilon \sum_{i}^{N} G_{i,i} + V(J_x - J_x^2). \tag{8}$$

J_x is the sum $[J_+ + J_-]/2$. Its eigenvalues are $E_n(c, J)$ [17,18].

For the AFP Hamiltonian matrix, please see Appendix A.

4. Working within the Gibbs Ensemble Framework

The procedure is described in detail in [35]. All thermal quantities of interest are deduced from the partition function Z [19]. We construct Z using probabilities assigned to the models' microscopic states. Their energies are E_i [19]. Some important macroscopic quantifiers are computed as in [19]. These indicators, together with Z, derive from the canonical probability distributions [19] $P_n(v, J, \beta)$. β is the inverse temperature. The pertinent expressions are given in [19]. We call the mean energy U and the free energy F:

$$P_n(v, J, \beta) = \frac{1}{Z(v, J, \beta)} e^{-\beta E_n(v,J)} \tag{9}$$

$$Z(v,J,\beta) = \sum_{n=0}^{N} e^{-\beta E_n(v,J)} \tag{10}$$

$$\begin{aligned} U(v,J,\beta) &= \langle E \rangle = -\frac{\partial \ln Z(v,J,\beta)}{\partial \beta} \\ &= \sum_{n=0}^{N} E_n(v,J) P_n(v,J,\beta) \\ &= \frac{1}{Z(v,J,\beta)} \sum_{n=0}^{N} E_n(v,J) e^{-\beta E_n(v,J)} \end{aligned} \tag{11}$$

$$S(v,J,\beta) = 1 - \sum_{n=0}^{N} P_n(v,J,\beta) \ln[P_n(v,J,\beta)] \tag{12}$$

$$F(v,J,\beta) = U(v,J,\beta) - T\,S(v,J,\beta). \tag{13}$$

The thermal quantifiers above provide much more information than the one obtained via just the quantum resources of zero temperature T [19]. Taking a low enough T, our quantifiers above yield a good representation of the $T = 0$ scenario [19]. Below, we will adopt the high enough $\beta = 20$ value.

A State's ρ Degree of Mixture C_f

As is well-known in quantum mechanics, the degree of mixture C_f of a given state represented by ρ is given by [36]

$$C_f = 1 - Tr\rho^2 = 1 - \sum_i p_i^2, \tag{14}$$

where $Tr\rho^2$ is the so-called "Purity" P_y. Note that we have $C_f = 0$ and $P_y = 1$ for pure states. C_f is a very important quantity for us here. Because the Tsallis practitioner will immediately recognize that Equation (14) is Tsallis' entropy of index $q = 2$, i.e., S_2. One encounters a direct link (equality) between S_2 and C_f.

In probability terms, one has $P_y = \sum_{n=0}^{N} (P_n(v,J,\beta))^2$ and $C_f = S_2 = 1 - P_y^2$.

5. Present Results for Our Main Quantifier S_2

5.1. Results as a Function of the Particle Number

Remember that we work at finite temperature but for very low T values, so that $T = 0$ remnants are very pronounced ones. In our first graph (Figure 1), we depict $S_2 = C_f$ versus the fermion number for several values of the coupling constant v. Remarkably enough, given the v value, for all N values but one, $S_2 = C_f = 0$, entailing *finite-temperature purity: T is not high enough to generate mixing*. This is an interesting result. However, given v, this happens for specific values of N and only for them.

This effect occurs for **all** v and we encounter a special N value ($= N_m$) for which S_2, and the mixing degree, suddenly grows. Here, we borrow the described "magic number" $N_m(v)$ from nuclear physics such that the system experiences a noticeable amount of mixing. Magic numbers are rather typical features of fermion systems. We discover that as v diminishes, N_m grows.

Let us now discuss the results depicted in Figure 2 below. One notices there that given N, C_f vs. v presents a peak at a particular value of v, where $C_f = 0.5$. We look at these special values in Figure 2:

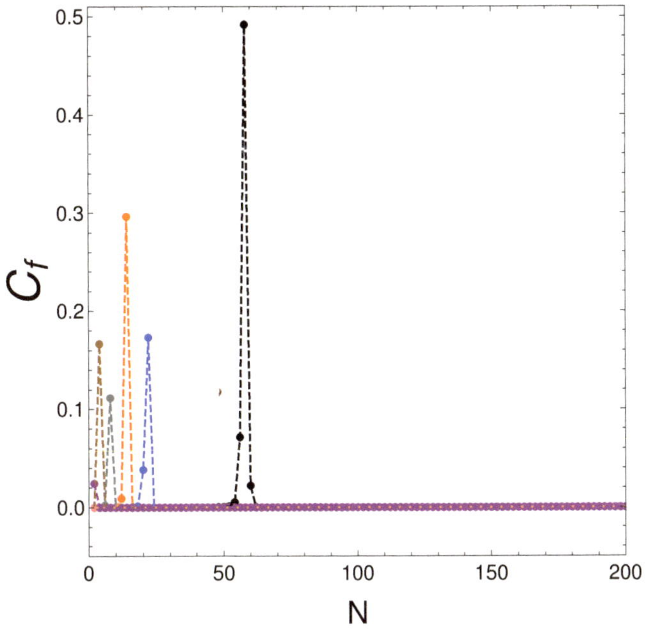

Figure 1. We plot $C_f = S_2$ vs. N for several v-values, with $\beta = 20$. Purity prevails, with intriguing exceptions. $v-$colors are assigned in this way: $v = 0.5$ (violet); $v = 0.3$ (rose); $v = 0.2$ (brown); $v = 0.1$ (grey); $v = 0.05$ (orange); $v = 0.03$ (blue); $v = 0.01$ (black); $v = 0.001$ (green); $v = 0$ (red).

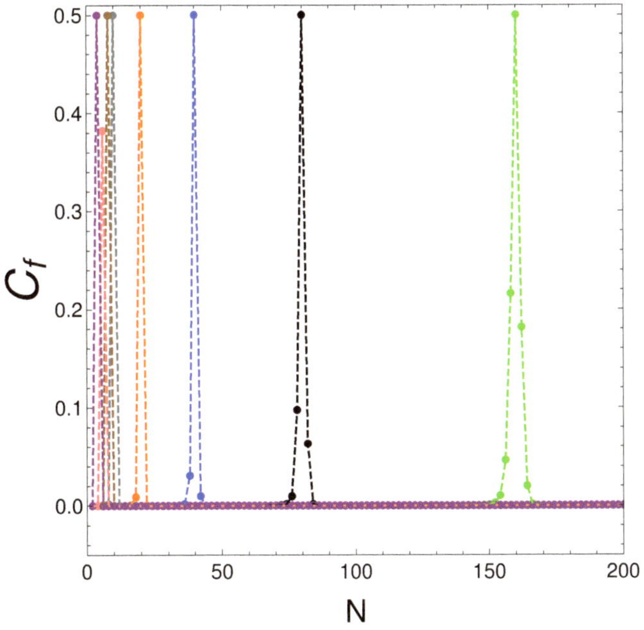

Figure 2. We plot C_f versus N for the v-values listed in Table 1. The peaks occur at the corresponding N values of Table 1. However, we see that C_f ceases to be zero for some fermion numbers that are neighbors of N_m, which are marked with dots in the graph.

5.2. Energetic Interpretation of the N_m

Let $E_0(N)$ stand for the energy of the ground state of our Hamiltonian matrix and, further, let $E_1(N)$ be the energy of the associated first excited state. Consider their difference, that is, the excitation energy of the first level above the ground state.

$$A(N) = E_1 - E_0. \tag{15}$$

We see in Table 1 that these two energies are much closer to each other for N_m than for N_{m-1} or N_{m+1}. With regard to Figure 1, we next list in Table 1 the energy differences A for several number-of-particles triplets, N_{m-2}, N_m, and N_{m+2}. These triplets are associated with the peaks in Figure 1, in the way we discuss next.

Table 1. Values of the energy difference $A(N) = E_1 - E_0$ for the number-of-particles triplets associated with the peaks in Figure 1. The values at the center of the triplet exhibit quasi-degeneracy as likely being responsible for the magic number peculiarity. That is, the two energies E_1 and E_2 are much closer to each other for N_m than for N_{m-1} or N_{m+1}.

Color Line	v	N_m	A_{m-2}	A_m	A_{m+2}
Black	0.01	58	0.1629	0.0129	0.2243
Blue	0.03	22	0.1959	0.1123	0.5503
Orange	0.05	14	0.2689	0.0755	0.6447

At N_m, we see that the energy difference A is very small, which in turn generates a sort of quasi-degeneracy of the two lowest-lying states of our Hamiltonian matrix, which favors mixing. A is instead larger for $N_{m\pm1}$ than for N_m.

5.3. Results as a Function of the Coupling Constant v

We now consider the behavior of the mixing degree $C_f = S_2$ as a function of the Hamiltonian's coupling constant v for different values of N. See Figure 3, which displays an illustrative example. Even if purity prevails overall, magic numbers become noticeable again, but this time with reference to v values. We have a magic number for every v.

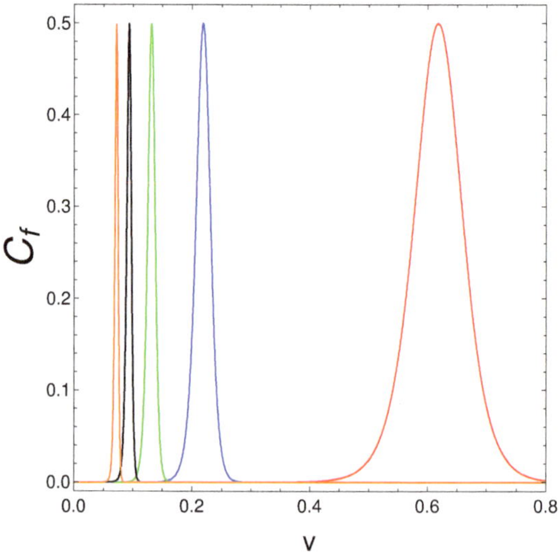

Figure 3. We plot $C_f = S_2$ vs. v for $\beta = 20$. Colors are as follows: $N = 2$ (red); $N = 4$ (blue); $N = 6$ (green); $= 8$ (black); $N = 10$ (orange). See that we confront here magic v-regions (windows), whose size diminishes as N grows. Outside these windows, the mixing degree vanishes.

5.4. Effects of the S_2 Peaks on Macroscopic Quantities

Let us compute the mean energy <U>, and the Shannon entropy S versus v. The results are depicted in Figure 4. The magic character manifests itself in slope changes for the mean energy and in peaks for the two entropies.

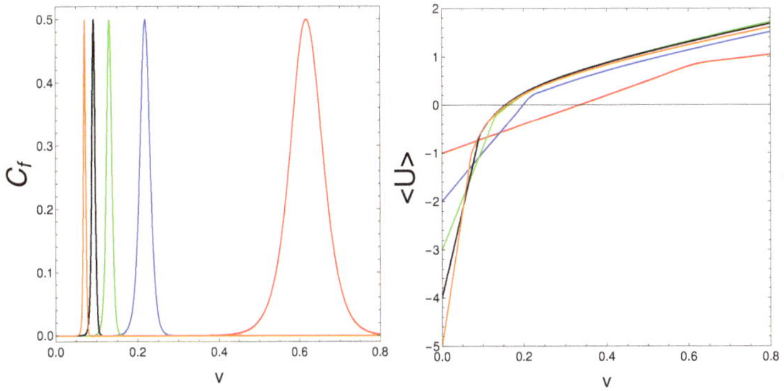

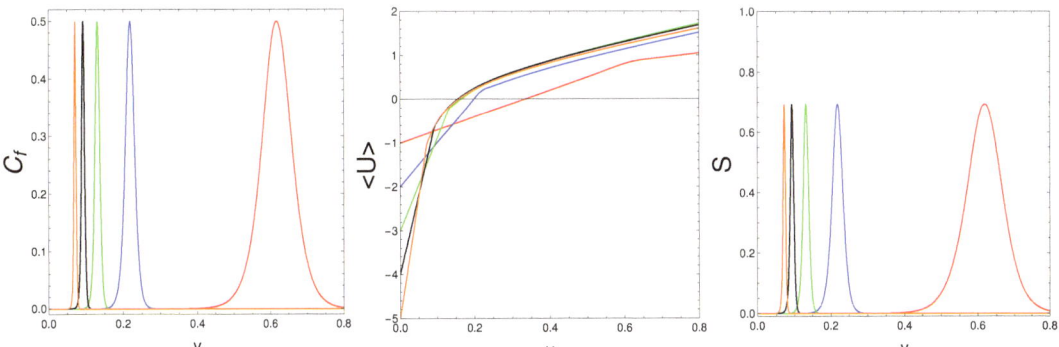

Figure 4. We find $C_f = S_2$ (**left**), <U> (**center**), and Shannon's S (**right**) confront vs. v for $N = 2, 4, \ldots, 10$, with $\beta = 20$. One sees that <U> displays slope changes at the v values associated with entropic peaks. Regarding the trait <U>, this fact shows the existence of critical values for the coupling constants at which the mean energy suffers a slope change. These critical values are found within the areas covered by the S_2 peaks.

6. Conclusions

Statistical mechanics often appeals to probability models so as to describe the behavior of systems composed of a large number of microscopic constituents. In this work, our constituents are interacting fermions and the ensembles are the canonical Gibbs ones. We work at very low temperatures so as to use results as useful proxies for many-body features at zero temperature. Remnants of these results survive very well at low T and are much easier to deal with than appealing directly to the many-fermions system's structural properties. We have appealed to a well-known exactly solvable many-fermion system so as to discuss exact results. More specifically, we have investigated fermion dynamical traits associated to the mixing degree of the pertinent many-body states using Tsallis entropy for $q = 2$.

There are two important quantities in this paper: the fermion number N (a quantity that in a sense defines the system (think of an atomic nucleus)) and the Hamiltonian's coupling constant v, which is a mere (although very important) parameter. Considering the system's microstates (MS) at a very low temperature, we find that, given the v-value, the MS remain pure, at our finite low T, for all N, but with the exception of a special one, which we call "magic" and denote by N_m. Magic numbers are typical in fermion systems [23]. Here, for each v, there is a corresponding N_m, which is smaller the larger the coupling constant is. Table 1 assigns responsibility for the existence of magic numbers to a quasi-degeneracy of the ground state and the first excited one. This happens, of course, at zero temperature, but remnants of such a trait persist at low temperatures. The special quantities, which we call magic, are discrete (of course). One has $C_f = 0.5$ at the peaks.

We emphasize that the magic mixing degree *is not caused by temperature*. It originates, as stated above, in a quasi-degeneracy of the Hamiltonian's two lowest-lying eigen-energies.

Author Contributions: Investigation, D.M., A.P. and A.R.P.; project administration, A.P.; writing—original draft, D.M., A.P. and A.R.P. All authors have read and agreed to the published version of the manuscript.

Funding: This research was partially supported by FONDECYT, grant 1181558, and by CONICET (Argentine Agency).

Data Availability Statement: Every thing needed is found in the manuscript.

Acknowledgments: We thank Conicet (Argentine Agency).

Conflicts of Interest: The authors declare no conflict of interest.

Appendix A. Our Hamiltonian Matrix

For the AFP, one deals with (see from Equation (6) of [33]) the Hamiltonian matrix:

$$\begin{aligned}\langle n'|H_{AFP}|n\rangle = \; & (n-J)\delta_{n',n} + \frac{1}{2}v\{2(2J^2+J+n^2-2Jn)\delta_{n',n} \\ & +2\sqrt{(2J-n)(n+1)}\delta_{n',n+1} + 2\sqrt{(2J-n+1)n}\delta_{n',n-1} \\ & -\sqrt{(2J-n-1)(n+2)(2J-n)(n+1)}\delta_{n',n+2} \\ & -\sqrt{(2J-n+2)(n-1)(2J-n+1)n}\delta_{n',n-2}\end{aligned} \tag{A1}$$

References

1. Tsallis, C. Possible generalization of Boltzmann-Gibbs statistics. *J. Stat. Phys.* **1988**, *52*, 479–487. [CrossRef]
2. Gell-Mann, M.; Tsallis, C. *Nonextensive Entropy: Interdisciplinary Applications*; Oxford University Press: Oxford, UK, 2004.
3. Tsallis, C. Entropy. *Encyclopedia* **2022**, *2*, 264–300. [CrossRef]
4. Tsallis, C. The nonadditive entropy S_q and its applications in physics and elsewhere: Some remarks. *Entropy* **2011**, *13*, 1765–1804. [CrossRef]
5. Tsallis, C. Beyond Boltzmann-Gibbs-Shannon in physics and elsewhere. *Entropy* **2019**, *21*, 696 [CrossRef]
6. Sánchez Almeida, J. The principle of maximum entropy and the distribution of mass in galaxies. *Universe* **2022**, *8*, 214. [CrossRef]
7. Tsallis, C. *Introduction to Nonextensive Statistical Mechanics—Approaching a Complex World*, 2nd ed.; Springer: Berlin/Heidelberg, Germany, 2023.
8. Curilef, S. On the generalized Bose-Einstein condensation. *Phys. Lett. A* **1996**, *218*, 11–15. [CrossRef]
9. Tirnakli, U.; Buyukkilic, F.; Demirhan, D. Some bounds upon the nonextensivity parameter using the approximate generalized distribution functions. *Phys. Lett. A* **1998**, *245*, 62. [CrossRef]
10. Uys, H.; Miller, H.G.; Khanna, F.C. Generalized statistics and high—Tc superconductivity. *Phys. Lett. A* **2001**, *289*, 264. [CrossRef]
11. Conroy, J.M.; Miller, H.G. Color superconductivity and Tsallis statistics. *Phys. Rev. D* **2008**, *78*, 054010. [CrossRef]
12. Silva, R.; Anselmo, D.H.A.L.; Alcaniz, J.S. Nonextensive quantum H-theorem. *Europhys. Lett.* **2010**, *89*, 10004. [CrossRef]
13. Biro, T.S.; Shen, K.M.; Zhang, B.W. Non-extensive quantum statistics with particle-hole symmetry. *Phys. A* **2015**, *428*, 410. [CrossRef]
14. Deppman, A.; Megias, E.; Menezes, D.P. Fractal Structures of Yang-Mills Fields and Non-Extensive Statistics: Applications to High Energy Physics. *Physics* **2020**, *2*, 455–480. [CrossRef]
15. Bengtsson, I.; Zyczkowsi, K. *Geometry of Quantum States: An Introduction to Quantum Entanglement*; Cambridge University Press: Cambridge, UK, 2006.
16. Jaeger, G. *Qantum Information: An Overview*; Springer: Berlin/Heidelberg, Germany, 2007.
17. Lipkin, H.J.; Meshkov, N.; Glick, A.J. Validity of many-body approximation methods for a solvable model: (I). Exact solutions and perturbation theory. *Nucl. Phys.* **1965**, *62*, 188. [CrossRef]
18. Co', G.; De Leo, S. Analytical and numerical analysis of the complete Lipkin–Meshkov–Glick Hamiltonian. *Int. J. Mod. Phys. E* **2018**, *27*, 5. [CrossRef]
19. Plastino, A.R.; Monteoliva, D.; Plastino, A. Information-theoretic features of many fermion systems: An exploration based on exactly solvable models. *Entropy* **2021**, *23*, 1488. [CrossRef] [PubMed]
20. Otero, D.; Proto, A.; Plastino, A. Surprisal Approach to Cold Fission Processes. *Phys. Lett. B* **1981**, *98*, 225. [CrossRef]
21. Satuła, W.; Dobaczewski, J.; Nazarewicz, W. Odd-Even Staggering of Nuclear Masses: Pairing or Shape Effect? *Phys. Rev. Lett.* **1998**, *81*, 3599. [CrossRef]
22. Dugett, T.; Bonche, P.; Heenen, P.H.; Meyer, J. Pairing correlations. II. Microscopic analysis of odd-even mass staggering in nuclei. *Phys. Rev. C* **2001**, *65*, 014311. [CrossRef]
23. Ring, P.; Schuck, P. *The Nuclear Many-Body Problem*; Springer: Berlin/Heidelberg, Germany, 1980.
24. Kruse, M.K.G.; Miller, H.G.; Plastino, A.R.; Plastino, A.; Fujita, S. Landau-Ginzburg method applied to finite fermion systems: pairing in nuclei. *Eur. J. Phys. A* **2005**, *25*, 339. [CrossRef]
25. de Llano, M.; Tolmachev, V.V. Multiple phases in a new statistical boson fermion model of superconductivity. *Phys. A* **2003**, *317*, 546. [CrossRef]
26. Xu, F.R.; Wyss, R.; Walker, P.M. Mean-field and blocking effects on odd-even mass differences and rotational motion of nuclei. *Phys. Rev. C* **1999**, *60*, 051301. [CrossRef]
27. Häkkinen, H.; Kolehmainen, J.; Koskinen, M.; Lipas, P.O.; Manninen, M. Universal Shapes of Small Fermion Clusters. *Phys. Rev. Lett.* **1997**, *78*, 1034. [CrossRef]

28. Hubbard, J. Electron Correlations in Narrow Energy Bands. *Proc. R. Soc. Lond.* **1963**, *276*, 237.
29. Liu, Y. Exact solutions to nonlinear Schrodinger equation with variable coefficients. *Appl. Math. Comput.* **2011**, *217*, 5866. [CrossRef]
30. Frank, R. Quantum criticality and population trapping of fermions by non-equilibrium lattice modulations. *New J. Phys.* **2013**, *15*, 123030. [CrossRef]
31. Lubatsch, A.; Frank, R. Evolution of Floquet topological quantum states in driven semiconductors. *Eur. Phys. J. B* **2019**, *92*, 215. [CrossRef]
32. Feng, D.H.; Gilmore, R.G. Self-organized criticality in a continuous, nonconservative cellular automaton modeling earthquakes. *Phys. Rev. C* **1992**, *26*, 1244. [CrossRef]
33. Bozzolo, G.; Cambiaggio, M.C.; Plastino, A. Maximum Overlap, Atomic Coherent States and the Generator Coordinate Method. *Nucl. Phys. A* **1981**, *356*, 48. [CrossRef]
34. Monteoliva, D.; Plastino, A.; Plastino, A.R. Statistical Quantifiers Resolve a Nuclear Theory Controversy. *Q. Rep.* **2022**, *4*, 127–134. [CrossRef]
35. Reif, F. *Fundamentals of Statistical Theoretic and Thermal Physics*; McGraw Hill: New York, NY, USA, 1965.
36. Pennini, F.; Plastino, A. Thermal effects in quantum phase-space distributions. *Phys. Lett. A* **2010**, *37*, 1927–1932. [CrossRef]

Article

Tsallis Entropy of a Used Reliability System at the System Level

Mohamed Kayid [1] and Mashael A. Alshehri [2,*]

[1] Department of Statistics and Operations Research, College of Science, King Saud University, P.O. Box 2455, Riyadh 11451, Saudi Arabia
[2] Department of Quantitative Analysis, College of Business Administration, King Saud University, Riyadh 11362, Saudi Arabia
* Correspondence: mealshehri@ksu.edu.sa

Abstract: Measuring the uncertainty of the lifetime of technical systems has become increasingly important in recent years. This criterion is useful to measure the predictability of a system over its lifetime. In this paper, we assume a coherent system consisting of n components and having a property where at time t, all components of the system are alive. We then apply the system signature to determine and use the Tsallis entropy of the remaining lifetime of a coherent system. It is a useful criterion for measuring the predictability of the lifetime of a system. Various results, such as bounds and order properties for the said entropy, are investigated. The results of this work can be used to compare the predictability of the remaining lifetime between two coherent systems with known signatures.

Keywords: coherent system; residual Tsallis entropy; Shannon entropy; system signature

---

Citation: Kayid, M.; Alshehri, M.A. Tsallis Entropy of a Used Reliability System at the System Level. *Entropy* **2023**, *25*, 550. https://doi.org/10.3390/e25040550

Academic Editors: Ugur Tirnakli, Christian Beck, Hans J. Herrmann, Airton Deppman, Henrik Jeldtoft Jensen, Evaldo M. F. Curado, Fernando D. Nobre, Angelo Plastino, Astero Provata and Andrea Rapisarda

Received: 10 February 2023
Revised: 19 March 2023
Accepted: 21 March 2023
Published: 23 March 2023

Copyright: © 2023 by the authors. Licensee MDPI, Basel, Switzerland. This article is an open access article distributed under the terms and conditions of the Creative Commons Attribution (CC BY) license (https://creativecommons.org/licenses/by/4.0/).

1. Introduction

For engineers, the performance and quantification of uncertainties over the lifetime of a system is critical. The reliability of a system decreases as uncertainty increases, and systems with longer lifetimes and lower uncertainty are better systems (see, e.g., Ebrahimi and Pellery, [1]). It has found applications in numerous areas described in Shannon's seminal work, [2]. Information theory provides a measure of the uncertainty associated with a random phenomenon. If X is a nonnegative random variable with an absolutely continuous cumulative distribution function (CDF) $F(x)$ and density function $f(x)$, the Tsallis entropy of order α, defined by (see [3]), is

$$\begin{aligned} H_\alpha(X) &= H_\alpha(f) = \frac{1}{1-\alpha}\left[\int_0^\infty f^\alpha(x)dx - 1\right], \\ &= \frac{1}{1-\alpha}[E(f^{\alpha-1}(X)) - 1] \end{aligned} \quad (1)$$

for all $\alpha > 0$, $\alpha \neq 1$, where $E(\cdot)$ denotes the expected value. In general, the Tsallis entropy can be negative, but it can also be non-negative if one chooses an appropriate value for α. It is obvious that $H(f) = \lim_{\alpha \to 1} H_\alpha(f)$ and thus reduces to the Shannon differential entropy. It is known that the Shannon differential entropy is additive in the sense that for two independent random variables X and Y, $H(X,Y) = H(X) + H(Y)$, where (X,Y) denotes the common random variable. However, the Tsallis entropy is non-additive in the sense that $H_\alpha(X,Y) = H_\alpha(X) + H_\alpha(Y) + (1-\alpha)H_\alpha(X)H_\alpha(Y)$. Because of the flexibility of Tsallis entropy compared to Shannon entropy, non-additive entropy measures find their justification in many areas of information theory, physics, chemistry, and engineering.

If X denotes the lifetime of a new system, then $H_\alpha(X)$ measures the uncertainty of the new system. In some cases, agents know something about the current age of the system. For example, one may know that the system is in operation at time t and is interested in measuring the uncertainty of its remaining lifetime, that is, $X_t = X - t|X > t$. Then

$H_\alpha(X)$ is no longer useful in such situations. Accordingly, the residual Tsallis entropy is defined as

$$H_\alpha(X_t) = \frac{1}{1-\alpha}\left[\int_0^\infty f_t^\alpha(x)dx - 1\right] = \frac{1}{1-\alpha}\left[\int_t^\infty \left(\frac{f(x)}{S(t)}\right)^\alpha dx - 1\right], \tag{2}$$

$$= \frac{1}{1-\alpha}\left[\int_0^1 f_t^{\alpha-1}(S_t^{-1}(u))du - 1\right], \ \alpha > 0, \tag{3}$$

where

$$f_t(x) = \frac{f(x+t)}{S(t)}, \ x,t > 0,$$

is the probability density function (PDF) of X_t, $S(t) = P(X > t)$ is the survival function of X and $S_t^{-1}(u) = \inf\{x; S_t(x) \geq u\}$ is the quantile function of $S_t(x) = S(x+t)/S(t)$, $x,t > 0$. Various properties, generalizations and applications of $H_\alpha(X_t)$ are investigated by Asadi et al. [4], Nanda and Paul [5], Zhang [6], Irshad et al. [7], Rajesh and Sunoj [8], Toomaj and Agh Atabay [9], Mohamed et al. [10], among others.

Several properties and statistical applications of Tsallis entropy have been studied in the literature, which you can read in Maasoumi [11], Abe [12], Asadi et al. [13] and the references therein. Recently, Alomani and Kayid [14] investigated some additional properties of Tsallis entropy, including its connection with the usual stochastic order, as well as some other properties of the dynamical version of this measure and bounds. Moreover, they investigated some properties of Tsallis entropy for the lifetime of a coherent and mixed system. It is suitable to study the behavior of the uncertainty of the new system in terms of Tsallis entropy. For other applications and researchers concerned with measuring the uncertainty of reliability systems, we refer readers to [15–18] and the references therein. In contrast to the work of Alomani and Kayid [14], the aim of this work is to study some uncertainty properties of a coherent system consisting of n components and having the property that at time t, all components of the system are alive. In fact, we generalize the results of the work published in the literature. To this end, we use the concept of system signature to determine the Tsallis entropy of the remaining lifetime of a coherent system.

The results of this paper are organized as follows: In Section 2, we provide an expression for the Tsallis entropy of a coherent system under the assumption that all components have survived to time t. For this purpose, we used the concept of system signature when the lifetimes of the components in a coherent system are independent and identically distributed. The ordering properties of the residual Tsallis entropy of two coherent systems are studied in Section 3 based on some ordering properties of system signatures even without simple calculations. Section 4 presents some useful bounds. Finally, Section 5 gives some conclusions and further detailed remarks.

Throughout the paper, "$\leq_{st}$", "$\leq_{hr}$", "$\leq_{lr}$" and "$\leq_d$" stand for stochastic, hazard rate, likelihood ratio and dispersive orders, respectively; for more details on these orderings, we refer the reader to Shaked and Shanthikumar [19].

2. Tsallis Entropy of the System in Terms of Signature Vectors of the System

In this section, the concept of system signature is used to define the Tsallis entropy of the remaining lifetime of a coherent system with an arbitrary system-level structure, assuming that all components of the system are functioning at time t. An n-dimensional vector $\mathbf{p} = (p_1, \ldots, p_n)$ whose i-th element $p_i = P(T = X_{i:n})$, $i = 1,2,\ldots,n$; is the signature of such a system where $X_{i:n}$ is the i-th order statistic of the n independent and identically distributed (i.i.d.) component lifetimes $\mathbf{X} = (X_1, \ldots, X_n)$, that is, the time of the i-th component failure, and T is the failure time of the system; (see Samaniego [20]). Consider a coherent system with independent and identically distributed component lifetimes $X_1, \ldots, X_n$ and a known signature vector $\mathbf{p} = (p_1, \ldots, p_n)$. If $T_t^{1,n} = [T - t | X_{1:n} > t]$, represents the remaining lifetime of the system under the condition that at time t, all components of the system are functioning, then from the results of Khaledi and Shaked [21] the survival function of $T_t^{1,n}$ can be expressed as

$$\begin{aligned} P(T_t^{1,n} > x) &= \sum_{i=1}^{n} p_i P(X_{i:n} - t > x | X_{1:n} > t), \\ &= \sum_{i=1}^{n} p_i P(T_t{}^{1,i,n} > x), \end{aligned} \tag{4}$$

where $T_t^{1,i,n} = [X_{i:n} - t | X_{1:n} > t]$, $i = 1, 2, \cdots, n$, denotes the remaining lifetime of an i-out-of-n system under the condition that all components at time t. The survival and probability density functions of $T_t^{1,i,n}$ are given by

$$P(T_t{}^{1,i,n} > x) = \sum_{k=0}^{i-1} \binom{n}{k} (1 - S_t(x))^k (S_t(x))^{n-k}, \; x, t > 0, \tag{5}$$

and

$$f_{T_t^{1,i,n}}(x) = \frac{\Gamma(n+1)}{\Gamma(i)\Gamma(n-i+1)} (1 - S_t(x))^{i-1} (S_t(x))^{n-i} f_t(x), \; x, t > 0, \tag{6}$$

respectively, where $\Gamma(\cdot)$ is the complete gamma function. It follows that

$$f_{T_t^{1,n}}(x) = \sum_{i=1}^{n} p_i f_{T_t^{1,i,n}}(x), \; x, t > 0. \tag{7}$$

In what follows, we focus on the study of the Tsallis entropy of the random variable $T_t^{1,n}$, which measures the degree of uncertainty contained in the density of $[T - t | X_{1:n} > t]$, in terms of the predictability of the remaining lifetime of the system in terms of Tsallis entropy. The probability integral transformation $V = S_t(T_t^{1,n})$ plays a crucial role in our goal. It is clear that $U_{i:n} = S_t(T_t^{1,i,n})$ follows from a beta distribution with parameters $n - i + 1$ and i with the PDF

$$g_i(u) = \frac{\Gamma(n+1)}{\Gamma(i)\Gamma(n-i+1)} (1-u)^{i-1} u^{n-i}, \quad 0 < u < 1, \; i = 1, \cdots, n. \tag{8}$$

In the forthcoming proposition, we provide an expression for the Tsallis entropy of $T_t{}^{1,n}$ by using the earlier transformation formulas.

Theorem 1. *The Tsallis entropy of $T_t{}^{1,n}$ can be expressed as follows:*

$$H_\alpha(T_t{}^{1,n}) = \frac{1}{1-\alpha} \left[\int_0^1 g_V^\alpha(u) f_t^{\alpha-1}(S_t^{-1}(u)) du - 1 \right], \; t > 0, \tag{9}$$

for all $\alpha > 0$.

Proof. By using the change of $u = S_t(x)$, from (2) and (6) we obtain

$$\begin{aligned} H_\alpha(T_t{}^{1,n}) &= \frac{1}{1-\alpha} \left[\int_0^\infty \left(f_{T_t^{1,n}}(x) \right)^\alpha dx - 1 \right] \\ &= \frac{1}{1-\alpha} \left[\int_0^\infty \left(\sum_{i=1}^{n} p_i f_{T_t^{1,i,n}}(x) \right)^\alpha dx - 1 \right] \\ &= \frac{1}{1-\alpha} \left[\int_0^1 \left(\sum_{i=1}^{n} p_i g_i(u) \right)^\alpha \left(f_t(S_t^{-1}(u)) \right)^{\alpha-1} dx - 1 \right] \\ &= \frac{1}{1-\alpha} \left[\int_0^1 g_V^\alpha(u) \left(f_t(S_t^{-1}(u)) \right)^{\alpha-1} du - 1 \right]. \end{aligned}$$

In the last equality $g_V(u) = \sum_{i=1}^{n} p_i g_i(u)$ is the PDF of V denotes the lifetime of the system with independent and identically distributed uniform distribution. □

In the specail case, if we consider an i-out-of-n system with the system signature $\mathbf{p} = (0, \ldots, 0, 1_i, 0, \ldots, 0)$, $i = 1, 2, \cdots, n$, then Equation (9) reduces to

$$H_\alpha(T_t^{1,i,n}) = \frac{1}{1-\alpha}\left[\int_0^1 g_i^\alpha(u)\left(f_t(S_t^{-1}(u))\right)^{\alpha-1} du - 1\right], \tag{10}$$

for all $t > 0$.

The next theorem immediately follows by Theorem 1 from the aging properties of their components. We recall that X has increasing (decreasing) failure rate (IFR(DFR)) if $S_t(x)$ is decreasing (increasing) in x for all $t > 0$.

Theorem 2. *If X is IFR (DFR), then $H_\alpha(T_t{}^{1,n})$ is decreasing (increasing) in t for all $\alpha > 0$.*

Proof. We just prove it when X is IFR where the proof for the DFR is similar. It is easy to see that $f_t(S_t^{-1}(u)) = u\lambda_t(S_t^{-1}(u))$, $0 < u < 1$. This implies that Equation (9) can be rewritten as

$$(1-\alpha)H_\alpha(T_t{}^{1,n}) + 1 = \int_0^1 g_V^\alpha(u)u^{\alpha-1}\left(\lambda_t(S_t^{-1}(u))\right)^{\alpha-1} du, \tag{11}$$

for all $\alpha > 0$. On the other hand, one can conclude that $S_t^{-1}(u) = S^{-1}(uS(t)) - t$, for all $0 < u < 1$, and hence we have

$$\lambda_t(S_t^{-1}(u)) = \lambda(S_t^{-1}(u) + t) = \lambda(S^{-1}(uS(t))),\ 0 < u < 1. \tag{12}$$

If $t_1 \le t_2$, then $S^{-1}(uS(t_1)) \le S^{-1}(uS(t_2))$. Thus, when F is IFR, then for all $\alpha > 1(0 < \alpha \le 1)$, we have

$$\begin{aligned}
\int_0^1 g_V^\alpha(u)u^{\alpha-1}\left(\lambda_{t_1}(S_{t_1}^{-1}(u))\right)^{\alpha-1} du &= \int_0^1 g_V^\alpha(u)u^{\alpha-1}\left(\lambda(S^{-1}(uS(t_1)))\right)^{\alpha-1} du \\
&\le (\ge) \int_0^1 g_V^\alpha(u)u^{\alpha-1}\left(\lambda(S^{-1}(uS(t_2)))\right)^{\alpha-1} du \\
&= \int_0^1 g_V^\alpha(u)u^{\alpha-1}\left(\lambda_{t_2}(S_{t_2}^{-1}(u))\right)^{\alpha-1} du,
\end{aligned}$$

for all $t_1 \le t_2$. Using (11), we obtain

$$(1-\alpha)H_\alpha(T_{t_1}{}^{1,n}) + 1 \le (\ge)(1-\alpha)H_\alpha(T_{t_2}{}^{1,n}) + 1,$$

for all $\alpha > 1(0 < \alpha \le 1)$. This implies that $H_\alpha(T_{t_1}{}^{1,n}) \ge H_\alpha(T_{t_2}{}^{1,n})$ for all $\alpha > 0$ and this completes the proof. □

The next example illustrates the results of Theorems 1 and 2.

Example 1. *Consider a coherent system with system signature $\mathbf{p} = (0, 1/2, 1/4, 1/4)$. The exact value of $H_\alpha(T_t{}^{1,4})$ can be calculated using the relation (9) given the lifetime distributions of the components. For this purpose, let us assume the following lifetime distributions.*

(i) *Consider a Pareto type II with the survival function*

$$S(t) = (1+t)^{-k},\ k, t > 0. \tag{13}$$

It is not hard to see that

$$H_\alpha(T_t{}^{1,4}) = \frac{1}{1-\alpha}\left[\left(\frac{k}{1+t}\right)^{\alpha-1} \int_0^1 u^{\frac{(\alpha-1)(k+1)}{k}} g_V^\alpha(u) du - 1\right],\ t > 0.$$

It is obvious that the Tsallis entropy of $H_\alpha({T_t}^{1,4})$ is an increasing function of time t. Thus, the uncertainty of the conditional lifetime ${T_t}^{1,4}$ increases as t increases. We recall that this distribution has the DFR property.

(ii) *Let us suppose that X has a Weibull distribution with the shape parameter k with the survival function*

$$S(t) = e^{-t^k},\ k, t > 0. \tag{14}$$

After some manipulation, we have

$$H_\alpha({T_t}^{1,4}) = \frac{1}{1-\alpha}\left[k^{\alpha-1}\int_0^1 \left(t^k - \log u\right)^{(1-\frac{1}{k})(\alpha-1)} u^{\alpha-1} g_V^\alpha(u)du - 1\right],\ t > 0.$$

It is difficult to find an explicit expression for the above relation, and therefore we are forced to calculate it numerically. In Figure 1 we have plotted the entropy of ${T_t}^{1,4}$ as a function of time t for values of $\alpha = 0,2$ and $\alpha = 2$ and $k > 0$. In this case, it is known that X is DFR when $\alpha = 0,1$. As expected from Theorem 2, it is obvious that $H_\alpha({T_t}^{1,4})$ is increasing in t for $\alpha = 0,1$. The results are shown in Figure 1.

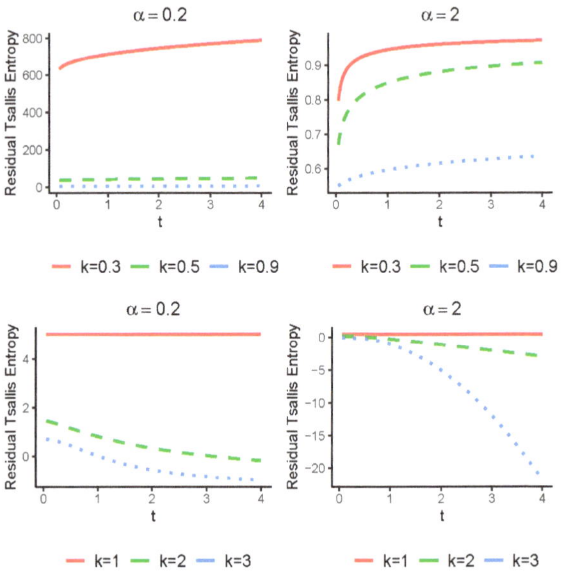

Figure 1. The exact values of $H_\alpha({T_t}^{1,4})$ with respect to t for the Weibull distribution for values of $\alpha = 0.2$ and $\alpha = 2$ when $k > 0$.

Below, we compare the Tsallis entropies of two coherent systems from their lifetimes and their residual lifetimes.

Theorem 3. *Consider a coherent system with independent and identically distributed IFR(DFR) component lifetimes. Then $H_\alpha({T_t}^{1,n}) \leq (\geq) H_\alpha(T)$ for all $\alpha > 0$.*

Proof. We prove it when X is IFR where the proof for DFR property is similar. Since X is IFR, Theorem 3.B.25 of Shaked and Shanthikumar [19] implies that $X \geq_d X_t$, that is

$$f_t(S_t^{-1}(u)) \geq f(S^{-1}(u)),\ 0 < u < 1,$$

for all $t > 0$. If $\alpha > 1$ $(0 < \alpha < 1)$, so we have

$$\int_0^1 g_V^\alpha(u) f_t^{\alpha-1}(S_t^{-1}(u))du \geq (\leq) \int_0^1 g_V^\alpha(u) f^{\alpha-1}(S^{-1}(u))du,\ t > 0. \tag{15}$$

Thus, from (9) and (15), we obtain

$$\begin{aligned} H_\alpha(T_t^{1,n}) &= \frac{1}{1-\alpha}\left[\int_0^1 g_V^\alpha(u) f_t^{\alpha-1}(S_t^{-1}(u))du - 1\right] \\ &\leq \frac{1}{1-\alpha}\left[\int_0^1 g_V^\alpha(u) f^{\alpha-1}(S^{-1}(u))du - 1\right] = H_\alpha(T). \end{aligned}$$

Therefore, the proof is completed. □

Theorem 4. *If X is DFR, then a lower bound for $H_\alpha(T_t^{1,n})$ is given as follows:*

$$H_\alpha(T_t^{1,n}) \geq \frac{H_\alpha(T)}{S(t)} + \frac{1}{1-\alpha}\left(\frac{1}{S(t)} - 1\right),$$

for all $\alpha > 0$.

Proof. Since X is DFR, then it is NWU (i.e., $S_t(x) \geq S(x),\ x, t \geq 0$.) This implies that

$$S_t^{-1}(u) + t \geq S^{-1}(u),\ t \geq 0,$$

for all $0 < u < 1$. On the other hand, it is known that when X is DFR, the PDF f is decreasing which implies that

$$f^{\alpha-1}(S_t^{-1}(u) + t) \leq (\geq) f^{\alpha-1}(S^{-1}(u)),\ 0 < u < 1,$$

for all $\alpha > 1$ $(0 < \alpha < 1)$. From (9), one can conclude that

$$\begin{aligned} H_\alpha(T_t^{1,n}) &= \frac{1}{1-\alpha}\left[\int_0^1 g_V^\alpha(u) \frac{f^{\alpha-1}(S_t^{-1}(u)+t)}{S(t)} du - 1\right] \\ &\geq \frac{1}{1-\alpha}\left[\int_0^1 g_V^\alpha(u) \frac{f^{\alpha-1}(S^{-1}(u))}{S(t)} du - 1\right] \\ &= \frac{1}{1-\alpha}\left[\frac{(1-\alpha)H_\alpha(T)+1}{S(t)} - 1\right], \end{aligned}$$

for all $\alpha > 0$, and this completes the proof. □

3. Entropy Ordering of Two Coherent Systems

Given the imponderables of two coherent systems, this section discusses the partial ordering of their conditional lifetimes. Based on various existing orderings between the component lifetimes and their signature vectors, we find some results for the entropy ordering of two coherent systems. The next theorem compares the entropies of the residual lifetimes of two coherent systems.

Theorem 5. *Let $T_t^{X,1,n} = [T - t | X_{1:n} > t]$ and $T_t^{Y,1,n} = [T - t | Y_{1:n} > t]$ denote the residual lifetimes of two coherent systems with the same signatures and n i.i.d component lifetimes $X_1, \ldots, X_n$ and $Y_1, \ldots, Y_n$ from cdfs F and G, respectively. If $X \leq_d Y$ and X or Y is IFR, then $H_\alpha(T_t^{X,1,n}) \leq H_\alpha(T_t^{Y,1,n})$ for all $\alpha > 0$.*

Proof. As a result of the relation (9), it is sufficient to demonstrate that $X_t \leq_d Y_t$. Due to the assumption that $X \leq_d Y$ and X or Y is IFR, the proof of Theorem 5 of Ebrahimi and Kirmani [22] means that $X_t \leq_d Y_t$, and this concludes the proof. □

Example 2. *Let us assume two coherent systems with residual lifetimes $T_t^{X,1,4}$ and $T_t^{Y,1,4}$ with the common signature $\mathbf{p} = (\frac{1}{2}, \frac{1}{4}, \frac{1}{4}, 0)$. Suppose that $X \sim W(3,1)$ and $Y \sim W(2,1)$, where $W(k,1)$ stands for the Weibull distribution with the survival function given in (14). It is easy to see* *that $X \leq_d Y$. Moreover, X and Y are both IFR. Thus, Theorem 5 yields that $H_\alpha(T_t^{X,1,4}) \leq H_\alpha(T_t^{Y,1,4})$ for all $\alpha > 0$. The plot of the Tsallis entropies of these systems is displayed in Figure 2.*

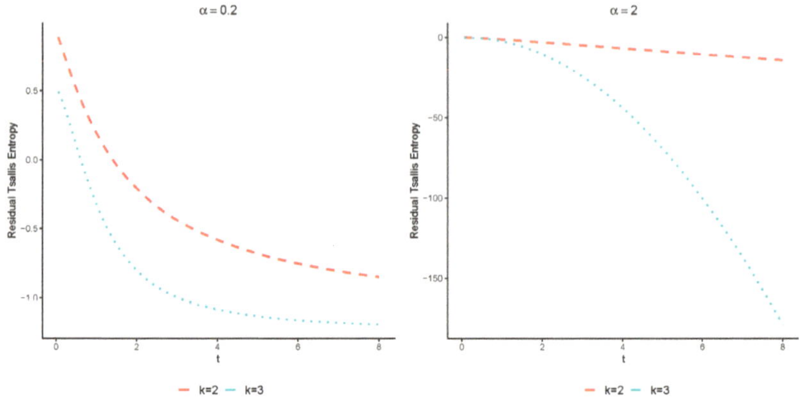

Figure 2. The exact values of $H_\alpha(T_t^{X,1,4})$ (blue color) and $H_\alpha(T_t^{Y,1,4})$ (red color) with respect to t for values of $\alpha = 0.2$ and $\alpha = 2$.

Next, we compare the residual Tsallis entropies of two coherent systems with the same component lifetimes and different structures.

Theorem 6. *Let $T_{1,t}^{1,n} = [T_1 - t|X_{1:n} > t]$ and $T_{2,t}^{1,n} = [T_2 - t|X_{1:n} > t]$ represent the residual lifetimes of two coherent systems with signature vectors $\mathbf{p_1}$ and $\mathbf{p_2}$, respectively. Assume that the system's components are independent and identically distributed according to the common CDF, F. Additionally, let $\mathbf{p_1} \leq_{lr} \mathbf{p_2}$. Then,*

(i) if $f_t(S_t^{-1}(u))$ is increasing in u for all $t > 0$, then $H_\alpha(T_{1,t}^{1,n}) \geq H_\alpha(T_{2,t}^{1,n})$ for all $\alpha > 0$.
(ii) if $f_t(S_t^{-1}(u))$ is decreasing in u for all $t > 0$, then $H_\alpha(T_{1,t}^{1,n}) \leq H_\alpha(T_{2,t}^{1,n})$ for all $\alpha > 0$.

Proof. (i) First, we note that the Equation (9) can be rewritten as follows:

$$(1-\alpha)H_\alpha(T_{t_i}{}^{1,n}) + 1 = \int_0^1 g_{V_i}^\alpha(u)du \int_0^1 g_{V_i}^\star(u)\Big(f_t(S_t^{-1}(u))\Big)^{\alpha-1}du, (i = 1,2), \tag{16}$$

where $V^\star$ has the PDF as

$$g_V^\star(u) = \frac{g_V^\alpha(u)}{\int_0^1 g_V^\alpha(u)du}, \; 0 < u < 1.$$

Assumption $\mathbf{s_1} \leq_{lr} \mathbf{s_2}$ implies $V_1 \leq_{lr} V_2$, and this means that $V_1^\star \leq_{lr} V_2^\star$, which means that

$$\frac{g_{V_2}^\star(u)}{g_{V_1}^\star(u)} \propto \left(\frac{g_{V_2}(u)}{g_{V_1}(u)}\right)^\alpha$$

is increasing in u for all $\alpha > 0$, and hence, $V_1^\star \leq_{st} V_2^\star$. When $\alpha > 1 (0 < \alpha < 1)$, we obtain

$$\int_0^1 g_{V_1}^\star(u)\Big(f_t(S_t^{-1}(u))\Big)^{\alpha-1}du \;\; \leq (\geq) \;\; \int_0^1 g_{V_2}^\star(u)\Big(f_t(S_t^{-1}(u))\Big)^{\alpha-1}du, \tag{17}$$

where the inequality in (17) is obtained by noting that the conditions $V_1^\star \leq_{st} V_2^\star$ imply $\mathbb{E}[\pi(V_1^\star)] \leq \mathbb{E}[\pi(V_2^\star)]$ for all increasing (decreasing) functions π. Therefore, relation (16) gives

$$(1-\alpha)H_\alpha(T_{t_1}{}^{1,n}) + 1 \leq (\geq)(1-\alpha)H_\alpha(T_{t_2}{}^{1,n}) + 1,$$

or equivalently, $H_\alpha({T_{1,t}}^{1,n}) \geq H_\alpha({T_{2,t}}^{1,n})$ for all $\alpha > 0$. Part (ii) can be similarly obtained. □

The next example gives an application of Theorem 6.

Example 3. *Let us consider the two coherent systems of order 4 displayed in Figure 3 with residual lifetimes* $T_{1,t}^{1,4} = [T_1 - t|X_{1:4} > t]$ *(left panel) and* $T_{2,t}^{1,4} = [T_2 - t|X_{1:4} > t]$ *(right panel). It is not hard to see that the signatures of these systems are* $\mathbf{p_1} = (\frac{1}{2}, \frac{1}{2}, 0, 0)$ *and* $\mathbf{p_2} = (\frac{1}{4}, \frac{1}{4}, \frac{1}{2}, 0)$*, respectively. Assume that the component lifetimes are independent and identically distributed according to the following survival function,*

$$S(t) = (1+t)^{-2},\ t > 0.$$

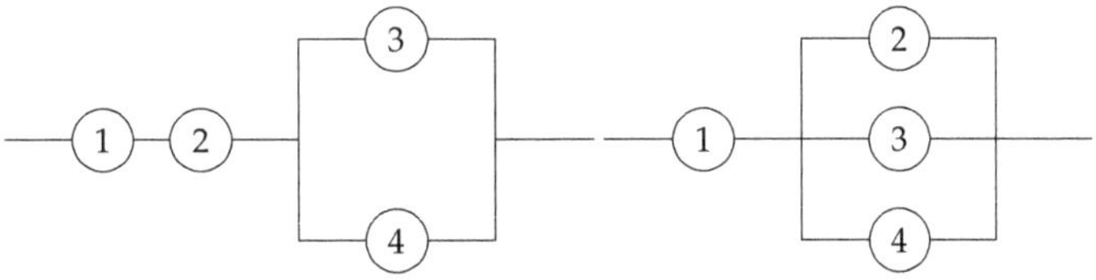

Figure 3. Two coherent systems with the likelihood ration ordered signature.

After some calculation, one can obtain $f_t(S_t^{-1}(u)) = \frac{2u\sqrt{u}}{1+t}$, $t > 0$. *This function is increasing in* u *for all* $t > 0$. *Hence, due to Theorem 6, it holds that* $H_\alpha(T_{1,t}^{1,4}) \geq H_\alpha(T_{2,t}^{1,4})$ *for all* $\alpha > 0$.

4. Some Useful Bounds

When the complexity is high and the number of components is large, it is difficult to compute the $H_\alpha(T_t^{1,n})$ of a coherent system. This situation is frequently encountered in practice. Under such circumstances, a Tsallis entropy bound can be useful to estimate the lifetime of a coherent system. To see some recent research on bounds on the uncertainty of the lifetime of coherent systems, we refer the reader, for example, to Refs. [15,16,23] and the references there. In the following theorem, we provide bounds on the residual Tsallis entropy of the lifetime of the coherent system in terms of the residual Tsallis entropy of the parent distribution $H_\alpha(X_t)$.

Theorem 7. *Let* $T_t^{1,n} = [T - t|X_{1:n} > t]$ *represent the residual lifetime of a coherent system consisting of n independent and identically distributed component lifetimes having the common CDF F with the signature* $\mathbf{p} = (p_1, \cdots, p_n)$. *Suppose that* $H_\alpha(T_t^{1,n}) < \infty$ *for all* $\alpha > 0$. *It holds that*

$$H_\alpha(T_t^{1,n}) \geq (B_n(\mathbf{p}))^\alpha H_\alpha(X_t) + \frac{(B_n(\mathbf{p}))^\alpha - 1}{1-\alpha}, \quad (18)$$

for all $\alpha > 1$ *and*

$$H_\alpha(T_t^{1,n}) \leq (B_n(\mathbf{p}))^\alpha H_\alpha(X_t) + \frac{(B_n(\mathbf{p}))^\alpha - 1}{1-\alpha}, \quad (19)$$

for $0 < \alpha < 1$ *where* $B_n(\mathbf{p}) = \sum_{i=1}^n p_i g_i(p_i)$, *and* $p_i = \frac{n-i}{n-1}$.

Proof. It can be clearly verified that the mode of the beta distribution with parameters $n-i+1$ and i is $p_i = \frac{n-i}{n-1}$. Therefore, we obtain

$$g_V(v) \leq \sum_{i=1}^n p_i g_i(p_i) = B_n(\mathbf{p}),\ 0 < v < 1.$$

Thus, for $\alpha > 1$ $(0 < \alpha < 1)$, we have

$$\begin{aligned} 1+(1-\alpha)H_\alpha(T_t^{1,n}) &= \int_0^1 g_V^\alpha(v) f_t^{\alpha-1}(S_t^{-1}(v))dv \\ &\leq (B_n(\mathbf{p}))^\alpha \int_0^1 f_t^{\alpha-1}(S_t^{-1}(v))dv \\ &= (B_n(\mathbf{p}))^\alpha[(1-\alpha)H_\alpha(X_t)+1]. \end{aligned}$$

The last equality is obtained from (3), from which the desired result follows. □

The bounds given in (18) and (19) are very valuable when the number of components is large or the structure of the system is complicated. Now, we obtain a public lower bound using properties of the Tsallis information measure and mathematical concepts.

Theorem 8. *Under the requirements of the Theorem 7, we have*

$$H_\alpha(T_t^{1,n}) \geq H_\alpha^L(T_t^{1,n}), \tag{20}$$

where $H_\alpha^L(T_t^{1,n}) = \sum_{i=1}^n p_i H_\alpha(T_t{}^{1,i,n})$ *for all* $\alpha > 0$.

Proof. Recalling Jensen's inequality for the convex function t^α (it is concave (convex) for $0 < \alpha < 1$ $(\alpha > 1)$), it holds that

$$\left(\sum_{i=1}^n p_i f_{T_t^{1,i,n}}(x)\right)^\alpha \geq (\leq) \sum_{i=1}^n p_i f^\alpha_{T_t^{1,i,n}}(x),\ t > 0,$$

and hence, we obtain

$$\left(\int_0^\infty f^\alpha_{T_t^{1,n}}(x)dx\right) \geq (\leq) \left(\sum_{i=1}^n p_i \int_0^\infty f^\alpha_{T_t^{1,i,n}}(x)dx\right). \tag{21}$$

Since $1-\alpha > 0$ $(1-\alpha < 0)$, by multiplying both sides of (21) in $1/(1-\alpha)$, we obtain

$$\begin{aligned} H_\alpha(T) &\geq \frac{1}{1-\alpha}\left[\sum_{i=1}^n p_i \int_0^\infty f^\alpha_{T_t^{1,i,n}}(x)dx - 1\right] \\ &= \frac{1}{1-\alpha}\left[\sum_{i=1}^n p_i \int_0^\infty f^\alpha_{T_t^{1,i,n}}(x)dx - \sum_{i=1}^n p_i\right] \\ &= \sum_{i=1}^n p_i \left[\frac{1}{1-\alpha}\left(\int_0^\infty f^\alpha_{T_t^{1,i,n}}(x)dx - 1\right)\right] \\ &= \sum_{i=1}^n p_i H_\alpha(T_t{}^{1,i,n}), \end{aligned}$$

and this completes the proof. □

Notice that the equality in (20) holds for i-out-of-n systems in the sense that we have $p_j = 0$, for $j \neq i$, and $p_j = 1$, for $j = i$, and then $H_\alpha(T_t^{1,n}) = H_\alpha(T_t^{1,i,n})$. When the lower bounds for $0 < \alpha < 1$ in both parts of Theorems 7 and 8 can be computed, one may use the maximum of the two lower bounds.

Example 4. Let $T_t^{1,5} = [T - t | X_{1:5} > t]$ represent the residual lifetime of a coherent system with the signature $\mathbf{p} = (0, \frac{3}{10}, \frac{5}{10}, \frac{2}{10}, 0)$ consisting of $n = 5$ independent and identically distributed component lifetimes having a uniform distribution in $[0, 1]$. It is easy to verify that $B_5(\mathbf{p}) = 2.22$. Thus, by Theorem 7, the Tsallis entropy of $T_t^{1,5}$ is bounded for $\alpha > 1$ $(0 < \alpha < 1)$, as follows:

$$H_\alpha(T_t^{1,n}) \geq \frac{2.22^\alpha(1-t)^{1-\alpha} - 1}{1-\alpha},$$

for all $\alpha > 1$ and

$$H_\alpha(T_t^{1,n}) \leq \frac{2.22^\alpha(1-t)^{1-\alpha} - 1}{1-\alpha},$$

for $0 < \alpha < 1$. Moreover, the lower bound given in (20) can be obtained as follows:

$$H_\alpha(T_t^{1,3}) \geq \frac{1}{1-\alpha}\left[(1-t)^{1-\alpha}\sum_{i=1}^{n} p_i \int_0^1 g_i^\alpha(u)du - 1\right], \; t > 0, \tag{22}$$

for all $\alpha > 0$. Assuming uniform distribution for the component lifetimes, we computed the bounds given by (19) (dashed line), as well as the exact value of $H_\alpha(T_t^{1,3})$ obtained directly from (9), and also the bounds given by (22) (dotted line). The results are displayed in Figure 4. As we can see, regarding the lower bound in (22) (dotted line) for $\alpha > 1$, it is better than the lower bound given by (19).

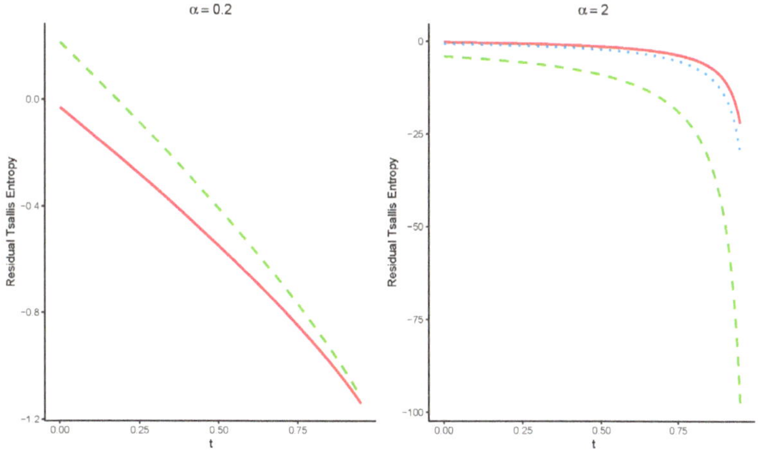

Figure 4. Exact value of $H_\alpha(T_t^{1,3})$ (solid line), as well as the corresponding lower bounds (18) (dashed line) and (19) (dotted line) for the standard uniform distribution concerning time t.

5. Conclusions

Intuitively, it is better to have systems that work longer and whose remaining life is less uncertain. We can make more accurate predictions when a system has low uncertainty. The Tsallis entropy of a system is an important measure for designing systems based on these facts. If we have some information about the lifetime of the system at time t, for example, that the system will still function at age t, then we may be interested in quantifying the predictability of the remaining lifetime. In this work, we presented a simple assertion for the Tsallis entropy of the system lifetime for the case where all components contained in the system are in operation at time t. Several properties of the proposed measure were discussed. In addition, some partial stochastic orderings between the remaining lifetimes of two coherent systems were discussed in terms of their Tsallis entropy using the concept of a system signature. Numerous examples were also given to illustrate the results.

Author Contributions: Conceptualization, M.K.; methodology, M.K.; software, M.A.A.; validation, M.A.A.; formal analysis, M.K.; investigation, M.A.A.; resources, M.A.A.; writing—original draft preparation, M.K.; writing—review and editing, M.A.A.; visualization, M.A.A.; supervision, M.A.A.; project administration, M.A.A.; funding acquisition, M.A.A. All authors have read and agreed to the published version of the manuscript.

Funding: This research was funded by Researchers Supporting Project number (RSP2023R392), King Saud University, Riyadh, Saudi Arabia.

Institutional Review Board Statement: Not applicable.

Informed Consent Statement: Not applicable.

Data Availability Statement: No new data were created or analyzed in this study. Data sharing is not applicable to this article.

Acknowledgments: The authors acknowledge financial support from King Saud University. This work was supported by Researchers Supporting Project number (RSP2023R392), King Saud University, Riyadh, Saudi Arabia.

Conflicts of Interest: The authors declare no conflict of interest.

References

1. Ebrahimi, N.; Pellerey, F. New partial ordering of survival functions based on the notion of uncertainty. *J. Appl. Probab.* **1995**, *32*, 202–211. [CrossRef]
2. Shannon, C.E. A mathematical theory of communication. *Bell Syst. Tech. J.* **1948**, *27*, 379–423. [CrossRef]
3. Tsallis, C. Possible generalization of Boltzmann-Gibbs statistics. *J. Stat. Phys.* **1988**, *52*, 479–487. [CrossRef]
4. Asadi, M.; Ebrahimi, N.; Soofi, E.S. Dynamic generalized information measures. *Stat. Probab. Lett.* **2005**, *71*, 85–98. [CrossRef]
5. Nanda, A.K.; Paul, P. Some results on generalized residual entropy. *Inf. Sci.* **2006**, *176*, 27–47. [CrossRef]
6. Zhang, Z. Uniform estimates on the Tsallis entropies. *Lett. Math. Phys.* **2007**, *80*, 171–181. [CrossRef]
7. Irshad, M.R.; Maya, R.; Buono, F.; Longobardi, M. Kernel estimation of cumulative residual Tsallis entropy and its dynamic version under ρ-mixing dependent data. *Entropy* **2021**, *24*, 9. [CrossRef]
8. Rajesh, G.; Sunoj, S. Some properties of cumulative Tsallis entropy of order $alpha$. *Stat. Pap.* **2019**, *60*, 583–593. [CrossRef]
9. Toomaj, A.; Atabay, H.A. Some new findings on the cumulative residual Tsallis entropy. *J. Comput. Appl. Math.* **2022**, *400*, 113669. [CrossRef]
10. Mohamed, M.S.; Barakat, H.M.; Alyami, S.A.; Abd Elgawad, M.A. Cumulative residual tsallis entropy-based test of uniformity and some new findings. *Mathematics* **2022**, *10*, 771. [CrossRef]
11. Maasoumi, E. The measurement and decomposition of multi-dimensional inequality. *Econom. J. Econom. Soc.* **1986**, *54*, 991–997. [CrossRef]
12. Abe, S. Axioms and uniqueness theorem for Tsallis entropy. *Phys. Lett. A* **2000**, *271*, 74–79. [CrossRef]
13. Asadi, M.; Ebrahimi, N.; Soofi, E.S. Connections of Gini, Fisher, and Shannon by Bayes risk under proportional hazards. *J. Appl. Probab.* **2017**, *54*, 1027–1050. [CrossRef]
14. Alomani, G.; Kayid, M. Further Properties of Tsallis Entropy and Its Application. *Entropy* **2023**, *25*, 199. [CrossRef] [PubMed]
15. Abdolsaeed, T.; Doostparast, M. A note on signature-based expressions for the entropy of mixed r-out-of-n systems. *Nav. Res. Logist. (NRL)* **2014**, *61*, 202–206.
16. Toomaj, A. Renyi entropy properties of mixed systems. *Commun. Stat.-Theory Methods* **2017**, *46*, 906–916. [CrossRef]
17. Toomaj, A.; Di Crescenzo, A.; Doostparast, M. Some results on information properties of coherent systems. *Appl. Stoch. Model. Bus. Ind.* **2018**, *34*, 128–143. [CrossRef]
18. Baratpour, S.; Khammar, A. Tsallis entropy properties of order statistics and some stochastic comparisons. *J. Stat. Res. Iran JSRI* **2016**, *13*, 25–41. [CrossRef]
19. Shaked, M.; Shanthikumar, J.G. *Stochastic Orders*; Springer Science & Business Media: Berlin/Heidelberg, Germany, 2007.
20. Samaniego, F.J. *System Signatures and Their Applications in Engineering Reliability*; Springer Science & Business Media: Berlin/Heidelberg, Germany, 2007; Volume 110.
21. Khaledi, B.E.; Shaked, M. Ordering conditional lifetimes of coherent systems. *J. Stat. Plan. Inference* **2007**, *137*, 1173–1184. [CrossRef]
22. Ebrahimi, N.; Kirmani, S. Some results on ordering of survival functions through uncertainty. *Stat. Probab. Lett.* **1996**, *29*, 167–176. [CrossRef]
23. Toomaj, A.; Chahkandi, M.; Balakrishnan, N. On the information properties of working used systems using dynamic signature. *Appl. Stoch. Model. Bus. Ind.* **2021**, *37*, 318–341. [CrossRef]

MDPI AG
Grosspeteranlage 5
4052 Basel
Switzerland
Tel.: +41 61 683 77 34

Entropy Editorial Office
E-mail: entropy@mdpi.com
www.mdpi.com/journal/entropy

www.ingramcontent.com/pod-product-compliance
Lightning Source LLC
LaVergne TN
LVHW072319090526
838202LV00019B/2313